# Game
# Programming
# Gems 2

# Game Programming Gems 2

### Edited by Mark A. DeLoura

**CHARLES RIVER MEDIA, INC.**

**Hingham, Massachusetts**

Publisher: Jenifer Niles
Production: Publishers' Design and Production Services
Printer: InterCity Press
Front Cover Image:  COURTESY OF LUCASFILM LTD. AND LUCASARTS ENTERTAINMENT COMPANY LLC

CHARLES RIVER MEDIA, INC.
20 Downer Avenue, Suite 3
Hingham, Massachusetts 02043
781-740-0400
781-740-8816 (FAX)
info@charlesriver.com
www.charlesriver.com

This book is printed on acid-free paper.

Mark DeLoura. *Game Programming Gems 2*.
ISBN: 1-58450-054-9

Library of Congress Cataloging-in-Publication Data

Game programming gems 2 / edited by Mark DeLoura.
        p. cm.
     Includes bibliographical references and index.
     ISBN 1-58450-054-9 (hardback w/CD-ROM)
     1. Computer games—Programming.   I. Title: Game programming gems
2. II. Title: Game programming gems two. III. DeLoura, Mark.
QA76.76.C672 G36 2001
794.8'1526—dc21
                              2001002803

Printed in the United States of America
01 02 7 6 5 4 3 2 First Edition

# Contents

# Preface

## Mark DeLoura

madsax@satori.org

**W**elcome to the second volume of *Game Programming Gems*! I'm proud to be able to offer you a book filled with 70 gems on diverse topics that you'll be able to take and insert into your own games.

When I first started planning this book, I wanted to make sure that it would be as useful and practical as possible. There aren't many things worse than a book full of theoretical technology that won't run in real time, or a book that is filled with ancient information. ("DirectX 7? What?!?") So, instead of organizing *Gems 2* on my own, I recruited experts for each subject in this volume, and asked them to choose the most relevant topics for their section. Fortunately, I was able to find incredible developers who had written for the original *Gems* volume, and were interested in devoting themselves to designing entire sections for *Gems 2*.

Here are the section editors for *Gems 2*. These fine folks dedicated many, many hours on top of their already busy schedules to ensure that the gems contained herein are worth your time.

Scott Bilas, Gas Powered Games—General Programming

Eddie Edwards, Naughty Dog—Mathematics

Steve Rabin, Nintendo of America—Artificial Intelligence

Eric Lengyel, C4 Engine—Geometry Management

D. Sim Dietrich Jr., Nvidia Corporation—Graphics Display

James Boer, Lithtech—Audio Programming

## Backstory

While I was organizing the original *Game Programming Gems*, I was a lead software engineer at Nintendo of America, and I was frustrated. All around me I saw companies in our industry creating more closed standards, more closed APIs, applying for software patents, and walling themselves off from everyone else. Frankly, I was pretty upset about the whole thing. Then, at 3:00 A.M. the night before sending *Gems* off to the publisher, I re-read the Preface that I had just finished writing in a stream of consciousness. I had written about how important it was to create open standards and share your knowledge with other people in the industry. In that moment, I realized a desire to dedicate myself to encouraging the spread of knowledge in our industry, and not just evangelizing another proprietary standard.

It wasn't long after this moment of clarity that, through a peculiar conspiracy of events and several deep conversations at E3, I agreed to take on the helm of editor-in-chief for *Game Developer* magazine. I now get to bring you a few gems every month!

## The Design of Gems 2

As I stated previously, this volume was designed as a collaboration of the six section editors and myself. Our intent was to make sure that the content of each section is valuable to you, the expert game developer. If you're an intermediate or even a beginner, we hope that you will read through the gems and learn, and then go to the references if you need more information about a particular topic. While many of the gems in this volume outline complex techniques, many of them also contain references to other resources where you can go for the backstory. Of course, there are also many great game development resources available online, including gamasutra.com, flip-code.com, and gamedev.net.

One issue I need to address is the use of APIs in this book. In the original *Game Programming Gems*, all of the gems used C/C++ and OpenGL. This was an attempt to ensure that the code would run on a wide variety of the currently available systems. In this volume, we've stepped back a bit. With the huge number of available game platforms today (including game consoles, computers, handhelds, the Web, and wireless devices), it is nigh-impossible to write code that will run on all of them. However, there is a subset of languages and APIs that every competent developer should know. These include C and C++ of course, x86 assembler if you're a PC engine programmer, and OpenGL and Direct3D if you're a 3D programmer. You likely also should be competent with Java and a few scripting languages. We assume that you as the expert game developer should have no trouble grokking any of these languages if they're used in this book, and we even go outside of those lines a bit here and there.

## The Industry

The game development industry has grown steadily for many years now. One of the statistics we all love to quote is that in the United States, our industry now generates more revenue than the movie industry. This sounds like a fabulous accomplishment, and we all should certainly stop coding for a moment and revel in it. However, keep in mind that the average movie costs about $8, while a game will run you about $40! Therefore, in actuality, we're only reaching one-fifth the number of people that the film industry is reaching.

We still have a lot of opportunity for growth. The day when you'll be able to download the latest Miyamoto game to your broadband set-top box and play collaboratively with your friends on the other side of the globe is not here yet. However, it's coming soon, perhaps in the next few years, and that will open up all sorts of new entertainment possibilities.

People all over the world are playing games, and making games. I've heard from developers in Russia, Croatia, Korea, Australia, New Zealand, Brazil, and many areas of Europe and North America. Games are a worldwide phenomenon that can bring people together through a shared experience. As you're designing your next title, consider thinking not only of cross-platform compatibility, but cross-culture compatibility!

One consideration about our expanding influence around the world is that we now reach enough people that we've become a concern to our cultural watchdogs. Whenever a troubled teen commits an act of senseless violence, we're now graciously included in the cadre of media that must somehow be responsible: movies, TV, music, and games. While on the surface this is aggravating, it does signal that games have become part of the public conversation: games are not just something for kids any more, they're an actual art form. As such, our industry has become subject to the same scrutiny as other art forms.

The question of whether violence in the media can cause people to become more violent will probably never be resolved, but there is a perception by the general public that this could be true. One of the most important things we can do as an industry to be responsible for this perception is to encourage the acceptance of the ESRB rating system. Giving parents the ability to choose what their kids play puts the responsibility where it belongs: in the hands of the parents.

Of course, you do learn something as you play a game. If you didn't, how would you get past that nasty monster on the 20th level? What that something that you learn is depends on the game. As the fidelity of our titles improves, the possibility for educating players increases. What will you teach your player?

## Open Standards

One of the most frustrating things to me these days is the growing number of languages and APIs, and how many of them are proprietary. It gets more and more challenging for independent developers to choose a platform, since it's hard to get accurate information on the development kits that are available. The trend in our industry toward keeping development systems secret is something that I don't understand.

This isn't as big of a problem on the PC. It seems that on the PC side, systems are actually becoming more open. And surprise, most technological innovation takes place on the PC. Several recent games have even opened up their source code shortly after they were launched.

There was a Harvard Business School study a few years ago that examined the researchers at Xerox PARC. In the study, they were hoping to determine the qualities that are most important in guaranteeing the success of a researcher. What they discovered is that the ability to communicate and share information successfully is one of the most important qualities to guarantee success. Those researchers who keep to themselves may do fine, but the researchers who really excel have a developed network of professionals with whom they often communicate.

This study is very applicable to our industry. Some of the most successful game development companies right now are the ones that are opening their games up and communicating with everyone. They're giving away their game's source code, the level editing tools, and the APIs. They're talking at the Game Developers Conference. Their game players get to create fantastic new levels and game mods, and aspiring game developers get to learn from the experts. Normally, when you give something away, you assume that you're losing something. However, in our industry, giving away your IP may be one of the wisest decisions you can make. If you can turn your game players into game developers, well, we all win.

# Acknowledgments

I want to acknowledge a few of the many great people who were involved with the production of this book. First and foremost, thanks to Dave Pallai and Jenifer Niles at Charles River Media for encouraging me to explore continuing the *Gems* series. Your tireless pursuit of excellence and consistent desire to make sure everything is taken care of are what made this book possible. Many thanks as well to Andrew Glassner for his original vision. I still have the *Graphics Gems* series on my shelf, and if you don't, dear reader, you should go buy those books right now.

The people who really created this book are the section editors and the gem authors. Most of them have full-time jobs; many of them even have crunch-time jobs, and yet they reserved large portions of their free time and sleep time in order to make sure everything in *Gems 2* was top notch. You all have my heartfelt appreciation. Thank you so much for sharing your expertise.

Finally, the third group of people I want to thank are my co-workers at Gama Network. Working with these people is absolutely amazing. Everyday I get to go to work and be with people who are solely dedicated to making sure that the game development industry is prospering. Being with people like Jennifer Pahlka, Alan Yu, Susan Marshall, Alex Dunne, and Dan Huebner each day is a true joy. They make sure that the Game Developers Conference, Gamasutra.com, and *Game Developer* magazine run smoothly and are useful and informative. I also want to thank my incredible edit staff on *Game Developer*: Laura Huber, Jennifer Olsen, and Tiger Byrd. These folks continually surprise me with their enthusiasm and professionalism. Thanks for helping this engineer learn how to be a successful editor-in-chief!

# About the Cover Image

## Andrew Kirmse

The picture on the cover is an in-engine shot from *Star Wars Starfighter*, a flight action game by LucasArts, which was released in February, 2000 for the Playstation 2. The terrain, islands, and waterfall were built in 3D Studio Max, and the buildings and enemies were then placed with the level editing tool. Vehicles use a second texture for reflection mapping, and the terrain uses a second detail texture. Particle systems simulate the mist at the bottom of the waterfall, the explosion and smoke, and boat wakes and laser strikes.

For this shot, the player's bomber (Nym's Havoc) destroyed an enemy ship, and gems were "glued" to the debris. A flying enemy may be performing terrain avoidance, targeting, dodging ships, and chasing the player simultaneously—too bad it can't avoid Nym's lasers!

# Author Bios

## Scott Bilas

scottb@aa.net

Scott Bilas is a code monkey at Gas Powered Games where he enjoys making boring back-end gaming systems. He also writes on occasion, and has been published in *Game Programming Gems* and *Game Developer* magazine. Scott recently began experimenting with time travel in an attempt to be a *Gems2* section editor, write some gems, do a GDC 2001 talk, and fill *Dungeon Siege* with bugs—all at the same time.

## James Boer

jimb@lithtech.com

James Boer is the audio programmer for Lithtech Inc., and has worked on such projects as *Deer Hunter I & II*, *Rocky Mountain Trophy Hunter*, *Microsoft Baseball 2000*, and *Tex Atomic's Big Bot Battles*.

## Charles Cafrelli

skywise@iquest.net

A graduate of Purdue University, Charles has worked on several games for Origin Systems (R.I.P.), including *Wing Commander 2*, *Privateer*, *Wing Commander 3*, and *Pacific Strike*. He has also developed software for blood-glucose meters at Boehringer-Mannheim, and is currently developing software for next-generation consumer electronics. His favorite games include Scott Adams' *Adventure*, Steve Meretsky's *Planetfall*, *Elite*, *Space Ace*, *Command and Conquer*, any game with Zelda in it, and *Final Fantasy*.

## Simon Carter

scarter@bigbluebox.com

Simon Carter has been working in the computer games industry since 1986, when he started out at the age of 11 helping his older brother Dene develop titles on the Sinclair ZX Spectrum. He started work at Bullfrog Productions Ltd. in 1994, cutting his programming teeth on *Magic Carpet*, and moved on to become the project leader and lead programmer on *Dungeon Keeper*. Simon and his brother started their own games company, Big Blue Box Studios, in 1999, where they are currently working on an as yet unannounced project for Microsoft's Xbox console.

## Peter Dalton

pdalton@xmission.com

www.xmission.com/~pdalton

Peter Dalton is currently working for Evans & Sutherland within the advanced displays group developing the next generation of visual displays. Most of his work is concentrated on improving the quality of flight simulators used to train fighter pilots.

## Bruce Dawson

bruced@humongous.com

www.cygnus-software.com/papers/

Bruce Dawson is the director of technology at Humongous Entertainment, which means that he gets to work on all the fun and challenging tasks that nobody else has time to do. Dawson also teaches part time at DigiPen. Prior to Humongous Entertainment, Dawson worked at Cavedog Entertainment, assisting various product teams. Dawson worked for several years at the Elastic Reality branch of Avid Technology, writing special effects software and video-editing plug-ins. In the distant past, he worked at Electronic Arts Canada, back when it was called Distinctive Software.

## Mark DeLoura

madsax@satori.org

www.satori.org/madsax

Mark is the editor-in-chief of *Game Developer* magazine, and the editor of the original *Game Programming Gems* and *Game Programming Gems 2*. Prior to joining *Game Developer* magazine, Mark worked for five years at Nintendo of America, where he was lead software engineer in the developer relations group, working on Gamecube and Nintendo 64. In a past life, Mark was involved with virtual reality research, and co-moderated several Usenet virtual reality newsgroups.

## D. Sim Dietrich Jr.

sdietrich@nvidia.com

D. Sim Dietrich Jr. has been doing real-time graphics since the Apple II+. He currently works in the technical developer relations group at Nvidia Corporation, helping PC developers push the state of the art in real-time 3D graphics. His current interests include per-pixel lighting and shadows, as well as using software engineering techniques to improve the productivity and creativity of the game development process.

## Nathan d'Obrenan

nathand@firetoads.com
www.firetoads.com/coding

Nathan has been programming video games since grade school and is entirely self-taught. Nathan is the lead programmer of Firetoad Software, Inc., a rebel game company in Calgary, Alberta, Canada. Those duties include researching and developing all new technologies to be used in their games. His hobbies include "sdrawkcab gniklat" and running around naked in the snow (it's an official sport in Canada).

## Carl Dougan

carl.dougan@gte.net

Carl Dougan has been in the industry for six years and is currently working on an XBox title for MassMedia game in California.

## Eric Dybsand

edybs@ix.netcom.com

Eric Dybsand was a contributor to the first *Game Programming Gems* book and has been involved with the computer game industry since 1987. He is currently developing race car AI for several racing games shipping in 2001. During 2000, he also consulted on the strategic AI for the space strategy game *Master of Orion 3*. Eric has also consulted on AI for baseball and wrestling games. He designed and developed the AI opponents for the Windward Studios RTS game *Enemy Nations*, and for the Fenris Wolfe FPS games *Rebel Moon Revolution* and *War In Heaven*. Eric has also been an AI roundtable moderator at the past five Game Developers Conferences as well as a CGDC lecturer, and is currently a moderator of the Gamasutra "AI Programming" and IGDA "AI in Games" forums on the Web. Eric lives in Glendale, Colorado where, when not working on a game, he is skiing, biking, hiking, and enjoying the great Colorado outdoors.

## Eddie Edwards

eddie@tinyted.net

Eddie Edwards studied mathematics at Cambridge University, and then did a brief stint as a software engineer before being seduced by the dark side. He worked on a variety of game projects in the UK, including ports of *Wolfenstein 3D* and *DOOM*, before joining Naughty Dog in California in 1999. He is currently a member of the programming team for their Playstation 2 game, due out Christmas 2001.

## Thomas Engel

tengel@factor5.com

Thomas Engel is director of technology and one of the founders of Factor 5, LLC. He has been working in the industry for more than 10 years, with his main focus being the technology behind the game play. One of his projects over the last years has been Factor 5's *MusyX* sound system. Thomas is currently busy developing both audio and graphics technologies for next-generation consoles such as the Nintendo Gamecube.

## Jeff Evertt

jeff@evertt.com

Jeff spent several years at Intel doing a combination of hardware and software design. He has also worked on several projects at Cavedog Entertainment, and can now be found developing the PC and Xbox renderers at Lithtech Inc.

## Mark Fischer

beach@beachsoftware.com

Mark Fischer founded Beach Software, which publishes encryption software. Mark also acts as an independent consultant, specializing in optimizing network software and deterministic software architectures.

## Tom Forsyth

tomf@muckyfoot.com

Obsessed by 3D graphics since seeing *Elite* on his ZX Spectrum, Tom has always tried to make hardware beg for mercy. He has written triangle-drawing routines on the Spectrum, Sinclair QL, Atari ST, Sega 32X, Saturn, Dreamcast, and PC, and he's tired of them now. He's very grateful that we have hardware to draw the things for him. After two excellent years writing 3D graphics card drivers at 3Dlabs, Tom moved to Mucky Foot Productions—a games company in Guildford, UK—and is currently trying to draw far more trees than any sane game should have.

## Dan Ginsburg

ginsburg@alum.wpi.edu

Dan Ginsburg currently works at ATI Research, Inc. as a software engineer in the OpenGL driver group. He is mainly responsible for implementing extensions, creating demos, and writing new extension specs. Prior to working at ATI, Dan spent almost two years at n-Space, Inc. working on *Die Hard Trilogy 2: Viva Las Vegas* for the Playstation and PC, and was a member of their engine group.

## Miguel Gomez

miguel@lithtech.com

Miguel Gomez is a lead engineer at Lithtech Inc., a developer of interactive application software, where he specializes in numerical analysis and physical modeling. His previous experience includes graphics and physics programming for Electronic Arts' *PGA Tour '96*, Activision's *Hyperblade*, Microsoft's *Baseball 3D*, and Psygnosis' *Destruction Derby 64*. He holds a bachelor's degree in physics from the University of Washington where he is currently pursuing a graduate degree in applied mathematics.

## Dave Gosselin

gosselin@ati.com

Dave Gosselin is currently a software engineer in the 3D application research group at ATI Research. He is involved in various demo and SDK work, and writing OpenGL extension specifications. Previously, he worked at several companies, including Oracle, Spacetec IMC, Xyplex, and MIT Lincoln Laboratory on varied projects from low-level networking and Web technologies to image processing and 3D input devices.

## Bryon Hapgood

bryonh57@hotmail.com

Bryon started life at Bullfrog Productions working on *Populous II* for the Amiga. He currently works for Kodiak Interactive as a programmer. In his spare time, Bryon enjoys writing short stories and annoying his wife with his devastating charm.

## Evan Hart

ehart@ati.com

Evan Hart is a software engineer in the 3D applications research group at ATI. His present focus is on OpenGL software and extensions. Before joining ATI, he worked on PC-based 3D simulations for Battelle.

## Pete Isensee

pkisensee@msn.com
www.tantalon.com/pete.htm

Pete has programmed games ranging from 7-CD titles, to multiplayer casual games, to console apps. He has a degree in computer engineering and spends his spare cycles researching C++ optimization techniques.

## John Isidoro

jisidoro@cs.bu.edu

John Isidoro works as a 3D graphics programming consultant for the Applications Research Group at ATI Technologies. He is also a graduate student working toward a Ph.D. in Computer Science at Boston University. It should also be mentioned that John really likes quaternions.

## Greg James

gjames@nvidia.com

Greg James is a software engineer with Nvidia's technical developer relations group, where he develops tools and demos for real-time 3D graphics. Prior to this, he was a research assistant in a high-energy physics laboratory. One night he got to feeling sorry for all of the protons being smashed around, so he left for a life in PC games and computer graphics, a hobby that began in his school days when Dad brought home a strange beige thing called an Amiga 1000.

## Lasse Staff Jensen

lasse@funcom.com
www.funcom.com

Lasse Staff Jensen has a computer engineering degree in system development from Trondheim College of Engineering, Norway. Before joining the game industry four years ago, he was working as an assistant teacher and system administrator at the Army College of Engineering. Lasse has in-depth computer graphics knowledge, and approximately 10 years of graphic application programming experience. He is currently the technical manager at Funcom, where he and his team of programmers are researching and developing Funcom's core technology.

## Yossarian King

yking@ea.com

Yossarian King is an engineer with Electronic Arts Canada. He is the lead programmer on the PC version of *FIFA Soccer*, and has previously worked on the Nintendo 64, 3DO, Sega Saturn, and, once upon a time, the Commodore 64. When not juggling bits and bytes, he juggles beanbags and clubs, and has been known to ride a unicycle.

## Andrew Kirmse

ark@alum.mit.edu

Andrew was the co-inventor and director of *Meridian 59* (1996), and the graphics programmer on *Star Wars: Starfighter* (2001). He has degrees in physics, mathematics, and computer science from MIT. Andrew now works at LucasArts Entertainment Company.

## Jesse Laeuchli

jesse@laeuchli.com

Jesse Laeuchli is a certified C/C++ and Windows programmer who now makes his home in Budapest, Hungary. As a child of a foreign service officer, he has lived in foreign countries such as China, Taiwan, Africa, and Saudi Arabia. He has written for several computer magazines and Web sites. His interests in computer programming are in computer graphics and operating systems. He is now studying Hungarian, and is working on developing an OpenGL 3D engine. He also runs a small network, and does general computer troubleshooting.

## Adam Lake

adam.t.lake@intel.com

Adam Lake is a senior software engineer in the graphics and 3D technologies group at the Intel Architecture Lab (IAL). He has a master's degree from the University of North Carolina at Chapel Hill.

## François Dominic Laramée

francoislaramee@videotron.ca
pages.infinit.net/idjy

François Dominic Laramée has plagued the game industry for almost a decade, during which he single-handedly wrecked over 20 titles released on consoles, personal computers, online networks, cable set-top boxes, and a handful of even weirder platforms. He has also waylaid thousands of readers with his articles on game design, programming, and production, and has somehow conned two different universities into granting him graduate degrees. (Well, one for sure, and one that he's still working on.) Read his hare-brained contribution at your own risk.

## Eric Lengyel

lengyel@c4engine.com

Eric Lengyel is the lead programmer for a project known as the *C4 Engine*. He is also the author of the book *Mathematics for 3D Game Programming & Computer Graphics* (Charles River Media, 2001). Previously, Eric has worked as a 3D engine architect at Sierra and as an OpenGL engineer at Apple Computer. He holds a master's degree in mathematics from Virginia Tech. When Eric's not scribbling down equations or writing code, he can usually be found running in the mountains surrounding Silicon Valley.

## Ian Lewis

ilewis@acclaim.com

Ian Lewis has worked in the computer entertainment industry since 1993. He is currently a network and sound programmer for Acclaim Studios in Salt Lake City, Utah.

## Noel Llopis

nllopis@mgigames.com
www.cs.unc.edu/~llopis/

Noel Llopis started writing games as a hobby on an Amstrad CPC in 1985. He obtained his undergraduate degree in computer engineering from the University of Massachusetts Amherst, and his master's degree in computer science from the University of North Carolina at Chapel Hill. A few years ago, he jumped ship from working on his Ph.D. to finally working in the games industry. He's now the lead software engineer for an undisclosed Xbox project at Meyer/Glass Interactive.

## John Manslow

jfm96r@ecs.soton.ac.uk

John Manslow graduated from the University of Northumbria (UK) in 1994 with a first-class honors degree in microelectronic engineering, specializing in the design of hardware artificial neural networks. After a brief period of contractual work at the University's communications research group, he joined Neural Computer Sciences, where he played a key role in developing a flexible object-oriented neural network library. In 1996, John enrolled for a Ph.D. with the University of Southampton's image, speech, and intelligent systems research group, applying AI techniques to the analysis of satellite imagery. Upon completion of his Ph.D., John joined Codemasters Software Company Limited in the role of AI research and development programmer, and worked on several projects aimed at introducing in-game learning into future Codemasters products. In early 2001, John moved to Neural Technologies Limited, where he uses advanced AI techniques in the detection of telecommunications fraud. Current interests include the application of AI in games and the evolution of artificial organisms.

## Herb Marselas

hmarselas@ensemblestudios.com
www.ensemblestudios.com

Herb Marselas is a 3D engine specialist working on the next "Age" of real-time strategy games at Ensemble Studios.

## Carl S. Marshall

carl.s.marshall@intel.com

Carl S. Marshall works in the graphics and 3D technologies group within Intel Architecture Labs. He has a master's degree in computer science from Clemson University where he did research in various areas of virtual reality. He spent a summer learning all about the gaming industry from Valve, a leading game development company. Carl is currently working on various aspects of the *Shockwave3D* graphics engine while pursuing research interests in artificial intelligence and creating real-time 3D non-photorealistic rendered virtual worlds and effects.

## Chris Maughan

cmaughan@nvidia.com

Chris has worked in the 3D graphics hardware industry for six years. Initially specializing in device drivers, he ran the DirectX driver team at 3Dlabs, before moving to NVIDIA and joining the developer relations group. Moving away from drivers and up the graphics pipeline a little has given him the chance to work on software that doesn't require a machine reboot every time he types in a bug. In the Nvidia developer relations team, Chris specializes in tools to assist in game development. His recent work has focused on debugging and generating shaders for DirectX.

## Jason L. Mitchell

jasonm@ati.com

Jason L. Mitchell heads the 3D application research group at ATI Research, where he has worked since 1996. The 3D application research group, which sits at the crossroads of hardware, application, and API development, interfaces with game developers, the OpenGL ARB, Microsoft's Direct3D team, and ATI's internal hardware architects. The group also develops novel rendering techniques and all of ATI's technical demos. Prior to working at ATI, Jason did work in human eye tracking for human interface applications at the University of Cincinnati, where he received his master's degree in electrical engineering. He received a bachelor's degree in computer engineering from Case Western Reserve University in 1994. In addition to the *Game Programming Gems* series, Jason has been published in *Game Developer* magazine and *Gamasutra.com*.

## Aaron Nicholls

aaron_feedback@hotmail.com

Aaron Nicholls is a development lead at Microsoft Corporation in Redmond, Washington. His interest in computer graphics and AI started at an early age, and he is always looking for new challenges in these areas. He welcomes your feedback and correspondence.

## John Olsen

infix@xmission.com

John Olsen graduated with a bachelor's degree from the computer science department of the University of Utah in 1989, and worked on graphics libraries and presentation software until moving into game development in 1997. He's been involved in several Playstation titles, including *Jet Moto 2*, and is now working for Microsoft developing a title for the Xbox. His interests include autonomous AI behaviors, networking, data organization and tracking, and going on jihads against special-case code.

## Javier F. Otaegui

jJavier@sabarasa.com.ar
www.sabarasa.com

Javier F. Otaegui is the CTO of Sabarasa Entertainment, a game development company of Buenos Aires. He has also been the game designer and lead programmer of *Malvinas 2032*, an RTS game that was commercialized in Argentina and in the United States, and will start European commercialization soon. Javier's current interests include 3D LOD landscapes, online multiplaying, highly addictive gameplay, and physical systems and simulations. Please check the company's web site for more information concerning *Malvinas 2032*, or drop Javier an e-mail.

## Kim Pallister

kim.pallister@intel.com

Kim Pallister is a technical marketing engineer and processor evangelist with Intel's solutions enabling group. He is currently focused on real-time 3D graphics technologies and game development. He welcomes mail from readers.

## Scott Patterson

scottp@tonebyte.com

Scott Patterson has worked for Naughty Dog, Midway, and Microprose over the last 10 years. During that time, he has done audio systems, graphics code, and development tools. He is now leading game engine development.

## Matt Pritchard

mpritchard@ensemblestudios.com

Matt Pritchard is a developer at Ensemble Studios, where he was one of the original programmers on the multimillion selling *Age of Empires* PC game, and has been deeply involved with all of the games that have since appeared in that series. In addition, he has somehow found the time to write numerous articles on game development topics such as optimization, graphics, and multiplayer cheating. Sensing that the production of *Game Programming Gems* might be too easy, he scheduled the birth of his first child for the same week his gem was due. When not involved in the production of cutting-edge game titles, he can be found at home with his family—which now includes a daughter and a black labrador retriever—or indulging in one of his hobbies such as collecting antique computers and video games. Feel free to e-mail him if you happen to be looking to get rid of an Atari 2600 *Quadrun* game, Exidy Sorcerer computer, or just want to send him feedback on his gems.

## Steve Rabin

steve_rabin@hotmail.com

Steve Rabin was a contributing author in the first *Game Programming Gems* book and is now the artificial intelligence section editor, as well as a contributing author, for *Game Programming Gems 2*. Steve is currently working at Nintendo of America in the Gamecube software development support group, where he writes demos, researches new techniques, and helps fellow developers. Before Nintendo, Steve worked for several small start-up companies as the AI engineer for three published games. In the past, he's spoken on the topic of AI at the Game Developers Conference and, in total, has been in the video game industry for 10 years. In addition, he received a bachelor's degree in computer engineering from the University of Washington, where he specialized in robotics.

## John W. Ratcliff

jratcliff@verant.com

John W. Ratcliff has been developing software and writing for over 20 years. John's products include *688 Attack Sub*, *SSN-21 Seawolf*, and *Scarab* for Electronic Arts, and *Cyberstrike 2* for 989 Studios. In addition to these games, John has developed numerous educational software titles with Milliken Publishing Company, and biomedical software systems for Cardiosoft. John has also been a technology contributor to hundreds of games with the development of *Digpak*, *Midpak*, and *Vidpak*. John is currently a senior technology architect for Sony Online Entertainment, working on *Planetside*, a massively multiplayer first-person shooter.

## Graham Rhodes

grhodes@sed.ara.com

Graham Rhodes is a senior scientist at the Quicksand Games division of Applied Research Associates, Inc. (ARA), an engineering R&D firm based in Albuquerque, New Mexico. Graham has over a decade of experience in computational geometry, interactive and real-time 3D graphics, and physics programming. While at ARA, he has participated in a wide variety of projects, including the development of real-time computational fluid dynamics for games and the nonlinear simulation of hand-thrown gliders and frisbees for interactive simulations in the *World Book Multimedia Encyclopedia*. From 1996 through 2000, Graham was the lead developer and software architect (under contract) of NASA's prototype Next Generation Revolutionary Analysis and Design Environment (NextGRADE) graphical user interface (also known as the Smart Assembly Modeler, SAM), for which he implemented computational geometry and topology algorithms.

## Jason Shankel

shankel@pobox.com

Jason Shankel is a game programmer for Maxis/EA. In addition to *Game Programming Gems*, he has written for *Dr. Dobbs Journal* and *DevJournal*.

## Greg Snook

gregsnook@home.com

Greg has been working in the video game industry for over six years. His career began in animation, but he was bitten by the coding bug and moved into programming soon after. Since that time, Greg has contributed to several PC and console titles as both an artist and a programmer.

## Bruno Sousa

gems2@fireworks-interactive.com
www.fireworks-interactive.com

Bruno has been programming for more than eight years, getting his first game programming job at age 17. He is currently in the process of creating his own company that specializes in developing low-cost tools for game development companies and budget games.

## Marco Tombesi

tombesi@infinito.it
digilander.iol.it/baggior/

Marco Tombesi is an Italian neo-graduated engineer who is great in C++, OpenGL, Java, and CORBA, who has managed some free game projects in his life, resulting in a huge amount of experience (but still not money!). He loves games, especially sports titles, so he is currently concentrating on the development of a wonderful new soccer game; maybe, in the future, this game will be out so everybody will enjoy his work.

## Paul Tozour

gehn29@yahoo.com

Paul Tozour is currently the AI developer for *Thief 3*. His most recent credits include the combat AI ("bots") for Microsoft's highly acclaimed *MechWarrior 4: Vengeance*.

## William van der Sterren

william@cgf-ai.com

William van der Sterren is an AI developer and owner at CGF-AI. He researches and develops tactical AI for games and simulations, and has spoken at the Game Developers Conference. William currently combines his AI work with an architect/scientist position at Philips Electronics Research Labs.

## Alex Vlachos

alex@vlachos.com
alex.vlachos.com

Alex Vlachos is currently part of the 3D application research group at ATI Research, where he has worked since 1998. Alex was the lead developer for *Radeon's Ark*, the launch demo for the ATI Radeon graphics processor, and continues to write 3D engines that showcase next-generation hardware features. In addition, he's also developed N-Patches (a curved surface representation that is part of Microsoft's DirectX 8). Prior to working at ATI, he worked at Spacetec IMC as a software engineer for the SpaceOrb 360, a six-degree-of-freedom game controller. Alex is a graduate of Boston University.

## Scott Wakeling

scott@chronicreality.com
www.chronicreality.com

Scott is a programmer at Virgin Interactive Ltd. and founder of Chronic Reality, an indie game group dedicated to exploring anything technical, useful or not, as long as it's fun. You can help him stay awake by sending him some e-mail.

## Keith Weiner

keith@dw.com

Keith Weiner is the CEO of DiamondWare, Ltd. He has architected audio products, engines, pipelines, and device drivers since 1994.

## Steven Woodcock

ferretman@gameai.com

www.gameai.com

Steven Woodcock's background in game AI comes from 18 years of ballistic missile defense work building massive real-time war games and simulators. He did a stint in the consumer arena, and then returned to the defense world to help develop the AI for the national missile defense system. His Web page is dedicated to game AI, and Steve is the author of a number of papers and publications on the subject. He now pursues game AI through a variety of contract work, and has had the honor of serving as contributor to and technical editor for several books in the field. Steve lives in gorgeous Colorado Springs at the foot of Pikes Peak with his lovely wyfe (sic) Colleen and an indeterminate number of pet ferrets. Hobbies include hiking, shooting, writing, and anything related to *Blakes Seven* (go figure).

## Thomas Young

thomas.young@bigfoot.com

Thomas Young is working as a freelance programmer from his home in the sunny south of France. He is currently working for Appeal (in Belgium), developing the path-finding system for *Outcast 2*. Before becoming a freelance programmer, he worked for many years at Gremlin Interactive in Sheffield coding AI and path-finding-type stuff for a number of projects, but most notably for *Soulbringer*. He misspent his youth coding hardware tricks for the Amiga custom chipset, but moved on to study for a bachelor's degree in artificial intelligence at Sussex University.

## Michael Zarozinski

michaelz@LouderThanABomb.com

www.LouderThanABomb.com

Michael Zarozinski owns and operates Louder Than A Bomb! Software, a company dedicated to "putting the AI in entertainment software." Michael has had a life-long interest in artificial intelligence. His early experiments resulted in an *Eliza* clone written for the TI-99/4A and many brushes with electrocution while building robots from old vacuum tube radios. You can read more about Michael—perhaps more than you need to know—at the "LouderThanABomb" Web site. In his spare time, Michael is webmaster for his own little piece of cyberspace: aiGuru.com, where you'll find information on all things AI, along with his rants and/or raves on AI and non-AI related subjects.

# GENERAL PROGRAMMING

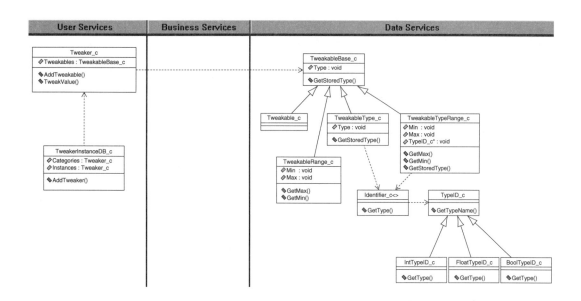

# Introduction

## Scott Bilas, Gas Powered Games

scottb@aa.net

**B**efore you start tearing into the gems that are waiting for you in this section, let's do a fun little exercise and try to get back to basics. Ask yourself a question: what is an engineer, or perhaps, what is it that you do? Is an engineer a person who writes code, someone who would, for example, make lots of triangles draw really fast? Not necessarily, of course. Plenty of engineers don't write much code at all. Engineering is about solving problems.

Let's put this in the context of a game, and ask a new question: what is an engineer's role at a game development studio? The answer is simple: an engineer's role is to serve the team. Setting aside for the moment our tendency to fill many roles at once, a typical team is divided up into three main groups. First, we have the designers, who figure out how the game is supposed to work and be fun. Next, we have the content developers, generally artists, composers, and level designers, who create the assets required to enact the design. And finally, we have the people who work down in the basement, taking far too long to accomplish their tasks as usual: the engineers. We are the ones who build the systems that connect the content assets with the game player. In other words, we, the engineers, spend all of our time serving the team by building tools. Serving? *Tools*?

What people generally think of as a "tool," such as a level editor, or a batch script processor, is only the obvious, visible part of the picture. *Everything* we create as engineers is a tool, whether it's the engine that plays back and blends the animations created by the artists, the in-game databases that manage the interactive content, or the debugging infrastructure that tracks memory usage patterns. Ultimately, what we do is create software tools for bringing a game's design to life.

Many of our tools live offline, and are used to create and preprocess data for efficient playback or simulation through the game engine. Examples of these are BSP compilers, texture compressors, resource assemblers, and level editors. These tools tend to remain in the hands of developers and mod makers and are not necessary to run the game, but are essential to create the game. Recently, games have started integrating tools such as these into the game engine itself. This is often done to speed up the development process by allowing significant portions of the content to be edited from within the game while it's running.

Other tools that we create live exclusively within the game itself. Some common examples of these are scripting engines, physics simulators, and the user interface. Each of these is, at its core, a command processor that receives instructions and does something useful with the information. In other words, these are tools that interpret and shape the content as dictated by design, and as such, they combine to form the game that the player experiences.

Sometimes, as engineers, we create tools for ourselves that live within the game. Modern games are so complex that they require vast levels of support by the game itself in order for us to effectively debug and optimize them. With tens of megabytes (and soon hundreds of megabytes) of memory at our disposal, the staggering quantities of content that we are churning through our games requires us to create complex support systems in order to keep our heads above water. We create debugging systems, profilers, type databases, utility libraries, stack-dumping exception handlers, logging utilities, self-check code, and, well, the list could fill a book. Conveniently, that's what the gems in this section of the book are all about. These gems will help build or enhance a solid foundation for game development. Enjoy!

# 1.1

## Optimization for C++ Games

### Andrew Kirmse, LucasArts Entertainment
ark@alum.mit.edu

**W**ell-written C++ games are often more maintainable and reusable than their plain C counterparts are—but is it worth it? Can complex C++ programs hope to match traditional C programs in speed?

With a good compiler and thorough knowledge of the language, it is indeed possible to create efficient games in C++. This gem describes techniques you can use to speed up games in particular. It assumes that you're already convinced of the benefits of using C++, and that you're familiar with the general principles of optimization (see Further Investigations for these).

One general principle that merits repeating is the absolute importance of profiling. In the absence of profiling, programmers tend to make two types of mistakes. First, they optimize the wrong code. The great majority of a program is not performance critical, so any time spent speeding it up is wasted. Intuition about which code is performance critical is untrustworthy—only by direct measurement can you be sure. Second, programmers sometimes make "optimizations" that actually slow down the code. This is particularly a problem in C++, where a deceptively simple line can actually generate a significant amount of machine code. Examine your compiler's output, and profile often.

## Object Construction and Destruction

The creation and destruction of objects is a central concept in C++, and is the main area where the compiler generates code "behind your back." Poorly designed programs can spend substantial time calling constructors, copying objects, and generating costly temporary objects. Fortunately, common sense and a few simple rules can make object-heavy code run within a hair's breadth of the speed of C.

- Delay construction of objects until they're needed.

  The fastest code is that which never runs; why create an object if you're not going to use it? Thus, in the following code:

```
void Function(int arg)
{
```

```
        Object obj;
        if (arg == 0)
            return;
        ...
    }
```

even when *arg* is zero, we pay the cost of calling *Object*'s constructor and destructor. If *arg* is often zero, and especially if *Object* itself allocates memory, this waste can add up in a hurry. The solution, of course, is to move the declaration of *obj* until after the *if* check.

Be careful about declaring nontrivial objects in loops, however. If you delay construction of an object until it's needed in a loop, you'll pay for the construction and destruction of the object on every iteration. It's better to declare the object before the loop and pay these costs only once. If a function is called inside an inner loop, and the function creates an object on the stack, you could instead create the object outside the loop and pass it by reference to the function.

• Use initializer lists.

Consider the following class:

```
class Vehicle
{
public:
    Vehicle(const std::string &name)  // Don't do this!
    {
        mName = name;
    }
private:
    std::string mName;
};
```

Because member variables are constructed before the body of the constructor is invoked, this code calls the constructor for the string *mName*, and then calls the = operator to copy in the object's name. What's particularly bad about this example is that the default constructor for *string* may well allocate memory—in fact, more memory than may be necessary to hold the actual name assigned to the variable in the constructor for *Vehicle*. The following code is much better, and avoids the call to *operator=*. Further, given more information (in this case, the actual string to be stored), the nondefault *string* constructor can often be more efficient, and the compiler may be able to optimize away the *Vehicle* constructor invocation when the body is empty:

```
class Vehicle
{
public:
    Vehicle(const std::string &name) : mName(name)
    {
    }
private:
```

```
        std::string mName;
    };
```

- Prefer preincrement to postincrement.

  The problem with writing $x = y++$ is that the increment function has to make a copy of the original value of $y$, increment $y$, and then return the original value. Thus, postincrement involves the construction of a temporary object, while preincrement doesn't. For integers, there's no additional overhead, but for user-defined types, this is wasteful. You should use preincrement whenever you have the option. You almost always have the option in *for* loop iterators.

- Avoid operators that return by value.

  The canonical way to write vector addition in C++ is this:

  ```
  Vector operator+(const Vector &v1, const Vector &v2)
  ```

  This operator must return a new *Vector* object, and furthermore, it must return it by value. While this allows useful and readable expressions like *v = v1 + v2*, the cost of a temporary construction and a *Vector* copy is usually too much for something called as often as vector addition. It's sometimes possible to arrange code so that the compiler is able to optimize away the temporary object (this is known as the "return value optimization"), but in general, it's better to swallow your pride and write the slightly uglier, but usually faster:

  ```
  void Vector::Add(const Vector &v1, const Vector &v2)
  ```

  Note that *operator+=* doesn't suffer from the same problem, as it modifies its first argument in place, and doesn't need to return a temporary. Thus, you should use operators like += instead of + when possible.

- Use lightweight constructors.

  Should the constructor for the *Vector* class in the previous example initialize its elements to zero? This may come in handy in a few spots in your code, but it forces every caller to pay the price of the initialization, whether they use it or not. In particular, temporary vectors and member variables will implicitly incur the extra cost.

  A good compiler may well optimize away some of the extra code, but why take the chance? As a general rule, you want an object's constructor to initialize each of its member variables, because uninitialized data can lead to subtle bugs. However, in small classes that are frequently instantiated, especially as temporaries, you should be prepared to compromise this rule for performance. Prime candidates in many games are the *Vector* and *Matrix* classes. These classes should provide methods (or alternate constructors) to set themselves to zero and the identity, respectively, but the default constructor should be empty.

As a corollary to this principle, you should provide additional constructors to classes where this will improve performance. If the *Vehicle* class in our second example were instead written like this:

```
class Vehicle
{
public:
    Vehicle()
    {
    }

    void SetName(const std::string &name)
    {
        mName = name;
    }

private:
    std::string mName;
};
```

we'd incur the cost of constructing *mName*, and then setting it again later via *Set-Name()*. Similarly, it's cheaper to use copy constructors than to construct an object and then call *operator=*. Prefer constructing an object this way—*Vehicle v1(v2)*—to this way—*Vehicle v1; v1 = v2;*.

If you want to prevent the compiler from automatically copying an object for you, declare a *private* copy constructor and *operator=* for the object's class, but don't implement either function. Any attempt to copy the object will then result in a compile-time error. Also get into the habit of declaring single-argument constructors as *explicit*, unless you mean to use them as type conversions. This prevents the compiler from generating hidden temporary objects when converting types.

- Preallocate and cache objects.

    A game will typically have a few classes that it allocates and frees frequently, such as weapons or particles. In a C game, you'd typically allocate a big array up front and use them as necessary. With a little planning, you can do the same thing in C++. The idea is that instead of continually constructing and destructing objects, you request new ones and return old ones to a cache. The cache can be implemented as a template, so that it works for any class, provided that the class has a default constructor. Code for a sample cache class template is on the accompanying CD.

    You can either allocate objects to fill the cache as you need them, or preallocate all of the objects up front. If, in addition, you maintain a stack discipline on the objects (meaning that before you delete object *X*, you first delete all objects allocated after *X*), you can allocate the cache in a contiguous block of memory.

## Memory Management

C++ applications generally need to be more aware of the details of memory management than C applications do. In C, all allocations are explicit though *malloc()* and *free()*, while C++ can implicitly allocate memory while constructing temporary objects and member variables. Most C++ games (like most C games) will require their own memory manager.

Because a C++ game is likely to perform many allocations, it must be especially careful about fragmenting the heap. One option is to take one of the traditional approaches: either don't allocate any memory at all after the game starts up, or maintain a large contiguous block of memory that is periodically freed (between levels, for example). On modern machines, such draconian measures are not necessary, if you're willing to be vigilant about your memory usage.

The first step is to override the global *new* and *delete* operators. Use custom implementations of these operators to redirect the game's most common allocations away from *malloc()* and into preallocated blocks of memory. For example, if you find that you have at most 10,000 4-byte allocations outstanding at any one time, you should allocate 40,000 bytes up front and issue blocks out as necessary. To keep track of which blocks are free, maintain a *free list* by pointing each free block to the next free block. On allocation, remove the front block from the list, and on deallocation, add the freed block to the front again. Figure 1.1.1 illustrates how the free list of small blocks might wind its way through a contiguous larger block after a sequence of allocations and frees.

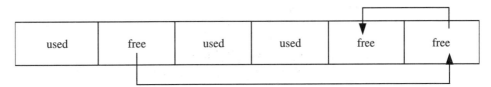

| used | free | used | used | free | free |
|------|------|------|------|------|------|

**FIGURE 1.1.1**   *A linked free list.*

You'll typically find that a game has many small, short-lived allocations, and thus you'll want to reserve space for many small blocks. Reserving many larger blocks wastes a substantial amount of memory for those blocks that are not currently in use; above a certain size, you'll want to pass allocations off to a separate large block allocator, or just to *malloc()*.

## Virtual Functions

Critics of C++ in games often point to virtual functions as a mysterious feature that drains performance. Conceptually, the mechanism is simple. To generate a virtual function call on an object, the compiler accesses the object's virtual function table, retrieves a pointer to the member function, sets up the call, and jumps to the member function's address. This is to be compared with a function call in C, where the compiler sets up the call and jumps to a fixed address. The extra overhead for the virtual function call is the indirection to the virtual function table; because the address of the call isn't known in advance, there can also be a penalty for missing the processor's instruction cache.

Any substantial C++ program will make heavy use of virtual functions, so the idea is to avoid these calls in performance-critical areas. Here is a typical example:

```
class BaseClass
{
public:
    virtual char *GetPointer() = 0;
};

class Class1 : public BaseClass
{
    virtual char *GetPointer();
};

class Class2 : public BaseClass
{
    virtual char *GetPointer();
};

void Function(BaseClass *pObj)
{
    char *ptr = pObj->GetPointer();
    }
```

If *Function()* is performance critical, we want to change the call to *GetPointer* from virtual to inline. One way to do this is to add a new protected data member to *BaseClass*, which is returned by an inline version of *GetPointer()*, and set the data member in each class:

```
class BaseClass
{
public:
    inline char *GetPointerFast()
    {
        return mpPointer;
    }

protected:
    inline void SetPointer(char *pData)
    {
        mpData = pData;
    }

private:
    char *mpData;
```

```
    };

    // class1 and class2 call SetPointer as necessary
    // in member functions

    void Function(BaseClass *pObj)
    {
        char *ptr = pObj->GetPointerFast();
    }
```

A more drastic measure is to rearrange your class hierarchy. If *Class1* and *Class2* have only slight differences, it might be worth combining them into a single class, with a flag indicating whether you want the class to behave like *Class1* or *Class2* at runtime. With this change (and the removal of the pure virtual *BaseClass*), the *GetPointer* function in the previous example can again be made inline. This transformation is far from elegant, but in inner loops on machines with small caches, you'd be willing to do much worse to get rid of a virtual function call.

Although each new virtual function adds only the size of a pointer to a per-class table (usually a negligible cost), the *first* virtual function in a class requires a pointer to the virtual function table on a per-*object* basis. This means that you don't want to have any virtual functions at all in small, frequently used classes where this extra overhead is unacceptable. Because inheritance generally requires the use of one or more virtual functions (a virtual destructor if nothing else), you don't want any hierarchy for small, heavily used objects.

## Code Size

Compilers have a somewhat deserved reputation for generating bloated code for C++. Because memory is limited, and because small is fast, it's important to make your executable as small as possible. The first thing to do is get the compiler on your side. If your compiler stores debugging information in the executable, disable the generation of debugging information. (Note that Microsoft Visual C++ stores debugging information separate from the executable, so this may not be necessary.) Exception handling generates extra code; get rid of as much exception-generating code as possible. Make sure the linker is configured to strip out unused functions and classes. Enable the compiler's highest level of optimization, and try setting it to optimize for size instead of speed—sometimes this actually produces faster code because of better instruction cache coherency. (Be sure to verify that intrinsic functions are still enabled if you use this setting.) Get rid of all of your space-wasting strings in debugging print statements, and have the compiler combine duplicate constant strings into single instances.

Inlining is often the culprit behind suspiciously large functions. Compilers are free to respect or ignore your *inline* keywords, and they may well inline functions without telling you. This is another reason to keep your constructors lightweight, so that objects on the stack don't wind up generating lots of inline code. Also be careful of overloaded operators; a simple expression like *m1* = *m2* * *m3* can generate a ton of inline code if *m2* and *m3* are matrices. Get to know your compiler's settings for inlining functions thoroughly.

Enabling runtime type information (RTTI) requires the compiler to generate some static information for (just about) every class in your program. RTTI is typically enabled so that code can call *dynamic_cast* and determine an object's type. Consider avoiding RTTI and *dynamic_cast* entirely in order to save space (in addition, *dynamic_cast* is quite expensive in some implementations). Instead, when you really need to have different behavior based on type, add a virtual function that behaves differently. This is better object-oriented design anyway. (Note that this doesn't apply to *static_cast*, which is just like a C-style cast in performance.)

## The Standard Template Library

The Standard Template Library (STL) is a set of templates that implement common data structures and algorithms, such as dynamic arrays (called vectors), sets, and maps. Using the STL can save you a great deal of time that you'd otherwise spend writing and debugging these containers yourself. Once again, though, you need to be aware of the details of your STL implementation if you want maximum efficiency.

In order to allow the maximum range of implementations, the STL standard is silent in the area of memory allocation. Each operation on an STL container has certain performance guarantees; for example, insertion into a set takes O(log n) time. However, there are no guarantees on a container's memory usage.

Let's go into detail on a very common problem in game development: you want to store a bunch of objects (we'll call it a list of objects, though we won't necessarily store it in an STL list). Usually you want each object to appear in a list only once, so that you don't have to worry about accidentally inserting the object into the collection if it's already there. An STL set ignores duplicates, has O(log n) insertion, deletion, and lookup—the perfect choice, right?

Maybe. While it's true that most operations on a set are O(log n), this notation hides a potentially large constant. Although the collection's memory usage is implementation dependent, many implementations are based on a red-black tree, where each node of the tree stores an element of the collection. It's common practice to allocate a node of the tree every time an element is inserted, and to free a node every time an element is removed. Depending on how often you insert and remove elements, the time spent in the memory allocator can overshadow any algorithmic savings you gained from using a set.

An alternative solution uses an STL vector to store elements. A vector is guaranteed to have amortized constant-time insertion at the end of the collection. What this means in practice is that a vector typically reallocates memory only on occasion, say, doubling its size whenever it's full. When using a vector to store a list of unique elements, you first check the vector to see if the element is already there, and if it isn't, you add it to the back. Checking the entire vector will take O(n) time, but the constant involved is likely to be small. That's because all of the elements of a vector are typically stored contiguously in memory, so checking the entire vector is a cache-friendly operation. Checking an entire set may well thrash the memory cache, as individual elements of the red-black tree could be scattered all over memory. Also consider that a set must maintain a significant amount of overhead to set up the tree. If all you're storing is object pointers, a set can easily require three to four times the memory of a vector to store the same objects.

Deletion from a set is O(log n), which seems fast until you consider that it probably also involves a call to *free()*. Deletion from a vector is O(n), because everything from the deleted element to the end of the vector must be copied over one position. However, if the elements of the vector are just pointers, the copying can all be done in a single call to *memcpy()*, which is typically very fast. (This is one reason why it's usually preferable to store pointers to objects in STL collections, as opposed to objects themselves. If you store objects directly, many extra constructors get invoked during operations such as deletion.)

If you're still not convinced that sets and maps can often be more trouble than they're worth, consider the cost of iterating over a collection, specifically:

```
for (Collection::iterator it = collection.begin();
    it != collection.end(); ++it)
```

If *Collection* is a vector, then ++*it* is a pointer increment—one machine instruction. But when *Collection* is a set or a map, ++*it* involves traversing to the next node of a red-black tree, a relatively complicated operation that is also much more likely to cause a cache miss, because tree nodes may be scattered all over memory.

Of course, if you're storing a very large number of items in a collection, and doing lots of membership queries, a set's O(log n) performance could very well be worth the memory cost. Similarly, if you're only using the collection infrequently, the performance difference may be irrelevant. You should do performance measurements to determine what values of n make a set faster. You may be surprised to find that vectors outperform sets for all values that your game will typically use.

That's not quite the last word on STL memory usage, however. It's important to know if a collection actually frees its memory when you call the *clear()* method. If not, memory fragmentation can result. For example, if you start a game with an empty vector, add elements to the vector as the game progresses, and then call *clear()* when the player restarts, the vector may not actually free its memory at all. The empty vector's memory could still be taking up space somewhere in the heap, fragmenting it. There are two ways around this problem, if indeed your implementation works this way. First, you can call *reserve()* when the vector is created, reserving enough space for the maximum number of elements that you'll ever need. If that's impractical, you can explicitly force the vector to free its memory this way:

```
vector<int> v;
// ... elements are inserted into v here
vector<int>().swap(v);  // causes v to free its memory
```

Sets, lists, and maps typically don't have this problem, because they allocate and free each element separately.

## Advanced Features

Just because a language has a feature doesn't mean you have to use it. Seemingly simple features can have very poor performance, while other seemingly complicated features can in fact perform well. The darkest corners of C++ are highly compiler dependent—make sure you know the costs before using them.

C++ strings are an example of a feature that sounds great on paper, but should be avoided where performance matters. Consider the following code:

```
void Function(const std::string &str)
{
}

Function("hello");
```

The call to *Function()* invokes a constructor for a string given a *const char \**. In one commercial implementation, this constructor performs a *malloc()*, a *strlen()*, and a *memcpy()*, and the destructor immediately does some nontrivial work (because this implementation's strings are reference counted) followed by a *free()*. The memory that's allocated is basically a waste, because the string "hello" is already in the program's data segment; we've effectively duplicated it in memory. If *Function()* had instead been declared as taking a *const char \**, there would be no overhead to the call. That's a high price to pay for the convenience of manipulating strings.

Templates are an example of the opposite extreme of efficiency. According to the language standard, the compiler generates code for a template when the template is instantiated with a particular type. In theory, it sounds like a single template declaration would lead to massive amounts of nearly identical code. If you have a vector of *Class1* pointers, and a vector of *Class2* pointers, you'll wind up with two copies of *vector* in your executable.

The reality for most compilers is usually better. First, only template member functions that are actually called have any code generated for them. Second, the compiler is allowed to generate only one copy of the code, if correct behavior is preserved. You'll generally find that in the vector example given previously, only a single copy of code (probably for *vector<void \*>*) will be generated. Given a good compiler, templates give you all the convenience of generic programming, while maintaining high performance.

Some features of C++, such as initializer lists and preincrement, generally increase performance, while other features such as overloaded operators and RTTI look equally innocent but carry serious performance penalties. STL collections illustrate how blindly trusting in a function's documented algorithmic running time can lead you astray. Avoid the potentially slow features of the language and libraries, and spend some time becoming familiar with the options in your profiler and compiler. You'll quickly learn to design for speed and hunt down the performance problems in your game.

## Further Investigations

Thanks to Pete Isensee and Christopher Kirmse for reviewing this gem.

Cormen, Thomas, Charles Leiserson, and Ronald Rivest, *Introduction to Algorithms*, Cambridge, Massachusetts, MIT Press, 1990.

Isensee, Peter, C++ Optimization Strategies and Techniques, www.tantalon.com/pete/cppopt/main.htm.

Koenig, Andrew, "Pre- or Postfix Increment," *The C++ Report*, June, 1999.

Meyers, Scott, *Effective C++, Second Edition*, Reading, Massachusetts: Addison-Wesley Publishing Co., 1998.

Sutter, Herb, Guru of the Week #54: Using Vector and Deque, www.gotw.ca/gotw/054.htm.

# Inline Functions Versus Macros

## *Peter Dalton, Evans & Sutherland*

pdalton@xmission.com

When it comes to game programming, the need for fast, efficient functions cannot be overstated, especially functions that are executed multiple times per frame. Many programmers rely heavily on macros when dealing with common, time-critical routines because they eliminate the calling/returning sequence required by functions that are sensitive to the overhead of function calls. However, using the *#define* directive to implement macros that look like functions is more problematic than it is worth.

## Advantages of Inline Functions

Through the use of inline functions, many of the inherent disadvantages of macros can easily be avoided. Take, for example, the following macro definition:

```
#define max(a,b) ((a) > (b) ? (a) : (b))
```

Let's look at what would happen if we called the macro with the following parameters: *max(++x, y)*. If *x = 5* and *y = 3*, the macro will return a value of 7 rather than the expected value of 6. This illustrates the most common side effect of macros, the fact that expressions passed as arguments can be evaluated more than once. To avoid this problem, we could have used an inline function to accomplish the same goal:

```
inline int max(int a, int b) { return (a > b ? a : b); }
```

By using the inline method, we are guaranteed that all parameters will only be evaluated once because they must, by definition, follow all the protocols and type safety enforced on normal functions.

Another problem that plagues macros, operator precedence, follows from the same problem presented previously, illustrated in the following macro:

```
#define square(x) (x*x)
```

If we were to call this macro with the expression *2+1*, it should become obvious that the macro would return a result of *5* instead of the expected *9*. The problem here is that the multiplication operator has a higher precedence than the addition operator has. While wrapping all of the expressions within parentheses would remedy this problem, it could have easily been avoided through the use of inline functions.

The other major pitfall surrounding macros has to deal with multiple-statement macros, and guaranteeing that all statements within the macro are executed properly. Again, let's look at a simple macro used to clamp any given number between zero and one:

```
#define clamp(a)            \
    if (a > 1.0) a = 1.0; \
    if (a < 0.0) a = 0.0;
```

If we were to use the macro within the following loop:

```
for (int ii = 0; ii < N; ++ii)
    clamp( numbersToBeClamped[ii] );
```

the numbers would not be clamped if they were less than zero. Only upon termination of the *for* loop when *ii == N* would the expression *if (numbersToBeClamped[ii] < 0.0)* be evaluated. This is also very problematic, because the index variable *ii* is now out of range and could easily result is a memory bounds violation that could crash the program. While replacing the macro with an inline function to perform the same functionality is not the only solution, it is the cleanest.

Given these inherent disadvantages associated with macros, let's run through the advantages of inline functions:

- Inline functions follow all the protocols of type safety enforced on normal functions. This ensures that unexpected or invalid parameters are not passed as arguments.
- Inline functions are specified using the same syntax as any other function, except for the inline keyword in the function declaration.
- Expressions passed as arguments to inline functions are evaluated prior to entering the function body; thus, expressions are evaluated only once. As shown previously, expressions passed to macros can be evaluated more than once and may result in unsafe and unexpected side effects.
- It is possible to debug inline functions using debuggers such as Microsoft's Visual C++. This is not possible with macros because the macro is expanded before the parser takes over and the program's symbol tables are created.
- Inline functions arguably increase the procedure's readability and maintainability because they use the same syntax as regular function calls, yet do not modify parameters unexpectedly.

Inline functions also outperform ordinary functions by eliminating the overhead of function calls. This includes tasks such as stack-frame setup, parameter passing, stack-frame restoration, and the returning sequence. Besides these key advantages, inline functions also provide the compiler with the ability to perform improved code optimizations. By replacing inline functions with code, the inserted code is subject to additional optimizations that would not otherwise be possible, because most compilers do not perform interprocedural optimizations. Allowing the compiler to perform global optimizations such as common subexpression elimination and loop invariant removal can dramatically improve both speed and size.

The only limitation to inline functions that is not present within macros is the restriction on parameter types. Macros allow for any possible type to be passed as a parameter; however, inline functions only allow for the specified parameter type in order to enforce type safety. We can overcome this limitation through the use of inline template functions, which allow us to accept any parameter type and enforce type safety, yet still provide all the benefits associated with inline functions.

## When to Use Inline Functions

Why don't we make every function an inline function? Wouldn't this eliminate the function overhead for the entire program, resulting in faster fill rates and response times? Obviously, the answer to these questions is *no*. While code expansion can improve speed by eliminating function overhead and allowing for interprocedural compiler optimizations, this is all done at the expense of code size. When examining the performance of a program, two factors need to be weighed: execution speed and the actual code size. Increasing code size takes up more memory, which is a precious commodity, and also bogs down the execution speed. As the memory requirements for a program increase, so does the likelihood of cache misses and page faults. While a cache miss will cause a minor delay, a page fault will always result in a major delay because the virtual memory location is not in physical memory and must be fetched from disk. On a Pentium II 400 MHz desktop machine, a hard page fault will result in an approximately 10 millisecond penalty, or about 4,000,000 CPU cycles [Heller99].

If inline functions are not always a win, then when exactly should we use them? The answer to this question really depends on the situation and thus must rely heavily on the judgment of the programmer. However, here are some guidelines for when inline functions work well:

- Small methods, such as accessors for private data members.
- Functions returning state information about an object.
- Small functions, typically three lines or less.
- Small functions that are called repeatedly; for example, within a time-critical rendering loop.

Longer functions that spend proportionately less time in the calling/returning sequence will benefit less from inlining. However, used correctly, inlining can greatly increase procedure performance.

## When to Use Macros

Despite the problems associated with macros, there are a few circumstances in which they are invaluable. For example, macros can be used to create small pseudo-languages that can be quite powerful. A set of macros can provide the framework that makes creating state machines a breeze, while being very debuggable and bulletproof. For an excellent example of this technique, refer to the "Designing a General Robust AI Engine" article referenced at the end of this gem [Rabin00]. Another example might be printing enumerated types to the screen. For example:

```
#define CaseEnum(a)    case(a) : PrintEnum( #a )
switch (msg_passed_in) {
    CaseEnum( MSG_YouWereHit );
        ReactToHit();
        break;
    CaseEnum( MSG_GameReset );
      ResetGameLogic();
      break;
}
```

Here, *PrintEnum()* is a macro that prints a string to the screen. The # is the stringizing operator that converts macro parameters to string constants [MSDN]. Thus, there is no need to create a look-up table of all enums to strings (which are usually poorly maintained) in order to retrieve invaluable debug information.

The key to avoiding the problems associated with macros is, first, to understand the problems, and, second, to know the alternative implementations.

## Microsoft Specifics

Besides the standard *inline* keyword, Microsoft's Visual C++ compiler provides support for two additional keywords. The *__inline* keyword instructs the compiler to generate a cost/benefit analysis and to only inline the function if it proves beneficial. The *__forceinline* keyword instructs the compiler to always inline the function. Despite using these keywords, there are certain circumstances in which the compiler cannot comply as noted by Microsoft's documentation [MSDN].

## References

[Heller99] Heller, Martin, *Developing Optimized Code with Microsoft Visual C++ 6.0*, Microsoft MSDN Library, January 2000.
[McConnell93] McConnell, Steve, *Code Complete*, Microsoft Press, 1993.
[MSDN] Microsoft Developer Network Library, http://msdn.microsoft.com.
[Myers98] Myers, Scott, *Effective C++, Second Edition*, Addison-Wesley Longman, Inc., 1998.
[Rabin00] Rabin, Steve, "Designing a General Robust AI Engine," *Game Programming Gems*. Charles River Media, 2000; pp. 221–236.

# 1.3

## Programming with Abstract Interfaces

### Noel Llopis, Meyer/Glass Interactive

nllopis@mgigames.com

The concept of abstract interfaces is simple yet powerful. It allows us to completely separate the interface from its implementation. This has some very useful consequences:

- It is easy to switch among different implementations for the code without affecting the rest of the game. This is particularly useful when experimenting with different algorithms, or for changing implementations on different platforms.
- The implementations can be changed at runtime. For example, if the graphics renderer is implemented through an abstract interface, it is possible to choose between a software renderer or a hardware-accelerated one while the game is running.
- The implementation details are completely hidden from the user of the interface. This will result in fewer header files included all over the project, faster recompile times, and fewer times when the whole project needs to be completely recompiled.
- New implementations of existing interfaces can be added to the game effortlessly, and potentially even after it has been compiled and released. This makes it possible to easily extend the game by providing updates or user-defined modifications.

### Abstract Interfaces

In C++, an abstract interface is nothing more than a base class that has only public pure virtual functions. A pure virtual function is a type of virtual member function that has no implementation. Any derived class must implement those functions, or else the compiler prevents instantiaton of that class. Pure virtual functions are indicated by adding = 0 after their declaration.

The following is an example of an abstract interface for a minimal sound system. This interface would be declared in a header file by itself:

```
// In SoundSystem.h
class ISoundSystem {
  public:
```

```
        virtual ~ISoundSystem() {};
        virtual bool PlaySound ( handle hSound ) = 0;
        virtual bool StopSound ( handle hSound ) = 0;
};
```

The abstract interface provides no implementation whatsoever. All it does is define the rules by which the rest of the world may use the sound system. As long as the users of the interface know about *ISoundSystem*, they can use any sound system implementation we provide.

The following header file shows an example of an implementation of the previous interface:

```
// In SoundSystemSoftware.h
#include "SoundSystem.h"

class SoundSystemSoftware : public ISoundSystem {
  public:
    virtual ~SoundSystemSoftware();
    virtual bool PlaySound ( handle hSound );
    virtual bool StopSound ( handle hSound );

    // The rest of the functions in the implementation
};
```

We would obviously need to provide the actual implementation for each of those functions in the corresponding .cpp file.

To use this class, you would have to do the following:

```
ISoundSystem * pSoundSystem = new SoundSystemSoftware();
// Now we're ready to use it
pSoundSystem->PlaySound ( hSound );
```

So, what have we accomplished by creating our sound system in this roundabout way? Almost everything that we promised at the start:

- It is easy to create another implementation of the sound system (maybe a hardware version). All that is needed is to create a new class that inherits from *ISoundSystem*, instantiate it instead of *SoundSystemSoftware()*, and everything else will work the same way without any more changes.
- We can switch between the two classes at runtime. As long as *pSoundSystem* points to a valid object, the rest of the program doesn't know which one it is using, so we can change them at will. Obviously, we have to be careful with specific class restrictions. For example, some classes will keep some state information or require initialization before being used for the first time.
- We have hidden all the implementation details from the user. By implementing the interface we are committed to providing the documented behavior no matter what our implementation is. The code is much cleaner than the equivalent code

full of *if* statements checking for one type of sound system or another. Maintaining the code is also much easier.

## Adding a Factory

There is one detail that we haven't covered yet: we haven't completely hidden the specific implementations from the users. After all, the users are still doing a *new* on the class of the specific implementation they want to use. The problem with this is that they need to *#include* the header file with the declaration of the implementation. Unfortunately, the way C++ was designed, when users *#include* a header file, they can also get a lot of extra information on the implementation details of that class that they should know nothing about. They will see all the private and protected members, and they might even include extra header files that are only used in the implementation of the class.

To make matters worse, the users of the interface now know exactly what type of class their interface pointer points to, and they could be tempted to cast it to its real type to access some "special features" or rely on some implementation-specific behavior. As soon as this happens, we lose many of the benefits we gained by structuring our design into abstract interfaces, so this is something that should be avoided as much as possible.

The solution is to use an abstract factory [Gamma95], which is a class whose sole purpose is to instantiate a specific implementation for an interface when asked for it. The following is an example of a basic factory for our sound system:

```
// In SoundSystemFactory.h
class ISoundSystem;

class SoundSystemFactory {
public:
  enum SoundSystemType {
    SOUND_SOFTWARE,
    SOUND_HARDWARE,
    SOUND_SOMETHINGELSE
  };

  static ISoundSystem * CreateSoundSystem(SoundSystemType type);
};


// In SoundSystemFactory.cpp
#include "SoundSystemSoftware.h"
#include "SoundSystemHardware.h"
#include "SoundSYstemSomethingElse.h"

ISoundSystem * SoundSystemFactory::CreateSoundSystem ( SoundSystemType
  _type )
{
  ISoundSystem * pSystem;
```

```
      switch ( type ) {
        case SOUND_SOFTWARE:
          pSystem = new SoundSystemSoftware();
          break;
        case SOUND_HARDWARE:
          pSystem = new SoundSystemHardware();
          break;
        case SOUND_SOMETHINGELSE:
          pSystem = new SoundSystemSomethingElse();
          break;
        default:
          pSystem = NULL;
      }

      return pSystem;
    }
```

Now we have solved the problem. The user need only include *SoundSystemFactory.h* and *SoundSystem.h*. As a matter of fact, we don't even have to make the rest of the header files available. To use a specific sound system, the user can now write:

```
    ISoundSystem * pSoundSystem;
    pSoundSystem = SoundSystemFactory::CreateSoundSystem
                    (SoundSystemFactory::SOUND_SOFTWARE);
    // Now we're ready to use it
    pSoundSystem->PlaySound ( hSound );
```

*We need to always include a virtual destructor in our abstract interfaces. If we don't, C++ will automatically generate a nonvirtual destructor, which will cause the real destructor of our specific implementation not to be called (and that is usually a hard bug to track down). Unlike normal member functions, we can't just provide a pure virtual destructor, so we need to create an empty function to keep the compiler happy.*

## Abstract Interfaces as Traits

A slightly different way to think of abstract interfaces is to consider an interface as a set of behaviors. If a class implements an interface, that class is making a promise that it will behave in certain ways. For example, the following is an interface used by objects that can be rendered to the screen:

```
    class IRenderable {
      public:
        virtual ~IRenderable() {};
        virtual bool Render () = 0;
    };
```

We can design a class to represent 3D objects that inherits from *IRenderable* and provides its own method to render itself on the screen. Similarly, we could have a terrain class that also inherits from *IRenderable* and provides a completely different rendering method.

```
class Generic3DObject : public IRenderable {
  public:
    virtual ~Generic3DObject();
    virtual bool Render();

    // Rest of the functions here
};
```

The render loop will iterate through all the objects, and if they can be rendered, it calls their *Render()* function. The real power of the interface comes again from hiding the real implementation from the interface: now it is possible to add a completely new type of object, and as long as it presents the *IRenderable* interface, the rendering loop will be able to render it like any other object. Without abstract interfaces, the render loop would have to know about the specific types of object (generic 3D object, terrain, and so on) and decide whether to call their particular render functions. Creating a new type of render-capable object would require changing the render loop along with many other parts of the code.

We can check whether an object inherits from *IRenderable* to know if it can be rendered. Unfortunately, that requires that the compiler's RTTI (Run Time Type Identification) option be turned on when the code is compiled. There is usually a performance and memory cost to have RTTI enabled, so many games have it turned off in their projects. We could use our own custom RTTI, but instead, let's go the way of COM (Microsoft's Component Object Model) and provide a *QueryInterface* function [Rogerson97].

If the object in question implements a particular interface, then *QueryInterface* casts the incoming pointer to the interface and returns *true*. To create our own *QueryInterface* function, we need to have a base class from which all of the related objects that inherit from a set of interfaces derive. We could even make that base class itself an interface like COM's *IUnknown*, but that makes things more complicated.

```
class GameObject {
  public:
    enum GameInterfaceType {
      IRENDERABLE,
      IOTHERINTERFACE
    };

    virtual bool QueryInterface (const GameInterfaceType type,
                                 void ** pObj );
    // The rest of the GameObject declaration
};
```

The implementation of *QueryInterface* for a plain game object would be trivial. Because it's not implementing any interface, it will always return false.

```
bool GameObject::QueryInterface (const GameInterfaceType type,
                                 void ** pObj ) {
   return false;
}
```

The implementation of a 3D object class is different from that of *GameObject*, because it will implement the *IRenderable* interface.

```
class 3DObject : public GameObject, public IRenderable {
  public:
    virtual ~3DObject();
    virtual bool QueryInterface (const GameInterfaceType type,
                                 void ** pObj );
    virtual bool Render();
    // Some more functions if needed
};

bool 3DObject::QueryInterface (const GameInterfaceType type,
                               void ** pObj ) {
  bool bSuccess = false;
  if ( type == GameObject::IRENDERABLE ) {
    *pObj = static_cast<IRenderable *>(this);
    bSuccess = true;
  }
  return bSuccess;
}
```

It is the responsibility of the *3DObject* class to override *QueryInterface,* check for what interfaces it supports, and do the appropriate casting.

Now, let's look at the render loop, which is simple and flexible and knows nothing about the type of objects it is rendering.

```
IRenderable * pRenderable;
for ( all the objects we want to render ) {
  if ( pGameObject->QueryInterface (GameObject::IRENDERABLE,
     (void**)&pRenderable) )
  {
    pRenderable->Render();
  }
}
```

Now we're ready to deliver the last of the promises of abstract interfaces listed at the beginning of this gem: effortlessly adding new implementations. With such a render loop, if we give it new types of objects and some of them implemented the *IRenderable* interface, everything would work as expected without the need to change the render loop. The easiest way to introduce the new object types would be to simply re-link the project with the updated libraries or code that contains the new classes. Although beyond the scope of this gem, we could add new types of objects at runtime through DLLs or an equivalent mechanism available on the target platform. This enhancement would allow us to release new game objects or game updates without the need to patch the executable. Users could also use this method to easily create modifications for our game.

Notice that nothing is stopping us from inheriting from multiple interfaces. All it will mean is that the class that inherits from multiple interfaces is now providing all the services specified by each of the interfaces. For example, we could have an *ICollidable* interface for objects that need to have collision detection done. A 3D object could inherit from both *IRenderable* and *ICollidable*, but a class representing smoke would only inherit from *IRenderable*.

A word of warning, however: while using multiple abstract interfaces is a powerful technique, it can also lead to overly complicated designs that don't provide any advantages over designs with single inheritance. Also, multiple inheritance doesn't work well for dynamic characteristics, and should rather be used for permanent characteristics intrinsic to an object.

Even though many people advise staying away from multiple inheritance, this is a case where it is useful and it does not have any major drawbacks. Inheriting from at most one real parent class and multiple interface functions should not result in the dreaded diamond-shaped inheritance tree (where the parents of both our parents are the same class) or many of the other usual drawbacks of multiple inheritance.

## Everything Has a Cost

So far, we have seen that abstract interfaces have many attractive features. However, all of these features come at a price. Most of the time, the advantages of using abstract interfaces outweigh any potential problems, but it is important to be aware of the drawbacks and limitations of this technique.

First, the design becomes more complex. For someone not used to abstract interfaces, the extra classes and the querying of interfaces could look confusing at first sight. It should only be used where it makes a difference, not indiscriminately all over the game; otherwise, it will only obscure the design and get in the way.

With the abstract interfaces, we did such a good job hiding all of the private implementations that they actually can become harder to debug. If all we have is a variable of type *IRenderable\**, we won't be able to see the private contents of the real object it points to in the debugger's interactive watch window without a lot of tedious casting. On the other hand, most of the time we shouldn't have to worry about it. Because the implementation is well isolated and tested by itself, all we should care about is using the interface correctly.

Another disadvantage is that it is not possible to extend an existing abstract interface through inheritance. Going back to our first example, maybe we would have liked to extend the *SoundSystemHardware* class to add a few functions specific to the game. Unfortunately, we don't have access to the class implementation any more, and we certainly can't inherit from it and extend it. It is still possible either to modify the existing interface or provide a new interface using a derived class, but it will all have to be done from the implementation side, and not from within the game code.

Finally, notice that every single function in an abstract interface is a virtual function. This means that every time one of these functions is called through the abstract interface, the computer will have to go through one extra level of indirection. This is typically not a problem with modern computers and game consoles, as long as we avoid using interfaces for functions that are called from within inner loops. For example, creating an interface with a *DrawPolygon()* or *SetScreenPoint()* function would probably not be a good idea.

## Conclusion

Abstract interfaces are a powerful technique that can be put to good use with very little overhead or structural changes. It is important to know how it can be best used, and when it is better to do things a different way. Perfect candidates for abstract interfaces are modules that can be replaced (graphics renderers, spatial databases, AI behaviors), or any sort of pluggable or user-extendable modules (tool extensions, game behaviors).

## References

[Gamma95] Gamma, Eric et al, *Design Patterns,* Addison-Wesley, 1995.
[Lakos96] Lakos, John, *Large Scale C++ Software Design,* Addison-Wesley, 1996.
[Rogerson97] Rogerson, Dale, *Inside COM.* Microsoft Press, 1997.

# 1.4

## Exporting C++ Classes from DLLs

### Herb Marselas, Ensemble Studios

hmarselas@ensemblestudios.com

**E**xporting a C++ class from a Dynamic Link Library (DLL) for use by another application is an easy way to encapsulate instanced functionality or to share derivable functionality without having to share the source code of the exported class. This method is in some ways similar to Microsoft COM, but is lighter weight, easier to derive from, and provides a simpler interface.

## Exporting a Function

At the most basic level, there is little difference between exporting a function or a class from a DLL. To export *myExportedFunction* from a DLL, the value *_BUILDING_MY_DLL* is defined in the preprocessor options of the DLL project, and not in the projects that use the DLL. This causes *DLLFUNCTION* to be replaced by *__declspec(dllexport)* when building the DLL, and *__declspec(dllimport)* when building the projects that use the DLL.

```
#ifdef _BUILDING_MY_DLL
#define DLLFUNCTION __declspec(dllexport) // defined if building the
                                          // DLL
#else
#define DLLFUNCTION __declspec(dllimport) // defined if building the
                                          // application
#endif

DLLFUNCTION long myExportedFunction(void);
```

## Exporting a Class

Exporting a C++ class from a DLL is slightly more complicated because there are several alternatives. In the simplest case, the class itself is exported. As before, the *DLLFUNCTION* macro is used to declare the class exported by the DLL, or imported by the application.

```
#ifdef _BUILDING_MY_DLL
#define DLLFUNCTION __declspec(dllexport)
#else
#define DLLFUNCTION __declspec(dllimport)
#endif

class DLLFUNCTION CMyExportedClass
{
   public:
      CMyExportedClass(void) : mdwValue(0)  {  }

      void setValue(long dwValue) { mdwValue = dwValue; }
      long getValue(void) { return mdwValue; }
      long clearValue(void);

   private:
      long mdwValue;
};
```

If the DLL containing the class is implicitly linked (in other words, the project links with the DLL's *lib* file), then using the class is as simple as declaring an instance of the class *CMyExportedClass*. This also enables derivation from this class as if it were declared directly in the application. The declaration of a derived class in the application is made normally without any additional declarations.

```
class CMyApplicationClass : public CMyExportedClass
{
   public:
      CMyApplicationClass(void)
      {
      }
   ...
};
```

There is one potential problem with declaring or allocating a class exported from a DLL in an application: it may confuse some memory-tracking programs and cause them to misreport memory allocations or deletions. To fix this problem, helper functions that allocate and destroy instances of the exported class must be added to the DLL. All users of the exported class should call the allocation function to create an instance of it, and the deletion function to destroy it. Of course, the drawback to this is that it prevents deriving from the exported class in the application. If deriving an application-side class from the exported class is important, and the project uses a memory-tracking program, then this program will either need to understand what's going on or be replaced by a new memory-tracking program.

```
#ifdef _BUILDING_MY_DLL
#define DLLFUNCTION __declspec(dllexport)
#else
#define DLLFUNCTION __declspec(dllimport)
#endif

class DLLFUNCTION CMyExportedClass
{
   public:
      CMyExportedClass(void) : mdwValue(0)  {  }

      void setValue(long dwValue) { mdwValue = dwValue; }
      long getValue(void) { return mdwValue; }
      long clearValue(void);

   private:
      long mdwValue;
};

CMyExportedClass *createMyExportedClass(void) {
     return new CMyExportedClass; }
void deleteMyExportedClass(CMyExportedClass *pclass) {
     delete pclass; }
```

## Exporting Class Member Functions

Even with the helper functions added, because the class itself is being exported from
the DLL, it is still possible that users could create instances of the class without calling
the *createMyExportedClass* helper function. This problem is easily solved by moving the
export specification from the class level to the individual functions to which the users
of the class need access. Then the application using the class can no longer create an
instance of the class itself. Instead, it must call the *createMyExportedClass* helper function to create an instance of the class, and *deleteMyExportedClass* when it wishes to
destroy the class.

```
class CMyExportedClass
{
   public:
      CMyExportedClass(void) : mdwValue(0)  {  }

      DLLFUNCTION void setValue(long dwValue) { mdwValue = dwValue; }
      DLLFUNCTION long getValue(void) { return mdwValue; }
      long clearValue(void);

   private:
      long mdwValue;
};

CMyExportedClass *createMyExportedClass(void) {
     return new CMyExportedClass; }
void deleteMyExportedClass(CMyExportedClass *pclass) {
     delete pclass; }
```

It should also be noted that although *CMyExportedClass::clearValue* is a public member function, it can no longer be called by users of the class outside the DLL, as it is not declared as *dllexported*. This can be a powerful tool for a complex class that needs to make some functions publicly accessible to users of the class outside the DLL, yet still needs to have other public functions for use inside the DLL itself. An example of this strategy in practice is the SDK for Discreet's 3D Studio MAX. Most of the classes have a mix of exported and nonexported functions. This allows the user of the SDK to access or derive functionality as needed from the exported member functions, while enabling the developers of the SDK to have their own set of internally available member functions.

## Exporting Virtual Class Member Functions

One potential problem should be noted for users of Microsoft Visual C++ 6. If you are attempting to export the member functions of a class, and you are not linking with the *lib* file of the DLL that exports the class (you're using LoadLibrary to load the DLL at runtime), you will get an "unresolved external symbol" for each function you reference if inline function expansion is disabled. This can happen regardless of whether the function is declared completely in the header.  One fix for this is to change the inline function expansion to "Only __inline" or "Any Suitable." Unfortunately, this may conflict with your desire to actually have inline function expansion disabled in a debug build. An alternate fix is to declare the functions virtual. The virtual declaration will cause the correct code to be generated, regardless of the setting of the inline function expansion option. In many circumstances, you'll likely want to declare exported member functions virtual anyway, so that you can both work around the potential Visual C++ problem and allow the user to override member functions as necessary.

```
class CMyExportedClass
{
   public:
      CMyExportedClass(void) : mdwValue(0)  {  }

      DLLFUNCTION virtual void setValue(long dwValue) { mdwValue =
dwValue; }
      DLLFUNCTION virtual long getValue(void) { return mdwValue; }
      long clearValue(void);

   private:
      long mdwValue;
};
```

With exported virtual member functions, deriving from the exported class on the application side is the same as if the exported class were declared completely in the application itself.

```
class CMyApplicationClass : public CMyExportedClass
{
   public:
      CMyApplicationClass(void)  {  }

      virtual void setValue(long dwValue);
      virtual long getValue(void);
};
```

## Summary

Exporting a class from a DLL is an easy and powerful way to share functionality without sharing source code. It can give the application all the benefits of a structured C++ class to use, derive from, or overload, while allowing the creator of the class to keep internal functions and variables safely hidden away.

# Protect Yourself from DLL Hell and Missing OS Functions

## *Herb Marselas, Ensemble Studios*

**hmarselas@ensemblestudios.com**

**D**ynamic Link Libraries (DLLs) are a powerful feature of Microsoft Windows. They have many uses, including sharing executable code and abstracting out device differences. Unfortunately, relying on DLLs can be problematic due to their standalone nature. If an application relies on a DLL that doesn't exist on the user's computer, attempting to run it will result in a "DLL Not Found" message that's not helpful to the average user. If the DLL does exist on the user's computer, there's no way to tell if the DLL is valid (at least as far as the application is concerned) if it's automatically loaded when the application starts up.

Bad DLL versions can easily find their way onto a system as the user installs and uninstalls other programs. Alternatively, there can even be differences in system DLLs among different Windows platforms and service packs. In these cases, the user may either get the cryptic "DynaLink Error!" message if the function being linked to in the DLL doesn't exist, or worse yet, the application will crash. All of these problems with finding and loading the correct DLL are often referred to as "DLL Hell." Fortunately, there are several ways to protect against falling into this particular hell.

## Implicit vs. Explicit Linking

The first line of defense in protecting against bad DLLs is to make sure that the necessary DLLs exist on the user's computer and are a version with which the application can work. This must be done before attempting to use any of their functionality.

Normally, DLLs are linked to an application by specifying their eponymous *lib* file in the link line. This is known as *implicit DLL loading*, or *implicit linking*. By linking to the *lib* file, the operating system will automatically search for and load the matching DLL when a program runs. This method assumes that the DLL exists, that Windows can find it, and that it's a version with which the program can work.

Microsoft Visual C++ also supports three other methods of implicit linking. First, including a DLL's *lib* file directly into a project is just like adding it on the link line. Second, if a project includes a subproject that builds a DLL, the DLL's *lib* file is automatically linked with the project by default. Finally, a *lib* can be linked to an application using the *#pragma comment ( lib "libname" )* directive.

The remedy to this situation of implicit linking and loading is to explicitly load the DLL. This is done by not linking to the DLL's *lib* file in the link line, and removing any *#pragma comment* directives that would link to a library. If a subproject in Visual C++ builds a DLL, the link property page of the subproject should be changed by checking the "Doesn't produce .LIB" option. By explicitly loading the DLL, the code can handle each error that could occur, making sure the DLL exists, making sure the functions required are present, and so forth.

## LoadLibrary and GetProcAddress

When a DLL is implicitly loaded using a *lib* file, the functions can be called directly in the application's code, and the OS loader does all the work of loading DLLs and resolving function references. When switching to explicit linking, the functions must instead be called indirectly through a manually resolved function pointer. To do this, the DLL that contains the function must be explicitly loaded using the *LoadLibrary* function, and then we can retrieve a pointer to the function using *GetProcAddress*.

```
HMODULE LoadLibrary(LPCTSTR lpFileName);
FARPROC GetProcAddress(HMODULE hModule, LPCSTR lpProcName);
BOOL FreeLibrary(HMODULE hModule);
```

*LoadLibrary* searches for the specified DLL, loads it into the application's process space if it is found, and returns a handle to this new module. *GetProcAddress* is then used to create a function pointer to each function in the DLL that will be used by the game. When an explicitly loaded DLL is no longer needed, it should be freed using *FreeLibrary*. After calling *FreeLibrary*, the module handle is no longer considered valid.

Every *LoadLibrary* call must be matched with a *FreeLibrary* call. This is necessary because Windows increments a reference count on each DLL per process when it is loaded either implicitly by the executable or another DLL, or by calling *LoadLibrary*. This reference count is decremented by calling *FreeLibrary*, or unloading the executable or DLL that loaded this DLL. When the reference count for a given DLL reaches zero, Windows knows it can safely unload the DLL.

## Guarding Against DirectX

One of the problems we have often found is that the required versions of DirectX components are not installed, or the install is corrupt in some way. To protect our game against these problems, we explicitly load the DirectX components we need. If we were to implicitly link to DirectInput in DirectX 8, we would have added the *dinput8.lib* to our link line and used the following code:

```
IDirectInput8 *pDInput;
HRESULT hr = DirectInput8Create(hInstance, DIRECTINPUT_VERSION,
                                IID_IDirectInput8,
                                (LPVOID*) & pDInput, 0);

if (FAILED(hr))
{
   // handle error - initialization error
}
```

The explicit DLL loading case effectively adds two more lines of code, but the application is now protected against *dinput8.dll* not being found, or of it being corrupt in some way.

```
typedef HRESULT (WINAPI* DirectInput8Create_PROC)
                   (HINSTANCE hinst, DWORD dwVersion, REFIID riidltf,
                    LPVOID* ppvOut,
                    LPUNKNOWN punkOuter);

HMODULE hDInputLib = LoadLibrary("dinput8.dll");
if (!hDInputLib)
{
   // handle error - DInput 8 not found. Is it installed incorrectly
   // or at all?
}

DirectInput8Create_PROC diCreate;
diCreate = (DirectInput8Create_PROC)
GetProcAddress(hDInputLib, "DirectInput8Create");

if (!diCreate)
{
   // handle error - DInput 8 exists, but the function can't be
   // found.
}

HRESULT hr = (diCreate)(hInstance, DIRECTINPUT_VERSION,
                        IID_IDirectInput8,
                        (LPVOID*) &mDirectInput, NULL);
if (FAILED(hr))
{
   // handle error - initialization error
}
```

First, a function pointer *typedef* is created that reflects the function *Direct-Input8Create*. The DLL is then loaded using *LoadLibrary*. If the dinput8.dll was loaded successfully, we then attempt to find the function *DirectInput8Create* using *GetProcAddress*. *GetProcAddress* returns a pointer to the function if it is found, or NULL if the function cannot be found. We then check to make sure the function pointer is valid. Finally, we call *DirectInput8Create* through the function pointer to initialize DirectInput.

If there were more functions that needed to be retrieved from the DLL, a function pointer *typedef* and variable would be declared for each. It might be sufficient to only check for NULL when mapping the first function pointer using *GetProcAddress*. However, as more error handling is usually not a bad thing. checking every *GetProcAddress* for a successful non-NULL return is probably a good thing to do.

## Using OS-Specific Features

Another issue that explicit DLL loading can resolve is when an application wants to take advantage of a specific API function if it is available. There is an extensive number of extended functions ending in "Ex" that are supported under Windows NT or 2000, and not available in Windows 95 or 98. These extended functions usually provide more information or additional functionality than the original functions do .

An example of this is the *CopyFileEx* function, which provides the ability to cancel a long file copy operation. Instead of calling it directly, *kernel32.dll* can be loaded using *LoadLibrary* and the function again mapped with *GetProcAddress*. If we load *kernel32.dll* and find *CopyFileEx*, we use it. If we don't find it, we can use the regular *CopyFile* function. One other problem that must be avoided in this case is that *CopyFileEx* is really only a *#define* replacement in the *winbase.h* header file that is replaced with *CopyFileExA* or *CopyFileExW* if compiling for ASCII or wide Unicode characters, respectively.

```
typedef BOOL (WINAPI *CopyFileEx_PROC) (LPCTSTR lpExistingFileName,
  LPCTSTR lpNewFileName, LPPROGRESS_ROUTINE lpProgressRoutine, LPVOID
  lpData, LPBOOL pbCancel, DWORD dwCopyFlags);

HMODULE hKernel32 = LoadLibrary("kernel32.dll");
if (!hKernel32)
{
   // handle error - kernel32.dll not found. Wow! That's really bad
}

CopyFileEx_PROC pfnCopyFileEx;
pfnCopyFileEx = (CopyFileEx_PROC) GetProcAddress(hKernel32,
   "CopyFileExA");

BOOL bReturn;
if (pfnCopyFileEx)
{
   // use CopyFileEx to copy the file
   bReturn = (pfnCopyFileEx)(pExistingFile, pDestinationFile, ...);
}
else
{
   // use the regular CopyFile function
   bReturn = CopyFile(pExistingFile, pDestinationFile, FALSE);
}
```

The use of LoadLibrary and GetProcAddress can also be applied to game DLLs. One example of this is the graphics support in a game engine currently under development at Ensemble Studios, where graphics support for Direct3D and OpenGL has been broken out into separate DLLs that are explicitly loaded as necessary. If Direct3D graphics support is needed, the Direct3D support DLL is loaded with *LoadLibrary* and the exported functions are mapped using *GetProcAddress*. This setup keeps the main executable free from having to link implicitly with either *d3d8.lib* or *opengl32.lib*.

However, the supporting Direct3D DLL links implicitly with *d3d8.lib*, and the supporting OpenGL DLL links implicitly with *opengl32.lib*. This explicit loading of the game's own DLLs by the main executable, and implicit loading by each graphics subsystem solves several problems. First, if an attempt to load either library fails, it's likely that that particular graphics subsystem files cannot be found or are corrupt. The main program can then handle the error gracefully. The other problem that this solves, which is more of an issue with OpenGL than Direct3D, is that if the engine were to link explicitly to OpenGL, it would need a typedef and function pointer for every OpenGL function it used. The implicit linking to the support DLL solves this problem.

## Summary

Explicit linking can act as a barrier against a number of common DLL problems that are encountered under Windows, including missing DLLs, or versions of DLLs that aren't compatible with an application. While not a panacea, it can at least put the application in control and allow any error to be handled gracefully instead of with a cryptic error message or an outright crash.

# 1.6

# Dynamic Type Information

## Scott Wakeling, Virgin Interactive

scott@chronicreality.com

As developers continue to embrace object orientation, the systems that power games are growing increasingly flexible, and inherently more complex. Such systems now regularly contain many different types and classes; counts of over 1000 are not unheard of. Coping with so many different types in a game engine can be a challenge in itself. A type can really mean anything from a class, to a struct, to a standard data type. This gem discusses managing types effectively by providing ways of querying their relations to other types, or accessing information about their type at runtime for query or debug purposes. Toward the end of the gem, an approach for supporting persistent objects is suggested with some ideas about how the method can be extended.

## Introducing the Dynamic Type Information Class

In our efforts to harness the power of our types effectively, we'll be turning to the aid of one class in particular: the dynamic type information (DTI) class. This class will store any information that we may need to know about the type of any given object or structure. A minimal implementation of the class is given here:

```
class dtiClass
{
private:
    char* szName;
    dtiClass* pdtiParent;
public:
    dtiClass();
    dtiClass( char* szSetName, dtiClass* pSetParent );
    virtual ~dtiClass();

    const char* GetName();
    bool SetName( char* szSetName );

    dtiClass* GetParent();
    bool SetParent( dtiClass* pSetParent );
};
```

In order to instill DTI into our engine, all our classes will need a *dtiClass* as a static member. It's this class that allows us to access a class name for debug purposes and query the *dtiClass* member of the class's parent. This member must permeate the class tree all the way from the root class down, thus ensuring that all game objects have access to information about themselves and their parents. The implementation of *dtiClass* can be found in the code on the accompanying CD.

ON THE CD

## Exposing and Querying the DTI

Let's see how we can begin to use DTI by implementing a very simple class tree as described previously. Here is a code snippet showing a macro that helps us define our static *dtiClass* member, a basic root class, and simple initialization of the class's type info:

```
#define EXPOSE_TYPE \
    public: \
        static dtiClass Type;

class CRootClass
{
public:
    EXPOSE_TYPE;
    CRootClass() {};
    virtual ~CRootClass() {};
};

dtiClass CRootClass::Type( "CRootClass", NULL );
```

By including the *EXPOSE_TYPE* macro in all of our class definitions and initializing the static *Type* member correctly as shown, we've taken the first step toward instilling dynamic type info in our game engine. We pass our class name and a pointer to the class's parent's *dtiClass* member. The *dtiClass* constructor does the rest, setting up the *szName* and *pdtiParent* members accordingly.

We can now query for an object's class name at runtime for debug purposes of other type-related cases, such as saving or loading a game. More on that later, but for now, here's a quick line of code that will get us our class name:

```
// Let's see what kind of object this pointer is pointing to
const char* szGetName = pSomePtr->Type.GetName();
```

In the original example, we passed *NULL* in to the *dtiClass* constructor as the class's parent field because this is our root class. For classes that derive from others, we just need to specify the name of the parent class. For example, if we were to specify a child class of our root, a basic definition might look something like this:

```
class CChildClass : public CRootClass
{
    EXPOSE_TYPE;
```

```
    // Constructor and virtual Destructor go here
};

dtiClass CChildClass::Type( "CChildClass", &CRootClass::Type );
```

Now we have something of a class tree growing. We can access not only our class's name, but the name of its parent too, as long as its type has been exposed with the EXPOSE_TYPE macro. Here's a line of code that would get us our parent's name:

```
// Let's see what kind of class this object is derived from
char* szParentName = pSomePtr->Type.GetParent()->GetName();
```

Now that we have a simple class tree with DTI present and know how to use that information to query for class and parent names at runtime, we can move on to implementing a useful method for safeguarding type casts, or simply querying an object about its roots or general type.

## Inheritance Means "IsA"

Object orientation gave us the power of inheritance. With inheritance came polymorphism, the ability for all our objects to be just one of many types at any one time. In many cases, polymorphism is put to use in game programming to handle many types of objects in a safe, dynamic, and effective manner. This means we like to ensure that objects are of compatible types before we cast them, thus preventing undefined behavior. It also means we like to be able to check what type an object conforms to at runtime, rather than having to know from compiler time, and we like to be able to do all of these things quickly and easily.

Imagine that our game involves a number of different types of robots, some purely electronic, and some with mechanical parts, maybe fuel driven. Now assume for instance that there is a certain type of weapon the player may have that is very effective against the purely electronic robots, but less so against their mechanical counterparts. The classes that define these robots are very likely to be of the same basic type, meaning they probably both inherit from the same generic robot base class, and then go on to override certain functionality or add fresh attributes. To cope with varying types of specialist child classes, we need to query their roots. We can extend the *dtiClass* introduced earlier to provide us with such a routine. We'll call the new member function *IsA*, because inheritance can be seen to translate to "is a type of." Here's the function:

```
bool dtiClass::IsA( dtiClass* pType )
{
    dtiClass* pStartType = this;
    while( pStartType )
    {
        if ( pStartType == pType )
        {
```

```
                return true;
            }
            else
            {
                pStartType = pStartType->GetParent();
            }
        }
        return false;
    }
```

If we need to know whether a certain robot subclass is derived from a certain root class, we just need to call *IsA* from the object's own *dtiClass* member, passing in the static *dtiClass* member of the root class. Here's a quick example:

```
CRootClass* pRoot;
CChildClass* pChild = new CChildClass();
if ( pChild->Type.IsA( &CRootClass::Type ) )
{
    pRoot = (CRootClass*)pChild;
}
```

We can see that the result of a quick *IsA* check tells us whether we are derived, directly or indirectly, from a given base class. Of course, we might use this fact to go on and perform a safe casting operation, as in the preceding example. Or, maybe we'll just use the check to filter out certain types of game objects in a given area, given that their type makes them susceptible to a certain weapon or effect. If we decide that a safe casting operation is something we'll need regularly, we can add the following function to the root object to simplify matters. Here's the definition and a quick example; the function's implementation is on the accompanying CD:

*ON THE CD*

```
// SafeCast member function definition added to CRootClass
void* SafeCast( dtiClass* pCastToType );

// How to simplify the above operation
pRoot = (CRootClass*)pChild->SafeCast( &CRootClass::Type );
```

If the cast is not safe (in other words, the types are not related), then the value will evaluate to nothing, and *pRoot* will be *NULL*.

## Handling Generic Objects

Going back to our simple game example, let's consider how we might cope with so many different types of robot effectively. The answer starts off quite simple: we can make use of polymorphism and just store pointers to them all in one big array of generic base class pointers. Even our more specialized robots can be stored here, such as *CRobotMech* (derived from *CRobot*), because polymorphism dictates that for any type requirement, a derived type can always be supplied instead. Now we have our vast array of game objects, all stored as pointers to a given base class. We can iterate over them safely, perhaps calling virtual functions on each and getting the more specialized (overridden) routines carried out by default. This takes us halfway to handling vast numbers of game objects in a fast, safe, and generic way.

As part of our runtime type info solution, we have the *IsA* and *SafeCast* routines that can query what general type an object is, and cast it safely up the class tree. This is often referred to as *up-casting*, and it takes us halfway to handling vast numbers of game objects in a fast, safe, and generic way. The other half of the problem comes with *down-casting*—casting a pointer to a generic base class safely down to a more specialized subclass. If we want to iterate a list of root class pointers, and check whether each *really* points to a specific type of subclass, we need to make use of the dynamic casting operator, introduced by C++.

The dynamic casting operator is used to convert among polymorphic types and is both safe and informative. It even returns applicable feedback about the attempted cast. Here's the form it takes:

```
dynamic_cast< type-id >(expression)
```

The first parameter we must pass in is the type we wish *expression* to conform to *after* the cast has taken place. This can be a pointer or reference to one of our classes. If it's a pointer, the parameter we pass in as *expression* must be a pointer, too. If we pass a reference to a class, we must pass a modifiable l-value in the second parameter. Here are two examples:

```
// Given a root object (RootObj), or pointer (pRoot) we
// can down-cast like this
CChildClass* pChild = dynamic_cast<CChildClass*>(pRoot);
CChildClass& ChildObj = dynamic_cast<CChildClass&>(RootObj);
```

ON THE CD

To gain access to these extended casting operators, we need to enable embedded runtime type information in the compiler settings (use the /GR switch for Microsoft Visual C++). If the requested cast cannot be made (for example, if the root pointer does not *really* point to anything more derived), the operator will simply fail and the expression will evaluate to *NULL*. Therefore, from the preceding code snippet, *pChild* would evaluate to *NULL* if *pRoot* really did only point to a *CRootClass* object. If the cast of *RootObj* failed, an exception would be thrown, which could be contained with a *try/catch* block (example is included on the companion CD-ROM).

The *dynamic_cast* operator lets us determine what type is really hidden behind a pointer. Imagine we want to iterate through every robot in a certain radius and determine which ones are mechanical models, and thus immune to the effects of a certain weapon. Given a list of generic *CRobot* pointers, we could iterate through these and perform dynamic casts on each, checking which ones are successful and which resolve to *NULL*, and thus exacting which ones were in fact mechanical. Finally, we can now safely *down-cast* too, which completes our runtime type information solution. The code on the companion CD-ROM has a more extended example of using the dynamic casting operator.

## Implementing Persistent Type Information

Now that our objects no longer have an identity crisis and we're managing them effectively at runtime, we can move on to consider implementing a persistent object solution, thus extending our type-related capabilities and allowing us to handle things such as game saves or object repositories with ease. The first thing we need is a barebones implementation of a binary store where we can keep our object data. An example implementation, *CdtiBin* can be found on the companion CD-ROM.

There are a number of utility member functions, but the two important points are the *Stream* member function, and the friend << operators that allow us to write out or load the basic data types of the language. We'll need to add an operator for each basic type we want to persist. When *Stream* is called, the data will be either read from the file or written, depending on the values of *m_bLoading* and *m_bSaving*.

To let our classes know how to work with the object repositories we need to add the *Serialize* function, shown here:

```
virtual void Serialize( CdtiBin& ObjStore );
```

Note that it is virtual and needs to be overridden for all child classes that have additional data over their parents. If we add a simple integer member to *CRootClass*, we would write the *Serialize* function like this:

```
void CRootClass::Serialize( CdtiBin& ObjStore )
{
    ObjStore << iMemberInt;
}
```

We would have to be sure to provide the friend operator for integers and *CdtiBin* objects. We could write object settings out to a file, and later load them back in and repopulate fresh objects with the old data, thus ensuring a persistent object solution for use in a game save routine. All types would thus know how to save themselves, making our game save routines much easier to implement.

However, child classes need to write out their data *and* that of their parents. Instead of forcing the programmer to look up all data passed down from parents and adding it to each class's *Serialize* member, we need to give each class access to its parent's *Serialize* routine. This allows child classes to write (or load) their inherited data before their own data. We use the *DECLARE_SUPER* macro for this:

```
#define DECLARE_SUPER(SuperClass) \
    public: \
        typedef SuperClass Super;
```

```
class CChildClass
{
    DECLARE_SUPER(CRootClass);
    // ...
}
```

This further extends our type solution by allowing our classes to call their immediate parents' versions of functions, making our class trees more extensible.

*CRootClass* doesn't need to declare its superclass because it doesn't have one, and thus its *Serialize* member only needs to cope with its own data. Here's how *CChildClass::Serialize* calls *CRootClass::Serialize* before dealing with some of its own data (added specifically for the example):

```
void CChildClass::Serialize( CdtiBin& ObjStore )
{
    Super::Serialize( ObjStore );

    ObjStore << fMemberFloat << iAnotherInt;
}
```

ON THE CD

A friend operator for the *float* data type was added to support the above. Note that the order in which attributes are saved and loaded is always the same. Code showing how to create a binary store, write a couple of objects out, and then repopulate the objects' attributes can be found on the companion CD-ROM.

As long as object types are serialized in the same order both ways, their attributes will remain persistent between saves and loads. Adding the correct friend operators to the *CdtiBin* class adds support for basic data types. If we want to add user-defined structures to our class members, we just need to write an operator for coping with that struct. With this in place, all objects and types in the engine will know precisely how to save themselves out to a binary store and read themselves back in.

## Applying Persistent Type Information to a Game Save Database

As mentioned previously, objects need to be serialized out and loaded back in the same order. The quickest and easiest method is to only save out one object to the game saves, and then just load that one back in. If we can define any point in the game by constructing some kind of game state object that knows precisely how to serialize itself either way, then we can write all our game data out in one hit, and read it back in at any point. Our game state object would no doubt contain arrays of objects. As long as the custom array type knows how to serialize itself, and we have all the correct *CdtiBin* operators written for our types, everything will work. Saving and loading a game will be a simple matter of managing the game from a high-level, all-encompassing containment class, calling just the one *Serialize* routine when needed.

## Conclusion

There is still more that could be done than just the solution described here. Supporting multiple inheritance wouldn't be difficult. Instead of storing just the one parent pointer in our static *dtiClass*, we would store an array of as many parents a class had, specifying the count and a variable number of type classes in a suitable macro, or by extending the *dtiClass* constructor. An object flagging system would also be useful, and would allow us to enforce special cases such as abstract base classes or objects we only ever wanted to be contained in other classes, and never by themselves ("contained classes").

## References

[Meyers98] Meyers, Scott D., *Effective C++ 2nd Edition,* Addison-Wesley, 1998.

[Wilkie94] Wilkie, George, *Object-Oriented Software Engineering,* Addison-Wesley, 1994.

[Eberly00] Eberly, David H., *3D Game Engine Design,* Morgan Kauffman, 1999–2000.

[Wakeling01] Wakeling, Scott J., *"Coping with Class Trees,"* available online at www.chronicreality.com/articles, March 12, 2001.

# 1.7

# A Property Class for Generic C++ Member Access

## Charles Cafrelli

skywise@iquest.net

Practically every game has a unique set of game objects, and any code that has to manipulate those objects has to be written from scratch for each project. Take, for example, an in-game editor, which has a simple purpose: to create, place, display, and edit object properties. Object creation is almost always specific to the game, or can be handled by a class factory. Object placement is specific to the visualization engine, which makes reuse difficult, assuming it is even possible to visually place an object on the map. In some cases, a generic map editor that can be toggled on and off (or possibly superimposed as a heads-up display) can be reused from game to game. Therefore, in theory, it should be possible to develop a core editor module that can be reused without having to rewrite the same code over and over again for each project. However, given that all games have unique objects, how does the editor know what to display for editing purposes without rewriting the editor code?

What we need is a general object interface that allows access to the internals of a class. Borland's C++ Builder provides an excellent C++ declaration type called a *property* that does this very thing, but alas, it is a proprietary extension and unusable outside of Borland C++. Interestingly enough, C#, Microsoft's new programming language developed by the creator of Borland C++ Builder, contains the same feature. Microsoft's COM interface allows runtime querying of an object for its members, but it requires that we bind our objects to the COM interface, making them less portable than straight C++. This leaves a "roll-your-own" solution, which can be more lightweight than COM, and more portable than proprietary extensions to the C++ language. This will allow code modules such as the in-game editor to be written just once, and used across many engines.

## The Code

ON THE CD

The interface is broken into two classes: a *Property* class and a *PropertySet* class. *Property* is a container for one piece of data. It contains a union of pointers to different data types, an enumeration for the type of data, and a string for the property name. The full source code can be found on the companion CD.

```cpp
class Property
{
protected:
    union Data
    {
        int* m_int;
        float* m_float;
        std::string* m_string;
        bool* m_bool;
    };

    enum Type
    {
        INT,
        FLOAT,
        STRING,
        BOOL,
        EMPTY
    };

    Data  m_data;
    Type  m_type;
    std::string m_name;

protected:
    void EraseType();
    void Register(int* value);
    void Register(float* value);
    void Register(std::string* new_string);
    void Register(bool* value);

public:
    Property();
    Property(std::string const& name);
    Property(std::string const& name, int* value);
    Property(std::string const& name, float* value);
    Property(std::string const& name, std::string* value);
    Property(std::string const& name, bool* value);
    ~Property();

    bool SetUnknownValue(std::string const& value);
    bool Set(int value);
    bool Set(float value);
    bool Set(std::string const& value);
    bool Set(bool value);

    void SetName(std::string const& name);
    std::string GetName() const;

    int GetInt();
    float GetFloat();
    std::string GetString();
    bool GetBool();
};
```

The example code shows basic data types being used and stored, although these could be easily expanded to handle any data type. Properties store only a pointer back to the original data. Properties do not actually declare their own objects, or allocate their own memory, so manipulating a property's data results in the original data's memory being handled. Setting a value via the *Set* function automatically defines the type of the property.

Properties are constructed and manipulated through a *PropertySet* class. The *PropertySet* class contains the list of registered properties, the registration methods, and the lookup method.

```cpp
class PropertySet
{
protected:
    HashTable<Property>m_properties;

public:
    PropertySet();
    virtual ~PropertySet();

    void Register(std::string const& name, int* value);
    void Register(std::string const& name, float* value);
    void Register(std::string const& name, std::string* value);
    void Register(std::string const& name, bool* value);

    // look up a property
    Property* Lookup(std::string const& name);

    // get a list of available properties
    bool SetValue(std::string const& name, std::string* value);
    bool Set(std::string const& name, std::string const& value);
    bool Set(std::string const& name, int value);
    bool Set(std::string const& name, float value);
    bool Set(std::string const& name, bool value);
    bool Set(std::string const& name, char* value);
};
```

The *PropertySet* is organized around a *HashTable* object that organizes all of the stored properties using a standard hash table algorithm. The *HashTable* itself is a template that can be used to hash into different objects, and is included on the companion CD.

We derive the game object from the *PropertySet* class:

```cpp
class GameObject : public PropertySet
{
    int m_test;
};
```

Any properties or flags that need to be publicly exposed or used by other objects should be registered, usually at construction time. For example:

```cpp
Register("test_value",&m_test);
```

Calling objects can use the *Lookup* method to access the registered data.

```
void Update(PropertySet& property_set)
{
    Property* test_value_property=
      property_set.Lookup("test_value");
    int test_value = test_value_property->GetInt();
    // etc
}
```

As all of the game objects are now of type *PropertySet*, and as all objects are usually stored in a master update list, it is a simple matter of handing the list pointer off to the in-game editor for processing. New derived object types simply have to register their additional properties to be handled by the editor. No additional coding is necessary because the editor is not concerned with the derived types. It is sometimes helpful to specify the type in a property name (such as "Type") to assist the user when visually editing the object. It's also useful to make the property required, so that the editor could, for example, parse the property list into a "tree" style display.

This process also provides the additional benefit of decoupling the data from its name. For instance, internally, the data may be referred to as *m_colour*, but can be exposed as "color."

## Additional Uses

These classes were designed around a concentric ring design theory. The *PropertySet* cannot be used without the *Property* class. However, the *Property* class can be used on its own, or with another set type (for example, *MultiMatrixedPropertySet*) without rewriting the *Property* class itself. This is true of the *HashTable* inside the *PropertySet* class as well. Smaller classes with distinct and well-defined purposes and uses are much more reusable than large classes with many methods to handle every possible use.

The *Property* class can also be used to publicly expose methods that can be called from outside code via function pointers. With a small amount of additional coding, this can also be used as a save state for a save game feature as well. It could also be used for object messaging via networks. With the addition of a *Send(std::string xml)* and *Receive(std::string xml)*, the *PropertySet* could easily encode and decode XML messages that contain the property values, or property values that need to be changed. The *Property/PropertySet* classes could also be rewritten as templates to support different property types.

Isolating the property data using "get" and "set" methods will allow for format conversion to and from the internal stored format. This will free the using code from needing to know anything about the data type of the property, making it more versatile at the cost of a small speed hit when the types differ.

## Additional Reading

Fowler, Martin, Kent Beck, John Brant, William Opdyke, Don Roberts, *Refactoring*, Addison-Wesley, ISBN: 0201485672.

Gamma, Erich, Richard Helm, Ralph Johnson, John Vlissides, Grady Booch, *Design Patterns*, Addison-Wesley, ISBN: 0201633612.

Lakos, John, *Large-Scale C++ Software Design*, Addison-Wesley, ISBN: 0201633620.

McConnell, Steve C., *Code Complete: A Practical Handbook of Software Construction*, Microsoft Press, ISBN: 1556154844 (anything by McConnell is good).

Meyers, Scott, *Effective C++: 50 Specific Ways to Improve Your Programs and Design (2nd Edition)*, Addison-Wesley, ISBN: 0201924889.

Meyers, Scott, *More Effective C++: 35 New Ways to Improve Your Programs and Designs*, Addison-Wesley, ISBN: 020163371X.

# 1.8

# A Game Entity Factory

## François Dominic Laramée

francoislaramee@videotron.ca

In recent years, scripting languages have proven invaluable to the game development community. By isolating the elaboration and refinement of game entity behavior from the core of the code base, they have liberated level designers from the code-compile-execute cycle, speeding up game testing and tweaking by orders of magnitude, and freed senior programmers' time for more intricate assignments.

However, for the data-driven development paradigm to work well, the game's engine must provide flexible entity construction and assembly services, so that the scripting language can provide individual entities with different operational strategies, reaction behaviors, and other parameters. This is the purpose of this gem: to describe a hierarchy of C++ classes and a set of techniques that support data-driven development on the engine side of things.

This simple framework was designed with the following goals in mind:

- **A separation of logical behavior and audio-visual behavior.** A single *Door* class can support however many variations of the concept as required, without concern for size, number of key frames in animation sequences, etc.
- **Rapid development.** Once a basic library of behaviors has been defined (which takes surprisingly little time), new game entity classes can be added to the framework with a minimum of new code, often in 15 minutes or less.
- **Avoiding code duplication.** By assembling bits and pieces of behavior into new entities at runtime, the framework avoids the "code bloat" associated with scripting languages that compile to C/C++, for example.

Several of the techniques in this gem are described in terms of patterns, detailed in the so-called "Gang of Four's" book *Design Patterns* [GoF94].

## Components

The gem is built around three major components: flyweight objects, behavioral classes and an object factory method. We will examine each in turn, and then look at how they work together to equip the engine with the services required by data-driven development. Finally, we will discuss advanced ideas to make the system even more flexible (at the cost of some code complexity) if a full-fledged scripting language is required by the project.

## Flyweight, Behavior, and Exported Classes

Before we go any further, we must make a distinction between the three types of "classes" to which a game entity will belong in this framework: its flyweight, behavioral, and exported classes.

- The *flyweight class* is the look and feel of the entity. In the code, the relationship between an entity and its flyweight class is implemented through object composition: the entity owns a pointer to a flyweight that it uses to represent itself audio-visually.
- The *behavioral class* defines how the object interacts with the rest of the game world. Behavioral classes are implemented as a traditional inheritance hierarchy, with class Entity serving as abstract superclass for all others.
- The *exported class* is how the object represents itself to the world. More of a convenience than a requirement, the exported class is implemented as an enum constant and allows an entity to advertise itself as several different object classes during its lifetime.

Let us now look at each in turn.

## Flyweight Objects

[GoF94] describes flyweights as objects deprived of their context so that they can be shared and used in a variety of situations simultaneously; in other words, as a template or model for other objects. For a game entity, the flyweight-friendly information consists of:

- **Media content**: Sound effects, 3D models, textures, animation files, etc.
- **Control structure**: Finite state machine definition, scripts, and the like.

As you can see, this is just about everything except information on the current status of the entity (position, health, FSM state). Therefore, in a gaming context, the term *flyweight* is rather unfortunate, because the flyweight can consume megabytes of memory, while the context information would be small enough to fit within a crippled toaster's core memory.

## SAMMy, Where Are You?

Much of a game entity's finite state machine deals with animation loops, deciding when to play a sound byte, and so forth. For example, after the player character is killed in an arcade game, it may enter the *resurrecting* state and be flagged as invulnerable while the "resurrection" animation plays out; otherwise, an overeager monster might hover about and score another kill during every frame of animation until the player resumes control over it. I call the part of the flyweight object that deals with this the *State And Media Manager*, or SAMMy for short:

```
class StateAndMediaManager
{
  // The various animation sequences available for the family
  // of entities
  AnimSequenceDescriptionStruct * sequences;
  int numAnimSequences;

  // A table of animation sequences to fire up when the entity's FSM
  // changes states out of SAMMy's control
  int * stateToAnimTransitions;
  int numStateToAnimTransitions;

public:
  // Construction and destruction
  // StateAndMediaManager is always constructed by its owner entity,
  // which is in charge of opening its description file. Therefore,
  // the only parameter the constructor needs is a reference to an
  // input stream from which to read a set of animation sequence
  // descriptions.
  StateAndMediaManager() : sequences( 0 ), numAnimSequences( 0 ),
    numStateToAnimTransitions( 0 ), stateToAnimTransitions( 0 ) {}
  StateAndMediaManager( istream & is );
  virtual ~StateAndMediaManager();
  void Cleanup();

  // Input-output functions
  void Load( istream & is );
  void Save( ostream & os );

  // Look at an entity's current situation and update it according
  // to the description of its animation sequences
  void FC UpdateEntityState( EntityStateStruct * state );

  // If the entity's FSM has just forced a change of state, the media
  // manager must follow suit, interrupt its current animation
  // sequence and choose a new one suitable to the new FSM state
  void FC AlignWithNewFSMState( EntityStateStruct * state );
};
```

ON THE CD

Typically, SAMMy is the product of an entity-crafting tool, and it is loaded into the engine from a file when needed. The sample on the companion CD-ROM is built into a text file for simplicity.

SAMMy can be made as powerful and versatile as desired. In theory, SAMMy could take care of all control functions: launching scripts, changing strategies, and so forth. However, this would be very awkward and require enormous effort; we will instead choose to delegate most of the high-level control structure to the behavioral class hierarchy, which can take care of it with a minute amount of code. (As a side effect of this sharing of duties, a single behavioral class like `SecurityGuard`, `Door` or `ExplosionFX` will be able to handle entities based on multiple related flyweights, making the system more flexible.)

## Behavioral Class Hierarchy

These are the actual C++ classes to which our entities will belong. The hierarchy has (at least) two levels:

- An abstract base class Entity that defines the interface and commonalities
- Concrete subclasses that derive from Entity and implement actual objects

Here is a look at Entity's interface:

```cpp
class Entity
{
  // Some application-specific data

  // Flyweight and Exported Class information
  int exportedClassID;
  StateAndMediaManager * sammy;

public:
  // Constructors
  ...

  // Accessors
  int GetExportedClass() { return exportedClassID; }
  StateAndMediaManager * GetFlyweight() { return sammy; }
  void SetExportedClass( int newval ) { exportedClassID = newval; }
  void SetFlyweight( StateAndMediaManager * ns ) { sammy = ns; }

  // Factory method
  static Entity * EntityFactory( int exportedClassRequested );

  virtual Entity * CloneEntity() = 0;
  virtual bool Updateself()
  {
    // Do generic stuff here; looping through animations, etc.
    return true;
  }

  virtual bool HandleInteractions( Entity * target ) = 0;
};
```

As you can see, adding a new class to the hierarchy may require very little work: in addition to constructors, at most three, and possibly only two, of the base class methods must be overridden—and one of them is a one-liner.

- `Clone()` is a simple redirection call to the copy constructor.
- `UpdateSelf()` runs the entity's internal mechanics. For some, this may be as simple as calling the corresponding method in SAMMy to update the current animation frame; for others, like the player character, it can be far more elaborate.

- HandleInteractions() is called when the entity is supposed to determine whether it should change its internal state in accordance to the behaviors and positions of other objects. The default implementation is empty; in other words, the object is inert window-dressing.

The companion CD-ROM contains examples of Entity subclasses, including one of a player character driver.

## Using the Template Method Pattern for Behavior Assignment

If your game features several related behavioral classes whose differences are easy to circumscribe, you may be able to benefit from a technique known as the Template Method pattern [GoF94]. This consists of a base class method that defines an algorithm in terms of subclass methods it calls through polymorphism.

For example, all types of PlayerEntity objects will need to query an input device and move themselves as part of their UpdateSelf() method, but how they do it may depend on the input device being used, the character type (a FleetingRogue walks faster than a OneLeggedBuddha), and so forth. Therefore, the PlayerEntity class may define UpdateSelf() in terms of pure virtual methods implemented only in its subclasses.

```
class PlayerDevice : public Entity
{
  // ...
  void UpdateYourself();
  void QueryInputDevice() = 0;  // No implementation in PlayerDevice
};

class JoystickPlayerDevice : public PlayerDevice
{
  // ...
  void QueryInputDevice();
};

void PlayerDevice::UpdateYourself()
{
  // do stuff common to all types of player devices
  QueryInputDevice();

  // do more stuff
}

void JoystickPlayerDevice::QueryInputDevice()
{
  // Do the actual work
}
```

Used properly, the Template Method pattern can help minimize the need for the dreaded *cut-and-paste programming*, one of the most powerful "anti-patterns" leading to disaster in software engineering [Brown98]!

## Exported Classes

The exported class is a convenience trick that you can use to make your entities' internal state information transparent to the script writer. For example, let's say that you are programming Pac-Man's `HandleInteractions()` method. You might start by looking for a collision with one of the ghosts; what happens if one is found then depends on whether the ghost is afraid (it gets eaten), returning to base after being eaten (nothing happens at all), or hunting (Pac-Man dies).

```
void PacMan::HandleInteractions( Entity * target )
{
  if ( target->GetClass() == GHOST && target->GetState() == AFRAID )
  {
    score += 100;
    target->SendKillSignal();
  }
}
```

However, what if you need to add states to the Ghost object? For example, you may want the ghost's SAMMy to include a "Getting Scared" animation loop, which is active for one second once Pac-Man has run over a power pill. SAMMy would handle this cleanly if you added a GettingScared state. However, you would now need to add a test for the GettingScared state to the event handler.

```
void PacMan::HandleInteractions( Entity * target )
{
  if ( target->GetClass() == GHOST &&
      ( target->GetState() == AFRAID ||
        target->GetState() == GETTINGSCARED ) )
  {
    ...
  }
}
```

This is awkward, and would likely result in any number of updates to the event handlers as you add states (none of which introduce anything new from the outside world's perspective) to SAMMy during production. Instead, let's introduce the concept of the *exported class*, a value that can be queried from an `Entity` object and describes how it advertises itself to the world. The value is maintained within `Update-Self()` and can take any number of forms; for simplicity's sake, let's pick an integer constant selected from an enum list.

```
enum { SCAREDGHOST, ACTIVEGHOST, DEADGHOST };
```

There is no need to export any information on transient, animation-related states like GettingScared. To Pac-Man, a ghost can be dead, active, or scared—period. Whether it has just become scared two frames ago, has been completely terrified for a while, or is slowly gathering its wits back around itself is irrelevant. By using an exported class instead of an actual internal FSM state, a `Ghost` object can advertise

itself as a dead ghost, scared ghost, or active ghost, effectively shape-shifting into three
different entity classes at will from the outside world's perspective, all for the cost of
an integer. Pac-Man's interaction handler would now look like this:

```
void PacMan::HandleInteractions( Entity * target )
{
  if ( target->GetExportedClass() == SCAREDGHOST )
  {
    score += 100;
    target->SendKillSignal();
  }
}
```

The result is cleaner and will require far less maintenance work, as the number of
possible exported classes for an Entity is usually small and easy to determine early on,
while SAMMy's FSM can grow organically as new looks and effects are added to the
object during development.

## The Entity Factory

Now that we have all of these tools, it is time to put them to good use in object creation.

A level file will contain several entity declarations, each of which may identify the
entity's behavioral class, flyweight class, exported class, starting position and velocity,
and any number of class-specific parameters (for example, hit points for monsters, a
starting timer for a bomb, a capacity for the player's inventory, etc.)  To keep things
simpler for us and for the level designer, let's make the fairly safe assumption that,
while a behavioral class may advertise itself as any number of exported classes, an
exported class can only be attached to a single behavioral class. This way, we eliminate
the need to specify the behavioral class in the level file, and isolate the class hierarchy
from the tools and level designers. A snippet from a level file could therefore look like:

```
<ENTITY Blinky>
<EXPORTEDCLASS ActiveGhost>
<XYZ_POSITION ...>
<PARAMETERS ...>
</ENTITY>
```

Now, let's add a *factory method* to the Entity class.

A factory is a function whose job consists of constructing instances of any number of classes of objects on demand; in our case, the factory will handle requests for all
(concrete) members of the behavioral class hierarchy. Programmatically, our factory
method is very simple:

- It owns a registry that describes the flyweights that have already been loaded into
  the game and a list of the exported classes that belong to each behavioral class.
- It loads flyweights when needed. If a request for an instance belonging to a flyweight class that hasn't been seen yet is received, the first order of business is to
  create and load a SAMMy object for this flyweight.

• If the request is for an additional instance of an already-loaded flyweight class, the factory will clone the existing object (which now serves as a *Prototype*; yes, another Gang of Four pattern!) so that it and its new brother can share flyweights effectively.

Here is a snippet from the method:

```
Entity * Entity::EntityFactory( int whichType )
{
  Entity * ptr;
  switch( whichType )
  {
    case SCAREDGHOST:
        ptr = new Ghost( SCAREDGHOST );
        break;

    case ACTIVEGHOST:
        ptr = new Ghost( ACTIVEGHOST );
        break;

    // ...
  }
  return ptr;
}
```

Simple, right? Calling the method with an exported class as parameter returns a pointer to an Entity subclass of the appropriate behavioral family.

```
Entity * newEntity = Entity::EntityFactory( ACTIVEGHOST );
```

ON THE CD

The code located on the companion CD-ROM also implements a simple trick used to load levels from standard text files: an entity's constructor receives the level file as an istream parameter, and it can read its own class-specific parameters directly from it. The factory method therefore does not need to know anything about the internals of the subclasses it is responsible for creating.

## Selecting Strategies at Runtime

The techniques described so far work fine when a game contains a small number of behavioral classes, or when entity actions are easy enough to define without scripts. However, what if extensive tweaking and experimentation with scripts is required? What if you need a way to change an entity's strategy at runtime, without necessarily influencing its behavioral classmates? This is where the *Strategy* pattern comes into play. (It's the last one, I promise. I think.)

Let's assume that your script compiler produces C code. What you need is a way to connect the C function created by the compiler with your behavioral class (or individual entity). This is where function pointers come into play.

### Using Function Pointers within C++ Classes

The simplest and best way to plug a method into a class at runtime is through a function pointer. A quick refresher: A C/C++ function pointer is a variable containing a memory address, just like any other pointer, except that the object being pointed to is a typed function defined by a nameless signature (in other words, a return type and a parameter list). Here is an example of a declaration of a pointer to a function taking two Entity objects and returning a Boolean value:

```
bool (*interactPtr) (Entity * source, Entity * target);
```

Assuming that there is a function with the appropriate signature in the code, for example:

```
bool TypicalRabbitInteractions( Entity * source, Entity * target )
{
  ...
}
```

then the variable `interactPtr` can be assigned to it, and the function called by dereferencing the pointer, so that the following snippets are equivalent:

```
Ok = TypicalRabbitInteractions( BasilTheBunny, BigBadWolf );
```

and

```
interactPtr = TypicalRabbitInteractions;
Ok = (*interactPtr) ( BasilTheBunny, BigBadWolf );
```

Using function pointers inside classes is a little trickier, but not by much. The key idea is to declare the function generated by the script compiler to be a `friend` of the class, so that it can access its private data members, and to pass it the special pointer `this`, which represents the current object, as its first parameter.

```
class SomeEntity : public Entity
  {
  // The function pointer
    void ( * friendptr )( Entity * me, Entity * target );

public:
  // Declare one or more strategy functions as friends
  friend void Strategy1( Entity * me, Entity * target );
  ...

  // The actual operation
  void HandleInteractions( Entity * target )
  {
    (*friendptr) ( this, target );
  }
};
```

Basically, this is equivalent to doing by hand what the C++ compiler does for you when calling class methods: the C++ vtable secretly adds "this" as a first parameter to every method. Because any modern compiler will inline the function calls, there should be no performance differential between calling a compiled script with this scheme and calling a regular method.

Note that picking and choosing strategies at runtime through function pointers is also a good way to reduce the number of behavioral classes in the hierarchy. In extreme cases, a single `Entity` class containing nothing but function pointer dereferences for strategy elements may even be able to replace the entire hierarchy. This, however, runs the risk of obfuscating the code to a point of total opacity—proceed with caution.

Finally, if an entity is allowed to switch back and forth between several alternative strategies depending on runtime considerations, this scheme allows each change to be implemented through a simple pointer assignment: clean, fast, no hassles.

## Final Notes

In simple cases, the techniques described in this gem can even provide a satisfactory alternative to scripting altogether. Smaller projects that do not require the full power of a scripting language and/or cannot afford the costs associated with it may be able to get by with a set of hard-coded strategy snippets, a simple GUI-based SAMMy editor, and a linear level-description file format containing key-value tuples for the behaviors attached to each entity.

```
<EntityName BasilTheBunny>
<ExportedClass Rabbit>
<StrategyVsEntity BigBadWolf Avoid>
<HandleCollision BigBadWolf Die>
...
```

ON THE CD

The companion CD-ROM contains several component classes and examples of the techniques described in this gem. You will, however, have to make significant modifications to them (for example, add your own 3D models to SAMMy) to turn them into something useful in your own projects.

Finally, the text file formats used to load SAMMy and other objects in the code are assumed to be the output of a script compiler, level editor, or other associated tools. As such, they have a rather inflexible structure and are not particularly human friendly. If they seem like gibberish to you, gentle readers, please take a moment to commiserate with the poor author who had to write and edit them by hand. ;-)

## References

[Brown98] Brown, W.H., Malveau, R.C., McCormick III, H.W., Mowbray, T.J., *Anti Patterns: Refactoring Software, Architectures and Projects in Crisis*, Wiley Computer Publishing, 1998.

[GoF94] Gamma, E., Helm, R., Johnson, R., & Vlissides, J. (1994), *Design Patterns: Elements of Reusable Object–Oriented Software*, Addison-Wesley, 1994.

[Rising98] Rising, L. ed., *The Patterns Handbook: Techniques, Strategies and Applications*, Cambridge University Press, 1998.

# Adding Deprecation Facilities to C++

## *Noel Llopis, Meyer/Glass Interactive*

nllopis@mgigames.com

During the lifetime of a piece of software, function interfaces are bound to change, become outdated, or be completely replaced by new ones. This is especially true for libraries and engines that are reused across multiple projects or over several years. When a function that interfaces to the rest of the project changes, the game (or tools, or both!) may not compile any more. On a team working on a large project, the situation is even worse because many people could be breaking interfaces much more often.

## Possible Solutions

There are different ways of dealing with this situation:

- **Don't do anything about it.** Every time something changes, everybody has to update the code that calls the changed functions before work can proceed. This might be fine for a one-person team, but it's normally unacceptable for larger teams.
- **Don't change any interface functions.** This is not usually possible, especially in the game industry where things change so quickly. Maybe the hardware changed, maybe the publisher wants something new, or perhaps the initial interface was just flawed. Trying to stick to this approach usually causes more harm than good, and ends up resulting in functions or classes with names completely unrelated to what they really do, and completely overloaded semantics.
- **Create new interface versions.** This approach sticks to the idea that an interface will never change; instead, a new interface will be created addressing all the issues. Both the original and the new interface will remain in the project. This is what DirectX does with each new version. This approach might be fine for complete changes in interface, or for infrequent updates, but it won't work well for frequent or minor updates. In addition, this approach usually requires maintaining the full implementation of the current interface and a number of the older interfaces, which can be a nightmare.

In modern game development, these solutions are clearly not ideal. We need something else to deal with this problem.

## The Ideal Solution

What we really want is to be able to write a new interface function, but keep the old interface function around for a while. Then the rest of the team can start using the new function right away. They may change their old code to use the new function whenever they can, and, after a while, when nobody is using it anymore, the old function can be removed.

The problem with this is how to let everybody know which functions have changed and which functions they are supposed to use. Even if we always tell them this, how are they going to remember it if everything compiles and runs correctly? This is where deprecating a function comes in. We write the new function, and then flag the old function as deprecated. Then, every time the old function is used, the compiler will generate a message explaining that a deprecated function is being called and mentioning which function should be used in its place.

## Using and Assigning Deprecated Functions

Java has a built-in way to do exactly what we want. However, most commercial games these days seem to be written mostly using C++, and unfortunately C++ doesn't contain any deprecation facilities. The rest of this gem describes a solution implemented in C++ to flag specific functions as deprecated.

Let's start with an example of how to use it. Say we have a function that everybody is using called *FunctionA()*. Unfortunately, months later, we realize that the interface of *FunctionA()* has to change, so we write a new function called *NewFunctionA()*. By adding just one line, we can flag *FunctionA()* as deprecated.

```
int FunctionA ( void )
{
  DEPRECATE ( "FunctionA()", "NewFunctionA()" )
  // Implementation
}

int NewFunctionA ( void )
{
  // Implementation
}
```

The line *DEPRECATE("FunctionA()", "NewFunctionA()")* indicates that *FunctionA()* is deprecated, and that it has been replaced with *NewFunctionA()*.

The users of *FunctionA()* don't have to do anything special at all. Whenever users use *FunctionA()* they will get the following message in the debug window when they exit the program:

```
****************************************************************
WARNING. You are using the following deprecated functions:
- Function FunctionA() called from 3 different places.
  Instead use NewFunctionA().
****************************************************************
```

## Implementing Deprecation in C++

*ON THE CD*

Everything is implemented in one simple singleton class [Gamma95]: *Deprecation-Mgr*. The full source code for the class along with an example program is included on the companion CD-ROM. In its simplest form, all *DeprecationMgr* does is keep a list of the deprecated functions found so far. Whenever the singleton is destroyed (which happens automatically when the program exits), the destructor prints out a report in the debug window, listing what deprecated functions were used in that session.

```
class DeprecationMgr
{
public:
  static DeprecationMgr * GetInstance ( void );
  ~DeprecationMgr ( void );

  bool AddDeprecatedFunction (const char * OldFunctionName,
                              const char * NewFunctionName,
                              unsigned int CalledFrom );
  // Rest of the declaration here
};
```

Usually, we won't have to deal with this class directly because the *DEPRECATE* macro will do all of the work for us.

```
#ifdef _DEBUG
#define DEPRECATE(a,b) { \
    void * fptr;   \
    _asm { mov fptr, ebp }    \
    DeprecationMgr::GetInstance()->AddDeprecatedFunction(a, b, fptr); \
}
#else
#define DEPRECATE(a,b)
#endif
```

Ignoring the first few lines, all the *DEPRECATE* macro does is get an instance to the *DeprecationMgr* and add the function that is being executed to the list. Because *DeprecationMgr* is a singleton that won't be instantiated until the *GetInstance()* function is called, if there are no deprecated functions, it will never be created and it will never print any reports at the end of the program execution. Internally, *Deprecation-Mgr* keeps a small structure for each deprecated function, indexed by the function name through an STL map collection. Only the first call to a deprecated function will insert a new entry in the map.

The *DeprecationMgr* class has one more little perk: it will keep track of the number of different places from which each deprecated function was called. This is useful so we know at a glance how many places in the code we need to change when we decide to stop using the deprecated function. Unfortunately, because this trick uses assembly directly, it is platform specific and only works on the x86 family of CPUs. The first two lines of the *DEPRECATE* macro get the *EBP* register (from which it is usually possible to retrieve the return address), and pass it on to *AddDeprecatedFunc-*

*tion()*. Then, if a function is called multiple times from the same place (in a loop for example), it will only be reported as being called from one place.

There is a potential problem with this approach for obtaining the return address. Typically, the address *[EBP-4]* contains the return address for the current function. However, under some circumstances the compiler might not set the register *EBP* to its expected value. In particular, this happens under VC++ 6.0, when compiler optimizations are turned on, for particularly simple functions. In this case, trying to read from *[EBP-4]* will either return an incorrect value or crash the program. There will be no problems in release mode, which is when optimizations are normally turned on, because the macro does no work. However, sometimes optimizations are also used in debug mode, so inside the function *AddDeprecatedFunction()* we only try to read the return address if the address contained in *[EBP-4]* is readable by the current process. This is accomplished by either using exception handling or calling the Windows-specific function *IsBadReadPtr()*. This will produce an incorrect count of functions that deprecated functions were called from when optimizations are turned on, but at least it won't cause the program to crash, and all the other functionality of the deprecation manager will still work correctly.

## What Could Be Improved?

One major problem remains: the deprecation warnings are generated at runtime, not at compile or link time. This is necessary because the deprecated functions may exist in a separate library, rather than in the code that is being compiled. The main drawback of only reporting the deprecated functions at runtime is that it is possible for the program to still be using a deprecated function that gets called rarely enough that it never gets noticed. The use of the deprecated function might not be detected until it is finally removed and the compiler reports an error.

## Acknowledgments

I would like to thank David McKibbin for reviewing this gem, and for identifying the problems caused by compiler optimizations and finding a workaround.

### References

[Gamma95] Gamma, Eric, et al, *Design Patterns,* Addison-Wesley. 1995.
[Rose] Rose, John, "How and When to Deprecate APIs," available online at java.sun.com/products/jdk/1.1/docs/guide/misc/deprecation/deprecation.html.

# 1.10

## A Drop-in Debug Memory Manager

### Peter Dalton, Evans & Sutherland

pdalton@xmission.com

**W**ith the increasing complexity of game programming, the minimum memory requirements for games have skyrocketed. Today's games must effectively deal with the vast amounts of resources required to support graphics, music, video, animations, models, networking, and artificial intelligence. As the project grows, so does the likelihood of memory leaks, memory bounds violations, and allocating more memory than is required. This is where a memory manager comes into play. By creating a few simple memory management routines, we will be able to track all dynamically allocated memory and guide the program toward optimal memory usage.

Our goal is to ensure a reasonable memory footprint by reporting memory leaks, tracking the percentage of allocated memory that is actually used, and alerting the programmer to bounds violations. We will also ensure that the interface to the memory manager is seamless, meaning that it does not require any explicit function calls or class declarations. We should be able to take this code and effortlessly plug it into any other module by including the header file and have everything else fall into place. The disadvantages of creating a memory manager include the overhead time required for the manager to allocate memory, deallocate memory, and interrogate the memory for statistical information. Thus, this is not an option that we would like to have enabled for the final build of our game. In order to avoid these pitfalls, we are going to only enable the memory manager during debug builds, or if the symbol *ACTIVATE_MEMORY_MANAGER* is defined.

### Getting Started

The heart of the memory manager centers on overloading the standard *new* and *delete* operators, as well as using *#define* to create a few macros that allow us to plug in our own routines. By overloading the memory allocation and deallocation routines, we will be able to replace the standard routines with our own memory-tracking module. These routines will log the file and line number on which the allocation is being requested, as well as statistical information.

The first step is to create the overloaded *new* and *delete* operators. As mentioned earlier, we would like to log the file and line number requesting the memory allocation. This information will become priceless when trying to resolve memory leaks, because we will be able to track the allocation to its roots. Here is what the actual overloaded operators will look like:

```
inline void*
            operator new(size_t size, const char *file, int line);
inline void*
            operator new[](size_t size, const char *file, int
line);
inline void operator delete( void *address );
    inline void operator delete[]( void *address );
```

It's important to note that both the standard and array versions of the *new* and *delete* operators need to be overloaded to ensure proper functionality. While these declarations don't look too complex, the problem that now lies before us is getting all of the routines that will use the memory manager to seamlessly pass the *new* operator the additional parameters. This is where the *#define* directive comes into play.

```
#define new new(__FILE__,__LINE__)
#define delete setOwner(__FILE__,__LINE__),false ? setOwner("",0)
          : delete
#define malloc(sz) AllocateMemory(__FILE__,__LINE__,sz,MM_MALLOC)
#define calloc(num,sz)
          AllocateMemory(__FILE__,__LINE__,sz*num,MM_CALLOC)
#define realloc(ptr,sz) AllocateMemory( __FILE__, __LINE__, sz,
          MM_REALLOC, ptr )
#define free(sz) deAllocateMemory( __FILE__, __LINE__, sz,
          MM_FREE )
```

The *#define new* statement will replace all *new* calls with our variation of *new* that takes as parameters not only the requested size of the allocation, but also the file and line number for tracking purposes. Microsoft's Visual C++ compiler provides a set of predefined macros, which include our required *__FILE__* and *__LINE__* symbols [MSDN]. The *#define delete* macro is a little different from the *#define new* macro. It is not possible to pass additional parameters to the overloaded *delete* operator without creating syntax problems. Instead, the *setOwner()* method records the file and line number for later use. Note that it is also important to create the macro as a conditional to avoid common problems associated with multiple-line macros [Dalton01]. Finally, to be complete, we have also replaced the *malloc()*, *calloc()*, *realloc()*, and the *free()* methods with our own memory allocation and deallocation routines.

The implementations for these functions are located on the accompanying CD. The *AllocateMemory()* and *deAllocateMemory()* routines are solely responsible for all memory allocation and deallocation. They also log information pertaining to the desired allocation, and initialize or interrogate the memory, based on the desired

ON THE CD

action. All this information will then be available to generate the desired statistics to analyze the memory requirements for any given program.

## Memory Manager Logging

Now that we have provided the necessary framework for replacing the standard memory allocation routines with our own, we are ready to begin logging. As stated in the beginning of this gem, we will concentrate on memory leaks, bounds violations, and the actual memory requirements. In order to log all of the required information, we must first choose a data structure to hold the information relevant to memory allocations. For efficiency and speed, we will use a chained hash table. Each hash table entry will contain the following information:

```
struct MemoryNode
{
size_t          actualSize;
size_t          reportedSize;
void            *actualAddress;
void            *reportedAddress;
char            sourceFile[30];
unsigned short  sourceLine;
unsigned short  paddingSize;
char            options;
long            predefinedBody;
ALLOC_TYPE      allocationType;
MemoryNode      *next, *prev;
};
```

This structure contains the size of memory allocated not only for the user, but also for the padding applied to the beginning and ending of the allocated block. We also record the type of allocation to protect against allocation/deallocation mismatches. For example, if the memory was allocated using the *new[]* operator and deallocated using the *delete* operator instead of the *delete[]* operator, a memory leak may occur due to object destructors not being called. Effort has also been taken to minimize the size of this structure while maintaining maximum flexibility. After all, we don't want to create a memory manager that uses more memory than the actual application being monitored.

At this point, we should have all of the information necessary to determine if there are any memory leaks in the program. By creating a *MemoryNode* within the *AllocateMemory()* routine and inserting it into the hash table, we will create a history of all the allocated memory. Then, by removing the *MemoryNode* within the *deAllocateMemory()* routine, we will ensure that the hash table only contains a current listing of allocated memory. If upon exiting the program there are any entries left within the hash table, a memory leak has occurred. At this point, the *MemoryNode* can be interrogated to report the details of the memory leak to the user. As mentioned previously, within the *deAllocateMemory()* routine we will also validate that the method used to allocate the memory matches the deallocation method; if not, we will note the potential memory leak.

Next, let's gather information pertaining to bounds violations. Bounds violations occur when applications exceed the memory allocated to them. The most common place where this happens is within loops that access array information. For example, if we allocated an array of size 10, and we accessed array location 11, we would be exceeding the array bounds and overwriting or accessing information that does not belong to us. In order to protect against this problem, we are going to provide padding to the front and back of the memory allocated. Thus, if a routine requests 5 bytes, the *AllocateMemory()* routine will actually allocate *5 + sizeof(long)\*2\*paddingSize* bytes. Note that we are using *longs* for the padding because they are defined to be 32-bit integers. Next, we must initialize the padding to a predefined value, such as *0xDEADC0DE*. Then, upon deallocation, if we examine the padding and find any value except for the predefined value, we know that a bounds violation has occurred. At this point, we would interrogate the corresponding *MemoryNode* and report the bounds violation to the user.

The only information remaining to be gathered is the actual memory requirement for the program. We would like to know how much memory was allocated, how much of the allocated memory was actually used, and perhaps peak memory allocation information. In order to collect this information we are going to need another container. Note that only the relevant members of the class are shown here.

```
class MemoryManager
{
public:
  unsigned int m_totalMemoryAllocations;
  unsigned int m_totalMemoryAllocated;      // In bytes
  unsigned int m_totalMemoryUsed;           // In bytes
  unsigned int m_peakMemoryAllocation;
};
```

Within the *AllocateMemory()* routine, we will be able to update all of the *MemoryManager* information except for the *m_totalMemoryUsed* variable. In order to determine how much of the allocated memory is actually used, we will need to perform a trick similar to the method used in determining bounds violations. By initializing the memory within the *AllocateMemory()* routine to a predefined value and interrogating the memory upon deallocation, we should be able to get an idea of how much memory was actually utilized. In order to achieve decent results, we are going to initialize the memory on 32-bit boundaries, once again, using *longs*. We will also use a predefined value such as *0xBAADC0DE* for initialization. For all remaining bytes that do not fit within our 32-bit boundaries, we will initialize each byte to *0xE* or *static_cast<char>(0xBAADC0DE)*. While this method is potentially error prone because there is no predefined value to which we could initialize the memory and ensure uniqueness, initializing the memory on 32-bit boundaries will generate far better results than initializing on byte boundaries.

## Reporting the Information

Now that we have all of the statistical information, let's address the issue of how we should report it to the user. The implementation that is included on the CD records all information to a log file. Once the user has enabled the memory manager and run the program, upon termination a log file is generated containing a listing of all the memory leaks, bounds violations, and the final statistical report.

The only question remaining is: how do we know when the program is terminating so that we can dump our log information? A simple solution would be to require the programmer to explicitly call the *dumpLogReport()* routine upon termination. However, this goes against the requirement of creating a seamless interface. In order to determine when the program has terminated without the use of an explicit function call, we are going to use a static class instance. The implementation is as follows:

```
class Initialize
    { public: Initialize() { InitializeMemoryManager(); } };
static Initialize InitMemoryManager;

bool InitializeMemoryManager() {
  static bool hasBeenInitialized = false;
  if (s_manager)                  return true;
  else if (hasBeenInitialized) return false;
  else {
    s_manager = (MemoryManager*)malloc(sizeof(MemoryManager));
    s_manager->intialize();
    atexit( releaseMemoryManager );
    hasBeenIntialized = true;
    return true;
  }
}
void releaseMemoryManager() {
  NumAllocations = s_manager->m_numAllocations;
  s_manager->release();    // Releases the hash table and calls
  free( s_manager );       //  the dumpLogReport() method
  s_manager = NULL;
}
```

The problem before us is to ensure that the memory manager is the first object to be created and the very last object to be deallocated. This can be difficult due to the order in which objects that are statically defined are handled. For example, if we created a static object that allocated dynamic memory within its constructor, before the memory manager object is allocated, the memory manager will not be available for memory tracking. Likewise, if we use the *::atexit()* method to call a function that is responsible for releasing allocated memory, the memory manager object will be released before the *::atexit()* method is called, thus resulting in bogus memory leaks.

In order to resolve these problems, the following enhancements need to be added. First, by creating the *InitMemoryManager* object within the header file of the memory manager, it is guaranteed to be encountered before any static objects are declared.

This holds true as long as we *#include* that memory manager header before any static definitions. Microsoft states that static objects are allocated in the order in which they are encountered, and are deallocated in the reverse order [MSDN]. Second, to ensure that the memory manager is always available we are going to call the *InitializeMemoryManager()* routine every time within the *AllocateMemory()* and *DeallocateMemory()* routines, guaranteeing that the memory manager is active. Finally, in order to ensure that the memory manager is the last object to be deallocated, we will use the *::atexit()* method. The *::atexit()* method works by calling the specified functions in the reverse order in which they are passed to the method [MSDN1]. Thus, the only restriction that must be placed on the memory manager is that it is the first method to call the *::atexit()* function. Static objects can still use the *::atexit()* method; they just need to make sure that the memory manager is present. If, for any reason, the *InitializeMemoryManager()* function returns *false*, then this last condition has not been met and as a result, the error will be reported in the log file.

Given the previous restriction, there are a few things to be aware of when using Microsoft's Visual C++. The *::atexit()* method is used extensively by internal VC++ procedures in order to clean up on shutdown. For example, the following code will cause an *::atexit()* to be called, although we would have to check the disassembly to see it.

```
void Foo() { static std::string s; }
```

While this is not a problem if the memory manager is active before the declaration of *s* is encountered, it is worth noting. Despite this example being completely VC++ specific, other compilers might differ or contain additional methods that call *::atexit()* behind the scenes. The key to the solution is to ensure that the memory manager is initialized first.

## Things to Keep in Mind

Besides the additional memory and time required to perform memory tracking, there are a few other details to keep in mind. The first has to deal with syntax errors that can be encountered when *#including* other files. In certain situations, it is possible to generate syntax errors due to other files redefining the *new* and *delete* operators. This is especially noticeable when using STL implementations. For example, if we *#include* "*MemoryManager.h*" and then *#include <map>*, we will generate all types of errors. To resolve this issue, we are going to be using two additional header files: *new_on.h* and *new_off.h*. These headers will simply *#define* and *#undefine* the *new/delete* macros that were created earlier. The advantage of this method includes the flexibility that we achieve by not forcing the user to abide by a particular *#include* order, and avoids the complexity when dealing with precompiled headers.

```
#include "new_off.h"
#include <map>
```

```
#include <string>
#include <All other headers overloading the new/delete operators>
#include "new_on.h"

#include "MemoryManager.h"  // Contains the Memory Manager Module
#include "Custom header files"
```

Another issue we need to address is how to handle libraries that redefine the *new* and *delete* operators on their own. For example, MFC has its own system in place for handling the *new* and *delete* operators [MSDN2]. Thus, we would like to have MFC classes use their own memory manager, and have non-MFC shared game code use our memory manager. We can achieve this by inserting the *#include "new_off.h"* header file right after the *#ifdef* created by the ClassWizard.

```
#ifdef _DEBUG
#include "new_off.h"                    // Turn off our memory manager
#define new DEBUG_NEW
#undef THIS_FILE
static char THIS_FILE[] = __FILE__;
#endif
```

This method will allow us to keep the advantages of MFC's memory manager, such as dumping *CObject*-derived classes on memory leaks, and still provide the rest of the code with a memory manager.

Finally, keep in mind the requirements for properly implementing the *setOwner()* method used by the *delete* operator. It is necessary to realize that the implementation is more complicated than just recording the file and line number; we must create a stack implementation. This is a result of the way that we implemented the *delete* macro. Take, for example, the following:

```
File 1: line 1: class B { B() {a = new int;} ~B() {delete a;} };
File 2: line 1: B *objectB = new B;
File 2: line 2: delete objectB;
```

The order of function calls is as follows:

```
1. new( objectB, File2, 1 );
2. new( a,       File1, 1 );
3. setOwner( File2, 2 );
4. setOwner( File1, 1 );
5. delete( a );
6. delete( objectB );
```

As should be evident from the preceding listing, by the time the *delete* operator is called to deallocate *objectB*, we will no longer have the file and line number information unless we use a stack implementation. While the solution is straightforward, the problem is not immediately obvious.

## Further Enhancements

*ON THE CD*

Within the implementation provided on the CD accompanying this book, there are several enhancements to the implementation discussed here. For example, there is the option for the user to set flags to perform more comprehensive memory tests. Options also exist for setting breakpoints when memory is deallocated or reallocated so that the program's stack can be interrogated. These are but a few of the possibilities that are available. Other enhancements could easily be included, such as allowing a program to check if any given address is valid. When it comes to memory control, the options are unlimited.

## References

[Dalton01] Dalton, Peter, "Inline Functions versus Macros," *Game Programming Gems II*, Charles River Media. 2001.

[McConnell93] McConnell, Steve, *Code Complete*, Microsoft Press. 1993.

[MSDN1] Microsoft Developer Network Library, http://msdn.microsoft .com/ library/devprods/vs6/visualc/vclang/_pluslang_initializing_static_objects.htm

[MSDN2] Microsoft Developer Network Library, http://msdn.microsoft .com/library/devprods/vs6/visualc/vccore/core_memory_management_with_mf c.3a_.overview.htm

[Myers98] Myers, Scott, *Effective C++, Second Edition*, Addison-Wesley Longmont, Inc. 1998.

# 1.11

# A Built-in Game Profiling Module

## Jeff Evertt, Lithtech, Inc.

jeff@evertt.com

This gem describes the architecture and implementation of a profiling module for low-overhead, real-time analysis that supports performance counter organization so that many consumers can work together in harmony. It is designed from a game engine perspective, with many of its requirements specifically pertaining to things typically found in games. At the time of this writing, the described module is in use by a commercially available game engine.

Profiling the performance of a game or engine is one of those things that everyone agrees is important, but just as often as not guesswork or quick hacks are substituted for a real game system that can gather solid data. In the long run, the time it takes to implement a clean profiling system is a wise investment. And, as with everything else, the earlier we plan for it, the easier it will be.

## Profiling Basics

The basic profiling mechanism is simple: take a timestamp at the beginning of the code of interest and again at the end. Subtract the first from the second, and voila, that's how long the code took to run. We need a high-resolution counter – the Windows multimedia timer and its millisecond resolution will not cut it. If the platform is Windows on a PC, there are two high-resolution API calls we can use: *QueryPerformanceCounter* and *QueryPerformanceFrequency*. However, because the overhead of these functions is fairly high, we will roll our own, which only requires a few lines of inline assembly:

```
void CWin32PerfCounterMgr::GetPerfCounter(
LARGE_INTEGER &iCounter) {
    DWORD dwLow,dwHigh;
    __asm {
        rdtsc
        mov dwLow, eax
        mov dwHigh, edx
    }
    iCounter.QuadPart = ((unsigned __int64)dwHigh << 32)
                        | (unsigned __int64)dwLow; }
```

To convert this number into seconds, we need to know the counter frequency. In this case it is equal to the CPU cycles per second. We can measure it once when the counters are enabled—take a time sample, sleep for at least 500ms, and then take another sample. Note that similar counters are available if the target platform is a game console.

## Commercially Available Tools

Performance tuning is definitely a case where choosing the right tool for the job can make all the difference. There are many time-tested commercial tools available for the PC that sample an application as it runs, then offline allow profile data to be viewed module-by-module, function-by-function, and just about any other imaginable way. Intel® VTune™ and Metrowerks® Analysis Tools both make use of the built-in CPU hardware counters to generate post-processed profiles of runtime sections of a game. Tuning assembly code by instruction ordering or pairing prediction is definitely a strength of VTune™.

The Intel® Graphics Performance Toolkit (GPT) provides some powerful scene analysis tools. It hooks in and snoops traffic at the layer between your application and Direct3D/OpenGL. Knowing exactly what is being drawn can at times be very helpful. Changing the order or the way in which the game renders can sometimes significantly affect performance. However, the GPT is written to a specific version of DirectX, so its releases usually trail that of DirectX. Also, taking any significant scene data will slow down the application, so relying on the performance characteristics of data taken when using the GPT can be dangerous.

Statistics-gathering drivers for graphics cards and hardware counters can be invaluable. Nvidia releases special drivers and a real-time data viewing application that hooks all of the function entry points of the drivers. If the graphics driver is taking a significant percentage of CPU time, this application will allow us to look inside and break it down further. Intel® provides counters in its drivers and hardware for its i740 chip, allowing optimization for stalls all the way down to the graphics chip level. Some of the game consoles also provide this ability. It can be very useful, as it is the only way to break down performance at this low level. It does, however, require a fair amount of knowledge about how the drivers and chips operate, and what the counters really mean.

## Why Roll Our Own?

Reason one: frame-based analysis. Games typically have a fairly high frame-to-frame coherency, but in just a matter of seconds can drastically change. Imagine a 3D shooter—a player starts facing a wall, runs down a long corridor, then ends it all in a bloody firefight with five AI-driven enemies. The game engine is running through many potentially different bottlenecks that can only really be identified with a frame-by-frame analysis. Looking at a breakdown of an accumulated sample over the entire interval gives an inaccurate view of what is really going on. Frame-based analysis allows focusing on one problem at a time.

Reason two: it can be done anytime and anywhere. At the end of a PC game development cycle, someone will probably be faced with performance problems that only manifest themselves on someone's brother's machine, on odd Tuesdays. There are typically a significant number of these types of problems. They can cost a lot of time and can very easily slip the release date. Although this type of problem is unique to PC games, console games still have to deal with the "shooting a missile in the corner of level three grinds the game to a slow crawl" types of problems. Once the problem is understood, figuring out the solution is usually the easy part. If we could walk over to that test machine and pop up a few counter groups, we would quickly nail down the culprit.

Reason three: customizability. Modern game engines are complicated. The ability to ignore all the other modules in the engine except for the one being working on is powerful. In addition, the only person that can organize the data exactly how they want it is the engineer actually doing the work.

## Profile Module Requirements

Requirement one: allow users to quickly and accurately profile the application.

Requirement two: be non-obtrusive (that is, have very low overhead). When the cost for taking samples and displaying the results becomes a significant portion of the frame time, it can actually change the application's behavior within the system. In general, slowing down the CPU will tend to hide stalls caused by graphics cards. While even a very small percentage can in some rare cases drastically change game performance, as a general rule, when the profiler is enabled, it should take less than five percent of the total CPU cycles. When disabled, it should be much less than one percent.

Requirement three: allow multiple users to work independently on their respective systems without having to worry about other engine modules.

Requirement four: when it's not needed, it should be well out of the way.

## Architecture and Implementation

A performance counter manager (*IPerfCounterMan*) keeps track of all active and inactive counters. The counters are organized into groups of similar type (for example, model render, world render, AI, physics) that are enabled and disabled together. This supports the notion of multiple groups working independently in an easy to understand grouping concept. Groups are useful for two reasons: for quickly determining if a counter needs to be sampled, and for enabling and disabling groups of counters to be displayed. We will make use of four-character codes (FourCC's) for the group ID and full text strings for counter names.

The entire system is organized into a module with an interface to the rest of the system. The basic component is a counter that is identified by a group ID (its

FourCC) and its string name. Each counter is given an integer ID on creation that uniquely identifies it. In typical usage, the game code creates counters on initialization and puts start/stop counter calls around the code to be profiled.

The basic functional unit interface for the module is as follows:

```
class IPerfCounterMan {
public:
// Add new counter (returns the ID, 0 is failure)
    int32       AddCounter(uint32 CounterGroup,
                                const char* szCounterName);

// Forget your counter's ID? (Zero is failure)
    int32       GetCounterID(uint32 CounterGroup,
                                const char* szCounterName);

// Delete the counter
    bool        DeleteCounter(uint32 CounterID);

// Start and Stop a counter.
    void        StartCounter(uint32 CounterID);
    void        StopCounter(uint32 CounterID);

// Draw the Counters onto the Screen (to be called once
// per frame near the end of the scene)
    void        DrawCounters();
};
```

*StopCounter* calculates the difference between the *StartCounter* and *StopCounter* calls and keeps a running total. On *DrawCounters*, all the running counters are cleared. A maximum value is also maintained and is set at the end of the frame in *DrawCounters*. Let's assume that our engine has a debug console that accepts text commands. It is a very convenient way to enable and disable counter groups and to allow customization of the display.

It is very helpful to allow as much configuration in the counter display as possible. We will most likely not want to refresh the counter display every frame (updates every 30 frames should be sufficient), but depending on what is being debugged, the ability to customize the refresh time can be very handy. In addition, displaying both the current percentage and the maximum percentage since last displayed is useful.

A bar graph is a good way to display the result. It gives the consumer a quick feel for the numbers and isn't hard to code. The ability to switch from percentage to actual time (in milliseconds), display the time or percentage as text values, and auto-scale the axes is also very useful. Be careful about switching the axis scale very often, especially without some kind of warning, because it will likely just confuse people.

## Implementation Details

The interface to the performance counter manager should be flexible and easy to use. Consumers of the profile manager will often find it easier to simply call *Add-Counter(...)* with the full string, get the ID, and start it up all at once instead of saving the counter ID at some one-time initialization point. Providing this mechanism can help out when doing some quick profiling. However, it's not as efficient, and calling it many times in a frame will add up quickly. Also, supplying a class that can be placed at the beginning of a function that calls *StartCounter* in the constructor and *StopCounter* in the destructor (when it goes out of focus) can be a handy way to instrument the counters.

When writing the profiling manager, it's best to provide some kind of *#define* macro that completely removes the profiler. When it comes down to getting peak performance out of a game, profiling code is often one of the first things to go. We need to provide macros for *AddCounter*, *StartCounter*, and *StopCounter* that completely compile out on an *#ifdef* change.

Also, it's best to use colors for visual cues. When the counters are being displayed, it's easier to read if we use different colors on each line.

## Data Analysis

Be sure to profile the release build, because it can have a very different set of bottlenecks from the debug version. If the target platform is the PC, it is also a good idea to pick two or three typical system configurations (low to high end) and profile each of them. Bottlenecks can vary greatly across system configurations.

The game should be profiled in the areas that have performance problems as well as during typical game play. We must break the problem down, try to focus on one thing at a time, and focus on the areas that will give the biggest bang for the buck. Just because a function is called the most often or takes the most CPU time doesn't mean it is the only place we should focus our efforts. Often, the only thing we can compare our cycle times with is our expectations, and realistic expectations are usually gained only through experience.

The profiler itself should also be profiled. If the act of profiling is intrusive, it changes the behavior of your game. There should be a counter around the profiler's draw routines.

## Implementation Notes

The described module has been implemented across multiple platforms. However, parts of it require platform-dependent functions. The actual timestamp query and the draw functions will mostly likely need to be implemented in platform-dependent code, so it's best to design a level of abstraction around those functions. The described implementation uses a set of debug geometry and text (which has a platform-dependent implementation) in the draw code so that it can be platform independent. You may need to write a macro to create your four character code values, as many compilers do not have support for them.

This same system can be used to take long running profiles of a game server to detect problems. All the counters go through one source, so data can easily be filtered down and saved to disk.

# Linear Programming Model for Windows-based Games

## *Javier F. Otaegui, Sabarasa Entertainment*

jJavier@sabarasa.com.ar

In the past, when DOS ruled the earth, we programmed our games in a mostly linear fashion. Then it was time to port our creations from DOS to DirectX, and this was a big jump because of the Windows message pump. Its architecture is simply not adequate for game programming. In this gem, we will cover an effective way to encapsulate the message pump, provide a linear programming model and, as a very desirable side effect, allow correct "*alt-tab*" application switching. We will also cover correct recovery of lost surfaces.

*If you have previously programmed linearly, you will easily understand the importance of the method introduced in this gem. If your experience in game programming started with Windows, then you might find the message pump a natural environment for game programming, but once you try linear programming, you will never go back to the message pump. It is far clearer and easier to follow and debug than a huge finite state machine is. You can save a lot of design, programming, debugging time, and thinking if you start working in a more linear way.*

## Updating the World

Modern games often have some sort of *UpdateWorld* function, located in the heart of the application in the message pump, and invoked whenever it is not receiving any messages. In a first attempt, coding an *UpdateWorld* function can be very simple: all the application variables, surfaces, and interfaces have already been initialized, and now we just have to update and render them. That should be an easy task, but only if we plan that our game will have only one screen, no cut-scenes, no menus, and no options.

The problem is that *UpdateWorld* must eventually finish and return to the message pump so we can process messages from the system. This prevents us from staying in a continuous *for* loop, for example. As old DOS games didn't have to return constantly to a message pump to process system requests, we could linearly program them, and our subroutines could have all the loops they needed, or delays, or cut-scenes. We simply had to insert the corresponding code into the subroutine. Now, however, with the message pump, which requires constant attention, we must return on every loop. As stated previously, the problem of returning in every single loop is when attempting to maintain several game screens.

The way to work around this is to make every subroutine of the application a finite state machine. Each subroutine will have to keep track of its internal state, and, according to this state, it must invoke several other subroutines. Each of these other subroutines is also a finite state machine, and when it finishes its execution (that is, it has no more states to execute), it must return a value to inform the invoking subroutine that it can proceed with its own following state. Of course, each subroutine, when it finishes, must reset its state to *0*, to allow the application to invoke it again.

Now if we imagine 30 or 40 of these subroutines, each with a couple dozen states, we will be facing a very big monster. Trying to debug or even follow this code will be difficult. This finite-state programming model is far more complicated that the simple model achieved by old linear DOS programs.

## The Solution: Multithreading

Here is a simple multithreading model that frees the game programmer from the message pump and its potentially undesirable finite-state programming model.

Windows supports multithreading, which means that our application can run several threads of execution simultaneously. The idea is very simple – put the message pump in one thread and the game into another one. The message pump will remain in the initial thread, so we can take out the *UpdateWorld* function from the message pump and return it to its simplest form (a linear programming scheme). Now we just need to add to the *doInit* function the code necessary to initiate the game thread.

```
HANDLE hMainThread;        // Main Thread handle

static BOOL
doInit( ... )
{
    ... // Initialize DirectX and everything else

    DWORD tid;

    hMainThread=CreateThread( 0,
        0,
        &MainThread,
        0,
        0,
        &tid);

    return TRUE;
}
```

MainThread is defined by:

```
DWORD WINAPI
MainThread( LPVOID arg1 )
{
    RunGame();
    PostMessage(hwnd, WM_CLOSE, 0, 0);
    return 0;
};
```

*MainThread* will invoke our *RunGame* function, and when it is finished, we just post a *WM_CLOSE* message to tell the message pump thread to finish execution.

### Initialization Code

Now we must choose whether to include initialization code (including the DirectX initialization code) in the *doInit* function or directly into our *RunGame* function. It may be more elegant to include it in the *doInit* function, as long as we include all terminating code in the response to *WM_CLOSE* in our message handler. On the other hand, we could include all the initialization code in the *RunGame* function, which means that we will handle all of the important parts of the code directly in our new linear game-programming function.

### The "Alt-Tab" Problem

Making a game truly multitasking under Windows is perhaps one of the most hazardous issues in game programming. A well-behaved application must be able to correctly switch to other applications. This means allowing the user to *alt-tab* away from the application, which some games attempt to disallow, but we will try to make things work correctly.

We could try using the standard *SuspendThread* and *ResumeThread* functions, but it's nearly impossible to get this to work properly. Instead, we will use a multithreaded communication tool: *events*. Events work like flags that can be used to synchronize different threads. Our game thread will check if it must continue, or if it must wait for the event to be set.

On startup, we must create a manual-reset event. This event should be reset (cleared) when the program is deactivated, and set when the program is reactivated. Then, in the main loop, we just have to wait for the event to be set.

To create the event, we need this global:

```
HANDLE task_wakeup_event;
```

To create and set the event, we need to include the following code during initialization:

```
task_wakeup_event =
    CreateEvent(
        NULL,     // No security attributes
        TRUE,     // Manual Reset ON
        FALSE,    // Initial state = Non signaled
        NULL      // No name
    );
```

Most games have a function in their main loop that is called every time the game needs to render a new screen; this is typically where DirectX is asked to flip the primary and back buffers. Because this function is called constantly, this is an ideal location to make the thread wait for the event in an idle state, using this code:

```
WaitForSingleObject( task_wakeup_event, INFINITE );
```

We must suspend the thread every time the operating system switches the active application. To do this, we must have our *WindowProc* function, and upon receiving an *APP_ACTIVATE* message, check whether the application is active. If the application has gone to an inactive state, we must suspend the game execution, which requires this call:

```
ResetEvent( task_wakeup_event );
```

and to resume it:

```
SetEvent( task_wakeup_event );
```

With this simple implementation, when the user hits *alt-tab*, the game will temporarily stop execution, freeing all the processor's time to enable the user to do other tasks. If the world update must continue executing even if the application loses focus, then we can just suspend the rendering pipeline, and continue updating the world. This event model can be used with any number of threads that the application may require, by inserting new events for each new thread.

### Handling Lost Surfaces

If we use video memory surfaces, we will face the problem of losing the surface information when the application loses focus. The problem that we now face is that with our new linear programming model, a program can be caught in the middle of a subroutine with all its surfaces lost.

There are many possible solutions to this situation, one of which is the Command pattern [GoF94]. Unfortunately, it obscures our code, and the main goal of this gem is to make things more clear. We can use a global stack of pairs of callback functions and *lpVoids*, which will be called when the surfaces need to be reloaded. When we need to restore the surfaces, we would invoke *callback_function( lpVoid )*. The *lpVoid* parameter can include pointers to all the surfaces that we need, so we can keep the surfaces local to our new linear subroutines.

Let's suppose that we have a subroutine called *Splash* that displays a splash screen in our game, which is a surface loaded from a file. If the user hits *alt-tab* while the splash screen is displayed and then comes back, we want our application to show the splash screen again (let's assume that the surface was lost while the application was inactive). Using our proposed method, we must do something like this:

```
int LoadSplashGraphics( lpvoid Params )
{
```

```
        Surface *pMySurface;
        pMySurface = (Surface *) Params;

        //  ...
        //  (load the graphic from the file)

        return 1;
    }

    int Splash()
    {
        Surface MySurface;

        // Push the function
        gReloadSurfacesStack.Push( &LoadSplashGraphics, &MySurface );

        // Do not forget to load graphics for the first time
        LoadSplashGraphics( &MySurface );

        // ... the subroutine functionality.

        // Pop the function
        gReloadSurfaceStack.Pop();
    }
```

We are using a stack so that each nested subroutine can add all the surface loading and generation code that it might need. The implementation could easily be changed to another collection class, but this is a classic stack-oriented problem due to its nested functionality, and so a stack works best here.

## References

[GoF94] Gamma, E., Helm, R., Johnson, R., & Vlissides, J. (1994), *Design Patterns: Elements of Reusable Object–Oriented Software.* Addison-Wesley. 1994.

Otaegui, Javier F., "Getting Rid of the Windows Message Pump," available online at www.gamedev.net/reference/articles/article1249.asp.

# 1.13

## Stack Winding

### Bryon Hapgood, Kodiak Interactive

bryonh57@hotmail.com

Stack winding is a powerful technique for assembly programmers that allows us to modify an application's stack to do weird and wonderful things that can be extended into C/C++ with very little work. While the days of writing every line of game code in hand-optimized machine language are over, sometimes it is worth the effort to dip into the realm of the arcane to get that extra bit of speed and elegance in a game.

In this gem, we cover one particular type of stack winding that I call the "temporary return." This is the bare minimum form that we will build upon in subsequent examples until we have a *thunked* temporary return. The code examples have been tested with Microsoft's MASM and Visual C++ compiler. I have personally used stack winding in a number of projects for the GameBoy Color, PC, and Xbox.

### Simple TempRet

Stack winding, as its name implies, is a technique for modifying the stack to make it do unexpected things. The term *stack winding* comes from the idea of inserting values in an existing stack frame to change its normal and expected behavior.

### Listing 1.13.1  The TempRet routine

```
0    .586
1    .model flat
2    .data
3    buffer dd ?
4    file_handle dd ?
5    filesize dd ?
6    .code
7
8    _TempRetEg:
9
10          call    fn0
11          call    fn1
12          ;
13          ;   before
14          ;
15          pop     edx
```

```
16          call   edx
17          ;
18          ;    after
19          ;
20          call   fn2
21          call   fn3
22          ret
23
24          A:  call   _TempRetEg
25          ret
26
27 end
```

In Listing 1.13.1, we see the first building block of stack winding: the TempRet routine. Let's take a function (call it MyFunc) and say it calls _TempRetEg. The latter then calls two functions: fn0 and fn1. It then hits the lines:

```
pop    edx
call   edx
```

Now we know that the way the CPU handles the assembly CALL instruction on line 24 is to push the address of the next line (25) and execute a JUMP to line 8. Line 15 *pops* that address off the stack and stores it in a CPU register. Now we CALL that address. This pushes line 20 onto the stack and executes a JUMP to line 25. The latter does nothing but execute a CPU return, which pops an address off the stack and jumps there.

The rest of _TempRetEg then continues and when *it* returns, we do not return to MyFunc but to whatever function called MyFunc in the first place. It is an interesting little trick, but why would it be important? The power comes when we consider the functions FN0 through FN3.

Let's say that FN0 opens a file, FN1 allocates a buffer and reads the file into memory, FN2 frees that memory, and FN3 closes the file. Thus, MyFunc no longer has to worry about the *release* steps. It doesn't have to close the file or worry about freeing up the memory associated with the file. Functionally the process of opening a file, reading it into memory, freeing that memory, and closing the file is all contained within a single block of code. MyFunc only has to call _TempRetEg, use the buffer, and return.

## TempRet Chains

The TempRet example comes of age when we chain functions together. Let's take a classic problem: the initialization and destruction of DirectX 7. This usually takes a number of steps, but it's incredibly important to release the components of DX in reverse order, which can sometimes become horribly complicated.

So, let's expand our first example to illustrate this:

## Listing 1.13.2   Winding multiple routines onto the stack

```
0   .586
1   .model flat
2   .code
3
4   TempRet macro
5   pop    edx
6   call   edx
7   TempRet endm
8
9   createWindow:
10    ; open the window
11    TempRet
12    ; close it
13    ret
14  setCooperativeLevel:
15    ; set to exclusive
16    TempRet
17    ; restore
18    ret
19  changeDisplayMode:
20    ; set 640x480 16 bpp
21    TempRet
22    ; restore
23    ret
24  createSurfaces:
25    ; create primary surface
26    ; get attached back
27    TempRet
28    ; release primary
29    ret
30  _SetupDX7:
31    call    createWindow
32    call    setCooperativeLevel
33    call    changeDisplayMode
34    call    createSurfaces
35    jmp     _SomeUserRunFunc
36
37
38  end
```

By performing numerous TempRets in succession we effectively have *wound* four routines onto the stack so that when _SomeUserRunFunc returns, we will bounce back through createSurfaces, changeDisplayMode, setCooperativeLevel, and createWindow at the line after the TempRet in reverse order.

So far, we've been using assembly language, but it's not necessary to write assembly modules to use this technique. We will cover two mechanisms in Microsoft's Visual C++ in the final section that aid us in stack winding: inline assembly and naked functions.

## Thunking

The ideas discussed so far need to be translated into C/C++. As stated previously, Visual C++ has a handy mechanism for doing this, but what about other compilers? If naked functions are not supported, then we will have to dip into assembly language because the presence of a stack frame *really* complicates things. It is not impossible, just difficult.

*Thunking* is a technique popularized by Microsoft for slipping a piece of code between two others. In effect, program flow is hurtling along through our code until *thunk!*—it crashes into that layer. Thunks are a great way of implementing a stack-winding paradigm in C++. Let's look at an example that performs the same task of setting up DirectX as we saw earlier:

## Listing 1.13.3   Visual C++ example using TempRet

```
#define TempRet\
__asm{pop edx}\
__asm{call edx}

#define NAKED void __declspec(naked)
#define JUMP __asm jmp
#define RET __asm ret

static NAKED createWindow(){
    // open the window
    TempRet
    // close it
    RET
}

static NAKED setCooperativeLevel(){
    // set to exclusive
    TempRet
    // restore
    RET
}

static NAKED changeDisplayMode(){
    // set 640x480 16 bpp
    TempRet
    // restore
    RET
}

static NAKED createSurfaces(){
    // create primary surface
    // get attached back
    TempRet
    // restore
    RET
}
```

```
NAKED SetupDX7(){
    createWindow();
    setCooperativeLevel();
    changeDisplayMode();
    createSurfaces();
    JUMP run
}
```

## Recursion

As a final example of the power of stack winding, we will explore a solution for a classic problem with recursive searching: how to roll back the recursion. In regular C we would simply *return* repeatedly, walking back through the stack until we reach the top. If our recursion is over 100 calls deep, however, this might take a little time. To fix this, here is a pair of utility functions called SafeEnter. Incidentally, the code works just as well from a C++ object as a global function.

### Listing 1.13.4   The SafeEnter and SafeExit functions that aid recursion

```
.586
.model flat
.code

public SafeEnter,SafeExit

; struct SAFE{
;     void*__reg[8];
;     void*__ret;
; }

; assembly for SafeEnter routine

_SafeEnter:

    pop edx ; return address
    mov eax,[esp]  ; safe
    ;
    ;
    ;
    mov [eax].safe.__ret,edx
    mov [eax].safe.__ebx,ebx
    mov [eax].safe.__ebp,ebp
    mov [eax].safe.__esp,esp
    mov [eax].safe.__esi,esi
    mov [eax].safe.__edi,edi
    ;
    ;
    ;
    pop     eax ; safe pointer
    pop     edx ; call function
    push    eax ; safe pointer
```

```
        mov     ebp,eax
        call    edx
        mov     eax,ebp
        jmp     sex

_SafeExit:

        pop     edx     ;    return
        pop     eax     ;    regs context
        ;
        ;
        ;
        mov     edi,[eax].safe.__edi
        mov     esi,[eax].safe.__esi
        mov     esp,[eax].safe.__esp
        mov     ebp,[eax].safe.__ebp
        mov     ebx,[eax].safe.__ebx
        mov     edx,[eax].safe.__ret
        mov     eax,[eax].safe.__eax
        ;
        ;
        ;
        jmp     edx

        end
```

SafeEnter works by saving off to a SAFE structure a copy of crucial CPU registers. It then calls our recursive function. As far as the function is concerned, no extra work is necessary. Now the cool part comes when we find the piece of data we're looking for. We simply call SafeExit() and pass it the register context we built earlier. We are instantly transported back to the parent function.

Now, if the unthinkable happened and the search routine did not meet its search criteria, then the function can simply return in the normal way, all the way up the chain.

## Listing 1.13.5   Recursive example using SafeEnter and SafeExit

```
static void search(SAFE&safe,void*v){
    if(<meets_requirement>)
      SafeExit(safe);
    // do stuff
    search(safe,v);
    return;
}

int main(){
    SAFE safe;
    SafeEnter(
      safe,
      search,
      <some_pointer>)
    ;
}
```

# .1.14

## Self-Modifying Code

### Bryon Hapgood, Kodiak Interactive

bryonh57@hotmail.com

Self-modifying code, also known as "RAM-code," is a fascinating technique that actually allows a program to alter its own code as it executes. It has been used in everything from genetic algorithms to neural networks with amazing results. In games it can be used as a powerful optimization technique. Recently I used this technique on a GameBoy Color title *Test Drive Cycles* to decompress artwork on the fly at 60 fps, decode 14 palettes of color information (instead of the standard eight), and enable multiple levels of parallax scrolling. In this gem, we will cover how to write self-modifying applications.

### The Principles of RAM-Code

RAM-code is a simple idea, but one that can take an inordinate amount of time to get just right. It is written for the most part in hexadecimal and can be difficult to debug. Let's look at a very simple case. We want to load a pointer from a 16-bit variable stored somewhere in RAM.

```
get_hl:
        ld  hl,ptr_var ; Load HL register with the address ptr_var
        ld  a,(hli)    ; Load A register with low byte
                       ; and increment HL
        ld  h,(hl)     ; Load L register with high byte of ptr_var
        ld  l,a        ; Save low byte into L
    ret                ; Return
```

This example can be improved by writing it as:

```
get_hl:
    db  $2a            ; ld hl,...
ptr_var
    dw  $0000          ; ...ptr_var
    ret
```

These two routines are logically no different from each other, but can you see the difference? The second example is stating the variable that stores the address to be loaded in HL as an immediate value! In other words, instead of physically going out and loading an address, we just load HL. It's quicker to load an immediate value than to access main memory, and because there are fewer bytes to decode, the code runs much faster. We can take that idea much further when it comes to preserving registers. Instead of pushing and popping everything, which can be expensive, we simply write the value ahead into the code. For example, instead of writing:

```
get_hl:
        ld      hl,ptr_var
        ld      a,(hli)
        ld      l,(hl)
        ld      h,a
        ld      a,(hl)
        push af  ; Save A register
        ;
        ; do something with A
        ;
        pop     af  ; Restore A register
    ret
```

this code can be optimized down to:

```
get_hl:
        db      $2a           ; ld hl,...
ptr_var
        dw      ptr_var       ; ...ptr_var
        ld      a,(hl)
        ld      (var1),a
        ;
        ; do something with A
        ;
        db      $2F           ; ld a,...
var1    db      $00           ; ...saved register value
        ret
```

This is not a huge saving, but it illustrates the point.

## A Fast Bit Blitter

In many games, it is often crucial to convert from one pixel format to another, such as from 16-bit (565) RGB to 24-bit RGB. Whether this is done in some offline tool or within the game itself can be satisfied with this one routine. We can define a structure (call it BITMAP) that contains information about an image. From this, our blitter can then use RAM-code techniques to construct an *execute-buffer*—a piece of code that has been allocated with malloc and filled with assembly instructions.

The blitter works by taking a routine that knows how to read 16-bit (565) RGB pixels and convert them to 32-bit RGBA values, and a routine that knows how to write them in another format. We can paste these two functions together, once for images with odd widths, or multiple times in succession to effectively unroll our loop. The example shown next takes the former approach.

So, let's define our bitmap structure and associated enumerated types.

```
enum Format{
    RGB_3x8=0,
    RGB_565=4,
    RGB_555=8,
    RGB_4x8=12,
    RGB_1x8=16
};

struct BITMAP{
    void *pixels;
    u32 w,h,depth;
    TRIPLET *pal;
    Format pxf;
    u32 stride;
    u32 size;
~   BITMAP();
    BITMAP(int,int,int,Format,int n=1);
    void draw(int,int,BITMAP&,int,int,int,int);
    operator bool(){
        return v!=NULL;
    }
};
```

Now, it's really important that we have the same structure defined on the assembly side of things.

```
BITMAP struct
pixels dd  ?
w      dd  ?
h      dd  ?
depth  dd  ?
pal    dd  ?
pxf    dd  ?
stride dd  ?
_size  dd  ?
BITMAP ends

PF_BGR_3x8  =    00h
PF_BGR_565  =    04h
PF_BGR_555  =    08h
PF_BGR_4x8  =    0Ch
PF_BGR_1x8  =    10h
```

The next step is to define our execute buffer.

```
execute_buffer db 128 dup(?)
```

For this code to work in C++, we must use a mangled C++ name for the member function BITMAP::draw. After that comes some initialization code:

```
?draw@BITMAP@@QAEXHHAAU1@HHHH@Z:

    push    ebp
    lea     ebp,[esp+8]        ;       get arguments address
```

```
            push    ebx
            push    edi
            push    esi

            mov edi,ecx                 ;dst bitmap
            mov esi,[ebp+8]             ;src bitmap
            mov eax,[esi].bitmap.pxf
```

The first thing we must decide is whether we *need* to do a conversion at all. Therefore, we test to see if the two pixel formats of the bitmap objects are the same. If so, we can further ask whether they are the same size. If that is the case, we can just do a fast string copy from one to the other. If not, but they're the same width, then we can still do the string copy. If the two have different widths, then we can do string copies line by line.

```
            mov edx,[edi].bitmap.pxf
            cmp eax,edx
            jne dislike
                ;
                ;   like copy
                ;
                mov ecx,[esi].bitmap._size
                cmp ecx,[edi].bitmap._size
                je  k3
                    mov   ecx,[edi].image.stride
                    mov   edx,[esi].image.stride
                    cmp   edx,ecx
                    jne   @f
                        ;
                        ;   same w different h
                        ;
                        mov edx,[edi].image.h
                        mov eax,[esi].image.h
                        cmp eax,edx
                        jl  k2
                            mov eax,edx
                        k2: mul ecx
                        mov ecx,eax
                        k3: mov esi,[esi].image.lfb
                        mov edi,[edi].image.lfb
                        shr ecx,2
                        rep movsd
                        jmp ou
@@:             ;
                ;   find smallest h -> ebx
                ;
                mov eax,[edi].image.h
                mov ebx,[esi].image.h
                cmp ebx,eax
                jl  @f
                    mov   ebx,eax
@@:             ;
                ;   calc strides
```

```
              ;
              add       ebp,12
              mov       eax,[ebp].rectangle.w
              mul       [esi].image.depth; edx corrupts
              mov       edx,[esi].image.stride
              sub       ecx,eax
              sub       edx,eax
              ;
              ;         calc offsets with intentional reg swap
              ;
              push      eax
              push      ecx
              push      edx
              call      calc_esdi
              pop       edx
              pop       eax
              pop       ecx
              ;
              ;         edx=dest pad
              ;
              shr       ecx,2
              mov       ebp,ecx
      @@:     rep       movsd
              lea       edi,[edi+eax]
              lea       esi,[esi+edx]
              mov       ecx,ebp
              dec       ebx
              jne       @b
      ou:     pop       esi
              pop       edi
              pop       ebx
              pop       ebp
              ret       1ch
```

If the two bitmaps have completely different pixel formats, we have no choice but to convert every single pixel from one format to the other. The following code shows this in action. There's another way to further improve this routine by unrolling the loop—this would be as simple as repeating the build step four or more times.

```
  dislike   :lea      eax,execute_buffer
             add       ebp,12
             push      ou
             push      eax
             push      edi
             push      esi
             push      ebp
             mov       ebx,edi   ; destination image
             mov       edi,eax
             ;
             ;         write "mov ebx,h"
             ;
             mov       al,0BDh
             stosb
             mov       eax,[ebp].rectangle.h
```

```
                stosd
                ;
                ;        write "mov ecx,w"
                ;
                mov      al,0B9h
                stosb
                mov      eax,[ebp].rectangle.w
                stosd
                ;
                ;        get read
                ;
                mov      edx,22
                mov      ebp,esi; source
                mov      eax,[ebp].image.pf
                mov      esi,rtbl_conv[eax]
                lodsd
                mov      ecx,eax
                add      edx,ecx
                rep      movsb
                ;
                ;        put write
                ;
                mov      eax,[ebx].image.pf
                mov      esi,wtbl_conv[eax]
                lodsd
                mov      ecx,eax
                add      edx,ecx
                rep      movsb
                ;
                ;        write tail
                ;
                mov      ecx,[esp]
                push     edx
                sub      dl,19
                neg      dl
                shl      edx,16
                or       edx,08D007549h
                mov      eax,edx
                stosd                            ; start of exec_tail
                mov      eax,[ecx].rectangle.w   ; args
                push     eax
                mov      ecx,[ebp].image.stride  ; source
                mul      [ebp].image.depth
                sub      ecx,eax
                jz       @f
                         mov      al,0B6h
                         stosb
                         mov      eax,ecx
                         stosd
                         jmp      pq
        @@:     ;
                ;        modify outer branch
                ;
                dec      edi
                mov      eax,[esp+4]
```

```
                  sub      eax,6
                  mov      [esp+4],eax
        pq:       pop      eax
                  mul      [ebx].image.depth
                  mov      ecx,[ebx].image.stride ; dest
                  sub      ecx,eax
                  jz       @f
                  mov      ax,0BF8Dh
                  stosw
                  mov      eax,ecx
                  stosd
                  pop      eax
                  jmp      pr
        @@:       pop      eax
                  sub      eax,6
        pr:       inc      al
                  neg      al
                  shl      eax,16
                  or       eax,0C300754Dh
                  stosd
                  pop      ebp
                  pop      esi
                  pop      edi
```

Another important step in this blitter is to correctly calculate the x and y offsets into the source and destination images. This routine does exactly that.

```
calc_esdi:        ;
                  ;        Destination
                  ;
                  mov      eax,[ebp-12].point.x       ; get dx
                  mul      [edi].image.depth          ; multiply by d
                  mov      ecx,eax                    ; store result
                  mov      eax,[ebp-12].point.y       ; get dy
                  mul      [edi].image.stride         ; multiple by stride
                  mov      edi,[edi].image.lfb        ; get target pixels
                  add      edi,ecx                    ; add x
                  add      edi,eax                    ; add y
                  ;
                  ;        Source
                  ;
                  mov      eax,[ebp].rectangle.x      ; get sx
                  mul      [esi].image.depth          ; multiply by d
                  mov      ecx,eax                    ; store result
                  mov      eax,[ebp].rectangle.y      ; get sy
                  mul      [esi].image.stride         ; multiple by stride
                  mov      edx,[esi].image.pal        ; palette info
                  mov      esi,[esi].image.lfb        ; get target pixels
                  add      esi,ecx                    ; add x
                  add      esi,eax                    ; add y
                  ret
```

For this whole RAM-code idea to work, we need some initialization that gets placed at the top of the RAM-code buffer. It simply loads the ECX register with the number of scan lines to copy.

```
exec_head      dd   5                                  ; (size)
               db   0B9h,000h,000h,000h,000h           ; mov   ecx,0
```

The next few routines are the actual read and write routines (RC and WC). The first byte tells us how many bytes make up the code in each subroutine.

```
RC_BGR_1x8     dd   18                                 ; (size)
               db   033h,0C0h                          ; xor   eax,eax
               db   0ACh                               ; lodsb
               db   08Bh,0D8h                          ; mov   ebx,eax
               db   003h,0C0h                          ; add   eax,eax
               db   003h,0C3h                          ; add   eax,ebx
               db   003h,0C2h                          ; add   eax,edx
               db   08Bh,000h                          ; mov   eax,[eax]
               db   025h,0FFh,0FFh,0FFh,000h           ; and   eax,-1

RC_BGR_3x8     dd   7                                  ; (size)
               db   0ADh                               ; lodsd
               db   025h,0FFh,0FFh,0FFh,000h           ; and   eax,-1
               db   04Eh                               ; dec   esi

RC_BGR_4x8     dd   1                                  ; (size)
               db   0ADh                               ; lodsd

RC_BGR_565:    dd   1                                  ; (size)
               lodsw

RC_BGR_555:    dd   1                                  ; (size)
               lodsw

WC_BGR_3x8     dd   6                                  ; (size)
               db   0AAh                               ; stosb
               db   0C1h,0E8h,008h                     ; shr   eax,8
               db   066h,0ABh                          ; stosw

WC_BGR_555     dd   28                                 ; (size)
               db   033h,0DBh                          ; xor   ebx,ebx
               db   0C0h,0E8h,003h                     ; shr   al,3
               db   0C0h,0ECh,003h                     ; shr   ah,3
               db   08Ah,0DCh                          ; mov   bl,ah
               db   066h,0C1h,0E3h,005h                ; shl   bx,5
               db   00Ah,0D8h                          ; or    bl,al
               db   0C1h,0E8h,013h                     ; shr   eax,13h
               db   066h,0C1h,0E0h,00Ah                ; shl   ax,0Ah
               db   066h,00Bh,0C3h                     ; or    ax,bx
               db   066h,0ABh                          ; stosw

WC_BGR_565     dd   28                                 ; (size)
               db   033h,0DBh                          ; xor   ebx,ebx
```

```
                    db   0C0h,0E8h,003h          ;  shr  al,3
                    db   0C0h,0ECh,002h          ;  shr  ah,2
                    db   08Ah,0DCh               ;  mov  bl,ah
                    db   066h,0C1h,0E3h,005h     ;  shl  bx,5
                    db   00Ah,0D8h               ;  or   bl,al
                    db   0C1h,0E8h,013h          ;  shr  eax,13h
                    db   066h,0C1h,0E0h,00Bh     ;  shl  ax,0Bh
                    db   066h,00Bh,0C3h          ;  or   ax,bx
                    db   066h,0ABh               ;  stosw

WC_BGR_4x8          dd   1                       ;  (size)
                    db   0ABh                    ;  stosd
```

Finally, we have a table that tells us which routine to use for every pixel format in BITMAP::pf.

```
rtbl_conv           dd   RC_BGR_3x8
                    dd   RC_BGR_565
                    dd   RC_BGR_555
                    dd   RC_BGR_4x8
                    dd   RC_BGR_1x8

wtbl_conv           dd   WC_BGR_3x8
                    dd   WC_BGR_565
                    dd   WC_BGR_555
                    dd   WC_BGR_4x8
                    dd   ?
```

# 1.15

## File Management Using Resource Files

### Bruno Sousa, Fireworks Interactive
gems2@fireworks-interactive.com

As games increase in size (I think the grand prize goes to *Phantasmagoria* with seven CDs), there is a need for organization of the game data. Having 10 files in the same directory as the executable is acceptable, but having 10,000 is not. Moreover, there is the directory structure, sometimes going five or more levels deep, which is a pain to work with. Because our games will hardly resemble Windows Explorer, we need to find a clean, fast way to store and organize our data. This is where resource files come into play. Resource files give us the power to encapsulate files and directories into a single file, with a useful organization. They can also take advantage of compression, encryption, and any other features we might need.

### What Is a Resource File?

We already use resource files all the time in our daily work—examples of these are WinZip, the Windows installer, and backup programs. A resource file is nothing more than a representation of data, usually from multiple files, but stored in just one file (see Listing 1.15.1). Using directories, we can make a resource file work just like a hard drive's file system does.

### Listing 1.15.1   Resource file structure.

```
Signature          = "SEALRFGNU" + '\0'
Version            = 1.0
Number of Files    = 58
Offset of First File = 19

[File 1]
[File 2]
[File 3]
[File .]
[File .]
[File .]
[File Number Of Files - 1]
[File Number Of Files]
```

Each lump (we will start calling files "lumps" from now on) in the resource file has its own structure, followed by all of the data (see Listing 1.15.2).

## Listing 1.15.2   File lump structure.

```
File Size = 14,340
Filename = "/bmp/Bob.bmp" + '\0'
Flags = COMPRESSED
FlagsInfo = 0xF34A400B
[Byte 1]
[Byte 2]
[Byte 3]
[Byte .]
[Byte .]
[Byte .]
[Byte File Size - 1]
[Byte File Size]
```

## Design

Before we do anything else, we'll need to name our resource system. We can then use the name to give each component a special naming scheme, one that will differentiate it from the other parts of the game. Let's call this system the "Seal Resource File System," abbreviated to SRFS, and use "sl" for class prefixes.

First, we need a resource file header. By looking at Listing 1.15.1, it's easy to see that we are keeping our system simple. However, that doesn't mean it isn't powerful, it means that it was designed to accommodate the most-needed features and still retain a fairly understandable syntax and structure.

Our resource file header gives us all the relevant information about the system. Multiple file types are used in games, and for each type, there is usually a file header that contains something unique to differentiate it from other file types. SRFS is no different, so the first data in its header is the file signature. This is usually a 5- to 10-character string, and is required so that we can identify the file as a valid Seal resource file. The version information is pretty straightforward—it is used to keep track of the file's version, which is required for a very simple reason: if we decide to upgrade our system by adding new features or sorting the lumps differently, we need a way to verify if the file being used supports these new features, and if so, use the latest code. Otherwise, we should go back to the older code—backward compatibility across versions is an important design issue and should not be forgotten. The next field in the header is for special flags. For our first version of the file system, we won't use this, so it must always be NULL (0). Possible uses for this flag are described in the *For the Future* section. Following this is the number of lumps contained in the resource file, and the offset to the first lump. This offset is required to get back to the beginning of the resource file if we happen to get lost, and can also be used to support future versions of this system. Extra information could be added after this header for later versions, and the offset will point to the first lump.

We now move to our lump header, which holds the information we need to start retrieving our data. We start with the lump size in bytes, followed by name and directory, stored as a fixed-length, NULL-terminated string. Following this is the flags member, which specifies the type of algorithm(s) used on the lump, such as encryption or compression. After that is information about the algorithm, which can contain a checksum for encryption or dictionary information for compression (the exact details depend on the algorithms). Finally, after all of this comes the lump information stored in a binary form.

Our system has only two modules: a resource file module and a lump module. To be able to use a lump, we need to load it from the resource file and possibly decrypt or decompress it into a block of memory, which can be accessed normally. Some systems prefer to encapsulate all functionality into the resource file module, and even allow direct access to lump data from within this module. This approach certainly has advantages, but the biggest disadvantage is probably that we need to have the whole resource in memory at once, unless we use only raw data or complicated algorithms to dynamically uncompress or decrypt our lump data to memory. This is a difficult process and beyond the scope of this gem.

We need functions to open the resource file, read the header, open individual lumps, read information from lumps, and get data from lumps. These are covered in the *Implementation* section.

## Implementation

ON THE CD

The sample code included in the CD is written in C++, but for the text, we will use pseudocode so it will be easy to implement in any language.

### The slCLump Module

Our lump module is similar to file streams in C++ or other language implementations of files in that we can write to it. Unfortunately, updating the resource file with a lump is very troublesome due to the nature of C++ streams. We can't add data to the middle of the stream—we can only replace it—and we can't modify the parent resource file.

```
DWORD           dwLumpSize;
STRING          szLumpName;
DWORD           dwLumpPosition;
BYTE [dwLumpSize] abData;
```

The variable *dwLumpSize* is a double word (32 bits) that specifies the size of the lump, *szLumpName* is a string describing the lump's name, *dwLumpPosition* keeps the lump's pointer position, and *abData* is an array of bytes with the lump information.

Here are the slCLump module functions:

```
DWORD   GetLumpSize (void);
STRING  GetLumpName (void);
```

```
DWORD    Read (BYTE [dwReadSize] abBuffer, DWORD dwReadSize);
DWORD    Write (BYTE [dwReadSize] abBuffer, DWORD dwWriteSize);
DWORD    Seek (DWORD dwSeekPosition, DWORD dwSeekType);
BOOLEAN IsValid (void);
```

GetLumpSize() retrieves the lump's size, and GetLumpName() retrieves the lump's name. Read() reads dwReadSize bytes into sbBuffer, and Write() does the exact opposite, writing dwWriteSize bytes to sbBuffer. Seek() moves the lump's pointer by a given number from a seek position, and IsValid() verifies if the lump is valid.

### The slCResourceFile Module

This module has all the functionality needed to load any lump inside the resource. The module members are nearly the same as those in the resource file header.

```
DWORD    dwVersion;
DWORD    dwFlags;
DWORD    dwNumberOfLumps;
DWORD    dwOffset;
STRING szCurrentDirectory;
FILE     fFile;
```

The use of these members has already been described, so here is a brief definition of each. *dwVersion* is a double word that specifies the file version, *dwFlags* is a double word containing any special flags for the lump, *dwNumberOfLumps* is the number of lumps in the resource, *dwOffset* gives us the position in bytes where the first lump is located, *szCurrentDirectory* is the directory we are in, and *fFile* is the actual C++ stream.

Now for the real meat of our system, the slCResourceFile functions—those that we use to access each lump individually.

```
void    OpenLump (STRING szLumpName, slCLump inOutLump);
void    IsLumpValid (STRING szLumpName);
void    SetCurrentDirectory (STRING szDirectory);
STRING GetCurrentDirectory (void);
```

Each of these functions is very simple. IsLumpValid() checks to see if a file with a given szLumpName exists in the resource. SetCurrentDirectory() sets the resource file directory to szDirectory. This directory name is prepended to each lump's name when accessing individual lumps within the resource file. GetCurrentDirectory() returns the current directory.

Now for our *Open* function. This function opens a lump within the resource file, and the logic behind the algorithm is described in pseudocode.

```
Check flags of Lump
    if Compressed
        OpenLumpCompressed (szLumpName, inOutLump)
    if Encrypted
```

```
        OpenLumpEncrypted (szLumpName, inOutLump)
    if Compressed and Encrypted
        OpenLumpCompressedEncrypted (szLumpName, inOutLump)
    else
        OpenLumpRaw (szLumpName, inOutLump)
end if
```

ON THE CD

Depending on the lump type, the appropriate function to open the lump is called, thus maintaining a nice design and simple code. The source of each function is included in the CD.

## Last Words about the Implementation

ON THE CD

Some support functions that are used to open the file or to keep track of information that can't be called directly are not represented in the preceding text. It is advisable to check the source code on the CD, which is well commented and easy to follow. The algorithms for compression and encryption are simple RLE compression and bit-wise encryption, the actual implementations of which are beyond the scope of this gem and must be researched separately. Information about useful public domain algorithms is at [Wotsit00], [Wheeler00], and [Gillies98].

## Conclusion

This system can be easily upgraded or adapted to any project. Some possibilities include supporting date and time validation, copy protection algorithms, checksums, a data pool, and better compression and encryption algorithms. There is no limit.

## References

[Hargrove98] Hargrove, Chris, "Code on the Cob 6," available online at www.loonygames.com/content/1.11/cotc/, November 2–6, 1998.

[Towner00] Towner, Jesse, "Resource Files Explained," available online at www.gamedev.net/reference/programming/features/resfiles/, January 11, 2000.

[Wheeler00] Wheeler, David J, et al, "TEA, The Tiny Encryption Algorithm," available online at www.cl.cam.ac.uk/ftp/users/djw3/tea.ps.

[Wotsit00] Wotsit.org, "The Programmer's File Format Collection: Archive Files," available online at www.wotsit.org, 1996–2000.

[Gillies98] Gillies, David A. G., "The Tiny Encryption Algorithm," available online at http://vader.brad.ac.uk/tea/tea.shtml, 1995–1998.

# 1.16

# Game Input Recording and Playback

## *Bruce Dawson, Humongous Entertainment*

bruced@humongous.com

The eighteenth-century mathematician and physicist Marquis Laplace postulated that if there was an intelligence with knowledge of the position, direction, and velocity of every particle of the universe, this intelligence would be able to predict by means of a single formula every detail of the total future as well as of the total past [Reese80]. This is *determinism*.

Chaos theory, Heisenberg's uncertainty principle, and genuine randomness in quantum physics have combined to prove determinism wrong. However, in the simplified universe of a game, Laplace's determinism actually works.

If you carefully record everything that can affect the direction of your game universe, you can replay your record and recreate what happened.

## What Exactly Is Input Recording Useful For?

Game input recording is useful for more things than many people realize: reproducing rare bugs, replaying interesting games, measuring optimizations, or creating game movies.

### Reproducing Bugs

Computer programs are deterministic and completely predictable, yet we frequently hear about people encountering bugs that are difficult to reproduce, and therefore difficult to fix. If computers are deterministic, how can bugs be difficult to reproduce?

Occasionally, the culprit is the hardware or OS. The timing of thread switching and the hard drive is completely consistent, so race conditions in your code can lead to rare crashes. However, the rare crashes are most frequently caused by a particular combination of user input that happens to be very rare. In that case, the bug is at least theoretically reproducible, if only we can reproduce the exact input sequence again.

Videotaping of testing helps track some of these bugs, but it doesn't help at all if the timing is critical. Why don't we put that computer predictability to work, by having the computer program record all input and play it back on demand?

The crucial step here is that if we are to use input recording to track bugs, we have to make sure that the input is recorded even when the game crashes—*especially* when the game crashes! On Win32, this is typically quite easy. By setting up a structured exception handler [Dawson99], we can arrange for our input buffer to be saved whenever the game crashes.

If we add an option to our game engine to "fast-forward" through game input (only rendering a fraction of the frames), we can get to the crash more quickly. If we also add an option to render frames at the exact same points in the game update loop, we can easily reproduce what are likely to be the relevant portions of the crash scenario.

Reproducing bugs is the one time when you will want to record and playback *all* of the user input, including the interactions with menu screens. Menu code is not immune to tricky bugs.

### Replaying Interesting Games

The most common use of game input recording is for players to record interesting games. These recordings are used to demonstrate how to play the game, to make tutorials, to test the performance of new computer hardware, or to share games.

The most important thing about recording games for users to play back later is that the recording must always be enabled. It is unrealistic to expect users to decide at the beginning of the game whether they want to record the game for posterity; they should be asked at the end whether they want to permanently store the recorded game.

### Measuring Optimizations

The most important thing to do when optimizing is to measure the actual performance, both before and after. Failing to do this leads to a surprisingly frequent tendency to check in "optimizations" that actually slow the code.

Measuring the performance of a game is tricky because it varies so much. Polygon count, texture set, overdraw, search path complexity, and the number of objects in the scene all affect the frame rate. Timing any single frame is meaningless, and a quick run-through is hopelessly unscientific.

Game input playback is a great solution. If you run the same playback multiple times, recording detailed information about game performance, you can chart your progress after each change to see how you're doing and where you still need work. Recording the average and worst-case frame rate and the consistency of the frame rate becomes easier and much more meaningful.

Testing optimizations with game input playback doesn't always work because your changes might affect the behavior—your wonderful new frame rate might just mean the player has walked into a closet. Therefore, when using game input playback for optimization testing, it is crucial that you record critical game state and check for changes on playback.

### Creating Game Movies

To create a demo reel, you can hook a VCR up to a video capable graphics card and play the game; however, the results will *not* be pretty. The VCR, the video encoder, and the variable frame rate of the game will lead to a blurry, jerky mess.

With game input recording, it's trivial to record an interesting game, and then play it back. With some trivial modifications to the engine you will be able to tell the game engine when you are at an interesting part of the playback, at which point you can switch from real-time playback to movie record playback. In this mode, the engine can render precisely 60 frames for each second of game play, and record each one to disk. The frame rate may drop to an abysmal two frames per second, but it doesn't matter because the canned inputs will play back perfectly.

### Implementing Multiplayer

A number of games—*X-Wing vs. TIE Fighter*, and *Age of Empires*—have used input recording and playback for their networking model [Lincroft99]. Instead of transmitting player status information, they just transmit player input. This works particularly well for strategy games with thousands of units.

## What Does It Take?

Game input recording is simple in theory, and can be simple in practice as well. However, there are a few subtleties that can cause problems if you're not careful.

### Making Your Game Predictable

For game input recording and playback to work, your game must be predictable. In other words, your game must not be affected by anything unpredictable or unknowable. For example, if your game can be affected by the exact timing of task switching, then your game is unpredictable.

Many games use variably interleaved update and render loops. Input is recorded at a set frequency. A frame is rendered and then the game update loop runs as many times as necessary to process the accumulated set of inputs.

This model implies that the number of times that the game update loop is run for each frame rendered is unpredictable; however, this needn't make the game itself unpredictable. If you are tracking down a bug in the renderer, then you may need to know the exact details of how the render loop and update loop were interleaved, but the rest of the time it should be irrelevant. It is worthwhile to record how many updates happened for each frame, but this information can be ignored on playback unless you are tracking a renderer bug.

However, if the render function does anything to change the state of the game, then the variably interleaved update loop and render function do make the game unpredictable, and input recording will not work. One example of this is a render function that uses the same random number generator as the update loop. Another example can be found in *Total Annihilation*. In this game, the "fog of war" was only updated when the scene was rendered. This was a reasonable optimization because it reduced the frequency of this expensive operation. While it ensured that the user only ever saw accurate fog, it made the game's behavior unpredictable. The unit AI used the same fog of war as the renderer; the timing of the render function calls would subtly affect the course of the game.

Another example of something that can make a game unpredictable is uninitialized local variables or functions that don't always return results. Either way, your game's behavior will depend on whatever happened to be on the stack. These are bugs in your code, so you already have a good reason to track them down.

One tricky problem that can lead to unpredictability is sound playback. This can cause problems because the sound hardware handles them asynchronously. Tiny variances in the sound hardware can make a sound effect occasionally end a bit later. Even if the variation is tiny, if it happens to fall on the cusp between two frames, then it can affect your game's behavior if it is waiting for the sound to end.

For many games, this is not a problem because there is no synchronization of the game to the end of these sounds. If you do want this synchronization, then there is a fairly effective solution: approximation. When you start your sound effect, calculate how long the sample will play—number of samples divided by frequency. Then, instead of waiting for the sound to end, wait until the specified amount of time has elapsed. The results will be virtually identical and they will be perfectly consistent.

**Initial State**

You also need to make sure that your game starts in a known state, whether starting a new game or loading a saved one. That usually happens automatically. However, each time you recompile or change your data you are slightly changing the initial state. Luckily, many changes to code and data don't affect the way the game will unfold. For instance, if you change the size of a texture, then the frame rate may change, but the behavior should not—as long as the game is predictable. If changing the size of that texture causes all other memory blocks to be allocated at different locations, then this should also have no effect—as long as your code doesn't have any memory overwrite bugs.

An example of a code or data change that could affect how your game behaves would be changing the initial position of a creature or wall, or slightly adjusting the probability of a certain event. Small changes might never make a difference, but they destroy the guarantee of predictability.

Floating-point calculations are one area where your results may unexpectedly vary. When you compile an optimized build, the compiler may generate code that gives slightly different results from the unoptimized build—and occasionally, these differences will matter. You can use the "Improve Float Consistency" optimizer setting in Visual C++ to minimize these problems, but floating-point variations are an unavoidable problem that you just have to watch for.

### Random Numbers

Random numbers can be used in a deterministic game, but there are a few caveats.

The reason random numbers can be used is that *rand()* isn't really random. *rand()* is implemented using a simple algorithm—typically a linear congruential method—that passes many of the tests for random numbers while being completely reproducible. This is called a pseudo-random number generator. As long as you initialize *rand()* with a consistent seed, you will get consistent results. If having the randomness in your game different each time is important, then choose a seed for *srand()* based on the time, but record the seed so that you can reuse it if you need to reproduce the game.

One problem with *rand()* is that it produces a single stream of random numbers. If your rendering code and your game update code are both using *rand()*—and if the number of frames rendered per game update varies—then the state of the random number generator will quickly become indeterminate. Therefore, it is important that your game update loop and your renderer get their random numbers from different locations.

Another problem with *rand()* is that its behavior isn't portable. That is, the behavior is not guaranteed to be identical on all platforms, and it is unlikely that it will be.

The third problem with *rand()* comes if you save a game and continue playing, and then want to reload the saved game and replay the future inputs. To make this work predictably, you have to put the random number generator back to the state it was in when you saved the game. The trouble is, there's no way to do this. The C and C++ standards say nothing about the relationship between the numbers coming out of *rand()* and the number you need to send to *srand()* to put it back to that state. Visual C++, for instance, maintains a 32-bit random number internally, but only returns 15 of those bits through *rand()*, making it impossible to reseed.

These three problems lead to an inescapable conclusion: don't use *rand()*. Instead, create random number objects that are portable and restartable. You can have one for your render loop, and one for your game update loop.

When implementing your random number objects, please don't invent your own random number algorithm. Random number generators are very subtle and you are unlikely to invent a good one on your own. Look at your C runtime source code, the sample code on the CD, Web resources [Coddington], or read Knuth [Knuth81].

### Inputs

Once you have restored your game's initial state, you need to make sure that you can record and play back all of the input that will affect your game. If your game update loop is calling OS functions directly to get user input—such as calling the Win32 function *GetKeyState(VK_SHIFT)* to find out when the Shift key is down—then it will be very hard to do this. Instead, all input needs to go through an input system. This system can record the state of all of the input devices at the beginning of each frame, and hand out this information as requested by the game update loop. The input system can easily record this information to disk, or read it back from disk, without the rest of the game knowing. The input system can read data from Direct-Input, a saved game, the network, or a *WindowProc*, without the update loop knowing the difference. As a nice bonus, isolating the game input in one place makes your game code cleaner and more portable.

Programmers have a habit of breaking all rules that are not explicitly enforced, so you need to prevent them from calling OS input functions directly. You can use the following technique to prevent programmers from accidentally using "off-limits" functions.

```
#define  GetKeyState Please do not use this function
#define  GetAsyncKeyState Please do not use this function either
...
```

Another important input to a multiplayer game is the network. If you want to be able to replay your game, then you need to record the incoming network data together with the user's input stream. This will allow you to replay the game, even without a network connection. The network data stream is the one type of data that can actually get quite large—a game running on a 56K modem could easily receive many megabytes of network data per hour. While this large data stream does make the recording more unwieldy, it is not big enough to be really problematic. The benefits of recording this stream are enormous, and the costs are quite small.

The final "input" that a game might use is time. You may want certain events to happen at a specific time, and it is important that these times are measured in game time, not in real time. Whenever your game needs to know the time—except for profiling purposes—it should ask the game engine for the current game time. As with the other input functions, it is a good idea to use the preprocessor to make sure that nobody accidentally writes code that calls *timeGetTime()* or other OS time functions.

It is a good idea to record inputs throughout the game. That lets you use input playback to track down bugs anywhere in the game, even in the pre-game menus. However, for many purposes you will want to store the record of the input during the game separately, so that you can play it back separately.

## Testing Your Input Recording

Game input recording should work on any well-written game. Even if your game is a multiplayer game, if you record every piece of input that you receive on your machine, then you should be able to reproduce the same game.

However, if your game playbacks are failing to give consistent results, it can be difficult to determine why. A useful option in tracking down these problems is recording part of the game state along with the input—perhaps the health and location of all of the game entities. Then, during playback, you can check for changes and detect differences before they become visible.

## Conclusion

Game input recording and playback is a valuable part of a game engine with many benefits. If it is planned from the beginning, then it is easy to add, and leads to a better-engineered and more flexible game engine. Here are some rules to follow:

- Route all game input, including keyboard, mouse, joystick, network, and time, through a single input system, to ensure consistency and to allow recording and saving of all input. This input should always be recorded. It should be stored permanently in case the game crashes or the user requests it at the end of the game.
- Watch for floating-point optimizations or bugs in your code that can occasionally lead to behavior that is different or unpredictable in optimized builds.
- The *rand()* function should be avoided; use random number objects instead.
- Never change the game's state in rendering functions.
- Store some of your game state along with the input so you can automatically detect inconsistencies. This can help detect race conditions, unintended code changes, or bugs.

ON THE CD

The sample code on the CD includes an imput system and a random number class.

## References

[Reese80] Reese, W.L., *Dictionary of Philosophy and Religion*. Humanities Press, Inc. 1980. p. 127.

[Knuth81] Knuth, Donald, *The Art of Computer Programming, Second Edition, Volume 2, Seminumerical Algorithms.*

[Coddington] Coddington, Paul, "Random Number Generators," available online at www.npac.syr.edu/users/paulc/lectures/montecarlo/node98.html.

[Dawson99] Dawson, Bruce, "Structured Exception Handling," *Game Developer* magazine (Jan 1999): pp. 52–54.

[Lincroft99] Lincroft, Peter, "The Internet Sucks: What I Learned Coding X-Wing vs. TIE Fighter," 1999 Game Developers Conference Proceedings, Miller Freeman 621–630.

# 1.17

# A Flexible Text Parsing System

## James Boer, Lithtech, Inc.

jimb@lithtech.com

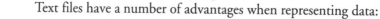

Nearly every modern game requires some sort of text parser. This gem, along with the sample code on the CD, demonstrates a powerful but easy-to-use text parsing system designed to handle any type of file format.

Text files have a number of advantages when representing data:

- They are easy to read and edit using any standard text editor. Binary data usually requires a custom-built tool that must be created, debugged, and maintained.
- They are flexible—the same parser can be used for simple variable assignment or a more complex script.
- They can share constants between code and data (more on this later).

Unfortunately, text data has a few drawbacks as well:

- Unlike most binary formats, text must first be tokenized and interpreted, slowing the loading process.
- Stored text is not space efficient; it wastes disk space and slows file loading.

Because many game parameters only need to be tweaked during development, it may be practical to use a text-based format during development, and then switch to a more optimized binary format for use in the shipping product. This provides the best of both worlds: the ease of use of text files, and the loading speed of binary data. We'll discuss a method for compiling text files into a binary format later in the gem.

## The Parsing System

Here's what our parser will support:

- Native support for basic data types: keywords, operators, variables, strings, integers, *floats*, *bools*, and GUIDs
- Unlimited user-definable keyword and operator recognition
- Support for both C (block) and C++ (single-line) style comments
- Compiled binary read and write ability
- Debugging support, able to point back to a source file and line number in case of error

- *#include* file preprocessing support
- *#define* support for macro substitution

Most of the preceding items are self-explanatory, but *#include* files and *#define* support may seem a bit out of place when discussing a text parser. We'll discuss how these features can greatly simplify scripts, as well as provide an additional mechanism to prevent scripts and code from getting out of sync.

## Macros, Headers, and Preprocessing Magic

Preprocessing data files in the same manner as C or C++ code can have some wonderful benefits. The concept is perhaps best explained by a simple example. Let's assume that we wish to create a number of unique objects using a script file, which will provide the necessary data to properly initialize each object and create unique handles for use in code. Here's what such a script might look like:

```
CreateFoo(1)    { Data = 10 }
CreateFoo(2)    { Data = 20 }
CreateFoo(3)    { Data = 30 }
CreateBar(4)    { Foo = 1 }
```

Assuming that the *CreateFoo()* keyword triggers the creation of a *Foo* object in code, we now have three *Foo* objects in memory, each with unique member data, created by a script. Also, assuming that we're referencing these objects with handles, we can now access these objects in code with the values of 1, 2, and 3 as unique handles. Note that in our example, the script can also use these numeric handles. The *Bar* class requires a valid *Foo* object as a data member, and so we use a reference to the first *Foo* object created when creating our first *Bar* object.

It could get easy to lose track of the various handle values after creating several hundred of them. Any time an object is added in the script, the programmer must change the same values in code. There are no safeguards to prevent the programmer from accidentally referencing the wrong script object. This problem has already been solved in C and C++ through the use of *header files* in which variables and other common elements can be designed for many source files to share. If we think of the text script as simply another source file, the advantages of a C-like preprocessor quickly become apparent. Let's look again at our example using a header file instead of magic numbers.

```
— Header File —

// ObjHandles.h
// Define all our object handles
#define SmallFoo    1
#define MediumFoo   2
#define LargeFoo    3
#define SmallBar    4
#define FooTypeX    10
```

```
#define FooTypeY    20
#define FooTypeZ    30

— Script File —

//
// Directs the parser to scan the header file
#include "ObjHandles.h"

CreateFoo(SmallFoo)              { Data = FooTypeX }
CreateFoo(MediumFoo)   { Data = FooTypeY }
CreateFoo(LargeFoo)              { Data = FooTypeZ }
CreateBar(SmallBar)              { Foo = SmallFoo }
```

In addition to this being much easier to read and understand without the magic numbers, both the text script and source code share the same header file, so it's impossible for them to get out of sync.

Because we're already performing a simple preprocessing substitution with *#define*, it's just one more step to actually parse and use more complex macros. By recognizing generic argument-based macros, we can now make complex script operations simpler by substituting arguments. Macros are also handy to use for another reason. Because macros are not compiled in code unless they are actually used (like a primitive form of templates), we can create custom script-based macros without breaking C++ compatibility in the header file.

Note that although we're processing macros and *#defines*, the parser does not recognize other commands such as *#ifdef*, *#ifndef*, and *#endif*.

## The Parsing System Explained

There are five classes in our parsing system: *Parser*, *Token*, *TokenList*, *TokenFile*, and *Macro*. The *Macro* class is a helper class used internally in *Parser*, so we only need to worry about it in regard to how it's used inside *Parser*. *TokenFile* is an optional class used to read and write binary tokens to and from a standard token list. This leaves the heart of the parsing system: *Parser*, *Token*, and *TokenList*. Because *Token* is the basic building block produced by the parser, let's examine it first.

### The *Token* Class

The basic data type of the parsing system is the *Token* class. There are eight possible data types represented by the class: keywords, operators, variables, strings, integers, real numbers, Booleans, and GUIDs. Keywords, operators, variables, and strings are all represented by C-strings, and so the only real difference among them is semantic. Integers, real numbers, and Booleans are represented by *signed integers*, *doubles*, and *bools*. For most purposes, this should be sufficient for data representation. GUIDs, or Globally Unique IDentifiers, are also given native data type status, because it's often handy to have a data type that is guaranteed unique, such as for identifying classes to create from scripts.

The *Token* class is comprised of a type field and a union of several different data types. A single class represents all basic data types. Data is accessed by first checking what type of token is being dealt with, and then calling the appropriate *Get()* function. Asserts ensure that inappropriate data access is not attempted.

Each of the data types has a role to play in the parser, and it's important to understand how they work so that script errors are avoided. In general, the type definitions match similar definitions in C++. All keywords and tokens are case sensitive.

### Keyword

Keywords are specially defined words that are stored in the parser. Two predefined keywords are *include* and *define*. User-defined keywords are used primarily to aid in lexicographical analysis of the tokens after the scanning phase.

### Operator

An operator is usually a one- or two-character symbol such as an assignment operator or a comma. Operators are unique in the fact that they act like white space regarding their ability to separate other data types. Because of this, operators always have the highest priority in the scanning routines, meaning that the symbols used in operators cannot be used as part of a keyword or variable name. Thus, using any number or character as part of an operator should be avoided. Operators in this parsing system also have an additional restriction: because of the searching method used, any operator that is larger than a single character must be composed of smaller operators. The larger symbol will always take precedence over the smaller symbols when they are not separated by white space or other tokens.

### Variable

A variable is any character-based token that was not found in the keyword list.

### String

A string must be surrounded by double quotes. This parser supports strings of lengths up to 1024 characters (this buffer constant is adjustable in the parser) and does not support multiple-line strings.

### Integers

The parser recognizes both positive and negative numbers and stores them in a signed integer value. It also recognizes hexadecimal numbers by the *0x* prefix. No range checking is performed.

### Floats

Floating-point numbers are called *floats* and are represented by a *double* value. The parser will recognize any number with a decimal point as a float. It will not recognize scientific notation, and no range checking is performed on the floating-point number.

### Booleans

Boolean values are represented as a native C++ *bool* type, and *true* and *false* are built-in keywords. As with C++, these values are case sensitive.

### GUIDs

By making use of the macro-expansion code, we can support GUIDs without too much extra work. Note that unless the macro is expanded with *ProcessMacros()*, the GUID will remain a series of separate primitive types. This function is described later.

### The *TokenList* Class

The *TokenList* class is publicly derived from a standard STL *list* of *Tokens*. It acts exactly like a standard STL *list* of tokens, and has a couple of additional features. The *TokenList* class allows viewing of the file and line number that any given token comes from. This is exclusively an aid for debugging, and can be removed with a compile-time flag.

### The *Parser* Class

This is the heart of the parsing functionality. We first create a parser object and call the *Create()* function. Note that all functions return a *bool* value, using *true* for success and *false* for failure. Next, we must reserve any additional operators or keywords beyond the defaults required for the text parsing.

After this comes the actual parsing. The parsing phase is done in three passes, handled by three functions. Splitting the functionality up gives the user more control over the parsing process. Often, for simple parsing jobs, *#include* file processing and macro substitution are not needed. The first pass reads the files and translates the text directly into a *TokenList* using the function *ProcessSource()*. The next function, *ProcessHeaders()*, looks for any header files embedded in the source, and then parses and substitutes the contents of those headers into the original source. The third function, *ProcessMacros()*, performs both simple and complex C-style macro substitution. This can be a very powerful feature, and is especially useful for scripting languages.

Let's see what this whole process looks like. Note that for clarity and brevity's sake, we are not doing any error checking.

```
// We need a Parser and TokenList object to start
TokenList toklist;
Parser parser;

// Create the parser and reserve some more keywords and tokens
parser.Create();
parser.ReserveKeyword("special_keyword");
parser.ReserveOperator("[");
parser.ReserveOperator("]");

// Now parse the file, any includes, and process macros
parser.ProcessSource("data\scripts\somescript.txt", &toklist);
parser.ProcessHeaders(&toklist);
parser.ProcessMacros(&toklist);
```

### The *TokenFile* Class

Because parsing and processing human readable text files can be a bit slow, it may be necessary to use a more efficient file format in the shipping code. The *TokenFile* class can convert processed token lists into a binary form. This avoids having to parse the text file multiple times, doing *#include* searches, macro substitutions, and so forth. Character-based values, such as keywords, operators, and variables, are stored in a lookup table. All numeric values are stored in binary form, providing additional space and efficiency savings. In general, this binary form can be expected to load five to ten times as fast as the text-based form.

Using the *TokenFile* class is simple as well. The *Write()* function takes a *TokenList* object as an argument, and creates the binary form using either the output stream or filename that was specified. The class can also store the file in either a case-sensitive or case-insensitive manner. If both the variable "Foo" and "foo" appear in the script, turning the case sensitivity off will merge them together in the binary format, providing further space savings. It defaults to off.

Reading the file is performed with the *Read()* function. Here's how it looks in code:

```
TokenFile tf;

// Write a file to disk
tf.Write("somefile.pcs", &toklist);

// Or read it
tf.Read("somefile.pcs", &toklist);
```

## Wrapping Up

Text file processing at its simplest level is a trivial problem requiring only a few lines of code. For anything more complex than this, however, it's beneficial to have a comprehensive text-parsing system that can be as flexible and robust as the job demands.

# 1.18

## A Generic Tweaker

### Lasse Staff Jensen, Funcom

lasse@funcom.com

**D**uring game development, one of the most frequent tasks we perform is tweaking variables until the game has just the right balance we need. In this gem, we will cover an easy-to-use "tweaker" interface and the design issues behind the implementation.

### Requirements Analysis

One of the primary goals of a generic tweaker interface is to make it as transparent and easy to use as possible. The user in this case is the programmer who exposes variables to be tweaked. Further requirements to emphasise are the size in memory, the ability to tweak a variable without too much added overhead, and the speed of actually tweaking a variable (because in some cases the tweaker will be used in the release build as well).

Let's try to break down the requirements in more detail, and see what the implementation really needs to do:

- It should be transparent to the coder, meaning that the variables we want to tweak shouldn't contain any additional data and/or functionality, and that the usage of these variables shouldn't need to know about the tweaker at all.
- It should be simple to use, meaning that the user should be able to define variables to be tweaked in less than 10 lines of code, and be able to tweak and get variables from a common database in typically two or three lines of code.

### Implementation

#### Design

Figure 1.18.1 contains the UML diagram of the classes to be presented in a bottom-up fashion in the rest of this gem. The type information and the tweakable hierarchy are the essence of this design.

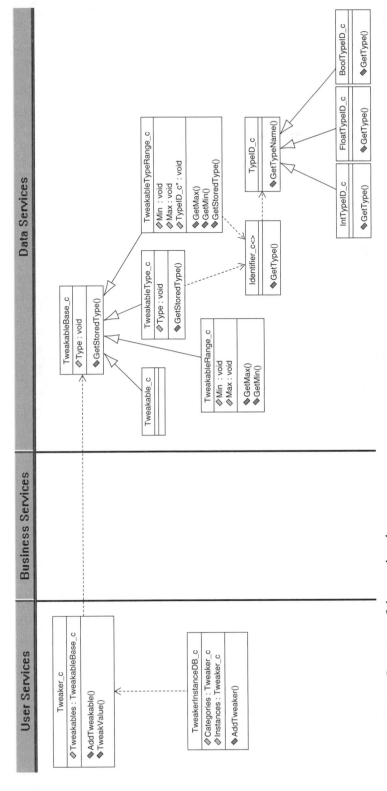

**FIGURE 1.18.1** *Overview of the tweaker classes.*

**Type Information**

We will use template specialization to provide type information that we can store in a uniform way. First is our base class *TypeID_c* that defines the interface for our type information class with a virtual function that returns a string with the type name:

```
class TypeID_c {
public:
  virtual const char* GetTypeName() const { return "Unknown"; }
};
```

Next, we create a template class that we can use to retrieve the correct type when given the variable. In this class, we add a member to get the pointer to our *TypeID_c* instance that can be tested directly for the stored pointer address.

```
template <class T>
class Identifier_c {
  public:
    static const TypeID_c* const GetType();
};
```

Now that we have this class declared, we will use template specialization to define each unique type. Each subclass of *TypeID_c* will exist as a singleton, and the pointer to that instance serves as the identifier of the type. For simplicity, all of these will be placed in the global scope through static members. We can make sure that the actual instances exist, if called from other static functions, by receiving the pointer from the *GetIdentification* method. The full implementation for *float* values follows:

```
class floatID_c : public TypeID_c {
public:
  virtual const char* GetTypeName() const { return "float"; }
  static TypeID_c* const GetIdentification();
};

template <>
class Identifier_c<float> {
public:
  static const TypeID_c* const GetType() {
   return floatID_c::GetIdentification();
  }
};

TypeID_c* const floatID_c::GetIdentification() {
    static floatID_c cInstance;
    return &cInstance;
}
```

To use these classes for type information, we can simply store the base pointer:

```
float vMyFloat;
...
const TypeID_c* const pcType = TweakableBase_c::GetTypeID( vMyFloat );
```

Here, the *TweakableBase_c* (more on this class later) has a template member that calls the correct *Identifier_c* specialization. Then we can test the address of the pointer:

```
if( Identifier_c<float>::GetType() == pcType ) {
  // We have a float!
}
```

**ON THE CD**

There are two macros for defining user types in the code on the accompanying CD, so all that's required for support of a new data type is to place a call to *DECLARE_DATA_TYPE* in the header and *DEFINE_DATA_TYPE* in the implementation file, and then recompile. (In addition, one might want to add a call to the macro DUMMY_OPERATORS() in case one doesn't want to support range checking.)

### TweakableBase_c

We have a clean and easy way to store type info, so let's continue by creating the base class to hold the pointer to the tweakable variable. This class also contains the template member for getting the type info mentioned earlier. Because one of our requirements is to keep memory overhead to a minimum, we will use RTTI for checking which specific types of tweakables we have stored in memory. We therefore make sure the class is polymorphic by adding a virtual function to get the type info stored (or NULL if none). Here is the implementation:

```
class TweakableBase_c {
public:

  TweakableBase_c( void* i_pData ) : m_pData( i_pData ) {;}
  ~TweakableBase_c() { /*NOP*/;}

  virtual const TypeID_c* const GetStoredType() const { return NULL; }

  template <class T>
  static const TypeID_c* const GetTypeID( const T& i_cValue ) {
    return Identifier_c<T>::GetType();
  }

protected:
    void* m_pData;

}; // TweakableBase_c
```

Now that we have the base class, we can create subclasses containing additional data such as type information, limits for range checking, a pointer for a call-back function, and any other data we might need to attach to the various tweakables, while keeping the memory to a minimum. Here is how one of the specific tweakable classes looks:

```
template <class T>
class TweakableType_c : public TweakableBase_c {
```

```
public:

  TweakableType_c( T* i_pxData, const TypeID_c* i_pcType ) :
    TweakableBase_c( reinterpret_cast<void*>( i_pxData ) ),
    m_pcType( i_pcType ) { /*NOP*/; }

  const TypeID_c* const GetDataType() const { return m_pcType; }
  virtual const TypeID_c* const GetStoredType() const {
    return m_pcType; }

private:
  const TypeID_c* const m_pcType;
}; // TweakableType_c
```

The great thing about this code is that the subclasses are implemented as templates, even though the base class was defined without them. This way, we can pass in the pointer to the actual data type, hiding the casting to *void* from the interface.

### Tweaker_c

We finally have all the building blocks we need to create the tweaker class itself. This class will store all of our tweakables and give the user functionality for tweaking the stored values. We will use an STL *map* to hold all of the pointers to our tweakables, using the name of each tweakable as the key. Simple template members provide all the functionality. An example of this is the *TweakValue* member:

```
template<class Value_x>
TweakError_e TweakValue( const std::string& i_cID, const Value_x&
                         i_xValue ) {
  TweakableBase_c* pcTweakable;
  iTweakableMap_t iSearchResult = m_cTweakable_map.find( i_cID );
  if( iSearchResult == m_cTweakable_map.end() ) {
    return e_UNKNOWN_KEY; }
  pcTweakable = (*iSearchResult).second;

#ifdef _DEBUG
  TweakableType_c<Value_x>* pcType;
  if( pcType = dynamic_cast< TweakableType_c<Value_x>* >(
      pcTweakable ) ) {
    assert( pcTweakable->GetTypeID( i_xValue ) ==
      pcType->GetDataType() );
  }
#endif

  TweakableTypeRange_c<Value_x>* pcTypeRange;
  if( pcTypeRange = dynamic_cast< TweakableTypeRange_c<Value_x>* >(
      pcTweakable ) )
  {
    assert( pcTweakable->GetTypeID( i_xValue ) ==
      pcTypeRange->GetDataType() );

    if( i_xValue < pcTypeRange->GetMin() ) { return e_MIN_EXCEEDED; }
    if( i_xValue > pcTypeRange->GetMax() ) { return e_MAX_EXCEEDED; }
```

```
    }

    *(reinterpret_cast<Value_x*>( pcTweakable->m_pData ) ) = i_xValue;
    return e_OK;
} // TweakValue
```

Because the member is a template, we can cast back to the given value directly, thereby completely hiding the ugly *void* casting. Note that if users decide to not store the type information, they could easily force us to do something bad, since we have no way of checking the origin of the *reinterpret_cast*!

### TweakerInstanceDB_c

In order to support grouping of tweakables and the ability to store several instances of a given variable, we have an instance database to hold different tweakers. The implementation is straightforward—an STL *multimap* holding all of the instances of different tweakers, and an STL *map* of these *multimap*s where the category is the key.

## Usage

Let's test our implementation against the requirements to verify that we have reached our goals. Defining a variable to be tweakable requires us to create a tweaker and add it to the tweakable instance database.

```
Tweaker_c* pcTweaker = TweakerInstanceDB_c::AddTweaker( "Landscape",
    TWEAKER_CREATE_ID( this ), "Graphics" );
```

Here we create a tweaker for the class *Landscape* (inside the constructor, for example) and put it in the Graphics category. The *TWEAKER_CREATE_ID* macro takes the *this* pointer and makes sure that each instance of the class *Landscape* gets a unique ID. Then, we simply add each variable to this (and other tweakers we make) by:

```
pcTweaker->AddTweakable( &m_vShadowmapScaleTop, "Shadowmap scale",
    0.0F, 68.0F );
```

Here we have added a variable, constrained it to the interval [0, 68], and called it "Shadowmap scale." It's vital to note that because of the template nature of the *AddTweakable* method, we must pass correct types to all of the arguments (for example, use 0.0F and not just 0). Defining a variable to be tweakable takes two lines of code, and is totally hidden from the users of the variable in question.

For tweaking this variable, all we need is the name, data type, and desired instance. Usually, we have the pointer to the tweaker instance itself, but in the GUI code, one would typically do something like:

```
TweakerInstanceDB_c::iConstCategoryMap_t iCategory =
    TweakerInstanceDB_c::GetCategory( "Graphics" );
Tweaker_c* pcTweaker =
    GetTweaker( iCategory->second, "Landscape", TWEAKER_CREATE_ID(
pcLandscape ) ) ;
```

Here we first get all of the instance maps that are stored under the "Graphics" category label. Then we search for the correct instance of the *Landscape* class (we assume the pointer *pcLandscape* points to the instance in question). Changing the value of a specific value is straightforward.

```
Tweaker_c::TweakError_e eError;
eError = pcTweaker->TweakValue( "Shadowmap scale", 20.0F );
```

So, tweaking a variable is one line of code, with additional lines for error handling (or simply asserting the return value). Receiving the stored value is done similarly:

```
float vShadowmapScale;
eError = pcTweaker->GetValue( "Shadowmap scale", &vShadowmapScale );
```

## Graphical User Interface

GUIs tend to be specific to each project, so I have left a general discussion of this topic out of this gem, although I will describe an existing implementation as a source for ideas. In Equinox, Funcom's next-generation 3D engine, we have implemented a directory structure, as shown in Figure 1.18.2, that can be browsed in a console at the top of the screen.

For tweaking values, we have defined input methods that can be assigned to the tweakables. That way, we can create specialized input methods such as the angle tweaker seen in Figure 1.18.3.

For saving and loading, in addition to the binary snapshots, we can save all of the tweakables in *#define* statements directly into *h* files. Because the number of instances of a variable could change over the lifetime of the application, we only save the first instance into the header file. This feature gives us the capability to add variables to be tweaked only in debug builds, and we then *#include* the header file to initialize the

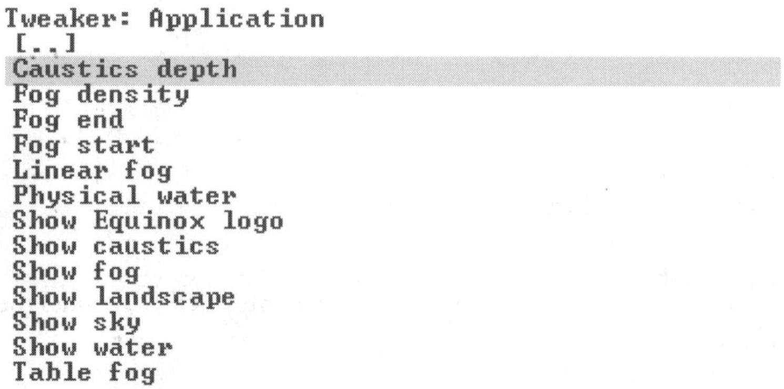

```
Tweaker: Application
 [..]
Caustics depth
Fog density
Fog end
Fog start
Linear fog
Physical water
Show Equinox logo
Show caustics
Show fog
Show landscape
Show sky
Show water
Table fog
```

**FIGURE 1.18.2**   *Screen shot from our GUI. The user can move up and down in the directories (categories in the code) and choose values to be tweaked.*

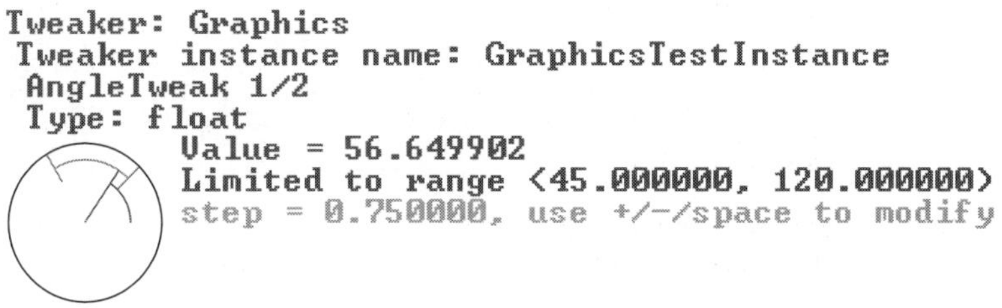

```
Tweaker: Graphics
Tweaker instance name: GraphicsTestInstance
AngleTweak 1/2
Type: float
      Value = 56.649902
      Limited to range <45.000000, 120.000000>
      step = 0.750000, use +/-/space to modify
```

**FIGURE 1.18.3**  *This specialized input gives the user the possibility to visually tweak angles in an intuitive way.*

variables to the latest tweaked value in the release build. Here is a sample of how this works for our *ShadowmapScale* variable:

```
landscape_tweakables.h:

...

#define SHADOWMAP_SCALE 43.5

...

landscape.cpp:

#include "landscape_tweakables.h"
...
m_vShadowmapScale = SHADOWMAP_SCALE;
...
```

## Note

It is possible to use the RTTI *typeid()* to replace the type information code detailed previously. There are pros and cons to using our type information code.

Pros:

- It takes up less space for the type information, since it is only required for classes that use it.
- One can add specific information to the *TypeID_c* class; for example, a way to load and store the type or a pointer to the GUI control.

Cons:

- We have to use macros for each unique type, while RTTI provides the type information automatically.

## Acknowledgment

I would like to thank Robert Golias for invaluable help and suggestions, and for implementing the Equinox tweaker GUI that was an excellent test of how simple the interface actually turned out!

# 1.19

## Genuine Random Number Generation

### Pete Isensee, Microsoft

pkisensee@msn.com

Computer games use random numbers extensively for rolling dice, shuffling cards, simulating nature, generating realistic physics, and performing secure multi-player transactions. Computers are great at generating pseudo-random numbers, but not so good at creating genuine random numbers. Pseudo-random numbers are numbers that *appear* to be random, but are algorithmically computed based on the previous random number. Genuine, or real, random numbers are numbers that not only appear random, but are unpredictable, nonrepeating and nondeterministic. They are generated without the input of the previous random number. This gem presents a method of creating genuine random numbers in software.

### Pseudo-Randomness

Pseudo-random number sequences eventually repeat themselves and can always be precisely reproduced given the same seed. This leads to distinct problems in gaming scenarios. Consider the common case of a game that initializes its random number generator (RNG) with the current tick count – the number of ticks since the machine was booted up. Now assume the player turns on their gaming console every time they begin playing this game. The level of randomness in the game is gated by the choice of seed, and the number of bits of randomness in the seed is unacceptably small.

Now consider the use of a pseudo-RNG to create secret keys for encrypting secure multiplayer game transmissions. At the core of all public key cryptographic systems is the generation of unpredictable random numbers. The use of *pseudo*-random numbers leads to false security, because a pseudo-random number is fully predictable—translate: easily hacked—if the initial state is known. It's not uncommon for the weakest part of crypto systems to be the secret key generation techniques [Kelsey98].

### Genuine Randomness

A genuine random number meets the following criteria: it appears random, has uniform distribution, is unpredictable, and is nonrepeating. The quality of unpredictability is paramount for security purposes. Even given full knowledge of the algorithm, an attacker should find it computationally infeasible to predict the output [Schneier96].

The ideal way of creating genuine random numbers is to use a physical source of randomness, such as radioactive decay or thermal noise. Many such devices exist; see [Walker(a)] for one example. However, PCs and video game consoles do not typically have access to these types of devices. In the absence of a hardware source, the technique recommended by RFC 1750 [Eastlake94] is "to obtain random input from a large number of uncorrelated sources and mix them with a strong mixing function." By taking input from many unrelated sources, each with a few bits of randomness, and thoroughly hashing and mashing them up, we get a value with a high degree of entropy—a truly random number.

## Random Input Sources

Examples of random input available on many PCs and game consoles include:

- System date and time
- Time since boot at highest resolution available
- Username or ID
- Computer name or ID
- State of CPU registers
- State of system threads and processes
- Contents of the stack
- Mouse or joystick position
- Timing between last N keystrokes or controller input
- Last N keystroke or controller data
- Memory status (bytes allocated, free, etc.)
- Hard drive state (bytes available, used, etc.)
- Last N system messages
- GUI state (window positions, etc.)
- Timing between last N network packets
- Last N network packet data
- Data stored at a semi-random address in main memory, video memory, etc.
- Hardware identifiers: CPU ID, hard drive ID, BIOS ID, network card ID, video card ID, and sound card ID

Some of these sources will always be the same for a given system, like the user ID or hardware IDs. The reason to include these values is that they're variable across machines, so they're useful in generating secret keys for transmitting network data. Some sources change very little from sample to sample. For instance, the hard drive state and memory load may only change slightly from one read to the next. However, each input provides a few bits of randomness. Mixed together, they give many bits of randomness.

The more bits of entropy that can be obtained from input sources, the more random the output. It's useful to buffer sources such as mouse positions, keystrokes, and network packets over time in a circular queue. Then the entire queue can be used as an input source.

## Hardware Sources

Some gaming platforms have access to physical sources of randomness. When these sources are available, they make excellent input sources. Examples of physical sources include:

- Input from sound card (for example, the microphone jack) with no source plugged in
- Input from a video camera
- Disk drive seek time (hard drive, CD-ROM, DVD)
- Intel 810 chipset hardware RNG (a thermal noise-based RNG implemented in silicon) [Intel99]

## Mixing Function

In the context of creating genuine random numbers, a strong mixing function is a function where each bit of the output is a different complex and nonlinear function of each and every bit of the input. A good mixing function will change approximately half of the output bits given a single bit change in the input.

Examples of strong mixing functions include:

- DES (and most other symmetric ciphers)
- Diffie-Hellman (and most other public key ciphers)
- MD5, SHA-1 (and most other cryptographic hashes)

Secure hashing functions such as MD5 are the perfect mixers for many reasons: they meet the basic requirements of a good mixing function, they've been widely analyzed for security flaws, they're typically faster than either symmetric or asymmetric encryption, and they're not subject to any export restrictions. Public implementations are also widely available.

## Limitations

Unlike generating pseudo-random numbers, creating genuine random numbers in software is very slow. For the output to be truly random, many sources must be sampled. Some of the sampling is slow, such as reading from the hard drive or sound card. Furthermore, the sampled input must be mixed using complex algorithms.

Game consoles have a more limited selection of input sources compared to PCs, so they will tend to produce less random results. However, newer consoles often have disk drives of some sort (CD-ROM, DVD, hard disk) that can be used as good hardware sources of entropy.

The randomness of the results depends solely on the level of entropy in the input samples. The more input samples and the more entropy in each sample, the better the output. Keep in mind that the more often this algorithm is invoked in quick succession, the less random the output, because the smaller the change in the input bits. To sum up, this technique is *not* a replacement for pseudo-RNG. Use this technique for the one-time generation of your RNG *seed* value or for generating network session keys that can then be used for hours or days.

## Implementation

ON THE CD

A C++ example of a genuine random number generator is provided on the accompanying CD. Any implementation of this algorithm will naturally be platform dependent. This particular version is specific to the Win32 platform, but is designed to be easily extensible to other platforms. It uses hardware sources of randomness, such as the Intel RNG and sound card input, when those sources are available. In the interests of efficiency and simplicity, it does not use all of the examples listed previously as input, but uses enough to produce a high level of randomness.

The primary functionality resides in the GenRand object within the TrueRand namespace. Here is an example use of GenRand to create a genuine seed value:

```
#include "GenRand.h" // Genuine random number header
unsigned int nSeed = TrueRand::GenRand().GetRandInt();
```

Here's another example showing the generation of a session key for secure network communication. The *Buffer* object is a simple wrapper around *std::basic_string<unsigned char>*, which provides the functionality we need for reserving space, appending data, and tracking the size of the sample buffer:

```
TrueRand::GenRand randGen;
TrueRand::Buffer bufSessionKey = randGen.GetRand();
```

The *GetRand()* function is the heart of the program. It samples the random inputs, and then uses a strong mixing function to produce the output. This implementation uses MD5 hashing, so the resulting buffer is the length of an MD5 hash (16 bytes). The *mCrypto* object is a wrapper around the Win32 Crypto API, which includes MD5 hashing.

```
Buffer GenRand::GetRand()
{
    // Build sample buffer
    Buffer randInputs = GetRandomInputs();

    // Mix well and serve
    return mCrypto.GetHash( CALG_MD5, randInputs );
}
```

The `GetRandomInputs()` function is the input sampler. It returns a buffer with approximately 10K of sampled data. This function can easily be modified to include more or less input as desired. Because the time spent in the function varies according to system (drive, sound card) access, we can use the hardware latency as a source of random input; hence, the snapshot of the current time at the beginning and end of the function.

```
Buffer GenRand::GetRandomInputs()
{
    // For speed, preallocate input buffer
    Buffer randIn;
    randIn.reserve( GetMaxRandInputSize() );

    GetCurrTime( randIn );        // append time to buffer
    GetStackState( randIn );      // stack state
    GetHardwareRng( randIn );     // hardware RNG, if avail
    GetPendingMsgs( randIn );     // pending Win32 msgs
    GetMemoryStatus( randIn );    // memory load
    GetCurrMousePos( randIn );    // mouse position

    // . . . etc.

    GetCurrTime( randIn );        // random hardware latency

    return randIn;
}
```

Finally, here's one of the input sampling functions. It extracts the current time, and then appends the data to the mRandInputs buffer object. `QueryPerformance-Counter()` is the highest resolution timer in Windows, so it provides the most bits of randomness. We can ignore API failures in this case (and many others), because the worst that happens is that we append whatever *random* stack data happens to be in PerfCounter if the function fails.

```
void GenRand::GetCurrTime( Buffer& randIn )
{
    LARGE_INTEGER PerfCounter;
    QueryPerformanceCounter( &PerfCounter ); // Win32 API
    Append( randIn, PerfCounter );
}
```

## How Random Is GenRand?

ON THE CD

There are many tests for examining the quality of random numbers. One test is the publicly available program ENT [Walker(b)], included on the accompanying CD, which applies a suite of tests to any data stream. Tests of GenRand() without using *any* sources of hardware input (including hard drive seek time), and generating a file of 25,000 random integers using GetRandInt() gives the following results:

- Entropy = 7.998199 bits per byte.
- Optimum compression would reduce the size of this 100,000-byte file by 0 percent.

- Chi square distribution for 100,000 samples is 250.13, and randomly would exceed this value 50 percent of the time.
- Arithmetic mean value of data bytes is 127.4918 (127.5 = random).
- Monte Carlo value for Pi is 3.157326293 (error 0.50 percent).
- Serial correlation coefficient is 0.000272 (totally uncorrelated = 0.0).

These results indicate that the output has a high degree of randomness. For instance, the chi square test—the most common test for randomness [Knuth98]—indicates that we have a very random generator.

## References

[Callas96] Callas, Jon, "Using and Creating Cryptographic-Quality Random Numbers," available online at www.merrymeet.com/jon/usingrandom.html, June 1996.

[Eastlake94] Eastlake, D., Network Working Group, et al, "Randomness Recommendations for Security," RFC 1750, available online at www.faqs.org/rfcs/rfc1750.html, December 1994.

[Kelsey98] Kelsey, J., et al, "Cryptanalytic Attacks on Pseudorandom Number Generators," available online at www.counterpane.com/pseudorandom_number .html, March 1998.

[Intel99] Intel Corporation, "Intel Random Number Generator," available online at http://developer.intel.com/design/security/rng/rng.htm, 1999.

[Knuth98] Knuth, Donald, *The Art of Computer Programming, Volume 2: Seminumerical Algorithms, Third Edition*. Addison-Wesley. 1998.

[Schneier96] Schneier, Bruce, *Applied Cryptography, Second Edition*. John Wiley & Sons. 1996.

[Walker(a)] Walker, John, "HotBits: Genuine Random Numbers Generated by Radioactive Decay," available online at www.fourmilab.ch/hotbits/.

[Walker(b)] Walker, John, "ENT: A Pseudorandom Number Sequence Test Program," available online at www.fourmilab.ch/random/.

# 1.20

# Using Bloom Filters to Improve Computational Performance

*Mark Fischer, Beach Software*

beach@beachsoftware.com

Imagine the desire to store Boolean information in a bit array—a very simple premise. Simply assign each element in the bit array to a specific meaning, and then assign it a value. In this scenario, it takes 1 bit in the array to store 1 bit of stored information. The bit array faithfully represents its relative value with 100-percent accuracy. This, of course, works best when the stored data is array oriented such as a transient over time or space. However, what if the data is not a linear transient-oriented data set?

## Bloom's Way

In 1970, Burton H. Bloom published a simple and clever algorithm [Bloom70] in the "Communications of the ACM." In his publication, Bloom suggests using a "Hash Coding with Allowable Errors" algorithm to help word processors perform capitalization or hyphenation on a document. This algorithm would use less space and be faster than a conventional one-to-one mapping algorithm. Using this example, a majority of words (90 percent, for example) could be checked using a simple rule, while the smaller minority set could be solved with an exception list used to catch the instances where the algorithm would report a word as simply solvable when it was not. Bloom's motivation was to reduce the time it took to look up data from a slow storage device.

## Possible Scenarios

A Bloom Filter can reduce the time it takes to compute a relatively expensive and routinely executed computation by storing a true Boolean value from a previously executed computation. Consider the following cases where we'd like to improve performance:

- Determine if a polygon is probably visible from an octree node.
- Determine if an object probably collides at a coordinate.
- Determine if a ray cast probably intersects an object at a coordinate.

133

All of these cases fit into a general scenario. Each case involves an expensive computation (CPU, network, or other resource) where the result is a Boolean (usually false) answer. It is important to note that that the word probably is used in each case because a Bloom Filter is guaranteed to be 100-percent accurate if the Bloom Filter test returns a false (miss), but is, at best, only probably true if the Bloom Filter returns true (hit).

A Bloom Filter can store the true result of any function. Usually, the function parameter is represented as a pointer to a byte array. If we wish to store the result of a function that uses multiple parameters, we can concatenate the parameters into a single function parameter. In cases where 100-percent accuracy is needed, we must compute the original expensive function to determine the absolute result of the expensive function, if a Bloom Filter test returns true.

## How It Works

There are two primary functions in a Bloom Filter: a function for storing the Boolean true value returned from an expensive function, and a function for testing for a previously stored Boolean true value. The storing function will accept input in any form and modify the Bloom Filter Array accordingly. The testing function will accept input in the same form as the storing function and return a Boolean value. If the testing function returns false, it is guaranteed that the input was never previously stored using the storing function. If the function returns true, it is likely that the input was previously stored using the storing function. A false positive is a possible result from the test. If 100-percent accuracy is desired, perform the original expensive function to determine the absolute value. A conventional Bloom Filter is additive, so it can only store additional Boolean true results from an expensive function and cannot remove previously stored values.

## Definitions

The high-quality operation of a Bloom Filter requires a high-quality hash function that is sometimes referred to as a message digest algorithm. Any high-quality hash function will work, but I recommend using the MD5 message digest algorithm [RSA01] from RSA Security, Inc., which is available in source code on the Net, and is also documented in RFC 1321. The MD5 hash function takes N bytes from a byte array and produces a 16-byte (128-bit) return value. This return value is a hash of the input, which means if any of the bits in the input change (even in the slightest), the return value will be changed drastically. The return of the hash function, in Bloom terminology, is called the Bloom Filter Key.

Bloom Filter Indexes are obtained by breaking the Bloom Filter Key into blocks of a designated bit size. If we choose a Bloom Filter Index bit size of 16 bits, a 128-bit Bloom Filter Key can be broken into eight complete 16-bit segments. If there are remaining bits left over from breaking the Key into complete segments, they are discarded.

The number of Bloom Filter Phases used in a Bloom Filter is the number of Bloom Filter Indexes used to store the Boolean value from the expensive function. For example, three phases might be used from a 128-bit key using a Bloom Filter Index bit size of 16 bits. The remaining five indexes will be discarded, in this example.

A Bloom Filter Array is used to store the expensive function's Boolean value. For example, if the Bloom Filter Index bit size is 16 bits, the Bloom Filter Array will be $2^{16}$ bits long, or 64K bits (8K bytes). The larger the array, the more accurate the Bloom Filter test.

The Bloom Filter Saturation of the Bloom Filter Array is the percentage of bits set to true in the bit array. A Bloom Filter Array is optimal when saturation is 50 percent, or half of the bits are set and half are not.

## Example 1

For an example, we will store the function parameter ("Mikano is in the park") using three phases with an index bit size of 16 bits into an array 64k bits long (8k bytes). In this instance, the expensive function was used to determine if Mikano was truly in the park and the result was yes (true). Although we used a string variable, in this case, any variable format will work. The format of the stored expensive function parameter data is independent of the Bloom Filter performance, accuracy, or memory usage.

First, the hash function is computed from the expensive function parameter data. Let's assume that the hash function returned the 128-bit value 0x10027AB30001BF 7877AB34D976A09667. The first three segments of 16-bit indexes will be 0x1002, 0x7AB3, and 0x0001. The remaining segments are ignored.

The Bloom Filter Array starts out reset (all false bits), before we begin to populate the bit array with data. Then, for each of these indexes, we will set the respective bit index in the Bloom Filter Array to true regardless of its previous value. As the array becomes populated, sometimes we will set a bit to true that has already been set to true. This is the origin of the possible false positive result when testing the Bloom Filter Array (Figure 1.20.1).

When we wish to examine the Bloom Filter Array to determine if there was a previously stored expensive function parameter, we proceed in almost the same steps as a store, except that the bits are read from the Bloom Filter Array instead of written to them. If any of the read bits are false, then the expensive function parameter was absolutely never previously stored in the Bloom Filter Array. If all of the bits are true, then the expensive function parameter was likely previously stored in the Array. In the case of a true result, calculate the original expensive function to accurately determine the Boolean value (Figure 1.20.2).

### Tuning the Bloom Filter

Tuning the Bloom Filter involves determining the number of phases and the bit size of the indexes. Both of these variables can be modified to change the accuracy and capacity of the Bloom Filter. Generally speaking, the larger the size of the bit array

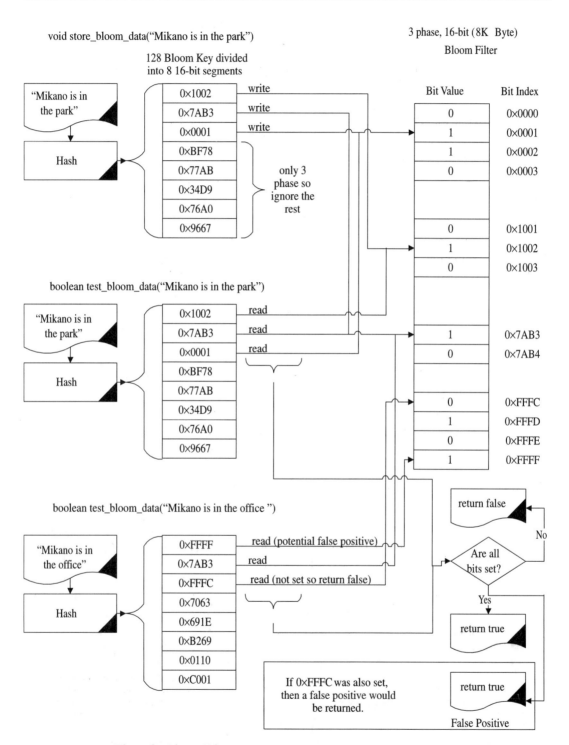

**FIGURE 1.20.1**  *Flow of a Bloom Filter.*

```
// returns a pointer to 16 bytes of data that represent the hash
void * compute_hash( pData, nDataLength );

// returns the integer value for the bits at nIndex for nBitLength long
int get_index_value( void * pData, int nBitIndex, int nBitLength );

// tests a bit in the Bloom Filter Array.
// returns true if set otherwise returns false
boolean is_bit_index_set( int nIndexValue );

// sets a bit in the Bloom Filter Array
void set_bit_index( int nIndexValue );

void store_bloom_data( void * pData, int nDataLength )
{
    void *pHash;
    int nPhases = 3, nPhaseIndex = 0, nBitIndexLength = 16;

    // returns pointer to 16 bytes of memory
    pHash = compute_hash( pData, nDataLength );

    // now set each bit
    while ( nPhaseIndex < m_nPhases )
    {
        nIndexValue = get_index_value( pHash, nPhaseIndex, nBitIndexLength );

        // if bit is not set, we have a miss so return false
        set_bit_index( nIndexValue );

        nPhaseIndex++;
    }
}

boolean test_bloom_data( void * pData, int nDataLength )
{
    void *pHash;
    int nPhases = 3, nPhaseIndex = 0, nBitIndexLength = 16;

    // returns pointer to 16 bytes of memory
    pHash = compute_hash( pData, nDataLength );

    // now test each bit
    while ( nPhaseIndex < m_nPhases )
    {
        nIndexValue = get_index_value( pHash, nPhaseIndex, nBitIndexLength );

        // if bit is not set, we have a miss so return false
        if ( !is_bit_index_set( nIndexValue ) ) return( false );

        nPhaseIndex++;
    }

    // all bits are set so we have a probably hit.
    return( true );
}
```

Theoretically, a different input parameter could return the same value but that is unprobable. Either way, the algorithm will still work.

compute_hash will always return the same 16 bytes of data when called with the same input parameters.

Return false as soon as we find a false bit. At this point, the expensive function has definitely not been previously stored.

**FIGURE 1.20.2** *Basic use of a Bloom Filter.*

(N) and the more phases, the less likely a false positive response will occur. Bloom asserted that the optimum performance of this algorithm occurs when saturation of the bit array is 50 percent. Statistically, the chance of a false positive can be determined by taking the array saturation and raising it to the power of the number of phases. Other equations are available to tune the Bloom filter algorithm.

The equation to calculate the percentage of false positives is:

$$percent\_false\_positive = saturation^{number\_of\_phases}$$

or expressed as a function of percent_false_positive:

$$number\_of\_phases = Log_{saturation}(percent\_false\_positive)$$

By assuming that the Bloom Filter Array is operating at optimum capacity of 50-percent saturation, Table 1.20.1 can be computed from the preceding formulas.

For example, if we want the false positive rate below half a percent (0.5 percent), eight phases must be used, which will return a worst-case scenario of 0.39-percent false positives.

Next, we calculate the Bloom Filter Array bit size.

$$array\_bit\_size = (number\_of\_phases * max\_stored\_inputs)/-ln(0.5)$$

The array_bit_size is usually rounded up to the nearest value where array_bit_size can be expressed as 2 to the power of an integer.

$$array\_bit\_size = 2^n$$

Finally, compute the index_bit_size from the array_bit_size.

$$array\_bit\_size = 2^{index\_bit\_size}$$

**Table 1.20.1  Percentage of False Positives Based on Number of Phases Used**

| percent_false_positive | number_of_phases |
|---|---|
| 50.00% | 1 |
| 25.00% | 2 |
| 12.50% | 3 |
| 6.13% | 4 |
| 3.13% | 5 |
| 1.56% | 6 |
| 0.78% | 7 |
| 0.39% | 8 |

## Example 2

Suppose we want to store a maximum of 9000 expensive function parameters with at least 95-percent accuracy when the Bloom Filter Array test returns true. From Table 1.20.1, we can determine that five phases will be necessary to obtain an accuracy of equal to or greater than 95 percent and a false positive of less than or equal to 5 percent.

*5 phases * 9000 expensive function parameters / -ln(0.5) = 64,921 bits*

Rounding up to the nearest $2^n$ gives us 64K bits (*8K bytes*), and because $2^{16}$ = 64K, the *index_bit_size* will be 16 bits.

## Final Notes

One way to improve performance is to use an exception list to prevent executing the expensive function, as Bloom did in his algorithm. An exception list contains all of the false positive cases that can be returned from testing a Bloom Filter. This can be computed at parameter storage or dynamically when false positives are detected (Figure 1.20.3).

Another way to improve performance is to dynamically build a Bloom Filter Array. If the range of expensive function parameters is too great, Bloom Filters can be calculated dynamically and optimized for repetitive calls to test the bit array. By dynamically building a Bloom Filter Array, the commonly tested expensive function parameters are calculated once, and untested function parameters do not waste space in the bit array.

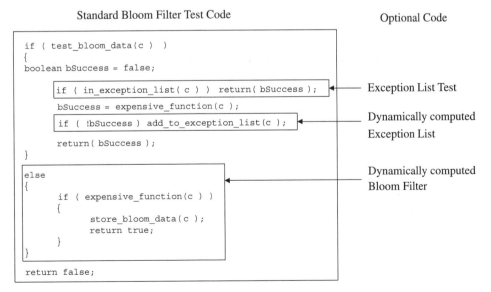

Standard Bloom Filter Test Code                     Optional Code

```
if ( test_bloom_data(c ) )
{
boolean bSuccess = false;

    if ( in_exception_list( c ) )  return( bSuccess );     ← Exception List Test

    bSuccess = expensive_function(c );
    if ( !bSuccess ) add_to_exception_list(c );            ← Dynamically computed
                                                             Exception List
    return( bSuccess );
}
else                                                       ← Dynamically computed
{                                                            Bloom Filter
    if ( expensive_function(c ) )
    {
        store_bloom_data(c );
        return true;
    }
}
return false;
```

**FIGURE 1.20.3**   *Bloom Filter configurations.*

Here are some interesting Bloom Filter characteristics:

- Two Bloom Filter Arrays can be merged together by bitwise ORing them.
- Bloom Filter Arrays can be shared among parallel clients.
- Optimized Bloom Filter Arrays are not compressible.
- Underpopulated Arrays are very compressible.
- Memory corruption in the array can be mended by setting unknown bits to true.

## Conclusion

Bloom Filters offer a method of improving performance of repeatedly called expensive functions at the expense of memory. While this method has been documented for a long time, it remains a relatively unused technique, although exceptions exist, such as Bloom Filter usage in the very popular Web-caching program *Squid* (www.squid-cache.org/) by Duane Wessels. Adding a Bloom Filter algorithm to a program can usually be done in less that 20K bytes of code. As with most performance-enhancing tricks, it is a good idea to add Bloom Filters to a project during the optimization stage, after the main functionality is finished.

## References

[Beach01] Beach Software, "Bloom Filters," available online at http://beachsoftware.com/bloom/, May 10, 2000.

[RSA01] RSA Security, "What Are MD2, MD4, and MD5," available online at www.rsasecurity.com/rsalabs/faq/3-6-6.html, March 4, 2001.

[Flipcode01] Flipcode, "Coding Bloom Filters," available online at "www.flipcode.com/tutorials/tut_bloomfilter.shtml, September 11, 2000.

[Bloom70] Bloom, Burton H., "Space/Time Trade-Offs in Hash Coding with Allowable Errors," Communications of the ACM, Vol. 13, No.7 (ACM July 1970): pp. 422–426.

# 1.21

# 3ds max Skin Exporter and Animation Toolkit

## Marco Tombesi

tombesi@infinito.it

ON THE CD

W e have seen wonderful special effects in modern films that have taken glorious monsters such as dinosaurs and made them move smoothly. We know how they did it (using software such as LightWave, 3ds max, Maya, etc.), but how do we use the same animation technology for our games?

This gem is intended as an introduction to a full toolset for that purpose, starting just after the creation of the animated character in 3ds max (and Character Studio), and ending with that object smoothly animating in a game's real-time scenes. Along the way, it passes through the export plug-in and is stored in a custom data format. In this gem, we will go into depth only about the export aspect; the rest is well explained by the code on the accompanying CD.

Let's talk about the necessary steps:

1. The animation is done with 3ds max 3.1 (hereafter simply called MAX) and Character Studio 2.2, using *Biped* and/or *bones* and the *Physique modifier*. It should be noted that although newer versions of these tools will become available, the algorithms required for any new versions should be similar.
2. The export plug-in creates a custom format file (.MRC), which consists of:
   - Mesh information (vertices, normals).
   - Skeletal structure (the bone tree).
   - Influence values (weighting) of each bone to vertices of the mesh (one vertex may be influenced by multiple bones).
   - Bone animation: For each bone, this consists of a set of translation and rotation keys (using quaternions), including the exact time in milliseconds from the animation start to when the transformation should be performed.
3. To read the .MRC file, we have a reusable DLL available, provided with full source code.
4. The renderer interpolates (linearly or better) between the sample keys and calculates the current transformation matrix to be applied to each bone.

This is done using the time elapsed from the animation start, obtaining a smooth and non-hardware-dependent animation.

5. At each frame, the renderer recalculates the position of each vertex and its normal. The calculation is based on the current transformation matrix and influence value that each bone has on a particular vertex. Most matrix operations can be done using the graphics hardware transformation and lighting features if they exist (for example, on the GeForce and Radeon cards).

*ON THE CD*

The process of exporting the animation data with a plug-in for MAX is not well documented. While there are many Web pages covering skinning techniques, few actually address the issue of exporting the data. Read and study the source code as well as all *Readme.txt* files in the project directories for this gem on the CD. More information is also available on the author's Web page [Tombesi01], where updates for MAX 4 will be available when it is released.

This gem is based on a hierarchical bone structure: a bone tree or a Biped, created using *Character Studio 2.2*. Build a low polygon mesh (about 5000 triangles). The mesh should be a single selectable object in MAX. Deform the mesh using the Physique modifier, based on the Biped previously created. The character animation should be created on the Biped.

## Exporting

First, we need a file format specification.

### The MRC File Format

*ON THE CD*

This is a simple file format for the purposes of this gem. It supports normals, bones, vertex weights, and animation keys. See Figure 1.21.1 for a self-explanatory schematic, and check the code on the CD for technical clarification.

### *Exporting to MRC with the MAX SDK*

*NOTE*

*If you are new to plug-in development and don't know how MAX works, be sure to refer to the MAX SDK documentation. In particular, study the following sections before proceeding:*

- *DLL, Library Functions, and Class Descriptors*
- *Fundamental Concepts of the MAX SDK*
- *Must Read Sections for All Developers*
- *Nodes*
- *Geometry Pipeline System*
- *Matrix Representations of 3D Transformations*

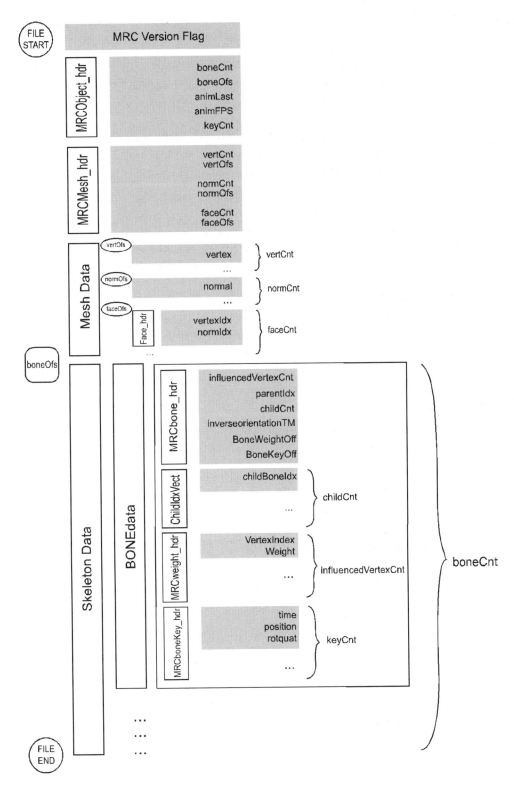

**FIGURE 1.21.1** *MRC file format description.*

### Working with Nodes

In our export plug-in, we must derive a class from *SceneExport* and implement some virtual methods, one of which is the main export routine.

```
class MRCexport : public SceneExport {
public:
    // Number of extensions supported
    int ExtCount()  {return 1;}

    // Extension("MRC")
    const TCHAR * Ext(int n)  {return _T("MRC");}
    ...

    // Export to an MRC file
    int DoExport(const TCHAR *name,
                 ExpInterface *ei,
                 Interface *i,
                 BOOL suppressPrompts=FALSE,
                 DWORD options=0);

    //Constructor/Destructor
    MRCexport();
    ~MRCexport();
    ...
};
```

Accessing scene data requires an *Interface* passed by MAX to the main export routine (the entry point of the plug-in). For every object in MAX, there is a node in the global scene graph, and each node has a parent (except *RootNode*) and possibly some children. We can access the root node and then traverse the hierarchy, or we can directly access a node if the user has selected it in MAX before exporting.

```
INode* pNode = i->GetSelNode(0);
INode* const pRoot = i->GetRootNode();
```

To navigate the node structure, we have these methods:

```
Int count = pNode->NumberOfChildren();
INode* pChNode = pNode->GetChildNode(i);
```

A node could represent anything, so we need to discriminate among object types via the node's class identifier (*Class_ID* or *SuperClassID*), and then appropriately cast the object. For our purposes, we need to check if a node is a geometric object (a mesh) or a bone (a Biped node or a bone).

```
bool IsMesh(INode *pNode)
{
    if(pNode == NULL)return false;
    ObjectState os = pNode->EvalWorldState(0);
    if(os.obj->SuperClassID() == GEOMOBJECT_CLASS_ID)
        return true;
    return false;
```

```
      }

      bool IsBone(INode *pNode)
      {
          if(pNode == NULL)return false;
          ObjectState os = pNode->EvalWorldState(0);
          if (!os.obj) return false;

          if(os.obj->ClassID() == Class_ID(BONE_CLASS_ID, 0))
              return true;

          if(os.obj->ClassID() == Class_ID(DUMMY_CLASS_ID, 0))
              return false;

          Control *cont = pNode->GetTMController();
              //other Biped parts
          if( cont->ClassID() == BIPSLAVE_CONTROL_CLASS_ID ||
              //Biped root "Bip01"
              cont->ClassID() == BIPBODY_CONTROL_CLASS_ID
          ) return true;
          return false;
      }
```

The previous example explains how to navigate MAX's nodes and check what they represent. Once we get a mesh node, we need to acquire the desired vertex data.

### Getting Mesh Data

For convenience later on, we'll store all vertex data in global coordinate space. MAX object coordinates are in object space, so we need a transformation matrix to be applied to each vertex and normal of the mesh.

We can grab this global transformation matrix at any time during the animation using *GetObjectTM(TimeValue time)*. This matrix is used to transform vectors from object space to world space and could be used, for example, if we want to get the world space coordinate of one mesh vertex. We could do this by taking the vertex coordinate in object space and multiplying it (post-multiply in MAX) by the matrix returned from this method. We are interested in mesh data at the animation start, so *TimeValue* is zero.

```
      Matrix3 tm = pNode->GetObjectTM(0)
```

*MAX uses row vector 1x3 and 4x3 matrices, so to transform a vector, we must premultiply it by the matrix.*

NOTE

Vertices and other data are not statically stored, but dynamically calculated each time. To access data, we must first perform the geometry pipeline evaluation, specifying the time at which we want to get the object state.

MAX has a modifier stack system, where every object is the result of a modification chain. Starting from a simple parametric primitive (such as a box) that is the base object, the final object is built, applying modifiers in sequence along the stack. This is the object pipeline and we will work with the result. The resulting object is a *Derived-Object* and has methods to navigate the stack of modifiers.

To get the result at a specified animation time, we must first retrieve an *Object-State*, which is done by invoking the method *EvalWorldState* on the node. This makes MAX apply each modifier in the pipeline from beginning to end.

```
ObjectState os = pNode->EvalWorldState(0);
```

*ObjectState* contains a pointer to the object in the pipeline and, once we have this object, we can finally get the mesh data. To do this, we must cast the generic object to a geometric one, which has a method to build a mesh representation.

```
Mesh& mesh = *(((GeomObject*)os.obj)->GetRenderMesh(0, pNode, ...));
```

Now it is easy to access the *mesh* members and finally put vertices, faces, and normals in memory, ready to be written to a file. These methods are available to accomplish this: *Mesh::getNumVerts()*, *Mesh::getNumFaces()*, *Mesh::getVert(i)*, and *Mesh::getNormal(i)*.

Listing 1.21.1 illustrates how to export mesh data to a file.

### Getting the Bone Structure

Now we need a way to write the skeleton's hierarchical structure to an output data file. Starting from the root node, we traverse depth-first through the tree, and for each bone, we need to get several things. First, we assign an index to any direct child and to the bone's parent, and then we grab the bone orientation matrix.

```
tm = pNode->GetNodeTM(0);
tm.Invert();
```

*Although very similar, the preceding matrix isn't the object matrix, but is related to the node's pivot point, which may not be the object's origin. Check with the SDK documentation to find a precise description. We will use this matrix to transform every mesh vertex from world space to related bone space, so it can move with the bone. Since we have to multiply any vertex by the inverse of this matrix, we can invert it now and save rendering time.*

### Getting the Bone Influences

Now we are at the most exciting part of this gem: getting the vertex bone assignment and influence value (weighting). The weighting is important when two or more bones influence the same vertex and the mesh deformation depends on both (see [Woodland00] for the theory). These assignments should be done using the Physique modifier in Character Studio 2.2. Note to the reader: Study the *Phyexp.h* header that comes with Character Studio for modifier interface help.

First, we must find the Physique modifier on the object's node that we wish to export (this is the same node we used earlier to get the mesh vertex data). We do this by accessing the referenced *DerivedObject* and then scanning each applied modifier on the stack until we find the Physique modifier (using a *Class_ID* check).

```
Modifier* GetPhysiqueMod(INode *pNode)
{
    Object *pObj = pNode->GetObjectRef();
    if(!pObj) return NULL;

    // Is it a derived object?
    while(pObj->SuperClassID() == GEN_DERIVOB_CLASS_ID)
    {
        // Yes -> Cast
        IDerivedObject *pDerivedObj =
            static_cast<IDerivedObject*>(pObj);

        // Iterate over all entries of the modifier stack
        int ModStackIndex = 0;
        while(ModStackIndex < pDerivedObj->NumModifiers())
        {
            // Get current modifier
            Modifier* pMod = pDerivedObj->
                GetModifier(ModStackIndex);

            // Is this Physique?
            if(pMod->ClassID() ==
                Class_ID(PHYSIQUE_CLASS_ID_A,
                    PHYSIQUE_CLASS_ID_B))
                return pMod;

            // Next modifier stack entry
            ModStackIndex++;

        }
        pObj = pDerivedObj->GetObjRef();
    }
    // Not found
    return NULL;
}
```

Now we enter the Bone assignment phase (see Listing 1.21.2; a code overview follows). Once we have the Physique modifier, we get its interface (*IPhysiqueExport*) and then access the Physique context interface (*IPhyContextExport*) for the object. This owns all of the methods with which we need to work. Each vertex affected by a modifier has an interface *IPhyVertexExport*. Grab this interface to access its methods, calling *GetVertexInterface(i)* on the Physique context interface.

We must check to see if a vertex is influenced by one or more bones (`RIGID_TYPE` or `RIGID_BLENDED_TYPE`, respectively). In the former case, the weight value is 1 and we have to find just a single bone (calling `GetNode` on the i-th vertex interface). In the latter case, we have to find every bone assigned to the vertex, and for each bone we must get its proper weight value by invoking *GetWeight(j)* on the i-th vertex interface, where j is the j-th bone influencing it. In addition, note that at the end, we must remember to release every interface.

Now we are ready for the last phase: bone animation data acquisition.

### Getting Bone Animation Keys

This is a simple step. At selected time intervals (default 100 milliseconds), grab the transformation matrix of each bone. In the MAX SDK, time is measured internally in "ticks," where there are 4800 ticks per second, so we must perform a conversion. Then we use this method:

```
tm = pNode->GetNodeTM(timeTicks);
```

It's more efficient to not store the complete matrix (16 floats), but instead only the translation (3 floats) and rotation data (4 floats), so we extract a position vector and a unit quaternion from the matrix.

```
Point3 pos = tm.GetTrans();
Quat quat(tm);
```

Once we have all the data collected in memory, we store everything to disk using the MRC file format. Now it is time to see how to use it all to perform smooth animation in our games.

## Put It to Use: The Drawing Loop

In our application, for each frame displayed, we should perform the following steps in sequence.

### Get the Exact Time

To make the animation very smooth and not processor dependent, getting the system time is necessary. We update the skeleton structure by cycling through the bone tree and, for each bone, work out the current transformation matrix by linearly interpolating between two sample keys. To find out which sample keys to interpolate between, we require the current real animation time (in milliseconds) from animation start.

### Moving the Skeleton

We determine actual bone position and rotation by linear (or better) interpolation and by quaternion interpolation (SLERP or better) between selected sample keys (sample times should enclose the current time). Then, given these data, you can build the current bone animation matrix from the translation and rotation. The math involved, especially in the quaternion calculations, is explained well in the previous *Game Programming Gems* book [Shankel00]. To take better advantage of graphics hardware, we perform all matrix calculations using OpenGL functions. This way we can exploit any advanced hardware features such as transformation and lighting, and performance will be much better!

### Recalculate the Skin

Once the skeleton is moved, it is time to deform the mesh accordingly, with respect to vertex weight assignments. See [Woodland00] for a good overview of this topic. It is convenient to check the vertices in bone-major order, traversing depth-first through the bone tree and doing the following passes for each bone. For each vertex influenced by the bone, we refer it to the bone's local coordinate system (multiplying by the bone inverse orientation matrix), and then transform it via the current bone animation matrix. Then, we multiply the vertex coordinates by the influence value (weight) this bone exerts on it. We add the result to the corresponding vertex value stored in a temporary buffer. Now this buffer contains the current vertex coordinates for the skin, at this point in the animation. To finish, we draw the computed mesh using vertex arrays (or better) to gain even more performance.

## Listing 1.21.1: Exporting the Mesh to a File

```
bool ExportMesh (INode* pNode, FILE *out)
{
    ...
    MRCmesh_hdr mHdr;
    Matrix3 tm = pNode->GetObjectTM(0);
    ObjectState os = pNode->EvalWorldState(0);
    int needDelete;
    Mesh& mesh = *(( (GeomObject*) os.obj)->GetRenderMesh (
        0, pNode, ...));
    ...

    // write the mesh vertices
    mHdr.vertCnt = mesh.getNumVerts();
    for(int i = 0; i < mHdr.vertCnt; i++)
    {
        Point3 pnt = mesh.getVert(i) * tm;     //premultiply in MAX
        ...
    }

    // write vertex normals
    mesh.buildNormals();
    mHdr.normCnt = mesh.getNumVerts();
    for(i = 0; i < mHdr.normCnt; i++)
    {
        Point3 norm = Normalize(mesh.getNormal(i));
        ...
    }

    // build and write faces
    mHdr.faceCnt = mesh.getNumFaces();
    for(i = 0; i < mHdr.faceCnt; i++)
    {
```

```
                    MRCface_hdr fHdr;
                    fHdr.vert[0] = mesh.faces[i].v[0];
                    fHdr.vert[1] = mesh.faces[i].v[1];
                    fHdr.vert[2] = mesh.faces[i].v[2];
                    ...
               }
               ...
          }
```

## Listing 1.21.2: Reading Bone Assignments

```
          bool GetPhysiqueWeights(INode *pNode, INode *pRoot,
                              Modifier *pMod, BoneData_t *BD)
     {
        // create a Physique Export Interface for given Physique Modifier
        IPhysiqueExport *phyInterface = (IPhysiqueExport*)
             pMod->GetInterface(I_PHYINTERFACE);
        if(phyInterface)
        {
           // create a ModContext Export Interface for the specific
           // node of the Physique Modifier
           IPhyContextExport *modContextInt = (IPhyContextExport*)
                phyInterface->GetContextInterface(pNode);

           // needed by vertex interface (only Rigid supported by now)
           modContextInt->ConvertToRigid(TRUE);

           // more than a single bone per vertex
           modContextInt->AllowBlending(TRUE);
           if(modContextInt)
           {
              int totalVtx = modContextInt->GetNumberVertices();
              for(int i = 0; i < totalVtx; i++)
              {
                 IPhyVertexExport *vtxInterface = (IPhyVertexExport*)
                      modContextInt->GetVertexInterface(i);
                 if(vtxInterface)
                 {
                    int vtxType = vtxInterface->GetVertexType();
                    if(vtxType == RIGID_TYPE)
                    {
                       INode *boneNode = ((IPhyRigidVertex*)vtxInterface)
                            -> GetNode();
                       int boneIdx = GetBoneIndex(pRoot, boneNode);
                         Insert
                       // Build vertex data
                       MRCweight_hdr wdata;
                       wdata.vertIdx = i;
                       wdata.weight = 1.0f;

                       //Insert into proper bonedata
                       BD[boneIdx].weightsVect.push_back(wdata);

                       // update vertexWeightCnt for that bone
```

```
                          BD[boneIdx].Hdr.vertexCnt
                               = BD[boneIdx].weightsVect.size();
                     }
                     else if(vtxType == RIGID_BLENDED_TYPE)
                     {
                          IPhyBlendedRigidVertex *vtxBlendedInt =
                               (IPhyBlendedRigidVertex*)vtxInterface;
                          for(int j = 0; j < vtxBlendedInt->GetNumberNodes()
                               ;j++)
                          {
                               INode *boneNode = vtxBlendedInt->GetNode(j);
                               int boneIdx = GetBoneIndex(pRoot, boneNode);

                               // Build vertex data
                               MRCweight_hdr wdata;
                               wdata.vertIdx = i;
                               wdata.weight = vtxBlendedInt->GetWeight(j);

                               // check vertex existence for this bone
                               bool notfound = true;
                               for (int v=0; notfound
                                    && v < BD[boneIdx].weightsVect.size();
                                    v++)
                               {
                                    // update found vert weight data for that
                                    // bone
                                    if ( BD[boneIdx].weightsVect[v].vertIdx
                                         == wdata.vertIdx )
                                    {
                                         BD[boneIdx].weightsVect[v].weight
                                              += wdata.weight;
                                         notfound = false;
                                    }
                               }

                               if (notfound)
                               {
                                    // Add a new vertex weight data into proper
                                    // bonedata
                                    BD[boneIdx].weightsVect.push_back(wdata);

                                    // update vertexWeightCnt for that bone
                                    BD[boneIdx].Hdr.vertexCnt
                                         = BD[boneIdx].weightsVect.size();
                               }
                          }
                     }
                }
           }
           phyInterface->ReleaseContextInterface(modContextInt);
      }
      pMod->ReleaseInterface(I_PHYINTERFACE, phyInterface);
 }
 return true;
}
```

## References

**SDK documentation file:**
[Discreet00] Max SDK Plug-in development documentation: *SDK.HLP*

**Web links:**
[Tombesi01] Tombesi, Marco's Web page: *http://digilander.iol.it/baggior/*

**Books:**

[Woodland00] Woodland, Ryan, "Filling the Gaps—Advanced Animation Using Stitching and Skinning," *Game Programming Gems*. Charles River Media 2000; pp. 476–483.
[Shankel00] Shankel, Jason, "Matrix-Quaternion Conversions" and "Interpolating Quaternions," *Game Programming Gems*. Charles River Media 2000; pp. 200–213.

# 1.22

# Using Web Cameras in Video Games

## Nathan d'Obrenan, Firetoad Software

nathand@firetoads.com

Most games nowadays have multiplayer capabilities; however, the only interaction that goes on among online gamers is the occasional text message. Imagine having the ability to see the expression on your opponent's face when you just pass them before reaching the finish line, or when they get fragged by your perfectly placed rocket. Web cams allow you that functionality, and with high-speed Internet slowly becoming standard, it's becoming feasible to send more data to more clients.

This gem demonstrates a straightforward approach to implementing Web cam methodologies into a game. We'll be using Video for Windows to capture the Web cam data, so Windows is required for the Web cam initialization function. We will cover numerous approaches for fast image culling, motion detection, and a couple of image manipulation routines. By the end, we will have a fully functional Web cam application that can be run and interacted with at reasonable frame rates.

## Initializing the Web Cam Capture Window

ON THE CD

The following code demonstrates how to use Video for Windows to set up a Web camera window in an application. Note to the reader: when dealing with video drivers from hardware vendors: You can never have too much error checking and handling code (review source code on CD for a more thorough implementation).

```
// Globals
HWND hWndCam = NULL;
BOOL cam_driver_on = FALSE;
int wco_cam_width = 160, wco_cam_height = 120;
int wco_cam_updates = 400, wco_cam_threshold = 120;

// WEBCAM_INIT
void webcam_init(HWND hWnd)
{
  // Set the window to be a pixel by a pixel large
  hWndCam = capCreateCaptureWindow(appname,
                             WS_CHILD | WS_VISIBLE |
                             WS_CLIPCHILDREN |
                             WS_CLIPSIBLINGS,
```

```
                                   0,0,
                                   1,1,
                                   hWnd,
                                   0);
    if(hWndCam)
    {
      // Connect the cam to the driver
      cam_driver_on = capDriverConnect(hWndCam, 1);

      // Get the capabilities of the capture driver
      if(cam_driver_on)
      {
        capDriverGetCaps(hWndCam, &caps, sizeof(caps));

        // Set the video stream callback function
        capSetCallbackOnFrame(hWndCam, webcam_callback);

        // Set the preview rate in milliseconds
        capPreviewRate(hWndCam, wco_cam_updates);

        // Disable preview mode
        capPreview(hWndCam, FALSE);

        // Initialize the bitmap info to the way we want
        capwnd.bmiHeader.biSize = sizeof(BITMAPINFOHEADER);
        capwnd.bmiHeader.biWidth  = wco_cam_width;
        capwnd.bmiHeader.biHeight = wco_cam_height;
        capwnd.bmiHeader.biPlanes = 1;
        capwnd.bmiHeader.biBitCount = 24;
        capwnd.bmiHeader.biCompression = BI_RGB;
        capwnd.bmiHeader.biSizeImage =wco_cam_width*wco_cam_height*3;
        capwnd.bmiHeader.biXPelsPerMeter = 100;
        capwnd.bmiHeader.biYPelsPerMeter = 100;

        if(capSetVideoFormat(hWndCam, &capwnd,
                             sizeof(BITMAPINFO)) == FALSE)
        {
          capSetCallbackOnFrame(hWndCam, NULL);
          DestroyWindow(hWndCam);
          hWndCam = NULL;
          cam_driver_on = FALSE;
        }
        else
        { // Assign memory and variables
          webcam_set_vars();
          {
            glGenTextures(1, &webcam_tex.gl_bgr);
            glBindTexture(GL_TEXTURE_2D, webcam_tex.gl_bgr);
            glTexImage2D(GL_TEXTURE_2D, O, 3, webcam_tex.size,
                         webcam_tex.size, O, GL_BGR_EXT,
                         GL_UNSIGNED_BYTE, webcam_tex.bgr);

            glTexParameteri(GL_TEXTURE_2D, GL_TEXTURE_WRAP_S,
                            GL_REPEAT);
```

```
                    glTexParameteri(GL_TEXTURE_2D, GL_TEXTURE_WRAP_T,
                                    GL_REPEAT);
                    glTexParameterf(GL_TEXTURE_2D, GL_TEXTURE_MIN_FILTER,
                                    GL_LINEAR);
                    glTexParameterf(GL_TEXTURE_2D, GL_TEXTURE_MAG_FILTER,
                                    GL_LINEAR);
                }
                {

                    glGenTextures(1, &webcam_tex.gl_grey);
                    glBindTexture(GL_TEXTURE_2D, webcam_tex.gl_grey);
                    glTexImage2D(GL_TEXTURE_2D, 0, 1, webcam_tex.size,
                                 webcam_tex.size, 0, GL_LUMINANCE,
                                 GL_UNSIGNED_BYTE, webcam_tex.greyscale);
                    glTexParameteri(GL_TEXTURE_2D, GL_TEXTURE_WRAP_S,
                                    GL_REPEAT);
                    glTexParameteri(GL_TEXTURE_2D, GL_TEXTURE_WRAP_T,
                                    GL_REPEAT);
                    glTexParameterf(GL_TEXTURE_2D, GL_TEXTURE_MIN_FILTER,
                                    GL_LINEAR);
                    glTexParameterf(GL_TEXTURE_2D, GL_TEXTURE_MAG_FILTER,
                                    GL_LINEAR);
                }
            }
        }
    }
    else
    {
        cam_driver_on = FALSE;
    }
}
```

The above function retrieves the handle to the Web cam window we're capturing from through the function *capCreateCaptureWindow()*. We then initialize it with windows properties such as its size, and whether it should be visible. In our case, we do want it to be visible; however, we're only going to set the window to a 1x1 pixel, so it's basically invisible. This is required because we don't actually want to display the image subwindow, but we want to receive the data updates from Windows through the callback function.

We then retrieve driver information, set the callback function (more on this later), the number of times per second we want to refresh the Web cam, and then reset all our variables.  The driver is then tested to see if it can handle returning the standard bitmap information in which we are interested. Upon success, we initialize all the memory for all our movement buffers, as well as the OpenGL texture. We pull a little trick when deciding how big to make this texture, which will come in handy later on. Based on whatever height we set up our Web cam window to be, we find and allocate our memory to the next highest power of 2. Even though we are allocating a bigger buffer than the Web cam image, we save ourselves an expensive texture resize operation, by just doing a *memcpy()* right into the larger buffer—at the cost of some small precision loss in the Web cam image.

### Retrieving Data

Once we have our video window initialized, we need a way to retrieve the data from the Web cam every frame. To let Windows know which callback function it should send the data to, we must call *capSetCallbackOnFrame()* with the address of the callback function. When Windows decides it's time to update the Web cam, it will pass us the bitmap information inside the *VIDEOHDR* structure.

In our case, we'll make the callback function process all the Web cam data to decide if we want to create a texture out of it. We can pass all of that data to the web-cam_calc_movement() function for further processing, which will determine if enough data has changed since the last frame, after which, we can update the texture.

```
// WEBCAM_CALLBACK
// Process video callbacks here
LRESULT WINAPI webcam_callback(HWND hwnd, LPVIDEOHDR video_hdr)
{
  // Calculate movement based off of threshold
  if(webcam_calc_movement(video_hdr,
                          webcam_tex.delta_buffer,
                          wco_cam_width,
                          wco_cam_height,
                          webcam_tex.size,
                          wco_cam_threshold))
  {
    webcam_make_texture(video_hdr, wco_cam_rendering);
  }

  return TRUE;
}

Windows defines the LPVIDEOHDR structure as:

typedef struct videohdr_tag
{
    LPBYTE      lpData;         // pointer to locked data buffer
    DWORD       dwBufferLength; // Length of data buffer
    DWORD       dwBytesUsed;    // Bytes actually used
    DWORD       dwTimeCaptured; // Milliseconds from start of stream
    DWORD       dwUser;         // for client's use
    DWORD       dwFlags;        // assorted flags (see defines)
    DWORD       dwReserved[4];  // reserved for driver
} VIDEOHDR, NEAR *PVIDEOHDR, FAR * LPVIDEOHDR;
```

Windows saves the Web cam data in the buffer called *lpData*. This is the primary variable we are interested in, but *dwTimeCaptured* and some of the flags may prove useful as well. Now that we've captured the data from the Web cam, let's test it to see if it's useful.

### Motion Detection

We now want to weed out any unnecessary frames which have barely changed so we can avoid unnecessary updates to our texture. Updating textures is a notoriously slow operation in a 3D API such as OpenGL.

The following source code compares delta buffers, and returns *true* or *false* if the given threshold has been breached. Note that returning early when the threshold has been exceeded could optimize this function further; however, that would hamper us from using the delta buffer later on. *Ectosaver* [Firetoad00] uses these unsigned bytes of delta movement to calculate the amplitude of the waves it causes, and to determine when there is no one moving around.

```
// GLOBALS
unsigned char wco_cam_threshold=128; // This is a good amount (0-255)

// WEBCAM_CALC_MOVEMENT
// This is a simple motion detection routine that determines if
// you've moved further than the set threshold
BOOL webcam_calc_movement(LPVIDEOHDR video_hdr,
                          unsigned char *delta_buff,
                          int webcam_width, int webcam_height,
                          int gl_size, unsigned char thresh)
{
  unsigned char max_delta=0;
  int i=0, j=0;
  int length;
  unsigned char *temp_delta = (unsigned char *)malloc(
      sizeof(unsigned char)* webcam_width * webcam_height);

  length = webcam_width * webcam_height;

  webcam_tex.which_buffer = webcam_tex.which_buffer ? 0 : 1;

  if(!video_hdr->lpData)
    return FS_TRUE;

  for(i=0; i<length; i++)
  {
    // Save the current frames data for comparison on the next frame
    // NOTE: Were only comparing the red channel (lpData is BGR), so
    // in theory if the user was in a solid red room, coated in red
    // paint, we wouldn't detect any movement....chances are this
    //isn't the case :)  For our purposes, it this test works fine
    webcam_tex.back_buffer[webcam_tex.which_buffer][i]
    = video_hdr->lpData[i*3];

    // Compute the delta buffer from the last frame
    // If it's the first frame, it shouldn't blow up given that we
    // cleared it to zero upon initialization
    temp_delta[i] =
    abs(webcam_tex.back_buffer[webcam_tex.which_buffer][i] –
        webcam_tex.back_buffer[!webcam_tex.which_buffer][i]);
```

```
  // Is the difference here greater than our threshold?
  if(temp_delta[i] > max_delta)
    max_delta = temp_delta[i];
}

// Fit to be inside a power of 2 texture
for(i=0; i<webcam_height; i++)
{
  memcpy(&delta_buff[i*(gl_size)],
         &temp_delta[i*(webcam_width)],
         sizeof(unsigned char)*webcam_width);
}

free(temp_delta);

if(max_delta > thresh)
  return TRUE;
else
  return FALSE;
}
```

## Manipulating Web Cam Data

### Get the BGR Pixels

Once we've performed all our testing and culling, we are ready to manipulate the data we were sent from Windows. For this, we will simply copy the pixels from the *VIDEOHDR* data struct (the native format Windows returns is BGR) into a buffer that we've allocated to have a power of 2. Note that this technique avoids resizing the texture data's pixels, as it simply copies the pixels straight over, preserving the pixel aspect ratio. The only drawback to this technique is that it will leave some empty space in our texture, so we're left with a bar of black pixels at the top of the image. We can eliminate that bar by manipulating texture coordinates (once mapped onto 3D geometry) or resizing the texture.

```
// WEBCAM_MAKE_BGR
void webcam_make_bgr(unsigned char *bgr_tex, unsigned char *vid_data,
int webcam_width,  int webcam_height, int glsize)
{
  int i;

  for(i=0; i<webcam_height; i++)
  {
    memcpy(&bgr_tex[i*(glsize*3)],
           &vid_data[i*(webcam_width*3)],
           sizeof(unsigned char)*webcam_width*3);
  }
}
```

### Convert to Grayscale

Once we've captured the BGR data, we could convert it to grayscale. This would result in an image that is one-third the size of our regular textures, which would be practical for users who have slow Internet connections, but still want to transmit Web cam data.

Here is a function that multiplies each RGB component in our color buffer by a scalar amount, effectively reducing all three color channels to one:

```
// WEBCAM_MAKE_GREYSCALE
void webcam_make_greyscale(unsigned char *grey,
                           unsigned char *color,  int dim)
{
  int i, j;

  // Greyscale = RED * 0.3f + GREEN * 0.4f + BLUE * 0.3f
  for(i=0, j=0; j<dim*dim; i+=3, j++)
  {
    grey[j] = (unsigned char)float_to_int(0.30f * color[i]   +
                                          0.40f * color[i+1] +
                                          0.30f * color[i+2]);
  }
}
```

### *Real–Life Cartoons*

Once we've successfully converted all our data to grayscale, we can manipulate the data to draw the picture in a cartoon-like fashion. This method splits the image into five different levels and six different colors, coloring different ranges of pixel values with solid values. All we have to do is perform some simple comparisons and evaluate each pixel based on our heat intensity constants.

The final result is compared against a lookup from either the grayscale buffer *or* our delta buffer. If we want to see the image every frame (single buffer), we will need to compare against the grayscale. To give different results, we'll assign random color intensities for each pixel based on our heat intensity constants.

```
// WEBCAM_INIT_CARTOON
void webcam_init_cartoon(cartoon_s *cartoon_tex)
{
  char i;

  for(i=0; i<3; i++)
  {
    // Pick random colors in our range
    cartoon_tex->bot_toll_col[i]  = rand()%255;
    cartoon_tex->min_toll_col[i]  = rand()%255;
    cartoon_tex->low_toll_col[i]  = rand()%255;
    cartoon_tex->med_toll_col[i]  = rand()%255;
    cartoon_tex->high_toll_col[i] = rand()%255;
    cartoon_tex->max_toll_col[i]  = rand()%255;
  }
}

#define  MIN_CAM_HEAT    50
```

```
#define   LOW_CAM_HEAT    75
#define   MED_CAM_HEAT   100
#define HIGH_CAM_HEAT   125
#define   MAX_CAM_HEAT   150

// WEBCAM_MAKE_CARTOON
void webcam_make_cartoon(unsigned char *cartoon,
                         cartoon_s cartoon_tex,
                         unsigned char *data, int dim)
{
  int i, j, n;

  for(i=0, j=0; j<dim*dim; i+=3, j++)
  {
    if(data[j] < MIN_CAM_HEAT)
    {
      for(n=0; n<3; n++)
        cartoon[i+n] = cartoon_tex.bot_toll_col[n];
    }
    if(data[j] > MIN_CAM_HEAT && data[j] < LOW_CAM_HEAT)
    {
      for(n=0; n<3; n++)
        cartoon[i+n] = cartoon_tex.min_toll_col[n];
    }
    if(data[j] > LOW_CAM_HEAT && data[j] < MED_CAM_HEAT)
    {
      for(n=0; n<3; n++)
        cartoon[i+n] = cartoon_tex.low_toll_col[n];
    }
    if(data[j] > MED_CAM_HEAT && data[j] < HIGH_CAM_HEAT)
    {
      for(n=0; n<3; n++)
        cartoon[i+n] = cartoon_tex.med_toll_col[n];
    }
    if(data[j] > HIGH_CAM_HEAT && data[j] < MAX_CAM_HEAT)
    {
      for(n=0; n<3; n++)
        cartoon[i+n] = cartoon_tex.high_toll_col[n];
    }
    if(data[j] > MAX_CAM_HEAT)
    {
      for(n=0; n<3; n++)
        cartoon[i+n] = cartoon_tex.max_toll_col[n];
    }
  }
}
```

### Uploading the New Texture

Now, all that's left is uploading the texture to OpenGL. The first step is to get the color values from Video for Windows. Once the new color values are calculated, we can go on to converting it to grayscale, and then go on to our cartoon renderer. Once all the image manipulation is finished, we call *glTexSubImage2D()* to get it into the appropriate texture. It is then ready for use in a 3D application as a texture.

```
// WEBCAM_MAKE_TEXTURE
void webcam_make_texture(LPVIDEOHDR video, webcam_draw_mode mode)
{
  // Build the color first
  webcam_make_bgr(webcam_tex.bgr,
video->lpData,
wco_cam_width,
wco_cam_height,
webcam_tex.size);

  if(mode == GREYSCALE || mode == CARTOON)
    webcam_make_greyscale(webcam_tex.greyscale,
                          webcam_tex.bgr,   webcam_tex.size);

  // Note: Could also pass in the delta buffer instead of
  // the greyscale
  if(mode == CARTOON)
    webcam_make_cartoon(webcam_tex.bgr,
                        webcam_tex.cartoon,
                        webcam_tex.greyscale,
                        webcam_tex.size);

/////////////////////////////////////////////////////////////////

  // Upload the greyscale version to OpenGL
  if(mode == GREYSCALE)
  {
    glBindTexture(GL_TEXTURE_2D, webcam_tex.gl_grey);
    glTexSubImage2D(GL_TEXTURE_2D,0,0,0,
                    webcam_tex.size, webcam_tex.size,
                    GL_LUMINANCE,
                    GL_UNSIGNED_BYTE, webcam_tex.greyscale);
  }
  // Upload the color version to OpenGL
  else
  {
    glBindTexture(GL_TEXTURE_2D, webcam_tex.gl_bgr);
    glTexSubImage2D(GL_TEXTURE_2D,0,0,0,
                    webcam_tex.size,  webcam_tex.size,
                    GL_BGR_EXT, GL_UNSIGNED_BYTE, webcam_tex.bgr);
  }
}
```

### Destroy the Web Cam Window

After we're done using the Web cam, we need to destroy the window and set our call-back function to *NULL*, so Windows knows to stop sending messages to it. In addition, we must free up all the memory we previously allocated to our color, grayscale, and delta buffers.

```
// WEBCAM_DESTROY
void webcam_destroy(void)
{
  if(cam_driver_on)
```

```
      {
    capSetCallbackOnFrame(hWndCam, NULL);
      DestroyWindow(hWndCam);
      hWndCam = NULL;

      if(webcam_tex.bgr)
        free(webcam_tex.bgr);

      if(webcam_tex.greyscale)
        free(webcam_tex.greyscale);

      if(webcam_tex.delta_buffer)
        free(webcam_tex.delta_buffer);

      if(webcam_tex.back_buffer[0])
        free(webcam_tex.back_buffer[0]);

      if(webcam_tex.back_buffer[1])
        free(webcam_tex.back_buffer[1]);
    }
  }
```

## Conclusion

Web cams have a lot of untapped potential that game developers may not realize. They have the ability to be used as input devices, as in the way a mouse is used, by tracking color objects and translating their rotations from 2D to 3D [Wu99]. It's even possible to replace your standard mouse using a Web cam, by performing data smoothing and color tracking algorithms on the input frames.

## References

Microsoft Developer Network Library http://msdn.microsoft.com/library/devprods/ vs6/visualc/vcsample/vcsmpcaptest.htm.

[Firetoad00] Firetoad Software, Inc., *Ectosaver*, 2000 www.firetoads.com.

[Wu99] Wu, Andrew, "Computer Vision REU 99" www.cs.ucf.edu/~vision/reu99/ profile-awu.html.

# MATHEMATICS

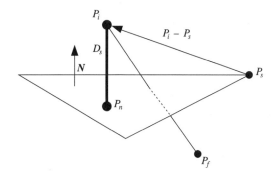

# Introduction

## *Eddie Edwards, Naughty Dog*

eddie@tinyted.net

Computers and mathematics have long been bedfellows. One of my earliest memories is seeing the Cray supercomputers that were used in the UK in the 1980s to try to predict the nation's notoriously unpredictable weather patterns. The computers were big—the size of a small room—and performed millions of floating-point calculations every second. At the time, my 6809-based microcomputer was struggling to display a wireframe cube in real time! Back then, mathematics was not something the average programmer would spend too much time worrying about. Meanwhile, the programmers of these gargantuan machines were busy solving some very tricky problems, with an array of hacks and tricks that would make any game programmer proud.

In 2001, the game console in our living room has enough computing power to put that Cray XMP to shame. The programmers of these diminutive machines are the readers of this book. However, we still don't know if it's going to rain in London tomorrow!

This section illustrates this evolution quite nicely. On the one hand, we have Yossarian King's excellent selection of floating-point hacks, which cleverly brings traditional game programming tricks up to date with modern floating-point technology. On the other hand, we have an article like the one by Alex Vlachos and John Isidoro that uses some quite sophisticated mathematics to derive a smooth but low-cost interpolation scheme for quaternions. And Steve Rabin's method for fast spatial grouping reminds us that, no matter how much computing power we have, some problems are just *hard* (although no longer *as* hard, thanks to his algorithm!).

The articles show another side to game programming, too. There is not a single piece here that does not show a high degree of inventiveness by its author. For instance, the mathematically sophisticated reader might be tempted to skip Jesse Laeuchli's introductory piece on fractals. If he or she did so, however, he or she would miss Jesse's main invention—a Perlin-like noise function that works at game speeds.

The other four articles should be of equal value to the reader. Aaron Nicholls solves a class of problems in projectile physics that could be useful in any 3D game. John Olsen provides an excellent summary of vector and plane tricks, giving simple equations for the most common vector calculations. Graham Rhodes provides an industrial-strength solution to the edge-edge intersection problem, and Carl Dougan describes a simple but highly stable curve-following algorithm (where a 3D object must track a curve).

In combination, these factors made it a great pleasure to edit this section. I hope you derive as much satisfaction from reading it.

# 2.1

## Floating-Point Tricks: Improving Performance with IEEE Floating Point

**Yossarian King, Electronic Arts Canada**

yking@ea.com

## Overview

Integers have fixed precision and fixed magnitude. Floating-point numbers have a "floating" decimal point and arbitrary magnitude. Historically, integers were fast and floats were slow, so most game programmers used integers and avoided floats. Integer math was cumbersome for general calculations, but the performance benefits were worth the effort. Hardware costs have come down, however, and today's PCs and game consoles can do floating-point add, subtract, multiply, and divide in a few cycles. Game programmers can now take advantage of the ease of use of floating-point math.

Although basic floating-point arithmetic has become fast, complex functions are still slow. Floating-point libraries may be optimized, but they are generally implemented for accuracy, not performance. For games, performance is often more important than accuracy.

This gem presents various tricks to improve floating-point performance, trading accuracy for execution speed. Table lookup has long been a standard trick for integer math; this gem shows generalized linear and logarithmic lookup table techniques for optimizing arbitrary floating-point functions.

The following sections discuss:

- The IEEE floating-point standard
- Tricks for fast float/int conversions, comparisons, and clamping
- A linear lookup table method to optimize sine and cosine
- A logarithmic method to optimize square root
- Generalized lookup table methods to optimize arbitrary floating-point functions
- The importance of performance measurement

## IEEE Floating-Point Format

The IEEE standard for floating-point numbers dictates a binary representation and conventions for rounding, accuracy, and exception results (such as divide by zero). The techniques outlined in this article rely on the binary representation, but are generally not concerned with the rounding and exception handling. If a computer or game console uses the standard binary representation, then these tricks apply, regardless of whether the floating-point handling is fully IEEE compliant. The Pentium III Streaming SIMD Extensions (SSE) and PS2 vector unit both implement subsets of the IEEE standard that do not support the full range of exception handling; however, since the binary representation follows the standard, the tricks in this gem will work with these instruction sets.

The IEEE standard represents floating-point numbers with a sign bit, a biased exponent, and a normalized mantissa, or significand. Single precision, 32-bit floating-point numbers (a "float" in C) are stored as shown in Figure 2.1.1.

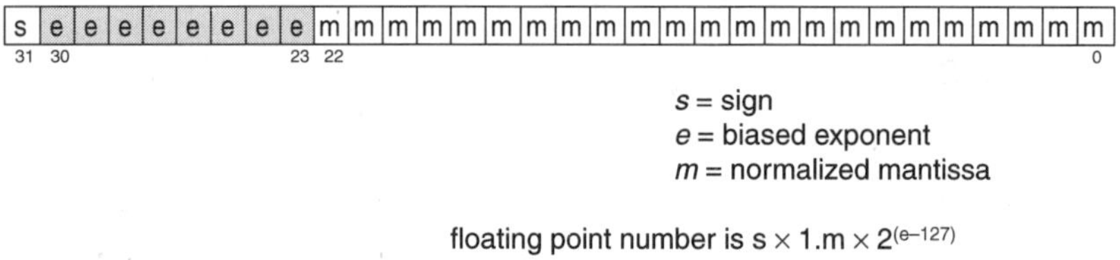

$s$ = sign
$e$ = biased exponent
$m$ = normalized mantissa

floating point number is $s \times 1.m \times 2^{(e-127)}$

**FIGURE 2.1.1** *IEEE 32-bit floating-point format has a 1-bit sign, 8-bit exponent, and 23-bit mantissa.*

The exponent is stored as a positive number in biased form, with 127 added to the actual exponent (rather than the more familiar two's complement representation used for integers). The mantissa is usually stored in normalized form, with an implied 1 before the 23-bit fraction. Normalizing in this way allows maximum precision to be obtained from the available bits.

A floating-point number thus consists of a normalized significand representing a number between 1 and 2, together with a biased exponent indicating the position of the binary point and a sign bit. The number represented is therefore:

$$n = s \times 1.m \times 2^{(e-127)}$$

For example, the number −6.25 in binary is −110.01, or $-1 \times 1.1001 \times 2^2$. This would be represented with $s = 1$, $e = 2 + 127 = 10000001$, $m = [1.]1001$, as shown in Figure 2.1.2.

Some additional "magic values" are represented using the exponent. When $e = 255$, $m$ encodes special conditions such as not-a-number (NaN), undefined result, or positive or negative infinity. Exponent $e = 0$ is used for denormalized numbers—numbers so tiny that the range of the exponent overflows 8 bits.

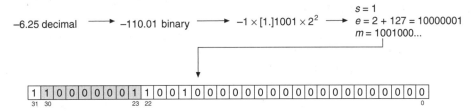

**FIGURE 2.1.2**  *The number –6.25 as stored in memory in 32-bit IEEE floating-point format.*

Double precision 64-bit floating-point numbers are stored using the same basic format, but with 11 bits for the exponent and 52 for the significand. The exponent is biased by 1023, rather than 127. Double precision numbers require twice the storage space and may be slower to load from memory and to process. For these reasons, double precision should generally be avoided in game code. This gem uses only single-precision floats.

## Floating-Point Tricks

Before getting to the lookup table techniques, this section discusses some useful floating-point tricks that help explain the games you can play with the bit patterns of floating-point numbers.

### Float/Int Conversions

The lookup table techniques that follow convert a floating-point number to an integer to generate lookup table indices. This operation can be slow; on a Pentium II, for example, casting a float to an int with "(int)f" takes about 60 cycles. This is because the ANSI C standard dictates that casting a float to an int should truncate the fraction, but by default, the FPU rounds to the nearest integer. Casting to an int becomes a function call to a routine that changes the FPU rounding mode, does the conversion, and then changes the rounding mode back. Nasty.

Note that the cost of casting between ints and floats is dependent on the compiler and processor with which you are working. As with all optimizations, benchmark this conversion trick against a regular typecast and disassemble the code to see what's actually happening.

The conversion can be performed much faster by simply adding $1 \times 2^{23}$ to the floating-point number and then discarding the upper exponent bits of the result. We'll look at the code first, and then analyze why it works.

To do this, it is helpful to define the following union, which lets us access a 32-bit number as either an integer or a float.

```
typedef union
{
        int        i;
        float      f;
} _INTORFLOAT;
```

The INTORFLOAT type is used in code snippets throughout this gem. Note that it makes access to the bit pattern of numbers look very simple—in practice, the compiler may be generating more code than you expect. On a Pentium II, for example, floating-point and integer registers are in separate hardware, and data cannot be moved from one to the other without going through memory; for this reason, accessing the members of the INTORFLOAT union may require additional memory loads and stores.

Here is how to convert a float to an int:

```
INTORFLOAT   n;       // floating-point number to convert
INTORFLOAT   bias;    // "magic" number

bias.i = (23 + 127) << 23;  // bias constant = 1 x 2^23
n.f = 123.456f;             // some floating-point number

n.f += bias.f;              // add as floating-point
n.i -= bias.i;              // subtract as integer
// n.i is now 123 – the integer portion of the original n.f
```

Why does this work? Adding $1 \times 2^{23}$ as a floating-point number pushes the mantissa into the lower 23 bits, setting the exponent to a known value (23 + 127). Sub-

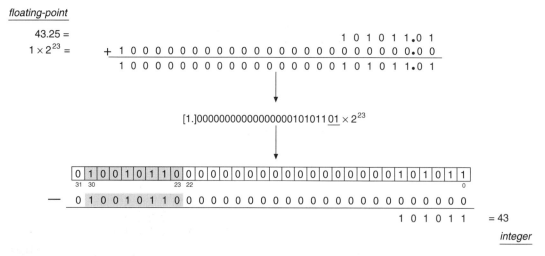

**FIGURE 2.1.3** *The number 43.25 is converted to an integer by manipulating the floating-point format. The underlined bits in the mantissa do not fit in memory and are discarded (with rounding).*

tracting the known exponent as an integer removes these unwanted upper bits, leaving the desired integer in the low bits of the result. These steps are illustrated in Figure 2.1.3 for the number 43.25.

On a Pentium II (with everything in cache), this reduces the conversion time from 60 cycles to about 5. Note that it is also possible to write inline assembly code to get the FPU to convert from float to int without changing the rounding mode—this is faster than typecasting, but generally slower than the biasing trick shown here.

This trick works as long as the floating-point number to be converted does not "overlap" the bias constant being added. As long as the number is less than $2^{23}$, the trick will work.

To handle negative numbers correctly, use $bias = ((23 + 127) << 23) + (1 << 22)$—the additional $(1 << 22)$ makes this equivalent to adding $1.5 \times 2^{23}$, which causes correct rounding for negative numbers, as shown in Figure 2.1.4. The extra bit is required so that the subtract-with-borrow operation does not affect the most significant bit in the mantissa (bit 23). In this case, 10 upper bits will be removed instead of 9, so the range is one bit less than for positive numbers—the number to be converted must be less than $2^{22}$.

To convert from a float to a fixed-point format with a desired number of fractional bits after the binary point, use $bias = (23 - bits + 127) << 23$. Again, to handle negative numbers, add an additional $(1 << 22)$ to $bias$. This is illustrated in Figure 2.1.5, which shows the conversion of 192.8125 to a fixed-point number with two fractional bits.

Note that you can use the "inverse" of this trick to convert from integer to floating-point.

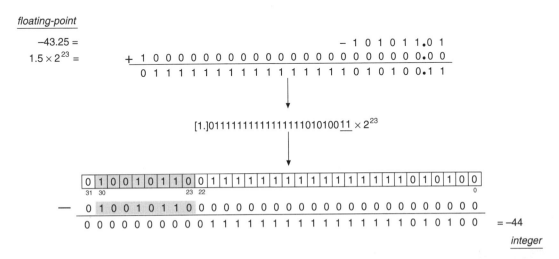

**FIGURE 2.1.4** *To convert a negative float to an integer is slightly different than for positive numbers. Here we see the conversion of –43.25. Observe how the rounding applied when the underlined bits are discarded yields the correct negative integer.*

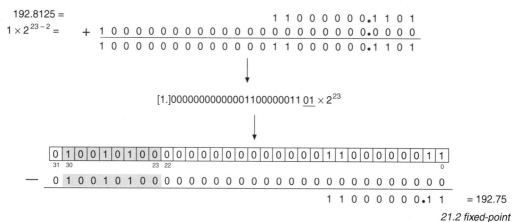

**FIGURE 2.1.5** *Fractional bits can be preserved during the conversion from float to integer. Here, 192.8125 is converted to a fixed-point number with two bits after the binary point.*

```
n.i = 123;          // some integer

n.i += bias.i;      // add as integer
n.f -= bias.f;      // subtract as floating-point
// n.f is now 123.0 — the original n.i converted to a float
```

Usually, int-to-float conversions using typecasts are fast, and thus less in need of a performance-optimizing trick.

### Sign Test

Because the sign bit of a floating-point number is in bit 31, the same as for integers, we can use the integer unit to test for positive or negative floating-point numbers. Given a floating-point number *f*, the following two code fragments are (almost) equivalent:

```
if ( f < 0.0f )     // floating-point compare
...

INTORFLOAT ftmp;
ftmp.f = f;
if (ftmp.i < 0)     // integer compare
...
```

Although they are equivalent, the integer compare may run faster due to better pipelining of the integer instruction stream. Try it and see if it helps your code. ("Almost" equivalent because negative 0 will behave differently.)

### Comparisons

Since the floating-point format stores sign, exponent, mantissa in that bit order, we can use the integer unit to compare floating-point numbers—if the exponent of *a* is greater than the exponent of *b*, then *a* is greater than *b*, no matter what the mantissas. The following code fragments may be equivalent:

```
if ( a < b )          // floating-point compare
...

INTORFLOAT atmp, btmp;
atmp.f = f; btmp.f = b;
if (atmp.i < btmp.i)   // integer compare
...
```

Again, the integer comparison will usually pipeline better and run faster. Note that this breaks down when *a* and *b* are both negative, because the exponent and mantissa bits are not stored in the two's complement form that the integer comparison expects. If your code can rely on at least one of the numbers being positive, then this is a faster way to do comparisons.

### Clamping

Clamping a value to a specific range often comes up in games programming, and often we want to clamp to a [0,1] range. A floating-point value *f* can be clamped to 0 (i.e., set $f = 0$ if $f < 0$) by turning the sign bit into a mask, as in the following code snippet:

```
INTORFLOAT ftmp;
ftmp.f = f;
int s = ftmp.i >> 31;    // create sign bit mask
s = ~s;                  // flip bits in mask
ftmp.i &= s;             // ftmp = ftmp & mask
f = ftmp.f;
```

*s* is set to the bits of *f* shifted right by 31—sign extension replicates the sign bit throughout all 32 bits. NOT-ing this value creates a mask of 0 bits if *f* was negative, or 1 bits if *f* was positive. AND-ing *f* with this value either leaves *f* unchanged or sets *f* to 0. Net result: if *f* was negative, then it becomes 0; if it was positive, it is unchanged.

This code runs entirely in the integer unit, and has no compares or branches. In test code, the floating-point compare and clamp took about 18 cycles, while the integer clamp took less than five cycles. (Note that these cycle times include loop overhead.)

Clamping positive numbers to 0 (set $f = 0$ if $f > 0$) is less useful but even easier, since we don't need to flip the bits in the mask.

```
INTORFLOAT ftmp;
ftmp.f = f;
int s = ftmp.i >> 31; // create sign bit mask
```

```
ftmp.i &= s;            // ftmp = ftmp & mask
f = ftmp.f;
```

Clamping to 1 (set $f$ = 1 if $f$ > 1) can be done by subtracting 1, clamping to 0, and then adding 1.

```
INTORFLOAT ftmp;
ftmp.f = f - 1.0f;
int s = ftmp.i >> 31;  // create sign bit mask
ftmp.i &= s;            // ftmp = ftmp & mask
f = ftmp.f + 1.0f;
```

Note that using conditional load instructions in assembly will generally increase the speed of clamping operations, as these avoid the need for branching, which kills the branch prediction logic in the instruction pipeline.

### Absolute Value

This one's easy: since floating-point numbers do not use two's complement, taking the absolute value of a floating-point number is as simple as masking the sign bit to 0.

```
INTORFLOAT ftmp;
ftmp.f = f;
ftmp.i &= 0x7fffffff;
f = ftmp.f;
```

Note that this is much faster than using a compare to determine if $f$ is less than 0 before negating it.

## Linear Lookup Tables for Sine and Cosine

Trigonometry is often useful in games—for calculating distances and angles, stepping along a circle, or animating a water mesh. The standard math library has all the normal trig functions, but they are slow, and they work on doubles, so they use more memory than needed. In a game, a low-precision calculation is often sufficient.

To efficiently compute sine and cosine, we can use a lookup table. A common approach is to use fixed-point math, with angles represented on an integer scale, say, 0 to 1023 to cover the full circle. However, this means that the game programmer needs to understand the library implementation of sine and cosine, and represent his or her angles in the format it requires. By using floating-point tricks for efficient indexing, we can create floating-point trig functions that use standard radians and do not require the programmer to know about implementation details.

### sin

Let's implement:

```
float fsin( float theta );
```

This can easily be done with a lookup table. A 256-entry table, covering the range of angles 0 to $2\pi$, is initialized as:

```
sintable[i] = (float)sin((double)i * 2.0*3.14159265/256.0)
```

which simply converts $i$ in the range 0–256 to floating-point radians in the range 0 to $2\pi$ and takes the sine of the resulting angle.

Given this table, the *fsin* function could be implemented as follows:

```
float fsin( float theta )
{
    i = (unsigned int)(theta * 256.0f/
        (2.0f*3.14159265f));return table[i];
    }
```

However, this has two problems: first, it uses the slow float-to-int typecast, and second, if theta is outside the range [0,$2\pi$), then the function will index out of the table.

Both of these problems are solved with this implementation:

```
#define FTOIBIAS    12582912.0f    // 1.5 * 2^23
#define PI          3.14159265f

float fsin( float theta )
{
    int    i;
    INTORFLOAT ftmp;
    ftmp.f = theta * (256.0f/(2.0f*PI)) + FTOIBIAS;
    i = ftmp.i & 255;
    return table[i];
}
```

This implementation uses the floating-point biasing trick described previously for fast conversion from floating-point to integer. It masks the integer with 255 so that the table index wraps around, always staying in the 0–255 range. Note that if $f$ exceeds $2^{22}$, then the float-to-integer conversion trick will fail, so it's still necessary to periodically reduce $f$ to the valid [0,$2\pi$) range.

This implementation of *fsin* takes about 10 cycles on a Pentium II (assuming all code and data is in primary cache), as compared with almost 140 cycles for the standard math library implementation of *sin* (even though *sin* uses the hardware sine instruction in the FPU).

A 256-entry floating-point table takes 1K, which should easily stay within cache for the duration of your inner loops. Accuracy is basically eight bits, as constrained by the lookup table size. The worst-case error can easily be determined from analyzing the lookup table (as is demonstrated in the code on the CD). Larger lookup tables increase the accuracy of your results, but will hurt cache performance.

ON THE CD

**cos**

The cosine function could be implemented in exactly the same way, with its own lookup table, but we can take advantage of the fact that $\cos(\theta) = \sin(\theta + \pi/2)$, and use the same lookup table. To do this, we just need to add 256/4 (since adding $\pi/2$ means we're adding a quarter of a circle to the angle) to the lookup table index, which we can do at the same time as biasing the exponent. This yields the following implementation:

```
float fcos( float theta )
{
    int    i;
    INTORFLOAT ftmp;
    ftmp.f = theta * (256.0f/(2.0f*PI)) + FTOIBIAS + 64f;
    i = ftmp.i & 255;
    return table[i];
}
```

Depending on the application, it is often useful to get both sine and cosine at the same time. This can be done more efficiently than computing each separately—simply look up sin, and then add 64 to the index and mask by 255 to look up cos. If you need to compute several sines or cosines at once, you can write custom code to interleave the calculations and make it faster still.

## Logarithmic Optimization of Square Root

Square roots are useful in games for operations such as computing distances, normalizing vectors, and solving quadratic equations. Despite the presence of a square root instruction built into the FPU, the *sqrt* function in the standard C library still takes about 80 cycles on a Pentium II CPU, making it another good candidate for optimization.

Square root optimization is an interesting use of floating-point bit fiddling, because the logarithmic, multiscale nature of square root allows us to decompose the square root calculation and manipulate the mantissa and exponent separately. Consider the square root of a floating-point number:

$$f = 1.m \times 2^e$$
$$sqrt(f) = sqrt(1.m \times 2^e)$$
$$= sqrt(1.m) \times 2^{e/2}$$

So, to compute the square root of $f$, we compute the square root of the mantissa and divide the exponent by 2. However, the exponent is an integer, so if the exponent is odd, then dividing by 2 loses the low bit. This is addressed by prepending the low bit of the exponent to the mantissa, so we have:

$$sqrt(f) = sqrt(1.m \times 2^{e_0}) \times 2^{\lfloor e/2 \rfloor}$$

where $e_0$ is the low bit of the exponent.

This is implemented with a 256-entry table for the square root of the truncated mantissa and some additional tweaking for the exponent calculation, as follows:

```
float  fsqrt( float f )
  {
  INTORFLOAT      ftmp;
  unsigned int    n, e;

  ftmp.f = f;
  n = ftmp.i;
  e = (n >> 1) & 0x3f800000; // divide exponent by 2
  n = (n >> 16) & 0xff;      // table index is e0+m22-m16

  ftmp.i = sqrttable[n] + e; // combine results

  return ftmp.f;
}
```

The table index is simply the upper bits of the mantissa and the low bit of the exponent ($e_0$). The lookup table contains the mantissa of the computed square roots.

The exponent of the square root is computed by shifting the exponent of $f$ by 1 to divide by 2. Since the exponent is biased, this divides the bias by 2 as well as the exponent, which is not what we want. This is compensated for by adding an additional factor to the entries of *sqrttable* to re-bias the exponent.

**ON THE CD**

This *fsqrt* function takes about 16 cycles on a Pentium II CPU—about five times faster than the C library implementation. Again, this is assuming that everything is in cache.

The algorithm is explained in more detail in the code on the CD.

## Optimization of Arbitrary Functions

Consider an arbitrary floating-point function of one variable:

$$y = f(x)$$

The techniques just discussed reveal two basic methods for table-based optimizations of general functions. For sine and cosine, the value of $x$ was linearly quantized over a known range and used as a table index to look up $y$. For square root, the value of $x$ was logarithmically quantized and used as a table index to look up a value. This value was scaled by a function of the exponent of $x$ to get the final value of $y$.

The linear approach rescales a floating-point number and converts it to an integer to generate a lookup table index via linear quantization. This is a simple technique very similar to integer lookup tables, the only wrinkle being the efficient conversion of a floating-point value into an integer index. The logarithmic approach uses the floating-point bit pattern directly as a table index, to achieve logarithmic quantization.

Both of these techniques can be generalized to the case of arbitrary functions. Depending on the function, the linear or logarithmic approach may be more appropriate.

## Linear Quantization

The *fsin* function in the previous section can be used as a template for optimizing general functions via linear quantization. Suppose we know that the function will only be used over a limited range $x \in [A, B)$. We can build a lookup table that uniformly covers this range, and efficiently calculate the correct index into the table for values of $x$ within the range. The optimized function $f$ is then implemented as:

```
#define FTOIBIAS       12582912.0f    // 1.5 * 2^23
#define TABLESIZE      256
#define INDEXSCALE     ((float)TABLESIZE / (B − A))

float flut( float x )
{
    int     i;
    INTORFLOAT ftmp;
    ftmp.f = x * INDEXSCALE + (FTOIBIAS − A * INDEXSCALE);
    i = ftmp.i & (TABLESIZE − 1);
    return ftable[i];
}
```

The lookup table is initialized with:

```
ftable[i] = f( (float)i / INDEXSCALE + A );
```

where *f* is the full-precision floating implementation of the function. The *flut* computation requires two floating-point operations (multiply and add), one integer bitwise mask, and a table lookup. It takes about 10 cycles on a Pentium II CPU.

Note that additional accuracy can be obtained for a few more cycles by linearly interpolating the two closest table entries. An API supporting this optimization for general functions is provided on the CD, including optional linear interpolation to increase accuracy.

## Logarithmic Quantization

The linear method treats the range $[A,B)$ uniformly. Depending on the function, a logarithmic treatment may be more appropriate, as in the square root optimization. The basic idea is that the bits of the floating-point representation are used directly as a lookup table index, rather than being manipulated into an integer range. By extracting selected bits of the sign, exponent, and mantissa, we can massage the 1:8:23 IEEE floating-point number into our own reduced precision format with as many bits as we like for the sign, exponent, and mantissa.

In the square root example, we extracted 8 bits to give a logarithmically quantized 0:1:7 representation. We used 1 bit of the exponent and 7 bits of the mantissa. The sign bit was discarded, since the square root of a negative number is undefined. The 0:1:7 format represents an 8-bit mantissa (remember the implied 1 in the IEEE representation) and a 1-bit exponent, so it can represent numbers between $[1].0000000 \times 2^0$ and $[1].1111111 \times 2^1$, which covers the range $[1,4)$.

The square root function was decomposed into an operation on the 0:1:7 quantized number (a table lookup) and an independent operation on the exponent (divide by 2). Additional trickery was employed to optimize the two independent operations and combine the mantissa and exponent into a 32-bit floating-point result.

Other functions can benefit from this method of logarithmic quantization. The IEEE format makes it easy to extract the least significant bits of the exponent with the most significant bits of the mantissa in a single shift and mask operation. To extract *ebits* of the exponent and *mbits* of the mantissa, simply do this:

*bits* = (*n* >> (23 − *mbits*)) & ((1 << (*ebits* + *mbits*)) − 1)

This shifts the number *n* to the right so that the desired bits of the mantissa and exponent are the rightmost bits in the number, and then masks off the desired number of bits.

The sign bit can be handled with some extra bit fiddling, depending on the function with which you are working. If you know that you are only dealing with positive numbers (for example, square root), or that your function always returns a positive result, then you can ignore the sign. If the sign of your result is the same as the sign of the input number (in other words, f(−x) = −f(x)), you can simply save and restore the sign bit.

For functions with a limited range of input values, masking out selected bits of the exponent and mantissa can give you a direct table index. For example, if you only care about your function over the range $[1,16)$, then you can use 2 bits of exponent and 4 bits of mantissa (for example). This 0:2:4 representation stores binary numbers between $1.0000 \times 2^0$ and $1.1111 \times 2^3$, or decimal 1.0 to 15.5. Mask out these bits and use the bits directly as an index into a precomputed 64-entry table. This requires very few cycles and is computationally fast. However, as you add more precision, the table grows and may become prohibitively large, at which point cache performance will suffer.

An alternative is to decompose the exponent and mantissa calculations, as was done in the square root example. If your function f(x) can be decomposed as:

$$f(x) = f(1.m \times 2^e) = f1(1.m) \times 2^{f2(e)}$$

then you can, for example, approximate f1 with a 256-entry lookup table, using 8 bits of the mantissa *m*, and perform the calculation of f2 directly, as an integer operation on the exponent *e*. This is essentially the technique used by the square root trick.

Logarithmic quantization is a powerful tool, but often requires function-specific bit fiddling to optimize a particular function. Fully general techniques are not always possible, but the methods described in this section should be helpful when tackling your specific optimization problem.

## Performance Measurement

When optimizing code, make sure you measure performance carefully before and after making the optimization. Sometimes an optimization that looks good on paper causes trouble when implemented, due to cache behavior, branch mispredictions, or poor handling by the compiler. Whenever you make changes, be sure that you are improving your performance—never assume.

Make sure compiler optimizations are enabled. Use inline functions where appropriate. Again, test your results when using inline functions or tweaking the compiler settings.

When benchmarking code, take care that compiler optimization isn't getting in the way of your tests. Disassemble your code and step through it to be sure it's running what you expected. When timing things, it's often helpful to run something in a loop—but if the body of your loop gets optimized out, then your timing won't be very accurate!

On Pentium computers, you can use the rdtsc (read time stamp counter) instruction to get the current CPU cycle count. Intel warns that this instruction should be executed a couple times before you start using the results. Intel also recommends using an instruction such as cpuid that will flush the instruction cache, so that you get more consistent timing results. To get absolute times, the cycle counts can be converted to seconds by dividing by the execution speed (MHz) of the processor.

Cycle counters are the most reliable way to measure fine-grain performance. Other tools such as VTune and TrueTime (on the PC) are useful for higher level profiling. For any benchmarking, make sure that memory behavior is realistic, as memory bottlenecks are one of the most serious impediments to high performance on modern processors. Be aware of how your benchmark is using the cache, and try to simulate the cache behavior of your game. For a benchmark, the cache can be "warmed up" by running the algorithm a couple of times before taking the timing measurements. However, a warm cache may not emulate the behavior of your game—best is to benchmark directly in the game itself. Disable interrupts for more reliable results, or take measurements multiple times and ignore the spikes.

ON THE CD

All the cycle times reported in this gem are from an Intel Pentium II 450-MHz machine. Each operation was repeated 1000 times in a loop, with the instruction and data cache warmed by running the test multiple times. Cycle counts include loop overhead. See the code on the CD for actual benchmarks used.

The lookup table techniques described in this article are appropriate if the lookup table remains in cache. This is probably true within the inner loop of your rendering pipeline or physics engine, but it's probably not true if you are calling these functions randomly throughout the code. If the lookup tables cannot be kept in cache, then techniques that use more computation and fewer memory accesses are probably more appropriate—methods such as polynomial approximation (see [Edwards00] for a good overview).

## Conclusions

This gem scratched the surface of floating-point optimization. Lookup tables are the primary method explored, and they often produce significant speedups. However, be aware of cache behavior, and always benchmark your results. Sometimes you can achieve the same result faster by using more computation but touching memory less—techniques such as polynomial approximation may be appropriate. The tricks shown here can be extended in a variety of ways, and many other tricks are possible. As a popular book title suggests, there is a Zen to the art of code optimization, and a short overview like this can't hope to cover all possibilities.

## References

[Abrash94] Abrash, Michael, *Zen of Code Optimization*, Coriolis Group, 1994.

[Edwards00] Edwards, Eddie, "Polynomial Approximations to Trigonometric Functions," *Game Programming Gems*, Charles River Media, 2000.

[Intel01] Intel Web page on floating-point unit and FPU data format. Good for PCs, but relevant to any IEEE-compliant architecture. Available at http://developer .intel.com/design/intarch/techinfo/Pentium/fpu.htm.

[Lalonde98] Lalonde, Paul, and Dawson, Robert, "A High Speed, Low Precision Square Root," *Graphics Gems*, Academic Press, 1998.

# Vector and Plane Tricks

## John Olsen, Microsoft

infix@xmission.com

**Y**our collision detection routine is running flawlessly now, returning a surface point and a normal back when you feed it a position and velocity vector. Now what? Actually, there are quite a few things you can do based on the data you have.

In general, you may want to have your collision routine generate the actual collision point, but the methods in this gem show how to handle collision results that show only the plane of intersection. Since a plane can be fully specified with a surface normal and any point on the plane, you can work your way through the math to find everything you need from there.

Data that goes into your collision code would be an initial point $P_i$ and a final point $P_f$, and the output in the case of a collision would be a plane that is defined by a unit vector surface normal $N$ and a point on the surface $P_s$. The point need not be the actual intersection point as long as it is on the plane.

For optimization purposes, you will probably want to build a subset of these calculations back into your collision code. Much of the information you need will have already been calculated during the collision tests. It will be much faster to reuse the already known information rather than recalculate it from scratch.

The plane equation $Ax + By + Cz + D = 0$ maps onto the supplied data, where $x$, $y$, and $z$ are the components of the normal vector $N$, and $D$ is the dot product $N \bullet P_s$.

## Altitude Relative to the Collision Plane

One of the most commonly used pieces of data when checking collisions is the altitude of one of your data points. If the altitude is positive, the point is above the surface and has not collided yet. If it is negative, you have collided and penetrated the surface.

Typical collision testing code will only return a hit if one of your test points is on each side of the test surface. This means that if you want to predict collisions, you need to pass along a position with an exaggerated velocity vector. That way, the exaggerated vector will intersect much earlier than your actual movement would allow.

Once you have tricked your collision code into returning a surface point and normal, you can get your altitude relative to that surface by using your initial position. The final position is not used for this altitude calculation.

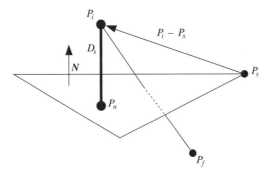

**FIGURE 2.2.1** *Determining the altitude.*

As shown in Figure 2.2.1, we want to find the length of the vector $(P_s - P_i)$ when it is projected onto the surface normal $N$. This gives us the distance of the shortest line from the point to the surface. This shortest vector is by definition perpendicular to the surface. This is exactly what the dot product gives us, so we are left with the scalar (nonvector) distance to the surface $D_s$ as shown:

$$D_s = (P_i - P_s) \cdot N$$

**Nearest Point on the Surface**

Once we have the distance to the surface, it takes just one more step to get the point on the surface $P_n$ that is closest to the initial point $P_i$ as also shown in Figure 2.2.1. We already know the point is distance $D_s$ from the starting point, and that distance is along the surface normal $N$. That means the point can be found with the following:

$$P_n = P_i - D_s N$$

The normal vector is facing the opposite direction of the distance we want to measure, so it needs to be subtracted from the starting point.

## Pinning Down the Collision Point

When you have one point on each side of a test surface, your vector must at some point intersect with it. Finding this intersection point $P_c$ will tell you where your vector pierces the surface. If your collision detection code has not already provided you with the exact point, here is how you would find it.

You know that the collision point must lie somewhere along the line. Knowing in advance that there is a collision makes it possible to take some shortcuts since we know there actually is a solution to the equation. If the test ray is parallel to the surface, the ratio cannot be calculated since it results in a divide by zero. We can take advantage of the calculation for $D_s$ in finding the collision point $P_c$. Figure 2.2.2 shows the information needed for this calculation.

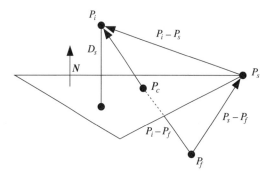

**FIGURE 2.2.2** *Finding the collision point* $P_c$.

Since we know the collision is between the two points, we can find it by calculating how far it is along the line from $P_i$ to $P_f$. This ratio can be written as:

$$R = ((P_i - P_s) \cdot N) / ((P_i - P_f) \cdot N)$$

Or, using our already computed $D_s$, it becomes:

$$R = D_s / ((P_i - P_f) \cdot N)$$

The two line segments are arranged to both point in the same direction relative to the surface normal, which guarantees that our ratio will be non-negative. Once we have this ratio, we can use it to multiply the length of the vector from $P_i$ to $P_f$ to tell how far from $P_i$ the collision occurs. In the special case of $R = 1$, you can avoid the calculation since it results in the point $P_f$. For $R = 0$, the point is $P_i$. Otherwise, the following equation is used:

$$P_c = P_i + R(P_f - P_i)$$

## Distance to the Collision Point

Although similar to $D_s$, this differs from the distance from the collision plane because the distance is calculated along the path of travel rather than along the surface normal. In the case of travelling near the surface but nearly parallel to it, your distance to collision will be very large when compared to your altitude.

This is the type of calculation you would want to use when calculating altitude for an aircraft, since you cannot guarantee the direction of a surface normal on the ground below. Rather than sending your actual velocity for a collision test, you would send your current position and a very large down vector, long enough to guarantee that it will intersect the ground. This works in the case of intersecting a small polygon

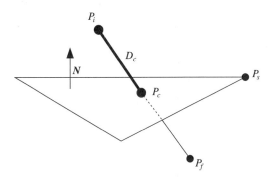

**FIGURE 2.2.3** *Calculating distance to the collision point.*

that happens to be aligned nearly perpendicular to the test vector. In that case, the altitude relative to the collision plane $P_n$ as calculated earlier would give a very small number.

Once you have the actual collision point, it's very easy to calculate the distance using Euclid's equation to find how far it is from the starting point to the collision point. Figure 2.2.3 shows the elements required. The distance to the collision point, $D_c$, is the magnitude of the vector from our starting point $P_i$ to the collision point $P_c$ that was calculated earlier:

$$D_c = \left| P_c - P_i \right|$$

Another way to describe the magnitude of this vector is that it is the square root of the sum of the squares of the differences of each component of the vector. Most vector libraries include a function call to find the magnitude or length of a vector. Vector magnitudes are never negative.

Another possible shortcut can be used when you know the ratio $R$ used to find the collision point as described in the previous section. The distance to the collision point is the length of the full line (which you may already have lying around) multiplied by the already computed ratio.

$$D_c = R \left| P_f - P_i \right|$$

## Reflecting Off the Collision Plane

The usual result of a collision is to bounce. The interesting part is figuring out the direction and position once you have rebounded off a surface. Figure 2.2.4 shows the elements used in calculating the reflected vector. The first two cases will perfectly

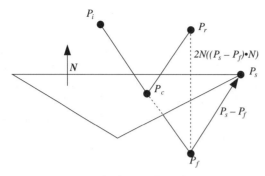

**FIGURE 2.2.4** *Calculating the reflected vector.*

preserve the magnitude of the velocity. In both cases, the result of the bounce will be the same distance from the plane as $P_f$.

One of the simplest ways to visualize reflecting a point relative to a plane is to imagine a vector from the below-ground destination point back up to the surface along the surface normal. The new reflected location is found by continuing that line an equal distance to the other side of the plane. You obtain the new location by adding to the final point twice the distance from the final point to the surface. Reusing our equation to find the distance perpendicular to the plane, we come up with the following. The distance is multiplied by the surface normal to turn it back into a vector since you cannot add a simple scalar value such as $D_s$ to a vector.

$$P_r = P_f + 2N((P_s - P_f) \cdot N)$$

The original and reflected vectors will have the same angle relative to the plane. Another way of looking at this is that if you normalize the vectors from your collision point going out to both your original start point and your reflected point, then find a dot product of each with your surface normal; they will be equal.

Vectors are normalized by dividing the vector by its length or magnitude, so the statement about reflected vectors in the previous paragraph can be written as:

$$\frac{P_c - P_r}{|P_c - P_r|} \cdot N = \frac{P_c - P_i}{|P_c - P_i|} \cdot N$$

Any point on the plane could be substituted for $P_c$ ($P_s$ works, for instance) in the preceding equation and the same result would hold since all we are saying here is that the ends of the unit vectors are the same distance from the plane.

A complication with reflections is that the newly determined end point needs to be tested all over again with your collision code to see if you have been pushed through some other surface. If you repeat the collision test, but with a vector from your collision point $P_c$ to the newly reflected point $P_r$, you will get a possible new collision. You will need to repeat this process until no collision occurs. At each pass, your vector will be smaller as it is chewed up by bouncing, as long as you do not try to bounce between two coincident planes.

There is one degenerate case you should also watch out for when chaining collisions together. Should you hit exactly at the intersection of two planes, your second test will be made with an initial point on the edge of the surface. This is easy to handle if you know about this problem and allow for it in advance by assuming anything exactly at the surface (or on the edge) has not yet collided, and is counted as above the surface for collision purposes. Collisions are reserved for penetration distances greater than zero.

Once you have completed your final reflection, a new velocity vector can be computed by normalizing the direction from the last collision to the final reflected location and multiplying it by the original velocity like this:

$$V = \frac{(P_r - P_c)\left|P_i - P_f\right|}{\left|P_r - P_c\right|}$$

**Kickback Collision**

Sometimes, rather than reflect off the collision plane, you want to kick the player back the way he or she came as shown in Figure 2.2.5. The calculations for this are simple once you have the collision point. Since this collision also preserves velocity, it is also perfectly elastic.

The point to which you are kicked back, $P_k$, is obtained by calculating the vector from your final point $P_f$ back to your collision point $P_c$ and adding it to the collision point.

$$P_k = P_c + (P_c - P_f)$$

We can combine terms to get:

$$P_k = 2P_c - P_f$$

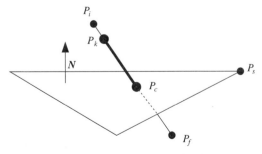

**FIGURE 2.2.5**  *Calculating a kickback vector.*

You can run into the same problems with kickback collisions as with reflections where the destination point leads to an additional collision. However, there is an early way out of the loop for kickback collisions in some cases. If the collision point is more than halfway from the initial point to the final point, the resulting kickback point will occur in an area that has already been checked for collisions, so no additional check is necessary.

## Collisions with Damping

Should you want to perform a collision with some sort of friction or damping, you will need to be careful of how you handle the vectors. You will need a scalar value $S$ that will be used as a multiplier to change your velocity at each impact. It will typically range from zero (the object stops on impact) to one (a completely elastic collision preserving velocity). Energy can be injected into the system by increasing the scalar above one. A kickback collision is the same as using a scalar of negative one.

To properly handle nonelastic collisions, you must scale only the portion of the vector from the collision point $P_c$ to the reflected point $P_r$ as shown in Figure 2.2.6, since that is the only portion of the flight that will have been slowed due to the impact. The following equation relies heavily on the earlier equations to determine what your new slowed point would be.

$$P_{slow} = P_c + (P_r - P_c)S$$

In coordination with this, you would need to multiply any separately stored velocity vector by the same scalar value, or your object will resume its full speed the next frame. In the case of a collision putting your point into another immediate collision as discussed earlier, this scale factor should be applied at each pass to simulate the damping effect of multiple bounces in a single frame.

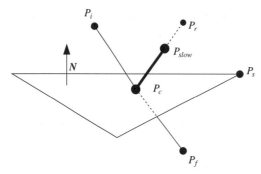

**FIGURE 2.2.6** *Calculating a damped reflection vector.*

**Interpolation Across a Line or Plane**

An interesting side note about lines and planes is that a weighted average interpolation between any set of points occupies the space defined by those points. For instance, starting with a line, you can assign weights to the end points where the weights sum to one, and all possible resulting points are on the line defined by the points. Adding another point to build a plane extends the rule so the sum of the three weights must equal one in order for the weighted sum to remain on the plane defined by the three points. Additional points on the plane may be added, and additional dimensions may also be added should you have need for a point on an n-dimensional plane.

This trick is related in a roundabout way to the reason we can often use $P_s$ and $P_c$ interchangeably in several of the previous equations. Either point is sufficient to fill the needs of the plane equation.

It's also interesting to note that the individual weights don't need to be between zero and one. They just need to all sum up to the value one, which allows the resulting point to be outside the line segment or polygon defined by the points while still being on the extended line or plane.

**Sphere-to-Plane Collision**

Colliding a ball with a surface is a little bit more complex than colliding a point against the surface. One way to approach it is through ratios. If you draw a line from the start point $P_i$ to the line-based collision point $P_c$ of the vector against the plane, the ball center $P_b$ will be somewhere on that line when the ball begins to intersect the plane.

When the ball just touches the surface, we can compare the line from $P_i$ to $P_c$ to the line $P_i$ to $P_n$ to gain the information we need. If you project the first line onto the second, the ball center is off the surface by exactly the ball radius $r$ on the line $P_i$ to $P_n$. Since the length of that line is known to be $D_s$, we can get a ratio of how far the ball is along the line. This is similar to the way we used a ratio to find the surface collision point $P_c$. This ratio is the same when applied to the line from $P_i$ to $P_c$, which leads to the equation:

$$\frac{(P_c - P_b)}{(P_c - P_i)} = \frac{r}{D_s}$$

The equation can be solved for the location of the ball $P_b$, resulting in:

$$P_b = P_c - \frac{(P_c - P_i)r}{D_s}$$

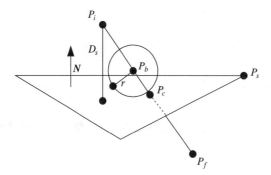

**FIGURE 2.2.7** *Colliding with a sphere.*

Figure 2.2.7 shows the relation graphically, indicating where the sphere is in relation to the vectors. Care must be taken to notice that the ball does not actually reach $P_c$ as the ball touches the surface unless the line from $P_i$ to $P_c$ is perpendicular to the surface. As the vector comes closer to being parallel to the plane, the ball will be farther from $P_c$ when it touches the plane.

# Fast, Robust Intersection of 3D Line Segments

## Graham Rhodes, Applied Research Associates

grhodes@sed.ara.com

The problem of determining the intersection of two line segments comes up from time to time in game development. For example, the line/line intersection problem can be beneficial in simple collision detection. Consider two objects in three-dimensional space that are moving in time. During a time step or animation frame, each object will move from one point to another along a linear path. The simplest check to see if the objects collide during the time step would be to see how close the two linear paths come to crossing, and if they are within a certain distance of each other (in other words, less than the sum of the radii of bounding spheres of the objects), then process a collision. Other common applications for line segment intersections include navigation and motion planning (for example, when combined with an AI system), map overlay creation, and terrain/visibility estimation.

This gem describes a robust, closed form solution for computing the intersection between two infinite lines or finite-length line segments in three-dimensional space, if an intersection exists. When no intersection exists, the algorithm produces the point along each line segment that is closest to the other line, and a vector between the two nearest points.

## What Makes This Algorithm Robust?

The algorithm presented here is robust for a couple of reasons. First, it does not carry any special requirements (for example, the line segments must be coplanar). Second, it has relatively few instances of tolerance checks. The basic algorithm has only two tolerance checks, and these are required mathematically rather than by heuristics.

## The Problem Statement

Given two line segments in three-dimensional space, one that spans between the points $\vec{A}_1 = [A_{1x} \quad A_{1y} \quad A_{1z}]^T$ and $\vec{A}_2 = [A_{2x} \quad A_{2y} \quad A_{2z}]^T$ and one that spans between the points $\vec{B}_1 = [B_{1x} \quad B_{1y} \quad B_{1z}]^T$ and $\vec{B}_2 = [B_{2x} \quad B_{2y} \quad B_{2z}]^T$, we would like to find the true point of intersection, $\vec{P} = [P_x \quad P_y \quad P_z]^T$, between the two segments, if it exists. When

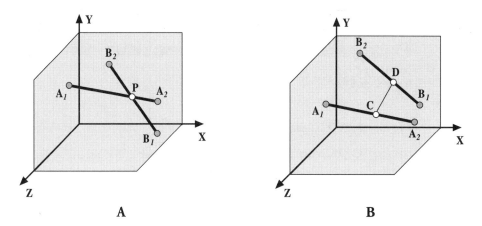

**FIGURE 2.3.1**  *Two line segments in three-dimensional space. A) An intersection exists. B) No intersecton.*

no intersection exists, we would like to compromise and find the point on each segment that is nearest to the other segment. Figure 2.3.1 illustrates the geometry of this situation.

The nearest points, labeled *C* and *D* respectively, can be used to find the shortest distance between the two segments. This gem focuses on finding the nearest points, which are identical to the true intersection point when an intersection exists.

### Observations

Before delving into how to solve the line intersection problem, it can be useful to make a few observations. What are the challenges to solving the problem correctly?

Consider an arbitrary, infinite line in space. It is likely that the line will intersect an arbitrary plane (if the line is not parallel to the plane, then it intersects the plane); however, it is unlikely that the line will truly intersect another line (even if two three-dimensional lines are not parallel, they do not necessarily intersect). From this observation, we can see that no algorithm designed to find only true intersections will be robust, capable of finding a result for an arbitrary pair of lines or line segments, since such an algorithm will fail most of the time. The need for a robust algorithm justifies the use of an algorithm that finds the nearest points between two lines, within a real-time 3D application such as a game.

Since every student who has taken a basic planar geometry class has solved for the intersection of lines in a two-dimensional space, it is useful to consider the relationship between the three-dimensional line intersection problem and the two-dimensional intersection problem. In two-dimensional space, any two nonparallel lines truly intersect at one point. To visualize what happens in three-dimensional space, consider a plane that contains both defining points of line A, and the first defining point of line

B. Line A lies within the plane, as does the first defining point of line B. Note that the point of intersection of the two lines lies on the plane, since that point is contained on line A. The point of intersection also lies on line B, and so two points of line B lie within the plane. Since two points of line B lie in the plane, the entire line lies in the plane.

The important conclusion here is that whenever there is a true intersection of two lines, those two lines do lie within a common plane. Thus, any time two three-dimensional lines have a true intersection, the problem is equivalent to a two-dimensional intersection problem in the plane that contains all four of the defining points.

### Naïve Solutions

A naïve, and problematic, solution to the intersection problem is to project the two segments into one of the standard coordinates planes (XY, YZ, or XZ), and then solve the problem in the plane. In terms of implementation, the primary difficulty with this approach is selecting an appropriate plane to project into. If neither of the line segments is parallel to any of the coordinate planes, then the problem can be solved in any coordinate plane. However, an unacceptable amount of logic can be required when one or both segments are parallel to coordinate planes. A variation on this approach, less naïve but still problematic, is to form a plane equation from three of the four points, $\vec{A}_1$, $\vec{A}_2$, $\vec{B}_1$, and $\vec{B}_2$, project all four points into the plane, and solve the problem in the plane. In the rare case that there is a true intersection, this latter approach produces the correct result.

One key feature that is completely lacking from the basic two-dimensional projected intersection problem is the ability to give a direct indication as to whether a three-dimensional intersection exists. It also doesn't provide the three-dimensional nearest points. It is necessary to work backwards to produce this vital information.

The biggest problem with either variation on the projected solution arises when the two lines pass close to one another, but do not actually intersect. In this case, the solution obtained in any arbitrary projection plane will not necessarily be the correct pair of nearest points. The projection will often yield completely wrong results! To visualize this situation (which is difficult to illustrate on a printed page), consider the following mind experiment. There are two line segments floating in space. Segment A is defined by the points (0, 0, 0) and (1, 0, 0), and segment B is defined by (1, 0, 1) and (1, 1, 1). When the lines are viewed from above, equivalent to projecting the lines into the XY plane, the two-dimensional intersection point is (1, 0, 0), and the three-dimensional nearest points are (1, 0, 0) and (1, 0, 1). These are the correct nearest points for the problem. However, if those two lines are viewed from different arbitrary angles, the two-dimensional intersection point will move to appear anywhere on the two line segments. Projecting the two-dimensional solution back onto the three-dimensional lines yields an infinite number of "nearest" point pairs, which is clearly incorrect. The test code provided on the companion CD-ROM is a useful tool to see

*ON THE CD*

this problem, as it allows you to rotate the view to see two line segments from different viewing angles, and displays the three-dimensional nearest points that you can compare to the intersection point seen in the viewport.

In the next section, I derive a closed-form solution to the calculation of points $C$ and $D$ that does not make any assumptions about where the two line segments lie in space. The solution does handle two special cases, but these cases are unavoidable even in the alternative approaches.

# Derivation of Closed-Form Solution Equations

## Calculating the Nearest Points on Two Infinite Lines

The equation of a line in three-dimensional space can be considered a vector function of a single scalar value, a parameter. To derive a closed-form solution to the nearest-point between two 3D lines, we first write the equation for an arbitrary point, $\vec{C} = [C_x \quad C_y \quad C_z]^T$, located on the first line segment, as Equation 2.3.1.

$$\vec{C} = \vec{A}_1 + s\vec{L}_A, \text{ where } \vec{L}_A = \left(\vec{A}_2 - \vec{A}_1\right) \tag{2.3.1}$$

Notice that Equation 2.3.1 basically says that the coordinates of any point on the first segment are equal to the coordinates of the first defining point plus an arbitrary scalar parameter $s$ times a vector pointing along the line from the first defining point to the second defining point. If $s$ is equal to zero, the coordinate is coincident with the first defining point, and if $s$ is equal to 1, the coordinate is coincident with the second defining point. We can write a similar equation for an arbitrary point, $\vec{D} = [D_x \quad D_y \quad D_z]^T$, located on the second line segment, as Equation 2.3.2:

$$\vec{D} = \vec{B}_1 + t\vec{L}_B, \text{ where } \vec{L}_B = \left(\vec{B}_2 - \vec{B}_1\right) \tag{2.3.2}$$

Here, $t$ is a second arbitrary scalar parameter, with the same physical meaning as $s$ with respect to the second line segment. If the parameters $s$ and $t$ are allowed to be arbitrary, then we will be able to calculate points $\vec{C}$ and $\vec{D}$ as they apply to infinite lines rather than finite segments. For any point on a *finite* line segment, the parameters $s$ and $t$ will satisfy $0 \leq s,t \leq 1$. We'll allow $s$ and $t$ to float arbitrarily for now, and treat the finite length segments later.

The two 3D line segments intersect if we can find values of $s$ and $t$ such that points $\vec{C}$ and $\vec{D}$ are coincident. For a general problem, there will rarely be an intersection, however, and we require a method for determining $s$ and $t$ that corresponds to the nearest points $\vec{C}$ and $\vec{D}$. The remainder of the derivation shows how to solve for these values of $s$ and $t$.

First, subtract Equation 2.3.2 from Equation 2.3.1 to obtain the following equation for the vector between points $\vec{C}$ and $\vec{D}$:

$$\vec{C} - \vec{D} = -\overrightarrow{AB} + s\vec{L}_A - t\vec{L}_B = \begin{bmatrix} 0 & 0 & 0 \end{bmatrix}^T,$$

where $\overrightarrow{AB} = \vec{B}_1 - \vec{A}_1$                                                                                           (2.3.3)

Here, since we would like for points $\vec{C}$ and $\vec{D}$ to be coincident, we set the vector between the points to be the zero vector. The right side of Equation 2.3.3 can then be represented by the following matrix equation:

$$\begin{bmatrix} L_{Ax} & -L_{Bx} \\ L_{Ay} & -L_{By} \\ L_{Az} & -L_{Bz} \end{bmatrix} \begin{bmatrix} s \\ t \end{bmatrix} = \begin{bmatrix} AB_x \\ AB_y \\ AB_z \end{bmatrix}$$                                      (2.3.4)

There are three rows in Equation 2.3.4, one for each coordinate direction, but only two unknowns, the scalar values $s$ and $t$. This is a classic over-determined or under-constrained system. The only way there can be an exact solution is if the coefficient matrix on the left side turns out to have rank 2, in which case the three equations are equivalent to just two independent equations, leading to an exact solution for $s$ and $t$. Geometrically, when there is an exact solution, the two lines have a true intersection and are coplanar. Thus, two arbitrary lines in three-dimensional space can only have a true intersection when the lines are coplanar.

The difference between the left side and right side of Equation 2.3.4 is equal to the vector representing the distance between $\vec{C}$ and $\vec{D}$. It is also the error vector of Equation 2.3.4 for any arbitrary values of $s$ and $t$. We determine the nearest points by minimizing the length of this vector over all possible values of $s$ and $t$.

The values of $s$ and $t$ that minimize the distance between $\vec{C}$ and $\vec{D}$ correspond to a linear least-squares solution to Equation 2.3.4. Geometrically, the least-squares solution produces the points $\vec{C}$ and $\vec{D}$. When we have the case of the segments being coplanar but not parallel, then the algorithm will naturally produce the true intersection point. Equation 2.3.4 can be written in the form:

$$M\vec{s} = \vec{b}, \text{ where } \vec{s} = \begin{bmatrix} s & t \end{bmatrix}^T$$                                                      (2.3.5)

One method for finding the least-squares solution to an over-determined system is to solve the *normal equations* instead of the original system [Golub96]. The normal equations approach is suitable for this problem, but can be problematic for general problems involving systems of linear equations. We generate the normal equations by premultiplying the left side and right side by the transpose of the coefficient matrix M. The normal equations for our problem are shown as Equation 2.3.6.

$$M^T M \vec{s} = M^T \vec{b}, \text{ where } M^T \text{ is the transpose of M.}$$                              (2.3.6)

Equation 2.3.6 has the desired property of reducing the system to the solution of a system of two equations, exactly the number needed to solve algebraically for values of $s$ and $t$. Let's carry through the development of the normal equations for Equation 2.3.4. Expanding according to Equation 2.3.6 , the normal equations are:

$$\begin{bmatrix} L_{Ax} & L_{Ay} & L_{Az} \\ -L_{Bx} & -L_{By} & -L_{Bz} \end{bmatrix} \begin{bmatrix} L_{Ax} & -L_{Bx} \\ L_{Ay} & -L_{By} \\ L_{Az} & -L_{Bz} \end{bmatrix} \begin{bmatrix} s \\ t \end{bmatrix} = \begin{bmatrix} L_{Ax} & L_{Ay} & L_{Az} \\ -L_{Bx} & -L_{By} & -L_{Bz} \end{bmatrix} \begin{bmatrix} AB_x \\ AB_y \\ AB_z \end{bmatrix} \qquad (2.3.7)$$

Carrying through the matrix algebra:

$$\begin{bmatrix} \vec{L}_A \cdot \vec{L}_A & -\vec{L}_A \cdot \vec{L}_B \\ -\vec{L}_A \cdot \vec{L}_B & \vec{L}_B \cdot \vec{L}_B \end{bmatrix} \begin{bmatrix} s \\ t \end{bmatrix} = \begin{bmatrix} \vec{L}_A \cdot \overrightarrow{AB} \\ -\vec{L}_B \cdot \overrightarrow{AB} \end{bmatrix} \qquad (2.3.8)$$

Or, simplifying by defining a series of new scalar variables:

$$\begin{bmatrix} L_{11} & L_{12} \\ L_{12} & L_{22} \end{bmatrix} \begin{bmatrix} s \\ t \end{bmatrix} = \begin{bmatrix} r_A \\ r_B \end{bmatrix} \qquad (2.3.9)$$

This is a simple 2×2 system, and to complete this section we will solve it algebraically to form a closed-form solution for $s$ and $t$. There are a number of ways to solve Equation 2.3.9, including Cramer's rule [O'Neil87] and Gaussian elimination [Golub96]. Cramer's rule is theoretically interesting, but expensive, requiring approximately $(n+1)!$ multiply and divide operations for a general-sized problem. Gaussian elimination is less expensive, requiring $n^3/3$ multiply and divide operations. There are other approaches to solving systems of linear equations that are significantly more reliable and often faster for much larger systems, including advanced direct solution methods such as QR factorizations for moderate-sized systems, and iterative methods for very large and sparse systems. I will derive the solution using Gaussian elimination, which is slightly less expensive than Cramer's rule for the 2×2 system. Here, we perform one row elimination step to yield an upper triangular system. The row elimination step is as follows. Modify row 2 of Equation 2.3.9 by taking the original row 2 and subtracting row 1 times $L_{12}/L_{11}$. to yield Equation 2.3.10.

$$\begin{bmatrix} L_{11} & L_{12} \\ L_{12} - L_{11}\dfrac{L_{12}}{L_{11}} & L_{22} - L_{12}\dfrac{L_{12}}{L_{11}} \end{bmatrix} \begin{bmatrix}  \\  \end{bmatrix} = \begin{bmatrix} r_A \\ r_B - r_A\dfrac{L_{12}}{L_{11}} \end{bmatrix} \qquad (2.3.10)$$

Simplify Equation 2.3.10 and multiply the new row 2 by $L_{11}$ to yield the upper triangular system shown in Equation 2.3.11.

$$\begin{bmatrix} L_{11} & L_{12} \\ 0 & L_{11}L_{22} - L_{12}^2 \end{bmatrix} \begin{bmatrix} s \\ t \end{bmatrix} = \begin{bmatrix} r_A \\ L_{11}r_B - L_{12}r_A \end{bmatrix} \tag{2.3.11}$$

Equation (2.3.11) immediately yields a solution for $t$,

$$t = \frac{L_{11}r_B - L_{12}r_A}{L_{11}L_{22} - L_{12}^2} \tag{2.3.12}$$

and then, for $s$,

$$s = \frac{r_A - L_{12}t}{L_{11}} \tag{2.3.13}$$

It is important to note that Equations 2.3.12 and 2.3.13 fail in certain degenerate cases, and it is these degenerate cases that require that we use tolerances in a limited way. Equation 2.3.13 will fail if line segment A has zero length, and Equation 2.3.12 will fail if either line segment has zero length or if the line segments are parallel. These situations lead to a divide-by-zero exception. I provide more discussion later in the section titled *Special Cases*.

In terms of computational expense for the 2×2 problem, the only difference between solving for $s$ and $t$ using Gaussian elimination and Cramer's rule, for this case, is that the computation of $s$ requires one multiply, one divide, and one subtraction for Gaussian elimination, but four multiplies, one divide, and two subtractions for Cramer's rule.

To summarize from the derivation, given line segment A from point $\vec{A}_1$ to $\vec{A}_2$ and line segment B from point $\vec{B}_1$ to $\vec{B}_2$, define the following intermediate variables:

$$\vec{L}_A = \left(\vec{A}_2 - \vec{A}_1\right); \quad \vec{L}_B = \left(\vec{B}_2 - \vec{B}_1\right); \quad \overrightarrow{AB} = \vec{B}_1 - \vec{A}_1 \tag{2.3.14}$$

and

$$L_{11} = \vec{L}_A \cdot \vec{L}_A; \qquad L_{22} = \vec{L}_B \cdot \vec{L}_B; \qquad L_{12} = -\vec{L}_A \cdot \vec{L}_B$$
$$r_A = \vec{L}_A \cdot \overrightarrow{AB}; \qquad r_B = -\vec{L}_B \cdot \overrightarrow{AB} \tag{2.3.15}$$

Compute the parameters $s$ and $t$ that define the nearest points as,

$$t = \frac{L_{11}r_B - L_{12}r_A}{L_{11}L_{22} - L_{12}^2} \tag{2.3.16}$$

and

$$s = \frac{r_A - L_{12}t}{L_{11}} \tag{2.3.17}$$

The point where the first segment comes closest to the second segment is then given by:

$$\vec{C} = \vec{A}_1 + s\vec{L}_A \qquad\qquad (2.3.18)$$

and the point where the second segment comes closest to the first segment is given by:

$$\vec{D} = \vec{B}_1 + t\vec{L}_B \qquad\qquad (2.3.19)$$

We can consider a point located halfway between the two nearest points to be the single point in space that is "nearest" to both lines/segments as:

$$\vec{P} = \left(\vec{C} + \vec{D}\right)\big/2 \qquad\qquad (2.3.20)$$

Of course, when the lines do intersect, point $\vec{P}$ will be the intersection point.

## Special Cases

When we talk about the nearest points of two infinite lines in space, there are only two possible special cases. The first case occurs when one or both lines are degenerate, defined by two points that are coincident in space. This occurs when point $\vec{A}_1$ is coincident with $\vec{A}_2$, or when $\vec{B}_1$ is coincident with $\vec{B}_2$. We'll call this the *degenerate line special case*. The second case occurs when the two lines are parallel, called the *parallel line special case*.

It is easy to relate the degenerate line special case to the equations developed previously. Note that variable $L_{11}$, defined in Equation 2.3.15, is equal to the square of the length of line segment $A$, and $L_{22}$ is equal to the square of the length of segment $B$. If either of these terms is zero, indicating that a line is degenerate, then the determinant of the matrix in Equation 2.3.9 is zero, and we cannot find a solution for $s$ and $t$. Note that when either $L_{11}$ or $L_{22}$ is zero, then $L_{12}$ is also zero.

One standard test to check and decide if line $A$ is degenerate is the following,

```
bool line_is_degenerate = L₁₁ < ε² ? true : false;
```

Here, $\varepsilon$ is a small number such as perhaps $10^{-6}$. It is wiser to choose a value for $\varepsilon$ such as $10^{-6}$ rather than a much smaller number such as machine epsilon.

When segments $A$ and $B$ are both degenerate, then point $\vec{C}$ can be selected to be equal to point $\vec{A}$, and point $\vec{D}$ can be selected to be equal to point $\vec{B}_1$. When segment $A$ alone is degenerate, then point $\vec{C}$ is equal to $\vec{A}_1$, and point $\vec{D}$ is found by computing the point on segment $B$ that is nearest to point $\vec{C}$. This involves computing a value for parameter $t$ only, from Equation 2.3.21.

$$-\vec{L}_B t = \overrightarrow{AB} \qquad\qquad (2.3.21)$$

Equation 2.3.21 is a simplification of Equation 2.3.4 for the case where segment *A* is degenerate, and again it requires that we find a least-squares solution. The least-squares solution, shown here using normal equations without derivation, is:

$$t = \frac{-\vec{L}_B \cdot \overrightarrow{AB}}{\vec{L}_B \cdot \vec{L}_B} = \frac{r_B}{L_{22}} \tag{2.3.22}$$

Point $\vec{D}$ can be calculated using Equation 2.3.2.

When segment B alone is degenerate, then point $\vec{D}$ is set equal to $\vec{B}_1$, and point $\vec{C}$ is found by computing the point on segment A that is nearest to point $\vec{D}$. This involves computing a value for parameter *s* only, from Equation 2.3.23, which is analogous to Equation 2.3.21.

$$\vec{L}_A s = \overrightarrow{AB} \tag{2.3.23}$$

Solving for *s* yields:

$$s = \frac{r_A}{L_{11}} \tag{2.3.24}$$

Note that Equation 2.3.24 is identical to Equation 2.3.13 with *t* set equal to zero. Since *t* equals zero at point $\vec{B}_1$, our derivation here is consistent with the derivation for nondegenerate lines.

Certainly, a nice way to handle the cases where only one segment is degenerate is to write a single subroutine that is used both when segment A alone is degenerate and when B alone is degenerate. It is possible to do this using either Equation 2.3.22 or Equation 2.3.24, as long as the variables are treated properly. The implementation provided on the companion CD-ROM uses Equation 2.3.24 for both cases, with parameters passed in such that the degenerate line is always treated as segment B, and the nondegenerate line is always treated as segment A.

It is also easy to relate the parallel line special case to the equations developed previously, although it is not quite as obvious as the degenerate case. Here, we have to remember that $L_{12}$ is the negative dot product of the vectors $\vec{L}_A$ and $\vec{L}_B$, and when the lines are parallel, the dot product is equal to the negative of the length of $\vec{L}_A$ times the length of $\vec{L}_B$. The determinant of the matrix in Equation 2.3.9 is given by $L_{11}L_{22} - L_{12}^2$, and this is equal to zero when $L_{12}$ is equal in magnitude to the length of $\vec{L}_A$ times the length of $\vec{L}_B$. Thus, when the line segments are parallel, Equation 2.3.9 is singular and we cannot solve for *s* and *t*.

In the case of infinite parallel lines, every point on line *A* is equidistant from line *B*. If it is important to find the distance between lines *A* and *B*, simply choose $\vec{C}$ to be equal to $\vec{A}_1$, and then use Equations 2.3.22 and 2.3.2 to find $\vec{D}$. Then, the distance between $\vec{C}$ and $\vec{D}$ is the distance between the two segments. We'll look at how to handle finite length segments in the next section.

### Coding Efficiency

For coding efficiency, you should check first for degenerate lines, and then for parallel lines. This approach eliminates the need to calculate some of the convenience variables from Equations 2.3.14 and 2.3.15 when one or both of the lines are degenerate.

## Dealing with Finite Line Segments

The previous two sections treated infinite lines. This is useful; however, there are perhaps many more situations in game development when it is required to process finite line segments. So, how do we adjust the results shown previously to deal with finite-length line segments?

### Line Segments that Are Not Parallel

If Equations 2.3.12 and 2.3.13 generate values of $s$ and $t$ that are both within the range $[0,1]$, then we don't need to do anything at all, since the finite length line segment results happen to be identical to the infinite line results. Whenever one or both of $s$ and $t$ are outside of $[0,1]$, then we have to adjust the results. For nonparallel lines, there are two possibilities: 1) $s$ or $t$ is outside of $[0,1]$ and the other is inside $[0,1]$; and 2) both $s$ and $t$ are outside of $[0,1]$. Figure 2.3.2 illustrates these two cases.

For the case when just one of $s$ or $t$ is outside of $[0,1]$, as in Figure 2.3.2a, all we need to do is:

1. Clamp the out-of-range parameter to $[0,1]$.
2. Compute the point on the line for the new parameter. This is the nearest point for the first segment.
3. Find the point on the other line that is nearest to the new point on the first line, with the nearest point calculation performed for a finite line segment. This is the nearest point for the second segment.

In the last step, just clamp the value from Equation 2.3.22 to $[0,1]$ before calculating the point on the other segment.

For the case when both $s$ and $t$ are outside of $[0,1]$, as in Figure 2.3.2b, the situation is slightly more complicated. The process is exactly the same except that we have to make a decision about which segment to use in the previous process. For example, if we selected line segment $A$ in Figure 2.3.2b, step 2 would produce point $\vec{A}_2$. Then, step 3 would produce point $\vec{B}_1$, the nearest point on segment $B$ to point $\vec{A}_2$. The pair of points, $\vec{A}_2$ and $\vec{B}_1$ clearly are *not* the correct points to choose for $\vec{C}$ and $\vec{D}$. Point $\vec{B}_1$ is the correct choice for $\vec{D}$, but there is a point on segment $A$ that is much closer to segment $B$ than $\vec{A}_2$. In fact, the point generated by step 3 will always be the correct choice for either $\vec{C}$ or $\vec{D}$. It is the point from step 2 that is incorrect. We can compute the other nearest point by just using the result from step 3. The process for both s and t outside of $[0,1]$ then becomes:

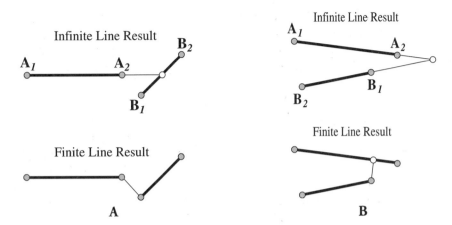

**FIGURE 2.3.2** *Finite-length line segments. A) Either s or t is outside of [0,1]. B) Both s and t are outside of [0,1].*

1. Choose a segment and clamp its out-of-range parameter to [0,1].
2. Compute the point on the line for the new parameter. This is *not guaranteed* to be the nearest point for the first segment!
3. Find the point on the other line that is nearest to the new point on the first line, with the nearest point calculation performed for a finite line segment. This is the nearest point for the second line segment.
4. Find the point on the first line segment that is nearest to the point that resulted from step 3. This is the nearest point for the first line segment.

If we select segment B in Figure 2.3.2b as our initial segment to correct, we would immediately select point $B_1$, and step 3 would give the point between $\vec{A}_1$ and $\vec{A}_2$. In this case, step 4 is not required. The implementation provided here does not bother to check for this situation.

### Line Segments that Are Parallel

There are two basic possible scenarios when the two segments are parallel, both of which are illustrated in Figure 2.3.3. First, there might be a single unique pair of nearest points, shown in Figure 2.3.3a. This always occurs when the projection of both segments into a line parallel to both do not overlap. Second, there might be a locus of possible nearest point pairs, shown in Figure 2.3.3b. Here, we could choose the two nearest points to be any pair of nearest points between the two vertical gray lines. The implementation provided on the accompanying CD-ROM selects the nearest points for finite length, overlapping parallel line segments to be halfway between the gray lines; that is, at the midpoint of the overlapping portion of each segment.

It is important to note that when the two segments are parallel, or almost parallel, the nearest points computed by this algorithm will often move erratically as the lines

**FIGURE 2.3.3** *Parallel line segments. A) Unique nearest point pair. B) Locus of nearest point pairs.*

are rotated slightly. The algorithm will not fail in this case, but the results can be confusing and problematic, as the nearest points jump back and forth between the ends of the segments. This is illustrated in Figure 2.3.4.

Shown in Figure 2.3.4a, the nearest points will stay at the far left until the lines become exactly parallel, at which point the nearest points will jump to the middle of the overlap section. Then, as the lines continue to rotate past parallel, the nearest points will jump to the far right, shown in Figure 2.3.4b. This behavior may be problematic in some game applications. It is possible to treat the behavior by using a different approach to selecting the nearest point when lines are parallel or near parallel. For example, you could implement a rule that arbitrarily selects the point nearest $\vec{A}_1$ as the nearest point on segment A when the segments are parallel within, say, 5 degrees of each other. To avoid the erratic behavior at the 5-degree boundary, you would need to blend this arbitrary nearest point with an algorithmically generated nearest point between, say, 5 and 10 degrees, with the arbitrary solution being 100% at 5 degrees and 0% at 10 degrees. This solution will increase the expense of the algorithm. There are certainly other approaches, including ones that may be simpler, cheaper, and more reliable. The implementation provided on the companion CD-ROM does not attempt to manage this behavior.

ON THE CD

**FIGURE 2.3.4** *Erratic movement of nearest points for nearly parallel line segments. A) Nearest points at the left. B) Nearest points at the right.*

## Implementation Description

The implementation includes four C-language functions, contained in the files *lineintersect_utils.h* and *lineintersect_utils.cpp*. The primary interface is the function *IntersectLineSegments*, which takes parameters defining the two line segments, and returns points $\vec{C}$, $\vec{D}$, and $\vec{P}$, as well as a vector between points $\vec{C}$ and $\vec{D}$. The function also takes a parameter indicating whether you want the line segments to be treated as infinite lines, and a tolerance parameter to be used to check the degenerate and parallel line special cases. The vector between $\vec{C}$ and $\vec{D}$ can be used outside of the implementation to determine a distance between the lines. It is important to note that the vector is not necessarily normal to either of the line segments if the lines are finite. If the lines are infinite and at least one is not degenerate, the vector will be normal to the nondegenerate line(s). The supporting functions are as follows:

- *FindNearestPointOnLineSegment* calculates the point on a line segment that is nearest to a given point in three-dimensional space.
- *FindNearestPointOfParallelLineSegments* calculates representative (and possibly unique) values for $\vec{C}$ and $\vec{D}$ for the case of parallel lines/segments.
- *AdjustNearestPoints* adjusts the values of $\vec{C}$ and $\vec{D}$ from an infinite line solution to a finite length line segment solution.

The code is documented with references to the text.

ON THE CD

A test program is also provided, called *line_intersection_demo*. The demo requires that you link to the GLUT library for OpenGL. Project files are present for Microsoft Visual C++ 6.0 for Windows. It should not be too difficult to port this to other systems that support OpenGL and GLUT.

## Opportunities to Optimize

The implementation source code was written carefully, but without any attempt to optimize for a particular processor or instruction set. There are a number of opportunities in every code to optimize the implementation for a given platform. In this case, perhaps the biggest opportunity is in the area of vectorization. There are numerous operations in this code that require a multiply or addition/subtraction operation on all three elements of a vector. These are prime opportunities to vectorize. Additionally, if you have an instruction set that supports high-level operations such as dot products, take advantage when evaluating Equation (2.3.15), for example. To truly maximize the performance, I strongly recommend that you use a professional code profiling utility to identify bottlenecks and opportunities for your target platform(s).

ON THE CD

The text presented here and the implementation provided on the accompanying CD-ROM is rigorous, and treats every conceivable situation. The code is generally efficient, but in the case where the infinite lines intersect outside of the range of the finite segments (in other words, one or both of $s$ and $t$ are outside of $[0,1]$), the true nearest points are not necessarily cheap to compute. In fact, the nearest point problem we've solved here is a minimization problem, and as is the case in general, the cost increases when constraints are applied to minimization problems. Beyond processor/platform-specific optimizations, it is certainly possible to remove parts of the implementation that are not required for your application. For example, if you do not need to treat finite length segments, remove everything that deals with finite length segments. Just have the main function return a bool that is true when the nearest point is found between the finite segment endpoints, and false when the nearest point is found outside the finite segment endpoints.

## Conclusions

The algorithm discussed here is rigorous and capable of handling any line intersection problem without failing. Depending on your particular use of line intersections, you may need to adjust the algorithm; for example, to manage the idiosyncrasies that arise when two finite segments are nearly parallel, or to remove the processing of finite segments when you only deal with infinite lines. I sincerely hope that some of you will benefit from this formal discussion of line and line segment intersections, along with ready-to-use source code.

## References

[Golub96] Golub, Gene H., and Charles F. van Loan, *Matrix Computations, Third Edition*, The Johns Hopkins University Press, 1996.

[O'Neil87] O'Neil, Peter V., *Advanced Engineering Mathematics, Second Edition*, Wadsworth Publishing Company, 1987.

# 2.4

# Inverse Trajectory Determination

## Aaron Nicholls, Microsoft

aaron_feedback@hotmail.com

A problem frequently faced in the development of games is that of calculating trajectories. In the most common case, we have a velocity and a direction for a projectile, and need to determine the location at a given time, and whether the projectile has collided with any other entities. This is a simple iterative problem, but it is not all that is required for most games. In many cases, we also need to solve the inverse of this problem; namely, given a number of constants (gravity, starting position, intended destination), we must calculate the proper yaw, pitch, and/or initial velocity to propel the projectile between the two points. In addition, once we have a solution for this problem, we can use this as a framework for solving more complex variants of the same problem.

This gem expects that the reader is familiar with fundamental 2D/3D transformations, basic integral calculus, and trigonometry.

## Simplifying the Problem at Hand

There are several ways to simplify the problem, and we can begin by reducing a three-dimensional problem to a two-dimensional one. Given an initial velocity and direction for a projectile, if the only acting force is gravity (which can usually be assumed to be constant), the trajectory of the projectile will be parabolic and planar. Therefore, by transforming this planar trajectory into two dimensions ($x$ and $y$), we can simplify the problem significantly. In addition, by translating the starting point to the origin, we can remove the initial $x$ and $y$ values from most of the equations, focusing on the destination coordinates. A sample trajectory, rotated into the $xy$ plane and translated to the origin, is shown in Figure 2.4.1.

In addition, we need to determine exactly what the problem is that we wish to solve. In this case, our variables are initial velocity, angle of elevation, and distance in $x$ and $y$ between the points. In the case where we know three of the four values (and thus have one unknown), our goal is to produce an equation that defines the value of the unknown in terms of the three known values.

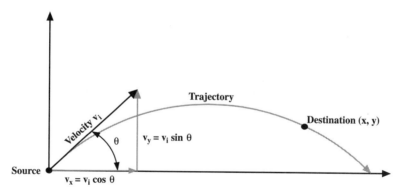

**FIGURE 2.4.1** *Trajectory between two points in two dimensions.*

However, it is very common to have to deal with multiple unknowns. In that case, the best solution is typically to get rid of some of the variables by setting their values to constants. For instance, we often know the locations of the two points, but need to provide an initial velocity and angle of elevation. In this case, we can eliminate initial velocity as a variable by setting it to the maximum possible velocity $v_{max}$. By doing so, we only have one unknown, and we simply need to determine the angle of elevation $\theta$ in terms of $v_i$, $x$, and $y$. This technique and guidelines for using it are discussed in further detail later in this gem, under *Solving for Multiple Variables*.

### Defining Position and Velocity as a Function of Time

Now that we have reduced the problem to two dimensions, we can identify the velocity and acceleration working in each dimension. Starting with initial velocity $v_i$, angle of elevation ?, and gravity $g$, we can express initial velocity along the $x$ and $y$ axes as follows:

$$v_{xi} = v_i \cos\theta$$

$$v_{yi} = v_i \sin\theta$$

Since the only force acting upon this system is gravity, we can assume that vertical velocity ($v_x$) stays constant, while gravity is acting upon horizontal velocity ($v_y$). The two can be expressed as follows:

$$v_x = v_i \cos\theta \tag{2.4.1}$$

$$v_y = v_i \sin\theta - gt \tag{2.4.2}$$

Next, we integrate the velocity equations to determine the position at a given time (assuming the origin as the starting point).

$$x = \int v_i \cos\theta \; dt$$

$$\rightarrow x = v_i t \cos\theta \qquad\qquad (2.4.3)$$

$$y = \int \left( v_i \sin\theta - gt \right) dt$$

$$\rightarrow y = v_i t \sin\theta - \frac{1}{2} gt^2 \qquad\qquad (2.4.4)$$

## A Special Case:

### Both Points at the Same Elevation

Before tackling the general case of this problem, let's examine a simpler case, which will give us insight into solving the more general problem. One of the common special cases is that in which both the start and end points have the same $y$ value. An example of this might be a game where the ground is flat, and a cannon on the ground is firing at a ground target. In this case, we know that $y$, the horizontal displacement between the two points, is zero. Therefore, we can simplify the horizontal position equation by setting $y=0$. This allows us to simplify Equation 2.4.4 to solve for time $t$, initial velocity $v_i$, or angle of elevation $\theta$ as follows:

$$y = v_i t \sin\theta - \frac{1}{2} gt^2 = 0$$

$$\rightarrow t = \frac{2v_i \sin\theta}{g}$$

$$\rightarrow v_i = \frac{gt}{2\sin\theta}$$

$$\rightarrow \theta = \sin^{-1}\left( \frac{gt}{2v_i} \right)$$

In addition, this leads to a simplified formula for calculating $x$ for this special case:

$$x = v_i \left( \frac{2v_i \sin\theta}{g} \right) \cos\theta$$

$$\rightarrow x = \frac{2v_i^2 \sin\theta \cos\theta}{g}$$

Using the trigonometric identity $sin\ \theta\ cos\ \theta = sin\ 2\theta$, we can simplify further as follows:

$$x = \frac{2v_i^2\ sin\ 2\theta}{g} \tag{2.4.5}$$

In addition, in the previous case where a ground-based cannon is firing at ground targets on flat terrain, this equation can be used to determine the maximum horizontal range of a cannon at angle of elevation $\theta$, given maximum projectile velocity $v_{max}$:

$$Range = \left| \frac{2v_{max}^2\ sin\ 2\theta}{g} \right| \tag{2.4.6}$$

## Solving for Angle of Elevation

Now that we have defined the equations that define the projectile's movement and solved for a special case, we can continue to solve for the more general case. First, we will analyze the case in which both points may not be at the same altitude, and we must determine the angle of elevation or velocity required to propel a projectile between the two points. Since we have expressed $x$ and $y$ in terms of $t$, we can begin by removing $t$ from the equation and defining $x$ and $y$ in terms of each other.

$$x = v_i t\ cos\ \theta \rightarrow t = \frac{x}{v_i\ cos\ \theta}$$

Next, we replace $t$ with $x\ /\ v_i\ cos\ \theta$ in the equation for $y$ to remove $t$ from the equation.

$$y = v_i t\ sin\ \theta - \frac{1}{2} gt^2$$

$$\rightarrow y = v_i (\frac{x}{v_i\ cos\ \theta})\ sin\ \theta - \frac{1}{2} g(\frac{x}{v_i\ cos\ \theta})^2$$

$$\rightarrow y = x\ tan\ \theta - \frac{gx^2}{2v_i^2\ cos^2\ \theta}$$

We then use the trigonometry identity $1/cos^2\ \theta = tan^2\ \theta + 1$ to reduce further.

$$y = x\ tan\ \theta - \frac{gx^2}{2v_i^2} (\frac{1}{cos^2\ \theta})$$

$$\rightarrow y = x \tan\theta - \frac{gx^2(\tan^2\theta + 1)}{2v_i^2}$$

$$\rightarrow \frac{gx^2}{2v_i^2}\tan^2\theta - x\tan\theta + \frac{gx^2}{2v_i^2} + y = 0 \qquad (2.4.7)$$

As odd as this final equation may look, it serves a purpose: this version of the equation fits into the quadratic equation as follows:

$$\tan\theta = \frac{-b \pm \sqrt{b^2 - 4ac}}{2a}$$

where

$$a = \frac{gx^2}{2v_i^2}$$

$$b = -x$$

$$c = \frac{gx^2}{2v_i^2} + y$$

Plugging the preceding values of $a$, $b$, and $c$ into the quadratic equation and solving for $\theta$, we obtain the following:

$$\theta = \tan^{-1}\left(\frac{-x \pm \sqrt{x^2 - 4\left(\frac{gx^2}{2v_i^2}\left(\frac{gx^2}{2v_i^2} + y\right)\right)}}{\frac{gx^2}{v_i^2}}\right)$$

$$\rightarrow \theta = \tan^{-1}\left(v_i^2\left(\frac{-x \pm \sqrt{x^2 - \frac{g^2x^4}{v_i^4} + \frac{2gx^2y}{v_i^2}}}{gx^2}\right)\right) \qquad (2.4.8)$$

The quadratic form provides us with a way to solve for θ, given a known initial velocity $v_i$, horizontal displacement $x$, and vertical displacement $y$. If $(b^2 - 4ac)$ is positive, we have two possible solutions, and if it is negative, there are no solutions for the given parameters. In addition, if the initial velocity is zero, we know that the trajectory is entirely vertical, so θ is irrelevant.

When dealing with two trajectories, it is important to remember that the flatter trajectory will yield a faster route to the target, and is thereby preferable in most cases. If both angles are between $-\pi/2$ and $\pi/2$, the angle closer to zero will yield the flatter trajectory for a given $v_i$. A case with two valid angles of elevation to reach a given target is shown in Figure 2.4.2. Here, Trajectory 2 is the fastest.

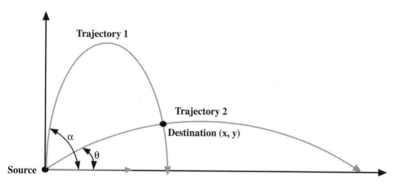

**FIGURE 2.4.2**   *Two angle of elevation solutions* α *and* θ *for a given* $v_i$.

### Solving for Initial Velocity

Now that we have the problem solved for the case where θ is unknown, we can change Equation 2.4.7 slightly to solve for initial velocity $v_i$, given a known angle of elevation θ, horizontal displacement $x$, and vertical displacement $y$ as follows:

$$\frac{gx^2}{2v_i^2} \tan^2 \theta - x \tan \theta + \frac{gx^2}{2v_i^2} + y = 0$$

$$\rightarrow \frac{gx^2}{2v_i^2} \tan^2 \theta + \frac{gx^2}{2v_i^2} = x \tan \theta - y$$

$$\rightarrow \frac{gx^2}{2v_i^2} (\tan^2 \theta + 1) = x \tan \theta - y$$

We then multiply both sides by $v_i^2/(x \tan \theta - y)$, thereby isolating initial velocity.

$$\frac{gx^2}{2(x \tan \theta - y)} (\tan^2 \theta + 1) = v_i^2$$

Solving for $v_i$, we get the following:

$$v_i = x \sqrt{\frac{g(\tan^2 \theta + 1)}{2(x \tan \theta - y)}} \tag{2.4.9}$$

Again, we can choose to use the trigonometric identity $1/cos^2 \theta = tan^2 \theta + 1$ to simplify the square root.

$$v_i = \frac{x}{\cos \theta} \sqrt{\frac{g}{2(x \tan \theta - y)}} \tag{2.4.10}$$

Again, since we are dealing with a square root, there are some cases that have no solution. An example would be when the slope of the initial trajectory is less than the slope to the target. One special case is where $\theta = \pi/2$ (straight upward), since there can be two solutions.

### Calculating Maximum Height for a Trajectory

Solving for peak height of a trajectory is straightforward: vertical peak is defined as the point where vertical velocity $v_y = 0$, given $\theta \geq 0$. Therefore, we simply solve the vertical velocity equation as follows:

$$v_y(t) = v_i \sin \theta - gt = 0$$

Solving for $t$, we get the following:

$$t = \frac{v_i \sin \theta}{g}$$

Now, to determine the maximum altitude, we substitute the preceding value for $t$ in the vertical position equation as follows:

$$y_{max} = v_i t \sin \theta - \frac{1}{2} gt^2$$

$$= \frac{v_i^2 \sin^2 \theta}{g} - \frac{g}{2} \left( \frac{v_i \sin \theta}{g} \right)^2$$

$$\rightarrow y_{max} = \frac{v_i^2 \sin^2 \theta}{2g} \tag{2.4.11}$$

As mentioned previously, this depends on $\theta \geq 0$. If the angle of elevation $\theta$ is negative (pointing downward), the vertical peak will be at $y=0$, since the projectile's initial downward velocity is only increased by gravity. This is somewhat of a special case, since vertical velocity is not necessarily zero at the vertical peak in this case.

### Calculating Flight Time

In order to determine time to destination, we can simply rewrite the horizontal position from Equation 2.4.3 in terms of $t$.

$$x(t) = v_i t \cos \theta \rightarrow t = \frac{x}{v_i \cos \theta}$$

However, in the case where $v_i = 0$ or $\cos \theta = 0$, $t$ is undefined if expressed in terms of $x$. In addition, in this case, $x$ will always be zero, and no solutions exist in this case if the two points are not at the same $x$ value. In implementation, these boundary cases are worth testing, since a mistake here can cause an engine to crash or behave erratically at times.

To solve for $t$ when $v_i = 0$ or $\cos \theta = 0$, we can use the vertical position equation from Equation 2.4.4 instead.

$$y(t) = v_i t \sin \theta - \frac{1}{2} g t^2$$

If $v_i = 0$, we can use the following equation to express $t$ in terms of $y$ and $g$.

$$y = -\frac{1}{2} g t^2 \rightarrow t = \sqrt{\frac{-2y}{g}}$$

However, if $\cos \theta = 0$ and $v_i > 0$, there can be one or two solutions (the latter happens only if $\theta \geq 0$, since $v_i \geq 0$ in practice). In addition, we know that if $\cos \theta = 0$, $\sin \theta = \pm 1$. This reduces the problem further, but we still need to express this in terms of $t$ as follows:

$$y = v_i t \sin \theta - \frac{1}{2} g t^2$$

$$\rightarrow \frac{1}{2} g t^2 - v_i t \sin \theta + y = 0 \tag{2.4.12}$$

This is a quadratic in terms of $t$, and the solution thereof is left to the reader.

### Solving for Multiple Variables

As mentioned near the start of this topic, it is very common that two or more values are unknown or need to be determined, usually $\theta$ and $v_i$ (since both points are usually known). In multivariate cases, the set of possible solutions expands greatly, so in order to solve the problem, the fastest approach is to eliminate some of the unknowns. In the most common case, we are given two points and a maximum initial velocity $v_{max}$, and need to solve for both $v_i$ and $\theta$.

When reducing variables in order to simplify to a single-variable problem, it is important to reduce in a manner that does not overly restrict possible solutions. In the previous case in which both $\theta$ and $v_i$ are unknown, restricting $\theta$ greatly reduces the number of solutions, and is undesirable. On the other hand, setting $v_i = v_{max}$ and varying $\theta$ preserves a larger set of landing points. This same logic can be extended to other forms of this problem, although there is not space to elaborate further within the scope of this gem.

## Optimizing Implementation

When implementing the previous equations in code, there are a few optimizations that can make a substantial difference in performance. This is because trigonometric functions have a very high overhead on most systems.

### Avoid Oversimplification

When deriving mathematical calculations, there is a tendency to reduce formulae to their simplest mathematical form, rather than the simplest or most optimal algorithm. For instance, in solving for initial velocity $v_i$, we came across Equations 2.4.9 and 2.4.10 as follows:

$$v_i = x \sqrt{\frac{g(\tan^2 \theta + 1)}{2(x \tan \theta - y)}}$$

$$= \frac{x}{\cos \theta} \sqrt{\frac{g}{2(x \tan \theta - y)}}$$

The tendency from a mathematical point of view would be to prefer the latter form, since it reduces the equation; however, in implementation, it is more efficient to precalculate *tan* $\theta$ and use it twice in the first equation, rather than calculating both *tan* $\theta$ and *cos* $\theta$ as is done in the latter formula. In addition, even if we choose to use the second equation (and not simplify to terms of *tan* $\theta$), leaving *cos* $\theta$ outside of the square root bracket means that two divisions need to be done: one inside the bracket and one outside. To optimize, one can either place the *cos* $\theta$ inside the divisor within the bracket as *cos²* $\theta$, or multiply x by *1/cos* $\theta$.

### Reduce Trigonometric Functions to
### Simpler Calculations

Rather than using the provided functions for *sin*, *cos*, and *tan*, it is much more efficient to use pregenerated lookup tables or take advantage of known relations between other variables. For instance, to calculate *tan* $\theta$, you can simply divide the initial value of $v_y$ by $v_x$, since they are defined in terms of *sin* $\theta$ *and cos* $\theta$, respectively, and are likely precomputed.

In addition, there is additional room for optimization—The purpose here is simply to alert the reader to the high computational cost involved with trigonometric calculation and the importance of optimization.

## Summary

Efficient trajectory production can enhance perceived AI quality and engine performance. Although the derivation can be math intensive, the resulting equations are relatively simple and easy to understand. In addition, once the process involved in deriving and simplifying the previous formulae is understood, it is easy to apply that knowledge to more complicated situations, such as moving targets, nonvertical acceleration, and other related problems.

# The Parallel Transport Frame

## *Carl Dougan*

Carl.dougan@gte.net

**M**any tasks in computer games require generating a suitable orientation as an object moves through space. Let's say you need to orient a camera flying along a looping path. You'd probably want the camera to turn with the path and point along the direction of travel. When the path loops, the orientation of the camera should change appropriately, to follow the loop. You wouldn't want it to suddenly flip or twist, but turn only to match the changes of the path. The *parallel transport frame* method can help provide this "steady" orientation.

You can also use this technique in the generation of geometry. A common operation in 3D modeling is *lofting*, where a 2D shape is *extruded* along a path curve, and multiple sections made from the shape are connected together to produce 3D geometry. If the 2D shape was a circle, the resulting 3D model would be a tube, centered on the path curve. The same criteria apply in calculating the orientation of the shape as did with the camera—the orientation should "follow" the path and shouldn't be subject to unnecessary twist.

The parallel transport method gets its stability by incrementally rotating a coordinate system (the frame) as it is translated along a curve. This "memory" of the previous frame's orientation is what allows the elimination of unnecessary twist—only the minimal amount of rotation needed to stay parallel to the curve is applied at each step. Unfortunately, in order to calculate the frame at the end of a curve, you need to iterate a frame along the path, all the way from the start, rotating it at each step. Two other commonly used methods of curve framing are the *Frenet Frame* and the *Fixed Up* method [Eberly01], which can be calculated analytically at any point on the path, in one calculation. They have other caveats, however, which will be described later.

## The Technique

A relatively simple numerical technique can be used to calculate the parallel transport frame [Glassner90]. You take an arbitrary initial frame, translate it along the curve, and at each iteration, rotate it to stay as "parallel" to the curve as possible.

Given:
 a curve **C**
 an existing frame **F1** at **t**-1
 a tangent **T1** at **t**-1  (the 1$^{st}$ derivative or velocity of **C** at **t**-1)
 a tangent **T2** at **t**

a new frame **F2** at the next time **t** can be calculated as follows:
 **F2**s position is the value of **C** at **t**.
 **F2**s orientation can be found by rotating **F1** about an axis **A** with angle α, where
 **A** = **T1** × **T2** and
 α = ArcCos((**T1** ·**T2**)/(|**T1**||**T2**|))

If the tangents are parallel, the rotation can be skipped  (i.e., if **T1** × **T2** is zero)
(Figure 2.5.1).

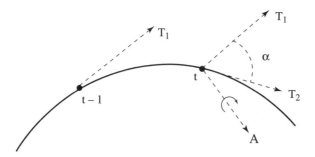

**FIGURE 2.5.1** *The frame at **t**-1 is rotated about **A** by α to calculate the frame at **t**.*

The initial frame is arbitrary. You can calculate an initial frame in which an axis
lies along the tangent with the Fixed Up or the Frenet Frame method.

In some cases, you may find it desirable to use parallel transport to generate
frames at a coarse sampling along the curve, and then achieve smooth rotation
between the sample frames by using quaternion interpolation. Using quaternions is
desirable anyway, since there is an efficient method of generating a quaternion from a
rotation axis and angle [Eberly01]. You can use the angle and axis shown previously to
generate a rotation quaternion, and then multiply it with the previous frame's quaternion to perform the rotation.

### Moving Objects

You can orient a moving object with a single parallel transport rotation each time the
object is moved, presumably once per frame. We need three pieces of information: the
velocity of the object at the current and previous locations, and the orientation at the previous location. The velocities correspond to the tangents **T1** and **T2** shown previously.

For some tasks, the parallel transport frame may be too "stable." For example, an
aircraft flying an S-shaped path on the horizontal plane would never bank. To achieve

realistic-looking simulation of flight, you may need to use a different solution, such as simulating the physics of motion. Craig Reynolds describes a relatively simple, and thus fast, technique for orienting flocking "boids" that includes banking [Reynolds99]. Reynolds' technique is similar to parallel transport in that it also relies on "memory" of the previous frame.

## Comparison

The details here show how the parallel transport method we have looked at so far compares with the Frenet Frame and Fixed Up methods of curve framing.

### The Frenet Frame

The Frenet Frame is built from three orthogonal axes:

- The tangent of the curve
- The cross-product of the tangent, and the second derivative
- Another vector generated from the cross-product of the prior two vectors

The Frenet Frame is problematic for the uses already discussed because it cannot be calculated when the second derivative is zero. This occurs at points of inflection and on straight sections of the curve [Hanson95]. Clearly, not being able to calculate a frame on a straight section is a big problem for our purposes. In addition, the frame may spin, due to changes in the second derivative. In the case of an S-shaped curve, for example, the second derivative points into the curves, flipping sides on the upper and lower halves. The resulting Frenet Frames on the S-shaped curve will flip in consequence. Figure 2.5.2 shows what this means graphically; instead of continuous

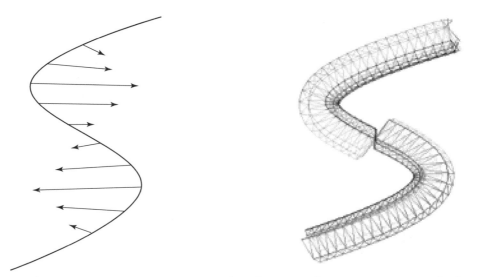

**FIGURE 2.5.2** *Second derivative on an S-shaped curve, and Frenet Frame generated tube from the same curve.*

geometry, we have a discontinuity where the second derivative switches sides. If this was a flock of birds, they would suddenly flip upside down at that point.

### *The Fixed Up Method*

In the case of the Fixed Up method, the tangent **T** and an arbitrary vector **V** (the Fixed Up vector) are used to generate three axes of the resulting frame, the direction **D**, up **U**, and right **R** vectors [Eberly01].

$$\mathbf{D} = \mathbf{T} / |\mathbf{T}|$$
$$\mathbf{R} = \mathbf{D} \times \mathbf{V} / |\mathbf{D} \times \mathbf{V}|$$
$$\mathbf{U} = \mathbf{R} \times \mathbf{D}$$

A problem with the Fixed Up method occurs when the tangent and the arbitrary vector chosen are parallel or close to parallel. When **T** and **V** are parallel, the cross-product of **D** and **V** is zero and the frame cannot be built. Even if they are very close, the twist of the resulting vector relative to the tangent will vary greatly with small changes in **T**, twisting the resulting frame. This isn't a problem if you can constrain the path—which may be possible for some tasks, like building the geometry of freeways, but may not be for others, like building the geometry of a roller coaster.

Figure 2.5.3 shows a comparison of a tube generated using parallel transport with one using the Fixed Up method. In the upper and lower sections of the curve, the cross-product of tangent and the Fixed Up vector is coming out of the page. In the middle section, it is going into the page. The abrupt flip causes the visible twist in the generated geometry.

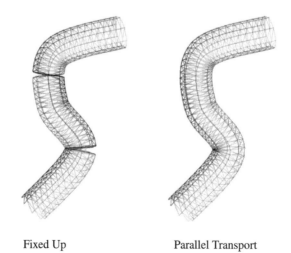

Fixed Up                        Parallel Transport

**FIGURE 2.5.3** *Comparison of Fixed Up and parallel transport.*

## Conclusion

For unconstrained paths—for example, flying missiles or looping tracks—parallel transport is one method that you can use to keep the tracks from twisting and the missiles from flipping.

## References

[Glassner90] Bloomenthal, Jules, "Calculation of Reference Frames Along a Space Curve," *Graphics Gems*, Academic Press, 1990: pp. 567–571.
[Eberly01] Eberly, David H., *3D Game Engine Design*, Academic Press, 2001.
[Hanson95] Hanson, Andrew J., and Ma, Hui, *Parallel Transport Approach to Curve Framing*, Department of Computer Science, Indiana University, 1995.
[Reynolds99] Reynolds, Craig, "Steering Behaviors for Autonomous Characters," available online at www.red3d.com/cwr/steer/gdc99/index.html.

# 2.6

# Smooth C² Quaternion-based Flythrough Paths

## Alex Vlachos, ATI Research;
## and John Isidoro

alex@Vlachos.com and jisidoro@cs.bu.edu

In this gem, we describe a method for smoothly interpolating a camera's position and orientation to produce a flythrough with $C^2$ continuity. We draw on several known methods and provide a C++ class that implements the methods described here.

## Introduction

Smoothly interpolating the positions of a flythrough path can easily be achieved by applying a natural cubic spline to the sample points. The orientations, on the other hand, require a little more attention. We describe a method for converting a quaternion in $S^3$ space (points on the unit hypersphere) into $R^4$ space (points in 4D space) [Johnstone99]. Once the quaternion is in $R^4$ space, any 4D spline can be applied to the transformed data. The resulting interpolated points can then be transformed back into $S^3$ space and used as a quaternion. In addition, a technique called *selective negation* is described to preprocess the quaternions in a way that produces the shortest rotation path between sample point orientations.

Camera cuts (moving a camera to a new location) are achieved by introducing phantom points around the camera cut similar to the way an open spline is padded. These additional points are needed to pad the spline to produce smooth results near the cut point. The code provided describes cut points as part of a single fly path and simplifies the overall code. Internally to the C++ class, the individual cut segments are treated as separate splines without the overhead of creating a spline for each segment.

## Position Interpolation

Let's now discuss position interpolation.

### Sample Points

There are two common ways to specify sample points. The first is to have each segment between control points represent a constant time (for example, each control point represents one second of time). The second is to use the control points only to define the shape of the camera path, and to have the camera move at a constant speed along this path. The code provided with this gem assumes a constant time between control points, although this code could easily be modified for the constant speed technique.

**Natural Cubic Spline**

A natural cubic spline is chosen due to the high degree of continuity it provides, namely C². However, it's important to note that any spline may be used in place of the natural cubic spline. Code for implementing this spline is widely available, including *Numerical Recipes In C* [Press97]. The sample code provided is modeled after this.

A natural cubic spline is an interpolating curve that is a mathematical representation of the original drafting spline. One important characteristic of this spline is its lack of local control. This means that if any single control point is moved, the entire spline is affected. This isn't necessarily a disadvantage; in fact, this functionality may be desirable. As you begin to use this spline, you'll see the advantages it has in smoothing out the camera movement when you sample the spline at a higher frequency.

It is important to differentiate between open and closed splines. In the case of a closed spline, the spline is specified such that the last point is the same as the first point. This is done to treat the camera path as a closed loop. To work around any possible discontinuities in the spline at the loop point, simply replicate the last four points of the spline to the beginning of the array, and the first four sample points to the end of the array. In practice, we've found that using four points was sufficient to eliminate any visual artifacts.

This replication eliminates the need for modulus arithmetic and also simplifies our preprocessing of the camera path. This is even more important when dealing with orientations using the selective negation method as described later (Figure 2.6.1).

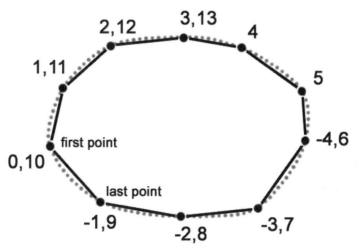

**FIGURE 2.6.1** *Replicating points for a closed spline.*

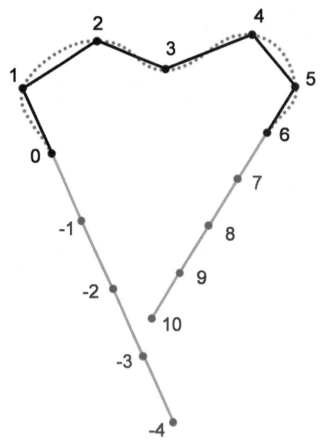

**FIGURE 2.6.2** *Creating phantom points for an open spline.*

In contrast, an open spline has a different beginning and end point. In order to sample the spline, you need to pad the spline with several "phantom" points at both the beginning and end of the open spline (Figure 2.6.2). A constant velocity is assumed for the phantom points before and after the open spline path. At the beginning of the spline in Figure 2.6.2, the vector $V_0 = P_1 - P_0$ is subtracted from $P_0$ to get the resulting point $P_{-1}$. Similarly, $V_0$ is subtracted from $P_{-1}$ to create $P_{-2}$, and so on. The trailing phantom points are calculated in a similar way.

## Orientation Interpolation

### Sample Points

Unit quaternions are used as the orientation data at the sample points. Quaternions can be very useful for numerous applications. The beauty of quaternions is that, for rotations, they take the form of a normalized 4-element vector (later referred to as a 3-element vector and a scalar component). This is exactly enough information to represent an axis of rotation and an angle of rotation around that axis [GPG1]. Quaternions give us everything we need to represent a rotation and nothing more.

For orientation, however, there is an ambiguity in using quaternions. Orientation can be thought of as a rotation from a base orientation. When using quaternions, there are two possible rotations that will bring you to the same orientation. Suppose there is a counterclockwise rotation $\theta$ about an axis $w$ that gives you the desired orientation. A rotation by $360°-\theta$ about the axis $-w$ also results in the same orientation. When converted into a quaternion representation, the second quaternion is simply the negation of the first one.

## Direction of Rotation and Selective Negation

When performing quaternion interpolation, there is one small nuance that needs to be considered. When representing an orientation, either a quaternion or its negation will suffice. However, when interpolating orientations (for example, performing a rotation), the positive and negative quaternions result in vastly different rotations and consequently different camera paths. If the desired result is to perform the smallest possible rotation between each pair of two orientations, you can preprocess the quaternions to achieve this.

Taking the dot product of two quaternions gives the cosine of half the angle of rotation between them. If this quantity is negative, the angle of rotation between the two quaternions is greater than 180 degrees. In this case, negating one of the orientation quaternions makes the angle between the two quaternions less than 180 degrees. In terms of interpolation, this makes the orientation spline path always perform the shortest rotation between the orientation key frames. We call this process *selective negation*.

The technique of selectively negating orientation quaternions can be incorporated as a preprocessing step for a camera flythrough path. For the preprocessing step, traverse the flythrough path from start to end, and for each quaternion $q_t$ on the path, negate it if the dot product between it and its predecessor is negative (in other words, if $(q_t \cdot q_{t-1})<0$). Using selective negation as a preprocessing step makes spline interpolation much more efficient by not requiring the selective negation math for every sample.

To preprocess a closed spline path, it is necessary to replicate the first four points of the spline path and append them to the end of the path prior to the selective negation. Note that the replicated points may have different signs than the original points. When dealing with an open spline, you need to create phantom quaternions (corresponding to the phantom control points) to pad the spline. The concept is similar in that you want to linearly interpolate the difference between the two quaternions closest to the beginning or end of the path. However, linearly interpolating quaternions doesn't suffice. Instead, we use the spherical linear interpolation (slerp) algorithm. Given quaternions $q_0$ and $q_1$, we need to generate four phantom quaternions—$q_{-1}$, $q_{-2}$, and so on— to pad the beginning of an open spline. We use the slerp function (spherical linear interpolation) to slerp from $q_1$ to $q_0$ with a slerp value of 2.0. This effectively gives us a linear change in rotation at our phantom points.

Once we have preprocessed our entire list of orientation quaternions for interpolation, it is straightforward to perform smooth spline-based quaternion interpolation techniques.

## Spline Interpolation for Quaternions

As seen for positional interpolation, splines can be used to give us much smoother interpolation than linear interpolation can. However, spline interpolation for quaternions is not so straightforward, and there are several techniques that can be used. One technique simply interpolates the raw quaternion values, and then renormalizes the resulting quaternion. However, this technique does not result in a smooth path and produces bizarre changes in angular velocity. Another idea is to use techniques based on the logarithms of quaternions. SQUAD (spherical quadrangle interpolation) [Shoemake91] is an example of this. A performance limitation is incurred when using these techniques because they require transcendental functions (sin, cos, log, pow, and so on). Other techniques involve blending between great 2-spheres laying on the unit quaternion hypersphere [Kim95], or involve some sort of iterative numeric technique [Neilson92]. While many of these techniques provide decent results, most of them do not provide $C^2$ continuity or are computationally prohibitive to use, especially when many flythrough paths are used (for game characters or projectiles, as an example).

However, there is a technique for quaternion spline interpolation that gives very good results and obeys derivative continuity requirements. This uses an invertible rational mapping [Johnstone99] M between the unit quaternion 4-sphere ($S^3$) and another four-dimensional space ($R^4$). In the following equations, $a$, $b$, and $c$ are the components of the vector portion of the quaternion, and $s$ is the scalar portion.

The transformation $M^{-1}$ from $S^3 \rightarrow R^4$ is:

$x = a/sqrt(2(1-s))$
$y = b/sqrt(2(1-s))$
$z = c/sqrt(2(1-s))$
$w=(1-s) /sqrt(2(1-s))$

The transformation M from $R^4 \rightarrow S^3$ is:

$s = (x^2 + y^2 + z^2 - w^2 ) / (x^2 + y^2 + z^2 + w^2)$
$a = 2xw / (x^2 + y^2 + z^2 + w^2)$
$b = 2yw / (x^2 + y^2 + z^2 + w^2)$
$c = 2zw / (x^2 + y^2 + z^2 + w^2)$

To use this for quaternion spline interpolation is straightforward. First, selective negation should be applied to the control quaternions to assure the shortest possible rotation between control points. After this, apply $M^{-1}$ to all the control quaternions to get their resulting value in $R^4$. This can be done as a preprocessing step and can be done in the flythrough-path building or loading stage of a program. This way, the square root does not have to be calculated when the flythrough path is being evaluated.

Next, the resulting 4-vectors can be interpolated using the spline of your choice. Because this is a continuous rational mapping, the continuity of the interpolated $S^3$ quaternion path has the same continuity as the spline used for interpolation in $R^4$ space.

In our application, we use natural cubic splines [Hearn94][Press97] for the interpolation in $R^4$ space.

This gives us $C^2$ continuous orientation interpolation as well. The qualitative effect of this is that the camera path does not have any sharp changes in angular acceleration.

After the desired point on the spline in $R^4$ is found, it can be converted back into a quaternion using M.

However, there is one mathematical nuance in using this technique that needs to be addressed.

## Singularity in the Rational Mapping

If your flythrough path contains orientation quaternions close or equal to (1,0,0,0), it will cause numerical instability when interpolated through in $R^4$ space, as $M^{-1}(1,0,0,0)$ = $(\infty,\infty,\infty,\infty)$. There are a few ways to handle this singularity. One possible option is to ignore it, and surprisingly, this is feasible in many cases. For example, if the z-axis of the world is pointing up, and you know the camera will never point straight up with the camera's up-vector pointing up the y-axis, the orientation quaternion (1,0,0,0) will never occur in the flythrough path, and the problem is solved.

If this is not the case, another option is to find a quaternion $q_f$ that is not within 30 degrees of any of the orientation quaternions, and use $q_f$ to rotate all of the quaternions into "safe" orientations that are not near the singularity [Johnstone 99]. The basic idea behind this is to perform the spline interpolation on a rotated version of your flythrough path, and then rotate the interpolated orientations back into their original coordinate frame. All that has to be done is to multiply all your orientation quaternions by $q_f$ after the selective negation step. Following, you transform the quaternions from $S^3$ space into $R^4$ space, apply the natural cubic spline, and transform the resulting $R^4$ values back into $S^3$ space. After this, we add the additional step of rotating each resulting quaternion by $q_f^{-1}$ before using it.

An easy way to find $q_f$ is to randomly generate unit length quaternions, until you find one that is not within 30 degrees of any of the selectively negated orientation quaternions.

## Camera Cuts

A *camera cut* is defined as moving the camera from one point in your scene to another. You can't just introduce a cut in the middle of a spline, and you can't simply step over

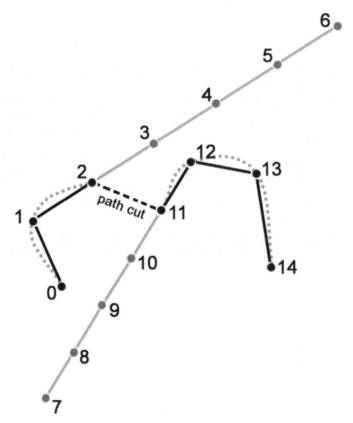

**FIGURE 2.6.3**  *Creating phantom points for a path cut segment.*

a segment of the spline. Instead, you segment your spline into two separate splines at a cut point, and process these splines as separate open splines. This is done simultaneously for both the position- and orientation-based splines. The code we supply deals with camera cuts in such a way that you don't need to explicitly create a separate path (see Figure 2.6.3).

## Code

The code accompanying this gem is a C++ class that implements most of the techniques explained in this article. It has member functions for creating and editing the control points manually, reading and writing path files, dealing with cut points, sampling the spline at a given time, and setting up vertex and index buffers for drawing the spline. The class assumes there is a constant time between control points as opposed to a constant velocity. In addition, the code does not solve the singularity problem, since we never saw the singularity in our project. Please see the source files for more information.

# References

[Press97] Press, William H., et al, *Numerical Recipes in C,* Cambridge University Press, 1997.

[Hearn94] Hearn, Donald, Baker, M. Pauline, *Computer Graphics Second Edition,* Prentice Hall, Inc. 1994.

[Johnstone99] Johnstone, J. K., Williams, J. P., "A Rational Quaternion Spline of Arbitrary Continuity," Tech Report: *www.cis.uab.edu/info/faculty/jj/cos.html,* 1999.

[GPG1] Edited by Mark DeLoura, *Game Programming Gems,* Charles River Media, 2000.

[Shoemake91] Shoemake, K., *Quaternion Calculus for Animation,* Math for SIGGRAPH (ACM SIGGRAPH '91 Course Notes #2), 1991.

[Neilson92] Neilson, G., and Heiland, R., "Animating Rotations Using Quaternions and Splines on a 4D Sphere," English Edition, *Programming and Computer Software,* Plenum Pub., New York. 1992.

[Kim95] Kim, M.S. and Nam, K.W., *Interpolating Solid Orientations with Circular Blending Quaternion Curves,* Computer-Aided Design, Vol. 27, No. 5, pp. 385–398, 1995.

# 2.7

## Recursive Dimensional Clustering: A Fast Algorithm for Collision Detection

### Steve Rabin, Nintendo of America

steve_rabin@hotmail.com

**B**asic collision detection can be a costly operation. The simplest method relies on treating each object as a sphere and comparin $n^2$ distances. Listing 2.7.1 shows the code for this simple brute-force comparison algorithm. However, a new technique called Recursive Dimensional Clustering (RDC) can take the typical case from $O(n^2)$ to something close to $O(nlog_2n)$.

### Listing 2.7.1   Brute-force comparison algorithm

```
// Slightly optimized O((n^2-n)/2) time complexity
for( i=0; i<num_objects; i++ ) {
   for( j=i+1; j<num_objects; j++ ) {
      if( Distance(i, j) < Radius(i) + Radius(j) ) {
         //in collision
      }
   }
}
```

The practical difference between RDC and the brute-force method is shown in Table 2.7.1. These times were calculated on a Pentium II 400 MHz with data containing only one collision. Note that the brute-force $O(n^2)$ algorithm was fully optimized to run at $O((n^2-n)/2)$ as in Listing 2.7.1 and compared positions using distance squared in order to avoid the costly square root operation.

What's interesting about Table 2.7.1 is that RDC increases almost linearly, while the brute force method increases exponentially. Although the results are remarkable, RDC only becomes useful if you are dealing with large numbers of objects that are usually not in collision.

**Table 2.7.1 The Difference between RDC and the Brute-Force Method**

| Objects | RDC | Brute Force |
|---|---|---|
| 10 | < 1 ms | < 1 ms |
| 50 | 2 ms | 6 ms |
| 100 | 4 ms | 18 ms |
| 200 | 7 ms | 67 ms |
| 300 | 11 ms | 150 ms |
| 400 | 15 ms | 263 ms |
| 500 | 19 ms | 406 ms |
| 1000 | 38 ms | 1596 ms (1.6 seconds) |
| 2000 | 81 ms | 6335 ms (6.3 seconds) |
| 5000 | 222 ms | 39380 ms (39.4 seconds) |
| 10000 | 478 ms | 157621 ms (2 minutes, 37.6 seconds) |

## Other Applications

One of the benefits of RDC is that it naturally finds groups of objects rather than single collision pairs. A group is a collection of objects that touch each other or are within a certain radius of each other. This definition also includes groups such that if A touches B and B touches C, then A, B, and C are all in the same group, meaning that every group member is not required to touch every other group member. Thus, RDC can be used to find simultaneous collisions of several objects or even groups of enemies on a battlefield.

One interesting application of RDC involves identifying metaball clusters in order to speed up geometry generation (*Marching Cubes* algorithm). In this use, RDC finds the clusters and then calculates the minimal axis-aligned bounding boxes (AABB) around those clusters. Minimal bounding boxes are critical for the *Marching Cubes* algorithm. This is because the computational speed is proportional to the volume of the boxes, which equates to an algorithm with $O(n^3)$ time complexity. Color Plate 1 shows an example.

### The RDC Algorithm

In order to understand how RDC works, the first step is to follow how it recognizes groups of objects in collision along a single dimension. Figure 2.7.1 shows a one-dimensional example with three objects.

As you can see, objects B and C overlap, while object A is by itself. Thus, a clustering algorithm would find two groups: one group containing A, and a second group containing both B and C. Although it's easy to figure this out visually, we need a systematic algorithm that achieves the same result.

The basic idea of this algorithm is to mark the boundaries of each object and then find groups of overlapping objects using that data. This is done by looping through all entities and storing the beginning and ending boundaries for a given dimension in a

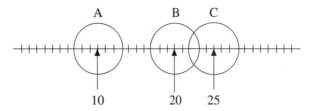

**FIGURE 2.7.1** *Three objects along one dimension.*

linked list. For example, the first object *A* has a left boundary of 7 and a right boundary of 13. In order to make this apply to any dimension, we can think of these boundaries in terms of brackets and label them open and close, instead of left and right. Figure 2.7.2 shows the resulting linked list created from the three objects.

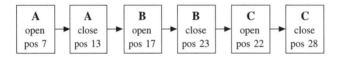

**FIGURE 2.7.2** *The boundary list.*

With the boundary list complete, the next step is to sort the list from lowest to highest position using your favorite sorting algorithm, such as *quicksort*. The sorted list is shown in Figure 2.7.3. In this example, only two elements were swapped.

Now that we have the sorted list of boundaries, we can find the groups. The algorithm for finding the groups is very similar to parser algorithms for matching brackets. The pseudocode in Listing 2.7.2 will go through the sorted list and extract each "bracketed" group.

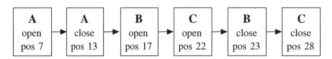

**FIGURE 2.7.3** *The list after sorting.*

## Listing 2.7.2   Algorithm for finding groups along one dimension

```
int count = 0;
Clear( currentGroup );
for( element in list )
{
    if( element is an "open bracket" ) {
        count++;
        Add entity to currentGroup;
    }
```

```
        else { //element is a "closed bracket"
           count--;
           if( count == 0 ) { //entire group found
              Store( currentGroup );
              Clear( currentGroup );
           }
        }
     }
  }
  assert( count == 0 );
```

At this point, you may have noticed that the algorithm arbitrarily groups objects that share boundaries. For example, if object *A* has a closed boundary at position 10, and object *B* has an open boundary at position 10, then any simple sorting algorithm would not distinguish between them. The result is that the algorithm in Listing 2.7.2 would inconsistently group these types of cases. However, there are many solutions to this problem. The easiest is to use floating-point values and to make sure that objects don't snap to integer locations. Another solution involves "puffing out" each object radius by a very tiny amount, thus causing identical boundaries to be offset from each other. You could also fix the problem in the sorting function; however, that would introduce extra overhead and increase the running time.

### RDC in Higher Dimensions

Clearly, this algorithm works well for finding groups along one dimension. However, it would only be useful if it worked in two or three dimensions. The trick for multiple dimensions is to first find groups along one axis, and then send each newly formed group to the next axis to be subdivided further.

Figure 2.7.4 shows a set of four objects in two dimensions. Again, it's easy to spot the groups visually, but this example will show how the algorithm determines groups in multiple dimensions.

The ordered linked list for Figure 2.7.4 along the x-axis is shown in Figure 2.7.5.

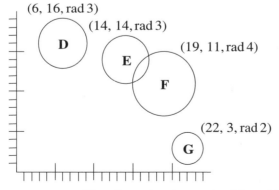

**FIGURE 2.7.4** *Two-dimensional example of four objects.*

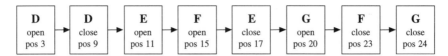

**FIGURE 2.7.5**  *The sorted boundary list for Figure 2.7.4.*

The groups in the x-axis are:

```
Group₀ = { D }, Group1 = { E, F, G }
```

We've now determined that there are at least two groups. The first group contains object *D*, and the second group contains *E*, *F*, and *G*. With the x-axis done, each new group is sent to the y-axis to be divided further. Since object *D*'s group has only one member, it doesn't need to be divided anymore and will simply be its own group. However, objects *E*, *F*, and *G* must now be analyzed along the y-axis. Figure 2.7.6 shows the ordered linked list for *Group₁* along the y-axis.

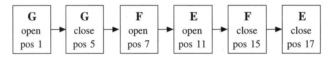

**FIGURE 2.7.6**  *The* Group₁ *y-axis sorted boundary list.*

The groups in the y-axis are:

```
Group₁ₐ = { G }, Group₁ᵦ = { E, F }
```

Now that we've gone through each dimension once, the final groups are:

```
Group₀ = { D }, Group₁ₐ = { G }, Group₁ᵦ = { E, F }
```

Figures 2.7.7a and 2.7.7b graphically show the boundaries of each object in each dimension and the resulting groups. When this algorithm is expanded to three dimensions, the groups are simply analyzed in one more dimension; namely, the z-axis. Following is a summary of the steps involved in the RDC algorithm.

## RDC Steps:

1.  Start with the x-axis.
2.  Construct a linked list of object boundaries in this dimension.
3.  Sort that list by boundary position, from lowest to highest.
4.  Find groups using the open/close "bracket matching" algorithm in Listing 2.7.2.

5.  For each group found in that dimension, repeat steps 2–5 in the next dimension.

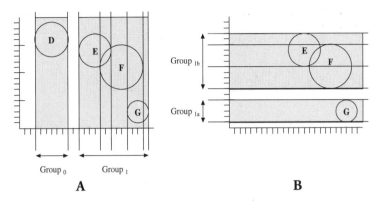

**FIGURE 2.7.7** *A) Groups found in the x-axis. B) Group₁ subdivided in the y-axis.*

## A Flaw in the Algorithm

Unfortunately, the algorithm described so far has a fatal flaw. When grouping objects along one axis, objects can get sucked into groups that aren't later separated by other dimensions. Figure 2.7.8 points out a problem configuration.

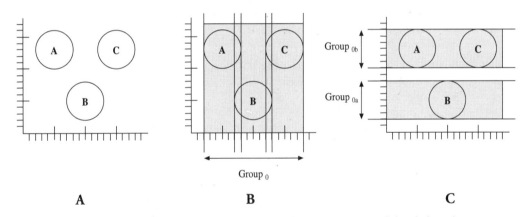

**FIGURE 2.7.8** *A) Flaw example. B) Groups in the x-axis. C) Group₀ subdivided in the y-axis.*

Figure 2.7.8b shows the first pass along the x-axis and finds that all three objects overlap. Thus, they are all assigned to the same group. Then the single group is analyzed along the y-axis, as in Figure 2.7.8c. This results in two groups being found, but it understandably fails to put object $A$ and object $C$ in separate groups.

The correct solution would be for each object to be in its own group. However, the result of the algorithm was only partially correct. The fix is to send the new groups found along the y-axis back to be analyzed again along the x-axis. When this is done, the correct groups are finally found.

This solution can be generalized in order to permanently correct the algorithm. The algorithm needs the following rule:

*When a group is subdivided along one dimension,*
*the resulting subgroups must be reanalyzed along all other dimensions.*

In the 2D case, a group that is broken up along the y-axis must be reanalyzed in the x-axis, and vice versa. In 3D, a group that is broken up along the y-axis must be reanalyzed in both the x-axis and the z-axis. This fix finally explains the recursive element of RDC. Following are the revised steps for RDC algorithm.

### RDC steps (revised):

1. Start with the x-axis.
2. Construct a linked list of object boundaries in this dimension.
3. Sort that list by boundary position, from lowest to highest.
4. Find groups using the open/close "bracket matching" algorithm in Listing 2.7.2.
5. For each group found in that dimension, repeat steps 2–5 in the other dimension(s) until the group no longer gets subdivided and all dimensions have been analyzed for that unique group.

## Finding Pairs in Collision

As presented so far, RDC only identifies groups or clusters of objects that touch each other. The effect is that a group can contain members who may or may not directly touch every other member in the group. While this has many great uses (simultaneous collisions, grouping info), general collision detection usually requires *pairs* that are in collision.

To find collision pairs, each final cluster group from RDC must be sent to the brute-force comparison algorithm. Hopefully, the clusters have very few objects at this point so that the $O((n^2-n)/2)$ algorithm runs sufficiently fast.

One way to find collision pairs even faster is to use the brute-force algorithm once a collision cluster gets below a certain number; for example, less than 10 objects. At this point, it would be simply faster to compare all of the objects rather than attempting to subdivide the group further with continued recursive calls.

### The RDC Implementation

As described, the algorithm is basically recursive and attempts to break groups up until the minimum clusters are found. The tricky part is designing a recursive function that chooses which dimensions to subdivide and when to end the recursion. In 3D, the function must at least try to subdivide the group along all three dimensions. However, if any of those dimensions results in subdivision, each subdivided group must then be sent recursively to the other two dimensions.

The easiest way to accomplish this is to let a recursive function take three arguments that determine which dimensions still need to be considered. When the function first gets called, all three dimensions appear as arguments. As each dimension is analyzed and not subdivided, the dimension argument list shrinks to zero and the recursion halts. However, it is mandatory for a subdivided group to be called recursively with two arguments (the other two dimensions). The complete function can be found in Listing 2.7.3.

## Listing 2.7.3   RDC algorithm (pseudocode)

```
void RDC( Pairs& pairs, Group& group,
          Axis axis1, Axis axis2, Axis axis3 )
{
  //"pairs" holds all final pairs that are in collision
  //"group" is the current group of objects to analyze
  //"axis1" is the axis to analyze within this function
  //"axis2", "a3" will be analyzed in recursive calls

  if( Size( group ) < 10 || axis1 == INVALID_AXIS )
  { //end recursion and test for collisions
    BruteForceComparison( pairs, subGroup );
  }
  else {
    //for this group, find the boundaries and sort them
    OpenCloseBoundaryList boundaries;
    FindOpenCloseBoundaries( axis1, group, boundaries );
    SortOpenCloseBoundaries( boundaries );   //O(nlogn)

    Group subGroup;
    unsigned int count = 0;
    Axis newAxis1 = axis2;
    Axis newAxis2 = axis3;
    Axis newAxis3 = INVALID_AXIS;
    bool groupSubdivided = false;

    //subdivide the group if possible and call recursively
    for( every curBoundary in boundaries list )
    {
      if( curBoundary is "open bracket" )
      { //this entity lies within a cluster group
        count++;
        AddToGroup( subGroup, curBoundary->entity );
      }
      else
      {
        count--;
        if( count == 0 )
        { //found the end of a cluster group - take subgroup
          //and call recursively on remaining axis'

          if( curBoundary != GetLastBoundary( boundaries ) )
          { //this group is being subdivided - remember
            groupSubdivided = true;
          }
```

```
        if( groupSubdivided )
        { //reconsider all other axis'
          if( axis1 == X_AXIS ) {
            newAxis1 = Y_AXIS;
            newAxis2 = Z_AXIS;
          }
          else if( axis1 == Y_AXIS ) {
            newAxis1 = X_AXIS;
            newAxis2 = Z_AXIS;
          }
          else if( axis1 == Z_AXIS ) {
            newAxis1 = X_AXIS;
            newAxis2 = Y_AXIS;
          }
        }
      }

      //recursive call
      RecursiveClustering( pairs, subGroup,
                    newAxis1, newAxis2, INVALID_AXIS );
      Clear( subGroup ); //clear the subGroup for the next group
    }
  }
 }
}
```

As you examine the RDC function, note that it has been augmented to find collision pairs. When the recursion halts and a minimal cluster is found, it then sends that cluster to the brute-force comparison function. It will also halt the recursion should a cluster fall below 10 members. At this point, it immediately compares the members with the brute-force function.

## Time Complexity

At first glance, this algorithm looks fairly time intensive. Your gut feeling probably tells you that it's an $O(n^2)$ algorithm—and you'd be pretty close. However, because of the physical restrictions of 3D space, certain worst-case configurations are extremely rare. Instead, the algorithm takes on average $O(n log_2 n)$, as long as most objects aren't in collision.

RDC performs badly in two extreme cases. One is when the objects' configuration causes RDC to recurse very deeply—this is the worst case of $O(n^2 log_2 n)$. The other is when the objects are all in collision with each other, in which case RDC does almost no work and the brute-force algorithm must be used with $O(n^2)$.

In the worst case, recursion gets very deep. Functionally, this happens when the object set is split completely asymmetrically, with one object in one group, and *n-1* objects in the other. The larger group is then sent to the function recursively. If this happens at each level of recursion, we get a total of *n–1* calls to the function. (This analysis applies to one dimension only. In three dimensions, we can get up to *3 + 2(n–1)* calls. In all cases, this is $O(n)$).

For these calls, the average group size $m$ is equal to $n/2$. The most complex part of the function is the sort that we assume to be $O(mlog_2m)$ or $O(nlog_2n)$. This gives the total time complexity of the worst case as $O(n) * O(nlog_2n)$, or $O(n^2log_2n)$.

Figure 2.7.8 shows the near worst-case scenario for time complexity (a true worst-case scenario might not be physically possible). Since Figure 2.7.9 is such an unlikely configuration, the worst-case time complexity of $O(n^2log_2n)$ is somewhat misleading. Interestingly, this particular configuration results in an actual time complexity of $O(n^{1.78}log_2n)$. In practice you should never expect anything nearly that bad, since this particular case is humorously rare and contrived.

A more likely bad case for RDC occurs when all objects are in collision with each other. In this situation, each dimension would be tested, and only one group would be found. This would take $O(3nlog_2n)$ time. Then the entire group would be sent to the brute-force comparison algorithm in order to find the final collision pairs. This would make the actual worst case be $O(3nlog_2n + (n^2-n)/2)$, or simply $O(n^2)$. Given that this time complexity is identical to the brute-force method and that no objects will ever be in collision with all other objects, it's almost always faster to use RDC.

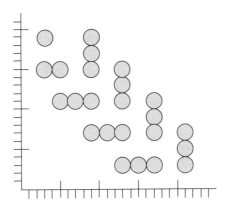

**FIGURE 2.7.9**  *Near worst-case configuration for RDC (24 objects).*

## Conclusion

Although Recursive Dimensional Clustering (RDC) isn't a complete collision detection solution, it's an impressive first-pass filter for determining groups of objects that might be in collision. It works with blazing speed, dramatically outperforming brute-force methods. While partitioning of the world space is the standard solution for speeding up collision detection, RDC has remarkable performance in the absence of such techniques. However, for practical purposes, RDC is best suited for analyzing large numbers of objects (25+) for collision, perhaps even after other partitioning algorithms have reduced the testable set.

# References

[Blow97] Blow, Jonathan, "Practical Collision Detection," Proceedings, (Computer Game Developers Conference 1997), also available online at http://142.104.104.232/eCOW/projects/Resources/practical_collision_detection.html.

[Bobic00] Bobic, Nick, "Advanced Collision Detection Techniques," available online at www.gamasutra.com/features/20000330/bobic_pfv.htm, March 30, 2000.

[Roberts95] Roberts, Dave, "Collision Detection," *Dr. Dobb's Sourcebook* (May/June 1995): pp. 7–11.

# 2.8

## Programming Fractals

### *Jesse Laeuchli*

jesse@laeuchli.com

Today, many 3D games and applications display randomized landscapes. Often, fractals are used to create these landscapes. Such landscapes are known for their quality and realism, but only recently has the computer power become available in game machines to play with them in real time.

There are a number of reasons why you might use fractals to make a landscape. If you created a completely random landscape, setting the heights of the valleys and hills to any height, it would look random, and unlike any real-life landscape. On the other hand, if you assigned the landscape heights with an orderly function—for example, sin—you would get a completely regular and predictable landscape, something not possible in real life. It is possible to use fractals to get a mix between the two: a landscape where there will not be impossibly wild mountains and valleys, or evenly spaced hills, but more life-like scenes that match the qualities of the physical landscapes we see around us.

A good non-mathematical definition of a *fractal* is something regular that has randomness added in a controlled way. Things modeled with fractals are not completely random, but they are not entirely orderly either. Fractals are most often used as textures, or to create geometric models. Things that are complex, but do not have any regularity (such as people) cannot be directly modeled with fractals.

This gem looks at the more useful fractals, and examines how they are used. Not all types of fractals will be examined, as many of them are highly mathematical and have little use in game programming currently. In games, fractals are usually stored as height-maps: a rectangular grid with numbers in each cell representing the fractal's value at that point. In the case of a fractal landscape, the value represents the height; in the case of a fractal cloud, it might represent the density. The value can be interpreted in many ways, some of which (no doubt) have yet to be invented, however, since height is the most frequent case, I shall refer to the "height" of a fractal at a point, rather than using the rather bland word *value*.

## The Plasma Fractal

One of the most common fractals is the *plasma fractal*. This is very easy to program, the sort of thing demo writers love to optimize, and you have probably seen hundreds of them (Figure 2.8.1).

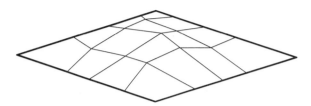

**FIGURE 2.8.1** *A small plasma fractal.*

To create a plasma, we create an empty height-map and assign heights to the four corners. Then, for each side, we linearly interpolate between each pair of corners. The center square's height is the arithmetic mean of the four corners' heights. We then repeat the process for each of the four squares we have defined with these new vertices, and recurse. This interpolation scheme generates a smooth curved surface between the four corners; in fact, it can be used alone to smoothly interpolate a height-map.

To make a fractal from this simple curved surface, we introduce a new step at each level of recursion. After generating the center vertex, we add or subtract a random amount from its height. At the next level of recursion, we do the same thing, but we reduce the range of the random numbers by a number $H$. Note that this factor is the only control available over the fractal. If H is 0, the height-map varies wildly; as H gets larger, the height-map gets less varied.

The main advantages of the plasma fractal are that it is extremely easy to understand and runs very fast. Unless speed is more important than results, though, this fractal should be avoided for two reasons. First, very little control is available over the fractal. Second, this fractal has very bad artifacts—very pronounced ridges along the edges.

## The Fault Fractal

Another common fractal is the *fault fractal*. This is also quite easy to program, but much slower than the plasma fractal. The fault fractal very roughly simulates the effect of severe earthquakes along random "fault lines."

To create this fractal, we again create an empty height-map. Then, we apply a series of "earthquakes" as follows: create a random line through the height-map, raise every cell on one side of the line up a small amount, and move every other cell down a small amount. This process is repeated until the landscape looks good enough.

This technique can create some very good fractals, but generating them is a slow process. Generally, 1000 to 10,000 fault lines are required before you get acceptable results. Therefore, the fractal cannot be done in real time! However, for offline processing, this fractal is very easy to implement and does not suffer from the same aliasing effects as subdivision fractals such as the plasma.

The fault fractal is one of the few fractals that work on a sphere. The lines become great circles on the sphere that split the sphere into two hemispheres. Then, each hemisphere is moved slightly on their common plane.

Fault fractals have no control parameters, other than the sequence of random numbers used, so it is difficult to generate them artistically.

## Fractal Brownian Motion

The methods given so far are rather *ad hoc* approaches to generating fractals. *Fractal brownian motion* (FBM) fractals have a more rigorous mathematical background and have very good mathematical properties, which makes them simple to work with.

An FBM fractal is a combination of noise functions, but each noise function is special. The key to this technique is understanding the different types of noise.

First, we have white noise, which is completely random. The static on a television not picking up a signal is akin to white noise. The heights in white noise change wildly, and are not related to the heights nearby.

Second, we have pink noise, which has a limit on how much its heights change from one point to another.

In computer graphics, when the term *noise* is used it usually means pink noise unless otherwise specified. Ken Perlin was the first to use pink noise in computer graphics, when he wrote his now-famous noise() function (known as Perlin Noise). He was also the first graphics programmer to win an Academy Award—for the aforementioned function. (I look forward to winning my Oscar for best call to fopen()!)

While we usually think of noise as a 1D function (e.g., sound) or a 2D function (e.g., a height-map), it can be generated in 3D, 4D, and even higher dimensions. This can be useful when one wishes to introduce a time component to an animating texture (which can simulate fire) or to an animating 3D density function (which can simulate boiling clouds).

To create pink noise, you take a regular grid (or higher-dimension array) and store random values in each cell. The fractal is then generated at every point on the surface by interpolating between these values. The defining feature of any such noise function is then the *frequency*, which is the inverse of distance between the grid points. The higher the frequency, the closer the pink noise gets to white noise.

Once you have created pink noise of various frequencies, it is easy to create an FBM fractal by mixing the heights returned by the noise function. The simplest case is just adding the noise functions together, but they can be multiplied or combined in other ways.

The FBM has a few more parameters than noise alone. In addition to the frequency, there are the *octave*, *amplitude*, and *H* parameters. The octave variable sets how many noises are added together. The amplitude is a variable that adjusts the overall height of the noise. H controls how much the amplitude changes over each octave. The frequency of each slice of noise must be chosen as well. To understand the effects of frequency on an FBM, we can consider fractal landscapes. When adding noises together, the lower frequency noise is responsible for hills and mountains, and the higher frequency noise creates roughness. This gives a tremendous amount of control over exactly how the fractal looks. In addition, it is possible to make the amount that you change the frequency differ from section to section of the noise function. This makes it possible to have some areas of your fractal rougher than others, so you could have a landscape that is rougher in the mountains, and smoother in the deserts.

It is also possible to multiply the noise functions instead of adding them together. Doing this will create more variety in your fractal. Multiplying noises together has the effect of damping out the lower parts of the noise, and accentuating the higher parts. If the resulting heightmap is used for a landscape, it will have planes, mountains, and foothills—if you just add the noises together, the landscape will have a uniform look. It is necessary to be careful when multiplying noises together, as it is easy to go to extremes and dampen and accentuate things too much, leaving just a flat plane with spikes in it!

## Implementation

Now that we have examined the theory of creating FBMs, the next step is to implement a noise generator. To generate noise, a source of random numbers to be interpolated has to be generated. The following is the code for my random number generator:

```
float random (int x , int y)
{
    int n=x+y*57;
    n=(n<<13)^n;
    float ret;
    ret= (1 - ( (n * (n * n * 19417 + 189851) + 4967243) & 4945007) /
3354521.0);
    return ret;
}
```

This function just multiplies, adds, and subtracts prime numbers from your numbers, and returns a pseudo-random value between −1 and 1. This is not the only way to generate random numbers, of course. Some systems use pregenerated random numbers. That method gives a small performance improvement, but then you must store large amounts of random numbers. With this method, all that needs to be remembered is the seed to regenerate the random numbers that were used.

Next, we need a function that interpolates these random values. A simple lerping function would work, and it would be fast, but it does not provide very good results. While some use spline interpolation, this is the slowest and most complex option. This article uses cosine interpolation to build our noise function. This has good quality, it is fast, and it is easy to understand. Note that this is not the only noise function possible, and it differs from Perlin Noise (which is much more complex). For a more complete list, see [Ebert98].

Here is some code for cosine interpolation:

```
double cosineinterpolation(double number1,double number2,double x)
{
    double ft;
    double f;
    double ret;
    ft = x * 3.1415927;
    f = (1 - cos(ft)) * .5;
    ret=number1*(1-f) + number2*f;
    return ret;
}
```

Now that there is a random number function, and an interpolation function, it is possible to create a noise function by creating random numbers and interpolating them.

```
float noise(float x, float y)
{
    int xinteger=x;
    float fractionx=x-xinteger;
    int yinteger=y;
    float fractiony=y-yinteger;
    float v1,v2,v3,v4,i1,i2;
    float ret;
    v1= randomnumber (xinteger, yinteger);
    v2= randomnumber (xinteger + 1, yinteger);
    v3= randomnumber (xinteger, yinteger + 1);
    v4= randomnumber (xinteger + 1, yinteger + 1);
    i1= cosineinterpolation (v1,v2,fractionx);
    i2= cosineinterpolation (v3,v4,fractionx);
    ret= cosineinterpolation (i1,i2,fractiony);
    return ret;
}
```

The preceding function takes two variables. Normally, the function is called for each point on the heightmap or grid in which you wish to store the results. Note that this is two-dimensional noise.

In some cases, it is better to smooth the noise. Smoothing reduces the frequency of your noise, and makes it look less square. It is pointless to smooth 1D noise, as the same effect is achieved by just reducing the frequency. If you want to smooth your noise, call smoothrandom instead of randomnumber in the noise function.

```
float smoothrandom(int x,int y)
{
    float corners=(randomnumber(x-1,y-1)+randomnumber(x+1,y-
1)+randomnumber(x-1,y+1)+randomnumber(x+1,y+1))/16;
    float sides   = (randomnumber(x-1, y)+randomnumber(x+1,
y)+randomnumber(x, y-1)+randomnumber(x, y+1) ) / 8;
```

```
float center  =  randomnumber(x, y) / 4;
float ret=corners+sides+center;
return ret;
}
```

This is equivalent to doing integration on the nine points around the center point.

After a noise function has been constructed, it is quite easy to create an FBM. This is how it is done:

```
float FBM(float x, float y, float octaves, float amplitude, float
frequency, float h)
{
    float ret=0;

    for(int i=0;i<(octaves-1);i++)
    {
        ret +=( noise (x* frequency, y* frequency)* amplitude);
        amplitude*=h;
    }
    return ret;
}
```

While the way the values change over each octave in this noise may work fine in many cases, sometimes it may be useful to change them. You can change the amount the frequency and amplitude change over each octave. You can even skip octaves. This control is another advantage to using FBMs (Figure 2.8.2).

A slight variation on FBMs are *multifractals*. Multifractals are like FBMs, except that instead of adding noise, noise is multiplied together. Here is how they are made:

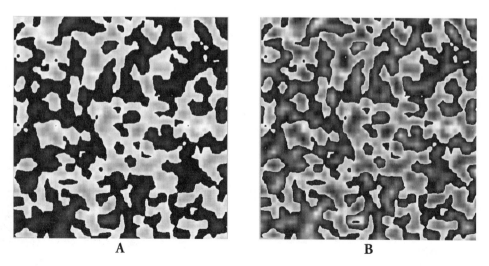

| A | B |

**FIGURE 2.8.2** *A) An FBM of just a few octaves. B) The same FBM after several more octaves.*

```
float Multifractal(float x, float y, float octaves, float amplitude,
float frequency, float h, float offset)
{
    float ret=1;

    for(int i=0;i<(octaves-1);i++)
    {
        ret *=(offset)*( noise (x* frequency, y* frequency)*
amplitude);
        amplitude*=h;
    }
    return ret;
}
```

The offset variable gives some control over the multiplication of the noise. You will notice that the resulting fractal has different kinds of hills and mountains, as well as planes.

## Using FBM

Let's learn how to make clouds with FBMs.

### Clouds

Clouds are quite easy to make with FBMs. You generate an FBM, then you interpret all the heights over zero as white, and assign them an alpha value greater than zero. To all heights lower than zero, assign an alpha value of zero. Map this texture to a quad or sphere, colored the way the sky would be at the time of day being modeled. Figure 2.8.3 shows some example cloud textures. See clouds.cpp for more details.

The example program uses OpenGL to map this texture to a quad. While it looks less realistic on a quad than on a sphere, it demonstrates the theory.

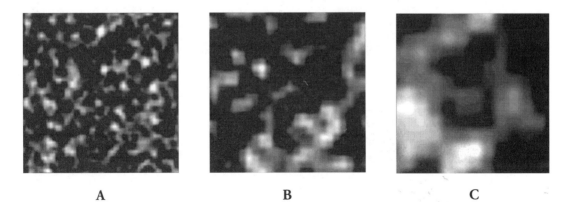

A                              B                              C

**FIGURE 2.8.3** *(A–C) Clouds generated with FBMs of decreasing frequency.*

## Landscapes

FBMs are also useful for creating landscapes; in fact, FBMs can create excellent landscapes. Just interpret the heightmap as heights for the landscape (hence, the name!). To render it, create a flat plane out of triangles, and at each triangle vertex, use a height from the heightmap (Figures 2.8.4 and 2.8.5). See landscape2.cpp for the complete listing.

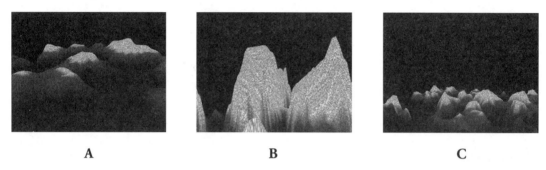

A                                    B                                    C

**FIGURE 2.8.4** *Various fractal heightmaps: the ground texture is a height-frequency FBM colored by height. A) Generated with a small frequency, small octave, and small amplitude. B) The same landscape with a much higher amplitude. C) Generated with a high frequency.*

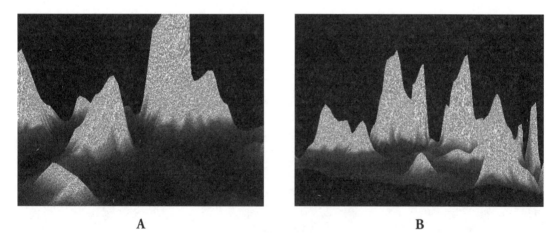

A                                                        B

**FIGURE 2.8.5** *Two multifractal landscapes. Note how there are valleys, plains, hills, and tall mountains all in the same landscape.*

## References

[Ebert98]. David S. Ebert, et al. Texturing and Modeling. San Diego: Academic Press, 1998.

# ARTIFICIAL INTELLIGENCE

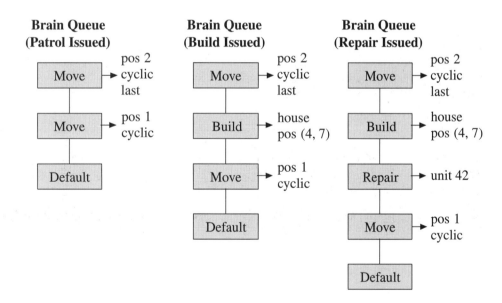

**Brain Queue (Patrol Issued)**

Move → pos 2 cyclic last

Move → pos 1 cyclic

Default

**Brain Queue (Build Issued)**

Move → pos 2 cyclic last

Build → house pos (4, 7)

Move → pos 1 cyclic

Default

**Brain Queue (Repair Issued)**

Move → pos 2 cyclic last

Build → house pos (4, 7)

Repair → unit 42

Move → pos 1 cyclic

Default

# Introduction

## *Steve Rabin, Nintendo of America*

steve_rabin@hotmail.com

**W**elcome to the AI section of *Game Programming Gems 2*! With the success of the first book, including the great reviews of the AI section in particular, this edition has a lot to live up to. Fortunately, the following gems are truly innovative and are testaments to the experience, wisdom, and hard work of each author. These are practical AI techniques that can be immediately applied to almost any game in development.

Although 11 different authors contributed to this section, no article stands by itself. Many of the gems build on each other, while several others follow up on concepts and techniques presented in the first *Game Programming Gems* book. Ideas are woven throughout the section and it really pays off to read each and every gem. The layout and organization of the section can be seen in Figure 3.I.1.

For many years, there was great excitement in the game community to experiment with advanced AI that grew from academic research, such as genetic algorithms, neural networks, and other exotic techniques. Since then, the pendulum has swung in

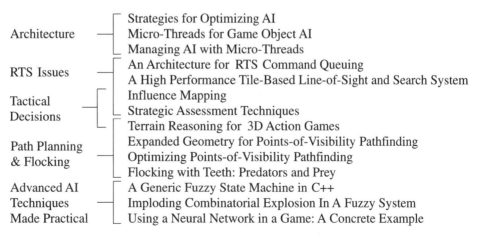

Architecture
- Strategies for Optimizing AI
- Micro-Threads for Game Object AI
- Managing AI with Micro-Threads

RTS Issues
- An Architecture for RTS Command Queuing
- A High Performance Tile-Based Line-of-Sight and Search System

Tactical Decisions
- Influence Mapping
- Strategic Assessment Techniques
- Terrain Reasoning for 3D Action Games

Path Planning & Flocking
- Expanded Geometry for Points-of-Visibility Pathfinding
- Optimizing Points-of-Visibility Pathfinding
- Flocking with Teeth: Predators and Prey

Advanced AI Techniques Made Practical
- A Generic Fuzzy State Machine in C++
- Imploding Combinatorial Explosion In A Fuzzy System
- Using a Neural Network in a Game: A Concrete Example

**FIGURE 3.I.1** *The organization of this section.*

the other direction, and most AI game programmers are now sticking with simpler, proven techniques that consistently work well.

Interestingly, this concentration on proven methods has driven AI game programmers to make their own leaps and bounds, independent of the academic community. This is not really surprising since the two groups have very different goals. Academic research is process oriented, concerned with how a problem is solved, while game programming is results oriented, concerned with the appearance of the final product. Because of this, game programming is often an inexact science that makes calculated concessions for the greater purpose of the game. Conversely, academic research strives to never cheat or compromise a solution, since the algorithm is the real prize. Neither one is "correct"; each group simply has different goals and motivations.

A good example of this disparity between the two groups is found in the A* search algorithm. This algorithm is frequently used in games to find a path for a character through a complicated environment. The academic community is interested in A* because it has the ability to find *the shortest* path with good computational speed. However, with a small modification to the heuristic, A* can be sped up significantly. Unfortunately, this modification results in paths that aren't guaranteed to be the shortest, yet still can be of excellent quality.

Since the shortest path is no longer guaranteed, academic researchers refer to this modified heuristic as *inadmissible*. This is a strong word that shows the disdain for close, but not perfect, results. Consequently, there is little academic investigation into using inadmissible heuristics. Yet, in games, this inadmissible heuristic is *exactly* what you want to use, since it's so much faster and gives almost identical results. A thorough discussion of this technique was described in the first *Game Programming Gems* book, in the article "A* Speed Optimizations."

As you can see, it's up to game programmers to push their field forward and make advancements that are in their own interest. It's wonderful when academic research can assist in the creation of AI systems in games, but game programmers need to do their own research as well. Thus, the need for books such as this one becomes that much clearer. On that note, journey forward and discover all of the great techniques, and useful *game development research*, that this book has to offer.

# 3.1

## Strategies for Optimizing AI

### *Steve Rabin, Nintendo of America*

steve_rabin@hotmail.com

Sophisticated AI requires significant computational power. The problem worsens when dozens or hundreds of autonomous agents must intelligently roam the world simultaneously. Yet this isn't your average optimization problem. Many domains within games deal with scalability, but AI has the extra wrinkle of supporting imaginary parallelism. This parallelism comes from each AI agent running its own piece of code with the illusion of all agents thinking at the same time.

As it turns out, parallelism is one of AI's greatest exploitable assets. This parallelism, along with other unique attributes of AI agents, can be manipulated to optimize most AI systems. As you read through the following optimization strategies, keep in mind a mental picture of hundreds of AI agents all having unique actions and agendas. When you consider this magnitude, it's more obvious why certain strategies make sense.

### Strategy #1: Use Event-Driven Behavior Rather than Polling

Ideally, autonomous agents should continuously monitor their world and react accordingly. Every frame they might poll the world for events or objects to which they should respond. This means everything from collision detection to noticing interesting things to look at. The problem with this approach is that it promotes an enormous amount of redundant computation. As a rule, individual polling is usually wasteful.

The alternative is to employ event-driven techniques whenever possible. For example, in a baseball game when the ball is initially hit, the ball could simply tell the fielders that it was hit. This is extremely more efficient than each fielder polling the situation to detect when the batter has hit the ball. Granted, this is an obvious use of event-driven behavior, but it still shows the magnitude of processing that can be saved by using an event-driven strategy.

Another example would be of an arrow flying through a battlefield. Normally, the arrow would be checking for collisions with characters. If the arrow strikes a character, it would then notify the character of the collision as well as the location. The character could then react appropriately, responding to where the arrow pierced him. While this is starting to be event driven, nothing too spectacular has happened yet.

Now consider if you wanted the character to anticipate the impact of the arrow, or even try to avoid the arrow. A polling solution would involve each character intermittently looking for nearby arrows. Conversely, the event-driven solution is to have the arrow predict future collisions, as part of its collision detection routine, and notify any characters that might get hit in the future. The characters can then do whatever they want with that info, including running away, ducking, or bracing for impact. The result is very deep behavior without the need to poll for every contingency.

A good example of an event-driven AI system can be found in the first *Game Programming Gems* book, in the article "Designing a General Robust AI Engine" [Rabin00a].

## Strategy #2: Reduce Redundant Calculations

The goal of this strategy is to reduce redundant calculations by sharing the results between several AI agents. Many times agents will individually recalculate the same information, even though they could have calculated it once and shared it. This is an easy optimization that can often save many cycles.

A simple example of this strategy is apparent in collision detection. If every object were to run its own simplistic collision checks, there would be $O(n^2-n)$ tests, or 9900 calculations for 100 objects. However, since a given pair of objects only needs to be tested once, an optimized collision algorithm would have only $O((n^2-n)/2)$ tests, or 4950 calculations for 100 objects. The savings come directly from eliminating redundant work.

Another example of reducing redundant computation is found in pathfinding. When a player grabs a bunch of units and orders them to all move to the other side of the map, each unit might expect to separately find a path. Instead, a faster and simpler solution is to let one unit find a path and then let the other units roughly follow him. This avoids the virtually identical path requests that would have normally taken place, thus saving a considerable number of cycles.

## Strategy #3: Centralize Cooperation with Managers

Agents often need to cooperate with other agents, whether they comprise a crack commando squad or a sports team. Cooperation among multiple agents can be made faster and simpler by having a manager entity make the complex decisions. These complex decisions usually determine each member's role, while the agent is left to autonomously execute that role.

For example, imagine a SWAT team that is infiltrating a building. The team needs to cooperate very tightly in order to secure each position and move on. If members had to determine their actions individually, it would be quite difficult to coordinate and would require an enormous amount of inter-member communication. Instead, a manager entity can plan out each step of the operation and instruct individual members as to their immediate goal. This simpler approach results in a more robust and efficient design. An example of how a manager can simplify the game of baseball can be found in [Rabin98].

It's important to remember that with this strategy, managers don't need to be represented on-screen. Usually these managers are just fictitious entities that organize the complex cooperation among AI agents. You can even imagine transient managers that dynamically form around groups of monsters that have banded together. If that group then divides or combines with another group, each newly formed group can be assigned its own manager. With these monster managers, individual monsters can be coordinated so that optimal targets are chosen and everyone doesn't mob the same enemy.

## Strategy #4: Run the AI Less Often

Rarely do AI agents need to run through all of their decision-making routines every frame. Many times, agents can run portions of code every couple frames or even every couple seconds. Since real creatures have reaction times, it's not unreasonable for AI agents to have less than lightning reflexes. This results in a handy way to cut down on AI processing.

Using an agent architecture that supports arbitrary timer callbacks is a great way to implement this strategy. If an agent can easily set a timer and be notified when it expires, flexible systems can be built that are easily tunable. The first *Game Programming Gems* book has a gem "Designing a General Robust AI Engine" [Rabin00a] that discusses a timer messaging system that is well suited for this strategy.

One problem with this strategy is the possibility of AI processing peaks. This would occur if a majority of the agents became synchronous in their callback executions, simultaneously executing every $N$ seconds or so. The simple solution is to randomize the window of processing for each agent. For example, an agent might execute his invader-detection code every 0.3 to 0.5 seconds, randomly picking a new delay within that window after each callback. This random window of execution virtually guarantees that agents won't become synchronous with each other, accidentally causing a processing peak.

## Strategy #5: Distribute the Processing over Several Frames

Typically, A* pathfinding is one of the dreaded algorithms that can eat up CPU cycles. Since situations rarely change much over a couple frames, it's possible for an agent to spread a pathfinding calculation over several frames. By saving the results from each frame and resuming the next frame, a path can be found over 2–4 frames. This results in a lower per-frame processing load. Any algorithm that can take an unspecified amount of time can be broken up in this manner.

This strategy can be implemented as a special case in a module, like a pathfinding module, or it can be part of an AI operating system. The next gem in this book, "Micro-Threads for Game Object AI," by Bruce Dawson, explains how you can implement a micro-thread strategy in order to minimize AI loads. This particular architecture makes it easier for an AI agent to spread calculations over many frames and can help keep processing loads under control. Following Bruce's gem is "Managing AI with Micro-Threads" by Simon Carter, which describes how to best structure your AI within a micro-thread environment.

## Strategy #6: Employ Level-of-Detail AI

The level-of-detail (LOD) concept is a clever optimization that has many uses outside of graphics. Currently, most game engines use graphical LODs in order to quickly render objects that are far off in the distance. The idea is to use a low polygon count model when an object is far from the camera, and use a high polygon count model when it's close. The effect is that the rendering time is greatly sped up with little or no visual loss to the game. An important realization is that the level-of-detail concept can also be applied to other game programming areas, such as AI.

Practically, the level-of-detail technique for AI comes down to three strategies. The first is to vary the processing frequency of an agent by how close it is to the camera, player, or action. The second is to vary the complexity of an agent's algorithms based on relevance, by doing things such as eliminating precise pathfinding when an agent is offscreen. The third is to represent multiple agents in a single simulation algorithm as their individual importance decreases to the player. An extreme example of the third variation is to simulate the outcome of a far-off military battle with a simple formula, while battles close to the player might simulate every single soldier and bullet.

Level-of-detail is all about trying to get away with less work without the player noticing. If the player can tell something is wrong or different, then the optimization needs to be scaled back, just as it would be with graphical LODs that visually "pop."

## Strategy #7: Solve Only Part of the Problem

When given a large problem, sometimes it suffices to only solve the part that you need right away. The rest of the solution can then be computed in the future when you actually need it. It might even be the case that the situation changes enough that the rest of the problem is irrelevant and never needs to be computed anyway. This strategy is extremely similar to *lazy evaluation*.

The best example of this strategy in action is probably hierarchical pathfinding. In hierarchical pathfinding, the path is found in two phases. First, the character's high-level, room-to-room path to the goal is calculated. Once that is computed, the micro path to get the character to the next room, toward the goal, can be computed as each new room is entered. If for some reason the character gets redirected, the remaining path is thrown away and never computed. This on-demand pathfinding results in a tremendous speed improvement that is critical for games that have large areas to navigate. See [Rabin00b] for a complete description of hierarchical pathfinding issues and implementation.

## Strategy #8: Do the Hard Work Offline

Sometimes, a problem is so difficult that you don't even have the CPU time to solve it. In the early years of game development, problems such as finding the cosine of an angle simply took too much time. This resulted in programmers precalculating cosine for a range of values and simply indexing a look-up table to get the answer. While today that technique is no longer relevant, the basic strategy is as useful as ever.

Current incarnations of this strategy can be found in precomputed BSPs, preanalyzed terrains, and carefully trained neural nets. Later, you'll find three gems that exemplify this strategy: "Terrain Reasoning for 3D Action Games" by William van der Sterren, "Expanded Geometry for Points-of-Visibility Pathfinding" by Thomas Young, and "Using a Neural Network in a Game: A Concrete Example" by John Manslow. Each gem exploits the bountiful offline time that can be used to analyze, refine, and store specialized information that can then be used at a moment's notice during runtime. This is surely one of the most powerful optimization strategies, since it can cram thousands of hours of wisdom into a few kilobytes of data and a trivial amount of CPU cycles.

## Strategy #9: Use Emergent Behavior to Avoid Scripting

This strategy has the opposite problem of the last strategy. Often, you don't have enough offline time to create the behavior or scripts for hundreds of background AI entities that might populate your world. The solution is to come up with very simple rules that result in intelligent, emergent behavior. Later in this book, the gem "Flocking with Teeth: Predators and Prey" by Steven Woodcock details how flocking can help create wonderfully complex behavior that is unscripted, yet interesting and lifelike.

Unfortunately, this strategy is a double-edged sword. While it cuts down on the amount of offline work, it has the potential for unintended consequences. In his gem, Steven describes a world full of creatures that feed off each other. This sometimes results in the predators completely wiping out the population of prey, causing the entire ecosystem to collapse. By its very nature, emergent behavior is unpredictable and can be hard to thoroughly test. Consequently, it might be best suited for noncritical AI entities that aren't pivotal to the progress or completion of a game, such as background wildlife.

## Strategy #10: Amortize Query Costs with Continuous Bookkeeping

Sometimes a lot of data needs to be collected in order to make an intelligent decision. If that data is gathered right when it's needed, then it might take an unacceptable amount of time to calculate. The solution is to continuously update a data structure with this data *as it changes*. Although more time and memory is spent keeping track of data, it's amortized over many, many frames. The result is that a simple query of the data no longer causes a hit to the frame rate.

Influence maps are an excellent example of this strategy at work. Influence maps are used to analyze general strategic patterns, and in doing so, speed up AI decisions. As a game progresses, the units keep their info updated within the influence map as they move, evolve, or disappear. This way, when a general strategic AI wants to analyze the world, the data is already available. This results in quick queries to the influence map without any significant speed hit. Further in this book, you'll find the gem "Influence Mapping" by Paul Tozour that explains influence maps and has some unique insights into making them even more powerful.

This strategy is also key in a later gem written by Matt Pritchard entitled "A High-Performance Tile-Based Line-of-Sight and Search System." In his gem, Matt uses this strategy of continuous bookkeeping to maintain the line-of-sight data for hundreds of agents in real time, which is not a simple task. Many RTS games fail to achieve this frame-by-frame accuracy for their fog-of-war, mini-map, and general intelligence; however, Matt fully explains the techniques and strategies that give the *Age of Empires* series that extra edge.

## Strategy #11: Rethink the Problem

Michael Abrash is well known as an optimization guru within the game development community, as well as one of the leading figures in graphics research. On many occasions, both in presentations and in print [Abrash00], he has stressed the importance of rethinking a problem in order to speed up code by orders of magnitude. His main premise is that optimizing specific sections of code will always result in marginal gains. The real way to optimize is to attack the problem from a slightly different perspective, with an alternate approach or algorithm.

This strategy is well illustrated later in the book by Michael Zarozinski in his gem "Imploding Combinatorial Explosion in Fuzzy Systems." In this gem, Michael explains an alternate algorithm, called the Combs Method, which completely circumvents the exponential nature of traditional fuzzy systems. Although the method doesn't produce identical results, the output is very comparable and sufficient for most purposes. In addition, it simplifies fuzzy logic implementation and planning to the point where anyone can *easily* incorporate it into a game.

Rethinking a problem from a different perspective is probably the best advice anyone can give for optimization. It's the seed from which every other optimization grows. Only through the process of redefining or abstracting the problem, creating an analogy, or changing your perspective, can you make the leaps that will allow you to truly optimize your code. While leaps don't come very often, you can learn from other's leaps by simply reading and learning as much as you can about how they solved similar problems.

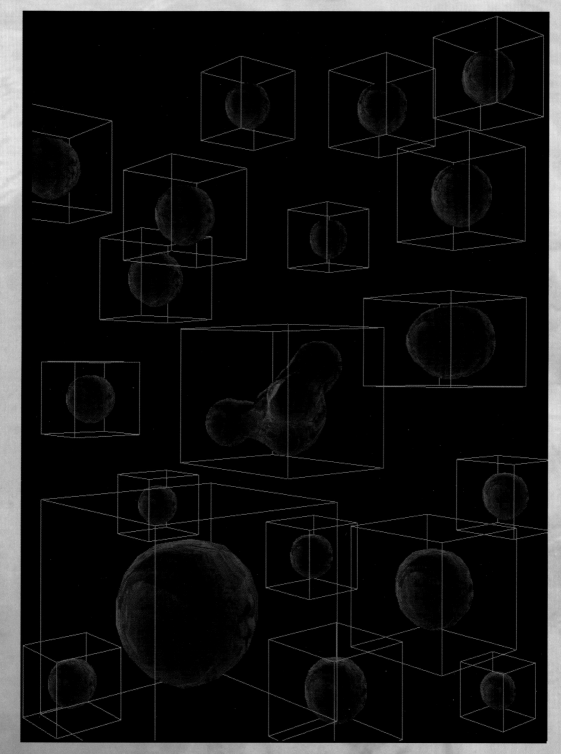

**Figure 1** An example of Axis-Aligned Bounding Boxes (AABBs) as used in recursive dimensional clustering. Courtesy Steve Rabin.

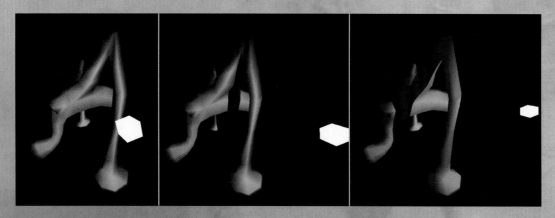

**FIGURE 3** The segmented model, rendered with shadows, from three different angles. Courtesy Alex Vlachos, David Gosselin, and Jason L. Mitchell.

**FIGURE 4**  A gouraud-shaded duck (left), inked duck with faces colored as background (center), and a flat-shaded duck using a painting algorithm (right). Courtesy Carl S. Marshall.

**FIGURE 5**
In this image the duck model has been shaded with a cartoon rendering technique. Courtesy Adam Lake.

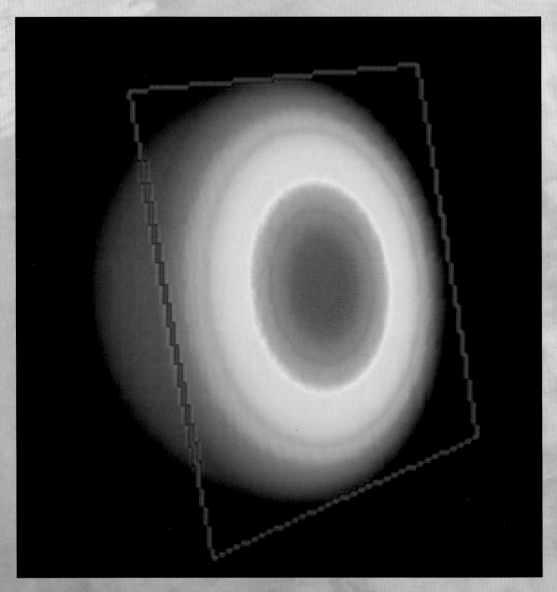

**FIGURE 6** A cross-section of a 3D lightmap. The actual lightmap is monochrome; this picture uses color-coding to clearly show the map fall-off. Red is highest intensity and blue is least. Courtesy Dan Ginsburg and David Gosselin.

**FIGURE 7** An example of a base texture map modulated by a 3D lightmap. Courtesy Dan Ginsburg and David Gosselin.

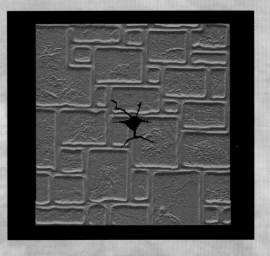

**FIGURE 8** A dot3 bump map texture generated from a heigthfield using the Sobel filter. Courtesy Dan Ginsburg and David Gosselin.

**FIGURE 9** An example of a base texture map modulated by a 3D lightmap and dot3 bump mapping. Courtesy Dan Ginsburg and David Gosselin.

**FIGURE 10** An example of a base texture map modulated by a 3D lightmap, dot3 bump mapping, and a cubemap normalizer. Courtesy Dan Ginsburg and David Gosselin.

**FIGURE 11** An example of dynamic procedural clouds. Courtesy Kim Pallister.

**FIGURE 12** A demonstration of lens flare texture masking in a tree grove. Courtesy Chris Maughan.

**FIGURE 13** Edge detection and image processing. A) is the original image. B) is the result of an edge detection in programmable pixel hardware. C) shows a 50% blend of a and b. D) is the original minus the difference between the original and a blur of the original. Courtesy Greg James.

## Conclusion

It takes a slightly different perspective to optimize the problems that face AI systems. Don't be afraid to scan the list of strategies the next time you're faced with trying to speed up a seemingly unoptimizable system. With so many ways to view a problem, it helps to refresh your memory and contemplate how each strategy applies to your unique situation. Here is a recap of all the strategies:

1. Use event-driven behavior rather than polling.
2. Reduce redundant calculations.
3. Centralize cooperation with managers.
4. Run the AI less often.
5. Distribute the processing over several frames.
6. Employ level-of-detail AI.
7. Solve only part of the problem.
8. Do the hard work offline.
9. Use emergent behavior to avoid scripting.
10. Amortize query costs with continuous bookkeeping.
11. Rethink the problem.

As you read the gems that follow, consider how these optimization strategies have been applied and exploited within each. While there are a wide variety of strategies, it's quite amazing how disparate problems can often be solved with the same strategy. The genius is in seeing those connections.

## References

[Abrash00] Abrash, Michael, "It's Great to Be Back! Fast Code, Game Programming, and Other Thoughts from 20 (Minus Two) Years in the Trenches," Conference Proceedings, (Game Developers Conference 2000). Text available online at www.gamasutra.com/features/20010117/abrash_01.htm. Video also available online at www.gamasutra.com/features/index_video.htm.

[Rabin98] Rabin, Steve, "Making the Play: Team Cooperation in Microsoft Baseball 3D," Conference Proceedings, (Computer Game Developers Conference 1998).

[Rabin00a] Rabin, Steve, "Designing a General Robust AI Engine," *Game Programming Gems*, Charles River Media, 2000: pp. 221–236.

[Rabin00b] Rabin, Steve, "A* Aesthetic Optimizations," and "A* Speed Optimizations," *Game Programming Gems*, Charles River Media, 2000.

# 3.2

## Micro-Threads for Game Object AI

### Bruce Dawson, Humongous Entertainment
bruced@humongous.com

**W**riting good AI can be very difficult. It took many years and millions of dollars before a computer program was able to beat the world's best chess players. Game AI doesn't have to play championship chess, but it does have to update many game objects per frame, in very little CPU time.

Adding to the essential complexity of writing good AI is the "accidental complexity" [Brooks95] introduced by the common methods of implementing AI for game objects.

As an example of accidental complexity in most games' code, let's say we want to make a "Janitor" object that wanders around our world cleaning up. This janitor's routine is very simple: choose a target, move toward it, dispose of it when you get close enough, and then repeat. Of course, since this is for a game we want to do it in small steps, one per update loop. Some C++ style pseudocode—without accidental complexity—might look like this:

```
void Janitor::Process() {
    while (true) {
        GameObject* target = GetNewTarget(this);
        while (Distance(this, target) > k_collisionTolerance) {
            WaitOneFrame();
            MoveABitTowards(this, target);
        }
        Dispose(this, target);
    }
}
```

However, that doesn't work very well in a game because it doesn't share the CPU with other entities in the world. Therefore, the traditional way to implement such a janitor object would be as a Janitor class with a virtual function that is called every frame, like this code, taken from the sample on the CD:

ON THE CD

```
Janitor::Janitor()
    : m_target(0), m_state(k_NeedsGoal) {
}
```

```
void Janitor::ProcessFrame(){
    switch (m_state) {
        case k_NeedsGoal:
            m_target = GetNewTarget(this);
            if (Distance(this, m_target) <= k_collisionTolerance) {
                m_state = k_DisposeObject;
                ProcessFrame();    // Call ourselves.
                return;
            }
            m_state = k_MovingTowardsTarget;
            // Intentionally missing break.
        case k_MovingTowardsTarget:
            MoveABitTowards(this, m_target);
            if (Distance(this, m_target) > k_collisionTolerance)
                break;
            else
                m_state = k_DisposeObject;
                // Intentionally missing break.
        case k_DisposeObject:
            Dispose(this, m_target);
            m_state = k_NeedsGoal;
            break;
    }
}
```

What a mess! Our AI code has gone from simple and elegant to a huge and unreadable state machine. Modifying the second version of the code will clearly be much more complex, and the state machine cannot be reused with another class, because it requires m_state and m_target. That's accidental, or nonessential complexity.

Central to the problem is that all of the state now has to be stored in the object. This is a profound change. In the first version of the code the "target" variable was declared as a local variable. It was created exactly when it was needed and fell out of scope when its job was done. Now, the target has to be recorded in the object. We also added another member variable to our Janitor class, m_state. Where did this variable come from? Why wasn't it needed in our first version of this routine?

In the first version of Process(), the state is implied by which line of code is executing. It's stored in the program counter. The program counter keeps track of the current state, the stack pointer points at the current set of variables, and life is easy. When we implement AI with callbacks, we have to simulate the instruction pointer and stack pointer and the benefits they bring us.

## A Simpler Method

At this point, it should seem obvious that using callbacks for our entity code is messy. Therefore, how do we turn our simple version of the janitor code into something that actually works? To do that we need to let the rest of the game loop and the other objects have some CPU time, and we need to synchronize the objects so they do exactly one update per frame. To do this we need to put each game entity into a separate thread and have the WaitOneFrame() function switch to the next thread. With such a system, the pseudocode of the first example can be compiled and run perfectly!

We could start an OS thread for each object. This lets each thread pretend that it owns the CPU, while the operating system manages the magic of swapping things around to change the CPU state. The WaitOneFrame() function would do the necessary work to switch to the next thread—see the sample code for details.

This sort of strategy works well for Web servers and other multi-threaded apps, but it's a poor option for games. Many games run in environments where there is no operating system support for threads—or no operating system at all. Even if there are threads, they are frequently too expensive for game purposes. Switching threads on Win32 takes thousands of machine cycles, and each thread uses up a minimum of 8 KB of memory—4 KB for the Thread Information Block and 4 KB for the smallest possible stack. Both allocations take 4 KB because, in order to keep threads independent and allow for stack growth, their allocations are put on separate memory management pages, and this forces a 4K granularity.

On Win32, there is also the option of using fibers—cooperatively multitasking threads. Fibers are a bit better for our purposes because the context switching is much faster and more easily controlled. However, the stack still takes at least 4 KB, and fibers don't work at all on Win95. On Win98, each fiber stack takes a minimum of 8 KB, making its memory footprint as bad as for regular threads.

## Micro-Threads

Let's step back and think about precisely what we want. We want to be able to write AI or other object-updating code that can pretend that it owns the CPU. After executing the code for one time slice update, we want to be able to call WaitOneFrame() to give the rest of the game some CPU time. When WaitOneFrame() returns we want execution to continue where it left off, one time slice later. We want this to be fast, and we want minimal memory overhead.

What do we have to do to switch from one thread of execution to another? The instruction pointer in a CPU is a register that points at the next instruction to be executed. If we were to write some code that changed the instruction pointer, we could easily jump from one thread to another. Changing the instruction pointer is easy—CPUs have many instructions for doing that. In a few lines of assembly language you can get the current instruction pointer, store it somewhere, and then jump to a new location. This will give the desired effect of jumping back into a previously running piece of code—but if that's all you do, you will be terribly disappointed.

The instruction pointer is not the only piece of state in a CPU and it is not the only thing that determines what function you are executing. Another important piece of the puzzle is the stack pointer. All of the local variables of a function are stored relative to the stack pointer (or the stack frame pointer, but let's ignore that for now). In fact, the stack pointer is even more important than the instruction pointer, because function return addresses—instruction pointers—are stored on the stack.

Let's imagine that we've written a piece of code that pushes the instruction pointer onto the stack, then changes the stack pointer, and then pops the instruction pointer off of the stack. Since the new instruction pointer is popped off of the *new* stack, changing the stack pointer has also changed the instruction pointer—*voilà*, we've changed threads. In fact, since calling a function pushes the instruction pointer, and returning from a function pops the instruction pointer, our thread switching function is just two instructions—move a new value into the stack pointer, then return!

Okay, it's not quite that easy. First, CPUs have more registers than just the stack pointer and the instruction pointer. No problem—we'll deal with them the same way. Push them all onto the stack at the beginning, change the stack pointer, and then pop them all at the end. It *just works*. The exact details vary from CPU to CPU, but any CPU that has enough flexibility in where you point the stack pointer can implement this system. Micro-threads have even been implemented on a Nintendo GameBoy! On an x86 CPU, a complete thread switch can be implemented in 12 assembly language instructions. In the micro-thread sample programs on the CD, that is all the assembly language that is used. Here is a sample SwapThreads() routine:

ON THE CD

```
SwapThreads
    // Preserve all of the registers that VC++ insists we preserve.
    // VC++ does not care if we preserve eax, ecx and edx.
    push    ebx
    push    ebp
    push    esi
    push    edi

    // Swap stack pointers
    mov     eax, esp
    mov     esp, s_globalStackPointer
    mov     s_globalStackPointer, eax

    // Restore all of the registers that we previously preserved.
    // Yes, they're coming off of a different stack - they were
    // carefully placed there earlier.
    pop     edi
    pop     esi
    pop     ebp
    pop     ebx
    ret
```

Is that all there is to it? That depends. On some CPUs, you may have to preserve floating-point or multimedia registers as well. On the Intel architecture, because of the, umm, *peculiar* arrangement of the floating-point registers, it is impractical for compilers to preserve them over function calls, so compilers always make sure that all floating-point numbers have been written to memory before calling any function, including your WaitOneFrame() function. You also don't need to preserve all of the integer registers, because compilers don't expect all of them to be preserved over function calls—consult your compiler documentation for details.

## Stack Management

But what, exactly, are we assigning to our stack pointer when we change threads? When we start an OS thread we are implicitly allocating and initializing a stack—now we have to do it ourselves. On Win32, the operating system allocates a 4 KB page of memory for each stack. It also reserves some extra address space—1 MB by default—so that the stack can grow. If you declare a large array in a function, or have deeply recursive function calls, the operating system automatically allocates more 4 KB pages of memory. If you go beyond the address space that was reserved, it stops you with a page fault.

We're trying to avoid allocating 4 KB of stack for each thread, so how much should we allocate? We might decide that we want to allocate no more than 100 bytes of stack per object; after all, we want to have hundreds or thousands of these things. We could use malloc or new to allocate 100-byte blocks and then, with a bit of careful array initialization, set up this stack so that we can switch to it with SwapThreads(). This method will work, but it's rather dangerous. If you write any game entity code that uses a bit too much stack, terrible things will happen. You will corrupt whatever block of memory comes before the thread stack, and your game will crash. If you decide to use this system, be sure to put some sort of marker at the far end of the stack, and check these markers after every thread switch to see if they have been overwritten. At least that way you will know when you have trashed memory.

A slightly different implementation of micro-threads can avoid these strict stack size limits. In this variation a large stack is allocated that all micro-threads share. When a micro-thread goes to sleep, the thread manager *copies* the contents of the stack to a resizable backup buffer. This buffer only needs to be reallocated when the thread's stack size increases, so the buffer allocation time is negligible. Therefore, the only additional overhead of this method is copying the contents of the stack back and forth. Interestingly enough, this copying is virtually free, because it primes the CPU caches and prepares them for running the thread.

So far, stack copying probably doesn't seem any better than allocating a fixed stack for each thread. However, the advantage with stack copying is that the stack usage only needs to be small when you switch threads. If your AI entities need to call a complex BSP pathfinding routine, a debug print function, or some other function that uses a lot of stack, they can do this with stack copying micro-threads. The temporarily large stack usage is harmless as long as you don't call WaitOneFrame() from deep within these utility functions. With fixed-stack micro-threads you can never use large amounts of stack—not even temporarily.

This is a *huge* advantage. If your AI routines are forced to use a tiny little stack with not much depth, you may end up with AI that has a tiny little brain with not much depth.

## Complications

### Loading and Saving Games

Compilers will sometimes generate stack frames for each function, which are used for easier addressing of local variables and parameters. These stack frames are tied together in a linked list on the stack. In other words, a typical stack contains pointers to itself. Therefore, the stack image cannot be used in a different location.

Stacks also contain return addresses—pointers to code. Therefore, if you save a stack buffer to disk you cannot load it up and expect it to work if you have recompiled your code—all of the code bytes will have moved.

Even if you deal with the problems of micro-thread stacks containing pointers to themselves and to code, the stacks will contain local variables, some of which will be pointers. When you have pointers in a structure you can still save and restore the structure if you are careful, but with micro-thread stacks, you don't know where the pointers are. Careful use of C++ pointer objects can manage this problem, but it is complicated.

Therefore, loading and saving of games that use micro-thread stacks is problematic. This may restrict their usage to games that don't need to load and save, or to console machines where the exact memory layout can be restored when saving.

### Structured Exception Handling

Win32 structured exception handling is a critical part of a debugging strategy, as it ensures that detailed crash information is recorded. It is also used to implement C++ exception handling. However, if you aren't careful, structured exception handlers will not get called for exceptions that happen inside micro-threads. That's because the OS handler that walks the linked list of exception handlers (another linked list on the stack) gives up if it notices an implausible pointer, such as a stack pointer outside of the current OS thread's known stack range [Pietrek97].

This can be avoided if you locate your temporary stack somewhere in the address range of your real stack, well below what you're actually using. Remember that it has to be in a fixed location because the linked lists on the stack won't work if it moves, and you have to make sure that your main thread's stack never goes down far enough to be overwritten by the micro-thread stacks.

### OutputDebugString

ON THE CD

On Windows NT, if you call OutputDebugString() from a micro-thread when you're not running under a debugger, your program may exit, due to the structured exception handling problem mentioned earlier. This is easily fixed by placing your stack appropriately or by using the OutputDebugStringW95() function on the companion CD-ROM, which detects whether you are running under a debugger and only uses OutputDebugString() when it is safe. It also looks for DBWin32, the freely available debug output monitoring program, and talks to it directly whenever possible.

## Conclusion

Threads are a simpler method of writing AI code for many independent entities. Micro-threads let us implement our game entities using threads without the high memory or CPU cost of other threading methods. Micro-threads can be easily implemented on any CPU architecture, with very little assembly language [Keppel01].

*ON THE CD*

A sample implementation of micro-threads for Win32 is on the companion CD-ROM. Also included is a simple game that uses micro-threads, and a test application for comparing micro-threads to Fibers and OS threads.

Micro-threads have also been implemented in several scripting languages used in games, such as Lua [Lua01], SCUMM (a proprietary Lucas Arts engine also used by Humongous Entertainment), and Python [Tismer01].

A micro-thread janitor can clean up your game code.

## References

[Brooks95] Brooks, Frederick P., Jr. *The Mythical Man-Month: Essays on Software Engineering, Anniversary Edition*, Addison-Wesley, 1995.

[Keppel01] Keppel, David, "QuickThreads distribution," available online at http://www.mit.edu/afs/sipb/project/scheme/src/guide-1.3/qt/, June5, 2001.

[Lua01] "The Programming Language Lua," available online at www.tecgraf.puc-rio.br/lua/about.html, February 22, 2001.

[Pietrek97] Pietrek, Matt, "A Crash Course on the Depths of Win32 Structured Exception Handling," *Microsoft Systems Journal* (Jan 1997).

[Tismer01] Tismer, Christian, "Stackless Python," available online at www.stackless.com/, February 23, 2001.

# 3.3

# Managing AI with Micro-Threads

## Simon Carter, Big Blue Box Studios

scarter@bigbluebox.com

A s discussed in the previous gem, AI in games is generally implemented through some form of state machine. State machine architecture has a number of advantages for AI. Most notably, the system can be suspended at any particular state, a facility that is critically important for any game that intends to have more than one AI entity. However, traditional implementations of state machines tend to be messy, unintuitive, prone to bugs, difficult to debug, and hard to read. Micro-threads offer a far more elegant way of implementing state machines and can lead to a very robust and extensible AI system. This gem attempts to give an idea of how to implement such a system and take full advantage of its flexibility.

## Piece by Piece

Micro-threads allow us to code up state machines using normal, everyday programming practices. Most of the "magic" goes on in the background, leaving us free to design our AI system as elegantly as we wish, without having to pander to background architecture issues. Although this is very liberating, it can be difficult to know where to start when so many restrictions are lifted.

Good artificial intelligence in games is all about organizing what can become a very complex system into manageable chunks, and to make these "modules" as intuitive and reusable as possible. An important design decision is the granularity of this modularization. By way of example, classic state machines by necessity tend to make each individual state a module, and it is this very low-level granularity that makes the system awkward. Micro-threads allow us to choose the granularity of our modules ourselves, and choose the level that makes the most sense conceptually.

From a design standpoint, it is far better to break complex AI into units of "behavior." In this context, "behavior" is the full set of tests and actions that are used to model an entity's responses to particular stimuli; for example, being hungry, being in a fight, being scared, and so forth. The more behaviors a particular entity has, the more rich and varied its resulting AI will appear to be. An ideal design scenario would be to have the ability to attach different suites of behaviors to different entities. In addition, it would be great to be able to reuse certain common behaviors between different types of entities, and hence minimize the amount of replicated code.

A system based on behavioral units will allow us to construct flexible AI out of these different modules, allowing us to rapidly build up different entity "brains" from reusable behaviors.

## Good Behavior

Here's how a general interface for a behavior module might look:

```
class CAIBehavior
{
    CAIEntity* PEntity;
public:
    CAIBehavior(CAIEntity* pentity);
    virtual bool IsRunnable(void) = 0;
    virtual void Update(void) = 0;
    virtual void OnActivate(void) = 0;
    virtual void Cleanup(void) = 0;
};
```

The IsRunnable method is responsible for stating whether the correct conditions are present for the behavior to run; for example, is there food nearby and is the entity hungry, for a "hunger" behavior. OnActivate is called whenever a particular behavior becomes "active." Cleanup is called whenever a behavior is deactivated and is responsible for making sure that the entity is put back cleanly into whatever state it was in before the behavior was activated.

Don't worry about these too much, as they are only necessary when we want to organize multiple behaviors later. For the moment, the most important method for our single unit of behavior is Update, as this is the method that performs the meat of our AI.

In general, a particular module of AI behavior will simply be a tree of conditional tests, which will resolve into different actions. For example, think about what a hungry creature might do.

```
CFood* pfood = FindPFood(PEntity->GetPos());
if(pfood!=NULL){
    //Move toward the food until we are near it
    while(!PositionsAdjacent(PEntity->GetPos(), pfood->GetPos())
        PEntity->MoveOneStepTowardsPos(pfood->GetPos());
    PEntity->EatFood(pfood); //Eat the food.
}
```

Here, the creature looks for food and, if it finds it, moves toward it one step at a time until it is adjacent. When it is near the food, it eats it. Unfortunately, if we ran this code, the game would freeze in the while loop; this is where micro-threads come in to save the day. Assuming this behavior class is being run in a micro-thread, all we have to do is add one magical line:

```
while(!PositionsAdjacent(PEntity->GetPos(), pfood->GetPos()){
    PEntity->MoveOneStepTowardsPos(pfood->GetPos());
    MicroThreadSleep(); // a call to suspend the micro thread.
}
PEntity->EatFood(pfood);
```

Suddenly, our simple AI process is a state machine! Now, after every step, the AI will suspend its processing, returning control to the main game.

## It's All in the Mind

Although it may not seem like we've achieved much yet, we are now able to construct a single module of AI behavior. In order to make an entity's life rich and varied, however, we need some way of organizing and prioritizing multiple, conflicting behaviors in such a way that only one is active at a time. This is where the brain class comes in.

```
class CAIBrain
{
    MicroThreadInfo*          PMicroThread;
    std::list<CAIBehavior>    Behaviors;
    std::list<int>            BehaviorPriorities;
    CAIBehavior*              PActiveBehavior;
    int                       ActiveBehaviorPriority;
public:
    void AddBehavior(int priority,  CAIBehavior& behavior);
    void Update(void);
};
```

Each AI entity in our game will have its own brain, and each brain has a micro-thread. Using the AddBehavior method, different types of entities can add different behaviors to the suite of possibilities. In addition, each behavior is given a priority, which can be used to help choose the behavior to run. It is the responsibility of the Update method of the brain to keep switching control to the micro-thread, which will in turn keep pumping the Update method of the active behavior.

Before that, however, we must make sure that there *is* an active behavior. When our entity has nothing to do, we need to run through all the available behaviors and choose the one with the highest priority that succeeds in the IsRunnable test. We take that chosen behavior, call OnActivate on it in case it has any special initialization code, and set it as our active behavior. Once that behavior has finished, we call Cleanup on it to run any uninitialization routines it may have, and then do the whole thing again.

In this way, a brain will make sure it always keeps an appropriate active behavior running. In practice, it is usually a good idea to give all entities some type of fallback idling behavior that will always pass the IsRunnable test, just so that it always looks like it is doing something.

There is a slight additional complication to this. Say our entity has decided it wants to go and run its Sleep behavior for a couple of minutes, because everything is quiet and its DefendSelf behavior, despite having a higher priority, has found no aggressors in the IsRunnable method. Unfortunately, while it is sleeping, the entity is attacked by some unscrupulous enemies. Using the system described previously, our sleeping AI character will be brutally murdered in his sleep, because he would only choose another active behavior when his current one finished.

What we need to do is periodically check our behavior list for an entry that succeeds on IsRunnable and is of a higher priority than the active behavior. If we find one, we unplug whatever is currently running—in this case, our Sleep behavior—and slap in our new, higher priority system—DefendSelf. In this particular instance, it would probably be the job of the Cleanup method of the Sleep behavior to ensure that the entity is awake, before the new and rather more violent behavior is plugged in. The code for the basics of this system is shown here:

```
void Update()
{
    CAIBehavior* pending = NULL;
    if(PActiveBehavior) {
        pending = FindNextBehavior(ActivePriority);
    }
    if(!pending && !PActiveBehavior)
        pending = FindNextBehavior(-1);
    if(pending){
        if(PActiveBehavior)
            TerminateActiveBehavior();
        PActiveBehavior = pending;
        PActiveBehavior->OnActivate();
    }
    if(PActiveBehavior)
        SwitchToMicroThread(PMicroThread);
}

void FindNextBehavior(int priority)
{
//Find a higher priority behavior that passes IsRunnable
}

static void MicroThreadFunction(void* pcontext)
{
    CAIBrain* pthis = (CAIBrain*)(pcontext);
    while(!pthis->TerminateThread){
        if(pthis->PActiveBehavior){
            pthis->ActiveBehaviorRunning = true;
            pthis->PActiveBehavior->Update();
            pthis->ActiveBehaviorRunning = false;
        }
        MicroThreadSleep();
    }
}
```

# Complications

### Dying Considerately

All of this so far has been deceptively simple. Brains run micro-threads, which in turn call update methods in behaviors. However, distributing processing across game turns has a number of important ramifications with which we need to deal. If we return to the simple hunger code we looked at earlier, there are a couple of hidden difficulties. First is the issue of tracked entity death; because the code is now spread across multiple game turns, somebody else may eat the food we are tracking by the time we reach it. If our food had simply been deleted from the game when it had been eaten, the code would crash since our pointer would be tracking invalid data.

Depending on how we handle entity deaths in our game, there are a number of ways to deal with this. Fundamentally, we have to make sure that any handles we have on game entities will be valid between game turns. In addition, we should be able to inquire whether the entity we are tracking has died. One solution is to force our persistent handles to be identifier numbers instead of pointers, unique to every entity that gets allocated in our game. That way, when an entity dies, our game code can simply tell us that our handle is invalid. Unfortunately, whenever we wish to access any part of the entity, we have to turn our handle into a reference to the actual data, which can result in bloated, inefficient code.

A better method is to write a special smart pointer system that deals with all of these issues automatically; a good set of guidelines for writing smart pointers is given by Scott Meyers [Meyers96]. Classic smart pointers conceptually have a degree of ownership over the objects they point to, through reference counting of some sort. What we want is the reverse, a pointer that passes ownership of itself to the special type of object at which it is pointing. Whenever a tracking pointer is pointed at one of our objects, it registers itself with it. Then, when the object dies, it can inform any tracking pointers that refer to it about its death and set them to a null value. Once we have this working, all we have to do in our AI code is make sure we check that the pointer is non-null before we use it. Example code on how to implement this "tracking pointer" system is provided on the companion CD-ROM.

ON THE CD

### Dying Cleanly

There is another issue with which we have to deal. What happens if the object whose AI we are running dies or is interrupted? If this occurs, then the active behavior needs to stop, all the objects we created on the heap need to be deleted, and we have to exit our AI code as quickly as possible. Again, depending on your preferences, there are a number of ways to handle this.

An elegant method is to use the C++ exception language facility. When an exception is thrown, behind-the-scenes C++ magic cleans up the stack and moves control back up the execution hierarchy, which is exactly the functionality we want. All the brain class needs to do is catch the exception and call the behavior's cleanup method. However, this is a fairly heavyweight approach, and some micro-thread implementations don't deal too kindly with exceptions.

A simpler approach, although rather more invasive, is to periodically check for whether we have been terminated, and return if we have. This does require some careful structuring of the AI code, but it is also a very lightweight solution. With some thought, this can even be packaged up to be only minimally invasive. In most cases, to be on the safe side, the brain will keep polling the micro-thread until it receives notification that the behavior has indeed stopped running, a technique with which you are familiar if you have used threads before.

```
void CAIBrain::TerminateActiveBehavior()
{
    if(PActiveBehavior){
        PActiveBehavior->SetTerminateFlag();
        while(ActiveBehaviorRunning)
            SwitchToMicroThread(PMicroThread);
        PActiveBehavior->Cleanup();
        PActiveBehavior->ClearTerminateFlag();
    }
}
```

## Actions Speak Louder

Taking all these modifications on board, let's see how our earlier example "hunger" behavior code might now look.

```
void Update()
{
    CTrackingPointer<CFood> pfood;
    pfood = FindPFood(PCreature->GetPos());
    if(pfood!=NULL){
        if(ActionMoveTowardsFood(pfood)==AI_OK)
            PEntity->EatFood(pfood);
    }
}

EAIReturn ActionMoveTowardsFood(CSmartPointer<CFood> pfood)
{
    while(pfood!=NULL && !PositionsAdjacent(PEntity, pfood-
>GetPos())){
        if(Terminated())
            return(AI_TERMINATE);

        PEntity->MoveOneStepCloserToPos(pfood->GetPos());
        MicroThreadSleep();
    }
    if(pfood!=NULL)
        return(AI_OK);

    return(AI_FAIL);
}
```

A special tracking pointer is used to track the food in case it dies. The `Action-MoveTowardsFood` method asks the brain to suspend the micro-thread after every step it takes toward the food. If the action finds that it has been "terminated" by the behavior's brain, it returns a value that lets the calling AI behavior know that it should cleanly exit. Likewise, if the food dies, it returns a code telling the behavior as much. In addition, all the code that deals with the problems of distributing the process across game turns has been packaged into a separate method. Structuring our code in this way has a number of important advantages:

- AI is effectively a tree of conditional tests that ultimately resolve into actual things to do. These "actions" are the only pieces of code that need to be distributed across game turns; hence, it makes sense to isolate them from the rest of the system.
- Since only actions need to suspend processing, only they need to do any testing for termination. Keeping the suspension and termination code together keeps things tidy and reduces the chances of forgetting to do one or the other.
- Action functions can be put into the behavior base-class and reused between different behaviors.

### Extensions

The system described here has been kept purposefully loose, as I have simply attempted to give an idea of the elegant architecture that micro-threads can provide for AI. Any number of favored AI tricks can be added, including:

- Giving each behavior a string name, which can be displayed for debugging purposes.
- Allowing brains to be assembled using an external data scripting language, to allow nonprogrammers to create and specialize entities. See Scott Bilas' excellent gem in this book on the topic.
- Using the "message" system described in *Game Programming Gems* to allow AI entities to enquire and send information about interesting events in the world [Rabin00].

## Conclusion

Micro-threads allow an enormous amount of flexibility for writing AI. Using this freedom properly, it is possible to create convincing, fast, lightweight, bug-free AI quickly and easily. Particular advantages that this system has over other methods include:

- Behaviors are grouped intuitively into modules. They can be reused between different types of entities trivially by adding them to different brains.
- There is no arbitrary jumping around spaghetti links between states, common in other state machine implementations. As such, when debugging, you can see the entire conditional tree that led to a particular problem, without having to trace through disparate states.

- Programmers can code using their favored programming techniques, without having to pander to a rigid architecture.
- Data specific to an entity and its behavior can be stored naturally between game turns in the behavior class.

## References

[Meyers96] Meyers, Scott, "Smart Pointers," *More Effective C++*, Addison Wesley, 1996.

[Rabin00] Rabin, Steve, "Designing a General Robust AI Engine," *Game Programming Gems,* Charles River Media, 2000.

# 3.4

# An Architecture for RTS Command Queuing

## Steve Rabin, Nintendo of America

steve_rabin@hotmail.com

**R**eal-time strategy games have a unique method of user interaction. Using a mouse, the player is able to assign multiple orders to individual units or groups of units. This interaction has matured over the years, with each new RTS building and improving on previous designs. One of the most evolved designs is a technique called *command queuing*. This gem describes how this method of interaction works, and how it can be directly woven into the underlying AI architecture.

## RTS Commands

The basic user interface for an RTS game involves selecting units and commanding them to do some task, such as attack an enemy or move to a particular spot. This is a fairly simple concept that doesn't require any great AI architecture to implement. However, it's important to first consider the range of simple commands that are available in most RTS games before discussing more complex combinations. The following is a list of common RTS commands.

- Attack a creature or building
- Build a structure or weapon
- Move to a spot
- Patrol to a spot
- Collect a resource (food, raw material, energy)
- Research a skill
- Repair a unit or building
- Reclaim a unit (recycle dead unit's material/energy)
- Guard a unit or building (attack anyone who attacks it)
- Hold position (attack anything in range but don't move)
- Stop
- Self-destruct

## Command Queuing

While playing an RTS game, you spend much of your time telling units where to move. Unfortunately, the pathfinding in most games isn't perfect and it often helps when the player assists in planning paths by setting waypoints. Waypoints are simply successive move commands that are queued up within a unit. The player queues up the move commands by holding some special button (like the Shift key) while clicking on the ground for each waypoint.

Waypoint queuing was an important step that has opened the door for a more powerful interface system. If you can queue waypoints, why not let the player queue any combination of commands? In effect, you could tell a unit to attack a creature, repair a wall, and then build a gun turret, all without waiting for any of the tasks to be completed. In addition, the player could decide, at a slightly later time, to queue even more commands onto the end of those. Generally, this idea is known as command queuing.

The trick is to think of every command as a task and to think of a unit's brain as a queue of tasks. The unit will always process the task that's at the front of the queue. Once that task is completed, it's destroyed and the next task is started. When there are no more tasks to process, a unit should have a default idle task. Figure 3.4.1 is an example of a unit's brain queue.

Figure 3.4.1 shows the result of queuing the commands attack, repair, and move. It also shows that each task has data associated with it, such as what to attack or where to move. New tasks to be queued are placed at the end of the list, but before the default task. The default task must always be the last task and it never completes and is never destroyed.

If the player commands a unit to do a new task without holding the "queuing" button, all tasks are destroyed and the new task is put in the queue. Thus, queued tasks can easily be replaced by a single, new command.

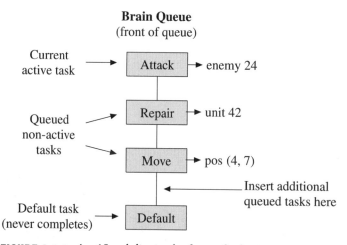

**FIGURE 3.4.1** *An AI task list in the form of a brain queue.*

With this architecture, a common behavior is to allow the player to "see" the command queue by selecting the unit and holding the "queuing" button. The on-screen result is that arrows show where the unit is planning to go and what they intend to do, such as build a structure. The elegant way to implement this is to let each task draw its contribution onto the screen. This allows the player to quickly see what's queued up in the unit and what additions might be appropriate.

This simple architecture is also blind to who put the commands in the queue. Obviously, the player can put commands there, but the game can also preload commands for a NPC (Non-Player Character) that might be patrolling or guarding a spot. The AI can also make high-level decisions about which units to attack by simply putting those commands in the queue. Even packets from over a network can be allowed to place commands in a unit's queue. It's a very elegant system that allows a lot of flexibility.

## Cyclic Commands

Patrolling is a cyclic command that presents some interesting consequences for the system described so far. When a player takes a unit and tells it to Patrol to a spot, the unit will remember his original spot and then walk back and forth between the two, indefinitely (or until an enemy is in sight). The player could also queue up several Patrol waypoints and the unit would similarly cycle through the waypoints forever. Figure 3.4.2 shows a three-point patrol that was initiated with two mouse clicks.

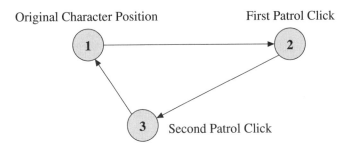

**FIGURE 3.4.2** *Patrol path for a unit.*

### Queuing the First Patrol Point

The first Patrol click from a player actually ends up placing two patrol commands on the queue. This is because the intent of the player is for the character to move to the position of the mouse click, and then move back to his original spot, repeating the cycle over and over again. Figure 3.4.3 shows the brain queue after just one Patrol command was issued by the player.

**Brain Queue**

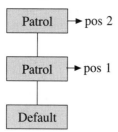

**FIGURE 3.4.3** *The brain queue after a single Patrol command was issued.*

Interestingly, a Patrol command is identical to a Move command, except that it gets cycled to the back of the queue. Therefore, our queuing system will work perfectly if a simple "cyclic" flag is set within a Move task in order to make it a Patrol task. When the Patrol task completes, rather than being destroyed (like a Move task), it's put onto the back of the queue (but before the default task). Figure 3.4.4 shows several iterations of the three-point patrol sequence from Figure 3.4.2.

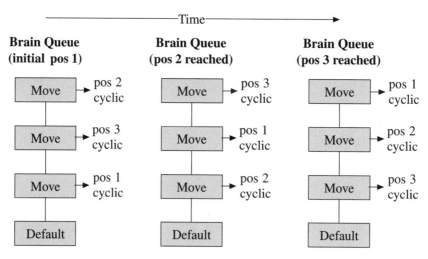

**FIGURE 3.4.4** *Three iterations of a patrol path.*

### Queuing Additional Commands

Some tricky issues arise when the player wants to queue extra commands when Patrol tasks exist in the queue. While the following might be slightly subjective, experimentally it's very close to what most players expect.

The first issue is where to put additional Patrol commands that are to be queued up. The player who is adding these extra Patrol points will probably expect that they're put after the first set of Patrol points (regardless of where the unit currently is in the brain queue). This is an important point since the unit could be anywhere along the patrol when the second set of Patrol commands are queued.

The solution is to mark the last Patrol command ever queued. This allows new Patrol commands to get queued after it. Once new Patrol commands are added, the "last" marker is moved. Figure 3.4.5 shows an example of three Patrol commands being queued successively.

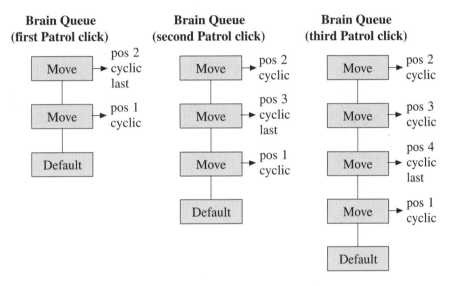

**FIGURE 3.4.5** *Three Patrol commands being queued in order.*

The second issue with queued Patrol commands involves queuing additional non-Patrol commands. In general, the player expects the command to be executed immediately after the current Patrol waypoint is achieved. This is tricky since the new commands must be placed after the current Patrol command, if there is one, and after any other noncyclic commands. Figure 3.4.6 shows a case of queuing several new non-Patrol commands.

As shown, Patrol commands throw several wrenches into the command queuing concept. The trick is to implement what the user expects to happen. The user will typically have a model in his or her head of how the system will work. Uncovering that model is not an easy task, but it will give you good insight into how to design the interaction and behavior of the command queuing system.

However, dealing with the users' mental model is a two-way street. It's also important to give the players immediate feedback, letting them know the result of

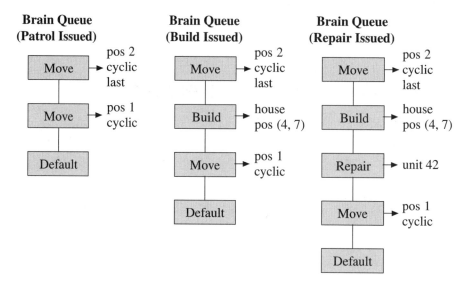

**FIGURE 3.4.6** *Queuing additional commands with Patrol tasks already queued.*

their input and how it was interpreted. That way, if the users' model is incorrect or flawed, they can quickly reconcile it with the correct model. A wonderful book that discusses the subject of mental models is "The Design of Everyday Things" by Donald Norman [Norman90].

## Conclusion

Command queuing is now a standard power feature that no RTS game can do without. By using the brain queue architecture to store tasks, many of the complexities of a command queuing system go away. In addition, you can think of the brain queue as a simple task list, or you can turn each task into its own neatly wrapped AI system that knows how to accomplish its job. Either way, your players should be able to queue up whatever they wish, and easily manage hundreds of units with this simple, yet powerful interface.

## References

[Norman90] Norman, Donald, A., *The Design of Everyday Things*, Currency/Double-day, 1990.

# 3.5

# A High-Performance Tile-based Line-of-Sight and Search System

## Matt Pritchard, Ensemble Studios

mpritchard@ensemblestudios.com

In the realm of strategy games, the concepts of Line-of-Sight (LOS) and Fog-of-War (FOW) for target identification and acquisition are often encountered. In traditional turn-based strategy games, using the brute-force approach of completely rebuilding a player's explored and visible maps has generally proven to be adequate. However, using the same approaches in a Real-Time Strategy (RTS) game quickly reveals performance issues, especially as the size of the game world or number of units increases. Still, many commercial RTS games, some very successful, have used this rebuild-all approach. Unfortunately, they have to make performance compromises such as forgoing the FOW altogether or not updating it every game turn, thus allowing inaccuracies to appear in the display. This gem presents an efficient implementation of a player visibility system for tile-based games that minimizes the performance impact, while providing support for fast searching as well as other game features.

## Overview

The first assumption is that internal to the program, sections of the game world area are represented by small chunks or tiles, which correspond to a two-dimensional array. Most real-time strategy games have rectangular game maps, but this implementation is easy to adapt to a hex-based world layout.

The goals of our player visibility system are as follows:

- The game's explored, visible, and fogged tiles must be fully accurate at all times.
- Units must be able to search very fast for other units or objects of interest, with respect to FOW and visibility.
- The system must support up to 16 players at a time, allowing for arbitrary information sharing between players.
- The system must scale well with respect to more units, larger maps, and larger search radii.

## Definitions

> **Tile**. The smallest discrete square- or hexagon-shaped portion of the game world.
>
> **World**. The total area in which the game takes place; internally a 2D array of tiles, also called the *map*.
>
> **Player**. A human or computer entity who controls a population of units. Each player has a unique set of visibility information.
>
> **Unit**. Any game entity that is owned or controlled by a player. It does not have to be movable.
>
> **Line-of-Sight (LOS)**. The area around a unit that is currently visible because of its presence.
>
> **LOS Radius**. The range of a unit's LOS area, measured in tiles.
>
> **Unexplored Tile**. A tile that the player's units have never seen within their LOS.
>
> **Fogged Tile**. A tile that has been explored but is not currently in the LOS of any of the player's units.
>
> **Visible Tile**. A tile that is currently in the LOS of one or more of the player's units.
>
> **Fog of War (FOW)**. The concept that if an explored tile is not currently in the LOS of a player's unit, then the player can't see other players' units on that tile.

In an RTS, we assume that for each player, the map starts out unexplored. As tiles fall into a unit's LOS, those tiles become explored for the player who owns that unit. When an explored tile is no longer in a unit's LOS, the tile becomes fogged for that player, yet will never revert to being unexplored. It's important to note that the tile states of unexplored, explored, and fogged are unique for each player.

## Component #1: Individual Player Visibility Maps

The first component of the player visibility system that needs to be implemented is a visibility count map for each player in the game. This is a rather simple structure: a 2D byte array with a one-to-one correspondence to the tile layout. Each array element contains a count of how many of the player's units can see that tile (in other words, how many units' LOS contain that tile).

Updating the visibility map is simple. When a unit is first created or moved into a new tile position, all of the visibility counts are incremented by one for the tiles in the unit's line of sight. When the unit is deleted, destroyed, or moves off a tile, all of the visibility counts are decremented by one for the tiles in the unit's LOS. The value in each visibility map element is nonzero if the tile is visible to the player. However, it is unclear if a zero value means an unexplored tile or a fogged tile. To solve this, we designate zero to mean fogged, and −1, or 255 in byte storage, to mean unexplored.

Unfortunately, when an unexplored tile is incremented for the very first time, the value will wrap to zero, which incorrectly means the tile is fogged. However, we can catch this special case and ensure that an increment that results in zero gets incremented again. This also provides a convenient place to add code for additional one-time processing on the explored tile, such as adding it to a mini-map, recording its type, or searching it for resources. Since most games do not ever revert a tile to unexplored, this special case will not appear in the decrement code. It's worth noting that the storage element size—in this case, a byte—sets an upper limit to the number of units that can see a specific tile at one time, which in this case is 254.

## Component #2: LOS Templates

In most strategy games, a unit's LOS is defined as a circular area around the unit, with the radius measured in the number of tiles. The simplest way to compute this shape, which many games have done, is to take a radius-sized box of tiles around the unit's position and see if the distance from each tile is less than the unit's LOS radius. However, from a performance standpoint, this is horribly inefficient. Given that this operation can be called a huge number of times each turn, this function begs for major optimization.

One of the best ways to optimize this is to precompute the LOS area for each possible LOS radius that is used in the game. This shape information can then be stored in a template structure with different templates used to represent different LOS radii.

The best implementation I have found is to store the LOS area as a series of horizontal strips, with start, stop, and vertical displacements relative to the unit's position, starting from the top and working down. The templates are processed horizontally under the assumption that elements in that axis of the array are stored linearly in memory, thus minimizing the number of cache accesses during processing. For units at the edges, clipping the LOS template shape to the game map just requires clamping the start and stop values in the outer loop. The following code shows a function to add a unit's LOS template to the visibility count map.

```
// This routine "explores" the game map in an area around the
// specified unit position using a line of sight template
// The template span data is an array of structs with 3 offset elements:
//   {vertical position, horizontal start, horizontal end}

void VisibilityMap::AddLOSTemplate(int XPosition, int YPosition,
LOSTemplate *template)
{
    int n, x, y, xStart, xEnd;

    for (n = 0; n < template->number_of_vertical_lines; n++)
    {
        y = Yposition + template->SpanData[n].Yoffset;
        if (y >= map_y_min_coord && y <= map_y_max_coord)
        {
            xStart = max(XPosition + template->lines[n].XStartOffset,
map_x_min_coord);
            xEnd = min(XPosition + template->lines[n].XEndOffset,
map_x_max_coord);

            for (x = xStart; x <= xEnd; x++)
            {
                if ((VisibleMap[y][x]++) == 0)
```

```
            {
                ExploreTileForFisrtTimeHandler(x, y);
                VisbleMap[y][x] = 1;
            }
        }
    }
  }
}
```

When a player's unit is removed from the game world, the game decrements the visibility count of its LOS area. If none of the player's other units have the tile in their LOS, it will be zero, indicating that the tile is no longer visible for the player, and is now fogged.

When a unit moves from one tile to an adjacent tile, which is normally a very common operation, it removes its LOS from the old position and adds it back in at the new position. Since this pair of function calls will be often made in tandem from the unit's movement code, another optimization is to combine the two operations into a single function. This new function takes both the old and new positions and only updates the portions of the player's visibility map where the increment and the decrement do not overlap. Another situation is when a unit's LOS radius changes. In that case, the remove LOS function is called with the old radius, followed by the add LOS function with the new radius. Properly written, the optimized update function should handle this case as well.

There are additional advantages to using LOS templates. The first is that different shapes can be created for different-sized objects with the same LOS radius. While a small game unit may occupy a single tile, larger units, such as immobile structures, might occupy several adjacent tiles and possibly even be nonsquare, such as rectangular or elliptical. An LOS template that appears centered on a one-tile unit would appear off center when used on the larger unit. Figure 3.5.1 shows a set of LOS template shapes for two different-sized objects, both with a radius of three tiles.

Another advantage of using templates is that nonsymmetrical LOS shapes can be made. Figure 3.5.2 shows an example of two rotations of a directional searchlight

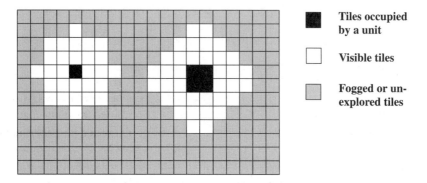

**FIGURE 3.5.1** *LOS shapes with the same radius for units of different size.*

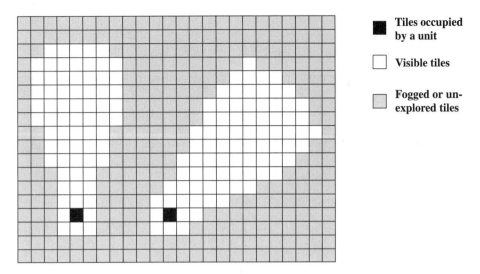

**FIGURE 3.5.2** *Noncircular LOS areas with two rotations of a searchlight pattern.*

shape. With a full set of rotated LOS templates, the searchlight unit could be easily animated to sweep a full circle, producing a cool game effect with very little specialized programming.

## Component #3: The Combined Visibility Map

So far, what's been implemented is more efficient, but it doesn't help with some of the other goals. This next component, called the *combined visibility map*, will tie the other structures together. This data structure will be accessed the most by the rest of the game code and will provide a big boost to the searching functions.

Like the individual player maps, the combined visibility map is a 2D array, sized the same as the tile grid. The difference is that there is only one combined visibility map for the entire game, and its elements are 32-bit DWORDs instead of bytes. Given its usage, it could be a good idea to make this globally available to the program.

The purpose of the combined visibility map is to contain all of the up-to-date visibility information in a single place for all of the players in the game. This is done by using just 2 bits per element for each player. One bit is to indicate that a player has explored the tile, and the other bit is used to indicate if the tile is currently visible to the player. This gives room for 16 players' worth of data in each DWORD.

The organization of the individual bits in a combined visibility map element is up to the user to implement. This should have no relevance on performance, as all updates should consist of a single binary OR, AND, or XOR operation on the entire 32-bit element, using mask values precomputed for each player.

In practice, the combined visibility map is initialized to all tiles as unexplored and fogged. It is then updated when any of the following events occurs for any player:

- A tile is explored for the first time.
- A tile transitions from unexplored or fogged to visible.
- A tile transitions from visible to fogged.

During the display of the game world or other structure such as a radar map, each player has a visibility mask value that contains the explored and visibility bits shifted into the correct position for that player. As each tile location is traversed by the various functions, the combined visibility map value for that location is ANDed with the current player's visibility mask. The result gives the visibility and explored status of that tile for the specified player, on which the code can then operate.

The first benefit of using the combined visibility map is that the player's visibility masks can be combined. This allows for various game effects such as sharing lines-of-sight and visibility with teammates, as well as spying on other players. The effects for each player can be added or removed at any time by simply updating the player's visibility mask and refreshing the display.

## Improved Searching

The direct approach to searching involves looking at the occupants of each tile in the searching unit's LOS area. As more units are added into the game, the number of searches each turn increases. In addition, as the radius for each search increases, such as with ranged units or LOS upgrades, the number of tiles searched rises very quickly. For example, a single ranged attack unit with a search radius of 10 tiles would have an area of about 350 tiles to be searched. Therefore, this direct approach results in a performance drop proportional to the number of tiles scanned.

Probably the biggest benefit of using the combined visibility map comes with this task of searching in a unit's LOS for enemy targets or other objects of interest. Rather than search the individual tiles, it's better to keep a running list of the other player's units in a given player's total combined LOS. This is where the combined visibility map comes into play. Each unit in the game accesses the combined visibility map entry for the tile it occupies. With this data, each unit knows which players can currently see that unit. By saving this information from the previous turn, a unit knows when it moves into and out of the LOS of every other player in the game, even if it is not moving. In addition, when a change occurs, the unit can add or remove itself from a list of units visible to the other player. The update overhead is only a single DWORD check per unit per turn, except for when the unit has actually transitioned in or out of another player's combined line-of-sight.

The list that the units add and remove themselves from can then be broken down further depending on what the unit represents to the player (for example, teammate, combat unit, infrastructure, etc.) The result is that each player will have a series of very small lists, often even empty, containing pointers to other players' units that are currently in the player's total LOS.

Once the lists are maintained, there is no longer a need to search large numbers of tiles, most of which probably won't contain possible targets. Instead, searching becomes a process of scanning a far smaller list that contains only possible targets. The search code can be simplified and the lists will cache better. The performance improvement can be an order of magnitude better, especially in situations that involve many long-range units.

The following code shows how a unit's update would process the changes in LOS visibility. This code determines for which players its visibility status has changed, and subsequently how to change them.

```
void GameUnit::TurnUpdateProcess(. . .)
{
    // Game specific unit processing code…
    . . .
    // Now we check to see if we've gone in or out of anyone's LOS
    DWORD CurrentlyVisibleTo =
            CombinedVisibilityMap[Yposition][Xposition];

    if ( CurrentlyVisibleTo != LastVisibleToValue)
    {
        // Get only the bits that have changed
        DWORD VisibilityChanges = CurrentlyVisibleTo ^
                LastVisibleToValue;
        LastVisibleToValue = CurrentlyVisibleTo;   // Save new value

        for (int playerNo = 0; playerNo < theGame->numOfPlayers;
            playerNo++)
        {
            DWORD PlayerMask = 0x0001 << playerNo;  // bit mask for
            player

            // Check to see if our visibility for this player has
changed
            if ((VisibilityChanges & PlayerMask) != 0)
            {
                if ((CurrentlyVisibleTo & PlayerMask) != 0)
                    AddUnitToPlayersVisibleList(playerNo, self);
                else
                    RemoveUnitFromPlayersVisibleList(playerNo, self);
            }
        }
    }
    // Continue with game processing
}
```

Another benefit of this method is that the searches will respect the player's total visibility and don't need to be restricted in range to the unit's LOS radius. As illustrated in Figure 3.5.3, each of the player's units at the bottom performs a target search with a search radius greater than its own LOS radius and finds the enemy units visible to the player on the upper-left side. However, they also failed to find the two enemy units in the upper right because they are on tiles that are currently fogged to the player. By respecting the combined LOS and using a search radius not tied to their LOS radius, more intelligent and humanlike AI decisions can be made.

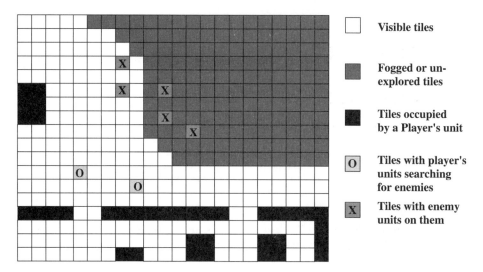

**Figure 3.5.3** *Demonstration of which enemy units can be seen by the player. By respecting the total LOS, the searching units will only see the enemy units on the left, even though the units in the FOW are closer.*

The same processing code can be used for large units that occupy more than one tile in the game world. The only difference is that the current visibility value is made by ORing together the combined visibility map values for each tile occupied, instead of taken from a single tile's value. This also makes it easy to do things like revealing the entire map area occupied by the unit, even if the player's LOS only falls on a corner of it.

Mirages are another game capability that the combined visibility map makes easy to implement. Mirages are ghost representations of units that appear visually in another player's fogged area, representing what that player last saw when he or she explored the area. Units that can generate mirages do so when they have transitioned out of another player's LOS. Also, the mirages know to remove themselves from the game when they detect that they are again fully visible to the other player, by checking the combined visibility map values.

## Conclusion

It never hurts to rethink a situation, even when it appears simple and straightforward. The development of this approach was the result of asking "why" and seeing how seemingly unrelated systems could lend each other a hand. The greatly improved searching capability is made possible because of the presence of the combined visibility map. This only works because the individual player visibility maps are always kept up to date, every game tick. Therefore, while the individual systems do their specific jobs, when joined together, more capabilities are exposed and greater optimizations are achievable.

# 3.6

# Influence Mapping

## *Paul Tozour*

gehn29@yahoo.com

We consider a game AI agent to be "intelligent" if it consistently makes decisions that we consider appropriate in a given context. Thus, we can say that the core of intelligent game AI is decision-making.

Everyday experience teaches that the key to effective decision-making is not merely having the best data, but presenting the data in the right way. Raw data is useless until converted to contextual information. An appropriate representation of the data will force the relevant underlying patterns to reveal themselves.

This and the subsequent gem on strategic assessment present techniques for giving AI agents a well-informed tactical and strategic perspective on the character of the game world and the current game state. We also discuss techniques relevant to different game genres and virtual environments.

## Influence Maps

Influence mapping is an invaluable and proven game AI technique for performing tactical assessment. Influence maps have been used most often in strategy games, but are also useful for many other types of games that require an aspect of tactical analysis. The general concepts of influence mapping are an essential part of any AI developer's toolkit.

An influence map is a spatial representation of an AI agent's knowledge about the world. It allows a computer player to develop a tactical perspective of the current game state layered on top of the underlying physical/geographical representation of the game environment. An influence map indicates where a computer player's forces are deployed, where the enemy is located or is most likely to be found, where the "frontier" between players lies, what areas remain to be explored, where significant battles have occurred, and where its enemies are most likely to attack it in the future. The structure of the influence map also makes it possible to make intelligent inferences about the characteristics of different locations in the environment. Influence maps can pick out areas of high strategic control, pinpoint weak spots in an opponent's defenses, identify prime "camping" locations or strategically vulnerable areas, find choke points on the terrain, and identify other meaningful features that human players would choose through intuition or practice.

There is no single, standard algorithm for creating influence maps, nor any single way to apply the technique. This gem describes several of the more popular influence mapping concepts, but it is only a starting point. The way you construct and employ influence maps will depend heavily on the specific strategic and tactical needs of your particular game and the design of the game world that your AI agents inhabit.

## A Simple Influence Map

An influence map can operate in almost any type of game world topography—a square grid, a hexagonal grid, or a fully 3D environment. For the sake of simplicity, most of this gem assumes a 2D grid, which is applicable to most strategy games. The final section of this gem discusses applications in more complex environments.

We begin with a set of square cells superimposed on our game world. All the cells are initialized with a value of zero. For each cell, we add a certain type of "influence" we wish to consider. For the sake of this example, we'll compute an estimate for "combat effectiveness." We'll add a positive value for each friendly unit, and a negative value for each enemy unit.

The specific value we add or subtract will be an estimate of the unit's combat effectiveness. For the moment, we'll assume that each unit has an effectiveness rating of 1, as shown in Figure 3.6.1.

The next step is to spread the influence of each cell to nearby cells. For now, let's assume that we propagate each cell's influence such that each time the influence is spread to a neighboring cell, it is diminished by 50 percent. Therefore, a value of 4 would add two points to each adjacent cell, one point to each cell two squares away, then 1/2, and so on.

Figure 3.6.2a shows how the influence of our two bugs spreads across the influence map. The influence of our two opponents—the sinister and nefarious agents of

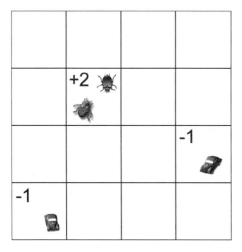

**FIGURE 3.6.1** *Initial influences.*

the dreaded Ford Motor Company—will propagate in a similar way (not shown), but their influence values will be negative because we hate them.

When we combine the influences of all the cars and bugs, we end up with Figure 3.6.2b. It should be immediately clear that this gives us an excellent sense of where each player wields influence. Darker cells belong to us; lighter cells belong to our opponent. More importantly, we can now trace a contour for the "frontier" between friendly and hostile assets. The frontier is defined as any part of the grid where two adjacent cells shift between negative and non-negative values. This is shown as an outlined white line in Figure 3.6.2b.

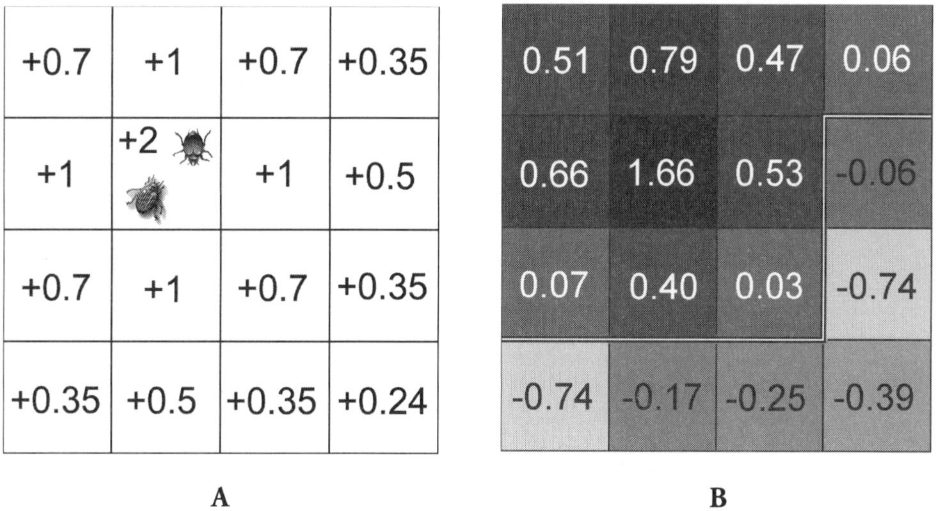

| +0.7 | +1 | +0.7 | +0.35 |
| +1 | +2 | +1 | +0.5 |
| +0.7 | +1 | +0.7 | +0.35 |
| +0.35 | +0.5 | +0.35 | +0.24 |

A

| 0.51 | 0.79 | 0.47 | 0.06 |
| 0.66 | 1.66 | 0.53 | -0.06 |
| 0.07 | 0.40 | 0.03 | -0.74 |
| -0.74 | -0.17 | -0.25 | -0.39 |

B

FIGURE 3.6.2  *A) Influence propagation. B) The final influence map.*

We can use this frontier to determine where to place our forces for offense or defense. By weighting the enemy's forces more heavily than our own (using a multiplier greater than one), we can pull the frontier closer to our own forces for a more defensive posture. If we weight our own forces more heavily, we push the frontier forward and develop toward a more aggressive posture.

## Influence Map Cell Data

The preceding example is clearly trivial. An influence map in a real game is considerably more sophisticated. Rather than simply containing a number, each of the influence map's "cells" is a repository for some amount of data about the game world. Each cell is, in effect, a miniature database of relevant data for all the units and resources that occupy that cell. Following are examples of some of the types of statistics that a cell will typically contain.

- **Combat strength**. This is the estimated combat effectiveness of the units currently in the cell. This should take into account factors such as attack/defense strength, current health or hit points, attack range, rate of fire, and so on. It may also be advisable to break units into categories in a manner appropriate to the design of your particular game; for example, to account for the relative strengths of ranged versus melee, infantry versus cavalry, or flying versus land-based versus aquatic units.
- **Vulnerable assets**. This is an estimate of the value of a player's current assets in the cell, such as a part of a village or military base in a typical strategy game.
- **Area visibility**. This is a number indicating how long the area has been visible or invisible to the player.
- **Body count**. Indicates how many units have died in the cell in the past, and when.
- **Resources**. The total resources still available for exploitation—gold, lumber, etc.
- **Passability**. An estimate of the difficulty of moving through the cell, possibly broken down by movement type (flying, walking, tracked, etc.)  This value is used to more accurately propagate a cell's influence to neighboring cells, and can factor into the cell's desirability for a given decision. A good variant is to separately store eight passability values, one for each of the directions exiting the cell.

An influence map will typically track these variables for each player in the game separately. Think of this as maintaining multiple parallel influence maps: each player updates an influence map for its own assets, plus an additional influence map to represent its own knowledge of every other player. This is useful as it allows you to distinguish the particular strengths and weaknesses of specific opponents, or to blend any set of friendly or enemy influences together as desired. Be warned, however, that performance can quickly get out of hand with more than three or four competing AI players.

Of course, you could also just keep a single influence map for everyone, and let every AI player access it. In a game with any kind of hidden map or fog-of-war (FOW), this constitutes "cheating," and it could produce suboptimal behaviors in some situations.

## Computing Desirability Values

Rather than using the basic statistics for each cell directly as a basis for decision-making, it's more useful to combine them into a "desirability value." This is a computed value which estimates the cell's "value" with regard to a certain decision. By comparing the desirability values of different cells, we can construct a ranking of which cells appear to be "better" for the task than others.

The most useful formula for desirability is often a simple weighted sum. Pick the variables from each cell that you consider relevant for the decision at hand, multiply each by a coefficient that roughly indicates that factor's relative utility in making the decision, and add the resulting values to determine desirability.

The specific parameters you select to calculate different desirability values will depend strongly on the particular needs of your game and the unique characteristics of your game design. The choice of appropriate coefficients is also subjective and is best achieved through careful tweaking and tuning. Simulated annealing or competitive evolutionary approaches are feasible, but probably not desirable. Be forewarned that you will also need to compensate for the different units of measurement that you use for statistics such as unit health/hit points, rate of fire, attack strength, and so on.

A short list of sample desirability values follows.

- **Attack and defense desirability**. We can typically compute a single "vulnerability" score to represent defense and attack capabilities for this player and his enemies, respectively. A high vulnerability score for an enemy means we can damage the assets in that area easily, so we should consider attacking the enemy in that cell; a high vulnerability score for this AI player means that we have significant assets in the cell that are susceptible to attack, and we should defend them more carefully.

  Vulnerable areas are typically those with many assets and key resources but minimal opposing military units nearby. Therefore, if an enemy player has a value of 80 for "assets" in a given cell (representing its base buildings and resources) and an enemy offensive value of 60 (representing the enemy forces that could potentially defend it), the final "vulnerability" rating is 20.

- **Exploration**. For strategy games that use a hidden map or FOW, a good AI player will dispatch scouts on a regular basis to refresh its view of the battlefield. A good heuristic for exploration is to rank the influence map cells that have gone unseen the longest as the most desirable for exploration. Other good factors in this decision are the enemy influence in a cell and the area's estimated passability (so your scouts can escape if attacked).

- **Defensive asset placement**. Immobile defensive assets should be placed in areas close to lots of vulnerable assets. They should be in areas vulnerable enough to be worth defending, but not so vulnerable that they can't be constructed.

  Choke points are also good spots for defensive assets. Terrain choke points can be easily identified on the influence map using precomputed passability values; choke points will be high-passability influence map cells that connect other high-passability areas but are surrounded by low-passability cells.

- **Resource-collection asset placement**. Assets that serve as resource collection points (Town Centers) are typically most effective in easily defensible areas that are as close as possible to the largest amounts of exploitable resources.

- **Unit-producing asset placement**. Unit-producing assets (such as a Barracks) should typically be placed in defensible areas closest to enemy forces.

- **Vulnerable asset placement**. Assets that need to be protected should be placed in the most defensible areas, and the farthest from potential threats. It's also usually a good idea to place such assets in less accessible areas to shield them from attack. For flat, rectangular game worlds, it's also often a good idea to consider that map corners have fewer avenues of approach and so are often less vulnerable, so you can weight the desirability values higher at the sides and corners of the map.

## Determining Optimal Cell Size

The size of the influence map cells is somewhat arbitrary. It's a trade-off between accuracy and efficiency. With cells that are too large, your influence maps will have a difficult time identifying small features, such as terrain choke points or weak spots in enemy defenses. If the cells are too small, things will get out of hand fast; you'll end up doing a lot of redundant computation and possibly using a lot of memory as well.

In practice, it's usually best to make the cells fairly large. Avoid the temptation to assume that smaller cells will make the AI smarter. For a typical strategy game, I recommend (as a starting point) making each cell large enough to fit 10–20 of your game's standard "units" side by side along the width or height of the cell, and carefully tune the cell size from there to obtain the best results in gameplay.

Some readers may note that the arbitrary positioning of the cells over the map could be problematic. A unit straddling two neighboring influence map cells will have a different effect depending on which of the two cells receives its influence. This will usually not be an issue due to the "influence propagation" described in the next section. However, a good way to handle the problem is to modulate the (X, Y) world-space offset of the entire influence map on a regular basis (perhaps each time you recalculate the influence map), using either a random or periodic offset. This is akin to a fishing net floating on the ocean that is washed back and forth by the waves.

## Influence Propagation

Once you have calculated an initial value for each cell of the influence map, the next step is to propagate the value of each cell to some number of nearby cells, as in the earlier example. This process is also referred to as *smoothing* or *blurring* as it has a lot in common with standard 2D image blurring techniques (see [Evans01]).

Influence propagation gives us a much more accurate picture of the current tactical situation. We don't care only about where units are and what they're doing; we care about what they might do—what areas they potentially "influence." If we have a pair of Archers in the field flanked by large battalions of Plasma Tanks on either side, we want our AI to perceive that the area the Archers occupy is really "owned" by the enemy. We need to propagate the Tanks' influence to the cell the Archers occupy.

Propagation is just a matter of spreading the influence of each cell to neighboring cells using a "falloff rule" that determines how the influence of a given cell decreases with distance as it spreads across the map. The selection of a particular falloff rule is subjective and there is no single accepted technique—as always, you will need to tweak and tune for optimal results. I typically find exponential falloff the most useful: pick a falloff constant between 0 and 1 (typically $0.6 < n < 0.8$), and each time you spread influence to a neighboring cell, use this constant as a multiplier. Given a falloff constant of 0.75 (=75%), a neighboring cell will have 0.75 = 75% of the original value. A cell two squares away will have $(0.75)^2 \approx 0.56 = 56\%$ of the original value, a cell three squares away will have $(0.75)^3 \approx 0.42 = 42\%$, and so on. The falloff constant should be proportional to the cell size: smaller influence map cells require a larger falloff value to spread the influence the same distance.

Other useful falloff rules include linear falloff (in which a cell's influence decreases by a constant value each time it spreads to a neighboring cell) and Gaussian filters (see [Evans01]).

Note that if you use floating-point numbers, your propagated influence values will never actually reach zero regardless of how far you spread them. This means that each cell will end up spreading its influence to every other cell in the entire influence map. The literature consistently refers to this phenomenon as "a bad thing." The simplest solution is to terminate propagation at a certain minimum influence value (usually a value beneath which the smoothed influence would be too tiny to make a difference anyway). This cutoff constant is best determined by experimentation.

Note, however, that it's usually a good idea to spread a cell's influence a fair distance. If your influence map consists of many small cells and the cells' influence is not propagated very far, you will likely end up with a lot of empty space (in other words, a lot of zeroes) in the influence map, and it will be difficult to determine exactly where the frontier lies. Use big cells, and spread their influence a good distance.

There is also an interesting alternative influence propagation technique based on quadtrees. All cells' values are passed up the quadtree to each higher layer, so higher-level quadtree cells can be used to obtain approximate "smoothed" values for their child cells. Unfortunately, this approach spreads cells' influence in a somewhat arbitrary fashion. The distance that a cell's influence is propagated is tightly bound to the structure of the quadtree, and influence might be propagated far more in some directions than others. I find this technique less flexible and often less accurate than the propagation technique described earlier.

## Accounting for Terrain

The propagation technique described here does not necessarily paint an accurate picture in all situations. Imagine that a powerful enemy wizard has a fortress on one side of a mountain range. The propagation technique will spread the influence of the fortress over the mountains even if the wizard has no way to attack us over the mountains, and cannot navigate any of his units over or around them.

There are several ways to account for the impact of terrain on the influence map. Probably the simplest is to use a precomputed passability value for each cell and use this as a multiplier for falloff values, as shown in Figure 3.6.3. Each cell contains either a single passability estimate or a set of four or eight passability values in the cardinal directions exiting the cell. We then spread the influence from the cell in a manner similar to a breadth-first search or the flood-fill algorithm. Although Figure 3.6.3 does not show it, this can also handle cells where influence is merely diminished and not blocked entirely.

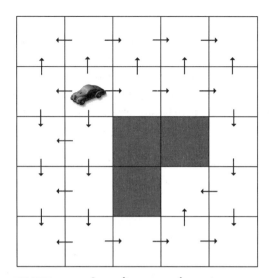

**FIGURE 3.6.3** *Spreading around terrain.*

A second technique involves precomputing all possible paths between nearby neighbors (Figure 3.6.4). For each cell, we perform a pathfinding step during map preprocessing that determines the shortest path from that cell to all neighbor cells up to a maximum path distance away. We can then store the computed distance to each target cell and use this as the actual "distance" to the neighboring cell when performing the propagation step. We consider a cell to be unavailable for influence propagation if no path exists.

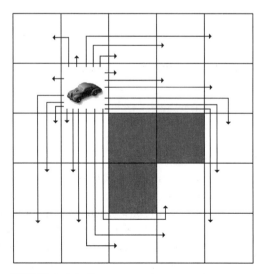

**FIGURE 3.6.4** *Precomputed propagation.*

The advantage of this technique is that it provides very accurate influence propagation. If there is an easy way to navigate around the mountain range, such as a pass through the center of the mountains, the influence map propagation will accurately reflect the fact that the mountains are not a significant tactical obstacle.

Unfortunately, this technique is difficult to apply to dynamic environments. If your game world allows players to build extended walls or to block off mountain passes, the precomputed propagation values no longer reflect reality, and it may be very difficult to update your influence map in real time. This method can also potentially require a lot of preprocessing time, as it requires us to perform pathfinding from each cell in the influence map to potentially dozens or hundreds of other cells.

## Special Considerations

Terrain will have different effects on different units. Flying units will not be stopped by mountains, and seafaring units will spread their influence over water but not over land. Therefore, it's important that each influence map cell track such different unit types separately (for example, track "flying" vs. "nonflying" assets in each cell), and propagate their values differently according to the terrain type.

Quite often, certain units will have very long firing ranges, and if a unit can fire a certain distance, then it can also fire that distance from any point to which it can move. A good way to account for this is for each influence map cell to separately track ranged-fire units according to the distance they can fire (possibly categorized as multiples of the width of an influence map cell). After spreading the influence for these ranged distance categories using propagation, we then spread the influence an extra $N$ cells from each influenced cell *without diminishing the value*. This way, we can account for a battleship's ability to strike far into the shore, even though it can't go on land.

You may also find it useful to add mobile units to the map based on their projected future positions rather than their current positions. This makes the influence map a bit more accurate, particularly if you don't recalculate the influence map very often. The simplest approach is dead reckoning—estimate each unit's position perhaps 5–10 seconds from now based on its velocity vector. Since you're presumably writing the AI, you might also simply look up each unit's future position if the unit is performing pathfinding (although of course this may constitute cheating if an AI player looks at other players' chosen routes).

## Refreshing the Influence Map

If your AI needs to analyze large portions of the influence map on a regular basis, it may make sense to recompute the entire influence map on a regular basis, perhaps every 1-10 seconds. Considering the pace of a typical strategy game, a faster refresh rate will probably not produce a more effective AI. Once the influence map is computed, you can then use it to perform many calculations extremely quickly.

A second approach is demand-based refreshing, a sort of lazy evaluation technique. This is a more flexible approach, and is more efficient when you need to perform less extensive influence map analysis. With this variant, you compute the values in a given cell only when the cell is actually queried, searching all the neighboring cells within a given maximum distance to see how their values propagate back to the original cell. This technique has the added advantage that you can specify the propagation parameters and desirability value coefficients at query time.

## Influence Maps in 3D Environments

This gem has focused thus far on applications in 2D environments. However, influence mapping and related approaches are also broadly applicable to more complex environments such as the 3D environments of typical action games.

Using a 2D grid for 3D influence mapping is usually a bad idea, as it will not accurately reflect the topography of our game environment. Fortunately, AI pathfinding in 3D environments is usually (though, alas, not always!) based on a navigation mesh approach (see [Snook00]). A navigation mesh consists of a graph of interconnected convex polygons that describe where characters can move in the game world. We can use each polygon of the navigation mesh as an influence map cell. The links between polygons can describe the avenues for influence propagation. Influence decreases according to the length "traveled" along each mesh node.

Because 3D game worlds are more topographically complex than 2D worlds and the emphasis is usually on individual combatants, terrain assessment is typically more important than the real-time player-versus-player tactical assessment that an influence map can provide. It's critical that our AI agents can pick out the tactical significance of different areas. The following list explains some of these tactical assessment factors.

- **Vulnerability ("cover")**. 3D action games typically involve firing powerful weapons over large distances, so it's critical to take into account the range of possible fire locations to and from each cell of the influence map. AI agents often need to determine the degree of "cover" in a given cell. A simple approach is to calculate an estimate for the degree of cover for each of the six faces of a cube projected from each influence map node.

  However, we often want to know whether a given cell (potential destination) can shoot or be shot from another cell (enemy position). A good line-of-fire representation would list the set of nodes that are "attackable" from any given node—but this could quickly get out of hand for large and highly interconnected environments that approach an $N^2$ degree of interconnectivity. A good solution is to package groups of influence map nodes into "zones," such that all nodes in a given zone are in the same "room" or "portal," and use this representation to determine which zones are potentially vulnerable from other zones.

- **Visibility**. This is similar to vulnerability, except that it disregards weapon distances, takes illumination levels into account, and can pass through certain surfaces that weapons fire cannot, such as reinforced glass. This calculation becomes tricky when dynamic lighting is used, and lights can be turned on and off.

- **Passability**. As before, this is an estimate of the difficulty of moving through an area. Tight passages are usually more difficult to move through, and elevators, ladders, and other such routes cause slow movement and thus have low passability.
- **Height advantage**. Locations with a high elevation relative to surrounding locations are usually tactically superior for both offense and defense, particularly if the game features hand grenades.

These are the basic precalculated statistics in our influence map cells. We can now whip out a few coefficients and compute desirability values.

The best locations for offense are typically those with high passability, high cover, and low visibility, but which also have a good line-of-fire to many areas of high visibility (and, ideally, low passability). Good offensive locations also usually have good cover locations nearby in case the agent comes under fire.

The best defensive locations are those with the highest cover and lowest visibility, and for which all the potential attacking locations have high visibility.

More to the point, if we precalculate these desirability values for all the nodes, we then can propagate these values to their neighbors using our standard influence mapping techniques and end up with a complete tactical assessment of the level.

Finally, note that we can also use the influence map to make inferences about our opponents—we can determine their respective levels of cover, visibility, passability, and height advantage. We can use this to select the best opponent to attack at any given moment, or to search for a destination that has an advantage over any or all of our opponents.

Another useful extension is to estimate opponents' most likely positions in the near future by finding the most desirable destinations available to them. This will allow us to prepare for our enemies' actions, and have the ambush already prepared.

## References and Additional Reading

[comp.ai.games95]  The seminal 1995 "influence mapping" thread on comp.ai.games (various authors) is reprinted at www.gameai.com/influ.thread.html.

[Evans01]  Evans, Alex. "Four Tricks for Fast Blurring in Software and Hardware," available online at www.gamasutra.com/features/20010209/evans_01.htm.

[Pottinger00]  Pottinger, Dave. "Terrain Analysis in Realtime Strategy Games," available online at www.gdconf.com/archives/proceedings/2000/pottinger.doc.

[Snook00]  Snook, Greg. "Simplified 3D Movement and Pathfinding Using Navigation Meshes" from *Game Programming Gems I* (Ed. Mark DeLoura, Charles River Media, 2000).

[Sterren01]  van der Sterren, William. "Terrain Reasoning for 3D Action Games."

[Zobrist69]  Zobrist, Albert L. "A Model of Visual Organization for the Game of Go." The seminal article on influence mapping. Proc. AFIPS 1969 Spring Joint Computer Conf. 34: pp. 103–112.

# 3.7

# Strategic Assessment Techniques

## Paul Tozour

gehn29@yahoo.com

**T**his gem describes a suite of useful techniques for strategic decision-making. Where the previous gem on influence mapping provided a means for tactical assessment on a geographical level, these data structures provide an AI agent or player with a means of assessing the current game state on a strategic and functional level.

These techniques are most clearly applicable to games that involve some aspect of economic management, resource-allocation decisions, and/or technological advancement, such as strategy games, economic simulations, and "god games." However, there are doubtless many potential applications to other genres as well.

## The Resource Allocation Tree

The *resource allocation tree* is a tree structure that represents the specific functional purpose of all the assets under a player's control. The tree breaks down all of the units and resources currently in play into a hierarchy of functional categories.

The usefulness of this representation derives from its ability to allow an AI player to evaluate the strategic strengths and weaknesses of all of the players in the game, itself included. The tree also provides an excellent basis for a wide variety of economic production and resource-allocation decisions. For example, it provides an immediate basis for determining what types of new units to produce and how to reallocate existing units into different functional roles.

At the top of the tree is a root node that represents a player's total assets. Directly beneath the root is a breakdown of the major different categories of assets available in the game.

Let's imagine we break this down into Military, Economic, and Intelligence. Each of these is broken down further into subcategories. Military might be broken down into Offense and Defense, for example, and each of these could be broken down into Ballistic, Ranged, and Melee to indicate different functional roles for military units. Economic would likely be broken down into Resource Gathering, Unit Production, Base Construction, Tech Advancement, and so on down the tree. Figure 3.7.1 illustrates a small slice of the resource allocation tree.

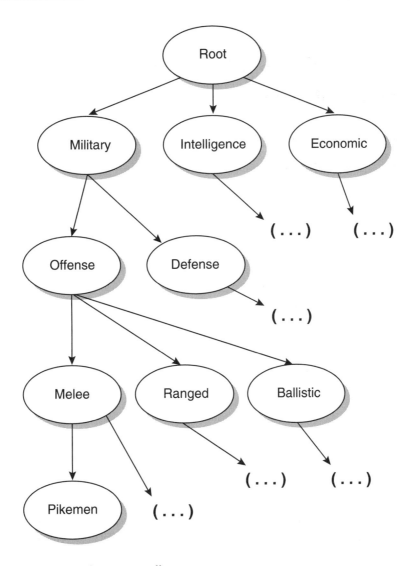

**FIGURE 3.7.1** *The resource allocation tree.*

The leaves of the tree are the specific types of units available. For example, "Pikemen" sits in Root/Military/Offense/Melee/Pikemen. The Pikemen node itself would likely include various statistics on all the Pikemen we've dedicated to an offensive capacity, such as the total quantity, total hit points, total number of Pikemen killed in combat, and so on.

Just as with an influence map, an AI player should maintain a separate instance of this data structure for each player in the game, including itself. The graphs for the other players will represent this player's current knowledge and best estimates of the functional breakdown of each player's current strategic assets.

A Pikeman is primarily a defensive unit, but it could also be used for attack or exploration. This raises the question of how to categorize a single species of unit that can participate in multiple functional roles.

An AI player will typically dedicate a given unit to only one functional role at any given moment, so I recommend categorizing units in terms of their current functional employment rather than attempting to split a single Pikeman into, say, 10% Exploration, 60% Defense, and 30% Offense. The Pikeman nodes beneath Offense, Defense, and Exploration should represent the Pikemen that are currently allocated to each of those functional roles.

It's also important to note that at any given moment, the resource allocation tree contains only those assets that I actually possess or am currently capable of producing. If I have no Mage Towers and can't currently build one, there is no reason to include it as a node in the tree.

## Calculating Desired Allocation

The structure of the resource allocation tree provides us with a very simple and natural means for determining appropriate resource allocation. We can rank the intended priority of each node in the tree by proceeding down the graph from the root.

Begin with a value of 1.0 at the root, indicating a desired 100% resource allocation. At each node, we split the current value into an appropriate fraction of the desired allocation for each child node. Starting from 1.0, we break this value down into Military = 0.3, Intelligence = 0.1, and Economic = 0.6. Under "Military," we break this 0.3 down further into 67% Defense and 33% Offense (Defense = 0.2 and Offense = 0.1). This process continues down the tree so that we calculate a "desired allocation" value for each tree node.

The algorithm for determining the numeric breakdown at each node will depend on the design of your game. Each nonleaf node will require custom logic code to continuously update the distribution to its child nodes in response to the evolving state of the game world. This is a matter of tweaking and tuning to achieve optimal results. Initially it's often a good idea to simply take a few guesses and use predetermined constants until you get a good sense of what specific factors should cause the computer player to change these weights as a given game session unfolds.

## Determining Current Allocation

Simultaneously, we can use the tree to calculate a "current allocation" value for each node. This gives us a breakdown of the assets we actually possess.

This calculation proceeds in the opposite direction, from the bottom of the tree up to the root. We iterate over all the Pikemen currently allocated to Defense, for example, and calculate some value indicating every defensive Pikeman's estimated value (say, by multiplying an attack strength value for Pikemen by that specific Pikeman's current hit points). We then add all these Pikemen's scores together and mark this as the current allocation value of the Pikeman node beneath Defense/Melee. We then pass this number up to the parent node (Melee), which adds together all of the numbers it receives from its children (such as all the Spearmen and Footmen we've allocated to Defense) and forwards this number up to its parent (in this case, Defense). Ultimately, the root node receives input from all of its children, and we end up with a fat floating-point number at the root that indicates the total current assets of all our possessions in the game world.

Once we've generated this value for "total assets," we can renormalize to values between 0 and 1. Revisit each node in the tree and divide its "current allocation" value by the root node's value, so that the root node again has a value of 1.0.

At this point, it should be obvious that we can directly compare the *current* allocation value in each tree node to the *desired* allocation value to trivially determine how far we are over or under budget in any particular capacity.

## Strategic Decision-Making

It should be apparent that the final allocation tree representation instantly provides us with an excellent way of organically maintaining the balance of our forces. If I'm in a battle and I lose all 20 of my Elephants, the Elephant node and all its parent nodes are now under-allocated relative to their desired allocation.

Of course, this won't necessarily mean that I replace all my Elephants with new Elephants. As the parent node of Elephant receives the resources it needs to fill in new child nodes, it may decide that the best course of action is to build a battalion of Plasma Tanks now that it's uncovered the requisite technologies.

The resource allocation tree is useful primarily for deciding which new units to construct and how to allocate existing units to the most appropriate roles. The first priority is usually to find those nodes that are most desperately in need of additional allocation, and then determine whether this is more appropriately addressed by reallocating existing units or by creating new ones.

The resource allocation tree also gives us a good way to design unique player personalities. Developing an expansionist, military-oriented "Genghis Khan," an economically obsessive capitalist, or a research-oriented technocrat is just a matter of tweaking the coefficients for the appropriate parts of the tree to favor or disfavor specific nodes. With a little tweaking at different parts of the tree, AI players can be made to favor individual species of units, different balances of growth versus defense, specific strategic categories of assets, or overall play styles.

Where combat is concerned, it's often a good idea to keep a precomputed "combat balancing table" of relative unit strengths, and use this for making decisions under the Military branch of the tree. This is essentially a 2D lookup table that allows you to determine the general effectiveness of any unit in combat against any other. By analyzing the functional asset tree that represents your knowledge of a particular enemy, you can determine the composition of his forces and emphasize the production of the assets that will be most effective against them.

Finally, the resource allocation tree is an excellent place to store all types of additional statistics. Several of the factors we would typically track in an influence map cell are also appropriate to a functional asset tree node.

It's also often a good idea to track which nodes in the tree have proven effective in the past, and which nodes have been attacked by enemy players. In the former case, it would allow me to detect that my Pikemen have served me well against another player, and to use this to direct my growth and development toward the functional roles that made my Pikemen victorious. In the latter case, it will allow me to detect that my enemy has a proclivity for attacking my resource-gathering units (for example), and to take additional steps to protect them in the future.

## Measuring Value

Probably the most significant challenge with this technique is finding an appropriate way to measure each unit's value in its particular branch of the tree. The numeric units used in each node need to be commensurate with all other units' values in their respective branches. Values under the Military branch should represent units' contributions in combat, and should take into account attack strength, rate of fire, movement speed, armor value, current hit points, and any other appropriate parameters. Values in the Intelligence branch should take into account factors appropriate for each unit's exploration ability, such as visibility range and movement speed, but probably not attack strength or hit points. Nodes in Resource Collection (under Economic) should take into account how quickly each resource-gatherer can collect resources, drop them off at the depot, and get back to the resources again. Finding an appropriate way to correlate these values is, like so much else in game AI, a matter of experimentation to find the optimal solution for your particular game.

Another potential challenge is handling economic systems with multiple resources. In games where different units cost different amounts of, say, gold, energy, and tiberium to produce, a single allocation value does not translate directly into a single resource. The potential solutions to this problem are beyond the scope of this gem.

## The Dependency Graph

The *dependency graph* is a data structure that models all the dependencies between the different types of assets in the game. The dependency graph encompasses all dependency-based relationships, such as a game's "tech tree" and "building tree."

The primary dependency type is a *creational* dependency. This indicates some number of conditions that must exist before a given species of asset can be constructed. For example, you must possess a Barracks before you can build a Pikeman. You must construct a Castle before you can reach the Imperial Age.

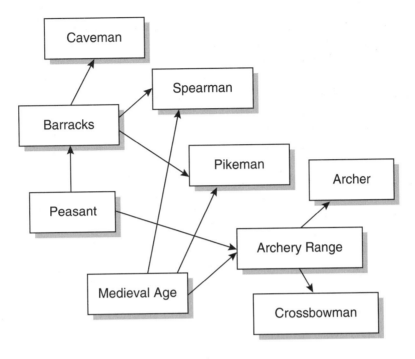

**FIGURE 3.7.2**  *The dependency graph.*

Creational dependencies can also include resource dependencies and other, more abstract dependencies. A Barracks requires gold and lumber. Gold and lumber come from the labors of peasants. Peasants get the gold from a gold mine and lumber from the forest.

Figure 3.7.2 shows a tiny sample dependency graph comprised solely of creational dependencies. A peasant can create Barracks and Archery Ranges, but the Archery Range can only be constructed after reaching the Medieval Age.

The second type of dependency is a support dependency. A Mage unit might require mana, which can only be generated by a Shrine. Without a shrine, the Mage will be essentially useless, as he cannot cast spells without a Shrine to feed him his precious mana.

As with the previously discussed data structures, an AI player should maintain several parallel dependency graphs, one for itself and one for each of the other players.

## Dependency Graph Nodes

A given node in a dependency graph will typically contain several different types of data. Useful categories include the total number of units of that type that the player currently possesses (or is believed to possess, if we are looking at another player); the total estimated value of those units; and the number of those assets currently in production (being created by a Barracks, for example). Given the overlap between their concerns, it may be possible for a "node" in the dependency graph to be similar to a "node" in the functional asset tree, or even be the same physical data structure. The main difference between the two is that the resource allocation tree tracks only the currently available assets, while the dependency graph tracks *all* possible assets.

## Economic Planning

The first and most obvious use for a dependency graph is building toward a goal. A computer player can use the dependency graph to determine what it needs to build in order to be able to produce a given asset. "I know I want to build a Wizards' Tower eventually, so to get there, I need to build a Library, and then secure a suitable source of mana, and then start building a Mage Hall . . . ."

The choice of which dependencies to fill in first is a trade-off between reacting to the present and planning for the future. A purely reactive AI will use the resource allocation tree to rank all the assets it can potentially create immediately and pick the best available node. A more planning-oriented AI will analyze all the nodes in the graph to find a long-term goal worth pursuing, query the functional asset tree to determine which dependencies are likely to be the most valuable, and build toward the most promising technology, however deep in the graph it may be.

Note that this process becomes tricky when there are several possible ways to fulfill a dependency—when either A or B will allow C. This seldom happens in practice, as game designers wisely avoid these types of dependencies. In a situation in which there are so many optional dependencies that the best route to a given node isn't obvious, any standard search algorithm should solve the problem quickly.

## Finding Vulnerable Dependencies

A dependency graph can be used to analyze strengths and weaknesses in a player's forces, and to pinpoint its opponents' most vulnerable dependencies. In *Red Alert 2,* the enemy AI will usually destroy my Barracks after taking out my War Factory. This is a clever and potentially devastating strategy as it forces me to spend precious time and money rebuilding the Barracks before I can consider rebuilding my War Factory.

There are three factors that generally determine whether a given node in the dependency graph is "vulnerable."

- **Intrinsic value**. Some assets are valuable of their own accord. A Nuclear Silo is valuable because it can attack the enemy directly. Assets deeper in the graph (farther along in the tech tree) usually have much higher intrinsic values.
- **Strong child dependencies**. Some assets are worth targeting because of what they can create or support. A War Factory can create tanks and other vehicles. A Library allows me to create the Mage Hall, which will eventually lead to Mages. A Fusion Plant supplies lots of electricity to a player's base (a support dependency).
- **Weak parent dependencies**. We can also eat away at parent dependencies, as with the Barracks destroyed after the War Factory. Graph nodes whose parents are

relatively weak (few instances of each supporting asset) and easy to attack (poorly defended) are more vulnerable to this type of attack.

We can use the same heuristic for both attack and defense. For attack, we often want to select the most valuable opposing player dependencies, and go after the War Factory first and the Barracks second. In defense, we use the graph to prepare for that exact possibility—we increase our defense and build duplicate buildings as backup.

## Strategic Inference

One subtle advantage of the dependency graph is that it provides a basis for making inferences about other players' current assets and likely strategies based on incomplete observations. For example, if I know my enemy has a Barracks, I can be confident that he either has Pikemen already or is capable of creating them in the near future. Similarly, if I see an enemy Pikeman, I can be 100-percent certain that he has a Barracks somewhere about (or at least, that he did when Pikeman unit was created—there's always the chance that the Barracks was destroyed after he created the Pikeman).

Inference works in two directions: forward and backward.

With forward inference, we know that the player in question possesses a given unit or resource, and we can project the likelihood that he will then fill in the child dependency. Each Barracks we observe makes the existence of Pikemen more likely.

With backward inference, we go back up the chain and assert that a given unit makes its dependencies nearly certain. Seeing a Pikeman makes us very confident of a Barracks, even if we've never observed it directly.

This kind of dependency-based inference can go a long way. If I see an enemy Grand Mage, I can assume there's a high probability that he also has a Mages' Arcanum building, High Magic upgrade, a Wizards' Tower, a Sages' Guild, a Library, and all the other dependencies leading up to the Grand Mage unit. Furthermore, I can then turn around and use forward inference on each of these nodes with their new probabilities. Since the Grand Mage allowed me to infer the existence of a Sages' Guild, I can assume that the player is probably capable of producing a Sage.

This process is a form of probabilistic inference and is broadly similar to a popular inference technique known as a "Bayes network" [see the *References* for details].

Interestingly, it's also possible to use inference to make certain nodes *less* probable. If we set an upper bound on the maximum possible size of a player's economy at a given point during the game—either on account of the amount of time he's had available to build up, or by reasoning based on inferences using data from the influence map—then certain dependencies make others less likely. Four minutes into the game, I know that the best player can build a Red Dragon Roost or a Nuclear Silo, but not both. Therefore, the presence of either makes the other less likely.

Of course, this is all a lot of work, and you can just as easily cheat and look at the other players' assets directly. As always, I leave this decision to your conscience and your opinion of how this decision would affect the entertainment value of your game.

## Player Personality

As with the functional asset tree, we can use the dependency graph to give AI players distinct personalities.

The vulnerability values for the various nodes in the dependency graph are a prime candidate for tweaking. By exaggerating or deflating the vulnerability values for different nodes, we cause our AI players to deflate or overvalue the significance of those assets. If we tweak the values on the dependency graphs we maintain for opposing players, we change the likelihood that we will target certain enemy assets rather than others. If we tweak the values on our dependency graph of our own assets, we change the way our economy develops and the specific technologies we embrace.

One simple technique for setting initial priorities is to pick a set of ultimate "goals" for a given AI player. Look at all the rightmost (deepest) nodes in the graph, find a suitable algorithm to rank these final dependencies by desirability, and come up with good final desirability values. You can then propagate these desirability values back toward the left side of the graph, and this will give the AI player a very clear indication of which technologies it should generally favor.

## Putting It All Together

Most of AI is decision-making, and a good representation of the game state can make an AI player's decisions vastly easier to make.

This gem and the previous one have described data structure foundations for this type of decision-making. Although not every game will be able to use all of these data structures, there are endless opportunities for intercommunication between whichever of these data structures you use for shared strategic and tactical decision-making. When the Influence Map, the Resource Allocation Tree, and the Dependency Graph communicate and share their data, we end up with a whole that is more than the sum of its parts. The Influence Map tells you where the enemy is, the Resource Allocation Tree tells you what you need to hit him with, and the Dependency Graph tells you how to build it and how to keep it full of gas once you're up and rolling.

## References and Additional Reading

[Ferber99] Ferber, Jacques, *Multi-Agent Systems*, Addison-Wesley, London, England, 1999. A useful perspective is to consider the cells/nodes of the data structures described here as hierarchical "agents" in a multi-agent system.

[Pearl88] Pearl, Judea, *Probabilistic Reasoning in Intelligent Systems: Networks of Plausible Influence*, Morgan Kaufman, San Francisco, CA, 1988. A must-read introduction to Bayes nets and probabilistic reasoning systems as they relate to AI.

[Russell95] Russell, Stuart and Norvig, Peter, *Artificial Intelligence: A Modern Approach*, Prentice Hall, Upper Saddle River, NJ, 1995. A comprehensive introduction to AI techniques—the "AI bible."

# 3.8

# Terrain Reasoning for 3D Action Games

## William van der Sterren, CGF-AI

william@cgf-ai.com

"Location! Location! Location!" This decree not only holds for real estate, but also for the virtual worlds in 3D action games. There, locations play a key role as sniper spots, strongholds, avenues of attack, bottlenecks, or "red armor" power-up areas. When locations are important in a game, they had better be important in the game AI as well.

This gem presents a technique for reasoning about locations and their role in the game. It shows how to translate location concepts to algorithms, so that the AI can compute and grasp these concepts. This helps the AI in picking good locations for its actions and in understanding the positions that other actors occupy. It literally puts the AI in a better position to assist or challenge the player.

First, we pick a terrain representation that the AI can handle efficiently: waypoint graphs. To illustrate waypoint-based reasoning, an example problem is introduced. Then, we identify tactical attributes and relate them to waypoint properties. We construct formulas to compute these waypoint properties, using static data such as the world geometry, and dynamic data such as actor activity. Finally, we discuss how to integrate terrain reasoning in our game and we look at various other applications of waypoint-based terrain reasoning.

## Representing Terrain to Reason About It

Reasoning about locations would be easy if there were only a few locations. However, today's game worlds feature tens of thousands of accessible polygons. In a game, multiple AI actors take into account both visible and invisible locations. If this were done in terms of raw polygons, that effort would probably consume more resources than the 3D graphics rendering.

To complicate matters further, the value of a location isn't so much determined by its own characteristics as it is its relationship with the surrounding locations. For example, is it easy to access the location? Is the location observable by many other locations? Are there any power-ups nearby? In addition, actual gameplay matters a lot: some locations (for example, near an objective) are frequently visited, whereas other areas are not.

Thus, to reason effectively and efficiently about terrain, we had better pick a representation that approximates the terrain using far less detail than the raw polygonal geometry. That representation should express relations between locations easily, and support capturing of location-based game activity. Ideally, the representation allows us to use precomputed intermediate results, leaving us some CPU time for more advanced AI or a faster game.

## Waypoints

Most 3D game AIs already have a terrain representation that is easy to handle. They use waypoints, or similar navigation aids such as grids, or cells (see [Snooke00], [Rabin00], [Reece00]). These waypoints represent the most relevant part of the terrain: the terrain that is accessible to the game actors. Each waypoint is a sample, an approximation, of its immediate surroundings. The number of waypoints is typically in the order of 250 to 2500.

Reasoning in terms of waypoints is attractive because many game AIs already use these waypoints to move around, to find paths, to mark the presence of special items and obstacles, and to receive hints from the level designer. Because the AI performs many of its actions with waypoints in mind, and because it thinks of players as being near waypoints, capturing gameplay data per waypoint is easy and almost free.

Before we start reasoning about the waypoint-based terrain representation, that representation needs to approximate the terrain and relevant properties well enough. The network of waypoints should be sufficiently dense to represent all relevant locations as well as any cover and concealment present. Typically, that means a larger number of waypoints than required for AI navigation and pathfinding.

Terrain reasoning often deals with other inter-waypoint relations than shortest path and movement. The need for these additional relations and the reasoning about waypoints are best illustrated using an example.

## Example Terrain and AI Needs

To illustrate waypoint-based terrain reasoning, let's look at the following example: in the area depicted in Figure 3.8.1, we want our AI actors to pick solid offensive and defensive tactical positions, both before and during a fight.

To support the AI in efficiently picking and visiting strong positions, we compute for each waypoint and for a number of directions, the offensive and defensive value of that waypoint. This value is computed using the waypoint graph and world geometry and improved with captured gameplay "experience." Such a "tactical'" understanding of each waypoint can be input for pathfinding, for flocking, to pick guard positions overlooking an objective, and so forth.

The example area features one objective and two entrances, and is populated by a dense grid of waypoints. Note that just the waypoints themselves (in Figure 3.8.1 center) already give you a good clue of the level's architecture.

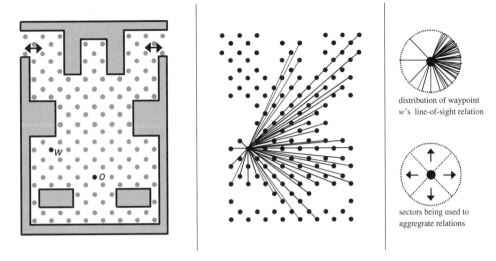

**FIGURE 3.8.1**  *(left) A top view of the example terrain, featuring two entrances/exits, and one objective* o. *The terrain is covered by a good number of waypoints, including waypoint* w. *(center) The waypoints in the example terrain, and the valid lines of sight from waypoint* w *to other waypoints. (right) The distribution of lines of sight from* w, *and the proposed sectors to aggregate them.*

## Tactical Analysis

In assessing the tactical value of a location, many factors need to be considered. A large number of these factors can be translated to properties of a waypoint, which in turn can be computed. Let's consider the example area from both a *Quake*-style capture-the-flag game and from a tactical simulation perspective.

In a fast capture-the-flag game, characterized by rapid movement, power-ups, nonlethal weapons, and rocket launchers, the tactical value of a location is largely determined by the following characteristics:

- Locations that provide for fast movement and freedom to move in any direction are essential for attackers.
- Locations near power-ups are valuable.
- Locations susceptible to rocket blasts aren't that attractive.
- Locations overlooking the path to the flag while being hard to spot when rushing to the flag make for good defensive positions.

In a tactical simulation, characterized by lethal weapons, slow movement, cover, stealth, and sniping, other characteristics become key.

- Nearby cover is important for offensive and defensive actions. Even partial cover or reduced visibility at a location can be a serious advantage.

- Locations where movement is slow or predictable (near the entrance, for example) make for bad offensive spots, whereas the locations overlooking them become more attractive for defense.
- As within the capture-the-flag game, locations that overlook the objective, and locations overlooking the main paths to and from the objective are important as well.

## From Tactical Values to Waypoint Properties

Now that we have identified a number of tactical characteristics that largely determine the offensive and defensive values of a location, we need to turn them into an evaluation function and output.

First, we look at the waypoint properties that we can use to express tactical characteristics. Figure 3.8.2 illustrates the different types of waypoint properties available.

A waypoint has properties that are local, such as the light level and the presence of a power-up or door. Another category of properties is determined by the waypoints' membership in a larger terrain representation (typically a group of waypoints). For example, the waypoint may be part of a room, a street, or a roof. Note that both the local properties and the group membership properties are nondirectional.

The relations between waypoints, however, are directional. For example, waypoint $w$ (in Figure 3.8.1) can see almost all waypoints to its east, and it will be hard to approach waypoint $w$ from the east without being observed. In a 3D world, height differences often cause a waypoint to be easily accessed from one direction, and much harder (read: taking a longer path and more time) from other directions.

A last, but essential, aspect is the distribution of the waypoint's relations. For example, if a waypoint overlooks many other locations in primarily one direction, the player or AI is able to focus on that direction and see all visible activity instantly, without having to worry about attacks from other directions. The concentration of relations in a sector is called *focus*.

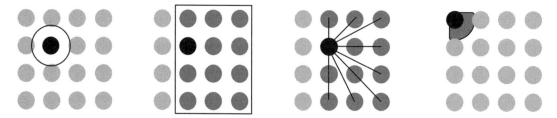

**FIGURE 3.8.2** *Waypoint properties: (from left to right) local properties, group membership, relations with other waypoints, and focus.*

## Computing Waypoint Properties

To compute a useful offensive or defensive rating for a given waypoint and direction, we need to implement each applicable tactical characteristic as a function of waypoint properties.

Many tactical characteristics can be decomposed into primitive functions about the waypoint graph, in effect dealing with linear distance, travel time, line-of-sight, line-of-fire, objectives, and obstacles. For example, an important characteristic of a good attack position is that it provides for rapid movement at that position. A "water" position does not allow rapid movement locally. A waypoint with a "water" local property should rate low in enabling rapid movement.

In small rooms and tunnels, it is difficult to dodge rockets and avoid the blast from a rocket or grenade. Locations that are more spacious thus offer an advantage. If a waypoint is part of an area (represented by a group of waypoints) that is a small room or tunnel, it should rate lower in being "open." Thus, the waypoint's group membership can be used to compute a tactical characteristic.

In the following code, two tactical characteristics are computed using a local waypoint property and a group membership property, respectively.

```
float GetLocalRapidMovement( waypointid wp )
{ // result in [0 .. 1], higher values meaning higher speeds
  return ( GetActorMovementSpeedAtWaypoint( wp )
          / GetMaxActorMovementSpeed( ) );
}
float GetOpenAreaMembership ( waypointid wp )
{ // result in [0 .. 1], higher values meaning more open
  return 1.0 - max( IsPartOfSmallRoom( wp ),
                    IsPartOfTunnel( wp ) );
}
```

It is more complicated to compute a directional relation for a waypoint. A specific relation for waypoint $w$, such as the availability of nearby cover from another waypoint $w_{to}$ that has a line of sight on $w$, is computed in the following function.

```
float GetCoverFromThreatsInDirection(waypointid w) {
  float        property [kMaxDirections];
  unsigned int entry[kMaxDirections];

  // set all property and entry values to 0
  ...

  // pass one: collect and interpret relations
  for (waypointid w_to = 0; w_to < kMaxWaypointId; w_to++ ) {
    direction dir = GetDirectionForWaypoints( w, w_to );

    // check for line-of-fire from w_to to w
    if ( (w_to != w ) && (HasLineOfFire(w_to, w)) ) {
      entry[dir]++;

      // get value for relation (value in [0..1])
      float value = GetCoverFromThreatsAt( w, w_to );
      property [dir} += value;
    }
  }

  // pass two: level result into [0 .. 1] range
  for ( direction dir = 0; dir < kMaxSectors; dir++ ) {
    if ( entry [dir] > 0 ) {
      property [dir] /= entry [dir];
    }
  }
}

float GetCoverFromThreatsAt(waypointid w, waypointid w_at) {
  for (waypointid w_n = 0; w_n < kMaxWaypointId; w_n++ ) {
    // check for lack of line-of-fire to neighbor of w
      if ( IsNeighborOf(w, w_n) && (!HasLineOfFire(w_at, w_n)) )
        return 1.0;
  }
  return 0; // no cover found
}
```

In a first iteration over all waypoints, solely those waypoints with a line of fire to *w* are considered. For each of these waypoints, the number of *w*'s relations is incremented, and the value of the nearby cover available is accumulated.

In a second iteration, the amount of "nearby cover" is divided by the number of relations, to return a value between 0 and 1. Rather than using the number of relations here, we will use the focus() function to deal with the concentration of relations in a certain direction. This focus() function is explained later.

In a function such as GetCoverFromThreatsAt() (the second function at bottom of the previous code listing), a very simple approximation is made. A more advanced approximation might use fuzzy logic to deal with such issues as the travel time to the nearest cover, the amount of cover available, and the weapon effectiveness over the distance between the waypoints.

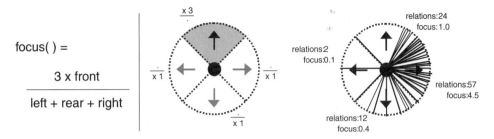

$$focus() = \frac{3 \times front}{left + rear + right}$$

**FIGURE 3.8.3** *Simple computation of the focus values for waypoint* w *in the example terrain. All relations are projected on a 2D dish with four 90-degree sectors. The focus of a sector is a weighted ratio of its relations versus the relations in other sectors.*

The focus of a waypoint reflects the concentration of relations over the various directions. Focus is particularly valuable in defense and when survival is important. In these cases, it is not sufficient for a location to offer great sniping opportunities in one direction. The location also needs to offer flank and rear protection; that is, have few line-of-sight/fire relations to the sides and to the rear.

The function `focus( w, d )` expresses the distribution of relations in one direction relative to the distribution in other directions. The exact implementation of `focus()` depends on the number of different directions considered (the sectors) and the type of relation for which the concentration is considered (often the line-of-sight). Figure 3.8.3 illustrates an implementation of focus for waypoint *w* in our example terrain, using simply four sectors to represent the various directions possible in a 3D sphere. When determining the focus, you should also deal with the exceptional case of a waypoint having relations solely in a single sector. Then, a default maximum should be used.

The `focus()` function assumes a more or less uniform distribution of waypoints across the terrain. However, the function is largely robust against moderate deviations in that distribution. When we have expressed every tactical characteristic in a number of waypoint property computations, we can combine them as follows:

```
rating( w, d ) = Σ kᵢ x local_propertyᵢ( w )
               + Σ kⱼ x group_membershipⱼ( w )
               + focus( w, d ) x Σ kₗ x relationₗ( w, d )
```

Note that for `focus()` to correctly emphasize or dampen the results from the `rela-tionx()` functions, these `relationₓ()` should all return positive values. This rating expresses the AI's a-priori understanding of a location and its role in the game. This rating, the tactical value of a location, is based on the waypoint graph and world geometry, and implicitly uses some static game constants such as actor movement speeds, weapon performance, and power-up locations. For the example area discussed, we are now able to automatically annotate each waypoint with its offensive and defensive values in a given direction (given some time for experimentation and tuning).

## Learning from Gameplay Experience

Obviously, not every value will be fully correct. Our terrain sampling, by means of waypoints, is an approximation, and so are the evaluation functions used to compute the values.

In addition, we have been ignoring actual gameplay. That mistake, however, is easily turned into an advantage.

Because the AI uses waypoints for its actions, and thinks of the players as being near waypoints, we can record their activity at a waypoint with little effort. We can use that information in two ways. We can use it to correct the outcome of our computations, and we can use it as additional input in the computations.

We can improve, for example, the defensive value of a waypoint in a direction by adding the damage done by an actor, and subtracting the damage received by an actor at that waypoint. In other words, we add a little reinforcement learning to the AI's understanding of the locations. That will correct part of the error present in our results. More importantly, it leads to an AI that will vary and adapt its choice of location based on its past successes and failures!

The captured gameplay data can also be input for our waypoint properties. For example, the more "hostile traffic" waypoints that can be seen from a location, the more useful that location will be for defense. Such a relation can be computed easily, if the required traffic data is available. When using gameplay data as input for the computations, the AI actually gains tactical understanding of the terrain.

## Putting Terrain Reasoning in the Game

So, our AI can analyze the example area by a series of computations, using geometry data, travel time, shortest paths, line-of-sight, line-of-fire, and waypoint-related gameplay data. These computations have $O(n^3)$ time complexity, because in computing some of the waypoint-to-waypoint relations, other nearby waypoints are also considered. In practice, the computations take some tens of seconds. This kind of waypoint reasoning is best done when preprocessing a level and possibly between missions, as a background thread.

Few resources are used by the results from the terrain reasoning algorithm. Typically, they consist of several tables per waypoint, each table containing a small number of bytes. The tables can quickly be read and contain knowledge about the terrain that would otherwise be almost impossible to obtain. In addition, the reinforcement learning based on gameplay data enables some varying and adaptive AI behavior at negligible costs.

In general, waypoint-based reasoning need not be CPU intensive. Terrain reasoning is quite feasible during gameplay, provided the AI considers a small set of waypoints, and has intermediate reasoning results available. Using small look-up tables for each waypoint to store both the nearby waypoints and the visible waypoints, the AI can, for example, efficiently plan paths that avoid locations under fire from threats.

Dynamic game terrain and entities, such as doors, vehicles, destructible terrain, and smoke do complicate the terrain reasoning, because these dynamics partially invalidate precomputed results. Notably the line-of-sight, line-of-fire, and paths will be affected by dynamic terrain. Nevertheless, it often remains attractive to use precomputed intermediate results. It is often more intelligent and efficient to use these results and try to correct for any dynamics than to use no reasoning at all.

The terrain reasoning discussed here is a set of heuristics. It takes a number of experiments and some analysis to find the right ingredients and weights for your AI terrain reasoning. To effectively tune and verify your algorithm, visualization of the (intermediate) reasoning output is essential. The output can be interpreted easily when projected onto the terrain within the game. Alternatively, you can export the results to a spreadsheet for further analysis.

## Other Applications

Waypoint-based terrain reasoning is presented here using a simple example, precomputing the offensive and defensive values of the game locations. The ideas behind the reasoning have a much wider use than that example. The idea of dissecting tactical guidelines and expressing them as evaluation functions per location is an approach that will work for many games where the AI needs to reason about locations.

Just ask yourself the question:

*"If I were to defend this base (or whatever the AI needs to do), why would I prefer location x over location y, and what does distance, travel time, line-of-fire, the type of area, (or whatever terrain property or game item you can come up with) have to do with it?"*

Waypoints, if placed in a sufficiently dense graph across the terrain, serve many more purposes than just navigation. Together with a few small lookup tables for nearby waypoints and visible waypoints, they enable the AI to predict out-of-sight opponent movement, and to find a nearby location providing a new line-of-sight.

Waypoints are a handy means to "host" additional costs for A* pathfinding. If we tag all waypoints that are visible from the assumed threat positions with extra costs, the A* pathfinder provides us a path offering cover from the threats where available. If we also tag all waypoints that restrict our movement, the path returned will be even more "tactical." These are just two of the many examples of waypoint-based reasoning. You can probably think of a few more that will put your AI in a strong position.

## Conclusion

Waypoint graphs provide an easy-to-use representation of the game terrain. You can translate many of the terrain-related tactics in your game to waypoint-related properties. As an example, this gem shows how to build a per-waypoint evaluation function that expresses the value of a location for general offense, general defense, or a particular tactic such as ambushing or sniping. This will provide your AI with a good understanding of the terrain.

You can extend and improve that evaluation function with captured gameplay data, resulting in an AI that becomes more varied and adaptive. There are many other ways your AI can reason about terrain using waypoints. Just try to relate the tactical guidelines to waypoint properties (that fit in a look-up table).

## References and Additional Reading

[Pottinger00] Pottinger, Dave, "Terrain Analysis in Realtime Strategy Games," Proceedings of Computer Game Developer Conference, 2000.

[Rabin00] Rabin, Steve, "A* Speed Optimizations," *Game Programming Gems*, Charles River Media, 2000: pp. 272–287.

[Reece00] Reece, Doug, et al, "Tactical Movement Planning for Individual Combatants," Proceedings of the 9th Conference on Computer Generated Forces and Behavioral Representation, 2000. Also available online at www.sisostds.org/cgf-br/9th/.

[Snook00] Snook, Greg, "Simplified 3D Movement and Pathfinding Using Navigation Meshes," *Game Programming Gems*, Charles River Media, 2000: pp. 288–304.

# 3.9

# Expanded Geometry for Points-of-Visibility Pathfinding

## Thomas Young

thomas.young@bigfoot.com

In *Game Programming Gems*, Bryan Stout and Steve Rabin described "points-of-visibility" pathfinding [Stout00], [Rabin00]. This is essentially a way to find the shortest path around polygonal obstacles.

As Steve pointed out, there are big advantages to the method. It enables you to create a minimal representation of the search space, resulting in very fast searches. In addition, paths found are perfectly direct.

In this gem I explain how to automate construction of expanded geometry from polygonal obstacles, and how to use this to implement points-of-visibility pathfinding. By using expanded geometry, we overcome most of the disadvantages of the technique.

- Points of visibility can be extracted directly from the expanded geometry without designer assistance.
- It is possible to support dynamic objects (such as characters, doors, moving blocks, and so on) by generating and integrating expanded geometry for those objects on the fly.
- The expansion can be parameterized to support characters of different sizes and formations.

For many games, pathfinding is fundamental to the AI. It is up to the pathfinder to guarantee certain aspects of character behavior. It is essential, for example, that AI characters do not get stuck against obstructions. Characters must not fail to find a path around obstacles when that path looks obvious to the player. When collision against obstructions is complicated, even these capabilities are difficult to guarantee.

If we accept some limitations on the collision model for character movement, we can use exactly the same model for both collision and pathfinding. By using expanded geometry we can build a pathfinding system that is exactly correct for this collision model. This system is guaranteed to understand correctly any position a character can reach, and returns paths that are guaranteed to be unobstructed, so characters can't get stuck.

Higher-level AI built on a "perfect" pathfinding system is much easier to code because you don't need to catch those tricky situations, such as a character getting stuck because no path can be found from its current position. By depending completely on the results of the pathfinding system, it is possible to build sophisticated movement-related AI with far fewer lines of code. It is also much more fun.

## Defining a Collision Model

A collision model precisely specifies character collision against the environment. We build our collision model around a "collision shape" for each character. The collision shape is a convex polygon chosen to best represent the shape and size of that character. The shape translates with the character's origin when the character moves, but doesn't rotate when it turns. The character is obstructed for positions where its collision shape overlaps the environment.

The environment is represented polygonally and can be comprised of convex and nonconvex polygons that mark obstructed areas, 2D meshes to represent unobstructed areas, or some combination of these representations (Figure 3.9.1).

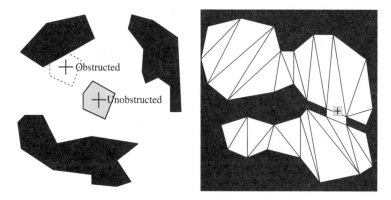

**FIGURE 3.9.1** *Collision shapes in polygonal environments.*

## Polygonal Pathfinding

Now that we have specified a collision model, it is the job of the pathfinder to find paths for a character that are unobstructed for this model. For simplicity, I consider only the traditional pathfinding constraint; that is, to find the shortest path from the start position to a given goal position. The problem can be restated as finding the shortest set of unobstructed line sections connecting start to goal.

## Expand and Conquer

The trick is to build an expanded geometry that combines our collision shape with the shape of the obstacles in the environment. This representation greatly simplifies the queries we require for our pathfinding system.

The expansion we use is a *Minkowski sum* of planar sets. Specifically, our expanded geometry will be a Minkowski sum between the environment and the negated collision shape. This is sometimes called a *Minkowski difference*.

The Minkowski sum of two sets A and B is the set of values that can be generated by adding some member of set A to some member of set B. A polygon can be viewed as a planar set; that is, the set of points inside that polygon.

Our expanded geometry represents the set of points that can be generated by subtracting some offset in our collision shape from some point inside the environment. This means that for each position in our expanded geometry, some point in the collision shape overlaps the environment. *Therefore, our expanded geometry represents the set of points where our character will be obstructed* (Figure 3.9.2).

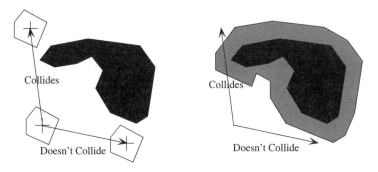

**FIGURE 3.9.2** *Collision shape in polygonal environment, point in expanded environment.*

Collision between a collision shape and the original polygonal environment is identical to collision between a point and the expanded geometry. To find out if a character can be placed at a position, we test whether that position is inside our expanded geometry. To find out if a line section is obstructed for a character, we simply test whether the line collides against our expanded geometry.

For points-of-visibility pathfinding, the set of convex corners in our expanded geometry gives us our points of visibility. Two points can be connected if the line between the points doesn't collide against our expanded geometry.

## Minkowski Sum of Convex Polygons

To build our geometry, we start by looking at the simpler case of a single convex polygon obstruction. The negated collision shape is also a convex polygon, so we must construct a Minkowski sum of two convex polygons.

For convex polygons C and O, this sum can be visualized as the space swept out by dragging the center of C around the perimeter of O (Figure 3.9.3a). This space will be bounded by a larger convex polygon. The sum can also be visualized as the shape

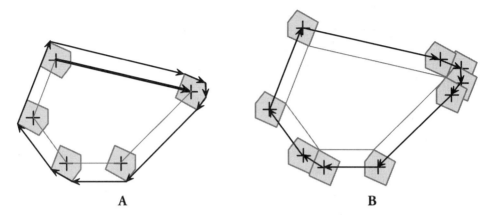

**FIGURE 3.9.3** *A) Sum of convex polygons. B) Alternative visualization.*

enclosed by the center of the (non-negated) collision shape as it slides around touching the perimeter of O (Figure 3.9.3b).

Edges in the expanded polygon are generated in three ways (see Figure 3.9.3b):

1. Directly from an edge in C, when C is placed at a corner of O.
2. By a corner of C as C moves along an edge in O.
3. By an edge in C as C moves along a parallel edge in O.

When there are no parallel edges, each edge in C and O is used exactly once, giving us a limit for edges in our expanded polygon equal to the edges in C plus the edges in O. This is useful for us to allocate space in advance for the expanded polygon.

It is fairly easy to build the expanded polygon. Vertices in C are numbered in a clockwise direction (Figure 3.9.4a). For each edge in O, we determine which of these vertices is used to expand the start and end points of that edge (Figure 3.9.4b). This

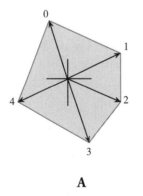

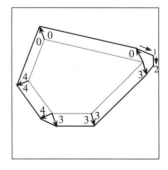

**FIGURE 3.9.4** *A) Vertices in C. B) Start and end points, interpolated vertices.*

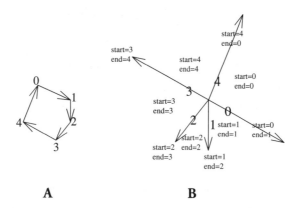

**A**                                   **B**

**FIGURE 3.9.5**  *Ordering by edge vectors, start and end expansion for an edge.*

gives us our type (2) or type (3) edges. Type (1) edges are constructed where the end point of one of these edges does not connect to the start point of the next, by interpolating vertices in C, if required, and adding edges (also Figure 3.9.4b). Interpolation is just a case of counting through vertices in C until we reach the vertex that expands the start of the next edge.

So, how do we determine the start and end expansions for each edge in the first place? We can define a circular ordering on vectors, based on the directions of the edges in C (Figure 3.9.5). For each edge in O, position in this ordering tells us which vertices in C expand the start and end points of that edge (also Figure 3.9.5). For a bit of extra speed, this position can be tracked incrementally as we loop through edges in O.

## Expanding Nonconvex Geometry

Now that we can expand a convex polygon, there is a straightforward way to extend this to a nonconvex polygon. We simply split the nonconvex polygon into convex parts and expand each part separately (Figure 3.9.6a). However, this can result in a large number of overlapping polygons with a lot of unnecessary edges and corners.

To make a well-formed Minkowski sum, we should detect intersections between expanded polygons and connect them together to make a single expanded shape. A fundamental problem with this approach is the fact that intersections may not fall exactly on points representable by the numbers we are using for coordinates. Moreover, if we use approximate points at intersections, then our pathfinder no longer corresponds exactly to our collision model, although this may not matter if our collision engine will also be built around the same expanded representation.

A good solution is to make a "lazy man's Minkowski sum." Here we are not concerned with the set of obstructed points, but rather with transitions from unobstructed areas into obstructed areas. This approach is more appropriate for external boundaries that can't be decomposed, as such, into convex polygons. This will also be more relevant if we need to make extensions in the future to support features such as overlapping geometry.

To build a "lazy man's Minkowski sum," we can use virtually the same method we used to expand a convex polygon. The difference is that we do not interpolate points at a concave corner. If the end point for the edge before the corner is not same as the start point for the edge after the corner, then we get an intersection and a discontinuity in the expanded edge list (Figure 3.9.6b).

This process is a lot easier to code and a lot faster than generating a true Minkowski sum. For a start, we don't have to perform any triangulation or detect intersections. For large collision shapes, we can still end up with unnecessary edges and corners, but this is usually not a big problem.

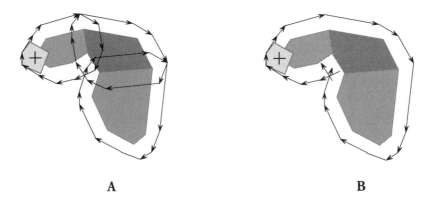

**A**　　　　　　　　　　　　　　　　　　　　　　**B**

**FIGURE 3.9.6** *A) Nonconvex polygon expanded as convex subparts. B) Lazy man's Minkowski sum.*

## Choosing a Collision Shape

The fact that our collision shape doesn't rotate is a major limitation for our collision model. Because the characters in our games will almost certainly need to rotate, we will want to use rotationally symmetrical collision shapes in order to get the most consistent collision behavior. A circle would be the best approximation, but we can't use a circle because the resulting expanded geometry would have no corners and hence no points of visibility. Instead, we must use an N-sided regular polygon to approximate a circle.

In general, the more edges we use in our collision shape, the more edges and corners we get in the resulting expanded geometry. With more edges and corners, pathfinding becomes more expensive (sometimes exponentially). Squares and octagons are obvious choices because they are relatively simple and because they can be aligned with the coordinate axes.

In the past, it was important to use axis-aligned collision shapes for performance reasons. For vector comparisons against horizontal, vertical or 45-degree lines, multiplication can often be avoided. Nowadays, branch prediction issues mean that it is better to simply go ahead and perform the same multiplications for all cases, so there is no longer any performance reason to only use axis-aligned shapes. For some platforms, avoiding multiplication may still be an important issue, however.

## Conclusion

I have shown how a pathfinding system can be constructed that is precise with respect to a reasonably interesting polygonal collision model. There is a trade-off to be made between sophisticated collision systems and collision systems that characters can "understand." For games where you are able to use this model for both character collision and pathfinding, there can be a big payback in reduced debugging and simplified AI.

## References

[Rabin00] Rabin, Steve, "A* Speed Optimizations," *Game Programming Gems*, Charles River Media, 2000.

[Stout00] Stout, Bryan, "The Basics of A* for Path Planning," *Game Programming Gems*, Charles River Media, 2000.

# 3.10

# Optimizing Points-of-Visibility Pathfinding

## *Thomas Young*

thomas.young@bigfoot.com

The "points of visibility" pathfinding method has a number of advantages (see Steve Rabin's article in *Game Programming Gems*, [Rabin00]). Also, with expanded geometry we can make this an exact method to guarantee correct paths with respect to a given polygonal obstruction set (see "Expanded Geometry for Points-of-Visibility Pathfinding" in this volume.) Complexity is independent of scale, so it is possible to efficiently compute paths over long distances, and by precalculating the network of connections between points of visibility, an extremely fast pathfinder can be constructed.

As map complexity increases, and with it the number of points of visibility, we find that the number of connections between these points can increase exponentially, particularly on maps with large open areas. Memory can become an issue, especially on console platforms. In addition, the need for interesting AI demands that pathfinders must support dynamic features such as moving objects, characters, doors, and so on. To support dynamic features such as these, we need to work with points of visibility that are generated on the fly, and obstacles that can move to invalidate connections. If we are not careful, the overhead for calculating visibility with these dynamic features can also increase exponentially.

I present some optimizations that enable us to quickly discard many potential paths and to greatly reduce the size of our network of connections. This results in faster searches and less overhead for dynamic objects. With these optimizations, our algorithm will scale better to handle increasingly complicated maps.

## Points-of-Visibility Pathfinding

For this gem, I assume that the pathfinding agent can be considered as a point agent in a polygonal environment. Section 3.9 explains how a more interesting collision model can be converted to this form.

Our pathfinder uses an A* algorithm with a set of points of visibility as possible intermediate states between start and goal. The points of visibility are derived directly from the convex corners in our polygonal environment. For an explanation of the A* algorithm, see Bryan Stout's article in *Game Programming Gems* [Stout00].

## Storing the Shortest Path to Each Point

An important first step to prevent exponential growth of our search tree is to ensure that only the shortest path to any intermediate point is retained for further consideration. This is not a specific optimization for points-of-visibility pathfinding as it should probably be standard behavior for any A* implementation. This needs to be stressed, however, because it makes a big difference to scalability.

In Bryan Stout's article, he describes the use of an open list and a closed list. At each step of the A* algorithm, these lists are searched to find any other paths that also end at the current point under consideration.

One important difference between tile-based pathfinding and points-of-visibility pathfinding is the number of potential intermediate locations we need to consider. Since we only consider the convex corners in our environment, this will tend to be an order of magnitude less than the number of tiles required to represent the same map for tile-based pathfinding.

This means that it is feasible to use an array (with one entry per point of visibility) to keep a record of the shortest path found so far to each point. Instead of searching through open and closed lists, we need only make a single lookup into this array. In fact, this means that there is no longer any need for a closed list at all.

The array must be cleared before each use, but on most platforms, there will be a fast memory clear routine readily available, so the time this takes is usually irrelevant. If there is a very large number of points and you expect to only use a small number of these for each search, then it might be worth keeping the closed list as a record of which points must be cleared after the search is complete.

## Connecting the Corners

Each step in the A* algorithm involves taking the best partial path found so far and generating a set of successor paths. Each successor is formed by connecting the end of the partial path to another point with a line section. The point can be either a point of visibility or the goal point. The straightforward approach is to generate a successor for every point in the world for which the line section will be unobstructed.

By preprocessing collision between all pairs of points of visibility and building a (possibly large) table, we can determine very quickly at runtime which other points of visibility can be reached from some source point of visibility. The start and goal positions will change at runtime, so line sections to and from these points cannot be preprocessed. The same is true for any points of visibility resulting from dynamic obstacles.

### Optimization #1: Only Consider Paths to Silhouette Points

As seen from some source point, each other point in the world can be classified as left silhouette, right silhouette, or not a silhouette (Figure 3.10.1).

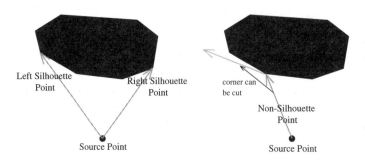

**FIGURE 3.10.1** *Silhouette points.*

This optimization is based on the observation that we don't need to consider path sections that connect to nonsilhouette points. Any path section going to a nonsilhouette point will result in a corner that can be cut to make a shorter path. (This is true unless that point coincides exactly with the goal point, or with another silhouette point. In both cases, there will be an alternative mechanism to generate that path.)

The optimization applies when we are generating the set of successors to a partial path. I will refer to the point at the end of this partial path as the current point. The points we consider using to extend the path are potential next points. We can simply discard any of these points that are not silhouettes as seen from the current point.

We discard nonsilhouette points because the resulting path can always be shortened by cutting a corner. To better visualize what is going on here, it is useful to understand that the shortened path will be realized as the search continues. This will happen either by connection directly from the current point or by connecting to a silhouette on a blocking object.

If we are using a visibility graph, then this optimization can also be applied directly to the connections in our visibility graph. Any connection can be removed from the graph where the destination point is not a silhouette from the source point.

### Optimization #2: Only Consider Paths that Go Around the Corner

This optimization is also applied when generating successors to a partial path.

For this optimization, we are interested in the line section at the end of our partial path. When generating successors for the first time, from the start position, the partial path is empty so this optimization does not apply. I will refer to the point at the start of this line section as the *previous* point. The point at the end of the partial path is our *current* point. As a result of our first optimization, the current point will always be a silhouette point as seen from the previous point.

The reasoning behind this optimization is similar to the reasoning behind the first optimization. Any path that does not go around the silhouette point will result in a corner that can be cut to make a shorter path. Figure 3.10.2 shows a silhouette point, a set of path sections that go around that point, and one example of a path that can be discarded. Again, the shortened path will be realized either by a direct connection from the previous point, or via another silhouette point if the direct connection is obstructed.

To implement this optimization, we use the vector from the previous point to the current point and the vector from the current point to the potential next point under consideration. At a left silhouette, the next vector must be on the right of the previous vector and to the left of the obstacle. At a right silhouette, the next vector must be on the left of the previous vector and to the right of the obstacle (Figure 3.10.2).

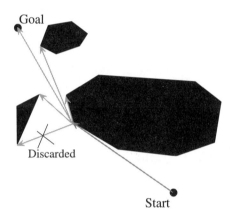

**FIGURE 3.10.2** *The path must go around each corner.*

## Silhouette Zones

For implementation, it is useful to define two zones relating to each point of visibility (Figure 3.10.3). Each point of visibility is positioned at a convex obstruction corner. The zones are formed by extension of the obstruction edges before and after that corner. The zones classify this point of visibility as seen from some arbitrary point. If that point is in the left silhouette zone, then our point of visibility is classified as left silhouette, and vice versa.

To go "around" the silhouette point, the next point must be in the opposite zone to the previous point, but it must also be inside the set of valid destinations bounded by the extension of the axis from the previous connection.

We can apply the second optimization to the connections in our visibility graph. Each connection in our graph has a source point and a destination point. When generating successors, these correspond to the current and next points, but there is no information in a simple visibility graph about the position of the previous point. This means that when we apply this optimization to the visibility graph, we must allow for

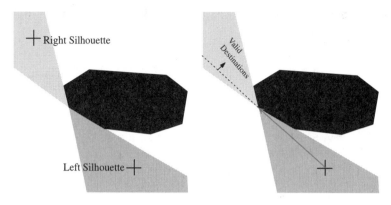

**FIGURE 3.10.3** *Silhouette zones at a corner.*

all possible positions for the previous point. This just means that our set of valid destinations becomes the set of points in either of our silhouette zones.

So, to apply this optimization to our visibility graph, we also discard connections where the destination point is not in one of the source point's silhouette zones. When we retrieve a connection from the visibility graph, we know the position of the previous point so we can make a more specific test to possibly discard that connection.

|  | Points | Connections before | Connections after |
|---|---|---|---|
| Environment 1 | 21 | 231 | 98 |
| Environment 2 | 96 | 1638 | 568 |

Figure 3.10.4 shows two examples of obstruction environments. The table above shows the number of connections in our visibility graph before and after using silhouette optimizations to discard connections.

**FIGURE 3.10.4** *Environment 1, Environment 2.*

### Using Silhouette Zones with Spatial Partitioning

The optimizations I have described enable us to reduce the number of connections in our visibility graph, and to reduce the size of our search tree. For dynamic points, we still need to test for connection to and from every other point in the world. We can quickly discard many of these connections, but connections that cannot be discarded need to be tested for collision.

The next step is to build a representation to quickly determine a minimal set of points that can potentially connect to or from a given dynamic point. Silhouette zones are a good starting point for building this representation. The zones for a given point of visibility give us an area within which dynamic points can potentially connect to that point of visibility. The exact nature of this representation should vary for different types of obstruction environments.

In maps with low visibility, built from rooms connected by portals, silhouette zones can be projected through portals to determine which rooms can potentially see the corresponding point of visibility.

For a more general system, silhouette zones can be clipped against the polygonal environment to determine the area in which a given point is visible. The resulting shapes can then be entered into some general spatial partitioning system. If the shape for one of these areas is represented exactly, then there is no need for any collision checking once it is known that a dynamic point is inside that shape. (Note that exact representation of the clipped area may depend on using an exact representation for line intersections.)

### Conclusion

There are many more details involved in building an efficient points-of-visibility pathfinding system. I have described some techniques for quickly discarding many connections and therefore reducing the total number of paths that must be considered. This is a good first step.

I have briefly mentioned how silhouette zones can be used with spatial partitioning to handle dynamic points efficiently. To support the addition of dynamic obstacles efficiently, a good spatial partitioning system is essential.

A final detail is the problem of testing for connection from one dynamic point to another. For the case with no dynamic obstacles, this only needs to be done once, for the potential connection from start point to goal point. With dynamic obstacles, this test may need to be performed a large number of times, so an efficient implementation becomes important.

### References

[Rabin00] Rabin, Steve, "A* Speed Optimizations," *Game Programming Gems*, Charles River Media, 2000.
[Stout00] Stout, Bryan, "The Basics of A* for Path Planning," *Game Programming Gems*, Charles River Media, 2000.

# Flocking with Teeth: Predators and Prey

## Steven Woodcock

### ferretman@gameai.com

**F**locking (sometimes called *swarming* or *herding*) is a technique first put forth by Craig Reynolds in a 1987 paper he did for SIGGRAPH entitled "Flocks, Herds, and Schools: A Distributed Behavioral Model" [Reynolds87]. In this paper, Reynolds defined the three basic rules (or steering behaviors) for flocking and explained how they interacted to give lifelike group behavior to creatures he called *boids*. In *Game Programming Gems*, I wrote a short gem introducing the subject [Woodcock00] and added another steering behavior to make what I called the "Four Rules of Flocking."

- **Separation**: Steer to avoid crowding local flockmates.
- **Alignment**: Steer toward the average heading of local flockmates.
- **Cohesion**: Steer to move toward the average position of local flockmates.
- **Avoidance**: Steer to avoid running into local obstacles or enemies.

**ON THE CD**

What's interesting about these four simple behavioral rules is how lifelike the resulting behavior of the boids can seem. Watching the original demo from the first book (also provided on the companion CD-ROM files for this chapter), one can see groups of boids coalesce and move in ripples around their world. When they approach boids belonging to another flock, they flee, breaking apart into smaller flocks, if necessary, to avoid contact with anybody not belonging to their flock. If split from their original flocks, individual boids eventually find fellows and form a new flock, which in turn would eventually find other flocks to join.

Another interesting aspect of flocking is that the movement algorithm itself is stateless—no information is maintained from movement update to movement update. Each boid reevaluates its environment at every update cycle. Not only does this reduce memory requirements that might otherwise be needed to provide a similar behavior using approaches besides flocking, it also allows the flock to react in real time to changing environmental conditions. As a result, flocks exhibit elements of emergent behavior—no one member of the flock knows anything about where the flock is going, but the flock moves as one mass, avoids obstacles and enemies, and keeps pace with one another in a fluid, dynamic fashion.

This technique has proven to be a valuable one for video games, having uses in everything from unit formations in an RTS, to realistic behavior of crowds in RPGs.

This gem builds on the original article in a number ways, borrowing from some of the suggested enhancements outlined there, together with one or two suggestions received by readers. I'll expand on the original demo, adding some features that somewhat individualize the boids, giving each boid a new feature—hunger. The world itself will be made a bit more difficult to navigate through the introduction of obstacles. I'll then introduce a new discriminator that gives our boids a reason to flee each other—some will be predators that actually *feed* on the others! Boids will now come in three flavors: hawks, sparrows, and flies. To this end, we'll be adding a "Fifth Rule":

- **Survival**: Steer to eat as needed, or to avoid being eaten if a predator is seen.

## A Whole New World

The original cube-shaped world of the first demo is a boring, empty place; nothing exists in that realm but the boids themselves. Left to itself (and assuming it didn't run into a boid from another flock), a given boid would pretty much fly around forever, wandering aimlessly. The only flocking-related code that might otherwise have influenced a boid's motion was a minor function I added to the flocking algorithm (in `CBoid::Cruising()`), and even that didn't contribute much. The world wrap code (which teleported boids flying off one side of the world to the other side) could screw up flocks a bit, but they always eventually found each other again.

More variety is needed if we're to make the lives of our creations more interesting and to provide an environment closer to one that might be found in an actual game. To help give our boids more to think about this time around, we've got to give them something new to deal with—*obstacles*.

### Obstacles

An obstacle is pretty much what it sounds like—something that's in the way. A new class of object called `CObstacle` has been added to create these. A `CObstacle` object forms an impenetrable cone-shaped barrier that all boids will try to avoid during their travels.

This class gives us a simple way to make the world a bit more interesting and provides them with some interesting navigational challenges. Obstacles can be created anywhere within the world with any arbitrary orientation, using either specified values or randomly determined ones. The `CObstacle::GetPosition()` method has been added to help us with collision detection and in determining if an obstacle is in the line of sight of a given boid, while `Cobstacle::GetRelativeDiameter()` will return the relative size of the obstacle at the boid's cruising altitude.

## Critters of All Kinds

Figure 3.11.1 shows how boids now come in three flavors, arbitrarily named *hawks*, *sparrows*, and *flies*, as they are all flying creatures. Each serves an important role in the ecology of our gem by hunting and feeding on each other.

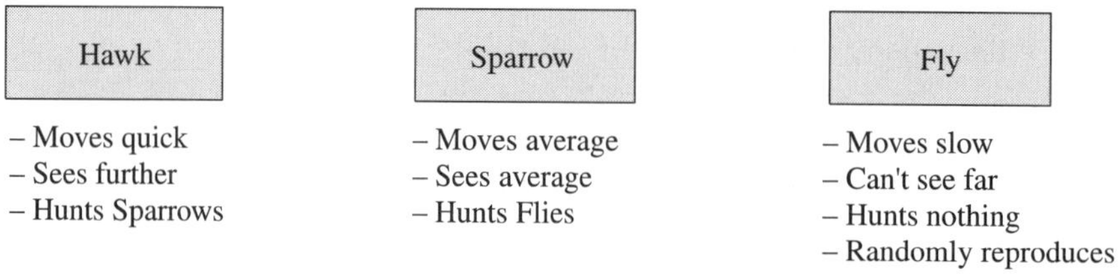

| Hawk | Sparrow | Fly |
|------|---------|-----|
| – Moves quick<br>– Sees further<br>– Hunts Sparrows | – Moves average<br>– Sees average<br>– Hunts Flies | – Moves slow<br>– Can't see far<br>– Hunts nothing<br>– Randomly reproduces |

**FIGURE 3.11.1** *Types of boids.*

## Every Boid Is a Bit Different

The original *Simple Flocking* demo initialized all boids with various parameters—range of sight, maximum speed of flight, etc.—which were identical for all boids anywhere in the world. There were no particular discriminators to distinguish one boid from another, beyond the flock to which it belonged. Boids belonging to other flocks were automatically enemies and avoided like the plague (if that switch was turned on).

The *Predators and Prey* flocking demo individualizes each boid a bit by allowing a randomized component upon boid creation. A boid thus created (via a new constructor added to the CBoid class) will now have some "personality," making each one a little bit different from its fellows. Some won't see well, while others will see farther than their brothers. Still others will want to maintain more distance from their fellows than the norm. Some will be hungrier than others, and so on.

Why do this? There are a couple of reasons, both of which add to the lifelike behavior of the creatures in our little world. First, providing each boid with slightly different capabilities is simply more realistic than an endless army of clones. Second, the differences will combine to provide some novel forms of *emergent behavior* as our boids interact, again providing what in the end is a more realistic representation of a group of creatures moving *en masse*. The tug and pull of two boids in the same flock, one of which wants to maintain a *cohesion* much tighter than its fellow, will make for some interesting group dynamics, as will a boid that can see an oncoming predator just a bit farther than any of his flockmates.

Additionally, the new demo adds some finer control over what types of boids are considered "enemies" and what types aren't. A new parameter has been added to the CBoid constructor that allows specification of that boid's type. This allows for simple tests to be added to the CBoid::SeeEnemies() and CBoid::FindFood() methods to compare types and determine if a given boid is a predator to be avoided or prey to be hunted.

Does this all add some overhead? Yes, though it's not much. The needs of the particular implementation, of course, will drive any such design decisions. For example, in an RTS game, every unit of archers might well be fairly generic, while in an FPS game, every squad-mate is an individual with unique characteristics.

## Feeding the Flock

It follows that if we're going to have classes of boids that feed on one another, we're going to need something to control that hunger. Nothing outside of the *Jaws* movies has an insatiable appetite, and our boids are no exception.

To represent this, both hawks and sparrows have a *hunger* rating that decrements a little each update cycle. When it reaches zero, our boid will become hungry and will begin to actively seek out prey to satisfy that hunger. In our demo, hawks hunt for sparrows, of course, while sparrow boids will seek out flies. Flies are at the bottom of the food chain and don't eat anything, but they will reproduce if there are enough of them in one flock. Each time a hawk or a sparrow eats, a random test will determine if it's still hungry by comparing its current hunger rating to its starting hunger rating. For example, if a hawk starts out with 10 hunger points and has eaten four sparrows, there's a 40-percent chance it will be satisfied and stop eating.

Since it isn't my desire to build a complicated feeding simulator, both hawks and sparrows "eat" when they successfully collide with their favorite food. A hawk will attempt to close with any sparrow boid it sees, while a sparrow boid will deliberately steer to intercept the nearest fly. Anything eaten is, of course, removed from the world.

## There's Always Another Fly

Since hawks feed on sparrows and sparrows feed on flies, flies are both at the low end of the food chain and arguably the most important members of it. If they die off, every other boid will too, sooner or later. To prevent this, flies have one feature that no other type of boid has—they can *reproduce*. To do this, I've added a *Reproduction* parameter to the CBoid class that controls the creation of new flies. When enough flies congregate in a flock, they can reproduce, creating a new fly boid every few seconds.

## Dinner on the Go

As mentioned previously, feeding is a pretty straightforward affair. When a hawk or sparrow is hungry (in other words, its *Hunger* rating has decremented down to zero), it will look for the nearest food it sees and try to collide with it. Any hawk that successfully intercepts a sparrow will gain one hunger point and then check to determine if it's eaten enough. The sparrow, on the other hand, is immediately removed from the world. Sparrows hunt flies in a similar fashion.

Since hawks are normally faster than sparrows, and sparrows are normally faster than flies, about the only thing that will prevent a given sparrow or fly from being eaten is a failure on the part of the predator to catch its prey. Each boid will, of course, automatically try to avoid any and all predators it sees, and so that natural motion will help somewhat. Interestingly, the biggest single frustrating factor for predators are the obstacles we'll be scattering about the world. Avoiding collision with them will often slow down a predator enough for an individual target to get away—for a while, anyway.

## Flocking with Teeth

ON THE CD

The results of all this effort can be seen in the *Flocking with Teeth* demo on the CD. The demo maintains the same control features of the original, with the user being able to pan and zoom as desired, turn on bounding bubbles to better visualize boid sight, avoidance, and cohesion distances, and so forth.

A few hawks (the larger delta-shaped objects) prowl in a world filled with obstacles of all sizes. Groups of sparrows (the medium-sized delta-shaped objects) flit between masses of flies (the masses of pixel-sized objects), eating them nearly as fast as they can reproduce. Every so often, a hawk becomes hungry and swoops towards the nearest flock of sparrows, causing them to scatter in all directions to avoid being eaten. Often an obstacle will frustrate either predator or prey, preventing capture or escape. Scattered flocks of sparrows and flies will seek the safety of others and form new flocks, and the whole cycle starts over again.

Depending on how the demo is set up, and to some degree blind luck, most demos end in one of two ways. The most likely outcome is what amounts to ecological disaster—the sparrows eat all the flies or the hawks eat all the sparrows. If all the flies die off, the sparrows also eventually die too from lack of food, and the hawks (left foodless) will follow soon after. If the sparrows all die because the hawks are just a bit too good at what they do, the hawks will eventually die as well, leaving a world filled with nothing but flies and obstacles. This seemed to happen quite a bit in most of my tests.

Another possibility is a sort of stasis between the sparrows and flies. The hawks might all die off through bad luck and not finding any sparrows to eat. If this happens, the sparrows will live on, feeding on the flies for an indefinite period. They might eventually kill off flies, which puts us back into the first scenario described earlier, but a balance is also possible, with the flies reproducing just fast enough to keep all the sparrows fed and happy.

If sparrows and hawks are allowed to reproduce (not the demo default, but an easy exercise for the reader), just about any outcome is possible. This is the most realistic way to configure the simulation, but it's also the most difficult to balance properly.

## Limitations and Potential Improvements

Although overall I'm fairly happy with the performance of the demo for the purposes of this gem, there are several improvements and enhancements that suggest themselves, particularly if one were to try to adopt this code for a game. Although only flies can reproduce in the demo, it's a simple matter to allow both sparrows and hawks to do so. Another potential improvement that could help "close the loop" ecology-wise might be to give the flies something to feed on as well, perhaps hawk feathers.

Vision is still handled very basically, with all boids having perfect 360-degree vision that enables them to see infinitely in any direction. In reality, most predators have rather keen and far-sighted forward vision, while most prey animals are fairly near-sighted with vision to the sides (compare the wolf to the sheep, for example). It wouldn't be too difficult to make vision in the demo more realistic and force hawks to actually search for sparrows rather than simply stumbling across them, although the additional overhead associated with limiting vision (line-of-sight tests, angle-of-vision tests, etc.) can add a lot of math overhead.

### Acknowledgments and Other Resources

Again, I'd like to thank Christopher Kline (Mitre Corporation) for his excellent method for computing roll/pitch/yaw (liberally adapted here), originally published in his *C++ Boids* implementation (available on his Web site [Kline96]). Another must-see site is the one maintained by the "father of flocking," Craig Reynolds [Reynolds00], where there are nearly a hundred pointers to uses of flocking in gaming and film, along with a huge resource of research on the topic. The author's Web site [Woodcock01] also maintains a number of pointers to flocking articles and pages.

One reader of the original *Game Programming Gems* built a great little flocking app that allows you to vary the influence of each steering behavior in real time [Grub01]. This is a great way to study how these behaviors affect the flock on an individual basis, and how their combination causes the emergent behavior that makes flocking so interesting.

Finally, an excellent book that addresses the topic of artificial life in general, in addition to discussing both flocking and boids, is Steven Levy's *Artificial Life* [Levy93].

## References

[Grub01] Grub, Tom, "Flocking Demo," www.riversoftavg.com/flocking.htm, March 6, 2001.

[Kline96] Kline, Christopher, maintains one of several excellent pages on flocking, together with many demos and sample code, at www.media.mit.edu/~ckline/cornellwww/boid/boids.html, August 14, 1996.

[Levy93] Levy, Steven, *Artificial Life: A Report from the Frontier Where Computers Meet Biology*, Vintage Books, 1993.

[Reynolds87] Reynolds, C. W. (1987) *Flocks, Herds, and Schools: A Distributed Behavioral Model*, in Computer Graphics, 21(4) (SIGGRAPH '87 Conference Proceedings) pp. 25–34.

[Reynolds00] Reynolds, Craig, maintains an extensive reference on flocking and steering behavior at www.red3d.com/cwr/boids/ and has presented a wide variety of papers at various conferences discussing the progress he's made in exploring and perfecting uses of this technology, December 6, 2000.

[Woodcock00] Woodcock, Steven, "Flocking a Simple Technique for Simulating Group Behavior," *Game Programming Gems*, Charles River Media, 2000.

[Woodcock01] Woodcock, Steven, maintains a page dedicated to game AI at www.gameai.com, 2001.

# 3.12

# A Generic Fuzzy State Machine in C++

## Eric Dybsand

edybs@ix.netcom.com

Fuzzy logic was ably presented in the original *Game Programming Gems* article titled "Fuzzy Logic for Video Games" by Mason McCuskey [McCuskey00]. Likewise, a generic Finite State Machine was introduced in that same book, in the article "A Finite-State Machine Class" written by me [Dybsand00]. This gem will serve to marry these two concepts into a generic Fuzzy State Machine (FuSM) C++ class that you can use in your games, and to provide you with an additional overview of fuzzy logic, as well as some ideas on how to use fuzzy logic in your games.

First, let's briefly review the FAQ definition of fuzzy logic:

> *"Fuzzy logic is a superset of conventional (Boolean) logic that has been extended to handle the concept of partial truth—truth values between "completely true" and "completely false" [FAQ97]."*

Thus, instead of the states of *ON* and *OFF*, or *TRUE* and *FALSE*, a fuzzy state machine can be in a state of almost *ON* or just about *OFF*, or partially *TRUE* or sort of *FALSE*. Or even both *ON* and *OFF* or *TRUE* and *FALSE*, but to various degrees.

What does this mean to a game developer? It means that a Non-Player Character (NPC), for instance, does not have to be just *MAD* at a player, but that the NPC can be almost *MAD*, or partly *MAD*, or really *MAD*, or raging *MAD* at a player. In other words, by using a FuSM (implementing fuzzy logic), a game developer can have multiple degrees of state assigned to a character (or a concept within the game—more on this later). This could also mean that states in a game do not have to be specific and discrete (often referred to in the fuzzy logic world as *crisp*), but can be, well, fuzzy (less determined). The real advantage to this is discussed in the next section.

Status in a FuSM is typically represented internally using the range of real numbers from 0.0 to 1.0; however, that is not the only way we can represent a fuzzy value. We can choose literally any set of numbers, and consider them fuzzy values. Continuing the NPC attitude example [Dybsand00], let us consider how to maintain the "dislike portion" of the attitude of an NPC toward a player within a FuSM. We could use the range of integers from 1 to 25 to indicate that an NPC has a variable feeling of

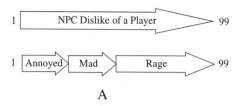

These values could even overlap

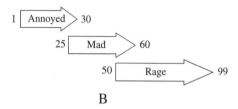

**FIGURE 3.12.1** *A) Fuzzy values for dislike attitudes toward player. B) Fuzzy values that overlap.*

*ANNOYANCE* toward a player, and the range of integers from 26 to 50 may reflect an NPC's variable feeling of *MAD* toward a player, while the range of integers from 51 to 99 may indicate the NPC's variable feeling of *RAGE*. Thus, within each type of attitude toward a player, the NPC may possess various degrees of dislike such as *ANNOYANCE, MAD* or *RAGE* (Figure 3.12.1).

Before we leave this brief introduction to FuSMs, let's clear up one common misconception often associated with fuzzy logic: there is no specific relationship between fuzzy values and probability. Fuzzy logic is not some new way to represent probability, but instead represents a degree of membership in a set. In probability, the values must add up to 1.0 in order to be effective. Fuzzy logic values have no such requirement (note the overlap example just presented). This does not mean that fuzzy logic values can't happen to add up to 1.0, it just means that they don't have to for a FuSM to be effective.

## Why Use a FuSM In a Game?

In this author's opinion, the number-one reason to use FuSMs in a computer game is that it is an easy way to implement fuzzy logic, which can broaden the depth of representation of the abstract concepts used to represent the game world and the relationships between objects in the game.

In essence, to increase gameplay!

How do FuSMs increase gameplay, you ask? FuSMs increase gameplay by providing for more interesting responses by NPCs, by enabling less predictable NPC behavior, and by expanding the options for choices to be made by the human player.

Thus, a player does not encounter an NPC that is just *MAD* or not *MAD* about being attacked by the player. Instead, the player must deal with an NPC that can be various degrees of being *MAD*. This broader array of considerations increases gameplay by adding to the level of responses that can be developed for the NPC, and seen by the human player.

Another effect of adding FuSMs to computer games is to increase the replayability of the game. By broadening the range of responses and conditions that the player may encounter in given situations during the game, the player will be more likely to experience different outcomes in similar situations.

## How To Use FuSMs in a Game

Actually, various forms of FuSMs have been used a lot in computer games!

One example of where a FuSM has been used in computer games is for the health or hit points of an NPC or agent. Instead of the agent simply being healthy or dead (finite states), using a range of hits points can reflect the agent being anything from completely healthy to partially healthy to almost dead to totally dead (fuzzy states). Another example of using a FuSM in a computer game can be found in the control process for accelerating or braking an AI-controlled car in a racing game. Using a FuSM in this case would provide various degrees of acceleration or braking to be calculated in lieu of the finite states of *THROTTLE-UP* or *THROTTLE-DOWN* and *BRAKE-ON* or *BRAKE-OFF* actions. And as our ongoing example of representing an attitude shows, a FuSM is perfect for representing NPC emotional status and attitude toward the player or other NPCs.

Applying fuzzy logic to states in a computer game is relatively straightforward, as noted in the previous examples. Those decision processes that can be viewed as having more than two discrete outcomes are perfect candidates for the application of fuzzy logic, and there are many of those processes to be found.

Now let's consider putting fuzzy logic into a generic C++ class, a FuSM.

## Review of *Game Programming Gems'* Generic Finite State Machine in C++

The original Generic FSM in C++ [Dybsand00] consisted of two classes: FSMclass and FSMstate. The FSMclass class object encapsulated the actual finite state machine process, maintained the current state of the FSM, supported the container for the various FSMstate class objects, and provided control for the state transition process.

The FSMstate class object encapsulated a specific state and maintained the arrays of input and output states for which a transition could be performed for the state of the object.

Inputs to the FSM were presented to FSMclass::StateTransition(), which determined the appropriate FSMstate object that was to handle the input (based on the current state), and then the input was passed to FSMstate::GetOutput() to obtain the new output state.

The new output state was returned to the FSM user process by `FSMclass::State-Transition()` and was also made the new current state of the `FSMclass` object. Thus, the generic FSM provided a crisp and discrete state transition in response to an input.

## Adapting the Generic FSM in C++ to FuSM in C++

There are only a few changes needed to transform the Generic FSM into a FuSM. The first is to add support to the `FSMclass` class object for multiple current states. The next change is to modify the `FSMstate` class to support degrees of being in a state. Finally, we need to modify the state transition process within both class objects to support a transition to multiple states and a degree of being in the new state. During this refinement process, we will morph *FSMclass* into `FuSMclass` and the `FSMstate` class into the `FuSMstate` class.

ON THE CD

The reader is invited to review the Fuzzy/Finite State Machine project found on the companion CD-ROM, and to follow along in that project code as the various classes are referenced.

The adaptation process begins with the `FuSMclass` class that, while similar to `FSMclass`, is now capable of supporting multiple current states (the new `FuSMclass` and `FuSMstate` class members are shown in bold.)  This capability is provided by the `FuzzyState_List m_list` member, which is an STL list object that contains pointers to `FuSMstate` objects. A pointer to any active fuzzy state (based on the current input value) object is saved in this list. This way, multiple current states can be supported. As in `FSMclass` before, `FuSMclass` also maintains an STL map object (the `FuzzyState_Map m_map` member) for containing pointers to all possible `FuSMstate` objects that could be considered by `FuSMclass`.

We continue the adaptation process by developing an access member function (called `GetNextFuzzyStateMember()`) that will provide an accessing service to the `FuSMclass` object. The `GetNextFuzzyStateMember()` member function maintains a pointer to the next `FuSMstate` pointer in the `FuzzyState_List m_list`, so that all active current states can be accessed by processes outside of `FuSMclass`. Thus, this service is how you can get access to the active current states by your program. By continuing to call `GetNextFuzzyStateMember()` until you receive a NULL pointer, your program can determine all the active fuzzy states.

The next step in the adaptation process is to modify the `FuSMstate` class to support various degrees of membership. This support is provided by adding the new member variables of `int m_iLowRange` and `int m_iHighRange`. For simplicity, this design views the fuzzy membership range as whole positive numbers, and could be easily adapted to view membership as a set of real numbers. For convenience, this adaptation also maintains two additional attributes of the `FuSMstate` object: the value of membership in the set for this `FuSMstate` object (`int m_iValueOfMemberShip`), and the degree of membership in the set (`int m_iDegreeOfMembership`).

Notice that the biggest difference between the finite state object (`FSMstate`) and our new fuzzy state object (`FuSMstate`) is that a state transition array is no longer needed. This is because in fuzzy logic, it is possible to be in one or more states at the same time; while in finite logic, it is possible only to be in one state at a time.

Concluding the adaptation process involves modifying the state transition process in both the `FuSMclass` and `FuSMstate` objects to support the possibility of multiple current states and to support various degrees of membership within a given state. For `FuSMclass`, this means modifying `StateTransition()` to process the `Fuzzy-State_Map m_map` member containing all possible states, giving each `FuSMstate` object an opportunity to effect a transition based on the accumulated input value (the `int m_iCurrentInput` member found in the `FuSMclass`). Those `FuSMstate` objects that do transition have their pointers saved off in the `FuzzyState_List m_list` member, thus indicating that the `FuSMstate object` is an active current state.

For the `FuSMstate` class object, the adaptation process involves replacing `FSM-state::GetOutput()` (from the FSM) with a new transition function. The new `FuSM-state::DoTransition()` member function accepts the input value maintained by `FuSMclass` and considers the degree of membership this input value represents. If membership within the fuzzy state exists, the member function returns a *TRUE* and maintains the status of membership for any future access.

ON THE CD

This completes the adaptation process. For more details and the code listings, see the FuSM project on the companion CD-ROM.

## Now Fuzzy Up Your Games!

Using the `FuSMclass` and `FuSMstate` classes as a guide, you are now ready to start making your games more fuzzy!  Doing so will enrich the gameplay experience of your players and broaden your own understanding of how to deploy one of the more flexible forms of artificial intelligence tools available to game developers.

## References

[Dybsand00] Dybsand, Eric, "A Generic Finite State Machine in C++," *Game Programming Gems*, Charles River Media, 2000.

[FAQ97] "What is fuzzy logic?" FAQ: Fuzzy Logic and Fuzzy Expert Systems 1/1 Monthly Posting, www.faqs.org/faqs/fuzzy-logic/part1/, 1997.

[McCuskey00] McCuskey, Mason, "Fuzzy Logic for Video Games," *Game Programming Gems*, Charles River Media, 2000.

# 3.13

## Imploding Combinatorial Explosion in a Fuzzy System

### Michael Zarozinski, Louder Than
### A Bomb! Software

michaelz@LouderThanABomb.com

Fuzzy logic, when you come right down to it, is just a bunch of "if-then" statements. One of the biggest problems in using fuzzy logic is that the number of "if-then" statements grows exponentially as you increase the number of fuzzy sets you "if" together. This is called *combinatorial explosion*, and can make fuzzy systems slow, confusing, and difficult to maintain. In games, speed is essential, and combinatorial explosion can make the use of fuzzy logic impractical.

For an introduction to fuzzy logic see "Fuzzy Logic for Video Games" by Mason McCuskey in the first *Game Programming Gems* [McCuskey00]. For this gem, we'll provide some definitions, as there is little agreement on fuzzy logic terminology.

- **Variable**. A fuzzy variable is a concept such as "temperature," "distance," or "health."
- **Set**. In traditional logic, sets are "crisp"; either you belong 100 percent to a set or you do not. A set of tall people may consist of all people over six feet tall, anyone less than six feet is "short" (or more appropriately, "not tall"). Fuzzy logic allows sets to be "fuzzy" so anyone over six feet tall may have 100-percent membership in the "tall" set, but may also have 20-percent membership in the "medium height" set.

### The Problem

Table 3.13.1 shows the effects of combinatorial explosion as more variables and/or sets are added to the system.

This exponential growth in the number of rules can bring any system to its knees if every possible rule must be checked on each pass.

**Table 3.13.1 The Effects of Combinatorial Explosion**

| Number of Variables | Sets Per Variable | Number of Rules |
|---|---|---|
| 2 | 5 | $5^2 = 25$ |
| 3 | 5 | $5^3 = 125$ |
| 4 | 5 | $5^4 = 625$ |
| 5 | 5 | $5^5 = 3{,}125$ |
| 6 | 5 | $5^6 = 15{,}625$ |
| 7 | 5 | $5^7 = 78{,}125$ |
| 8 | 5 | $5^8 = 390{,}625$ |
| 9 | 5 | $5^9 = 1{,}953{,}125$ |
| 10 | 5 | $5^{10} = 9{,}765{,}625$ |

## The Solution

William E. Combs, an engineer at Boeing, developed a method for turning the exponential growth shown above into linear growth known, appropriately enough, as the "Combs Method." This results in a system with 10 variables and 5 sets per variable having only 50 rules, as opposed to 9,765,625 rules.

It is important to note that the Combs Method is not an algorithm for converting existing "if-then" rules to a linear system. You should start from the bottom up, creating rules that fit in with the Combs Method.

If you're interested in the theory behind the Combs Method, see the proof at the end of this gem.

### The Real World

To bring this theory into the real world, we'll look at a trivial system for calculating the *aggressiveness* of a unit in a game. For now, we'll consider a one-on-one battle with three variables, ignoring any surrounding units (friend or foe):

- Our health
- Enemy health
- Distance between us and the enemy

The *health* variables have three sets:  Near death, Good, and Excellent.

The *distance* variable has three sets:  Close, Medium, and Far.

Finally, our output (*aggressiveness*) has three sets:  Run away, Fight defensively, and All-out attack!.

### Traditional Fuzzy Logic Rules

If we were using a traditional fuzzy logic system, we'd start creating rules in a spreadsheet format as shown in Table 3.13.2.

**Table 3.13.2 Some Traditional Fuzzy Logic Rules**

| Our Health | Enemy Health | Distance | Aggressiveness |
|---|---|---|---|
| Excellent | Excellent | Close | Fight defensively |
| Excellent | Excellent | Medium | Fight defensively |
| Excellent | Excellent | Far | All-out attack! |
| Excellent | Good | Close | Fight defensively |
| Excellent | Good | Medium | All-out attack! |
| Excellent | Good | Far | All-out attack! |
| Excellent | Near death | Close | All-out attack! |
| Excellent | Near death | Medium | All-out attack! |
| Excellent | Near death | Far | All-out attack! |
| | | . | |
| | | . | |
| | | . | |
| Good | Good | Close | Fight defensively |
| Good | Near death | Close | Fight defensively |
| | | . | |
| | | . | |
| | | . | |
| Near death | Excellent | Close | Run away |
| Near death | Excellent | Medium | Run away |
| Near death | Excellent | Far | Fight defensively |

Note that Table 3.13.2 only shows 14 of the 27 possible rules. While a trivial example such as this is fairly manageable, combinatorial explosion quickly comes into play. In a game, we may need to take into account more variables such as the relative health of our forces and the enemy forces that may join in the battle. If we were to represent these two additional variables (bringing the total number of variables to five), the table would grow from 27 rules to 243 rules. This can quickly get out of hand. Fortunately, the Combs Method only needs 15 rules to deal with the same five variables.

## Combs Method of Fuzzy Logic Rules

Building rules in the traditional system, we look at how the combination of input sets relates to the output. To build rules using the Combs Method, we look at each individual set's relationship to the output and build the rules one variable at a time (Table 3.13.3).

In a Combs Method system, it is recommended that all variables have the same number of sets as the output variable. This is not an absolute rule, but it gives each output set the chance to be paired with an input set for each variable.

**Table 3.13.3 Each Individual Set's Relationship to the Output**

| Our health | Aggressiveness |
| --- | --- |
| Excellent | All-out attack! |
| Good | Fight defensively |
| Near death | Run away |

| Enemy health | Aggressiveness |
| --- | --- |
| Excellent | Run away |
| Good | Fight defensively |
| Near death | All-out attack! |

| Distance | Aggressiveness |
| --- | --- |
| Close | Fight defensively |
| Medium | Fight defensively |
| Far | All-out attack! |

## Concrete Example

To test the system, we'll use the following values:

- Our health: 76.88
- Enemy health: 20.1
- Distance: 8.54

Figures 3.13.1 through 3.13.3 show the "Degree of Membership," or DOM, for the input values in the system (note that the DOMs for a variable do not have to sum to 100 percent).

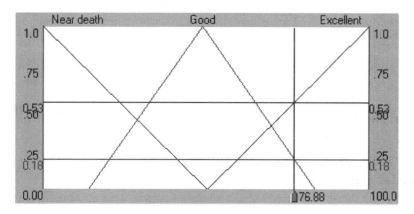

**FIGURE 3.13.1** Our Health *for a value of 76.88. Near death: 0%, Good: 18%, Excellent: 53%.*

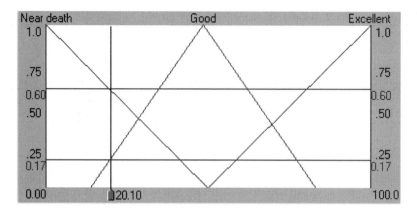

**FIGURE 3.13.2** Enemy Health *for a value of 20.1. Near death: 60%, Good: 17%, Excellent: 0%.*

Figures 3.13.1 through 3.13.4 were taken from the Spark! fuzzy logic editor, which allows you to visually create a fuzzy logic system, integrate it into your game, and change the AI in real time without having to recompile.

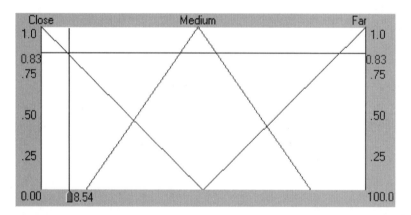

**FIGURE 3.13.3** Distance *for a value of 8.54. Close: 83%, Medium: 0%, Far: 0%.*

### Concrete Example with the Traditional System

Using the rules we created earlier, the rules listed in Table 3.13.4 are activated in the traditional system.

The DOM of the input sets are ANDed together to get the output set's DOM. The ANDing is logically equivalent to taking the MINIMUM of the three input values.

The defuzzification method we're using—center of mass—takes the MAXIMUM value for the output set then finds the center of mass for the output sets (Figure 3.13.4).

**Table 3.13.4 These Rules Are Activated in the Traditional System**

| Our Health | Enemy Health | Distance | Aggressiveness |
|---|---|---|---|
| Excellent (53%) | Good (17%) | Close (83%) | Fight defensively (17%) |
| Excellent (53%) | Near death (60%) | Close (83%) | All-out attack! (53%) |
| Good (18%) | Good (17%) | Close (83%) | Fight defensively (17%) |
| Good (18%) | Near death (60%) | Close (83%) | Fight defensively (18%) |

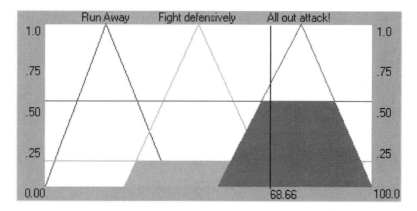

**FIGURE 3.13.4** *Traditional system output. Fight defensively: 18%; All-out attack: 53%; Aggressiveness: 68.66.*

### Concrete Example Using the Combs Method

Using the same input values, the Combs Method rules are listed in Table 3.13.5.

The Combs Method result of 60.39 is not exactly the same as the traditional method (68.66), but we wouldn't expect it to be as we're using a different inference method. The Combs Method is ORing the values together, which is the same as taking the MAXIMUM (Figure 3.13.5). Traditional fuzzy logic ANDs values together, which takes the MINIMUM; hence, the difference in the *fight defensively* output sets.

Note that (in this case) if we took the MINIMUM of the output sets (and there is no rule saying we can't) we would get the exact same result as the traditional fuzzy logic method. This is a result of the rules we selected for the Combs Method. Since there is not an algorithm to convert traditional fuzzy logic rules to the Combs Method, we cannot say that by simply taking the MINIMUM you will always get the same results as in the traditional method.

### The Proof

It is not essential that you understand why the Combs Method works in order to use it. Formal logic can be confusing, so this proof is provided for the reader who wishes to have a deeper understanding of the theory behind the Combs Method. The Combs

**Table 3.13.5 Combs Method system output. Fight defensively: 83%;
All out attack: 53%; Aggressiveness: 60.39.**

| Our Health | Aggressiveness |
| --- | --- |
| Excellent (53%) | All-out attack! (53%) |
| Good (18%) | Fight defensively (18%) |

| Enemy Health | Aggressiveness |
| --- | --- |
| Good (17%) | Fight defensively (17%) |
| Near death (60%) | Fight defensively (60%) |

| Distance | Aggressiveness |
| --- | --- |
| Close (83%) | Fight defensively (83%) |

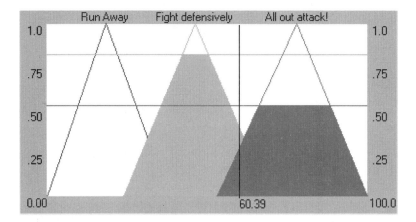

**FIGURE 3.13.5** *Combs Method system output. Fight defensively: 83%, All out attack:
53%. Aggressiveness: 60.39.*

Method is based on the fact that the logical proposition ($p$ and $q$) then $r$ is equivalent
to ($p$ then $r$) or ($q$ then $r$).

Since fuzzy logic is a superset of formal logic, we can ignore "fuzziness" and just
prove the equivalence of the Combs Method to the traditional method. In Table
3.13.6, $p$ and $q$ are antecedents and $r$ is the consequence. The antecedents are statements such as "if Jim is tall" or "if Jim is healthy." The consequence is a *potential*
result such as "Jim can play basketball".

This proof is straightforward, except for the $x$ then $y$ type clauses. These are standard formal logic propositions, but their truth table is confusing—especially when $x$
and $y$ are false but the proposition is true. See [aiGuru01] for some examples that will
help clarify this proposition's truth table.

**Table 3.13.6 Antecedents and Consequences**

| $p$ | $q$ | $p$ and $q$ | $r$ | ($p$ and $q$) then $r$ | $p$ then $r$ | $q$ then $r$ | ($p$ then $r$) or ($q$ then $r$) |
|---|---|---|---|---|---|---|---|
| T | T | T | T | **T** | T | T | **T** |
| T | T | T | F | **F** | F | F | **F** |
| T | F | F | T | **T** | T | T | **T** |
| T | F | F | F | **T** | F | T | **T** |
| F | T | F | T | **T** | T | T | **T** |
| F | T | F | F | **T** | T | F | **T** |
| F | F | F | T | **T** | T | T | **T** |
| F | F | F | F | **T** | T | T | **T** |

If you need visual proof, the Venn diagrams are shown in Figures 3.13.6 and 3.13.7. Since Venn diagrams can only show AND, OR, and NOT relationships, the following conversions are made by material implication:

- Traditional Logic: ($p$ and $q$) then $r$ is equivalent to (not ($p$ and $q$)) or $r$
- Combs Method: ($p$ then $r$) or ($q$ then $r$) is equivalent to ((not $p$) or $r$) or ((not $q$) or $r$)

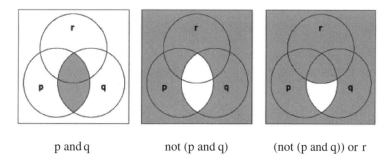

p and q          not (p and q)          (not (p and q)) or r

**FIGURE 3.13.6** *Venn diagram for Traditional Logic.*

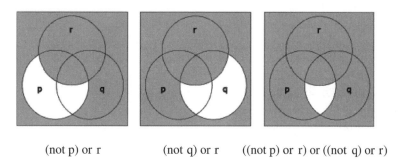

(not p) or r          (not q) or r     ((not p) or r) or ((not q) or r)

**FIGURE 3.13.7** *Venn diagram for Combs Method.*

## Conclusion

If forced to make a choice between fast and intelligent game AI, fast will win almost every time (ignoring turn-based games). The Combs Method allows you to create AI that is not only fast, but also complex enough to result in rich, lifelike behavior, thus providing a more engaging experience for the player.

Next time you're faced with creating a complex behavior system, give the Combs Method a try. You may be surprised by the depth of the behavior you can get with such a small number of rules.

## References

[aiGuru01]   Zarozinski, Michael, "if p then q?" available online at www.aiGuru.com/logic/if_p_then_q.htm, March 5, 2001.

[Andrews97] Andrews, James E., "Taming Complexity in Large-Scale Fuzzy Systems," PC AI (May/June 1997): pp.39–42.

[Combs99]   Combs, William E., *The Fuzzy Systems Handbook 2nd Ed*, Academic Press, 1999.

[McCuskey00] McCuskey, Mason, "Fuzzy Logic for Video Games," *Game Programming Gems*, Charles River Media, 2000.

# 3.14

## Using a Neural Network in a Game: A Concrete Example

### John Manslow, Neural Technologies Limited

jfm96r@ecs.soton.ac.uk

The original *Game Programming Gems* book included a contribution that gave a broad and comprehensive overview of the field of neural networks [LaMothe00]. This gem complements that by providing a concrete illustration of the application of one of the most useful and widely applied neural networks, the multiplayer perceptron (MLP). In so doing, it describes how to identify problems that can be solved by the MLP, and highlights the steps required to produce a solution.

## The Game

To provide a concrete illustration of the application of the MLP for this gem, it was necessary to construct an application that was sufficiently simple that the role of the neural network was clear, but not so trivial as to have any obvious alternative solution. The application that was settled upon was a simple tank game where two tanks are placed on a randomly generated side-view landscape, with the leftmost tank controlled by the player, and the rightmost tank by the computer.

The tanks take turns firing at each other, and the first one to score a hit is declared the winner. Each tank aims by adjusting the inclination of its barrel—a task made especially difficult because the tank's shell decelerates as it travels (due to drag) and is affected by wind (which, for simplicity, maintains a constant speed and direction for the duration of the shell's flight). The main challenge for the AI is thus how to set the inclination of its tank's barrel to hit the enemy tank. This gem will show how an MLP can be taught, by example, to solve this problem.

## The Multilayer Perceptron

The MLP is a type of neural network that became popular in the mid-1980s as a result of the discovery of a particularly efficient way of teaching it. Since then, the technique has grown rapidly in popularity and is currently one of the most widely applied neural network architectures in industry, and has even been used in a number of games (such as Codemasters' *Colin McRae Rally 2.0*).

Although more advanced techniques are now common in academia, the MLP remains popular because it is one of the easiest to understand, easiest to code, easiest to apply, and offers robust performance even in the hands of relatively inexperienced users. The MLP is thus a good starting point for people new to the field of neural networks and a powerful tool for more experienced users.

A neural network such as an MLP is really just a complex nonlinear function with a number of adjustable parameters that can be changed to control its shape. The process of teaching the network (or *training* it, as it is more commonly called) is simply one of adjusting its parameters so that the function it represents takes on a desired shape. Although polynomials and splines can be used to address similar problems to the MLP, the structure of the MLP makes it particularly robust.

The shape of the function to be learned is indicated by pairs of input-output samples and thus neural network training consists of nothing more than curve fitting—adjusting the parameters in the network so that it fits roughly through the samples. This process will be familiar to many readers from science class, where it was often necessary to draw smooth curves through data collected from experiments.

Since neural networks often represent quite complex equations, they are frequently visualized in terms of directed graphs. For example, Equation 3.14.1 is the formula for the output $y$ of an MLP with one linear output, $N$ inputs, $x_1$ to $x_N$, and $M$ hidden neurons, and Figure 3.14.1 is its graphical representation. Although the MLP is represented by a directed graph, arrows are usually omitted from the network diagram since information flow is always in the direction of input to output.

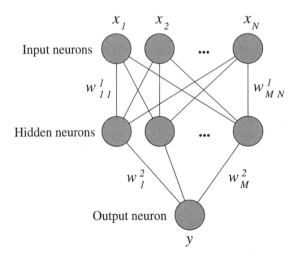

**FIGURE 3.14.1** *The graphical representation of the MLP in Equation 3.14.1. The ellipses indicate that the number of inputs and hidden neurons can vary.*

$$y = b^2 + \sum_{m=1}^{M} \left( w_m^2 \frac{1}{1 + \exp\left( -b_m^1 - \sum_{n=1}^{N} w_{mn}^1 x_n \right)} \right) \qquad (3.14.1)$$

The adjustable parameters of the network are the $w$'s (weights) and $b$'s (biases), the distinction being that weights connect neurons together, whereas the biases excite or inhibit individual neurons even in the absence of other activity in the network. The biases are not shown in Figure 3.14.1 since each can be considered to be part of the internal make-up of an individual neuron. A detailed examination of the structure of neural networks is given in [LaMothe00] and [Haykin94] and will not be repeated here.

For the purposes of this gem, it is sufficient to understand that an MLP represents the function given in Equation 3.14.1, and that that function will be used to calculate the inclination of the AI tank's barrel that is required to hit the player's tank. The $w$'s and $b$'s in Equation 3.14.1 are adjustable parameters that we can use to fit the MLP to a set of samples that illustrate how the inclination of the barrel should be set, and that those parameters are found using some curve-fitting procedure, otherwise known as training.

So, in order to train the MLP, we need a set of samples that consists of input-output pairings that are examples of how the AI tank's barrel should be set to hit the player's tank. Clearly, from the problem we're trying to solve, we want the network's output to be the inclination of the AI tank's barrel, but what should the inputs be? This often complex question is considered in the next section.

## Input Selection

Before the input-output samples that are required to train the network can be collected, it is necessary to decide what inputs the MLP is going to need. Clearly, the inputs must contain the information necessary for the MLP to calculate the correct output; in this case, the inclination of the tank's barrel that is required to hit the player's tank.

The selection of inputs is often difficult in practice, since a wide range of information can usually be extracted from the game world, and the problem being solved is often too complex or poorly understood to specify exactly what information is useful. In this case, much time can be spent training many different networks with different combinations of input variables to see which perform best. To minimize the effort required to find good combinations, the following guidelines should be followed:

- Use prior knowledge about the problem you're trying to solve. Make educated guesses about what information in the game world is likely to be relevant. If you think the network output should depend on a particular function of variables, add that function into the set of network inputs.

- Abstract variables derived as a function of much simpler ones often provide more precise information than any of their constituent parts. For example, in a strategy game, a single indicator of enemy strength may be more useful than lots of individual indicators relating to different aspects of it.

- Use variables that provide as different information about the game world as possible, because this lets you convey the same amount of information with fewer inputs. For example, no benefit would be gained in giving the relative positions of the player's tank and the AI tank in both polar and Cartesian coordinates since they contain no unique information.

- Try using combinatorial search algorithms to look for good combinations of inputs. For example, forward selection takes a large set of candidate inputs and repeatedly adds single inputs to the network, at each stage adding the one that improves performance the most. Such techniques require minimal human intervention, but are slow and may fail to find the best combination.

Although it is tempting to avoid the laborious process of input selection by providing the network with access to all variables that may be of relevance, this is likely to result in a network that performs poorly and in unpredictable ways. Input selection is the most labor-intensive part of developing a neural network application, and finding a small set of inputs that is rich in relevant information is crucial to success.

Fortunately, our prior knowledge is sufficient to say exactly what information is required to work out the inclination of the AI tank's barrel—the displacement between the tanks (expressed, say, as two inputs, $x$-displacement and $y$-displacement), and the wind speed and direction (expressed as a single signed input). The drag on the shell is fixed, and hence the network does not need to be told the strength of drag, but will learn its effect during training. Now that it has been decided what inputs to use, it is possible to collect the samples that will be used during training.

## Collecting Data

The simplest and most obvious way to generate samples that show how to set the inclination of the AI tank's barrel is for a player to control the AI tank, and to record the selected input variables (relative positions of the tanks and wind speed) and the inclination of the AI tank's barrel every time the player controlling the AI tank scores a hit. This process is repeated until a sufficiently large set of samples is available for training. Since a human player typically hits the enemy tank only in around one in five shots, the many hundreds or thousands of samples required for training can take a long time to collect.

To generate the samples used in this gem, the data collection process was automated by performing simple random searches for the correct inclination. This was done by setting the AI tank's barrel to random inclinations until, by chance, it scored a hit. At this point, the relative positions of the tanks, the wind speed, and the inclination that achieved the hit were recorded, and the process repeated for new, randomly placed tanks and a random wind speed.

Although this was highly inefficient, it required no human intervention and was left running until a sufficiently large data set had been generated. In addition, the simulation of the game world need not be run at normal speed and may be accelerated by, for example, disabling rendering, provided that this does not change its behavior. Overnight, this process achieved around 1200 hits and hence created a data set of roughly 1200 samples.

One important question that needs to be asked when collecting data is, "How much data should I collect?" Unfortunately, there is no simple answer to this, because it depends on the complexity of the problem you're trying to solve. In practice, provided that the number of hidden neurons is kept small (the 10 used in this gem would normally be considered quite a large number), good performance can be achieved with as few as $10^I$ training samples for a network with $I$ inputs.

One important hazard in developing neural network solutions is that the last-minute tweaking of a game engine that is often done to fine-tune game play can, if it changes the behavior of the game world, cause the neural network to perform poorly. This can be overcome by repeating the data collection and training processes to produce a new set of parameters for the network. Provided that the changes in the behavior of the game weren't too drastic, the difficult problem of input selection will not normally have to be repeated. Now that we've decided what the network is going to control and the inputs it needs, and we've collected some training data to show it what to do, we're ready to train it.

## Training the MLP

As has already been described, the MLP is a nonlinear function that is fit to a series of samples by adjusting its parameters. This training process is achieved by using an optimization algorithm to search for the parameters that minimize a measure of the error with which the MLP reproduces each output sample given their associated input. The mean squared error is the most commonly used error measure and is calculated from the sum of the squares of the differences between the MLP's outputs and the corresponding outputs in the samples, divided by the number of samples.

Although the gradient descent optimization algorithm is usually used to fit an MLP to the training samples, this article uses a rarely applied technique called the *perturbation search* because it is easier to code, easier to understand, and easier to apply (for example, it is guaranteed to be stable). In addition, the perturbation search does not require gradient information,

- Making it easy to experiment with a wide range of network structures, nonlinearities, and error functions.
- Eliminating common bugs that result from the incorrect calculation of gradient information or propagation of that information through the network structure.

- Allowing integer versions of networks (aimed at low-end platforms) to be optimized directly, avoiding some spurious behaviors that can result from the conversion of floating-point networks to integer form.
- Permitting the inclusion of discontinuous functions in the network.

The basic perturbation search can be summarized as follows: Measure the performance of the MLP. Perturb the MLP's parameters by adding a small amount of random noise to each one, and remeasure its performance. If its performance deteriorated, restore the parameters to their original values. Repeat this process until some stopping criterion is met.

Since all of the techniques that can be used to train an MLP will indefinitely improve its performance (if only incrementally), some decision must be made as to when to stop training. To this end, the MLP's performance should periodically be evaluated in the game, and training should stop either when the measured performance is adequate, or when further training fails to improve performance.

When evaluating the performance of the MLP in the game, great care must be taken to exercise the game in a way that is representative of how the game will actually be played. This ensures that the environment that the MLP is presented with during this testing phase is similar to the one that it will encounter once the game has shipped, and hence guarantees that the measured performance is a useful guide to the how the MLP will perform in the final product. If the MLP's performance in the game fails to reach a useful level, consider the following causes:

- The optimization algorithm has hit a plateau or a local minimum [Bishop95]. Try restarting training from a random set of parameters.
- The input samples contain insufficient information about their associated outputs for the network to reproduce them. Repeat the input selection process to find new inputs that contain more relevant information.
- The network is too simple to learn the relationship between the inputs and outputs in the sample data. Consider transformations of the inputs that might simplify the relationship, or increase the number of hidden neurons in the network (but keep them to an absolute minimum).
- The samples are not representative of the environment that the network encounters in game. The behavior of the game world must not change after the training samples have been collected, and the samples must contain everything that the network will encounter in-game in the right proportions.

**Computational Issues**

Since game AI operates in an environment in which CPU time is at a premium, it is important to consider the computational cost associated with neural networks. Unfortunately, training an MLP is processor intensive, making the MLP poorly suited to in-game learning and, in most cases, much simpler learning mechanisms can almost always be employed. In contrast, computing the output of a trained MLP requires very little processor time, particularly since all internal quantities can be modeled using integers and nonlinear functions replaced by look-up tables. Such optimizations have allowed the MLP to be used in several real-time titles on the PC and Playstation.

## Results

Following the steps outlined in the preceding sections, an MLP was created that had three inputs, two consisting of a Cartesian representation of the relative positions of the player's tank and the AI tank, and one representing wind speed. We collected 1207 examples of successful shots, and the MLP was trained for around two-and-a-half hours on a PC with a 500MHz Intel Celeron processor. At this time, training was stopped because the MLP's performance was as good as was required, achieving a 98-percent hit rate in the game.

## Conclusion

ON THE CD

This gem described the steps taken to produce the neural network AI that is used in the simple tank game that is included on the CD. The interested reader is strongly encouraged to pursue important issues such as input selection and overfitting in references such as [Haykin94] and [Bishop95], which are able to provide both a broader introduction and greater detail than is possible here. Finally, there is no substitute for practical experience—experiment with the MLP class that accompanies this article and apply it to your own problems. Follow the development process that was outlined, and you'll discover neural networks to be a flexible and powerful tool.

## References

[Bishop95] Bishop C. M., *Neural Networks for Pattern Recognition*, Oxford University Press Inc., 1995.

[Haykin94] Haykin S., *Neural Networks: A Comprehensive Foundation*, Macmillan College Publishing Company, 1994.

[LaMothe00], LaMothe, A., *Game Programming Gems*, Edited by DeLoura, M., Charles River Media, Inc, 2000.

[Sarle01] Sarle, W. S., "Neural Network FAQ" available online at www.ci.tuwien .ac.at/docs/services/nnfaq/FAQ.html, February 15, 2001.

# GEOMETRY MANAGEMENT

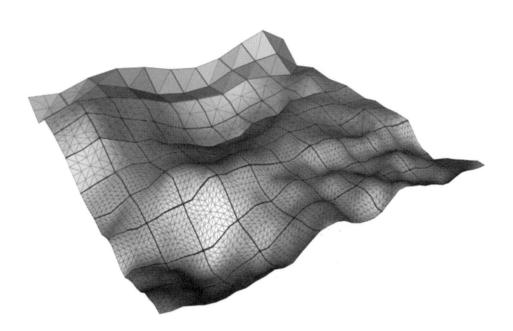

# Introduction

## Eric Lengyel

lengyel@c4engine.com

This section presents gems that deal with the geometry of the 3D models that are rendered to the screen. This geometry can be manipulated on many different levels. Several of the gems in this section describe techniques that operate at the polygon and vertex levels to achieve special effects. Others describe methods used for large-scale geometry management and level-of-detail algorithms.

It can be argued that geometry management is the single most important factor in a 3D engine's performance. Determining the smallest amount of data that is necessary to send to the graphics card, both in terms of visible geometry and level of detail, can make a larger difference in speed than almost anything else. Tom Forsyth's gem, "Comparison of VIPM Methods," and Greg Snook's gem, "Simplified Terrain Using Interlocking Tiles," describe techniques for smoothly reducing the level of detail in a scene.

The structures used to organize geometry in a scene are as important as the objects in the scene themselves. A method for managing moving objects within a sphere tree, which can be used for visibility testing, is described in John Ratcliff's gem, "Sphere Trees for Fast Visibility Culling, Raytracing, and Range Searching." Techniques for making organizational structures smaller, faster, and better are detailed in Miguel Gomez's gem, "Compressed Axis-Aligned Bounding Box Trees," and in Matt Pritchard's gem, "Direct Access Quadtree Lookup."

Vertex and polygon manipulation techniques enable an endless list of special effects and handy tricks. Alex Vlachos and Evan Hart present two gems, "Approximating Fish Tank Refractions" and "Rendering Print Resolution Screenshots," which describe how the modelview and projection matrices can be modified to alter vertex positions for specific purposes. Eric Lengyel's gem, "Applying Decals to Arbitrary Surfaces," demonstrates how surface markings can be applied to a model by clipping the surface's polygon mesh.

This section also includes a few miscellaneous gems. Information about setting up a skybox containing distant scenery is conveyed by Jason Shankel in his gem, "Rendering Distant Scenery with Skyboxes." The gem, "Self-Shadowing Characters," by Alex Vlachos, David Gosselin, and Jason Mitchell presents a new technique for generating shadows that a character can cast on itself. Finally, Steve Rabin's gem, "Classic Super Mario 64 Third-Person Control and Animation," describes methods by which user input can control the geometry of an animating character.

# 4.1

## Comparison of VIPM Methods

### Tom Forsyth, Mucky Foot Productions

tomf@muckyfoot.com

View-Independent Progressive Meshing (VIPM) has moved from the status of an interesting research project, to promising new technology, to sensible addition to all the best engines, and now into the Direct3D graphics API itself. It is now becoming almost required for any engine, and its inclusion in the Direct3DX library means that one form of VIPM is relatively easy to add.

However, in an effort to push the performance of VIPM, and in particular to drive the hardware as efficiently as possible, several new forms have been developed, each with their own tradeoffs and characteristics. This gem is intended as a guide to some of the more promising versions, and should help people decide which of the many variants to use in particular situations.

This gem does assume a basic familiarity with VIPM, and there is no space for a thorough introduction here. However, there are several good guides both in print and online. The two best known are Jan Svarovsky's gem in *Game Programming Gems* [Svarovsky00] and Charles Bloom's Web site [Bloom01], both of which have excellent step-by-step guides to implementations of the "vanilla" VIPM method. All of the methods discussed here use the same basic collapse/split algorithm, but implement it in different ways.

### Considerations

There are a few main points on which the various methods need to be judged. Different situations demand different choices, and the different ways each object type in a game is used may mean that different methods of VIPM are used. Things to consider include:

- **Global memory cost**. How much memory is taken up just by the mesh representation of the model? This memory is shared between all onscreen instances.
- **Instance memory cost**. How much memory is used for each instance of the object drawn onscreen? This memory is duplicated for each instance and cannot be shared.
- **Streaming or referenced memory cost**. This is the amount of data actually referenced on each frame. There may be a large amount of existing data for an

object that is mainly left on CD or swapped out to a hard drive by virtual memory. However, on each frame the actual amount of data referenced may be small, allowing the data to be streamed and/or handled efficiently by the virtual memory system. This is especially important for consoles that typically have limited memory.

- **CPU cost**. How many clock cycles does the algorithm take, in terms of user code? This includes both single-frame rendering costs and the cost of changing the level of detail from frame to frame.
- **API interface efficiency**. How many CPU cycles are used in driver and API interfaces getting data down to the graphics card?
- **Bus bandwidth**. How much data must be sent to the graphics card? On a PC, this means the AGP bus bandwidth.
- **Vertex–cache coherency**. Modern graphics cards try to fetch, transform, and light each vertex only once, even though the vertex will be used by multiple triangles. To do this, they have a vertex cache that holds the most recently used vertices, and applications need to try to use vertices in this cache as often as possible to get maximum performance. An algorithm that uses more triangles than another may still be faster because it has a higher vertex cache hit rate.

Vertex cache coherency will be quoted in terms of the number of vertices loaded or processed per triangle drawn, or "vertices per triangle." Current triangle reordering algorithms for static (i.e., non-VIPM) meshes using modern vertex caches of around 16 entries can get numbers down to around 0.65. For an example, see [Hoppe99]. This gives suitable benchmark figures to compare efficiencies when the mesh is converted to a VIPM one. Also note that when calculating the vertices per triangle using triangle strips, only drawn triangles should be counted, not degenerate ones. The degenerate triangles are a necessary evil—they add nothing to the scene.

Algorithms that are good at streaming allow the application to draw huge worlds that are mostly stored on disk, and to degrade image quality gracefully if the streaming of data hits a limit somewhere along the way, such as available disk bandwidth or available memory on the machine.

This also helps systems with virtual memory; if the data is accessed linearly, the virtual memory manager can swap out data that has yet to be accessed, or has not been accessed for a long time. Static data can be optimized even further and made into a read-only memory-mapped file. This also ensures that irritating "loading level" messages are no more tedious than absolutely necessary. The object data does not all need to be loaded at the beginning; the player can start playing the level with low-resolution data and as the detailed models are needed, they will be loaded.

All the methods discussed here are based around implementations of the same fundamental algorithm. Single operations are done that collapse a single vertex onto another vertex along one of its triangle edges. No new "average" vertex is generated, and no collapses between vertices that do not share an edge are allowed. These are worth looking into; however, the current consensus is that they involve a higher runtime cost for equivalent error levels on most current hardware. Of course, things change, and new algorithms are always being invented.

A note on the terminology used: The *resolution* of a mesh is proportional to the number of triangles in it. Thus, a high-resolution mesh undergoes edge collapses and becomes a lower-resolution mesh. The opposite of an edge collapse is an edge *split*, where a single vertex splits into two separate vertices. For a given edge collapse, there is a *kept* vertex and a *binned* vertex. The binned vertex is not used in any lower-resolution meshes, whereas the kept vertex is. For a given edge collapse, there are two types of triangles. Those that use the edge being collapsed will not be in any lower-resolution mesh and are binned. For a typical collapse, there are two binned triangles, although there may be more or less for complex mesh topologies. Those that are not binned but use the binned vertex are "changed" triangles, and changed so that they use the kept vertex instead of the binned vertex. When performing an edge split, the previously binned vertex and triangles are "new," although they are often still called binned because there are typically no split data structures, just collapse data structures that are done in reverse. Most of the perspective is in the collapsing direction, so words like *first*, *next*, *before*, and *after* are used assuming collapses from a high-triangle mesh to a low-triangle mesh. Again, splits are done by undoing collapses.

This gem will be talking in a very PC and DirectX-centric way about CPUs, AGP buses, graphics cards ("the card"), system/video/AGP memory, index, and vertex buffers. This is generally just a convenience—most consoles have equivalent units and concepts. Where there is a significant difference, it will be highlighted. The one term that may be unfamiliar to the reader is the *AGP bus*; this is the bus between the main system memory (and the CPU) and the graphics card with its memory. There are various speeds, but this bus is typically capable of around 500Mbytes/sec, which makes it considerably smaller than the buses between system memory and the CPU, and between the graphics chip and its video memory. Some consoles have a similar bottleneck; others use a unified memory scheme that avoids it. In many cases, this is the limiting factor in PC graphics.

## Vanilla VIPM

This is the best-known version of VIPM, and the version used by the Direct3DX8 library. It has a global list of static vertices, arranged in order from last binned to first binned. Each time a collapse is done, the vertex being binned by the collapse is the one at the end of the list, and the number of vertices used is decremented by one. This ensures that the used vertices are always in a single continuous block at the start of the vertex buffer, which means that linear software T&L pipelines always process only the vertices in use.

The triangles are also ordered from last binned to first binned. Each edge collapse generally removes two triangles, although they may actually remove anywhere from zero upward for meshes with complex topologies.

Triangles that are not binned but are changed during a collapse simply have the index to the binned vertex changed to that of the kept vertex. Since the index list changes as the level of detail changes, the triangle index buffer is stored as per-instance data. The index buffer is comprised of indexed triangle lists (each triangle defined by three separate indices), rather than indexed triangle strips.

Each record of collapse data has the following format:

```
struct VanillaCollapseRecord
{
    // The offset of the vertex that doesn't vanish/appear.
    unsigned short wKeptVert;
    // Number of tris removed/added.
    unsigned char  bNumTris;
    // How many entries in wIndexOffset[].
    unsigned char  bNumChanges;
    // How many entries in wIndexOffset[] in the previous action.
    unsigned char  bPrevNumChanges;
    // Packing to get correct short alignment.
    unsigned char  bPadding[1];

    // The offsets of the indices to change.
    // This will be of actual length bNumChanges,
    // then immediately after in memory will be the next record.
    unsigned short wIndexOffset[];
};
```

This structure is not a fixed length—wIndexOffset[] grows to the number of vertices that need changing. This complicates the access functions slightly, but ensures that when performing collapses or splits, all the collapse data is in sequential memory addresses, which allows cache lines and cache prefetching algorithms to work efficiently. It also allows the application to stream or demand-load the collapse data off a disk very easily. Because it is static and global, it can also be made into a read-only memory-mapped file, which under many operating systems is extremely efficient.

Although at first glance bPrevNumChanges doesn't seem to be needed for collapses, it is needed when doing splits and going back up the list—the number of wIndexOffset[] entries in the previous structure is needed so they can be skipped over. Although this makes for convoluted-looking C, the assembly code produced is actually very simple.

To perform a collapse, the number of vertices used is decremented since the binned vertex is always the one on the end. The number of triangles is reduced by bNumTris; again, the binned triangles are always the ones on the end of the list.

The changed triangles all need to be redirected to use the kept vertex instead of the binned one. The offsets of the indices that refer to the binned point are held in wIndexOffset[]. Each one references an index that needs to be changed from the binned vertex's index (which will always be the last one) to the kept vertex's index—wKeptVert.

```
VanillaCollapseRecord *pVCRCur = the current collapse;
iCurNumVerts—;
iCurNumTris -= pVCRCur->bNumTris;

unsigned short *pwIndices;
// Get the pointer to the instance index buffer.
pIndexBuffer->Lock ( &pwIndices );
for ( int i = 0; i < pVCRCur->bNumChanges; i++ )
{
    ASSERT ( pwIndices[pVCRCur->wIndexOffset[i]] ==
        (unsigned short)iCurNumVerts );
    pwIndices[pVCRCur->wIndexOffset[i]] = pVCRCur->wKeptVert;
}
// Give the index buffer back to the hardware.
pIndexBuffer->Unlock();
// Remember, it's not a simple ++
// (though the operator could be overloaded).
pVCRCur = pVCRCur->Next();
```

Note that reading from hardware index buffers can be a bad idea on some architectures, so be careful of exactly what that ASSERT() is doing—it is mainly for illustration purposes (Figure 4.1.1).

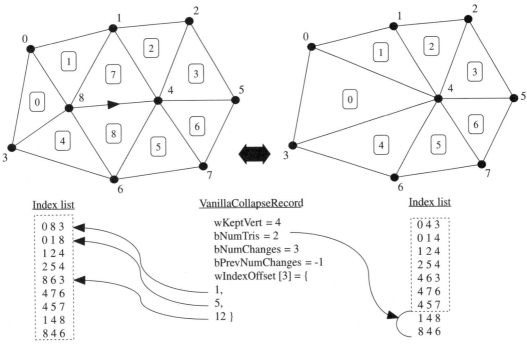

**FIGURE 4.1.1** *An edge collapse with before and after index lists and the* VanillaCollapseRecord.

Doing a split is simply a matter of reversing the process.

```
VanillaCollapseRecord *pVCRCur = the current collapse;
pVCRCur = pVCRCur->Prev();
unsigned short *pwIndices;
pIndexBuffer->Lock ( &pwIndices );
for ( int i = 0; i < pVCRCur->bNumChanges; i++ )
{
    ASSERT ( pwIndices[pVCRCur->wIndexOffset[i]] ==
        pVCRCur->wKeptVert );
    pwIndices[pVCRCur->wIndexOffset[i]] =
        (unsigned short)iCurNumVerts;
}
iCurNumTris += pVCRCur->bNumTris;
iCurNumVerts++;

pIndexBuffer->Unlock();
```

Note that in practice, and for arbitrary historical reasons, in the sample code the VertexCollapseRecords are stored last first, so the Prev() and Next() calls are swapped.

Vanilla VIPM is simple, easy to code, and has decent speed. It should probably be the first version used for any evaluation of VIPM, because it is so simple, and even this will give good scalability, streaming, and so on.

The good thing about vanilla VIPM is that it streams very well. Collapse information and index buffer data is completely linear in memory and ordered by collapse, so implementing a streaming system with fallbacks for when data is not immediately available is extremely easy.

However, there are many bad things about vanilla VIPM. Vertex cache coherency is poor. Because triangle order is strictly determined by collapse order, there is no way to reorder triangles for better vertex caching.

Another problem is the relatively large per-instance memory use. The whole index data chunk needs to be replicated for each instance. This can be reduced by only allocating as many indices as are actually currently being used, and growing or shrinking as needed (along with a bit of hysteresis to prevent calling malloc() and free() all the time), but it is still large if there are lots of objects onscreen.

Finally, vanilla VIPM only works with indexed triangle lists, which can be a poor choice for hardware that prefers strips.

## Skip Strips

*Skip strips* is a slightly overloaded name. It was borrowed from a paper on View-Dependent Progressive Meshing (VDPM) [El-Sana99]. VDPM is significantly more complex and requires some fairly extensive data structures to achieve good efficiency, and a *skip list* is one of those data structures. However, the section that inspired this VIPM method was the bit that noted that to bin a triangle, it does not have to fall off the end of the index list, as in vanilla. There is not much wrong with simply making it degenerate by moving one of its vertices (usually the binned vertex) to another one (usually the kept vertex), and leaving it in the list of drawn triangles. Hardware is very good at spotting degenerate triangles, and throws them away very quickly without trying to draw any pixels.

This means that the order of triangles is no longer determined by collapse order; they can be ordered using some other criteria. The cunning thing that the original skip strips paper pointed out is that triangles can now be ordered into strip order, and indeed converted into strips. This is great for hardware that prefers its data in strip order. Since this VIPM method was inspired by the paper, it inherited the name, despite it being somewhat inaccurate.

The ability to reorder triangles increases vertex cache coherency. Strips are naturally good at this—they have an implicit 1.0 vertices per triangle efficiency (for long strips with no degenerates), and with the right ordering and a decent-sized vertex cache, they can get much lower values.

One cunning thing about the implementation is that the collapse/split routines and data structures are virtually identical to vanilla VIPM. The only change is that the number of drawn triangles does not change with collapses and splits. Triangles simply become degenerate; they do not fall off the end of the list.

However, this shows a big problem with skip strips. After many collapses, there are many degenerate triangles in the list. Although they are rejected by the hardware quickly, they still take some time to reject, and their index data still has to be sent to the card. This eats into the bus bandwidth, and lowers the visible triangle throughput in triangles/second.

After many collapses, the vertex cache efficiency also drops. The nice neat strips will have been bent and broken by the collapses, which disrupts the cache efficiency. Moreover, as triangles become degenerate, the number of indices referring to one of the remaining vertices increases. A collapse that bins that vertex must change all the indices that refer to it, including the degenerate triangles. Therefore, the more collapses that are done, the more expensive each collapse becomes, because the size of `wIndexOffset[]` grows. This does not scale with the number of triangles drawn, which is no good since that is the whole point of VIPM—things at lower detail should take less time to render.

## Multilevel Skip Strips

Fortunately, there is a solution to most of skip strip's woes. After a certain number of collapses, simply stop, take the current geometry with all of its collapses done, throw away the degenerate triangles, and start making a completely new skip strip from scratch. Continue collapses with this new skip strip until it too becomes inefficient, and so on.

When creating each new skip strip level, all of the degenerate triangles are thrown away, which reduces the number of triangles (both visible and degenerate) that are sent to the card. The triangles are also reordered to make lists that are again vertex-cache optimal. New collapses don't need to change lots of degenerate triangle indices each time, each instance only needs to copy the skip strip level that it actually uses, and they become shorter with decreasing detail.

The different index lists can be stored globally since when switching to a new list, a new copy is taken and then refined with collapses to exactly the number of triangles wanted. Therefore, the fact that there are now multiple index lists is not too bad—it's global data. This also restores some of the nice streaming friendliness that the vanilla method has. The granularity is a bit coarser; the whole of an index list must be grabbed before anything can be rendered using that level, but at least it's no longer an all-or-nothing thing, and the lower-resolution index lists are actually very small.

For a bit more efficiency, two versions of the index lists can be stored in global space: fully collapsed (before switching to a lower-resolution list, that is) and fully uncollapsed. This means that a single-collapse oscillation across the boundary between two index lists is still fairly efficient. If only the uncollapsed versions are held, each time the level of detail increases, the higher-resolution index list must be copied, and then all of its collapses need to be performed to draw the next frame. Having the collapsed versions stored as well means that a change in the level of detail of $n$ collapses only actually requires $n$ collapses (and sometimes fewer).

The actual collapse/split code and structures are the same as for standard skip strips, except that there is a global array of structures holding the premade index lists, the collapse lists for each one, and the number of collapses in each. Before doing any collapses or splits, the code checks to see if it needs to change levels, and if so, copies the new level's index list and starts doing collapses/splits until it reaches the right level of detail within that level.

So, this has fixed all the bad things about skip strips when compared to vanilla in exchange for an increase in global (but easily streamed or swapped) memory.

Skip strips also have an equivalent using triangle lists instead of triangle strips. The principle is exactly the same, but use a different primitive. Some algorithms require lists rather than strips, and some vertex cache routines can obtain slightly higher caching rates with lists than strips. No separate implementation was done in the sample code, because they are so similar.

## Mixed-Mode VIPM

One of the problems with the types of VIPM mentioned so far is that the whole index list needs to be copied for each instance of the object. This can be quite a burden in some cases, especially on machines with limited memory, notably consoles, where everything has to be shoehorned into memory that is usually half the size that the programmers would like, even before VIPM is mentioned. It would be excellent if some of this index list could be moved to global (i.e., static and shared between instances) memory instead of having to be copied for each instance.

On a multilevel skip strip, many of the triangles are not affected, even when that level is fully collapsed. Therefore, there is no need to copy those triangles per instance;

they can be global and shared between instances. In fact, for this algorithm, indexed lists are used—the indexed strip case will be discussed later as a variant. At each level, the triangles are split into four lists:

- The triangles that are not affected by any collapses.
- The triangles that are binned by collapses, but not modified by any before they are binned.
- The triangles that are modified by collapses, but not binned.
- The triangles that are first modified by one or more collapses and then binned.

Lists 2 and 4 are each sorted by bin order, just as for vanilla VIPM. Lists 1 and 3 are sorted into whatever order gives the highest vertex cache efficiency. Then list 2 is appended to list 1, and the combined list is put into a global index buffer that is static and shared by all instances. List 4 is appended to list 3, and the combined dynamic list is copied into instances when they use that level. This list is then modified at run-time using exactly the same modification algorithm as vanilla VIPM.

To draw the mesh, the required collapses and splits are done to the dynamic per-instance list, and the list is drawn. Then the associated level's static list is drawn, with the only modification being that the number of triangles drawn will change as static triangles are collapsed.

The code and structures needed are based on the multilevel skip list, except that for each level there are two lists: the copied dynamic one and the shared static one. The other change is that there are two triangle counts, one for each list, and a collapse may alter either or both of these numbers. Therefore, the bNumTris member is replaced by bNumStaticTris and bNumDynamicTris, and the appropriate increments and decrements are added.

This means that a large proportion of each mesh is being drawn from a static index buffer that is tuned for vertex cache coherency (list 1). It is not quite as good as it could be, since the triangles in this list only make up part of the object. There will be "holes" in the mesh where triangles have been moved to the other three lists, and this decreases both the maximum and the actual vertex per-triangle numbers that are obtained. Some of the dynamic buffer is also ordered for optimal vertex cache behavior (list 3), although collapses can interfere with this efficiency, and the mesh for list 3 is usually far from usefully connected, so there is a limit to what any reordering can do.

Like all multilevel methods, it is streaming friendly; although in this case, since the lists are ordered by collapse order, the granularity is even finer at the triangle level, not just the list level. Whether this is terribly exciting is a different question—the finer control is probably not going to make much of a difference in performance.

This does require two DrawIndexedPrimitive() calls to Direct3D (or equivalent API), although on most platforms, this is not a bottleneck and does not affect rendering speed. It may be important for very low-triangle meshes, and for these, switching to another method may be appropriate.

## Mixed-Mode Skip Strips

Mixed-mode skip strips are identical to mixed-mode lists, except that strips are used, and instead of the dynamic list being done with vanilla VIPM, it is done using the skip strips algorithm. As with skip strips, using strips means that ordering by collapse order is too inefficient, and this means that list 2 triangles now have to be binned by being made degenerate. This forces them to become dynamic instead of static, and they join lists 3 and 4. The triangles from these three lists are merged and treated as a skip strips —reordered for optimal vertex cache efficiency, copied for each instance, and modified by collapse information.

The disadvantages with this method are that there is now more data being copied for each instance, and because the triangles are ordered by strip order and not collapse order, triangles cannot be binned entirely by simply dropping them off the end of the index list. However, both these factors are only mildly worse than the list version, and if the hardware needs to be fed strips, this is still an excellent method.

## Sliding Window

Sliding window VIPM introduces the idea of fully static and global index buffers, with no editing of indices, and therefore a tiny amount of per-instance memory.

Sliding window notes that when a collapse happens, there are two classes of triangles: binned triangles and modified triangles. However, there is no real need for the modified triangles to actually be at the same physical position in the index buffer before and after the collapse. The old version of the triangles could simply drop off the end of the index buffer along with the binned triangles, and the new versions added on at the other end.

Therefore, instead of an example collapse binning two triangles and editing three others, it actually bins five triangles and adds three new ones. Both operations are performed by just changing the first and last indices used for rendering—sliding a "rendering window" along the index buffer (Figure 4.1.2).

The index buffer is split into three sections. At the beginning are triangles added as a result of changes, in reverse collapse order. In the middle are triangles not affected by collapses, in any (vertex cache-optimal) order. At the end are triangles binned or changed by collapses, again ordered in reverse collapse order—first collapse at the end. Note that a triangle modified as the result of a collapse cannot then be involved (either binned or changed) in another collapse. To be modified by a second collapse would mean that triangle would have to fall off the end of the index buffer. It has already been added to the beginning so it cannot then also fall off the end—the chance of the ordering being just right to allow this are incredibly slim.

Once a triangle has been modified by a collapse, the only way it can be involved in another collapse is if a new index buffer is started that has all the same triangles as the previous (collapsed) one. The ordering of this new one is not constrained by the previous collapses, and so can be sorted by new collapses. Again, the multilevel con-

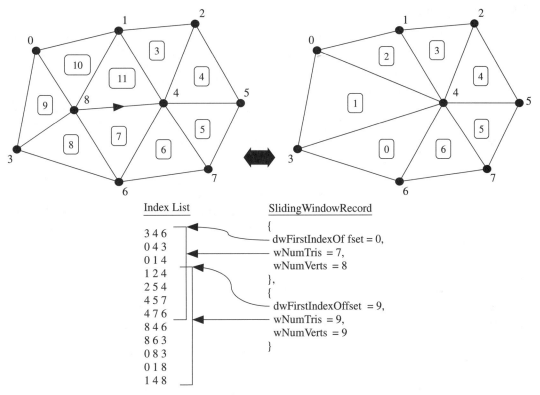

**FIGURE 4.1.2** *A collapse showing the index list and the two windows.*

cept is used, but in this case because further collapses cannot happen without it, not simply for efficiency.

The problem with this at face value is that algorithms such as QEM give an ordering for collapses. If this ordering is strictly followed, the QEM frequently wants to do a new collapse that involves a triangle that has already been modified by a previous collapse. This forces a new level to be made, and the index buffer needs to be copied. Since only a few collapses have been done, this copy is almost as big as the original. If only a few collapses are done before having to make a copy, the memory used for all the index buffers is going to be huge.

However, there is actually no need to strictly follow the order of collapses that QEM decides. Progressive meshing is not an exact science, since it ignores everything but the distance of the camera from the object, and the whole point is to simply be "good enough" to fool the eye. Therefore, there is no real need to precisely follow the collapse order that QEM decides—it can be manipulated a bit.

The way to do this is to follow the QEM collapse order until it decides to do a collapse that involves triangles that have already been modified. Doing this collapse would force a new level, and so this is put off for as long as possible. For the moment this collapse is ignored, and the best one that can be done without creating a new level is found. The errors of the two collapses are compared, and if they are within a certain tolerance, then doing them out of strict order is not going to affect visual quality all that much, and the collapse that will not force a new level is done.

Once the difference in error levels is too great, then doing the wrong collapse first is going to affect image quality significantly, and the algorithm bites the bullet and creates a new level. There have now been a decent number of collapses done before this copy happens, the triangle count has been significantly reduced, and thus far, fewer levels are needed before they collapse down to the minimum level of detail.

The sample code uses a fairly small tolerance level of 10 percent of the average collapse error, and even this small tolerance reduces the number of levels dramatically. Using a larger error tolerance can reduce the memory use even more, although only to a point. After a while, the algorithm simply runs out of triangles that have not already been involved in a collapse. Most meshes can only lose around 20 percent of their triangles before this happens, but this still keeps memory use at sensible levels.

Since no runtime modification is made to the index or vertex lists, all the data can be made global, and there is almost zero per-instance memory use. There is also almost zero CPU time used to change level of detail—each time, a simple table look-up is made to decide the index list to use, the start and end index to draw from that index list, and how many vertices are used. In practice, the index lists are concatenated together, so that the first index also implies the index list to use. The table is composed of this structure:

```
struct SlidingWindowRecord
{
    unsigned int    dwFirstIndexOffset;
    unsigned short  wNumTris;
    unsigned short  wNumVerts;
};
```

Although the number of triangles and vertices is known to be less than 64k (this is a limit in all currently known hardware), because the index list is a concatenation of many lists, it may easily be greater than 64k indices in length, so 32 bits are required for it. This does mean that the structure is nicely padded to 8-byte alignment, though. The rendering code is amazingly simple:

```
SlidingWindowRecord &pswr = swrRecords[iLoD];
d3ddevice->DrawIndexedPrimitive (
    D3DPT_TRIANGLELIST, // Primitive type
    0,                  // First used vertex
    pswr->wNumVerts,    // Number of used vertices
    pswr->dwFirstIndexOffset,// First index
    pswr->wNumTris );   // Number of triangles
```

There is no code to do splits or collapses as with all the other methods—the current level of detail is just looked up in the SlidingWindowRecord table each time the object is rendered. This also means that with hardware transform and lighting cards, the CPU time required to render objects is fixed and constant per object, whatever their level of detail. The phrase "constant time" is always a good one to find lurking in any algorithm.

The major problem with sliding window VIPM is that it forces the ordering of the triangles at the beginning and end of each level's index lists. This has two effects: it makes strips hard to use—only triangle lists really handle fixed ordering well—and vertex cache efficiency is affected.

Fortunately, it is not as bad as it first seems. When an edge collapse is performed, all of the triangles that use the binned vertex are removed, so they all go on the end of the triangle list. This is typically from five to seven triangles, and they form a triangle fan around the binned vertex. Then the new versions of the triangles are added. These need to go together at the beginning of the index list, there are typically three to five of them, and they form a triangle fan around the kept vertex. These fans can be ordered within themselves to get the best cache coherency. The middle of the index list that is not affected, and thus has no set order, can be reordered for the vertex cache. This gets much better cache coherency than vanilla. Although it is still quite a bit short of the theoretical ideal, it is not unreasonably poor.

Vertex cache coherency can be raised by having a larger middle index list section in each level—by having fewer collapses per level. This takes more memory, but the extra performance may be worth it, especially as it is global memory.

Hardware that requires strips rather than lists can still use this method, although it does require many degenerate triangles to join the different parts. In practice, this does not increase the number of indices required, it actually reduces it—strips have one index per triangle, compared to a list's three. The vertex cache efficiency per drawn triangle is exactly the same. The raw triangle throughput is increased a lot (roughly doubled), but since all of these extra triangles are just degenerate, most hardware will reject them very quickly. If there is a choice, which of the two primitives used depends on whether the hardware is limited by index bandwidth (in which case, strips are optimal) or triangle throughput (in which case, lists are optimal).

## Summary

VIPM seems to be coming of age. It is now mainstream, it has been incorporated into a major API, and for discrete objects it has beaten off VDPM and static level of detail methods for the most visual bang for the CPU buck (although it is worth noting that VDPM methods are still challengers for large landscapes, especially regular-height-field ones). In addition, it now has a plethora of methods from which to choose, each with its own advantages and disadvantages. Innovation certainly won't stop there—there are already some interesting paths for future investigation, but this roundup should give a fairly good guide to some of the issues and options when choosing which VIPM method to implement.

**Table 4.1.1 Summary of Strengths and Weaknesses of Each VIPM Method**

|  | Vanilla | Skip Strips | Mixed-Mode | Sliding Window |
|---|---|---|---|---|
| Vertex cache use | Poor | Excellent | Good | Good |
| Global memory use | Low | Medium | Medium | High |
| Instance memory use | High | High | Medium | Low |
| LoD-change CPU cost | Medium | Medium | Medium | Tiny |
| API efficiency | Good | Good | Good | Excellent |
| List efficiency | Poor | Excellent | Good | Good |

Table 4.1.1 shows the results of each method with their relative strengths and weaknesses. Note that "skip strips" refers to multilevel skip strips—the single-level version is not actually a sensible method in practice, for the reasons given.

# References

[Svarovsky00] Svarovsky, Jan, "View-Independent Progressive Meshing," *Game Programming Gems*, Charles River Media, 2000, pp. 454–464.

[Bloom01] Bloom, Charles, VIPM tutorial, and various VIPM thoughts gathered from many sources. www.cbloom.com/3d/index.html.

[Hoppe99] Hoppe, Hugues, "Optimization of Mesh Locality for Transparent Vertex Caching," Computer Graphics (SIGGRAPH 1999 proceedings) pp. 269–276. See also www.research.microsoft.com/~hoppe/.

[El-Sana99] J. El-Sana, F. Evans, A. Varshney, S. Skiena, E. Azanli, "Efficiently Computing and Updating Triangle Strips for View-Dependent Rendering," *The Journal of Computer Aided Design*, vol. 32, no. 13, pp. 753–772. See also www.cs.bgu.ac.il/~el-sana/publication.html.

# 4.2

## Simplified Terrain Using Interlocking Tiles

### Greg Snook

gregsnook@home.com

With recent advancements in 3D rendering hardware, it seems that everyone is bringing his or her game to the great outdoors. Far horizons and mountainous landscapes, once hidden by fog and far clipping planes, are now an obtainable reality. Game programmers once consumed with the BSP tree and span-based rendering methods are now trading in tired old buzzwords for shiny new acronyms like ROAM and VDPM.

ROAM (*Real-time Optimally Adapting Meshes*) [Duchaineau] and VDPM (*View Dependent Progressive Meshes*) [Hoppe98] are outlined elsewhere in great detail (see the References), so I'll just give them a quick overview here. Both of these methods do an amicable job of reducing the polygon count (and therefore the rendering load) on those parts of the terrain that do not require a great deal of geometry, such as reasonably flat plains or areas far off in the distance. In turn, they allow more detailed terrain to exist closer to the camera, or on very rough surfaces, where additional polygons are needed. Essentially, they are two rather complex ways to achieve the same simple goal: more polygons where you need them, less where you don't.

The trouble for some applications is that methods such as ROAM and VDPM tend to rely on procedurally generated geometry to achieve a smooth transition from low- to high-detail areas. ROAM uses a binary tree of triangle intersections to construct the actual terrain geometry from a given height field. VDPM achieves a similar effect by using a coarse mesh to represent the low-detail terrain and applying a set of successive vertex splits to further divide the terrain polygons where necessary. In most cases, these continuous triangulations disrupt the speed advantage of hardware transform and lighting, which relies on static geometry for optimum speed.

The main reason for this is that these methods work almost too well. They have the power to analyze the terrain down to the poly level, hand-picking those that stay and those that get collapsed. This can result in many minute changes to the terrain geometry over time, and requires reprocessing of the entire method should the terrain change. By sacrificing that finite level of control over the geometry, we can remain hardware friendly by working over larger areas of static geometry and remain flexible to changes in the terrain over time.

What this gem proposes is a far simpler method that most applications can take advantage of with a minimal amount of coding. It is not intended to wrestle with the visual quality that ROAM or VDPM methods can produce; instead, it serves to create a simple terrain with the benefits of dynamically adapting detail levels and animation flexibility. It does this while maintaining a data system that is perfectly suited for hardware transform and lighting.

## Tiles Revisited

Many moons ago, game programmers used 2D tiles to represent the playfield. This was done for one simple reason: less artwork was easier to create and manage. Early games simply did not have the memory to afford a large amount of pixel data, so smaller pictures were tiled to create the illusion of a larger area. These small tiles were also easier to draw and push around, so smooth-scrolling 2D games could easily be created out of little 32×32 pixel tiles.

The terrain method presented here works on the same basic principle by dividing the terrain into smaller, reusable tiles. The same advantages apply: smaller bits of data are easy to push around, drawing can be optimized, and memory is used more efficiently. The obvious difference is that we are no longer dealing with pixel data within the tiles. The terrain tiles are represented as index buffers that link together the vertices of the terrain.

Think of the 3D tiles as a grid being projected down on the landscape from above. Each grid square represents a single tile in the terrain system. On the surface, it may not appear as if the terrain tiles ever repeat, given that terrain is a pretty random set of geometry. The truth is the terrain may never repeat *on the surface*, but behind the scenes, there is ample data to tile and reuse.

Consider each terrain tile in the form of a vertex and index buffer. While each tile may contain a unique set of vertex data, the index buffers used to draw the tiles can be made to repeat rather frequently. In fact, by careful planning of the vertex data, we can create a finite set of index buffer "tiles" to use throughout the entire terrain.

We do this by taking advantage of a few refinements in the geometry of our tiles. First, each tile must contain an identical number of vertices, sharing the edge vertices with its neighbors. These vertices represent the highest level of detail possible for the tile. Second, the vertices of the tile are arranged in a regular grid on the *x-y* plane, using *z* to represent the vertices' height above sea level. Last, we store the vertices of each tile in an identical order so our index buffers can be used on any tile. Have a look at the sample tile shown in Figure 4.2.1. Here we have a 17×17 vertex tile showing the grid-aligned positioning of each vertex, each of which has a unique height value sampled from the terrain bitmap.

The reason for this vertex organization is simple. Since the vertex data always appears in a regular grid and in an identical order, a fixed set of index buffers can be created for the entire terrain. Using the proper index buffer, a given tile can be rendered at any level, ranging from full detail down to a simple pair of triangles. Index

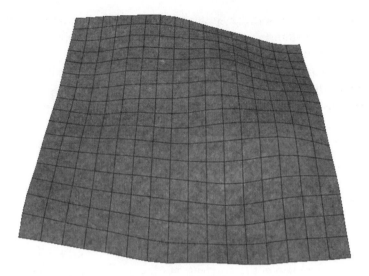

**FIGURE 4.2.1** *A sample terrain tile of 17×17 vertices.*

buffers that use more of the available vertices create a higher detailed representation of the tile. Similarly, index buffers using less vertices render tiles with reduced triangle counts. Figure 4.2.2 illustrates this by showing a sample tile rendered at different detail levels.

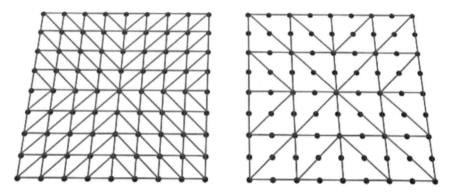

**FIGURE 4.2.2** *Using index buffers to create two separate detail levels from the same set of vertices.*

## Map Making

In order to create the landscape tiles, we need a set of source data from which to pull. A common method is to read elevation data from a height map. This map is simply a grayscale bitmap of the terrain, where the luminance of the pixel is used to represent the elevation at a given position. The height map has the added advantage that it is already arranged in a regular grid, so it can be easily translated into terrain vertex data. It can also serve as an animation resource, adjusting the pixel values to affect the terrain height at different locations.

Creating the tile vertices is simple. Since each tile vertex has a known 2D position on the *x-y* grid, all that remains is to sample the corresponding height pixel from the terrain bitmap and translate it to a *z* value for the terrain vertex. For each terrain tile, a corresponding block of pixels in the height map can be sampled to create a unique vertex buffer for the tile. In the case of an animating height map, this process must be repeated periodically to update the terrain vertices.

## Tile Templates

The index buffer can be thought of as a drawing template cast over the tile vertices. As we saw in Figure 4.2.2, the index buffer defines how we pull triangles out of the tile, controlling how detailed a version of it we draw. Following our key rules, each tile's vertex buffer has been laid out in an identical order so the index buffers can be used interchangeably. For an example 9×9 vertex tile, we can create a global set of index buffers to draw all possible detail levels for any 9×9 set of vertices, skipping vertices in the grid to create the level geometry. The top-level index buffer uses all 81 vertices to draw 128 triangles, while the lowest level uses only the four corner vertices to draw a two-triangle quad. In addition, there are two additional detail levels representing 32 and 8 triangles, respectively.

The next requirement is a method to determine which of our four detail levels each tile needs to use when being drawn. This determination can range from a simple function of the distance between the tile and the camera, to a full heuristic taking into account the viewing angle and perceived roughness of the tile. The best method to use depends on the game terrain and camera movement. Hugues Hoppe's paper on the VDPM method [Hoppe] sheds more light on heuristic ideas that can be used to select detail levels for each terrain location. The sample application on the companion CD-ROM, *SimpleTerrain*, uses the distance from the tile to the camera for simplicity. Once the detail level is known, drawing is a simple matter of sending the tile's vertex buffer along with the desired index buffer into your chosen rendering API for drawing.

ON THE CD

## Ugly, Ugly, Ugly

We have the basic terrain system in place, but it is by no means a smooth terrain. What we have now is a terrain that changes abruptly as tiles of different detail levels are drawn side by side. In addition to that, seams can appear in the gaps created by two tiles of different detail levels. In short, we have made a mess, but there is still hope.

The key to this method is having tiles that interlock. That is, creating tiles that mesh together perfectly, regardless of the differences in detail levels between neighboring tiles. To do this, a different set of index buffers is required to merge tiles of different levels together without gaps and seams. These index buffers can be broken into

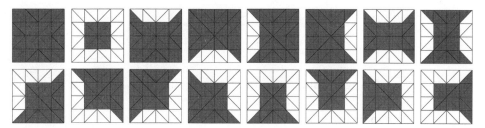

**FIGURE 4.2.3** *The 16 basic tile bodies. Unshaded areas show where linking pieces must be placed.*

two groups: bodies and links. Bodies represent a major portion of a tile at a given detail level, with areas removed to provide space for linking pieces. Links, as the name suggests, link the bodies of different detail levels together seamlessly.

Figure 4.2.3 shows the 16 possible body types for a tile of any given detail level. To keep things under control, we specify that tiles only link downward, meaning that tiles at higher detail levels must use link pieces to fit together with lower-detail neighbors. Looking at Figure 4.2.3, the unshaded areas of each body type then represent spaces where links are required to connect to a neighbor tile at a lower detail level.

Linking pieces are smaller index buffers that fit into the spaces left vacant by the body tiles. These index buffers arrange triangles to step down from a tile using a higher number of vertices to an adjacent one using less. Figure 4.2.4 shows an example link tile used to connect two body tiles. Since we only link downward in detail levels, each detail level needs enough link pieces to connect to the details levels below it. For the example 9×9 vertex tile, we would need three linking pieces for each side of our highest-detail level, since it must be able to link to three lower-detail levels. Our lowest-detail level, the simple quad tile, needs no linking pieces, since all higher-detail levels must do the work to link down to it.

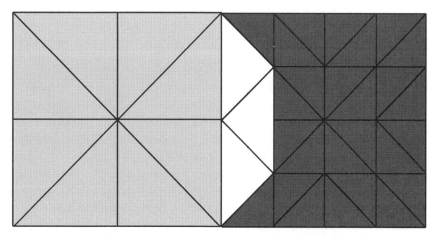

**FIGURE 4.2.4** *An example link piece used to join two tiles of different detail levels.*

**Table 4.2.1 All Index Buffers Required for Our Sample of Four Detail Levels**

| Detail Level | Body Pieces Required | + | Linking Pieces Required | = | Total |
|---|---|---|---|---|---|
| 4 | 16 | | 3 for each side | | 28 |
| 3 | 16 | | 2 for each side | | 24 |
| 2 | 15 | | 1 per side | | 19 |
| 1 | 1 | | 0 | | 1 |
| | | | | Grand Total: | 72 |

Given our example of a 9×9 vertex tile with four detail levels, we can calculate that the total number of index buffers required amounts to a grand total of 48 "body" pieces and 24 "linking" pieces. Table 4.2.1 shows the full table of index buffers required to smooth out our terrain. As can be seen, increasing the number of detail levels increases the index buffer count, but since these are relatively small in size and can be used throughout the entire terrain, they still remain rather efficient.

## Better, Faster, Stronger

Using the new body and linking pieces means we need to change our rendering method. For each tile, we now need to examine the tile's neighbors. We choose a body tile that contains a notched side for each neighbor that is at a lower detail level than the current tile. Then, we select the necessary linking pieces that fill the notches and connect us with the adjacent tiles. Each of these index buffers is then sent to the rendering API along with the tile's vertex buffer for drawing. In the worst case, we send five index buffers per tile (one body, four linking), but in the best case, we still send only one (the full body tile).

Organizing the index buffers into triangle strips and fans can further optimize the method. For larger tiles (33×33 vertices and up), this will greatly reduce rendering time. In addition, the order of the vertices in the tile can be adjusted for better cache performance when rendering. The exact order will depend on which index buffers the tile will be rendered with most often.

## Conclusion

ON THE CD

Figure 4.2.5 shows the final output of the rendering method. The sample program *SimpleTerrain* demonstrates the method using DirectX 8.0. Full source code for the sample program is available on the companion CD-ROM. In this image, the wireframe of the terrain is exposed to show the various body tiles and linking tiles in use. Ground textures have been removed for readability.

The intent of this gem was to provide an alternative to the popular procedural methods for rendering dynamic terrain while fully enabling hardware transform and lighting. By using this method, a dynamic terrain system can be up and running quickly without severely impacting the application's frame rate. While the final terrain may not rival that of a well-written ROAM or VDPM system, it does provide the

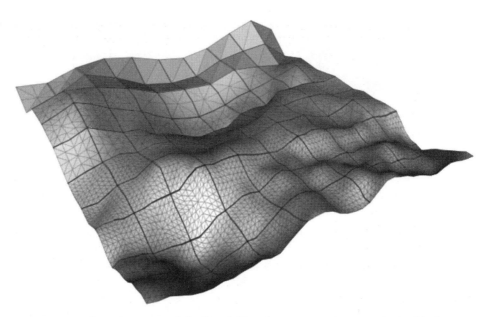

**FIGURE 4.2.5** *Sample output of the* SimpleTerrain *program showing tiles and linking pieces in use.*

same basic advantages of those methods with the potential of greater rendering speed in hardware.

## References

[Duchaineau] Duchaineau, M., Wolinski, M., Sigeti, D., Miller, M., Aldrich, C., and Mineev-Weinstein, M., "ROAMing Terrain: Real-time Optimally Adapting Meshes" (www.llnl.gov/graphics/ROAM).

[Hoppe98] Hoppe, H. "Smooth View-Dependent Level-of-Detail Control and Its Application to Terrain Rendering" *IEEE Visualization 1998*, October 1998, pp. 35–42. (www.research.microsoft.com/~hoppe).

# 4.3

# Sphere Trees for Fast Visibility Culling, Ray Tracing, and Range Searching

## John W. Ratcliff, Sony Online Entertainment

jratcliff@verant.com

**W**hile there are many data structures for storing static 3D objects, including quadtrees, octrees, and BSP trees, they are not always ideal for large numbers of dynamic objects. This gem presents an algorithm and demonstration application that manages thousands of objects in motion that are continuously maintained as a collection of hierarchical bounding spheres in a *SphereTree*.

The design goal for this algorithm has been to make the 99-percentile case spend almost no CPU time updating an object in motion within the tree structure. Queries against the SphereTree perform more tests than other data structures, but this is mitigated by the fact that the tree can be maintained using very little CPU time. This data structure is ideally suited for gross culling of massive numbers of moving objects in a large world space. It doesn't matter if the objects are moving at widely disparate speeds, or even if many of them are not in motion at all. It also has a very low cost when objects are inserted and removed from the tree with great frequency.

## Bounding Spheres

There are certain limitations when using a bounding sphere as a culling primitive. A bounding sphere does not necessarily fit very tightly around an object, especially if it is tall and thin. On the other hand, this over-described bounding sphere can be seen as a feature, not necessarily a limitation. A bounding sphere must encompass the complete extent of an object in all orientations. This includes taking into consideration all possible animation poses that might be applied. Additionally, this bounding sphere is presumed to encompass all child objects that are attached to the parent. This allows for the assumption that whatever the visibility state of the parent is also considered true for its children. Another advantage of an over-described bounding sphere is that it can be used to cull animations, shadows, and other associated effects. This extra slop around an object can be an effective tool to determine when to treat an object, its children, and its associated effects as active or inactive. Culling shadows, animations, and special effects are just as critical as culling geometry alone.

## Using Sphere Trees

Every object in the simulation, whether it is in motion or not, uses the class `SpherePack` to maintain itself inside a valid `SphereTree`. When an object changes position using the method `NewPos()`, `SpherePack` simply computes the squared distance between the new position and the center of the parent node. If it is still contained within the radius of the parent sphere, which is designed to be true almost all of the time, the routine immediately returns. This method is implemented inline for maximum performance. This is the only calculation performed for the vast majority of all objects in motion, even if there are thousands of them. For static objects, nothing is done beyond their initial insertion into the tree.

When a new position would cause an object to pierce the skin of its parent sphere, then that child is removed from the parent and inserted into the root node of the tree. This involves only a couple of pointer swaps to instantly maintain a completely valid tree. When a child node is detached from its parent, it is placed into the reintegration FIFO queue. The parent is added to the recomputation FIFO queue to maintain an optimally balanced tree. At each frame, the simulation performs the process method on the `SpherePackFactory` so that the reintegration and recomputation FIFO queues can be flushed.

One problem with a quadtree or an octree is that it is possible for a single leaf node to be contained in multiple nodes of the tree. If an object crosses a quadtree boundary, it needs to be represented in both nodes. The `SphereTree` does not have this property. No leaf node can ever be contained in more than one `SuperSphere`. What is true for the `SuperSphere` is automatically true for all children. If a `SuperSphere` is outside the view frustum, then all of its children are outside the view frustum as well. The same is true for range tests and ray trace tests.

This makes the sphere tree an ideal data structure for these kinds of queries. When performing visibility culling with a sphere tree, each node keeps track of the state it was in on the previous frame. Callbacks occur only when a node undergoes a state change, which allows the simulation to efficiently maintain a list of only those objects in the view frustum.

## Demonstration Application

This algorithm is demonstrated in the Windows application `SphereTest.exe`. `SphereTest.exe` will create a `SphereTree` containing 1000 spheres in motion. Even though this demonstration application is in 2D, the `SphereTree` is a completely 3D data structure. The rather large `SphereTree` displayed runs at a low frame rate since rendering all of this data is fairly slow under Windows. The `SphereTest` application demonstrates building a SphereTree and performing a variety of high-speed queries against it while running a simulation that models the type of situations seen in games.

The number of spheres created by the simulation can be passed as a command-line argument. With fewer spheres, it will be much easier to visualize the SphereTree that is built. If a SphereTree of 5000 to 10,000 items is created, queries will still be seen taking place very quickly, with most of the CPU time burned just calling Windows graphics routines to render the results. If the application is begun with a very large number of items, there will be a pause while the initial tree is built and balanced, after which it will run fairly quickly.

ON THE CD

The example simulation models the type of situations one would see in an actual game. In this simulation, 25 percent of the objects are in stasis, and the other 75 percent are always attempting to clump toward one of 16 different attraction points. In an actual game, objects are not usually evenly distributed across the address space. The example simulation demonstrating the use of the SpherePackFactory class is contained in the files Circle.cpp and Circle.h on the companion CD-ROM.

Figure 4.3.1 shows the class diagram for the SpherePack system.

To use the SpherePack system in a simulation, we simply instantiate a SpherePackFactory class with the maximum number of spheres, the size of the root node, the size of the leaf node, and the amount of gravy around each SuperSphere. The gravy factor acts as a bit of slop in our coordinate space to prevent objects from detaching from their parent SuperSphere too frequently. For each object in the simulation, we call the AddSphere() method to create a SpherePack instance. Whenever an object changes position, we invoke the NewPos() method. If the object changes both position and radius, we invoke the NewPosRadius() method. When an object in the

**SpherePack System**

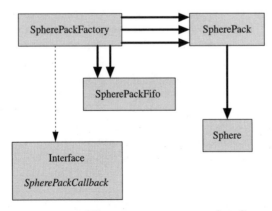

**FIGURE 4.3.1** *The* SpherePack *system class diagram.*

simulation is destroyed, we invoke the Remove() method on the `SpherePackFactory` class.

The `SpherePackFactory` class maintains the complete `SphereTree` hierarchy and contains the two integration FIFO queues. When performing queries, an interface called `SpherePackCallback` is used to extract information from the `SphereTree`. The leaf node `SpherePack` inherits the properties of a `Sphere` class.

# 4.4

# Compressed Axis-Aligned Bounding Box Trees

*Miguel Gomez, Lithtech*

miguel@lithtech.com

The axis-aligned bounding box (AABB) tree structure has proven to be very useful for accelerating intersection queries on sets of geometry. The data structure is easy to implement, the built structure is numerically well conditioned, and like all binary trees, they have $O(log\ n)$ search time [Sedgewick90]. This gem explains several techniques that can be used to lower the overall memory footprint of an AABB tree to 11 bytes per triangle.

## A Brief Survey of Hierarchical Sorting Methods

This section covers quadtrees, k-d trees, BSP trees, bounding volume trees, and axis-aligned bounding boxes, data structures for sorting three-dimensional sets of triangles.

### Quadtrees, k-d Trees, and BSP Trees

Some of the most popular data structures for sorting three-dimensional sets of triangles are the octree, k-d tree, and BSP tree. While the octree is probably the simplest to implement, the more sophisticated k-d and binary space partitioning (BSP) trees adapt better to specific sets of geometry. All of these structures use planes to separate space into convex regions, which leads to some serious side effects. First, any triangle that straddles a separating plane must either be split into two pieces, which increases the set of data and can create problematic "slivers," or included in multiple nodes, which removes any upper bound on the size of the node structure. Second, octrees and k-d trees do not separate geometry adaptively, so they may need arbitrary thresholds to terminate a recursive build algorithm. For example, if many triangles share the same vertex, the octree recursion may never achieve one triangle per node and will have to be terminated based on tree depth. This can lead to unnecessarily deep trees. BSP trees that adaptively use the planes of individual triangles for separation do not have this problem, but they still can have problems introduced by splitting.

### Bounding Volume Trees

Bounding volume trees approach the problem differently. Instead of dividing space, bounding volume trees recursively divide a set of triangles into two subsets and find a bounding volume that encloses each subset. This approach avoids having to split triangles or include them in multiple nodes, and building a tree simply stops when a subset has only one remaining triangle. For more information on bounding volume trees, see [vandenBergen99].

### Axis-Aligned Bounding Boxes

An axis-aligned bounding box has a position (its center) and extents. As its name implies, the sides of an AABB are parallel to the $x$-, $y$-, and $z$-axes. Figure 4.4.1 shows how an AABB fits a single triangle.

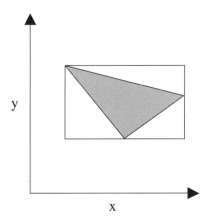

**FIGURE 4.4.1**  *The sides of an AABB are parallel to the coordinate axes.*

## AABB Trees

The bounding boxes in an AABB can and often do overlap. Figure 4.4.2 shows a shallow tree for a set of two connected triangles, L and R. Notice that the left and right AABBs overlap.

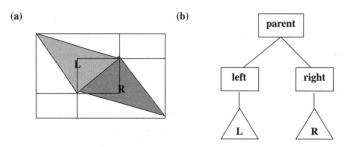

**FIGURE 4.4.2** *A) The AABBs for two connected triangles will always intersect. B) The AABB tree structure for this particular geometry.*

## Building AABB Trees

An AABB tree is built to by successively dividing a set of triangles into two subsets until each subset contains only one triangle. The basic algorithm for building an AABB tree is:

- Find the AABB that encloses the entire set.
- Divide the set into two subsets. This can be done by classifying the centroid of each triangle along the major (longest) axis of this AABB. If one subset is empty, arbitrarily create two subsets of approximately equal size.
- If a subset contains only one triangle, create a leaf.
- Otherwise, repeat the same process on each subset.

## Compressing AABB Trees

In most applications, 4-byte floats have sufficient precision (seven digits) for specifying box extents, requiring $6 \times 4 = 24$ bytes at each node. Any binary tree requires exactly $2n - 1$ nodes to sort $n$ elements, allowing an array of nodes to be allocated before building the tree. If the data set is large, it might be necessary to specify the indices of the child nodes with 4-byte unsigned integers. To avoid having to store yet another 4-byte integer for a triangle index at each node, we can exploit the fact that the $0^{th}$ node (the root) is never referenced by another node. Therefore, if one of the child node indices is zero, we can consider the node a leaf, and the other integer must index a triangle. This trick gives us a grand total of 32 bytes per node, or about 64 bytes per triangle as $n$ becomes large. If we are willing to limit our triangle count to $2^{15}$ (giving a node count of $2^{16} - 1$), unsigned 2-byte integers can be used for child node indices. This reduces the footprint to 28 bytes per node, or about 56 bytes per triangle. Since most applications can divide triangle sets into chunks of $2^{15}$, 56 bytes per triangle will be used as a reference value.

There are two important properties of AABB trees that can be exploited to minimize storage. First, child AABB nodes are fully contained by their parent. This allows us to store child extent values as unsigned 8-bit integer offsets relative to their parent's extents. Second, *at most*, six extent values of the child nodes are *not* identical to those of the parent node. This means that we only need to store six values to fully describe the two children.

## Approximating Extents

In order to use unsigned bytes as relative extent values for nodes, we must keep track of the floating-point extent values of the parent as the tree is built. By scaling the child extents relative to the parent AABB and then truncating to an integer value, we get a conservative estimate for the child AABB extents (Figure 4.4.3).

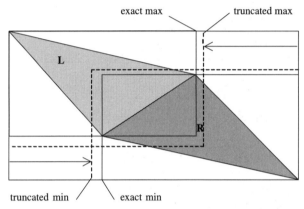

**FIGURE 4.4.3** *When approximating extents with unsigned 8-bit integers, min values are measured from the left, while max values are measured from the right.*

The error of any extent value relative to its parent is never more than $1/255 \approx 4 \times 10^{-3}$. To put this in perspective, if the extents of the parent node are one meter on each side, we get a resolution of about four millimeters for the child extents. Keep in mind that these numbers scale as the nodes become smaller. The equations for calculating relative offset values are:

$$i_{\min} = \mathrm{trunc}\left(255\,\frac{\min_{child} - \min_{parent}}{\max_{parent} - \min_{parent}}\right),$$

$$i_{\max} = \mathrm{trunc}\left(255\,\frac{\max_{parent} - \max_{child}}{\max_{parent} - \min_{parent}}\right),$$

$$i_{\max}, i_{\min} \in \left[0, 255\right].$$

Using 1 byte instead of 4 bytes to store an extent value immediately brings the memory consumption down to 10 bytes per node, or 20 bytes per triangle.

## Exploiting Redundancy

In order to store only six extent values for both children, we must take a bold step and store both the left and the right child information within one node structure. In this structure, a bit field is used to indicate which extent belongs to which child. A *true* bit means that the unique extent value belongs to the *left* child (so the parent's extent value belongs to the right child), and a *false* bit indicates the opposite situation. This requires only 6 bits, so the other 2 bits are used to indicate which nodes are leaves. When information for both children is stored at a single node, the node only consumes 11 bytes (Figure 4.4.4).

| flags (1 byte) | |
|:---:|:---:|
| extents (6 bytes) | |
| left node/triangle index (2 bytes) | right node/triangle index (2 bytes) |

**FIGURE 4.4.4**  *The compressed AABB node structure consumes only 11 bytes per node.*

In addition, only *n* nodes (including the root) are required to sort *n* triangles, so the tree now needs only 11 bytes of storage per triangle. (Some architectures may require a 12-byte structure for alignment.) This is almost 50 percent less than if relative values were used alone, and about one-fifth the storage of our reference value. As an added bonus, we can now keep track of twice as many triangles ($2^{16} - 1$ instead of $2^{15}$) (Figure 4.4.5).

In practice, the root node is a separate data type that specifies the floating-point extents of the entire triangle set and is not part of the actual node array, which contains $n - 1$ nodes.

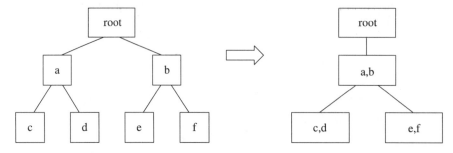

**FIGURE 4.4.5**  *For a set of four triangles, the uncompressed tree requires seven nodes, whereas the tree on the right requires only four.*

## Runtime Efficiency

The runtime cost of converting the 8-bit values back to floating-point values is minimal. An experiment in which a line segment was tested for possible intersection with 16K randomly distributed triangles showed that the compressed structure was about 10 percent slower than the full floating-point representation. It seems that the ability of the significantly smaller data set to fit in the cache nearly compensates for the overhead of converting integers to floating point values.

## Future Work

The compressibility of AABB trees gives them a clear advantage over other structures; however, it may be possible to apply the same techniques to compress other bounding volume tree structures, such as OBB trees. The fact that child AABB nodes are fully contained by their parent volume allows us to easily scale and share extent values. This same property does not hold for OBB trees [Gottschalk96]. The lack of this property may make it impossible to share redundant extent values; however, it may still be possible to store scaled 8-bit extent values and 8-bit orientation values for OBB trees by propagating the expanded dimensions back up the tree to the root node.

## References

[Gottschalk96] Gottschalk, S., Lin, M. C., and Manocha, D., "OBBTree: A Hierarchical Structure for Rapid Interference Detection," SIGGRAPH Proceedings, 1996, pp. 171–180.

[Sedgewick90] Sedgewick, Robert, *Algorithms in C*, Addison-Wesley, 1990.

[vandenBergen99] van den Bergen, G., *Collision Detection in Interactive 3D Computer Animation*, Ph.D. Thesis, Eindhoven University of Technology, 1999.

# 4.5

## Direct Access Quadtree Lookup

### Matt Pritchard, Ensemble Studios

mpritchard@ensemblestudios.com

Quadtrees are versatile and well-known constructs for spatially managing large amounts of two-dimensional data. In games programming, they are a favorite for managing object locations in a game world, offering good search performance and flexible implementation possibilities. In cases where the game data is static, quadtrees can be precalculated, and from a performance standpoint, they are quite efficient.

But what about a highly dynamic case, such as in a real-time strategy (RTS) game when large numbers of objects are constantly in motion and coming into and out of existence in the game world (quadtree)? During the implementation and subsequent profiling of such a scenario, I found that my quadtree update routines were showing up surprisingly high on the list of CPU-consuming code. This behavior for a constantly updating data set led me to ask where the time was actually going, and to look for more efficient ways to get the same job done. The result is the technique that I present here.

This technique is a general-purpose optimization for quadtree access that improves performance in three ways over the traditional implementations: 1) by eliminating node traversal and the unnecessary cache-misses it causes, 2) by requiring fewer instructions and CPU cycles overall vs. a best case traditional approach, and 3) by doing so in a compact amount of time and with minimal memory accesses regardless of what depth in the tree the target node resides in. Because it is general purpose in nature, many ways can be found to tweak and adapt this technique to suit the particular uses that may arise.

### Where the Performance Goes

Examining my original quadtree traversal routines (similar to those in Listing 4.5.1) showed almost no fat in the code itself after the compiler optimizations. The search routine was just a few lines of code that checked the bounding box of each child node and called itself recursively if necessary. Generating a CPU cycle count estimate of the number of calls assuming the worst case where it would recurse to the bottom level of the quadtree every time, didn't even begin to add up to the time that the profiles indicated.

It turns out that the performance drag was much the result of modern computer architecture. The code was constantly touching data through pointers, and then moving on to other data that wasn't adjacent in memory. The result of this was an extremely high cache miss rate. If all of the quadtree updates were queued up sequentially, most of the upper nodes toward the root node of the quadtree would eventually be in the CPU cache. When the updates weren't queued together, much of the previously cached quadtree node data would be flushed between calls.

To further degrade performance, the code in Listing 4.5.1 is comprised almost entirely of comparison functions which, when compiled, result in a large number of branch, jump, and call instructions, and a large number of possible data paths for each iteration. On modern CPUs, this stalls the instruction pipeline every time a branch or jump is mispredicted. Due to the nature of the data, this happens more often than one might think because, unlike most loops, the branch chosen in a previous iteration has no relevance to the likelihood of it being taken again.

## Eliminating the Middlemen

Basically, the compact C++ code in Listing 4.5.1 was spending more time waiting on data and instructions than actually executing. Upon further reflection, the vast majority of the data actually being looked at was not needed other than to be eliminated from consideration. Therefore, the question became: how to get the resultant quadtree node without actually examining the quadtree nodes themselves?

It is the asking of, or more specifically the answering of, this question that would eliminate most of the performance hit on the quadtree access routines. Of course, the implementation counts too, and what is presented here is an interesting and very efficient way to calculate the answer, but it is by no means the only possible solution.

## Conditions and Requirements

There are two limitations to this technique. First, the quadtree has to be regular; that is, each node is split exactly in the middle on each axis, making all nodes at a particular depth in the tree represent the same size area. Fortunately, most quadtrees are implemented this way. Second, the program has to select in advance the maximum depth (number of subdivisions) of the quadtree. Again, this is not unusual. Considering these limitations, one might conclude that the area represented by the quadtree then needs to be perfectly square, but that's not the case as will be explained later.

The only requirement is that the program needs to have array ordered access to the nodes at each level in the tree. This means that either all of the quadtree node pointers are placed in a linear array ordered by their spatial position, or if the quadtree node elements themselves are a fixed size, then they are stored in an array. Put another way, given the x and y node coordinates on a specific level, the address of the quadtree data can be obtained without having to traverse through other nodes.

## Determining the Tree Level

The first step in directly finding the target quadtree node is determining at what level in the tree the target resides. Once that is known, the coordinates of the search object will provide the row and column at which to directly look up the target node. For the rest of this gem, when we talk about objects, we are usually referring to their bounding volumes.

Consider that an object will reside in the root node of a quadtree if its volume crosses the nodes midline for either axis. If it doesn't touch the midlines, it can therefore be wholly contained in one of the node's children (Figure 4.5.1). It is assumed that it already passed the root volume area contain test. The process is repeated until either it gets to the bottom level of the quadtree, or it finds a node where the object crosses the midlines. The area check never has to worry about the outer edges, because they were the previous level's midlines and other edges.

Consider just one axis of the area represented by the quadtree if the total length was an exact power of 2, say 256.0 for example, and had nine levels where the lowest leaf nodes represented an area 1.0 by 1.0. The midline of the root node would be at 128.0, the midlines of the next level nodes would be at 64.0 and 192.0. Level 3 midlines would be 32.0, 96.0, 160.0, and 224.0. See a pattern here? The transition point for each level is at a different power of 2 that directly corresponds to the level depth on the tree.

Now take the same axis of the search object's bounding area, which gives a line segment $(x_1, x_2)$. What we want to know is the largest power of 2 that it spans, because that indicates the lowest level of the quadtree in which it can be wholly contained. Now, "spanning" a power of 2 simply means that the range from $x_1$ to $x_2$ transitions from below the power of 2 value to greater than (or equal to) the value. Since our storage requirement is that the object be fully contained inside a quadtree node, the quadtree level to store the object is actually one level higher than the level where the node area size is the specific power of 2 that is crossed.

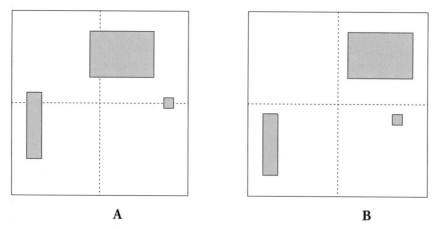

|   A   |   B   |
|:-----:|:-----:|

**FIGURE 4.5.1** *A) Objects that cross the node's midlines cannot be stored in child nodes. B) Objects that don't cross the midlines are stored in child nodes.*

Since the spanning of the value can be represented as a binary transition from 0 to 1, the program quickly can determine where the spanning occurs by taking the integral portions of our range $(x_1, x_2)$ and XORing them together. Each bit in the result indicates that the range crosses a point at the corresponding power of 2, returning 1 if there was a transition at that position. The lower the position of the first "1" bit of the result, the lower (deeper) in the quadtree the span can be stored. If a zero result occurs (i.e., no "1" bits in the result), then the range can be stored at the very lowest level in the quadtree. Therefore, the bit position of the highest "1" bit indicates how many levels above the bottom of the quadtree the range $(x_1, x_2)$ can first be properly placed.

Here are some examples using a nine-level, 256.0-length axis that illustrate this power of 2 property. Figure 4.5.2 shows a 2D representation of each example, using the *x*-axis.

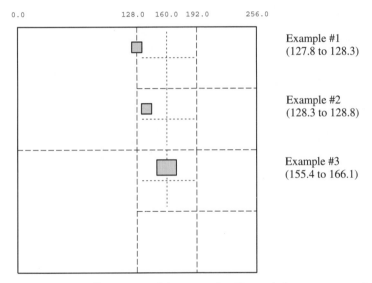

**FIGURE 4.5.2** *Illustration of the examples. Example boxes not to scale for illustrative purposes.*

**Example #1**

Object bounding line (127.8, 128.3). This object is sitting in the middle of the root node and only fits at the top level. Integer values for $(x_1, x_2)$ are (127, 128).

```
X1=            127 = 01111111
X2=            128 = 10000000
-------------------------
XOR result 255 = 11111111
```

The first "1" in the result is bit 7 ($2^7$) or the 8th position. 9 − 8 (number of tree level minus position) gives us 1, or the first level (root level) in the quadtree.

### Example #2

Object bounding line (128.3, 128.8). The object in Example #1 has been nudged just off the centerline and should fall all the way down to a leaf node (level 9). Integer values for $(x_1, x_2)$ are (128, 128).

```
X1=          128 = 10000000
X2=          128 = 10000000
- - - - - - - - - - - - - - - - - - - - - - - -
XOR result     0 = 00000000
```

There is no "1" bit in the result, so we get 0 for the position. $9 - 0 = 9$th level in the quadtree.

### Example #3

Object bounding line (155.4, 166.1). This is a very big object centered at about 60 percent of the range. Because of its size compared to the smallest node, it will be at least four levels above the bottom nodes (level 9). Integer values for $(x_1, x_2)$ are (155, 166).

```
X1=          155 = 10011011
X2=          166 = 10100110
- - - - - - - - - - - - - - - - - - - - - - - -
XOR result    61 = 00111101
```

The first "1" is at bit position 6. $9 - 6 = 3$rd level in the quadtree.

## Mapping to the Situation

Now that we know how to determine the level for a one-dimensional tree, moving the process to two dimensions is as simple as repeating the process for each axis and choosing the highest level (in the quadtree) result.

While the preceding examples work because they assume the storage range is a power of 2, in most situations the area represented by a quadtree is not going to be an even power of 2, and the smallest nodes are not going to just happen to represent an area 1.0 by 1.0 in size. Fortunately, the solution is as simple as transforming coordinate values from the game or application's measuring system to a scale that represents the quadtree's dimensions. This can be accomplished by computing a scale factor for each axis during initialization, and multiplying the coordinates by the scale before converting them to integers. For the quadtree scale, 1.0 represents the size of the leaf nodes on each axis. (Note that each axis can be independently scaled, allowing rectangular areas to map to a square node). Thus, the scaled coordinates for an $n$ level quadtree will be in the range 0 to $2^{n-1}$ for each axis.

After scaling and converting the coordinates to integers, we XOR together the start and end positions of each axis. There are several ways to determine which bit position contains the highest "1" bit. The simplest and most portable is a shift loop to count the bits, but a look-up table may work better for quadtrees with six or fewer levels. Even better, there are platform-specific solutions such as the Pentium's BSR instruction and the PowerPC's cntlzw instruction that bit-scan a value, removing looping and branching in the process. See Listing 4.5.2 for an example of code that determines the quadtree level using this method and a while loop.

## Determining the Location

Once the level in the quadtree has been determined, the only step remaining is to take the scaled coordinates and extract the row and column positions of the target node. If the target node is on the bottom level, no scaling will be necessary. For each level up the tree, the target coordinates have to be scaled down by 2 to reflect the smaller number of nodes on that level. This scaling can be done simply by right-shifting the integer coordinates by the number of levels the target is from the bottom level. This gives the row and column positions to plug into the array lookup for nodes on that level of the quadtree. Listing 4.5.3 shows an example function that puts all of this together.

## Traversing the Quadtree

If, after locating the search node, there still is a need to traverse the quadtree, all that is required is to save the tree level and array row and column positions. By shifting the position values right or left, a program can go up and down the tree levels, and by incrementing and decrementing the array positions, it can move adjacently on the current tree level.

## Tuning the Quadtree

Here are a couple of quick tips for getting the most out of a quadtree that apply to any quadtree access implementation.

The first is to make sure that items are being positioned as far down in the tree as possible. Improper edge boundary conditions can cause items to be placed much higher than they should be. In the example used of a 256 by 256 tree, an object that spanned position 128.0 would be placed in a root node. However, what about objects that only touch, but don't actually span, such as 1.0 sized "tiles" that sit at 127.0 to 128.0? In this case, switching ">=" or "<=" for ">" or "<" or tweaking the object coordinates with a tiny value can make the difference between root node placement and leaf node placement.

The next tip is to make sure that the program picks the correct number of levels for the quadtree. If it picks too few, the nodes will be overloaded with items to be searched, when the whole idea is to reduce the size of the search set in the first place. Too many tree levels can be just as bad. Many nodes may go empty, wasting space, and too much node traversal may be taking place during various operations. It's a good idea to add performance counters and statistics to the nonrelease versions of a quadtree implementation, and analyze the results using real data, as the optimal settings will be dependent on the actual data that is encountered.

Finally, I don't see any reasons why this technique couldn't be adapted to octrees. Perhaps someone out there will try this and let me know how well it works.

## Listing 4.5.1 Simple implementation of quadtree search

```cpp
// Two C++ classes, one to represent the QuadTree and one to
// Represent each individual node.
// all variables are class members unless defined

QuadNode* QuadTree::GetNodeContaining(const rect &ObjBounds)
{
    if (RootNode->Contains(ObjBounds))
      return(RootNode->GetNodeContaining(ObjBounds));
    else
        return(NULL);
}

QuadNode* QuadNode::GetNodeContaining(const rect &ObjBounds)
{
    if (!isLeafNode)
    {
      if (ULNode->Contains(ObjBounds)
          return(ULNode->GetNodeContaining(ObjBound));

      if (URNode->Contains(ObjBounds)
          return(URNode->GetNodeContaining(ObjBound));

      if (LLNode->Contains(ObjBounds)
          return(LLNode->GetNodeContaining(ObjBound));

      if (LRNode->Contains(ObjBounds)
          return(LRNode->GetNodeContaining(ObjBound));
    }
    return(this);

}

bool QuadNode::Contains(const rect &ObjBounds)
{
    return(ObjBounds.top    >= y1 && ObjBounds.left  >= x1 &&
           ObjBounds.bottom <= y2 && ObjBounds.right <= x2);
}
```

## Listing 4.5.2  Code to determine the level of the target quadnode

```
int QuadTree::GetNodeLevelContaining(const rect &ObjBounds)
{
    int   xResult = ((int) (ObjBounds.left * QuadXScale)) ^
                    ((int) (ObjBounds.right * QuadXScale));

    int   yResult = ((int) (ObjBounds.top * QuadYScale)) ^
                    ((int) (ObjBounds.bottom * QuadYScale));

    int   NodeLevel = NumberOfTreeLevels;

    while (xResult + yResult != 0 )    //Count highest bit position
    {
        xResult >>= 1;
        yResult >>= 1;
        NodeLevel--;
    }

    return (NodeLevel);
}
```

## Listing 4.5.3  Code to determine the level of the target quadnode

```
QuadNode* QuadTree::GetNode1Containing(const rect &ObjBounds)
{

    int   x1 = (int) (ObjBounds.left * QuadXScale);
    int   y1 = (int) (ObjBounds.top  * QuadYScale);

    int   xResult = x1 ^ ((int) (ObjBounds.right * QuadXScale));
    int   yResult = y1 ^ ((int) (ObjBounds.bottom * QuadYScale));

    int   NodeLevel = NumberOfTreeLevels;
    int   shiftCount = 0;

    while (xResult + yResult != 0 )    //Count highest bit position
    {
        xResult >>= 1;
        yResult >>= 1;
        NodeLevel--;
        ShiftCount++;
    }

    // Now lookup the node pointer in a 2D array stored linearly

    x1 >>= shiftCount;               // Scale coordinates for
    y1 >>= shiftCount;               // quadtree level

    QuadNode** nodes = NodeLevelPointerArray[NodeLevel];

    return (nodes[y1<<(NodeLevel-1)+x1]);
}
```

# 4.6

# Approximating Fish Tank Refractions

## *Alex Vlachos, ATI Research*

alex@vlachos.com

This gem briefly explains a method for approximating the refraction effect seen when looking through the side of a fish tank. The majority of this gem explains how to construct the transformation matrix that will be applied to the geometry inside the tank to simulate the refraction effect.

## Fish Tank Observations

Have you ever had a long wait at a seafood restaurant and spent any time staring at the fish tanks by the lobby? If so, you probably noticed the unique way in which the internal shape of the tank seems to change. Through observation, you'll notice that as you walk by the tank from one side to the other, the back wall of the tank seems to shear in the left and right directions. Simultaneously, the tank seems to flatten almost to a 2D image when you're at the far left or far right of the tank. Further observations (and common sense) show that the height of your head also affects the appearance of the internal shape of the tank in a similar way. An obvious way to simulate this movement is to concatenate a shear and scale matrix to simulate these observations.

Although there are surely more mathematically savvy methods using Snell's Law for computing refraction rays and so on, this gem focuses on approximating this visual effect based solely on empirical observation. It is important to note that this gem refers to fish tanks instead of shark tanks, the difference being the size of the tank relative to the viewer. This algorithm assumes that the viewer is, for the most part, not standing extremely close to the front of the glass. The phrase "extremely close" is obviously a relative one. If you imagine a fish tank that is approximately 3 feet by 2 feet, a person walking by that tank is the scale at which this gem is aimed. If you picture that same person walking in front of a shark tank measuring 30 feet by 10 feet, you'll realize that the person is spending most of his or her time directly in front of the tank relatively close to the glass. Although this algorithm doesn't break down, the visual effects are best noticed when the viewer is moving relative to the glass as opposed to standing directly in front of it. Environment mapping makes a similar assumption, so this is nothing new to real-time graphics.

## Precomputations

Given a fish tank whose front face has dimensions *width* and *height*, the transformation matrix that places the center of the front face of the tank at the origin in a certain orientation can be precomputed (e.g., back of the tank extends down the positive *z*-axis with the positive *y*-axis as the up vector). The reason the center of the front face is placed at the origin is to facilitate the scale and shear transformations. Once the transformation matrix has been generated, the position of the camera can be transformed into the space of the fish tank with a simple matrix multiply. This will allow all of the computations to happen in that common space (tank space). It's important to note that this method is based solely on the position of the camera relative to the tank. The view direction of the camera does not affect the visual results.

## Scale Factor

The scale factor for the tank needs to be computed per frame, which can be visualized by bringing the far face of the tank toward the near face (the face through which the viewer is looking). When the viewer is standing directly in front of the glass, no scaling should take place. When the viewer is standing off to the side of the tank looking across the face of the glass, the tank is scaled in quite a bit. The effect of this left to right motion is shown in Figure 4.6.1.

Given the viewer's position in tank space and the center of the glass, the angle to the surface of the tank is computed while taking into account the ratio of the *width*

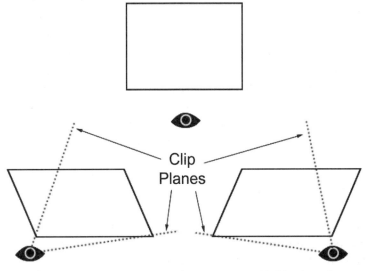

**FIGURE 4.6.1** *Three shearing and scaling examples based on the viewer's position. The user clip planes are created based on the viewer's position and the edges of the tank glass.*

and *height* of the tank's glass. If the glass dimensions aren't taken into account, the results across different shapes of glass will be inconsistent.

The scale factor is computed using the following method:

1. Transform the viewer's position into fish tank space. This puts the center of the tank's glass at the origin.
2. Calculate the vector from the center of the glass (the origin) to the camera, but do not normalize it.
3. Divide the x- and y-coordinates of the vector by the width and height of the glass, respectively.
4. Divide the z-coordinate of the vector by the depth of the tank (distance from near to far glass).
5. Normalize the vector.
6. Compute the dot product of this vector and the face normal of the glass in tank space (0, 0, −1). This scalar value clamped 0.0 to 1.0 will serve as the scale factor.

Assuming the tank was transformed to the origin as explained previously, the scale would take place along the z-axis.

### Shear Factor

The shear factor must also be computed per frame. Two separate shear values need to be generated: one for the x-axis and one for the y-axis. For the shear along the x-axis, we create a 2D vector composed of the x- and z-coordinates of the vector computed for the scale factor and normalize it. The x-component of the normalized 2D vector is used for the shearing along the x-axis. Similarly, we create a 2D vector composed of the y- and z-coordinates, normalize it, and use the x-component of the normalized 2D vector for the shearing along the y-axis. Experimentation has shown that limiting the shear values in x to 0.75 and in y to 0.25 helps reduce unwanted effects.

### Composing the Matrix

The scale and shear factors can be placed into a single matrix:

$$\begin{bmatrix} 1 & 0 & shear_x & 0 \\ 0 & 1 & shear_y & 0 \\ 0 & 0 & scale & 0 \\ 0 & 0 & 0 & 1 \end{bmatrix}$$

### User Clip Planes and the Stencil Buffer

When visualizing what happens to the geometry after the shear and scale transformations are applied, it becomes apparent that the geometry ends up touching pixels that were never intended to be modified. To solve this problem, if the fish tank glass is rectangular in shape, enabling four user clip planes from the position of the viewer to the four borders of the glass will solve the problem (Figure 4.6.1). This will clip all of the sheared geometry that could otherwise be seen from the outside of the tank. If the glass is circular or some other nonrectangular shape, the stencil buffer will need to be used in place of user clip planes to stencil out the pixels that don't belong to the fish tank glass.

## Improving the Reality

So far, this method describes how to make the geometry on the inside of the tank look as if it's filled with water. There is still much room for improvement. The first improvement that can be done is to apply caustic textures. In short, caustics are the patterns of light that appear on the bottom of a water-filled volume. These patterns are caused by light refracting as it passes from outside the tank through the surface of the water at the top. While it is nice to have caustic effects that correspond roughly to the simulation of the water surface, acceptable caustics can be created by simply scrolling two caustic textures across all of the geometry in the tank using projective textures.

The next obvious visual cue that is missing is making the outside of the glass reflective. A simple way to get nice reflections on glass is to render the reflected geometry of the glass into a renderable texture and then texture from that to give the illusion of a transparent reflective surface.

To give the viewer the ability to see through the water at the top of the tank, we could use another renderable texture to render what could be seen if there were no water in the tank. We could then apply environment-mapped bump mapping (or any other applicable pixel shader that uses dependent texture reads) to that renderable texture to give the illusion of animated water.

Obviously, this algorithm can be applied to each separate face of the fish tank. In addition, higher order culling can be performed if the vertices defining each side of the glass are outside the current view frustum. This method for culling large groups of polygons can be applied to each individual pane of glass.

## Conclusion

Simulating refractions through a planar surface can be very simple to fake. When combined with other real-time rendering techniques, it is possible to create a very convincing approximation to the real world.

# 4.7

## Rendering Print Resolution Screenshots

### Alex Vlachos and Evan Hart,
### ATI Research

alex@vlachos.com and ehart@ati.com

With the recent advances in real-time graphics technology, games have become fantastically rich in visual quality. While these images are great for display on a computer monitor that is typically 72 dots per inch (dpi), they are somewhat less appealing when displayed in print. Print resolution is typically a minimum of four times finer than monitor resolution in each dimension. Thus, a one-to-one mapping of the screen pixels to the dots on the printed page results in postage-stamp-sized screenshots. One solution to this problem is to enlarge the source image in the page layout software, but this results in blocky images that sell the original content short.

The simple solution to this problem is to take the screen shots at a higher frame buffer resolution. Naturally, the larger buffer can be an offscreen surface, so that it is not tied to the monitor's supported resolutions. This still poses problems, as most accelerators are only designed to render to the maximum resolution of monitors, leaving the programmer with at best a 2048 by 2048 screenshot. Although this resolution may sound sufficient, it won't cover a full magazine page at 300 dpi. This approach also takes up 32MB of graphics memory for a single color buffer and a depth buffer.

The solution proposed here is to break the task into the rendering of several smaller subimages. These subimages can then be pasted together to form a screen shot of arbitrary resolution. This gem focuses on the projection matrix tricks required to do this seamlessly.

### Basic Algorithm

Since current graphics hardware cannot render the resolutions required for print, the desired final image must be divided into a grid of subimages and pasted together. In the example code later in this gem, the dimensions for each of the subimages are assumed to be equal to the frame buffer dimensions. Although the subimages must be a supported rendering resolution by the graphics hardware, setting the viewport size to anything smaller than the frame buffer will allow this method to handle arbitrary dimensions.

Figure 4.7.1 shows how an image can be segmented into a grid of subimages. Six frustum planes define a projection matrix: near, far, left, right, top, and bottom. For each subimage, new left, right, top, and bottom planes are computed that will define a unique projection matrix for rendering that subimage.

Taking the screen shot involves three steps:

1. Calculate the frustum planes.
2. Determine the intermediate planes.
3. Render each subimage using its own frustum composed of the intermediate planes.

First, the frustum planes for the projection matrix are computed as six scalars. The near and far values are simply the distance from the eye to the near and far planes, while the left, right, top, and bottom values are defined by the points at which planes intersect the near plane. Section 3.5 of *Real-Time Rendering* has an excellent description of the meaning of these values [Möller99].

Next, the intermediate plane values $H_n$ and $V_n$ are computed by linearly interpolating the top and bottom values and the left and right values, respectively.

Finally, the frustum for each subimage is composed of the bordering $H_n$ and $V_n$ values for the left, right, top, and bottom. The projection matrix can be generated by

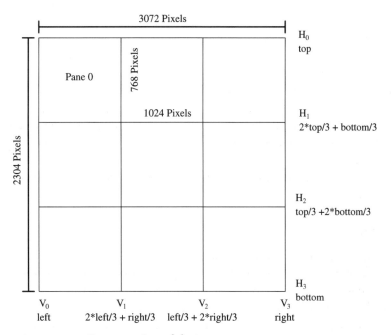

**FIGURE 4.7.1** *Segmentation of the image.*

calling either `glFrustum()` or `D3DXMatrixPerspectiveOffCenter()`. When rendering into each of the subimages, the entire scene is rendered normally.

Following is a simple code example for manually building the projection matrix for both OpenGL and Direct3D for a 3×3 grid of subimages.

```
const float GPG_PI = 3.14159265f;
inline float GpgDegToRad(float D) { return ((D) * (GPG_PI/180.0f)); }
void GpgPerspective (double fovy, double aspect, double Near, double
    Far, int subrect)
{
    double fov2, left, right, bottom, top;

    fov2 = GpgDegToRad(fovy) * 0.5;

    top = Near/(cos(fov2)/sin(fov2));
    bottom = -top;
    right = top*aspect;
    left = -right;

    if (subrect == -1)      //Regular full screen
       GpgFrustum (left, right, bottom, top, Near, Far);
    else if (subrect == 0) //UL
       GpgFrustum(left, left/3.0, top/3.0, top, Near, Far);
    else if (subrect == 1) //UC
       GpgFrustum(left/3.0, right/3.0, top/3.0, top, Near, Far);
    else if (subrect == 2) //UR
       GpgFrustum(right/3.0, right, top/3.0, top, Near, Far);
    else if (subrect == 3) //ML
       GpgFrustum(left, left/3.0, bottom/3.0, top/3.0, Near, Far);
    else if (subrect == 4) //MC
       GpgFrustum(left/3.0, right/3.0, bottom/3.0, top/3.0, Near, Far);
    else if (subrect == 5) //MR
       GpgFrustum(right/3.0, right, bottom/3.0, top/3.0, Near, Far);
    else if (subrect == 6) //BL
       GpgFrustum(left, left/3.0, bottom, bottom/3.0, Near, Far);
    else if (subrect == 7) //BC
       GpgFrustum(left/3.0, right/3.0, bottom, bottom/3.0, Near, Far);
    else if (subrect == 8) //BR
       GpgFrustum(right/3.0, right, bottom, bottom/3.0, Near, Far);
}

void GpgFrustum (double left, double right, double bottom, double
    top, double zNear, double zFar)
{
    float matrix[16] = { 1.0f, 0.0f, 0.0f, 0.0f,
                         0.0f, 1.0f, 0.0f, 0.0f,
                         0.0f, 0.0f, 1.0f, 0.0f,
                         0.0f, 0.0f, 0.0f, 1.0f };

#ifdef GPG_OPENGL_API
    matrix[0]  = (float)(2.0*zNear/(right-left));
    matrix[5]  = (float)(2.0*zNear/(top-bottom));

    matrix[8]  = (float)((right+left)/(right-left));
```

```
    matrix[9]  = (float)((top+bottom)/(top-bottom));
    matrix[10] = (float)(-(zFar+zNear)/(zFar-zNear));
    matrix[11] = (float)(-1.0);

    matrix[14] = (float)(-(2.0*zFar*zNear)/(zFar-zNear));
#else //Direct3D
    matrix[0]  = (float)(2.0*zNear/(right-left));
    matrix[5]  = (float)(2.0*zNear/(top-bottom));

    matrix[8]  = (float)((right+left)/(right-left));
    matrix[9]  = (float)((top+bottom)/(top-bottom));
    matrix[10] = (float)(-(zFar)/(zFar-zNear));
    matrix[11] = (float)(-1.0);

    matrix[14] = (float32)(-(zFar*zNear)/(zFar-zNear));
#endif

    //Now set this matrix as the current projection matrix
}
```

## Caveats and Concerns

As with any rendering algorithm, the programmer must pay attention to how this technique interacts with any special tricks performed by the graphics engine. The programmer should be aware that the utilization of multiple images to create the screen shot could affect Gouraud shading in the case of very large polygons in the scene. Due to the multiple projections, large polygons can possibly be clipped at all the subimage boundaries, resulting in lighting artifacts. Additionally, the programmer should take care to handle any special effects that require rendering into textures. The resolution for these images may also need to be increased for optimal results. Of course, if anything in the scene is animated, one should make sure that the same exact time is used in the animation when each of the subimages is rendered.

While we have referred to the Direct3D and OpenGL graphics APIs directly and implied the use of PC hardware, this technique would work equally well on game consoles where the screen shot problem is the worst. On these devices especially, gaming magazines are forced to jump through all sorts of hoops to get terrible screen grabs from NTSC signals.

Is this technique cheating? No. This method is equivalent to running your game at a higher resolution. You're not misrepresenting your work by providing large print-resolution screenshots to a gaming magazine. We have used this technique for color plates in *Real-Time Rendering* and *Game Programming Gems* and have been very pleased with the results.

## Conclusion

We have presented a technique for rendering print-resolution screenshots using graphics hardware. Since it is not possible to directly render the high-resolution images required for print, we have shown how to divide the desired final image into a grid of subimages that are rendered separately. This allows content developers to show their games in the best light in print media.

## References

[Möller99] Möller, Tomas, and Eric Haines, *Real-Time Rendering*, AK Peters, 1999.

# 4.8

## Applying Decals to Arbitrary Surfaces

### Eric Lengyel, C4 Engine

lengyel@c4engine.com

**M**any games need to render special effects such as scorch marks on a wall or footprints on the ground that are not an original part of a scene, but are created during gameplay. These effects are commonly implemented by creating a new object, which we will call a *decal*, which coincides with an existing surface, and rendering it using some type of depth offset technique (for example, see [Lengyel00]). Applying a decal to the interior of a planar surface is simple, but difficulties arise when applying decals to the more complex surfaces used in today's games to represent curved objects and terrain patches. This gem presents a general method for applying a decal to an arbitrarily shaped surface and concurrently clipping the decal to the surface's boundary.

### The Algorithm

We begin with a point P that lies on an existing surface and a unit normal direction N that is perpendicular to the surface at that point. The point P represents the center of the decal and may be the point at which a projectile has impacted the surface or the point where a character's foot has stepped on the ground. A unit tangent direction T must also be chosen in order to determine the orientation of the decal. This configuration is illustrated in Figure 4.8.1.

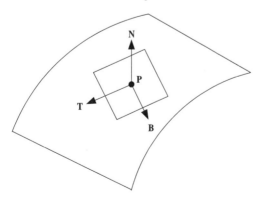

**FIGURE 4.8.1** *Configuration of a decal.*

Given the point P and the directions N and T, we have an oriented plane that is tangent to the surface geometry at P. We can carve a rectangle out of this plane that represents the area of our decal by constructing four boundary planes that are parallel to the normal direction N. Let $w$ and $h$ be the width and height of the decal. Then the 4D vectors corresponding to the four border planes are given by

$$left = \left( \mathbf{T}, \frac{w}{2} - \mathbf{T} \bullet \mathbf{P} \right)$$

$$right = \left( -\mathbf{T}, \frac{w}{2} + \mathbf{T} \bullet \mathbf{P} \right)$$

$$bottom = \left( \mathbf{B}, \frac{h}{2} - \mathbf{B} \bullet \mathbf{P} \right)$$

$$top = \left( -\mathbf{B}, \frac{h}{2} + \mathbf{B} \bullet \mathbf{P} \right) \tag{4.8.1}$$

where $\mathbf{B} = \mathbf{N} \times \mathbf{T}$. We will generate a triangle mesh for the decal object by clipping nearby surfaces to the four boundary planes. We also want to clip to front and back planes to avoid bleeding through to parts of the same surface mesh that may be inside the boundary planes, but far in front of or behind the point P. The 4D vectors corresponding to the front and back planes are given by

$$front = \left( -\mathbf{N}, d + \mathbf{N} \bullet \mathbf{P} \right)$$

$$back = \left( \mathbf{N}, d - \mathbf{N} \bullet \mathbf{P} \right) \tag{4.8.2}$$

where $d$ is the maximum distance that any vertex in the decal may be from the tangent plane passing through the point P.

The algorithm proceeds as follows. First, we identify which surfaces in the world may potentially be affected by the decal. This may be determined by locating any surfaces whose bounding volume reaches within a certain distance of the point P. For each potentially affected surface, we individually examine each triangle in the surface's mesh. Let M denote the unit normal direction corresponding to the plane of a triangle in the mesh. We throw out any triangles for which $\mathbf{N} \cdot \mathbf{M} < \varepsilon$ for some fixed positive value $\varepsilon$, since these triangles are facing away from the decal's normal direction N. Remaining triangles are clipped to the planes given by Equations 4.8.1 and 4.8.2 and stored in a new triangle mesh.

When a triangle overlaps any of the planes and needs to be clipped, we interpolate the normal vectors as well as the vertex positions so that we can later apply coloring to the clipped vertices that reflects the angle between each vertex's normal and the decal's normal direction. This has the effect of smoothly fading the decal texture in relation to each triangle's orientation relative to the plane of the decal. We assign an alpha value to each vertex using the equation

$$alpha = \frac{\dfrac{\mathbf{N} \cdot \mathbf{R}}{\|\mathbf{R}\|} - \varepsilon}{1 - \varepsilon} \tag{4.8.3}$$

where R is the (possibly unnormalized due to interpolation) normal corresponding to the vertex. This maps the dot product range $[\varepsilon,1]$ to the alpha value range $[0,1]$.

Texture mapping coordinates are applied to the resulting triangle mesh by measuring the distance from the planes passing through the point P and having normal directions T and B. Let Q be the position of a vertex in the decal's triangle mesh. Then the texture coordinates $s$ and $t$ are given by

$$s = \frac{\mathbf{T} \cdot (\mathbf{Q} - \mathbf{P})}{w} + \frac{1}{2}$$

$$t = \frac{\mathbf{B} \cdot (\mathbf{Q} - \mathbf{P})}{h} + \frac{1}{2} \tag{4.8.4}$$

## Triangle Clipping

Each triangle belonging to a surface that is potentially affected by the decal is treated as a convex polygon and is clipped to each of the six boundary planes one at a time. Clipping a convex polygon having $n$ vertices to a plane results in a new convex polygon having at most $n + 1$ vertices. Thus, polygons that have been clipped against all six planes may possess as many as nine vertices. Once the clipping process is complete, each polygon is treated as a triangle fan and added to the decal's triangle mesh.

To clip a convex polygon against an arbitrary plane, we first classify all of the vertices belonging to the polygon into two categories: those that lie on the negative side of the plane, and those that lie on the positive side of the plane or on the plane itself. If all of the polygon's vertices lie on the negative side of the plane, the polygon is discarded. Otherwise, we visit every pair of neighboring vertices in the polygon looking for edges that intersect the clipping plane. As shown in Figure 4.8.2, new vertices are added to the polygon where such intersections occur, and vertices lying on the negative side of the plane are removed.

Suppose that the vertex $V_1$ lies on the positive side of the clipping plane C, and that the vertex $V_2$ lies on the negative side of C. A point $V_3$ lying on the line segment connecting $V_1$ and $V_2$ can be expressed as

$$V_3 = V_1 + t(V_2 - V_1) \tag{4.8.5}$$

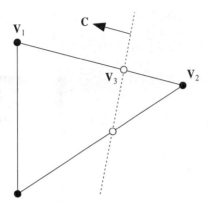

**FIGURE 4.8.2** *Clipping a polygon against a plane.*

where the parameter $t$ satisfies $0 \le t \le 1$. We would like to know for what value of $t$ the point $v_3$ lies on the plane C. If we treat the $V_i$ as a homogeneous vectors having $w$-coordinates of one, then we simply need to find the value of $t$ for which the 4D dot product $C \cdot V_3$ is zero. Plugging in the right side of Equation 4.8.5 for $V_3$ and solving for $t$ gives us

$$t = \frac{C \cdot V_1}{C \cdot \left(V_1 - V_2\right)} \tag{4.8.6}$$

(Note that the difference $V_1 - V_2$ has a $w$-coordinate of zero.) Substituting this value of $t$ back into Equation 4.8.5 gives us our new vertex.

## Implementation

**ON THE CD**

The source code on the companion CD-ROM demonstrates the algorithm presented in this article through the implementation of a C++ class called Decal. The constructor of this class takes the decal center P, the normal direction N, and the tangent direction T as parameters, as well as the width, height, and depth of the decal. After calculating the boundary planes using Equations 4.8.1 and 4.8.2, the constructor clips all potentially affected surfaces to these planes and stores the resulting mesh in a new triangle array. Vertex colors and texture mapping coordinates are then assigned using Equations 4.8.3 and 4.8.4. The source code generated the scorch marking decal shown in Figure 4.8.3.

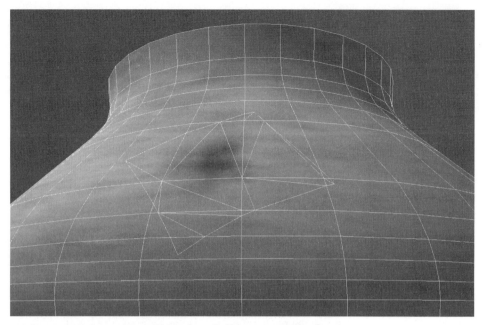

**FIGURE 4.8.3** *A scorch mark decal applied to a curved surface.*

## References

[Lengyel00] Lengyel, Eric, "Tweaking a Vertex's Projected Depth Value," *Game Programming Gems*, Charles River Media, 2000, pp. 361–365.

# 4.9

## Rendering Distant Scenery with Skyboxes

### Jason Shankel, Maxis

shankel@pobox.com

Consider a game that takes place on a Tibetan mountaintop. In the distance, we can see the ridge of the Himalayas, clouds in the sky, and a village down in the valley. Or, consider a game in deep space, with the Eagle and Orion nebulae shining from light-years away. Such imagery can heighten the beauty and sense of immersion of a 3D game.

Rendering distant scenery in 3D can be accomplished with skyboxes. This gem explains the principle of skyboxing and describes alternative means for rendering a skyboxed scene.

## Basic Technique

The idea behind a skybox is very simple. Distant scenery is rendered onto six textures, each of which is applied to one side of a cube. The camera is placed at the center of the cube. The camera can rotate freely within, but never move from the center of this cube. When the scene is rendered, the images projected on the walls of the skybox give the impression of distant scenery much in the same way images projected onto the ceiling of a planetarium give the impression of the night sky (Figure 4.9.1).

## Skybox Resolution

Ideally, one texel in the skybox object should map to one pixel on the screen. The following formula can be used to determine the ideal skybox resolution for a given screen resolution

$$skyboxRes = \frac{screenRes}{\tan(\texttt{fov}/2)}$$

where *skyboxRes* is the resolution of one side of the skybox in texels, *screenRes* is the width of the screen in pixels, and *fov* is the angle of the horizontal field of view. For example, a scene with a 90-degree field of view running at 640×480 would have an ideal skybox resolution of 640 texels.

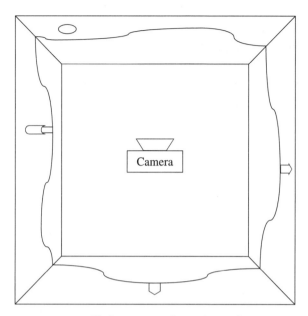

**FIGURE 4.9.1** *Skybox as seen from above: distant terrain is rendered on the sides of the box, and the camera is placed at the center.*

Some 3D systems limit texture resolution to 256×256 texels. This means that the skybox textures may be stretched noticeably when rendered to the screen. For some applications, this stretching may be acceptable. Others may wish to subdivide each skybox face to increase texture resolution (Figure 4.9.2).

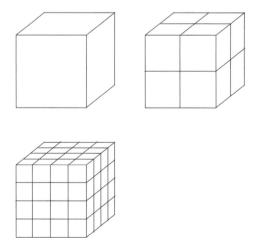

**FIGURE 4.9.2** *Subdividing the skybox's faces will improve image quality at the cost of increased texture memory and polygon count. Upper left) One texture per side. Upper right) Four textures per side. Lower left) Sixteen textures per side.*

## Skybox Size

Because the camera is always at the center, it does not matter how big we make the skybox as long as it falls within the viewing frustum. As the size of the skybox increases, its walls become proportionally more distant, keeping the same portion in frame.

The skybox dimensions should be chosen so that the farthest points, the corners, are closer to the camera than the far clipping plane. The following formula can be used to calculate the maximum skybox size:

$$\text{skyboxWidth} \leq \frac{2\sqrt{3}}{3} z_{\text{far}}$$

where *skyboxWidth* is the length of one edge of the skybox in world units, and $z_{\text{far}}$ is the distance to the far clipping plane in world units.

## Rendering the Scene

The simplest technique for drawing a skybox is to render an ordinary textured cube, aligned to the world axes and centered on the camera's world position. The skybox should be the first thing rendered. There is no need to clear the color buffer first, as the skybox will always fill the entire screen.

When rendering a skybox, both depth testing and depth writing should be disabled, as the skybox geometry will not intersect properly with the other geometry in the scene. Lighting, fogging, and any other similar effects should also be disabled. The skybox images should be rendered without any atmospheric modification.

As noted earlier, a simple one-texture-per-face cube may produce significant texture stretching. Texture filtering can be used to reduce the effect of this stretching. Texture filtering reduces the jagginess of stretched images by sampling neighboring texels and blending them together.

Texture filtering may cause seams to appear along the edges of the skybox, where two textures meet. These seams are caused by improper texture wrapping. Texture wrapping determines how the texture filter decides which texels "neighbor" the texels at the edge of a texture. If texture wrapping is set to repeat (GL_REPEAT in OpenGL), texels on one edge will be combined with texels on the opposite edge, causing seams between textures to stand out.

In OpenGL, texture wrapping should be set to GL_CLAMP_TO_EDGE_EXT, if possible. This will clamp filtering to the edge the texture, eliminating interference from border texels. GL_EXT_texture_edge_clamp is an OpenGL extension, so it might not be available on all systems. If the GL_CLAMP_TO_EDGE_EXT mode is not available, texture filtering should be set to GL_CLAMP, which combines edge texels with the texture's constant border color.

## Cube Environment Mapping

Cube environment mapping is an alternative to traditional skybox rendering. Cube environment mapping combines all six sides of a skybox into a single texture.

Traditionally, texture coordinates are specified as offsets into a two-dimensional texture map, with (0,0) being one corner of the texture, and (1,1) being the opposite corner. In cube environment mapping, six textures are combined to form a cube, and texture coordinates are specified as three-dimensional vectors, pointing outward from the center of the cube to a point on its surface (Figure 4.9.3).

Cube environment mapping can be used to render distant scenery, and to cast reflections of the skybox on nearby shiny objects.

Cube environment mapping limits skyboxes to one 2D texture per face, so subdividing faces to increase resolution is not possible. Fortunately, most cube environment mapping systems support texture resolutions above 256×256.

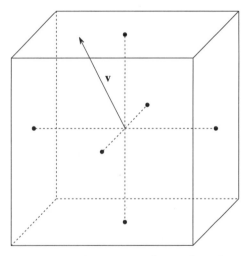

**FIGURE 4.9.3** *Texture coordinates for cube environment maps are specified as vectors pointing to the surface of a cube centered on the origin.*

## Generating Skybox Textures

Some software packages provide direct support for generating skyboxes. For those that don't, manually generating skybox images is simple.

The size of the output image should be set to texture resolution (e.g., 256×256) and the camera's field of view set to 90 degrees. Six renderings are generated, with the camera looking up and down each of the three cardinal axes (left, right, up, down, forward, and back).

## Conclusion

A sense of place is critical to most 3D games. Rendering distant scenery not only increases visual beauty, it also provides players with a means of orienting themselves in the virtual environment. Skyboxes provide an economical and effective way to render distant scenery.

## Source Code

*ON THE CD*

Sample source code is provided using OpenGL and GLUT. The sample program demonstrates both 2D and cube environment map rendering.

Cube environment mapping is supported in OpenGL via the `GL_ARB_texture_cube_map` extension. The sample code checks for the presence of this extension at startup. In cube environment map mode, a shiny object is placed in the camera's view, demonstrating reflectance.

Skybox textures were generated with Terragen (Copyright © 1997–2000 Planet-side Software).

# 4.10

# Self-Shadowing Characters

## *Alex Vlachos, David Gosselin, and*
## *Jason L. Mitchell; ATI Research*

alex@vlachos.com, gosselin@ati.com,
jasonm@ati.com

Rendering self-shadowing characters is an important visual cue missing from most real-time games. This gem presents a projective texture approach, which enables self-shadowing of convex subsections of characters in real time. After breaking the character into convex subsections, the subsections are rendered into a texture with varying alpha values from the point of view of the light source. When the character is rendered from the viewer's point-of-view, this texture is projected back onto the convex subsegments of the character, simulating the occlusion of each subsegment with respect to the light source. Being map based rather than stencil-volume based, this technique requires no additional work to be compatible with higher-order surface tessellation techniques.

## Previous Work

Projective techniques for shadowing started with [Williams78] and have been refined in many papers. This gem breaks with the depth-based shadow mapping and uses a technique similar to the priority buffers of [Hourcade85]. [Lengyel00] also uses a similar segmented technique.

## Segmenting Character Geometry

The first step in this algorithm is grouping the character geometry. The artist tags bones to form groups of geometry that will shadow the other groups of geometry. These groups should be selected to reduce the segmenting of the model but retain the shadowing relationships. During preprocessing, the dominant bone for each polygon will be determined by finding the bone that has the largest blending weight. The tag will then be extracted from this bone and the polygon will be placed in the appropriate group. See Figure 4.10.1 for an example of a segmented model.

**FIGURE 4.10.1** *Segmented model.*

## Rendering the Texture

Once the character has been logically divided into convex subsegments, these groups are sorted from front to back with respect to the light source. Since there are usually a relatively small number of groups in a given character, this sorting is an insignificant computational burden. The character in Figure 4.10.2, for example, has only six groups to sort. Then a view matrix is computed from the light's point of view such that is centered on the center of the bounding box surrounding the object. A perspective projection matrix is also generated to have the character fill as much of the renderable texture as possible.

The basic steps are:

1. Compute light matrix.
2. Clear renderable texture with (255, 255, 255, 255).
3. Draw each of the subsegments into the alpha texture from front to back (from the light's point of view) with increasing alpha values: 0, 1, 2, 3, 4, ... 254. (255 is reserved as the alpha clear color.)

Note that the rate of increasing the alpha values can be spread out to cover the entire range of alpha values available based on the number of groups being rendered. This will help to remove rendering artifacts, which is explained in the next section.

## Rendering the Character

Once the shadow map is created, the next step is to render the character into the frame buffer using the shadow map. In a brute-force approach, this is accomplished in three passes. The first pass renders a fully lit character into the frame buffer. The second pass renders each of the subsegments of the character with an alpha test of less than the alpha value that was used to draw the subsegment into the shadow buffer. This is done for two reasons. The first reason is to use only those parts of the shadow buffer that would be shadowing the character. Since the shadow buffer was segmented using the alpha values, setting the alpha test of less than retrieves the shadows of all the previous groups (the ones closer to the light). The second reason for using the alpha test is to effectively shrink the shadows by half a pixel in order to avoid pulling unwanted alpha values in from bilinear texture fetching. The texture matrix is set to take the world space position of the object and transform it by the light's view and projection matrix that was calculated when rendering to the texture. The pixels that pass the alpha test are drawn in black, effectively masking out the lighting in the first pass. The final pass draws the character with its base color modulated by a small ambient term to brighten the areas in shadow by an ambient term. Figure 4.10.2 shows the results of this rendering over several frames of animation. This is obviously a brute-force approach and can be optimized using pixel shaders.

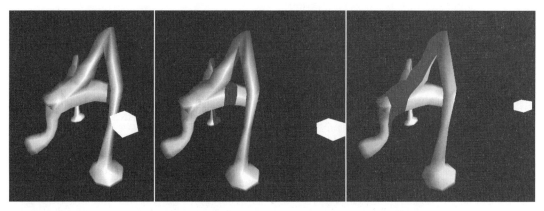

**FIGURE 4.10.2** *Character rendered with shadows from three different angles.*

## Conclusion

We presented a way to render animated characters with self-shadowing using a projective texture technique. By segmenting the character into convex subsegments, we avoided the aliasing found in purely depth-based approaches. The approach is also general enough to be used by any graphics hardware that supports rendering to textures and projective texture mapping.

## References

[Hourcade85] Hourcade, J. C., and Nicolas, A., "Algorithms for Antialiased Cast Shadows," *Computers and Graphics*, vol. 9, no. 3, pp. 259–264.

[Lengyel00] Lengyel, Jerome E., "Splatting for Soft-Edged Shadows," Microsoft Technical Report, 2000.

[Williams78] Williams, Lance, "Casting Curved Shadows on Curved Surfaces," *Computer Graphics* (SIGGRAPH 78 Proceedings), vol. 12, no. 3, 1978, pp. 270–274.

# 4.11

## Classic Super Mario 64 Third-Person Control and Animation

### Steve Rabin, Nintendo of America

steve_rabin@hotmail.com

The classic *Super Mario 64* control scheme has easily become one of the most intuitive ways to control a 3D character from a third-person perspective. While the game *Super Mario 64* didn't invent the technique, it did manage to polish it and popularize it with millions of gamers. It's routinely used as the measuring stick of an extremely playable control scheme. However, the real beauty is that it makes sense to even a first-time player, which is no small accomplishment.

This gem will deal with the basic issues of controlling and animating a character from a third-person perspective. While it seems straightforward enough (just copy *Super Mario 64*), it's not as trivial as it first appears. There are many small nuggets of wisdom that can often take weeks of trial and error to discover.

## The Setup

The classic *Super Mario 64* control incorporates a free-floating camera that follows the character around wherever he may go. Imagine the camera hovering behind him attached by a bungee cord to his body. As the character moves from a stand to a run, the camera smoothly accelerates toward the character trying to maintain a fixed distance from him. As the character turns, the camera gently circles around trying to stay behind him.

The key to this control scheme is that the character will go whichever way we tell him, as if we were sitting inside the camera. Therefore, if we press up on the controller, the character will move away from the camera. If we press right, the character moves rightward from the camera's perspective. The tricky part is that the camera is always moving and that this camera-oriented control needs to be mapped onto the world's coordinate system, where the character actually moves around.

## Converting the Controller Input

The basic programming problem involves converting the player's input (up, down, right, left) from the camera's perspective to the world orientation. In order to do this, we need a vector that corresponds to the camera's forward direction, and a vector that corresponds to the camera's rightward direction.

These vectors become useful because any up/down controller movements get directly mapped into translations along the camera's forward vector. Similarly, any right/left controller movements get mapped into translations along the camera's right vector. However, since the character basically moves on a flat plane, these camera vectors shouldn't contain any height information (traditionally represented by the $y$-axis). Figure 4.11.1 shows how we can think of the controller input in relation to the camera and the character.

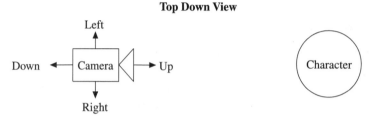

FIGURE 4.11.1 *Controller relationship to character with respect to the camera.*

The forward vector of the camera is easy to find since it's simply the direction the camera is facing. Once we have it, we zero out the vertical axis and renormalize it. Now we can get the camera's right vector with the following relationship:

```
right.x = forward.z
right.z = -forward.x
right.y = 0.0
```

Since controller input traditionally comes in the form of numbers, a brief explanation is necessary. We can expect that the user input on an analog stick will basically vary from –1.0 to 1.0 along each axis. In reality, most input schemes use integers and vary from –128 to 127 or –32768 to 32767, but for our purposes, we'll need to convert those to a floating-point number within the –1.0 to 1.0 range. However, it's important to realize that *Up* and *Right* are both positive. The layout of a controller is shown in Figure 4.11.2.

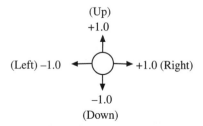

FIGURE 4.11.2 *Values from an analog controller.*

Armed with the camera's forward and right vectors, we can now remap the input from the controller to get the final world vector. The following relationship gives the direction the character should move, in world coordinates.

```
final.x = (inputLtRt * right.x) + (inputUpDn * forward.x)
final.z = (inputLtRt * right.z) + (inputUpDn * forward.z)
final.y = 0
```

Once this final vector is normalized, it can be applied to the character so that he moves in the proper direction. It's important to remember that for every frame, a new forward and right vector must be calculated, since the camera can move at any time.

## Rotating the Character

The user input at any instant gives a desired direction. By sampling the magnitude of the directions over time, the speed of the character can be determined. A simple model for moving the character is to maintain both a direction and a speed separately. It helps to keep them separate, instead of representing both as a single vector, so that a speed of zero still retains a direction. Obviously, bad things would happen if we try to orient the character using a zero vector.

As the input is sampled over time, the character's direction should converge on the user's desired direction. For example, if the character is facing north and the player turns him east, the character should turn toward the east using some kind of dampening. A very pleasing dampening effect comes from simply adding a proportion of the desired direction to the current direction, based on frame rate. In Figure 4.11.3, notice how the character initially rotates quickly and then slowly dampens toward the final desired direction over a short period of time.

The soft dampening shown in Figure 4.11.3 results in a smooth, responsive feel when controlling the character. The rate at which it converges on the desired direction can be carefully tuned to get the desired feel. The dampening function in Figure 4.11.3 can be represented by the following formula:

```
new_dir = (old_dir * 0.5) + (desired_dir * 0.5)
Normalize( new_dir )
```

By taking into account frame rate, the dampening function can be made to be fairly resilient to frame rate fluctuations. Unfortunately, wild frame rate fluctuations

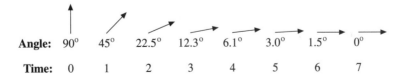

| Angle: | 90° | 45° | 22.5° | 12.3° | 6.1° | 3.0° | 1.5° | 0° |
| Time: | 0 | 1 | 2 | 3 | 4 | 5 | 6 | 7 |

**FIGURE 4.11.3** *Character rotation over time with exponential dampening.*

of 100 percent or so are not dealt with properly. The following is a dampening formula that is semi-resilient to frame rate changes (within a certain window).

```
new_ratio = 0.9 / FPS
old_ratio = 1.0 - new_ratio
new_dir = (old_dir * old_ratio) + (desired_dir * new_ratio)
Normalize( new_dir )
```

This new dampening formula will now rotate the character 90 percent toward the desired direction after one second, regardless of frame rate. The percentages need to be tuned, but whatever frame rate it's tuned to becomes the center of our frame rate window. However, as the frame rate wanders too far from that center, the "feel" will slowly distort and become either too sensitive or too sluggish. If the frame rate varies too much, we can consider decoupling this calculation with the graphics update in order to maintain a steady rate.

When a character is told to move 180 degrees from the current direction, smooth rotation is not always the best solution. Since there is such a large angle to cover, it results in an extended rotation that can feel clunky and unnatural. Instead, it's better to use a transition animation to make large changes in direction. In *Super Mario 64*, this occurs when Mario is at a full run and told to go in the opposite direction. This results in a skidding stop followed by a seamless 180-degree in-place turn. However, during this process, there's a speed penalty that stalls him for a split second before he can move again.

The method of rotation described up to this point is fairly touchy feely and *is* ultimately susceptible to frame rate issues, even though they have been reduced. For example, if you record a player's input and feed it back to the game at a slightly different frame rate, the result will be slightly different. This has grave consequences if you record a game, using input alone, and plan to replay it back from a different camera angle (perhaps causing the frame rate to vary). The solution is either to lock the simulation rate or use a highly controlled method of rotation, such as clamping to a particular angular velocity. However, this would give up some of the smooth acceleration effects in return for higher predictability.

## Translating the Character

With the character smoothly turning, we now need to actually move the character. This is done by taking the character's current direction and translating him forward by the current speed. The smooth rotation of the character basically points the hips in the proper direction, and the current speed moves him forward.

We'll want some type of dampening function, just like with the rotation, to control the speed. However, the speed needs to be clamped to a top speed, unlike the rotation. We'll also want to penalize the current speed for 180-degree turns and turns in general. The dampening function should quickly converge (faster than 1/10th of a second) to the desired speed in order to make the control feel responsive.

Responsiveness is a funny thing. Ideally, a character should respond instantaneously to a player's input. However, this is both unrealistic and abrupt. By adding an exponential dampening, the edge is taken off transitions while maintaining responsiveness. Note that this implies that there are no physics taking place. Characters have tremendous control over their movement and actually don't accelerate and decelerate like a car or rocket ship. Figure 4.11.4 shows the speed of a character under controller input. Notice how responsiveness equates to quickly advancing to the desired speed and then smoothly converging on it.

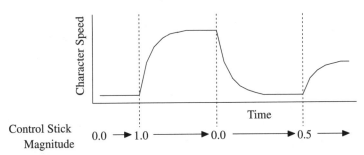

**FIGURE 4.11.4**  *Character speed based on controller input with exponential dampening.*

## Animating the Character

The simplest animation scheme is to have two different animation loops: standing and running. When the character's speed is zero, play the stand animation. When the character's speed is above zero, play the running animation. Obviously, most characters should have more elaborate animations, but this is a good starting place.

Here are some tricks to making the animation look reasonable:

1. Match the speed of the animation (the movement of the feet) with the top speed of the character. When moving, the character will spend most of the time at the top speed, so the loop should look the best at this speed. At this speed, the feet should meet the ground and appear to stick until they're lifted back up.

2. The speed of the animation can be changed to match the speed of the character, but most animations only look reasonable at a tiny range of speeds. There is a little room to vary the speed, but not the full range from 0 to 8 m/s for a decent run. A run can usually be varied from 5 to 8 m/s, a trot can be varied from 3 to 5 m/s, and a walk can vary from 1 to 3 m/s. Actual ranges can only be found experimentally with the actual animation data and are extremely subjective.

3. When the character is turning sharply at high speeds, the character should algorithmically lean into the turn. This helps emphasize speed and looks more

natural. Another turning enhancement is to have the character algorithmically rotate his head slightly in the direction of the turn. This further adds to the realism, since characters generally anticipate and look toward future positions.

4. Transition animations (stand to run, walk to run) are tricky to implement. Usually they tend to get in the way of responsiveness. A simple, clean solution is to algorithmically construct a single in-between frame when transitioning. This takes the edge off transitions without getting in the way of the look or feel. Calculating in-between frames is a well-known problem that can be referenced in many animation programming books.

5. The transition from a stand to a walk or run can be virtually seamless by designing the walk or run loop correctly. Figure 4.11.5 shows what the first frame of the loop should look like. Notice how the left foot is on the ground while the right foot is barely being lifted into the air. This particular keyframe minimizes the jar when changing animations from a stand to the walk or run. However, since a moving character can potentially stop at any time, this doesn't help smooth the transition to a stand. Transitioning to a stand can be dealt with by quickly interpolating the character to the stand position, paying careful attention not to let the feet pierce the ground.

6. A more elaborate transition system can be devised where there are actual transition animations, such as a stand-to-run and a run-to-stand. When the player commands the character to start moving, the stand-to-run animation is played and then followed by the run loop. When the player tells the character to stop, the character must somehow transition smoothly to the run-to-stop animation regardless of the current frame of the run loop. A simple way to solve this is to have two different run-to-stand animations, each beginning with a different foot in front. This way, the run loop at most

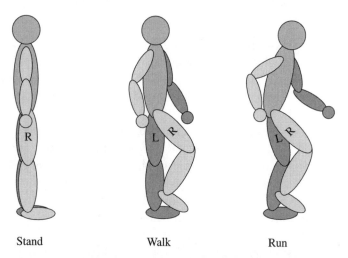

Stand                    Walk                    Run

**FIGURE 4.11.5** *First frame for smooth transitions.*

needs to play out half the run cycle before it can seamlessly transition into the run-to-stand animation. Unfortunately, some responsiveness is sacrificed if animations are forced to play out longer than necessary in order to line up transitions. Also, transition animations need to be lightning quick or else responsiveness is compromised even further. Depending on the desired look and feel of the game, it will take experimentation with both canned and algorithmic transitions in order to find the proper mix.

## *Super Mario 64* Animation Analyzed

The following tables list the animation behavior that can be found in *Super Mario 64*. This info was created by observing the game without any knowledge of actual implementation. Certainly, any game can be analyzed in this way in order to deconstruct the control and animation techniques.

| Speed | Animation |
| --- | --- |
| Stand | Several idle animations |
| Medium | Trot |
| Fast | Run with forward lean |
| Very Fast | Run with pronounced forward lean |

| Transitions | Animation |
| --- | --- |
| Stand to Tip-toe | Single Walk cycle followed by Tip-toe |
| Stand to Trot | Pop into Trot |
| Stand to Run | Pop into Run with puff of smoke |
| Tip-toe to Stand | Pop into Stand |
| Trot to Stand | Pop into Stand |
| Run to Stand | Pop into skidding stop, then seamlessly into Idle |
| Tip-toe to Trot | Pop into Trot |
| Trot to Run | Pop into Run (matching the foot cycle) with puff of smoke |
| Trot to Tip-toe | Pop into Tip-toe |
| Run to Tip-toe | Pop into Tip-toe |
| Run to Trot | Pop into Trot (matching the foot cycle) |

| Action | Resulting Behavior |
| --- | --- |
| Any turn during Stand | Pop into direction |
| 180° turn during Tip-toe | Smooth tight u-turn |
| 180° turn during Trot | Smooth tight u-turn |
| 180° turn during Run | Skid to stop with smooth about-face |
| < 180° turn during Tip-toe | Smooth rotation |
| < 180° turn during Trot | Smooth rotation |
| < 180° turn during Run | Smooth rotation |
| Turning during Run | Lean into turn |

## Conclusion

Undoubtedly, many great games have implemented the classic *Super Mario 64* third-person control, even before *Super Mario 64* ever existed. However, before trying to code something, find an example to model and become intimately familiar with it. Try to notice every nuance of what happens under different controller inputs. Notice the transitions, the acceleration/deceleration of the motion/rotation, the different speeds of walks/trots/runs, the shallow and sharp turns, and the decay after completely letting go of the controller. Having a good example to model is important so that you have a stable target to copy and ultimately improve upon.

## References

[Maestri99] Maestri, George, *Digital Character Animation 2: Essential Techniques*, New Riders Publishing, July 1999.

SECTION

# 5

# GRAPHICS DISPLAY

# Introduction

## D. Sim Dietrich Jr., Nvidia Corporation

sdietrich@nvidia.com

Our main goal with the Graphics Display section was to supply readers with practical, innovative techniques for real-time graphics. In addition, we strove to present enough information so readers could understand how the techniques work, and how to extend or modify the techniques to suit their particular needs. A further objective was to present techniques that would remain relevant for the next five years or so. Time will tell if we have succeeded on all counts, but I am cautiously optimistic.

The Graphics Display section covers several different aspects of real-time 3D graphics, but many of the Gems ended up sharing a particular technique: render-to-texture capability. This was not an intentional bias, but one that emerged due to its flexibility and utility. I believe this indicates that render-to-texture is one of the primitive operations on which much of future real-time graphics will be based, because it leverages the incredible power of modern graphics hardware to produce effects that were previously impossible in real time.

I'm sure I speak for the other authors when I express our thanks for the opportunity to contribute to the *Game Programming Gems* series, and our hope that we can continue to contribute to the state of the art in this golden age of real-time graphics.

# 5.1

# Cartoon Rendering: Real-time Silhouette Edge Detection and Rendering

## *Carl S. Marshall, Intel Architecture Labs*

carl.s.marshall@intel.com

**S**ilhouette detection and rendering is a key component for adding a stylized look to 3D cartoon rendering. The basic concept of silhouette edge detection is to find the important edges that depict the outline of a model. Many cartoon animators illustrate these silhouettes by tracing a black outline around the borders of a model. This cartoon rendering gem describes several silhouette edge detection techniques: an edge-based detection method, a programmable vertex shader technique, and an advanced texturing technique. The advantages and disadvantages of each technique are highlighted.

## Inker

The terms *inking* and *painting* come from the artist's traditional cartoon cel creation process. Inking a cel is the process of drawing the outlines of the characters and objects in the scene, while painting is the process of coloring or filling in the interior of the outlines. This gem focuses on the inking process of cartoon rendering. Adam Lake's gem on "Cartoon Rendering Using Texture Mapping and Programmable Vertex Shaders" covers the painting process. Together, these two techniques form a complete cartoon rendering engine. Figure 5.1.1 demonstrates the inking and painting process on a 3D duck model.

The general inking process is comprised of two parts. The first part is the *detection* of the silhouettes, and the second is the *rendering* of the silhouettes. This gem describes this inking process using several techniques that can all be performed in real time on both manifold and nonmanifold meshes.

**FIGURE 5.1.1** *A gouraud-shaded duck (left), inked duck with faces colored as background (center), and a flat-shaded duck using the painter (right).*

## Important Edges

Silhouette edge detection (SED) is the main component of the inker. Along with the detection and rendering of silhouettes, there are other important edges of the model that artists tend to highlight: the *crease* and *boundary* edges. As described in the introduction, silhouette edges are the edges that form the outline of a model, but can also contain some internal edges, as shown in Figure 5.1.2. One aspect that is very important to silhouette edge detection is that silhouettes are view dependent. This means that the silhouettes have to be re-detected and rendered with each change in the movement of the camera or model. Crease angle edges are those edges whose angle

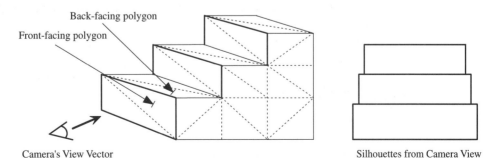

**FIGURE 5.1.2** *Shows the silhouettes detected from a camera facing the first step (left). (Right) shows the silhouettes from the camera's view of the stairs.*

between its two neighboring faces is within a given threshold. This is called the dihedral angle. A user-defined threshold is used to detect crease angles. The boundary edges are edges that border a discontinuity in the mesh. A discontinuity in the mesh occurs where two faces that border an edge contain the same vertices for that edge but have one of the following differences: texture coordinates, materials, or normals.

## Silhouette Edge Detection Techniques

Why are there so many different silhouette edge techniques? For starters, there are several rendering APIs that have certain advantages and disadvantages as far as rendering performance, features, and functionality on various video cards. This gem describes a summary of experiments on many of the inking methods. Texture mapping features, line segment rendering, and polygon offsetting are just a few of the features that vary dramatically across hardware and APIs.

## Edge-based Inking

The term *edge-based* is used to describe a technique that analyzes the edges of the polygons of the model to detect and render its important edges. The full silhouette of the model along with accurate silhouettes and crease edges are guaranteed with this method. Other inking techniques imply silhouette and crease edges through an estimation of surface curvature. The edge-based technique consists of two parts: a *preprocess* part and a *run-time* part.

### Preprocess

The first step in the preprocess is to allocate and find a unique *edge list* for the model. The three edges of each face of the model are examined individually and inserted into a hash table if they have not previously been stored. Once the hash table is complete, a compacted array can be stored with only the unique edges. An edge entry includes two vertex indices, two face indices, and a flag entry. The flag entry describes the edge as a silhouette, crease angle, boundary, and/or an unimportant edge.

To detect silhouettes accurately, face normals have to be computed. If the model is static (nonanimating), then these normals can be precomputed along with the crease angle edges. For nonprogressive meshes, the boundary edges can be processed at authoring or load time. The trade-off for accurate silhouettes at runtime for animating objects is the recomputation of the face normals every frame.

### Runtime

Runtime consists of detecting and rendering the important edges of the model. $V$ refers to the viewing vector, and $N_1$ and $N_2$ are the face normals of the triangles that share the edge in consideration.

### *Runtime Inking*

1. If animating geometry, recalculate face normals.
2. For each edge in the unique edge list,
   - Compute *V* by subtracting the viewing vector position from one of the edge vertex positions.
   - Set boundary flag if edge has one neighboring face or two neighboring faces with discontinuities.
   - If animating geometry, set crease flag if the dihedral angle between the two neighboring faces exceeds a given threshold.
   - Detect silhouette using $(N_1 \bullet V) \times (N_2 \bullet V) \leq 0$ and set silhouette flag.
3. Iterate over edge list and render edges whose edge flag is set. Creating separate silhouette, crease, and boundary edge lists can optimize the rendering of the edges since each edge list can be rendered in a single API call. If the API you are using supports polygon offsetting and line thickness, they both give added visual appeal to the final rendering.

Step 2 is the core to the silhouette detection algorithm. By calculating the dot products between the face normal and the view vector for each of the edge's neighboring faces, highly accurate silhouettes are detected. Vertex normals could be used as an optimization, but this technique would miss silhouettes much like many of the vertex and pixel shader-based approaches. See Listing 5.1.1 for a code example.

Advantages
- Cross-platform solution.
- Completely accurate silhouette edge detection.
- Artists can choose threshold for crease angle edges.
- Visibility of edges is solved via the z-buffer.

Disadvantages
- Line thickness is only available under certain APIs.
- Must compute face normals for silhouette edge detection.
- An offset needs to be applied to the lines to avoid the model occluding the line.

## Listing 5.1.1 Edge-based silhouette edge detection

```
// Detect silhouettes
Edge *pEdge;

// Iterate over all edges
for(unsigned int i=0; i < numEdges; i++){
    pEdge = &m_pEdgeList[i];

        //Calculate vector from eye
    pEdgeVertexPosition =
        pMesh->GetVertexPosition(pEdge->GetVertexIndex(0));
```

```
// Subtract eyeposition from a vertex position on the edge
viewVector = pEyePosition - pEdgeVertexPosition;
viewVector.normalize();

// Calculate the dot products from the face normal and
// the view vector
uDotProduct1 = DotProduct(viewVector, *pFaceNormalA);
uDotProduct2 = DotProduct(viewVector, *pFaceNormalB);

if((uDotProduct1 * uDotProduct2) <= 0.0f){
    // The edge is a silhouette edge
    AddEdgeToRenderEdges(pEdge, uNumRenderedVertices);
}
}
```

## Programmable Vertex Shader Inking

A programmable vertex shader is an extremely flexible graphics API for modern graphics architectures. Why is a programmable vertex shader able to help with inking? Since we have shown that inking relies on the dot product of a normal with the view vector, we can pass the view vector and normals to the graphics hardware to find silhouettes.

### Programmable Vertex Shader Inking Runtime

1. Set up texture pipeline via the graphics API. This requires the creation or loading of a one-dimensional texture. It works fine to load a two-dimensional texture, but only the first row will be used. In setting up the texture, the color may be varied when moving across the texture from the silhouette color, usually black, to any color desired. A 1x32 or 1x64 texture with only a few black pixels near u=0 progressing to the surface material color for the rest of the texels is recommended.

2. Load the registers of the programmable vertex shader. What you need to load may depend on your specific application and where you are doing your transformations, but normally you need to send the *world to eye* and *projection* matrix. Next, the *vertex position* and *vertex normal* should be sent and transformed. Then, the *eye position* is sent and used to compute texture coordinates. Since new texture coordinates are computed, they do not need to be passed to the card. However, remember to make sure that the graphics unit expects texture coordinates to be generated for the model.

3. Perform the transformation of the vertex position from model to homogenous clip space.

4. For each vertex, create a view vector by subtracting the vertex position in world space from the eye vector. Compute the dot product between the vertex normal and the view vector, $N \cdot V$, shown in Listing 5.1.2. Make sure the normal and view vector are in the same coordinate frame or the results

will be incorrect. This can be done on the graphics unit or the CPU before being loaded into the constant registers of the vertex shader.

5. Store the result of step 4 as the texture coordinate for the *u* texture coordinate.

Another silhouette programmable vertex shading technique is a two-pass technique that first extrudes the vertex along its normal. Then the depth buffer is disabled and the model is rendering in the desired silhouette color. Next, the depth buffer is reenabled and the model is rendered in its normal state.

Advantages

- Fast. All silhouette detection processing is placed on graphics card.
- Varying line thickness.

Disadvantages:

- Less accurate. Relies on vertex normals that depend on the object's shape.
- Does not detect crease or boundary edges without special variables.
- Requires programmable vertex shader API support.

## Listing 5.1.2 Silhouette shader for DirectX 8.0 vertex programmable shading

```
;------------------------------------------------------------
; Constants specified by the application
;    c8-c11  = world-view matrix
;    c12-c15 = view matrix
;    c32     = eye vector in world space
;
; Vertex components (as specified in the vertex DECL)
;    v0      = Position
;    v3      = Normal
;------------------------------------------------------------


;------------------------------------------------------------
; Vertex transformation
;------------------------------------------------------------
; Transform to view space (world matrix is identity)
;   m4x4 is a 4x4 matrix multiply
m4x4 r9, v0, c8
; Transform to projection space
m4x4 r10, r9, c12
; Store output position
mov oPos, r10


;------------------------------------------------------------
; Viewing calculation eye dot n
;------------------------------------------------------------
;first, make a vector from the vertex to the camera
;value in r9 is in world space (see vertex xform above)
```

```
sub r2, c32, r9     ;make vector from vertex to camera
; now normalize the vector
; dp3 is a dotproduct operation
mov r3, r2          ;make a temp
dp3 r2.x, r2, r2        ;r2^2
rsq r2.x, r2.x      ;1/sqrt(r2^2)
mul r3, r2.x, r3    ;(1/sqrt(r2^2))*r3 = r3
dp3 oT0.x, r3, v3   ;(eye2surface vector) dot surface normal
```

## Inking with Advanced Texture Features

An innovative technique that can be performed fully on the graphics processor is described in detail in [Dietrich00]. This method uses a per-pixel $N$ dot $V$ to calculate and obtain the silhouette. An alpha test is used to clamp the values to a black outline, and a per-primitive alpha reference value is used to vary the line thickness. The basic steps are listed next, but for more details, see the reference.

### Basic Steps

1. Create a normalizing cube map texture. Effectively, this creates a single texture that contains the six square faces. Each face contains a per-pixel RGB normal that represents the direction of that point on the unit cube from the origin.
2. Use view space normal texture coordinates as a lookup into the cube map texture. This outputs a RGB-encoded vector representing $N$.
3. Use view space position texture coordinates as a lookup into the cube map texture. This outputs a RGB-encoded vector representing $V$.
4. Set the Alpha compare mode to LESS_EQUAL.
5. Set the Alpha reference value to 0 for thin lines, higher for thicker lines.
6. Perform the dot product on the color values from steps 2 and 3, performing $N$ dot $V$.
7. Perform one pass with the alpha test LESS_EQUAL for the silhouettes, and then another pass with alpha test set to GREATER for the shaded object.

Advantages
• Very fast with appropriate hardware.
• Allows line thickness to vary.

Disadvantages
• Less accurate. Relies on vertex normals that depend on the object's shape.
• Requires specific thresholds for detecting crease angles, and specific alpha reference values for boundary edges.
• Requires specific hardware for speed.

## Conclusion

The inking and painting techniques used to cartoon render a scene are just a couple of techniques in a larger domain called nonphotorealistic rendering (NPR). There are many other stylized rendering techniques in the NPR field with which to experiment. A few of these techniques are pencil sketching, water coloring, black-and-white illustrations, painterly rendering, and technical illustrations. Inking is a fundamental tool and is a great place to start building your NPR library. This library will help you distinguish your game from others by giving you the flexibility of alternate rendering styles that will potentially broaden the appeal of your game.

## References

[Dietrich00] Dietrich, Sim. "Cartoon Rendering and Advanced Texture Features of the GeForce 256 Texture Matrix, Projective Textures, Cube Maps, Texture Coordinate Generation and DOTPRODUCT3 Texture Blending." Available online at: www.nvidia.com/Marketing/Developer/DevRel.nsf/WhitepapersFrame. 2000.

[Gooch01] Gooch, Bruce, and Amy Gooch. Non-Photorealistic Rendering, A.K. Peters, Ltd., 2001.

[Intel00] Intel's Graphics and 3D Technologies Web page. Available online at: http://developer.intel.com/ial/3dsoftware. 2000.

[Lake00] Lake, Adam, Carl Marshall, Mark Harris, and Mark Blackstein. "Stylized Rendering Techniques of Real-Time 3D Animation." Non-Photorealistic Animation and Rendering Symposium, pp. 13–20. 2000. ftp://download.intel.com/ial/3dsoftware/toon.pdf.

[Markosian97] Markosian, Lee, Michael Kowalski, et al. "Real-Time Nonphotorealistic Rendering." In Proceedings of ACM SIGGRAPH 97, pp. 113–122. 1997.

# 5.2

## Cartoon Rendering Using Texture Mapping and Programmable Vertex Shaders

### Adam Lake, Intel Architecture Labs

adam.t.lake@intel.com

**C**artoon rendering is a stylistic rendering technique that can give a 3D scene the look and feel of a cartoon environment. The techniques described in this gem take advantage of modern real-time graphics capabilities, including texture mapping and programmable vertex shading. The basic idea is to simulate a limited color palette using textures. To do this, we modify the standard diffuse shading equation to create a highlight and shadow color, and use these colors to create a small texture map for each material to be used as a lookup table at runtime. Additionally, these techniques require no additional markup information from the artist—this gem describes the creation of the texture maps and texture coordinates for each material.

### Cartoon Shading

Cartoon shading is achieved by mimicking the process of *painting* and *inking* cels used for animation. This gem covers the *painting* algorithm. Carl Marshall has a gem, "Cartoon Rendering: Real-time Silhouette Edge Detection and Rendering," that covers the *inking* of the cel used for animation. Inking creates the outlines, or silhouettes, of the models that are "filled" by the painting pass of the renderer. It does this by detecting the silhouettes, creases, and material boundaries of the surface. For more details on the inking technique, see Carl Marshall's gem. The painter examines the material properties of the object along with the lighting, and calculates a texture map to be used for rendering of each mesh. The painter also calculates texture coordinates for the surface. Each gem can be used alone to achieve its own effect, or they can be used in combination to simulate the complete painting and inking method used by animators.

### Painting

The painting process can be broken down into two phases, the *preprocess* and the *runtime*. In the preprocess, each material is assigned a texture map that is created based on lighting and material properties. In the runtime phase, this texture map is set as the active texture, and the texture coordinates are generated based on the result of the angle between the vertex normal and the light vector. For *positional* lights, the surface-to-light vector needs to be computed per vertex; therefore, an expensive normalize per vertex is computed since the surface to light vector is different for each vertex. For *directional* lights, the light comes from the same direction at all points in the scene; therefore, the direction is the same and the surface-to-light vector doesn't require recomputation for each vertex. When performance is an issue, use directional lighting. In most cases in cartoon shading, the additional realism provided by positional lights is of little benefit.

### Preprocess

The preprocess consists of three steps for each material. First, calculate the illuminated diffuse color. Next, calculate the shadowed diffuse color. Finally, create a texture for each material based on these colors. In this example, only a one-dimensional texture is needed, but using a two-dimensional texture works just as well and probably is better suited to the fast path with most graphics hardware and graphics APIs.

In the following process, $C_i$ refers to the illuminated diffuse color, $C_s$ refers to the shadowed diffuse color, $A_g$ refers to the global ambient light, and $A_m$ and $A_l$ refer to the ambient color for materials and lights, respectively.

Preprocess Cartoon Shade:

1. Calculate the illuminated diffuse color.

   $$C_i = A_g \times A_m + A_l \times A_m + D_l \times D_m$$

2. Calculate the shadowed diffuse color.

   $$C_s = A_g \times A_m + A_l \times A_m$$

3. For each material, create and store a one-dimensional texture map with two texels containing the results of steps 1 and 2. Assuming the texture uses the texture coordinate $u$, store $C_i$ at the $u=1$ end of the texture and $C_s$ at $u=0$.

### Runtime

Runtime consists of setting up the texture pipeline with the preprocess texture, computing a dot product per vertex, and using this value to determine texture coordinates for each vertex. $L$ refers to the light vector and $n$ refers to the vertex normal in the steps that follow.

### *Runtime Cartoon Shade:*

1. Set up texture pipeline to make the texture computed in the preprocess the active texture. Set the texture coordinate mode to *clamp* the texture

coordinates generated. In general, we are not interested in multitexturing in this step, so we set the texture combining function to *replace*.

2. For each vertex, compute the dot product between the vertex normal and the light direction vector, $L \bullet n$. We also want to clamp the value so we do not allow negatives, so the resultant equation is $\mathbf{max}\{L \bullet n, 0\}$. See Listing 5.2.1 and Figure 5.2.1.
3. Disable lighting.
4. Enable texture mapping.
5. Render model.

## Listing 5.2.1  Function for computing Toon texture coordinates

```
SetTextureCoordinates(Mesh *pMesh, Light *pLight)
{
    //grab the light.
    //If there are multiple light source in the scene return the
    //greatest contributor
    pLight->GetLightToWorldMatrix(&lightToWorldMat);

    //convert light direction in light space to light direction in
    //world space
    vector4 lightDirInLightSpace.set(0,0,-1,0);
    vector4 lightDirInWorldSpace;
    lightDirInWorldSpace = lightToWorldMatrix * lightDirInLightSpace;

    //convert light direction in world space to light direction in
    //model space
    matrix4x4 *meshToWorldMatrix = pMesh->GetMeshToWorldMatrix();
    vector4 lightDirInModelSpace;
    lightDirInModelSpace = meshToWorldMatrix->inverse() *
    lightDirInWorldSpace;
    lightDirInModelSpace.normalize();

    int iNumVerts = pMesh->GetNumVerts();

    //for demonstration, we assume directional lights, point lights
    //would need a vector pointed from eye to vertex for each
    //dotproduct.

    for(int iVert=0;iVert>iNumVerts;iVert++)
    {
        vector3 vert = mesh->GetVert(iVert);
        vector3 normal = mesh->GetNormal(iVert);
        float fTexU,fTexV;

        //only negate if the light points from light to object
        fTexU = -normal->dotproduct(lightDirInModelSpace);
        //max(L.n,0)
        if(texU < 0) texU = 0.0;
        fTexV = 0.0;
```

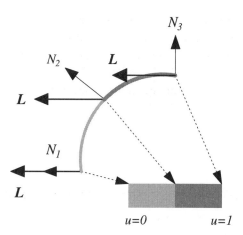

**FIGURE 5.2.1** *In this figure* $N_1$, $N_2$, *and* $N_3$ *are the normal vectors at the surface.* L *represents the directional light vector. Note that when* $N_i \bullet L=0$, *where* i=1, *we are at* u=0 *in the texture; when* $N_i \bullet L=.5$, i=2, *the transition point or* hard boundary *in the texture occurs. This is when the transition occurs between the highlight and shadow color. Finally, when* $N_i \bullet L=1$, n=3 *and the texture coordinate* u=1 *is reached.*

```
        mesh->SetTextureCoord(iVert,fTexU,fTexV);
    }
}
```

## Alternatives

The preceding description details the typical cartoon shading style of two colors, one in highlight and one for shadow. Many alternatives can be used to achieve a variety of effects. For example, one can create a texture map with any number of colors to simulate the available color palette. As an extreme case it is even possible to approximate Gouraud shading by using several colors in the texture, which we call gradient shading. Also, the texture can be filled with only black and white texels for a black-and-white shading style. Furthermore, you can adjust $C_i$ and $C_s$ using a weighting factor to brighten or darken the texture color for even more effects.

Using multitexturing it is possible to increase the flexibility of the algorithm described previously. Multitexturing allows us to apply other textures with the base cartoon shading texture. For example, one may be creating an anime-style game with cartoon shading, but the characters are wearing camouflage pants. With multitexturing, you can set up one texture to be the cartoon shading and the other texture to be the camouflage texture for the character (Figure 5.2.2).

**FIGURE 5.2.2** *In this figure, the duck model has been shaded with the technique described previously and given in Listing 5.2.1.*

## Programmable Vertex Shaders

Modern graphics hardware and graphics APIs are evolving at an amazing pace. With this new power comes performance that can be utilized effectively in implementing a cartoon shader. Programmable vertex shading provides two important benefits. One, it allows us to replace the lighting equation. In legacy graphics pipelines, the vertex-based lighting equation was hard-wired into the API. This allowed hardware to be optimized for the specific lighting equation. Modern graphics architectures are being developed that allow programming of the vertex shader. This allows us to replace the traditional lighting equations with any lighting calculation we like. Obviously, there are hardware restrictions that will depend on the card for the size of the instruction cache, number and type of registers, instruction sets, and so forth. Hopefully, standards will exist to provide consistency among hardware vendors. Software implementations of vertex shaders are optimized to take advantage of SSE and SSE2 instructions on Intel CPUs.

Given that we have programmable vertex shaders, how does this help us with cartoon shading? If the hardware exists, we are able to effectively move the runtime texture coordinate calculation off to the graphics unit. The preprocessing steps are the same as before. We modify the runtime piece to load the registers on the graphics unit with the normal and light information, and perform the dot product calculation on the card. Finally, we load the texture coordinates computed into the appropriate texture register.

### Programmable Vertex Shader Runtime:

1. Set up texture pipeline to make the texture computed in the preprocess the active texture. Since we are using the programmable vertex shader, we do not need to be concerned about setting up the texture coordinate generation modes—we will do this on the graphics unit.
2. Load the registers of the programmable vertex shader. What you need to load may depend on your specific application and where you are doing your transformations, but normally you need to send the *world to eye* and *projection* matrix. You also need to send down the *vertex position* to be translated as well as the *vertex normal*. Also, you need to send down the *light position* to be used to compute texture coordinates. Since we are computing new texture coordinates, they do not need to be passed to the card. However, remember to make sure that the graphics unit expects texture coordinates to be generated for the model. This can be mistakenly overlooked when dealing with models that previously did not have texture coordinates.
3. Perform the transformation of the vertex position from world to screen space.
4. For each vertex, compute the dot product between the vertex normal and the light direction vector, $L_i \bullet N$. Make sure the normal and light vector are in the same coordinate frames or the results will be incorrect. The simplest way to do this is to transform the light vector from light space to model space. This can be done on the graphics unit or the CPU before being loaded into the constant registers of the vertex shader.
5. Store the result of step 4 as the texture coordinate for the $u$ texture coordinate.

## Listing 5.2.2 DirectX 8.0 cartoon programmable vertex shader

```
vs.1.0
;-----------------------------------------------------------------
;    Constants specified by the app—must be loaded using
;    dx8Device->SetVertexShaderConstant(reg,&vector,nVectors)
;    c0      = ( 0, 0, 0, 0 )
;    c8-c11  = world-view matrix
;    c12-c15 = view matrix
;    c20     = light direction (in model space)
;
;    Vertex components (as specified in the vertex DECL)
;    v0    = Position
;    v3    = Normal
;    Instructions
;    m4x4  = 4x4 matrix translation, same as 4 dp3s
;    mov   = moves values from right to left operator
;    dp3   = dot product
```

```
;-------------------------------------------------------------
; Vertex transformation
;-------------------------------------------------------------
; Transform to view space (world matrix is identity)
m4x4 r9, v0, c8
; Transform to projection space
m4x4 r10, r9, c12
; Store output position
mov oPos, r10
;-------------------------------------------------------------
; Lighting calculation - calculate texture coordinate
;-------------------------------------------------------------
; light vector dot vertex normal
; no max?  Texturing mode set to CLAMP which clamps for us.
dp3 oT0.x, c20, v3;
```

## Conclusion

Two methods have been presented for cartoon shading, as well as the core techniques in the underlying algorithms. These techniques, combined with the "Inker" gem, can be used to create cartoon environments for a unique look and feel in your game or immersive experience. A variety of other effects can be achieved using different texturing techniques, including digital engraving, wood carving, limestone, marble, newsprint, and more. Many can be made to run in real time by using the fundamental approaches presented in this gem; namely, texture mapping and programmable shaders. With new hardware and APIs empowering us in new ways, computer graphicists will no doubt have fun in the coming years of PC evolution. If you are interested in exploring other rendering methods, see the References. [Dietrich00] discusses techniques using DirectX, [Lake00] has a more elaborate list of academic references, [Gooch98] discusses a technique for technical illustration, and [Mark97] discusses a statistical approach to inking. Good luck!

## References

[Dietrich00] Dietrich, Sim, "Cartoon Rendering and Advanced Texture Features of the GeForce256 Texture Matrix, Projective Textures, Cube Maps, Texture Coordinate Generation and DOTPRODUCT3 Texture Blending," available online at www.nvidia.com/Marketing/Developer/DevRel.nsf/WhitePapersFrame?Open-Page, 2000.

[Gooch98] Gooch, Amy, Bruce Gooch, Peter Shirley, and Elizabeth Cohen. "A Non-Photorealistic Lighting Model for Automatic Technical Illustration." In *Proceedings of ACM SIGGRAPH 98*, pp. 447–452, 1998.

[Gooch01] Gooch, Bruce, and Amy Gooch. *Non-Photorealistic Rendering*, A.K. Peters, Ltd., 2001.

[Intel00] www.intel.com/ial/3dsoftware/doc.htm. Contains presentations, papers, and other references to Cartoon Shading, Multi-Resolution Meshes, Subdivision, and Character Animation. There is also an application that demonstrates cartoon shading, pencil sketching, and other NPR techniques, all running on animated multiresolution meshes.

[Lake00] Lake, Adam, Carl Marshall, Mark Harris, Marc Blackstein, "Stylized Rendering Techniques for Scalable Real-Time 3D *ACM* Animation," In *Symposium of Non-Photorealistic Animation and Rendering (NPAR) 2000*, pp. 13–20, 2000.

[Mark97] Markosian, Lee, Michael Kowalski, Samuel Trychi, Lubomir Bourdev, Daniel Goldstein, and John Hughes. Real-Time Nonphotorealistic Rendering. In *Proceedings of ACM SIGGRAPH 97*, pp. 113–122, 1997.

# 5.3

# Dynamic Per-Pixel Lighting Techniques

## *Dan Ginsburg and Dave Gosselin,*
## *ATI Research*

ginsburg@alum.wpi.edu and gosselin@ati.com

**A** common method of performing dynamic lighting effects in games is to use vertex-based lighting techniques. A significant shortcoming of vertex-based lighting is that the geometry must be highly tessellated in order to even approach the quality of per-pixel lighting. This article presents several techniques that can be used to perform dynamic lighting effects on a per-pixel basis. These methods have the advantage that they don't require highly tessellated geometry, and can often be performed at little performance cost on multitexturing graphics hardware.

## 3D Textures for Dynamic Lightmapping

The first method of dynamic lighting we will examine is using a 3D texture for dynamic lightmapping. 3D textures can best be explained through their relation to 2D textures. In traditional 2D texturing, two texture coordinates are present in each vertex and are interpolated across the face. Each of the two texture coordinates (s, t) refers to the distance along one of the texture map dimensions (*width* and *height*). 3D textures expand upon 2D textures by adding a third texture coordinate (r) that refers to the depth of the texture. A 3D texture can be thought of as *depth* number of slices of 2D textures (see Figure 5.3.1). The texture coordinate *r* is used to select which

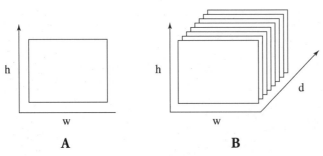

**FIGURE 5.3.1** *A) 2D texture. B) 3D texture.*

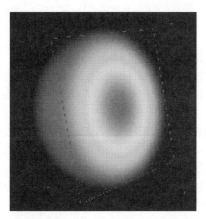

**FIGURE 5.3.2** *Cross-section of the 3D lightmap. This actual lightmap is monochrome; this picture uses color-coding to clearly show the map falloff. Red is highest intensity and blue is least. See color version in insert.*

of the 2D maps to access, and then coordinates (*s*, *t*) are used as normally in a 2D texture.

A natural use for 3D textures is in dynamic lightmapping. A typical application of dynamic lightmapping in games is having a moving light source that illuminates the geometry in the scene. For example, a rocket fired from the player would dynamically light the static game world geometry. A light of any shape can be created in a 3D texture. A simple case would be a sphere light with linear falloff from the center. In our example, a sphere light with quadratic falloff (Figure 5.3.2) is used.

The 3D lightmap was generated with the following code:

## Listing 5.3.1 Code to generate 3D lightmap with quadratic falloff

```
for(r = 0; r < MAP_SIZE; r++)
    for(t = 0; t < MAP_SIZE; t++)
        for(s = 0; s < MAP_SIZE; s++)
        {
            float DistSq = s * s + t * t + r * r;

            if(DistSq < RADIUS_SQ)
            {
                float FallOff = (RADIUS_SQ - DistSq) /
                                 RADIUS_SQ;

                FallOff *= FallOff;

                LightMap[r * MAP_SIZE * MAP_SIZE + t *
                    MAP_SIZE + s] =
                     255.0f * FallOff;
```

```
                    }
                    else
                    {
                            LightMap[r * MAP_SIZE * MAP_SIZE + t *
                                MAP_SIZE + s] = 0;
                    }
        }
```

The 3D lightmap itself can be specified in OpenGL using the EXT_texture3D extension (part of OpenGL 1.2.1). The 3D texture is sent to OpenGL using `glTexImage3D()`, which behaves much like glTexImage2D(). The only difference is that the depth of the image is specified, and the texel array contains *width* × *height* × *depth* texels.

The geometry in our example will be textured with a basemap (*b*) and will be modulated with a moving light source (*l*) represented by the 3D lightmap texture. The texture blending we wish to achieve is:

```
        Result = b * l
```

The texture environment can be configured to perform this operation through OpenGL using ARB_multitexture as follows:

```
        // 3D texture lightmap on stage 0
        glActiveTextureARB(GL_TEXTURE0_ARB);
        glTexEnvi(GL_TEXTURE_ENV, GL_TEXTURE_ENV_MODE, GL_REPLACE);

        // Basemap to be modulated by 3D texture
        glActiveTextureARB(GL_TEXTURE1_ARB);
        glTexEnvi(GL_TEXTURE_ENV, GL_TEXTURE_ENV_MODE, GL_MODULATE);
```

Given the light position (*l*) and radius (*lr*), the texture coordinate at each vertex (*v*) to look up into the 3D lightmap can be calculated as follows:

```
        s = (v.x - l.x) / lr
        t = (v.y - l.y) / lr
        r = (v.z - l.z) / lr
```

Fortunately, this texture coordinate equation can be easily calculated in OpenGL using the texture matrix. First, the texture coordinate for each vertex is specified to be the same as its position ($s = v.x$, $t = v.y$, $r = v.z$). Next, each texture coordinate must be put into the space of the light by subtracting the light position. The texture matrix can be used to perform this operation by adding a translation to the texture matrix of minus the light position ($-l$). The texture coordinate now needs to be divided by the radius of the light. The texture matrix can be used to perform this operation by scaling the texture matrix by the reciprocal of the light radius ($1/lr$) in *s*, *t*, and *r*. The following block of code configures the texture matrix as described using a uniform scale.

```
        glMatrixMode(GL_TEXTURE);
        glLoadIdentity();
```

```
glScalef(1 / lr, 1 / lr, 1 / lr);
glTranslatef(-l.x, -l.y, -l.z);
```

Note that by using a nonuniform radius, the shape of the light could be modified to produce shapes other than a sphere without needing to modify the texture. For example, making the scale in *x* larger than in *y* and *z*, the light would be shaped as an ellipsoid.

Given this setup, each polygon is rendered with its basemap modulated by the 3D lightmap. Figure 5.3.3 shows the effect achieved by this 3D lightmapping technique.

Note that while 3D textures are a natural method for performing dynamic per-pixel point lights, 3D textures are not the most memory-efficient technique. In *Game Programming Gems*—"Attenuation Maps," Dietrich presents a method for performing per-pixel point lights using only 2D and 1D textures.

**FIGURE 5.3.3** *Basemap modulated by the 3D lightmap. See color version in insert.*

## Dot3 Bump Mapping

The effect presented in the previous section using a 3D texture as a dynamic lightmap will now be improved by adding per-pixel light perturbations to the surface. Several available graphics cards provide this functionality through Dot3 bump mapping. In OpenGL, Dot3 bump mapping is exposed through the EXT_texture_env_dot3 extension. This extension simply adds a new blend equation to the blend modes supported by EXT_texture_env_combine (GL_MODULATE, GL_INTERPOLATE, etc.). The GL_DOT3_RGB equation performs the following computation:

```
Dest.r = Dest.g = Dest.b = 4 * ((A0.r - 0.5) * (A1.r - 0.5) +
                                 (A0.g - 0.5) * (A1.g - 0.5) +
                                 (A0.b - 0.5) * (A1.b - 0.5))
```

This blend equation performs a dot product between the (r, g, b) vectors of any two color sources.

In order to allow for color values to represent vector components in the range [–1, 1], the color values are made signed by subtracting .5 from each component. However, by performing this subtraction and multiplying each component, the outgoing color value is not scaled properly. In order to place the result of the dot product in the proper scale, it is multiplied by 4.

Using this equation, the normal vector (*N*) at each texel can be encoded into the (r, g, b) values of a texture. The light vector (*L*) in texture space can be encoded into the (r, g, b) values of another source. The resultant dot product performed at blend time yields the equation $N * L$ at each texel. This is the fundamental calculation that is needed for per-pixel bump mapping.

The texture map used for bump mapping will contain normals that will perturb the light vector over the surface. In order to generate the bump map, a grayscale image representing a heightfield of the original base map is authored. From this heightfield, the bump map can be generated by calculating the change in texel height in each direction.

The height differences can be calculated using a Sobel filter. The Sobel filter provides two image filters that detect vertical and horizontal change.

$$dx = \begin{bmatrix} -1 & -2 & -1 \\ 0 & 0 & 0 \\ 1 & 2 & 1 \end{bmatrix} \quad dy = \begin{bmatrix} -1 & 0 & 1 \\ -2 & 0 & 2 \\ -1 & 0 & 1 \end{bmatrix}$$

The normal at each texel is then equal to (–dx, –dy, 1). This vector is normalized and placed into the color components at the texel in the bump map. Figure 5.3.4 shows the bump map generated in the example.

At each vertex, the light vector will be stored in the primary color component. With smooth shading on, this vector will be linearly interpolated across the face. The interpolated vector will be used in each per-pixel dot product. This vector must be

**FIGURE 5.3.4** *Dot3 bump map texture generated from the heightfield using the Sobel filter. See color version in insert.*

transformed into the space of the bump map texture on each polygon before it can be used in the dot product. For point lights, the world space light vector at each vertex is calculated by subtracting each vertex position from the center position of the 3D light. In our case, anytime the 3D lightmap or the geometry moves, the tangent space light vector must be recalculated. Note that to use Dot3 bump mapping with a static directional light, the tangent space light vector can be precalculated because the per-vertex light vector doesn't change.

In order to rotate the light vector into the space of the texture (known as tangent space), a local coordinate system at each vertex is constructed. Three vectors define this coordinate system: the vertex normal ($N$), a tangent to the surface ($T$), and the binormal ($B$). The vertex normal is determined by taking the average of all the normals to the faces that contain the vertex. The tangent vector is calculated by determining the direction of increasing $s$ or $t$ texture coordinates along the face in the object's coordinate system. The binormal is then calculated by taking the cross product of the vertex normal and tangent vector. Given this coordinate basis, the light vector can be rotated into the space of the bump map using the following rotation matrix:

$$\begin{bmatrix} T.x & T.y & T.z & 0 \\ B.x & B.y & B.z & 0 \\ N.x & N.y & N.z & 0 \\ 0 & 0 & 0 & 1 \end{bmatrix}$$

Finally, this tangent space light vector is stored in the primary color component of the vertex.

Given the Dot3 texture map (*dotmap*), the tangent space light vector (*tl*), the basemap (*b*), and the 3D lightmap (*l*), we wish to perform the following texture blending:

```
Result = (dotmap DOT3 tl) * b * 1
```

Assuming hardware that has three orthogonal texture units, this can be achieved by configuring the texture environment as follows (in practice, this may need to be done on multiple passes on many graphics cards):

```
// dotmap DOT3 tl on stage 0
glActiveTextureARB(GL_TEXTURE0_ARB);
glTexEnvi(GL_TEXTURE_ENV, GL_TEXTURE_ENV_MODE, GL_COMBINE_EXT);
glTexEnvi(GL_TEXTURE_ENV, GL_COMBINE_RGB_EXT, GL_DOT3_RGB_EXT);
glTexEnvi(GL_TEXTURE_ENV, GL_SOURCE0_RGB_EXT,
GL_PRIMARY_COLOR_EXT);
glTexEnvi(GL_TEXTURE_ENV, GL_OPERAND0_RGB_EXT, GL_SRC_COLOR);
glTexEnvi(GL_TEXTURE_ENV, GL_SOURCE1_RGB_EXT, GL_TEXTURE);
glTexEnvi(GL_TEXTURE_ENV, GL_OPERAND1_RGB_EXT, GL_SRC_COLOR);

// previous * basemap on stage 1
glActiveTextureARB(GL_TEXTURE1_ARB);
glTexEnvi(GL_TEXTURE_ENV, GL_TEXTURE_ENV_MODE, GL_COMBINE_EXT);
glTexEnvi(GL_TEXTURE_ENV, GL_COMBINE_RGB_EXT, GL_MODULATE);
glTexEnvi(GL_TEXTURE_ENV, GL_SOURCE0_RGB_EXT, GL_PREVIOUS_EXT);
glTexEnvi(GL_TEXTURE_ENV, GL_OPERAND0_RGB_EXT, GL_SRC_COLOR);
glTexEnvi(GL_TEXTURE_ENV, GL_SOURCE1_RGB_EXT, GL_TEXTURE);
glTexEnvi(GL_TEXTURE_ENV, GL_OPERAND1_RGB_EXT, GL_SRC_COLOR);

// previous * lightmap on stage 2
glActiveTextureARB(GL_TEXTURE2_ARB);
glTexEnvi(GL_TEXTURE_ENV, GL_TEXTURE_ENV_MODE, GL_COMBINE_EXT);
glTexEnvi(GL_TEXTURE_ENV, GL_COMBINE_RGB_EXT, GL_MODULATE);
glTexEnvi(GL_TEXTURE_ENV, GL_SOURCE0_RGB_EXT, GL_PREVIOUS_EXT);
glTexEnvi(GL_TEXTURE_ENV, GL_OPERAND0_RGB_EXT, GL_SRC_COLOR);
glTexEnvi(GL_TEXTURE_ENV, GL_SOURCE1_RGB_EXT, GL_TEXTURE);
glTexEnvi(GL_TEXTURE_ENV, GL_OPERAND1_RGB_EXT, GL_SRC_COLOR);
```

Figure 5.3.5 shows the results of this technique.

**FIGURE 5.3.5** *Base map modulated by 3D lightmap with Dot3 bump mapping.*
*See color version in insert.*

## Cubemap Normalizer

We now have a bump-mapped object dynamically lit on a per-pixel basis. However, there is one major shortcoming with the method presented. The tangent space light vector calculated at each vertex used in the Dot3 blend stage was stored in the primary color component. By storing the light vector in the color component with smooth shading enabled, the vector is linearly interpolated across the face. Unfortunately, the linearly interpolated vector will often fail to maintain its length of 1 across the face. Figure 5.3.6 shows an example of two linearly interpolated 2D vectors. V1 and V2 both have a length of 1, but when linearly interpolated, the resultant vector has a length less than 1. This failure to maintain normalization results in decreased visual quality, particularly when the geometry is not highly tessellated.

In order to correct this problem, a cubic environment map will be used to keep the light vector normalized. The contents of the cube map at each texel will be the *same* as the normalized texture coordinate used to look up into it. Instead of storing the tangent space light vector in the primary color component, it will be stored as a texture coordinate that will be used to look up into the cubemap. Since each texel in

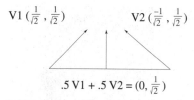

**FIGURE 5.3.6** *The linear interpolation of two normalized vectors resulting in a vector whose length is less than 1.*

the map contains the normalized vector of the texture coordinate, the light vector will stay normalized when interpolated across the face.

The Dot3 operation using the cubemap can be done using two texture units by configuring the texture environment as follows:

```
// Cubmap normalizer on stage 0, just pass it through
glActiveTextureARB(GL_TEXTURE0_ARB);
glTexEnvi(GL_TEXTURE_ENV, GL_TEXTURE_ENV_MODE,
          GL_COMBINE_EXT);
glTexEnvi(GL_TEXTURE_ENV, GL_COMBINE_RGB_EXT, GL_REPLACE);
glTexEnvi(GL_TEXTURE_ENV, GL_SOURCE0_RGB_EXT, GL_TEXTURE);
glTexEnvi(GL_TEXTURE_ENV, GL_OPERAND0_RGB_EXT, GL_SRC_COLOR);

// dotmap DOT3 cubemap on stage 1
glActiveTextureARB(GL_TEXTURE1_ARB);
glTexEnvi(GL_TEXTURE_ENV, GL_TEXTURE_ENV_MODE,
          GL_COMBINE_EXT);
glTexEnvi(GL_TEXTURE_ENV, GL_COMBINE_RGB_EXT,
          GL_DOT3_RGB_EXT);
glTexEnvi(GL_TEXTURE_ENV, GL_SOURCE0_RGB_EXT,
          GL_PREVIOUS_EXT);
glTexEnvi(GL_TEXTURE_ENV, GL_OPERAND0_RGB_EXT, GL_SRC_COLOR);
glTexEnvi(GL_TEXTURE_ENV, GL_SOURCE1_RGB_EXT, GL_TEXTURE);
glTexEnvi(GL_TEXTURE_ENV, GL_OPERAND1_RGB_EXT, GL_SRC_COLOR);
```

Figure 5.3.7 shows the improved results by using the cubemap normalizer.

## Per-Pixel Spotlights

In addition to per-pixel point lights as we have implemented using a 3D lightmap, another useful dynamic lighting technique is per-pixel spotlights. Instead of using a 3D lightmap, we will use 2D texture to represent the light and project it onto each face. The contents of the 2D texture will be a cross-section of the spotlight cone containing the attenuation falloff from the center. As with point lights, a tangent space light vector from the spotlight will be placed in the color component of the vertex. A falloff factor based on the distance from the tip of the cone to the vertex is placed in the alpha channel. The tangent space light vector will be Dot3'd with the vectors in

**FIGURE 5.3.7** *Base map modulated by 3D lightmap with Dot3 bump mapping and cubemap normalizer. See color version in insert.*

the normal map. The interpolated alpha in the vertex color is modulated with the color to perform the distance attenuation.

The result of this Dot3 calculation now need to be modulated by the projected spotlight texture. The spotlight can be projected onto the face by configuring the texture matrix to perform the projection. The texture matrix is first set to represent the view from the spotlight by calculating the "look-at" matrix based on its position, direction, and any vector perpendicular to the direction. The "look-at" texture matrix must finally be multiplied by a matrix that represents the frustum created by the spotlight. The texture coordinates for the spotlight texture will then simply be the world coordinates of the vertex. The result of this texture look-up is modulated with the DOT3 calculation to get the final lighting.

## References

[Blythe98] Blythe, David, "Advanced Graphics Programming Techniques Using OpenGL" available online at www.sgi.com/software/opengl/advanced98/notes/notes.html

[DeLoura00] DeLoura, Mark, *Game Programming Gems*, Charles River Media, 2000.
Dietrich, Sim, "Attenuation Maps," pp. 543–548.
Dietrich, Sim, "Hardware Bump Mapping," pp. 555–561.
[Mitchell] Mitchell, Jason, "Radeon Bump Mapping Tutorial," available online at www.ati.com/na/pages/resource_centre/dev_rel/sdk/RadeonSDK/Html/Tutorials/RadeonBumpMap.html
ARB_multitexture, EXT_texture_env_combine, and EXT_texture_env_dot3 spec available online at http://oss.sgi.com/projects/ogl-sample/registry/

# Generating Procedural Clouds Using 3D Hardware

## Kim Pallister, Intel

kim.pallister@intel.com

A great number of the games we play take place in outdoor environments, and most of those take place in environments that attempt to look much like the world around us. Because of this, the realistic rendering of terrain has become something of a holy grail for many game developers. Unfortunately, the modeling of the sky, and the clouds therein, does not get nearly as much attention, and is often added as an afterthought. Clouds usually end up being modeled with one or more layers of static scrolling textures. At first glance, these look OK, but they quickly give away their repetitive nature when looked at for an extended period.

In this gem, we'll set out to procedurally generate cloud textures that possess some of the properties that real clouds exhibit. In addition, because textures typically reside in graphics subsystem memory, we'll aim to generate the procedural clouds almost entirely using the graphics hardware. Finally, we'll address some ways to scale the technique's quality and performance requirements in order to accommodate a range of target machines.

## Properties of Clouds

By taking note of the characteristics of real clouds, it's possible to come up with a prioritized feature list for the simulation. As with all real-time techniques, we may need to forsake some of these features in the interest of speed, but we'll worry about that later.

Here are a few things that we notice at first glance:

- Clouds are animated. They both move across the sky as the wind pushes them along, and change shape or "evolve" with time (as can be seen in any time-lapse footage of clouds). Additionally, the amount of cloud in the sky changes with time. This gives us a hint that there are three variables we'll need: the simulation rate, the wind speed, and something describing how overcast it is.
- As the clouds change shape over time, small details change frequently, while larger details take longer to change.
- Clouds exhibit a great deal of self-similarity in their structure.

- The level of cloud cover can also vary from a completely overcast sky to a clear blue sky with only a few isolated clouds (or none at all). As the level of cloud cover changes, so does the appearance of the clouds. In overcast conditions, clouds become gray and dark; in clear skies, clouds tend to be bright white against the blue backdrop of the clear sky.
- Clouds are three-dimensional entities. They are lit by the sun on one side and fall in shadow on the other. On a smaller scale, it's much more complex than that, with clouds self shadowing and scattering light in all directions.
- Clouds are lit much differently at sunrise and sunset, as the light of the sun tends to illuminate them from an orthogonal angle, or even from underneath.
- Clouds tend to float at a common altitude, forming a cloud layer. Sometimes there are multiple layers. Since each of these layers is a constant altitude above the earth's curved surface, we'll likely use some kind of curved geometry for the layers of clouds.

. . . and this is just some of what we see from the ground. In an application such as a flight simulator, where we could fly up and into the clouds, a whole new set of difficulties comes up. For this gem, we'll stick to the view from the ground.

## Random Number Generation

As with almost any procedural texture, a good place to start is with the generation of some noise. *Noise* is a term used to describe a primitive that is random in nature. The noise primitive is a function that for a given input series (e.g., 1, 2, 3…), produces a *seemingly* random series of results (e.g., 0.52, –0.13, –0.38…). I say *seemingly* random because it must always produce the same result for a given input. This makes it *pseudo-random*, allowing us to recreate the same result for a given input seed value. Additionally, noise is often referred to as having a certain dimensionality (e.g., 2D noise, 3D noise, etc). This just refers to the number of inputs that are used to map into the random number function, much as one does a lookup into a multidimensional array. One of the dimensions is scaled by some factor (usually a prime number) large enough to keep repetitive patterns of results from showing up in an obvious fashion.

The generation of random numbers (or pseudo-random numbers) is a subject of much study. All approaches contain trade-offs between the complexity of the function and the quality of the result. A random number generator of high quality generates a good distribution of the random values, and does not repeat for a very long time.

Luckily, for the purposes of this gem, the results of a very simple random number generator will suffice. When we cover the specifics of the technique later, we'll be calling the random number generator multiple times per pixel with different input "seed" values. The cumulative result of this will mask any obvious repetition that occurs.

The pseudo-random number generator (PRNG) we'll start with is shown in Listing 5.4.1. It works by using the input parameter x as the variable in a polynomial, where each term of the polynomial is multiplied by large prime number. By scaling each term of the polynomial differently, we get a long series before it repeats. The sign bit is then masked off, and the number is divided down to the 0–2 range, and is subtracted from 1, to give us a range of –1 to 1.

## Listing 5.4.1 A simple pseudo-random number generator

```
float PRNG( int x)
{
    x =   (x<<13)^x;

    int Prime1 = 15731;
    int Prime2 = 789221;
    int Prime3 = 1376312589;


    return (1.0f — ((x * (x*x*Prime1 + Prime2) + Prime3)
    & 7fffffff ) / 1073741824.0)
}
```

In cases where multiple octaves are being used, you can increase the "randomness" of the PRNG by constructing an array of prime numbers and using different ones for Prime1 and Prime2, depending on the octave. For the purposes of this gem, using the single set of primes in Listing 5.4.1 is sufficient

Since we want to implement this in graphics hardware, and graphics hardware doesn't allow us to do all of the code shown in Listing 5.4.1, we'll create a lookup table of the function in a 512x512 texture map. Using a 512x512 texture map gives us ~260 thousand entries before the function repeats. We'll use this texture as a random number generator by copying part of this texture into a target texture, using a software-generated random number to offset the texture coordinates. This is illustrated in Figure 5.4.1. The copying is done using the graphics hardware to render our random number series texture to a quad in the target texture.

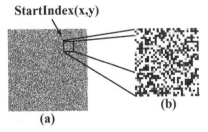

**StartIndex(x,y)**

(a)          (b)

**FIGURE 5.4.1** *A) The random number lookup table texture. B) The generated 32x32 noise texture.*

### Band-Limited Noise

Ken Perlin pioneered the technique of using *band-limited* noise as a rendering primitive. Band-limited means that the noise is limited to a certain frequency range, which can be thought of as its maximum rate of change between samples. For our purposes, this means that we want to be able to produce a series of random values spaced out according to the frequency range, with intermediate points interpolating between these random samples. We do this simply by indexing into our random number lookup table and upsampling by the desired amount, using the graphics hardware's bilinear filtering to do the interpolation for us. Getting rid of the high frequency components will make for a procedural primitive with smoother, more natural-looking transitions. This is illustrated in Figure 5.4.2.

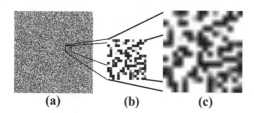

    (a)            (b)          (c)

**FIGURE 5.4.2** *A) Sampling the random number lookup table texture to create an array of noise. B, C) Using upsampling and filtering to create band-limited noise at the target resolution (the target frequency range).*

It's worth noting here than in some cases when using noise to create procedural content, bilinear interpolation is insufficient, and a higher order filtering is needed to produce adequate results. Luckily, this is one case where the lower quality bilinear filtering produces sufficient results.

An array of noise created in this fashion gives us a single noise primitive of a given frequency. We'll refer to this as an octave of noise, since we will later combine multiple octaves (multiples of the same frequency) together. First, though, we need to be able to animate our array of noise.

## Animating an Octave of Noise

If we want to animate an octave of noise, we can look at time as a third dimension that we can use to index into our random number generator. The way we'll implement this using the graphics hardware is to periodically save off our noise texture, create a new one, and then interpolate between the two from one update to the next. The rate at which we update the texture determines the frequency in this third dimension.

The interpolation is illustrated in Figure 5.4.3. This is one case where using linear interpolation results in some artifacts, as the noise becomes more "focused" at the

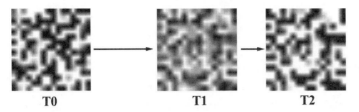

T0                                    T1                                    T2

**FIGURE 5.4.3.** *Interpolating between noise updates to animate an octave of noise. Result = PreviousUpdate \* (1-(T1-T0)/(T2-T0)) + NewUpdate \* (T1-T0)/(T2-T0). T0 is the previous update time, T2 is the new update time, and T1 is the current time between updates.*

actual sample points. Again, this artifact is not apparent after the noise is incorporated into the final effect, as we'll see. Still, it's worth keeping in mind. If we were willing to sacrifice enough fill rate, we could maintain octaves for multiple points in time and use a higher order interpolation scheme to achieve a better result.

### Summing Octaves into Turbulent Noise

A commonly used technique in procedural texture generation is to use a fractal sum, which is a summation of scaled harmonics of the basic noise function. This is referred to as fractional Brownian motion, or fBm, and is used in all types of procedural rendering techniques, such as fractal terrain, many types of procedural textures, and so forth. The fractal sum is shown in Equation 5.4.1. In it, $a$ determines how we step across the frequency spectrum ($a$ is most commonly 2, giving us f, 2f, 4f, …), and $b$ determines the amplitude of the contribution of each component in the series.

$$Noise(x) = \sum_{k=0}^{N-1} \frac{Noise(a^k x)}{b^k} \tag{5.4.1}$$

Fortunately, a value of 2 for $a$ is both commonly used in the generation of procedural textures, *and* is well suited to our hardware implementation, as we can simply implement the octaves of noise as a series of texture maps whose sizes are a series of powers of 2.

Using a value of 2 for b is also both commonly used and makes our implementation easier. The composition of the octaves of noise can be done by performing multiple render passes using a simple blend, as shown in the pseudocode in Listing 5.4.2.

## Listing 5.4.2 Noise octave composition

```
//note that ScaleFactor is needed to keep results in the
// 0-1 range, it changes {1 + 1/2 + 1/4 + …} to {1/2 + 1/4 + …}
```

```
float ScaleFactor  = 0.5
float FractalSum = 0.0
for i = 1 to NumOctaves
{
    FractalSum = FractalSum*0.5 + ScaleFactor *
    NoiseOctave(NumOctaves−i)
}
```

Figure 5.4.4 illustrates the process of animating the different octaves between updates, and building the composited turbulent noise texture.

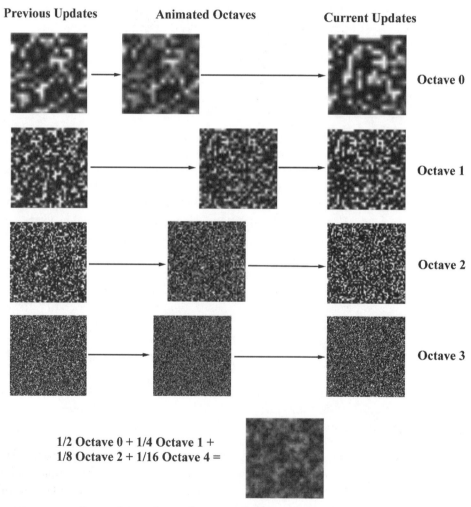

**FIGURE 5.4.4** *Composition of several octaves of animated noise.*

### Making Clouds from "Vapor"

Now that we have a texture map of animated, turbulent-looking noise, we need to do a few steps to turn it into clouds. Ideally, we'd like to use the noise as input to some sort of exponential function, giving us a sharp "condensation level" above which clouds would be visible, below which they would not. However, since this is an operation not available to us in a graphics chip, we'll have to use another method. There are several ways to tackle this.

The simplest way is to do a subtraction. Subtracting a fixed value from the texture clamps the texture at 0 where the noise was below that fixed value, isolating some clouds. This is illustrated in Figure 5.4.5.

**FIGURE 5.4.5** *Subtracting a fixed value to get isolated clouds.*

Unfortunately, we lose some of the dynamic range in the remaining clouds. We can compensate for this, however, by oversaturating and modulating with vertex colors and varying this. This is the method we use in the accompanying sample code.

Another way would be to have all the layers of texture that we have talked about so far have an alpha channel. This would let you do the subtraction and the clamping as in the previous test, but only on the alpha, and then do an alpha test to mask off the region without clouds without losing any dynamic range in the clouds themselves. A different problem occurs here, however. Since the alpha test is done before any filtering, rough jagged edges occur unless we use a really high-resolution destination texture.

Another way that may be better still would be to use some sort of dependent texture lookup, where one texture's color value affects the location from which a texel is fetched in a subsequent stage. One example of a texture- dependent lookup is the BumpEnvMap render state supported by some hardware under DirectX. In the future, as more hardware supports this type of operation, it may become feasible to encode an exponential function in a texture map and simply look up the result.

## Mapping It to the Sky Geometry

Having prepared the cloud texture in Figure 5.4.5, we can map it to the sky geometry. Your choice of geometry depends on your application. The sample application uses something we've called a "skyplane," which is simply a rectangular grid of triangles, with the vertices pulled down over the radius of a sphere. You can imagine this as dropping a piece of cloth over the surface of a beach ball. It's not perfect, but makes mapping the texture easy. The skyplane is illustrated in Figure 5.4.6.

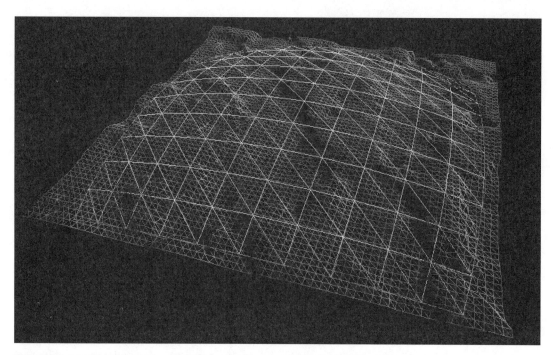

**FIGURE 5.4.6** *Terrain geometry and the skyplane used for the cloud texture.*

## Feature Creep

At this point, we can do many things to the clouds, depending on how much application time and graphics hardware fill-rate we want to consume. Some of these are implemented in the sample code; others are listed to provide you with ideas for your own implementation. Some of the things that can be added include:

- Noise-driven wind direction, cloud cover. Some dramatic results can be achieved by using other noise functions to modify some of our other variables over time, so that, for example, the wind can change direction and the level of cloud can increase or decrease over hours or days.
- Embossing the clouds to give them a 3D appearance. This will require an extra pass, and will require some modification of the vertex UV values. The vertices are given a second set of texture coordinates and are offset/scaled according to the direction of the sun. The clouds are darkened on the side away from the sun, and brightened on the side toward the sun.
- The clouds can cast shadows on the ground simply by using the end result texture with a subtractive blend. Your terrain will need to have another set of texture coordinates, or will have to use texture projection in order to do this.
- Modify lighting and/or lens flare intensity. Since we know how the texture is mapped to the geometry, and we know the angle of our sun, we can calculate the

exact texel or group of texels corresponding to where the sun is in our line of sight. We can use this to vary the level of lighting on our terrain, or to fade out a lens flare temporarily. Note that when modifying lighting, increased cloud cover should decrease the intensity of the directional light of your "sun" in the scene, but should *increase* the ambient level, since in reality the clouds will scatter the sunlight in all directions.

## Hardware Limitations

Allowing the graphics hardware to do much of the grunt work in this technique allows us to achieve better performance than we'd be able to achieve if we had to manually lock and modify the texture at every frame. Unfortunately, it comes with some drawbacks as well. The drawbacks fall in four areas:

- **Render-to-texture support**. The technique spelled out in this gem uses this capability extensively. However, support for rendering to texture surfaces is far from ubiquitous. Detecting support for the capability has become easier with more recent API releases, but can still be tricky. In cases where rendering to texture surfaces is not supported, a workaround of copying from frame buffer to texture can be used, but performance may suffer.
- **Limited precision**. Current hardware stores texture and render target values as integers, usually in 32 or 16 bits per pixel. Because we are essentially working in "monochrome," generating a texture in shades of gray, we are limited to 8 bits per pixel, and in the worst case, 4! The latter gives noticeable artifacts. Note that this means that the high-frequency octaves are only contributing a few bits of color data to the final result due to this problem.
- **Limited dynamic range**. Because the integer values represent data in the 0-1 range, we are forced to scale and offset values to fit in this range. Since our noise function originally returned values in the –1 to 1 range, we had to compress these to fit them into our available range. This requires extra work, and also amplifies the artifacts from the limited precision
- **Limited hardware instruction set and capabilities**. The limited instruction set of the graphics hardware limits us in terms of what we are able to do. It would have been nice to feed the turbulent noise texture into a power function, perhaps as the exponent, to generate some interesting results, but we are instead limited to simple arithmetic operations. As well, we make much use of render-to-texture, which isn't available on all hardware. In the future, as hardware capabilities increase, this will be less of an issue.

## Making It Scale

If we want to use this technique in a commercial game project, and are targeting a platform such as the PC, where performance can vary from one machine to the next, then we need to worry about scalability of the technique. Even if targeting a fixed platform, the game may have a varying load, and we may want to scale back the quality and performance requirements of the technique in heavy load situations.

There are several ways in which the technique can be scaled:

- **Texture resolution**. The resolution of the textures used at the various intermediary stages could be reduced, saving memory and fill-rate consumption. Note that scaling color depth is most likely not an option here, since the artifacts show up pretty quickly when using 16bpp textures.
- **Texture update rate**. Not every texture need be updated per frame. Particularly if the simulation rate is slow, the interpolating textures do not need to be updated at every frame as we did in the sample code.
- **Number of octaves used**. The sample code uses four octaves of noise, but using three might provide an acceptable result. Similarly, five octaves might give slightly better quality on systems that have the horsepower.

## Conclusion

Figure 5.4.7 displays the final result of the procedural cloud example program.

**FIGURE 5.4.7** *Final result of procedural cloud example program.*

We hope this technique has provided you with some insight into procedural texture generation, using clouds as an example, and how to get graphics hardware to do much of the per-pixel work needed in generating dynamic procedural textures.

As hardware grows more capable, so will the techniques in which we can generate these textures in real time. We encourage you to try your own experiments and share them with the development community.

## References

[Ebert et al, 98] Ebert, David S., et al, *Texturing and Modeling: A Procedural Approach*, AP Professional Inc., 1999. ISBN: 0-12-228730-4.

[Elias99] Elias, Hugo, "Cloud Cover," available online at http://freespace.virgin.net/hugo.elias/models/m_clouds.htm, offers a software-only technique similar to this one.

[Pallister99] Pallister, Kim, "Rendering to Texture Surfaces Using DirectX 7", available online at www.gamasutra.com/features/19991112/pallister_01.htm

# 5.5

# Texture Masking for Faster Lens Flare

## Chris Maughan, NVIDIA Corporation

cmaughan@nvidia.com

This gem introduces a novel way in which to generate texture information from pixels already rendered to the frame buffer. The technique can be used in several different ways, but is presented here as a solution to the common problem of occluded lens flare. Many games attempt to read back pixels generated in the frame buffer in order to determine exactly what was visible in the final scene. I will present a technique that works without CPU assistance, and does not require reading data from the graphics card. I will also outline the reasons why reading back information from the graphics card can be a costly operation and should be avoided if possible.

## Lens Flare Occlusion

Many modern games add lens flare to the scene to increase realism. The lens flare is usually applied as the last item in the scene, using a 2D texture map rendered as a billboard over the frame. A complication with this technique is that objects in the scene can occlude the sun image, and in this case, the correct visual result is a lessening of the lens flare intensity. A good way to visualize this is to imagine yourself driving along a road lined with trees on a sunny day; if the sun is below the tree line, you will experience a flickering as your viewpoint through the trees changes and the amount of light reaching your eyes varies.

The usual approach to detecting the occlusion of the sun is to first render the objects in the scene, including the sun itself. Then we read back the frame buffer data around where the sun pixels would be and deduce the amount of sun visible in the scene. We can do this in two ways: we can read back the color buffer and look for values that match our sun color, or we can read back the Z-buffer and look for Z values that are as far away as the sun. The ratio of visible to occluded sun pixels gives us a handy approximation of the intensity of the lens flare. We are now ready to draw our lens flare by blending it onto the final scene using an alpha value to set its intensity.

## Hardware Issues

The preceding approach is generally taken when rendering lens flare in games. While it can work well, it causes unnecessary stalls in the graphics pipeline that can seriously impair performance.

Modern graphics pipelines are very deep. Polygon data is not only queued inside the graphic chip pipeline, but it is also queued in a large "staging" buffer. Typically, many thousands of polygons will be queued in the staging buffer by the game, and the graphics chip will drain the buffer as it draws polygons into the frame buffer. In a good parallel system, the game can be doing useful work on the CPU, such as physics, AI, and so forth, while the graphics chip (GPU) is draining the staging buffers. Indeed, this is to be encouraged if the maximum performance of the system is to be achieved. Figure 5.5.1 illustrates a system with optimal parallelism.

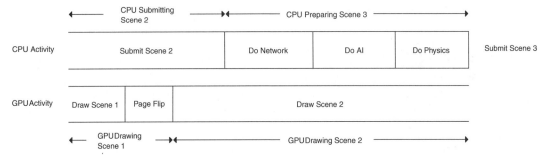

**FIGURE 5.5.1** *Parallelism of the GPU/CPU in an ideal game engine.*

Now consider the situation that occurs when the game has submitted all the polygons for the current scene to the graphics chip. Much of the scene may still be queued in staging buffers and will not be drawn for some time. The next thing our game wants to do is to read back the contents of the scene to determine the sun visibility for the lens flare calculation. Here lies the first part of our problem. In order to read the completed scene from the frame buffer, we must wait for the rendering to complete, and in order for this to happen, the whole pipeline must be flushed. While waiting for this to occur, the CPU is effectively unused, as it is simply idle inside the graphics card driver waiting for the rendering to complete. Ideally, we want the GPU and the CPU to be concurrently active at all times. One potential solution to this problem is to insert our physics/AI code after the scene render, but before the lens flare calculation. In this way, the CPU will be busy while the GPU is rendering the polygons.

In this case, if our CPU work is more than the GPU work, then we do not have a problem—although arguably the system is unbalanced because the GPU is waiting for the CPU to finish its work, when it could be doing more rendering (Figure 5.5.2).

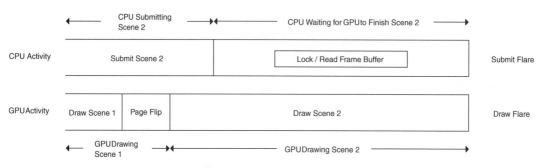

**FIGURE 5.5.2** *Pipeline stall caused by flush at end of rendering.*

If our CPU work is less than the GPU work, we will again stall when we try to read back the lens flare data. This is undesirable because ideally we would like to be preparing the next frame of the game on the CPU while the last one completes on the GPU (Figure 5.5.3). Parallelism is the key here, and inserting any stalls can hurt it considerably.

The story does not, however, end here. After losing our concurrency, there is another problem. Reading back data from a current generation graphics card is a slow operation, and in some cases cannot be done at all.

While most graphics cards run at AGP 2x/4x speeds when written to, reading back from them is still limited to PCI speeds—this is inherent in the nature of the AGP bus design as it stands today. The result is that for a 32-bit frame buffer, we can only read pixels at a maximum rate of 66Mhz, with no caching or bursting behavior. Therefore, reading an area of 256 * 256 from the graphics card will take

$$1 / (66,000,000 / (256 \times 256)) = \sim1 \text{ millisecond.}$$

This assumes a 256-square pixel area of the sun projected onto the screen. If we are standing nearer to the light source—for example, a street-lamp—then the projected area can vary quite considerably until the read back becomes very significant. Even if we are willing to take this hit in performance, there is no guarantee that the

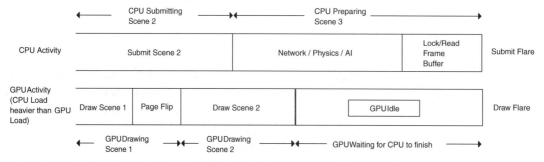

**FIGURE 5.5.3** *Pipeline stall caused by flush before end of frame, after CPU work.*

graphics card will allow us to read back the data at all; in fact, many do not. Most will not allow reading of the Z-Buffer, many do not allow reading of the frame buffer, and none will allow reading of an antialiased buffer.

## Texture Masking

How can we alleviate the stalls caused by reading the frame buffer? We arrive at the solution through a bit of lateral thinking. We know that we cannot pass a value down from the CPU to modulate the lens flare brightness, for the reasons outlined previously. This leaves only one possibility: that we modulate the lens flare value with data already generated in the graphics memory on the card. Such a value must be in the form of a texel in a texture map, and this texel needs to contain either a luminance color value or an alpha value. We know that we can render to a texture map in Direct3D or OpenGL. The remaining problem is how we actually generate this texel based on a set of source pixels. The solution lies in the alpha blending capabilities of the GPU. The alpha blending unit is basically an adder, which adds a value in the GPU to one on the frame buffer, and can be used to accumulate color information. Add to that the realization that objects in our scene are rendered in a color of our choosing, and a suitable solution presents itself. The following steps show how to achieve the result we need.

### Step 1

Create a texture map of 16x16 texels. Call this the *sun map*. We will be rendering the sun itself and the occluding geometry onto this map. The surface format should have at least 8 bits per color component. On typical graphics hardware, this equates to a 32-bit ARGB surface. The sun map is chosen to be 16x16 because it contains 256 texels. As we will see later, we are not limited to a 16x16 size, and can play tricks with filtering to reduce it if necessary.

### Step 2

Create a 1x1 texture map. This is the *intensity map*. This is the final destination of our intensity data. We only need a single texel of information, but of course, this texture can be as big as needed to satisfy particular hardware requirements. Again, the format of this surface should be at least 8 bits per color component.

### Step 3

Render the portion of the scene containing the sun into the sun map. There are many ways to do this, but we choose a simple approach. We orient the viewer to look directly at the center of the sun. We also set the projection matrix so that the sun fills the viewport. The front plane is just beyond the eye; the back plane is just behind the sun. The sun map is cleared to black. We render one of two colors to the sun map. The image of the sun itself is rendered in white. The occluding geometry is rendered in black, thus covering any of the sun values already rendered. If the sun is rendered first, Z-Buffering is not required, as we are just interested in the occlusion, not the depth ordering. The sun map now contains 256 values, some of which are white, some of which are black. In 32-bit color, this means that the frame buffer contains 0xFFFFFFFF or 0x00000000. Note that for consistency, I set up the alpha channel in the same way as the color channels, enabling the option of alpha blending or color blending.

### Step 4

Render 256 pixels to the 1x1 intensity map. Draw them using point-lists or point-sprites if the API/hardware supports them, as they require less transform work than full triangles or quads. Set texture coordinates so that each sun map texel is referenced once. Set the alpha blend unit to add the color information of each of the source sun map texels to the destination intensity map. We also want to sample only one texel at a time from the sun map, so we set texture sampling to point sampling mode. Note that we are writing to a single destination pixel multiple times, with different source texels. One further step is that we blend each sun map texel with a constant value of 0x01010101. This is actually 1/255 in each of the color channels. The result is that the modulated sun map values will either be 0x01010101 if the source sun map texel is white, or 0 if the source sun map texel is black. I choose white and black as values in the sun map because these are generally easy to achieve during rendering, and can be displayed for diagnostic purposes in the demo.

The trick here is that we are adding 256 values from the sun map, to form a possible range of 256 values in the intensity map. The brighter the pixel in the intensity map, the more visible sun pixels there are in the sun map, and hence the scene itself. We have "masked" out the texture results of a previous rendering and added them together. As we will see later, this texture masking approach can be very useful for various applications.

The whole process has used the GPU to generate lens flare intensity from information in the frame buffer. Because the GPU pipeline is serialized, we know that the intensity information will be written before we generate our lens flare, and that the pipeline does not require a flush during the operations discussed earlier. Further, because we have decoupled lens flare intensity generation from scene rendering, we can perform these steps at any point, and potentially use the resulting value during rendering of the actual scene rather than at the end. We could perhaps use this value to modify the ambient intensity of the scene to simulate the viewer's pupils' reaction to the light—an option that is not open to us with the lock method unless we want to render the entire scene twice.

## Performance Considerations

The presented algorithm may seem like a lengthy procedure, but is in fact a relatively inexpensive operation when compared to reading the frame buffer and flushing the pipeline. Consider that we are adding a little GPU work at the end of the frame, which can continue to run in parallel with the rest of our engine. The caveat is that the rendering of the sun map must be quick. We can ensure that this is the case by considering that the sun is usually above ground, and that the field of view to the sun is actually very small. This considerably reduces the number of objects we have to consider, and allows quick rejection of those that we do via frustum culling. We can do early-out rejection if we determine that any of our objects completely occlude the sun, and hence we do not draw the lens flare at all. A further option would be to render the potential occluders with less geometric detail.

Another performance concern may be the rendering of the 256 blended polygons we use to find the intensity result, but this isn't a problem because a modern GPU can render about 40 million points per second—a fraction of the time it will take to read back a potentially large amount of data from the frame buffer, issues of concurrency aside. In addition, reading back data from the frame buffer involves the CPU, which we are trying to free up for nongraphics tasks.

## Improvements

The preceding scheme works well, and it gives a good approximate result. One obvious criticism of the technique is that the sun is typically a circular object and the sun map we are using is a square texture. In fact, this is not a problem, as we can sample any texels we like from the source sun map, including a circular sampling pattern. Of course, we need to make the sun map larger in order for it to cover the required number of samples.

If we wish, we can only sample a selection of the sun map texels. To do this, we simply sample the required number of texels in the sun map, and change the modulate operation we use when writing to the intensity map to scale up our results.

Note that we are solving the lens flare problem as an example, but many of the techniques are reusable in other situations. Perhaps the intensity value could be used to darken the scene to mimic overexposure effects, or to add silhouettes or halos to characters. In fact, once we realize that the GPU has great flexibility as a mathematical solver, we can modify our algorithm in a number of ways, using the GPU as a general parallel mathematics engine. For example, we can use texture filtering to sample four texels at a time, giving an average result for four samples. In our previous example, we only need to draw 64 points to get our intensity map results if we rely on bilinear filtering to get the average intensity of the four samples. We can also do several mathematical operations by varying the blending operation, such as using modulation to scale values. This is useful if we wish to accumulate more samples in the intensity map, because we can use the modulation to add scaling to our intensity map results at the expense of dynamic range.

## Sample Code

ON THE CD

The sample demo on the companion CD-ROM gives a good idea of the performance difference between the locking and texture masking techniques, and shows how to implement the algorithm as described. Options are also available on the menu to enable the display of the sun map and the intensity map.

When running the demo on my target system, I take about a 50-percent frame-rate hit for using the lock method versus the texture masking method. The performance delta also increases the larger the frame buffer becomes. Typical numbers for the opening scene are as follows:

Texture Masking (600×500×32bits) = 53.5 fps
Frame Buffer Locking (600×500×32bits) = 27.8fps

ON THE CD

The source is heavily commented and should be easy to follow. I used Direct3D version 8 to write the demo, but the concepts are identical for OpenGL. See the README included with the application on the CD for more information on how to run the demo and analyze the results. Detail is also included on how to use the "Increase CPU Work" option in the demo to study the hit to system parallelism from using the lock call versus the texture masking technique.

## Alternative Approaches

There are two alternative approaches to lens flare that should be mentioned for completeness:

- Sometimes, a geometry-based approach is taken to determine the visibility of the flare. The approach is to scan the geometry and do ray intersection tests to determine visibility of a grid of sun pixels. While this works, it can be costly in terms of CPU compute time, and is not a useful approach when using billboards, as the source textures have to be scanned for "holes."
- Some graphics cards have the ability to do asynchronous readback of the frame buffer data. In this case, the light source area is uploaded in parallel with the rendering of the rest of the scene. This can be useful assuming that there is a suitable point in the scene after occlusion objects are drawn in which to start the readback, but before the rest of the scenery or lighting work is done. This method does of course rely on the support from the API to read back the data asynchronously, and support from the hardware to upload the data. At the time of writing, this support is not available in Direct3D or OpenGL, although extensions to both APIs have been proposed.

## References

[King00] Yossarian King, "2D Lens Flare," *Game Programming Gems*, Charles River Media Inc. 2000: pp. 515–518.

# 5.6

# Practical Priority Buffer Shadows

## *D. Sim Dietrich Jr., Nvidia Corporation*

sdietrich@nvidia.com

As game graphics become more sophisticated in certain areas, others begin to look primitive by comparison, thus breaking the consistency so essential to an immersive experience. One example of this phenomenon is the advent of detailed per-pixel lighting, which can be applied to the entire scene in real time (see the "Dynamic Per-Pixel Lighting" gem). Unfortunately, the visual complexity of the lighting outshines the shadow techniques employed by many games. This gem presents a set of techniques to improve the utility of *priority buffers*, first introduced in [Hourcade85]. Along the way, we will explore other shadow techniques, and close by discussing how to create useful hybrid techniques.

Shadows are very tricky in real-time graphics, because they are truly a scene-graph level problem, perhaps most naturally solved on the CPU. However, to achieve the detailed results and performance we seek, we must leverage graphics hardware to solve the shadow test on a per-pixel basis. Some graphics hardware currently has native shadow support, including priority buffers and *shadow depth buffers*. However, since none of these are available through a single standard interface, we will concentrate on generic techniques that should work with modern PC graphics hardware through either Direct3D or OpenGL.

Some of the shadow techniques employed by modern games are *shadow volumes*, *depth buffer shadows*, and *priority buffer shadows*. Each has various advantages and disadvantages, briefly outlined in Table 5.6.1.

Shadow depth buffers [Williams78] work by using the Z-buffer or a texture that represents per-pixel depth from the light. We will focus on techniques that work with texturing, to maximize the utility of the techniques across graphics hardware. Shadow depth buffers work like so:

***Buffer Creation Phase:***

```
For each Light
   Clear Depth Buffer Texture to 0xff
   For each Object in Light's Viewing Frustum
```

## Table 5.6.1 Comparison of Real-Time Shadow Techniques

| | Priority Buffers | Depth Buffers | Shadow Volumes |
|---|---|---|---|
| CPU Work | **Very Low**<br>Per-Light Setup<br>Object Sorting | **Very Low**<br>Per-Light Setup | **High**<br>Per-Light Setup<br>Per-Object Shadow<br>Volume Creation |
| Render To Texture Required | **Yes** | **Yes** | **No** |
| Fill Requirements | **Medium**<br>Depends on size of<br>shadow map | **Medium**<br>Depends on size of<br>shadow map | **High**<br>Depends on complexity<br>of shadow volume and<br>camera position |
| Self Shadowing | **Partial**<br>Only convex pieces can<br>self-shadow properly | **Yes** | **Yes** |
| Precision | Typically 8–24 bits of<br>ID<br>Range independent | 8–24 bits of ID<br>Typically spread across<br>lights' range | No limit to accuracy |
| Directional Lights | **Yes** | **Yes** | **Yes** |
| Spot Lights | **Yes** | **Yes** | **Yes** |
| Point Lights | **Yes** | **Yes**<br>With less precision | **Yes** |
| Aliasing Artifacts | **Yes**<br>Between Adjacent<br>Objects | **Yes**<br>Depending on Depth<br>Precision & Light Range | **No** |
| GPU Complexity | O( N * M * R * P )<br>N = Vertices of caster<br>R = Vertices of receiver<br>P = Number of receivers<br>M = Size of shadow map | O( N * M * R * P )<br>N = Vertices of caster<br>R = Vertices of receiver<br>P = Number of receivers<br>M = Size of shadow map | O( N * R * P * E )<br>N = Vertices of caster<br>R = Vertices of receiver<br>P = Number of receivers<br>E = Depth complexity<br>of shadow volume |

```
Compute Per-Pixel Depth from Light from 0x0 to 0xff
Render Object into Texture, using Depth as the color
```

### Shadow Testing Phase:

```
For each light
  Create texture matrix to move vertices from view space to
  Light's view space
  For each Object in Player's Viewing Frustum
    Compute Per-Pixel Depth exactly as above
    Select Depth Buffer as a Texture
    For each vertex
      Project vertices to the Depth Buffer Texture
    For each pixel of Object
      Compare Computed Depth to Closest Projected Depth
```

```
If Computed Depth > Closest Projected Depth
   Pixel is in Shadow
Else
   Pixel is Lit
```

Priority buffers work by first assigning each "Object" a unique ID from 0x0 to 0xFE. An object is defined as something that can't shadow itself. Examples of objects with perfect shadowing through this technique are convex objects and individual triangles. Priority buffer shadows work like so:

### Buffer Creation Phase:

```
For each Light
   Set Priority Buffer Texture as the Render Target
   Clear Priority Buffer Texture to 0xff
   For each Object in Light's Viewing Frustum
     Assign ID from nearest to Light = 0x0 to farthest from Light
        <=0xFE
     Render Object into Texture, using ID as the color
```

### Shadow Testing Phase:

```
For each light
   Create texture matrix to move vertices from view space to
    Light's view space
   For each Object in Player's Viewing Frustum
      Select ID as a constant color
      Select Priority Buffer as a Texture
      For each vertex
        Project vertices to the Priority Buffer Texture
      For each pixel of Object
        Compare constant ID to Closest Projected ID
        If Constant ID > Closest Projected ID
          Pixel is in Shadow
        Else
          Pixel is Lit
```

## Comparing Priority Buffers to Depth Buffers

Priority buffers and depth buffers are very similar techniques—we could even use the same pixel shader program or texture stage setup to perform either method.

Depth buffers have the advantage that each pixel is treated individually by having its own depth value measured from the light. This allows this technique to perform self-shadowing.

One downside of depth buffer shadows is that the depth from the light is typically computed over the light's entire range of influence. If we use an 8-bit color or alpha channel to represent depth from the light as in our previous example, only 8 bits are available for the entire light's range. This is not adequate precision for many scenes to support both proper inter-object shadows as well as intra-object self-shadowing (Figure 5.6.1).

At Light ┣━━━━━━━━━━━━━━━▶┫ At Light's Maximum Range

**FIGURE 5.6.1** *Depth from light.*

Priority buffers overcome this difficulty by assigning each object its own ID, based on its sort order in terms of distance from the light. This way, the precision is effectively infinite over the entire range. Any range can be equally accommodated, at the cost of losing self-shadowing. Because each object has its own ID, individual sections of the object can't shadow each other.

Figure 5.6.2 is an example where two chairs are rendered with different IDs from the point of view of the light. The background is normally white, but is cleared to black to make the chairs show up better.

**FIGURE 5.6.2** *Priority buffer from light's view point.*

There are several ways to overcome the self-shadowing problem without specialized hardware. One way is to break up the model into convex pieces, perhaps each hierarchy level of an animated model or even down to the individual triangle level. One natural approach for static geometry is to break up the world into convex pieces using OctTree or BSP nodes, and assign an ID to each node. Unfortunately, this approach exacerbates a serious problem—aliasing.

## Resolving Aliasing Problems

Aliasing artifacts most obviously occur when two nonoverlapping objects with different object IDs shadow each other. This occurs due to the simple fact that the back buffer and priority buffer texture are at different resolutions and different orientations. This causes a point sample of the priority buffer to fall somewhere within one texel of the desired sampling location. Sometimes the sample selects the desired texel, sometimes one of its neighbors (Figure 5.6.3).

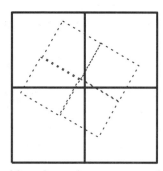

**FIGURE 5.6.3** *The dashed line shows the texture sample positions lined up with the priority buffer. This mismatch of size and orientation causes aliasing.*

Bilinear filtering is used for texture mapping in order to reduce this type of aliasing by performing a weighted average of a 2x2 footprint of texels. Unfortunately, averaging object IDs makes no sense. If we have texels with object ID 100 and 200, and we average them, we get object ID 150. This object ID may represent a completely different object, so we see that straight bilinear filtering won't do the trick.

One way to solve the aliasing problem is to offset the texture by half a texel so that the sample falls exactly in between a 2x2 area of texels. Then, perform the shadow test four times, and only allow a shadow when all four samples agree that the pixel should be in shadow. This solves the aliasing problem, but costs four texture fetches, and multiple passes on dual-texture hardware.

An improvement to this technique is to "pre-jitter" the priority buffer. After creating the priority buffer as we did earlier, by putting the object ID in the alpha channel of the priority buffer, we perform another render-to-texture pass into a texture the same size as the original priority buffer. With this pass, we perform the "pre-jitter" by taking the four texels that neighbor the original sample location in the priority buffer, and replicating them into R, G, B, and A of the destination color.

This way, during the shadow testing phase, a single texture fetch of the "pre-jittered priority buffer" gives all four neighboring samples. With a bit of per-pixel math, all four shadow tests can be computed at once, their results combined, and the aliasing eliminated, by only shadowing the pixel if all four tests agree it should be in shadow (Figure 5.6.4).

This pre-jitter technique is useful because there is only one jitter step per frame, but many shadow testing operations, so it exploits coherency for faster rendering.

Figure 5.6.5 is a pre-jittered version of Figure 5.6.4. Note how the chairs have a colored outline, which indicates that the R, G, and B channels represent different IDs after jittering.

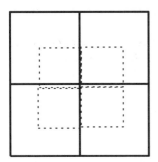

**FIGURE 5.6.4** *The dashed line shows the texture sample positions lined up with the four nearest neighbors of the priority buffer.*

**FIGURE 5.6.5** *Pre-jittered priority buffer from the light's view point.*

## Hybrid Approaches

Perhaps the best use of priority buffer shadows is to use them for inter-object shadows between objects that don't come close to intersecting, and thus won't alias, and use another technique altogether to handle self-shadowing. So, if two objects are far enough apart such their bounding spheres don't intersect, the priority buffer method is used to shadow the further one with the closer one. In the case where the bounding spheres do intersect, there is a chance that the objects may alias with each other, so they use the same object ID, and they must be shadowed with the self-shadow test.

One approach that combines priority buffers for inter-object shadows and depth buffers for self-shadowing is to encode the 8-bit object ID into the red channel of a texture in a vertical ramp, and an 8-bit depth in the green channel in a horizontal ramp. The idea here is that the 8-bit depth buffer is only used for self-shadowing within a single object, so the 8 bits can be spread across a single object's range. This gets around a major problem with standard depth buffer shadows: limited precision across the light's range (Figure 5.6.6).

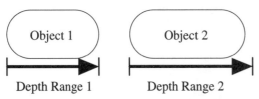

**FIGURE 5.6.6** *Depth measured across each object.*

The technique to perform this dual shadow test is a subtraction and a dot product, replicated into the alpha channel. Alpha testing can be used to determine whether a pixel is in shadow, thus allowing this technique to work on any hardware with dual texturing and a dot product operation.

Another hybrid approach is to use stencil shadow volumes only for self-shadowing. After computing the shadow volume edges, we can extrude them only to the edge of the object's bounding box, instead of extending them to the limit of the light's range. This reduces the impact of the major drawback to stencil shadow volumes—the fill rate cost when the shadow volume extends across the camera's view plane. By restricting them to self-shadowing only, we also have the benefit that we can completely skip the self-shadowing test for objects outside the viewing frustum.

Yet another way to achieve self-shadowing with priority buffers is to perform ray casts of each vertex to the light source on the CPU, and check for the ray intersecting the object. If the ray intersects a solid portion of the object, set the alpha channel of the vertex diffuse color to zero. During the lighting process, modulate this alpha value with the lighting contribution of the light. As shown previously, this could be performed only on objects in the viewing frustum, and even dropped altogether for distant objects. A variant on this approach is to perform the test only on chunks of the model—say, one for each model hierarchy level—like the shoulder or forearm. This makes a nice level-of-detail option for distant and/or unimportant models.

## Summary

Priority buffers are a great way to get inter-object shadows that bypasses the issue of limited precision across a light's range. Although standard priority buffers are not ideal for handling self-shadowing, other techniques can be paired with them to achieve a complete shadowing solution for real-time games.

## References

[Dietrich00] Dietrich, D. Sim, "GDC 2001 Presentation—Shadow Techniques," www.nvidia.com/marketing/developer/devrel.nsf/bookmark/0419FBACDE043 ABF88256A1800664C06.

[Hourcade85] Hourcade, J.C., and A. Nicolas, "Algorithms for Antialiased Cast Shadows," *Computers and Graphics*, vol. 9, no. 3, pp. 259–265, 1985.

[Williams78] Williams, Lance, "Casting Curved Shadows on Curved Surfaces," Computer Graphics (SIGGRAPH '78 Proceedings), vol. 12, no.3, pp. 270–274, August 1978.

# 5.7

## Impostors: Adding Clutter

### Tom Forsyth, Mucky Foot Productions
tomf@muckyfoot.com

*Impostoring* is a term that is probably not familiar to many reading this. However, the concept may be—it has surfaced in various forms many times in the history of 3D graphics. Simply put, it is about using sprites in a 3D scene, but instead of an artist drawing or rendering the sprites beforehand, they are updated on the fly. (In fact, the academic version of impostoring started when rendering things such as cityscapes for VR fly-throughs, and was not updated dynamically—that came in later versions. However, the dynamic update version is far more interesting to games, since by their nature they deal with scenes that change.)

Instead of rendering a high-triangle object every frame, the high-triangle object is occasionally rendered to a texture—usually on the order of once every 5 to 50 frames. Every frame this texture is mapped onto a much lower-triangle object which is drawn in place of the complex object.

The main target for impostors is scenes with lots of small static objects in them—clutter. Each of these objects will use an impostor, and most will be redrawn at a much lower rate than the main scene's frame rate. By doing this, the perceived triangle density is far higher than the actual density, and the visual quality allowed by all these incidental objects considerably increases the realism of the scene. The main difference between an office or house in a computer game and the real thing is the amount of clutter present.

Although newer cards have huge triangle throughput, using impostors is still of great benefit. The bus bandwidth (in the case of the PC, this is the AGP bus) is usually a bottleneck, and reducing this for some objects allows greater triangle detail to be used on others. An impostor is a single texture, whereas rendering the object normally may require multiple textures and multiple texture layers—changing texture flushes the hardware's texture cache and may require extra texture management from the driver, the API, or the application. Drawing the object each frame requires that it be lit each frame, even if the lighting has not changed, and as lighting techniques become more sophisticated, lighting becomes more expensive. Finally, there is usually plenty of application overhead associated with drawing an object, even before a single API call is made—using impostors can avoid much of that work.

## The Whole Process

Impostoring involves a few key parts, which will be addressed separately:

- Rendering the impostor texture on the screen each frame. I call this "rendering" the impostor.
- Rendering the impostor's mesh at low speeds to the texture. I call this "updating" the impostor.
- Deciding when to update the impostor, and when to leave it.
- Driving the hardware efficiently.

## Rendering the Impostor:

### ONE:INVSRCALPHA

An impostor is essentially a color picture with an alpha channel that defines that picture's opacity in some way. Given that, there are basically two choices for this sort of blending: premultiplied alpha and "normal" blended alpha.

Normal alpha is the standard SRCALPHA:INVSRCALPHA style. The other style is premultiplied alpha—the ONE:INVSRCALPHA style.

Which one to use depends on which produces the correct result when rendering an alpha-blended object into an impostor, and then rendering the impostor to the screen. A pixel P is rendered to an impostor texture (which is cleared to black) to produce an impostor pixel I, and then that is rendered on top of the existing framebuffer pixel F, to produce result pixel R.

If using non-premultiplied alpha, the desired result is:

$$R = P \times P_\alpha + F \times (1 - P_\alpha)$$

The render to the impostor produces the result:

$$I = P \times P_\alpha + 0 \times (1 - P_\alpha)$$
$$I_\alpha = P_\alpha \times P_\alpha + 0 \times (1 - P_\alpha)$$

And rendering this to the framebuffer produces:

$$R = I \times I_\alpha + F \times (1 - I_\alpha)$$
$$= P \times P_\alpha \times P_\alpha \times P_\alpha + F \times (1 - P_\alpha \times P_\alpha)$$

This is pretty useless, and very little like the desired result. With premultiplied alpha, the desired result is:

$$R = P + F \times (1 - P_\alpha)$$

The render to the impostor produces this result:

$$I = P + 0 \times (1 - P_\alpha)$$
$$I_\alpha = P_\alpha + 0 \times (1 - P_\alpha)$$

Rendering to the framebuffer produces this:

$$R = I + F \times (1 - I_\alpha)$$
$$= P + F \times (1 - P_\alpha)$$

which is perfect. Premultiplied alpha is not used by many apps, but it is fairly simple to adapt an existing engine to use it.

One thing to note is that it is now important to be precise about the alpha-channel result even when rendering opaque triangles, since the result will be written to the impostor, and will influence the result when the impostor is rendered to the screen. Non-alpha-blended (i.e., opaque) rendering to the impostor must ensure that the alpha result is 1, or the background will show through. Fortunately, this is fairly easy to do, but it does require more care with the alpha-channel result than is normally taken.

One problem with impostoring is that alpha-blend effects rendered into an impostor must be capable of expressing their effect within the premultiplied alpha scheme. This means that effects such as multiplicative color blends (basically, anything with a COLOR argument in the alpha-blend) will not work as intended, because the impostor has only a single alpha channel to express the amount of background to allow through. Fortunately, these sorts of effects are rarely used on objects that are suitable for impostoring. Note that this only applies to actual translucent effects—opaque multipass rendering that uses alpha blending to combine the passes (e.g., light maps, detail maps, etc.) will be fine, as long as the final alpha-channel value is carefully controlled.

### Billboard Quad

The most obvious way to render the impostor is to simply render a quad representing the impostored object. This gives a perfect result as long as the neither the object or the camera move.

Unfortunately, pixels are not all the app has to worry about in a 3D scene; there is also depth to consider. A quad can only represent a single plane of depth, but the object it represents will cover multiple depths.

So, for the quad, the app needs to decide at what depth to draw. Unfortunately, for some of the most common applications, there is no single depth that is appropriate. As can be seen in Figure 5.7.1, our impostored hero is standing between two walls. Unfortunately, his feet are sticking through the near wall, and his head has vanished through the far wall. Quads are no good if an impostored object is going to be close to other objects. They may be quite good for flying objects that don't usually get too close to things, though, such as aircraft in a flight simulation.

### Cuboid

The next approximation is a bounding box. Instead of a quad, the object-space bounding box of the object is drawn, with the impostor texture projected on it.

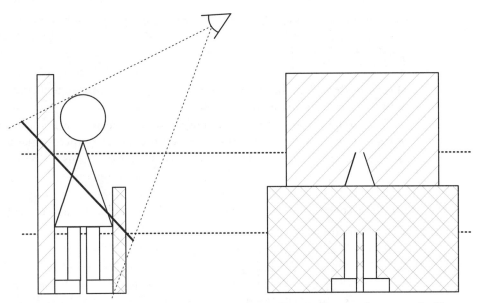

**FIGURE 5.7.1** *Side view and rendered view of a billboard impostor showing Z-buffer problems.*

Because the bounding box is a real 3D object, its Z-buffer properties can be controlled far better than those of a screen-aligned quad. In particular, its Z-buffer properties are now independent of the camera position—they only depend on the object position and orientation, which is one less thing the app has to worry about.

Bounding boxes actually work quite well. Most things in everyday life fill their bounding boxes nicely, and artifacts from intersections between bounding boxes are rare. Note that only the front or back of the bounding box is drawn. Either can be used, but I recommend the front, because many objects fill their bounding boxes, so using the front side gives a parallax shift that is similar to the real object when the camera moves.

Although a bounding box is more complex than a quad, it's not much more complex—12 tris is not going to break the triangle budget now that typical scenes have hundreds of thousands of triangles. The increase in Z-buffering stability compared to a single quad is definitely worth the effort.

### Bounding Object

There are plenty of objects for which a bounding box is not a good enough approximation, and using one leads to unnecessary Z-buffer clashes. Another factor to consider in choosing the shape of the impostor is parallax error. Most 3D scenes have a large number of elements that are stationary, but the camera will still be moving through that scene. A box painted with a picture of something on it is not going to look like that something for long when the camera starts moving. Although increasing the rate at which the impostor is updated can help, this just burns pixel and triangle rates far faster for not all that much benefit—the eye very quickly notices the lack of parallax as it moves.

Using an impostor object that is closer to the real shape of the object, although still with a very low triangle count, can give a good improvement over a bounding box. The main restriction on the shape is that it needs to fully enclose the object; otherwise, the impostor image may be bigger onscreen than the impostor object being used, and the edge of the image will not get drawn. The other restriction is that the object must usually be convex to prevent self-sorting problems, because the impostor texture is drawn with alpha blending.

### Image Warping

One of the problems with the impostor object is that it must be both convex and larger than the thing it represents. The former is required to prevent pixels being rendered twice, and the latter to prevent some pixels not being rendered at all. However, this inevitably means that the parallax as the object rotates (or the camera moves) is not going to be correct, because the impostor object is bound to be larger than the image it represents. Using a higher-tri impostor object can help reduce this in the case of entirely convex source objects. However, for nonconvex source objects, this does not noticeably improve matters—the impostor object must remain convex, and no amount of tris will allow it to match a concave object.

Another way to deal with this is to move the texture coordinates at each vertex each frame. The tri counts involved are fairly low, so a bit more work at each vertex is unlikely to hurt performance much. The principle is fairly simple—figure out where on the real object (and thus the impostor texture image) each impostor object's vertex lies when viewed from a certain angle. As this viewing angle changes, the texel that the vertex lies over will change. Therefore, for a new viewing angle, trace the line from the viewer through the impostor object vertex to the original object. Then work out which texel this part of the object was originally drawn to, and set the UV coordinates of this vertex accordingly.

### Nice Theory, What Can We Get Away With?

This is expensive and fiddly to implement. It also has loads of problem cases, such as the vertex raytrace falling down a visually insignificant "chasm" in the object and, because of the low density of vertices in the impostor object, producing large warps over the image. Another problem is what to do with vertices at the edge of the impostor object that do not map to any part of the real object at all—what happens to them? Some type of interpolation seems to be needed from the visible edges of the object out to these vertices. This is the type of work that an app does not want to be doing at runtime, however few vertices it involves.

In practice, what I have found to be far simpler, and works just fine, is to give each vertex a "parallax factor"—the number of image texels to move per degree of viewer movement. This is a factor usually tweaked by hand, and easily determines the vertex's texel coordinates at runtime. This factor is only done once for each impostor object vertex, and hand-tweaking around 8 to 10 vertices per object does not take long.

Alternatively, to generate these parallax values automatically for most real-world objects, find the nearest real-object vertex to each bounding object vertex. This distance is then proportional to the parallax factor required. The actual value depends on exactly how the factor is applied to the UV values, which depends on how the texture is mapped to the impostor object. For more complex objects, such as highly irregular, spiky, holed, or multilayered objects, it may still be better to hand-tweak the factors. This method finds the nearest vertex, but for these objects, it may be more appropriate to use some sort of average instead.

Even this simple method may not be possible because the objects are generated dynamically; for example, through animation. In this case, using a bounding cuboid and assuming an ellipsoid object inside works remarkably well for such a primitive approximation. It certainly works better than having no texture coordinate changes at all.

## Update Heuristics

On each frame, for each impostor, the decision needs to be made whether to update it that frame. A number of factors contribute to this decision. In all these cases, some sort of screen-space error estimate is made for each factor, and the factors summed. If this sum is over a global factor (which may be static, object-specific in some way, or dynamic to try to maintain a certain frame rate), the impostor is updated.

### Animation

Animation changes the appearance of the object, and at some point the error is going to grow too great. This can be quantified by a delta between the animation frame the impostor was rendered with, and the animation frame that would have been used if the object were not impostored. Doing this precisely requires the object to be animated each frame, even if an update is not needed. This can be quite a large part of the expense of rendering an object, and it is a good idea to try to avoid a complete animation step. The easiest way I have found is to do a preprocessing step on each animation and find the largest distance that any vertex moves during the animation. Divide by the length (in time) of the animation, and thus find a "maximum error per second" measure for the animation. This is easy to do in a brute-force way, and since it is a preprocessing step, this is perfectly reasonable.

Note that the human eye is absolutely superb at extracting humanoid movement from images just a few pixels high. Impostoring this motion, effectively reducing its effective frame rate, can be surprisingly noticeable, even at very slight levels. It is a good idea to have an extra bias on these animations that can place even more emphasis on them than simple mathematical screen-space error. This effectively rules out impostoring for anything but slight animations on distant objects.

### Lighting

If the lighting changes significantly on the object, it will need to be updated. Since lighting systems are extremely varied between 3D engines, this requires fairly engine-specific routines to decide what the equivalent screen-space error is. Lighting a point at the center of the object using the six cardinal normals and comparing RGB differences between the current conditions and those when the impostor was created gives a fairly good idea of how the lighting has changed. Multiplying this by object size and dividing by the distance from the camera then gives a rough screen-space error.

### Viewing Angle

Changing the viewing angle is probably the most obvious factor that decides an impostor update. Note that what is important is the vector from the camera to the object in object space. This will change when the object rotates, and also when the camera moves, both of which are important. The camera's direction of view is unimportant—unless an enormous field of view is used, the object does not change appearance much when the camera rotates, only when it moves.

### Camera Distance

As well as the direction from the object to the camera, the distance between the two is also important. Although it does not change the actual appearance of the object, as the camera moves directly toward the object, the impostor texture gradually enlarges. After a while, it becomes obvious that this is just an image that is being enlarged by bilinear filtering, and not a real polygonal object, and so needs updating. This update will render to a larger texture, and so give more detail.

### Game-Specific Heuristics

Many games also have specific heuristics that can be used to tweak these update rates. A common one for FPS games is that objects near the center of the view are usually the ones the player is looking at. These should get a slight boost to their update rates by dropping the acceptable screen error.

For mouse-driven games such as god games and RTS games, a similar tweak can be made to objects underneath the mouse cursor, for exactly the same reasons.

A distinction can also be made between "scenery" and "important" objects. Items that are purely in the scene to create an ambience, but are not usually involved in the gameplay, can be assigned a relatively large screen error. The player will not be examining them terribly closely—his or her attention is likely to be elsewhere. Therefore, these objects can be "more wrong" before the player notices the error.

## Efficiency

The main efficiency hit on most cards is changing the render target. This causes flushing of many internal caches and states, and on some cards causes a flush of the entire rendering pipeline. The main efficiency aim is to minimize these changes. The best way to do this is to wait until the end of the current scene, batching up the required updates to the impostor textures, rather than doing them as they are needed. Use large render targets, and at the end of the scene, pick the emptiest render target and render multiple impostor images to subregions of that texture.

## Prediction

When updating an impostor, the current state of the object is rendered to the texture. This is then faded in over a few frames, and then preserved for a few frames more, before in turn being replaced by a newer render. This does mean that what is visible onscreen is always out of date.

This can be improved by doing some forward prediction of impostor state. The idea is to predict what the impostor is going to look like halfway through its lifetime. If an object is currently being updated every sixth frame, when updating the impostor, the state of the impostor (orientation, position, lighting, animation, etc.) should be forward-predicted by three frames.

With games such as first-person-shooters, objects in the world are basically split into two distinct categories: those that almost never move (walls, furniture, clutter), and those that move erratically (players). The movement of the players is notoriously hard to predict, and it is probably a waste of time trying to impostor players.

On the other hand, impostoring the scenery and furniture is a far more viable proposition. Prediction for them is trivial—they almost never move. And when they do move, they usually move under control of a player; in other words, erratically. The easiest thing is to simply disable impostoring for the duration of the movement.

For god games and Real-Time Strategy (RTS) games, the problems are similar, but the movement of the camera is very different. It is usually a bird's-eye view, and most of the time it is either static (while issuing orders to units), or moving at constant speed over the map to get to a different area. Small, erratic movements are rare, which is fortunate since these are extremely hard to predict. Prediction of moving objects can also be very useful in these games, since most of them are AI-controlled. Much of the time, the objects are either stationary or walking in straight lines to a destination, both of which are easy to predict. However, both camera movement and object movement can change abruptly, and when they do, the best thing is to flag the impostor for an update very soon, or even to temporarily disable impostoring altogether.

## Summary

Impostoring is useful when trying to draw scenes with lots of fairly static objects in them. The raw triangle count will overwhelm any bus and graphics device that tries to render them at top detail, and progressive mesh methods can only do a certain amount to reduce the workload—texture changes and animation are extremely difficult to reduce in this way.

Impostoring is most effective on static objects some distance from the camera. Introducing this sort of clutter into games increases the visual quality substantially, especially since each object is still a real independent 3D object that players can interact with if they wish. It also allows key objects to be "hidden in plain sight" amongst a lot of other objects—something that has been extremely difficult to do with existing techniques and the limited number of objects available in a scene.

Even an implementation using a bounding box and some simple math produces good results for the incidental objects that are currently missing from games, but produce far more realistic scenes.

# Operations for Hardware-Accelerated Procedural Texture Animation

*Greg James, NVIDIA Corporation*

gjames@nvidia.com

Consumer-level 3D accelerators have come a long way in recent years. Today's most advanced chips sample four textures per pass and offer powerful texture addressing and pixel processing operations. Among these are dependent texture reads, where the color value sampled from one texture is used to perturb the coordinates of a subsequent texture read. Dependent texture reads combined with the ability to render to a color buffer and use that buffer as a source texture in later rendering make it possible to generate interesting textures and texture animations entirely on the graphics processor. With texel sampling rates close to one billion per second, these procedural texture effects run very fast and are practical for real-time 3D-accelerated scenes.

Techniques for procedural texture generation have been with us from the early days of computer graphics. There are various algorithms for mimicking natural phenomena and generating complex emergent patterns [Ebert98]. Procedural texture animation is excellent for a wide range of effects while using a tiny fraction of the memory and storage that a prerendered or "canned" animation would require. Memory to hold two or three full frames is often all that is required to generate an endless non-repeating animation. User input can be applied to these animations on the fly, and this interactivity enables richer and more engaging virtual scenes.

This gem covers a few fundamental operations for generating procedural animations, and puts these to use in specific examples that simulate fire, smoke, water, or perform image processing. With today's consumer hardware, we can even run complex cellular automata programs entirely within the rendering of a 3D accelerator and put the resulting animations to use in various effects.

## Hardware Operations

We will focus on two rendering operations that give rise to interesting procedural texture effects. The first is four-sample texture sampling from adjacent texels of an image, and the second is 2D dependent green-blue texture addressing. These operations are supported in the two most common APIs: OpenGL and Microsoft's

DirectX8. For the four-way multisampling, we will use a vertex program that is loaded into the graphics processor and operates on the incoming vertex position and texture coordinates. These vertex programs are DirectX8's "Vertex Shaders" [DX8'00] and what is currently the NVIDIA `NV_vertex_program` extension to OpenGL [NVExt2001]. For our examples, this vertex program establishes the appropriate coordinates for neighbor texel sampling in each of the four texture stages that feed the pixel engine. This pixel engine will combine the samples for various effects, and can also further manipulate the samples with the dependent texture addressing operations. The pixel engine is also programmable as exposed through DirectX 8's "Pixel Shader" programs and NVIDIA's `NV_texture_shader` extension. First, we examine the vertex processing operations.

### Neighbor Sampling for Blur, Convolution, and Physics

Many procedural texture algorithms rely on sampling a texel's neighbors and filtering or blurring these samples to create a new color value. We can accomplish this neighbor sampling for all the texels of a source texture by rendering it into a color buffer of the same resolution as the texture while using four-texture multisampling. The source texture is selected into all texturing units, and a vertex program generates four sets of independent texture coordinates, each offset by the distance to one of the texel's neighbors. By rendering a single quad with texture coordinates from 0.0 to 1.0, which exactly covers the render target, and setting each texture coordinate offset to zero, each texel of the destination would sample from its single source texel four times. We would end up with an exact copy of the source texture. By offsetting each texture coordinate by a vector to a neighboring texel, each pixel of the destination samples from four of its neighbors in the source. We can convolve the samples (combine them with various scale factors) in the pixel engine however we like.

If we use point sampling, four-sample multitexturing hardware gives us up to four neighbor samples per pass. If we enable bilinear filtering, each offset sample draws upon four texels, so we could potentially sample 16 neighbors per pass. The weighting of texels within each 2x2 bilinear sample is determined by the precise texture coordinate placement. For example, we could grab and average all eight of a texel's nearest neighbors by placing four bilinear samples exactly between pairs of neighboring texels. Figure 5.8.1b shows this, and Listing 5.8.1 presents code for neighbor sampling on four-sample multitexturing hardware. The 'X' of Figure 5.8.1 denotes the texel being rendered to the destination, and the dots indicate the sample locations from the source texture used to render it. We can select between various sets of sample locations (A or B in this case) by using the vertex shader indexing variable `a0.x`. The value of the indexing variable is loaded from a shader constant value that is set before rendering.

Offsets A          Offsets B

**FIGURE 5.8.1** *Texel sampling for the code of Listing 5.8.1, showing the sample pattern when the texel marked by the X is being rendered. The vertex program's texture coordinates as iterated in each texture unit T[0-3] are marked with dots. The hollow circle marks where a sample of texture coordinate offset (0.0, 0.0) would fall, illustrating the need for the* s_off *and* t_off *half-texel offsets. Each texel is of dimension (s1, t1) according to Listing 5.8.1.*

## Listing 5.8.1. Code and vertex program for sampling each texel's neighbors

RenderFullCoverageQuad() renders a single quad with input texture coordinates from 0.0 to 1.0 in each axis, which exactly covers the render target. These coordinates are offset four ways into the four output oT[0-3] texture coordinates so that as each pixel is rendered, it draws upon neighboring texels for its result. All-caps variables are #defines to appropriate indices into vertex shader constant memory.

```
float s1 = 1.0f / texture_resolution_x;  // one texel width
float t1 = 1.0f / texture_resolution_y;  // one texel height
float s_off =  s1 / 2.0f;     // to sample texel center
float t_off =  t1 / 2.0f;

// s,t,r,q offsets for 4 nearest neighbors (bilinear or point)
float offset_a1[4] = { -s1  + s_off, 0.0f  + t_off, 0.0f,
                  0.0f};
float offset_a2[4] = {  s1  + s_off, 0.0f  + t_off, 0.0f,
                  0.0f};
float offset_a3[4] = { 0.0f + s_off,  t1   + t_off, 0.0f,
                  0.0f};
float offset_a4[4] = { 0.0f + s_off, -t1   + t_off, 0.0f,
                  0.0f};

// s,t,r,q offsets for 8 surrounding neighbors (use bilinear)
float offset_b1[4] = {  s1/2.0f + s_off,  t1      + t_off, 0.0f,
                  0.0f};
float offset_b2[4] = { -s1      + s_off,  t1/2.0f + t_off, 0.0f,
                  0.0f};
float offset_b3[4] = { -s1/2.0f + s_off, -t1      + t_off, 0.0f,
                  0.0f};
```

```
float offset_b4[4] = {  s1        + s_off, -t1/2.0f + t_off, 0.0f,
                        0.0f};

SetVShaderConstants((T0_BASE .. T3_BASE) + SET_A, offset_a1 ..
                    offset_a4);
SetVShaderConstants((T0_BASE .. T3_BASE) + SET_B, offset_b1 ..
                    offset_b4);
SetVShaderConstants( OFFSET_TO_USE,  use_a ? SET_A : SET_B );
RenderFullCoverageQuad();
```

### Vertex Program

```
; v0 = vertex position
; v1 = vertex texture coordinate

; Transform vertex position to clip space.  4-vec * 4x4-matrix
dp4 oPos.x, v0, c[ WORLDVIEWPROJ_0 ]
dp4 oPos.y, v0, c[ WORLDVIEWPROJ_1 ]
dp4 oPos.z, v0, c[ WORLDVIEWPROJ_2 ]
dp4 oPos.w, v0, c[ WORLDVIEWPROJ_3 ]

; Read which set of offsets to use — set A or B
mov a0.x, c[OFFSET_TO_USE ].x

; Write S,T,R,Q coordinates to all four texture stages, offsetting
;   each by either offset_a(1-4) or offset_b(1-4)
add oT0, v1, c[ a0.x + T0_BASE ]
add oT1, v1, c[ a0.x + T1_BASE ]
add oT2, v1, c[ a0.x + T2_BASE ]
add oT3, v1, c[ a0.x + T3_BASE ]
```

It is important to note that for this case of rendering a full coverage quad to a buffer with the same resolution as the source texture, a texture coordinate offset of (0,0) would sample from the upper left (lowest coordinate point) of each texel. To sample from the exact texel center, we must either add half a texel width and height to the offset or move the quad by half a pixel in each axis. Listing 5.8.1 chooses to add half a texel width and height. It is essential to understand these half-texel offsets when using bilinear filtering. Without this, the bilinear sample will grab potentially undesired neighbors and produce very different results. It is essential to test and know exactly where texture samples are placed for procedural texture algorithms to work as expected. Conway's "Game of Life" described later in this gem makes a good test case.

The four resulting texture samples can be combined in the programmable pixel engine for various effects. By using the resulting image as a new source texture and applying the neighbor sampling again and again to create subsequent frames, a wide variety of interesting texture animations is possible. If the four samples are averaged, the result is a blurring of the source image. By introducing an additional $(s,t)$ scrolling amount to the offsets presented previously, we can blur and scroll a source image over successive frames. As we blur and scroll, we can jitter the scrolling vector used in each frame and multiply each sample color by various RGBA values to fade or alter the color. If we supply a steady input to the blur and upward scroll by first rendering

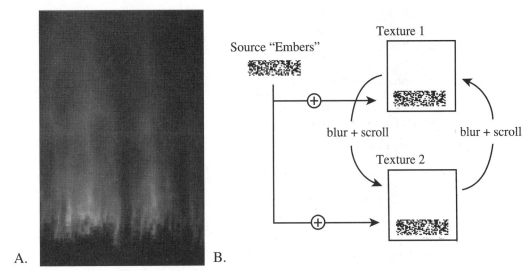

**FIGURE 5.8.2** *Fire and smoke animation using Listing 5.8.1's offsets A with a scroll offset. The bright "embers" at the bottom are rendered to the texture each frame before blurring and scrolling upward. B) shows the progression of rendering operations.*

bright source pixels or "embers" in the bottom of the texture for each frame, the result is the fire and smoke effect of Figure 5.8.2. Using just two 128x128 32-bit textures, this effect runs endlessly without repetition at over 500 frames per second on a modern graphics card. Because we cannot simultaneously render to a texture and use it as a source, we must use two textures and ping-pong back and forth between them. One is used as the previous frame source, and the other as the current frame destination.

Rather than averaging neighbor samples to blur, we can compute the differences between samples and raise this to a power for high contrast. Using Listing 5.8.1's offsets A and reducing the magnitude of the offsets to partially sample the center texel, we can perform edge detection in a hardware pixel shader program, as implemented by Matthias Wloka [Wloka2000] and shown in Figure 5.8.3. Another curious "frosted glass" effect is produced by blurring the source and differencing this blur from the original image. Figure 5.8.3d shows the result of ( src DIFF ( src DIFF( BLUR(src) ) ) ), where DIFF is the absolute value of the difference in RGB color.

Neighbor sampling and differencing can also be used to implement the physics of height-field-based water in successive render-to-texture operations. An algorithm for height-field water with vertex geometry on the CPU is presented in *Game Programming Gems* [Gomez00]. We can develop this into a series of rendering operations that use textures to represent the water height, velocity, and force. Each texel takes the place of a vertex in Gomez's implementation. Instead of sampling neighboring vertices on the CPU, we sample neighboring texels on the graphics processor. Our implementation involves six textures. Two textures represent the height of the water as

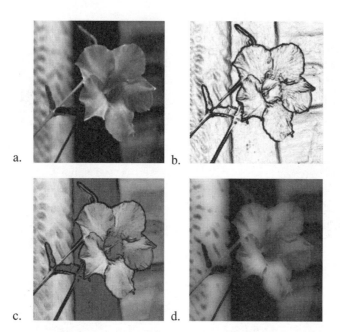

a.

b.

c.

d.

**FIGURE 5.8.3** *Edge detection and image processing. A) is the original image. B) is the result of an edge detection in programmable pixel hardware. C) shows a 50-percent blend of a and b. D) is the original minus the difference between the original and a blur of the original.*

grayscale color values (height maps), with one texture for the heights at the current time step and one for the heights at the previous time step. Similarly, two textures represent the velocity of the water, and two are used to accumulate the nearest-neighbor forces acting on each texel. Figure 5.8.4 shows four frames in the progression of an animation using this technique, and despite the use of six 256x256 32-bit textures and four rendering passes per time step, the animation maintains a rate of over 450

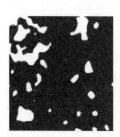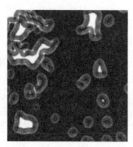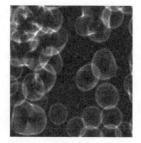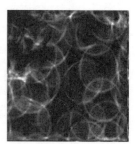

**FIGURE 5.8.4** *Initial condition and three frames of height-based water animation in the pixel processing of a 3D accelerator. Six textures are used in generating subsequent time steps, although only the output height texture is shown here.*

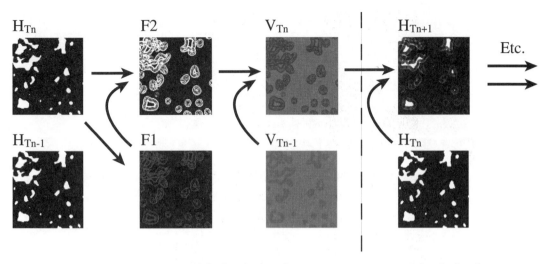

**FIGURE 5.8.5** *Six state textures used for height-based water animation. $H_{tn}$ is height for the most recent time step. F1 and F2 are used to accumulate the force that will act on each texel height. The resulting F2 is applied to the previous time step's velocity $V_{tn-1}$, and the resulting velocity $V_{tn}$ is applied to the height to create the height field at the next time step $H_{tn+1}$. Scale factors for "mass" and "time" that are multiplied into the texel values are not shown.*

time steps per second. Figure 5.8.5 shows the progression of textures used in generating one time step.

The hardware used for this example operates internally on 9-bit per component signed color values, and this gives rise to inaccuracy. Low bit values are easily lost, producing rounding errors in the physics that cause the system to decay to zero or grow to saturation. The nearest-neighbor sampling can also produce high-frequency oscillation between texel values that appears as noise. These problems are lessened by damping the system with blurring and adding a restoring force that pulls all heights gently to a midrange value. The blurring is accomplished by using bilinear filtering with neighbor offsets slightly greater than one texel width or height. The system can be driven by occasionally rendering seed droplets to the texture at random locations. By experimenting with the scale factors at which blurring, force, and velocity are applied, a stable endless animation is not difficult to achieve.

Animated grayscale height maps are useful, but we can go a step farther and use nearest-neighbor sampling to create an RGB normal map from the grayscale map. This normal map can then be used for realistic dot product bump mapping [Moller99]. The normal map can be created in a single render-to-texture pass on the graphics processor, and this avoids costly CPU work, texture memory copies, and graphics pipeline stalls. Creating normal maps in hardware this way is an elegant means of updating and animating the surface detail they represent. Grayscale height features such as bullet holes, cracks, and so forth can be rendered into the height map as the game is running, and this is then converted to a normal map on the fly. The conversion is comparable in speed to the fire and smoke effect discussed earlier. Listing 5.8.2 shows a pixel program for creating an RGB normal map from a grayscale height map in a single pass on four-sample multitexture hardware. It uses an approximation in normalizing the resulting RGB texels, and the result works very well for lighting and reflection calculations. Two passes and a dependent texture read operation could be used to produce exactly normalized RGB vectors.

Use texel offsets A from Listing 1.

## Listing 5.8.2 Code for RGB normal map creation in hardware from a grayscale height texture. The grayscale image is selected into all four texture stages, and offsets A from Listing 5.8.1 are used.

**Pixel Program:**

```
// Creates an RGB normal map from an input grayscale height map
// Pairing of RGB and Alpha instructions is not used
//   Normal map parameterization is [0,1] so 0.5 = zero component
//   along that axis (value of 127 stored in the texture).
//      Red   = positive S axis
//      Green = positive T axis
//      Blue  = positive R axis (up out of page)

// Declare pixel shader version
ps.1.1


def c5, 1.0, 0.0, 0.0, 1.0    // red mask for s axis component
def c6, 0.0, 1.0, 0.0, 1.0    // green mask for t axis component
def c4, 0.0, 0.0, 1.0, 1.0    // blue mask for r axis component
                              // (blue = up out of texture)
def c2, 0.5, 0.5, 0.0, 0.0    // 0.5 bias for red & green
def c1, 1.0, 1.0, 0.0, 0.0    // color mask for red & green


; get colors from all 4 texture stages
; t0 = -s,  0
; t1 = +s,  0
; t2 =  0, +t
; t3 =  0, -t


// Select source grayscale texture into all 4 texture stages
// Sample all 4 texture stages
tex t0              // t0 = RGBA texel at coordinate offset by
                    //      (-s, 0)
tex t1              // t1 = (+s, 0)
tex t2              // t2 = ( 0,+t)
tex t3              // t3 = ( 0,-t)
```

```
sub_x4 r0, t0, t1    // r0 = (t0-t1)*4 = s axis height slope
                     // Use _x4 to increase low contrast grayscale
                     // input
mul    t0, r0, c5    // t0 = r0 * red mask = red component only
                     // Use t0 as temp storage

sub_x4 r1, t3, t2    // r1 = (t3-t2)*4 = t axis height slope
mad    r0, r1, c6, t0    // r0 = r1.green + t0  = s and t result in
red,green
mul    t1, r0, r0    // t1 = square s and t components
                     // Use t1 as temporary storage

dp3_d2 r1, 1-t1, c1  // r1.rgb = (1 - s^2 + 1 - t^2 )/2
                     // (1-s^2) is approx sqrt(1-s^2) for small s
add r0, r0, c2       // r0 = r0 + 0.5 red + 0.5 green
                     // shifts signed values to [0,1]

mad r0, r1, c4, r0   // RGB = (r+0, g+0, 0+blue )
                     // output = r0
```

**Dependent Texture Addressing**

We have seen that a simple multisample operation can go a long way to produce various effects. There are other more sophisticated and powerful texture operations at our disposal. Dependent texture address operations enable us to fetch texture samples from one texture based on the colors of another texture, or to fetch based on the dot products of iterated texture coordinates and texture colors. This gem covers only one of the more simple dependent texture operations: the dependent green-blue texture addressing operation expressed as DX8's `texreg2gb` instruction, or the `GL_DEPENDENT_GB_TEXTURE_2D_NV` extension to OpenGL.

Dependent green-blue addressing is a straightforward process. For the pixel being rendered, the hardware fetches the source texture's color at that pixel. The green component of this color is used as the S (horizontal) coordinate of a fetch into another texture. The blue component is used as the T (vertical) coordinate. Figure 5.8.6 illustrates this with a 3x3 source texture.

Texture 2 can have any size relative to Texture 1; however, if Texture 1 holds 8-bit green and blue values, then any resolution of Texture 2 greater than 256 is pointless, as the fine resolution cannot be accessed by the coarse 8-bit values. Texture 2 provides an arbitrary lookup table for the Texture 1 input, and this can be used with render-to-texture operations to run some very sophisticated programs entirely within in the pixel hardware. We'll refer to Texture 1 as the "input" texture, and Texture 2 as the "rules" texture, because Texture 2 determines how an input color maps to a result.

With render-to-texture operations, we can use one or several texture maps to store intermediate logic results. We can also generate the input and rules maps on the fly based on previous results or user input. As you can imagine, there's quite a lot of flexibility here, and we haven't even considered dependent alpha-red lookups or the dot product address operations! Since the green-blue addressing operation relies on

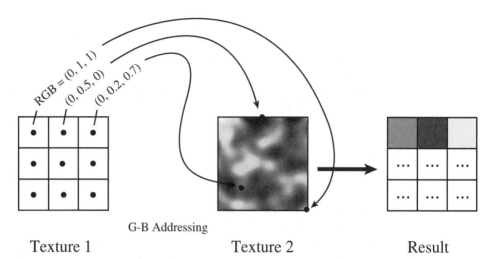

FIGURE 5.8.6 *Dependent green-blue texture addressing. The Texture 1 source is sampled at the points indicated. Each texel of Texture 1 determines the coordinate at which to sample from Texture 2, the "rules" texture. The resulting color from Texture 2 is output as the result.*

specific texture colors that are probably not the best colors for displaying in a scene, it is a good idea (and trivial) to add a second dependent lookup into a color table. This second operation maps the results of the procedural texture to any RGBA values for display in the scene. It creates a final output texture, so the user never sees the underlying green-blue textures driving the calculations. Our final example involves combining neighbor sampling and dependent lookups to run Conway's "Game of Life" on a graphics processor.

### Conway's "Game of Life" in Hardware

John Conway's "Game of Life" [Gardner70] is a popular cellular automata program. Though it does not at first seem relevant or of much use to the average computer game, it is familiar territory in which to work, and the basic operations of running the game on a graphics chip are applicable to other procedural techniques. The game can produce interesting patterns of correlated noise that are useful in driving other effects; for example, the embers in the fire and smoke effect shown previously. Implementing this game on your own platform is a good way to verify that the hardware is doing exactly what you expect. The game has easily recognizable cyclical patterns and depends sensitively on proper texel sample placement, making it easy to determine when you have your sampling correct.

In Conway's "Game of Life," each cell begins as either "on" or "off," which we represent by a texture map of white or black texels, respectively. The rules for creating the next generation are, for every cell on the map:

1. If a cell is on and has two or three neighbors on, the cell remains on in the next generation.
2. If a cell is on and has fewer than two or greater than three neighbors on, the cell is turned off in the next generation.
3. If a cell is off and has three neighbors on, the cell is turned on in the next generation.

The game requires that we sample eight neighbors and the center cell, and apply logic to the result of the sampling. The OpenGL "Red Book" [Neider93] outlines a technique for running the game using a hardware stencil buffer, but we can implement it in a more flexible manner using fewer passes with hardware capable of dependent texture addressing.

Our approach is to create a render target color buffer of the same resolution as the field of cells. Beginning with black at each texel of this buffer, we render colors additively from the source cell field for each of the eight neighbor texels and the center texel. Each neighbor texel of the source is multiplied by 1/8 green and added to the destination, and the center texel is multiplied by full blue and added in. In practice, we use bilinear sampling and the B offsets of Listing 5.8.1 to sample two neighbors at once, and multiply the sample by 1/4 green. A second pass samples the center texel multiplied by blue. The result is a color that encodes the condition of each source texel in relation to the rules of the game. Each cell's neighbor count ranges from 0 to

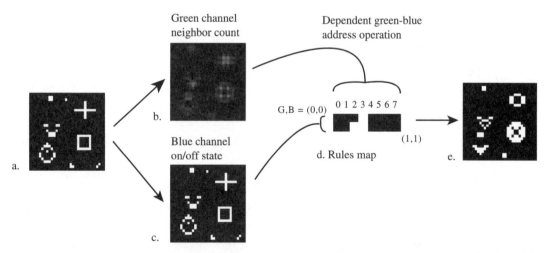

**FIGURE 5.8.7** *Steps in the production of the next generation of cells in Conway's "Game of Life." A) is the initial cell field. B) is the green component of the condition texture that is each cell's number of active neighbors. C) is the blue component of the condition that reflects whether the cell is on or off. D) is an 8x2 pixel texture that encodes the rules of the game. E) is the resulting generation of cells that will be used again as the new input a.*

1.0 in green, and the cell's "on" or "off" state is 0 or 1 in blue. Each green-blue texel is then used as the input for a dependent green-blue address operation. The operation reads from an 8x2 pixel rules texture that determines the color (white or black) of the texel in the next generation. This rules texture is black at all texels except those at (2,1), (3,1), and (3,0), which are white. These white pixels are those that the rules of the game determine to be "on" in the next generation. Figure 5.8.7 shows an initial generation source texture, the green-blue condition rendered from it, the rules texture, and the subsequent generation produced.

This simulation depends on the source texels being white and the intermediate being green-blue. We could easily perform an additional dependent texture read from the source or intermediate into an arbitrary color ramp to create a separate texture for use in rendering the scene. Also, there is no need to limit the rules texture to 8x2 pixels. Any size texture could be loaded, and this texture could encode highly complex rules, or rules that spawn pixels of any RGB value. See the online examples and source code mentioned below for a glimpse of the possibilities.

## Future Work

As graphics processors draw more texture samples per rendering pass, the 8-bit color components and internal pixel processing operations of today's hardware are squeezed for precision. It is all too easy to end up with color banding or other rendering artifacts. Future generations of hardware will almost certainly need higher precision formats, and with 16 or 32 bits per color component, there are great opportunities for hardware-accelerated procedural texture effects.

Problems of limited precision were mentioned earlier in the water simulation. 16-bit floating point values would virtually eliminate these. Higher precision floating-point values in textures and pixel calculations could enable fluid flow simulations and lattice grid-based Navier-Stokes algorithms to run in graphics hardware [Witting99]. CPU implementations of these algorithms are already close to real time in special effects houses and graphics research. Increased precision of render target buffers will also enable hardware-accelerated advanced lighting calculations that involve simple Fresnel integrals, wave propagation, and diffraction effects [Feynman85][Stam99].

Cellular automata programs give rise to a wealth of interesting animations and patterns with various degrees of correlation. Cellular automata programs do have the disadvantage of being difficult to control and engineer to a specific pattern or effect, but collections of discovered programs and convenient browsing programs exist on the Internet. Work on lattice gas automata (generally 2D surface simulations) may also provide useful animated patterns.

The future of real-time procedural texturing and animation is filled with promise. There is a vast landscape of techniques and effects to explore, and these certainly have the power to bring added realism and variety to interactive 3D games.

## Acknowledgments

Special thanks to Matthias Wloka for his work on multisampling and hardware image convolution, and to my co-workers at Nvidia for inspiring and enabling such amazing graphics hardware.

## Code Samples

DirectX 8 code for the preceding examples is posted on Nvidia's public Developer Web site (www.nvidia.com/Developer/DX8) for you to download and experiment with. The samples can be run in the DX8 SDK's reference rasterizer or on hardware that supports DX8 Vertex Shaders v1.1 and Pixel Shaders v1.1.

## References

[Ebert98] Ebert, David S., et al, *Texturing and Modeling: A Procedural Approach*, Academic Press, 1998 [ISBN 0-12-228739-4].

[DX8'00] Microsoft Corporation, *DirectX8* SDK, available online at http://msdn.microsoft.com/directx/, November, 2000.

[NVExt2001] Nvidia Corporation, "Nvidia OpenGL Extensions Specifications" (nvOpenGLSpecs.pdf), available online at www.nvidia.com/opengl/OpenGLSpecs, March 2001.

[Wloka2000] Wloka, Matthias, "Filter Blitting," available online at www.nvidia.com\Developer/DX8, November 2000.

[Gomez2000] Gomez, Miguel, "Interactive Simulation of Water Surfaces," *Game Programming Gems*, Charles River Media Inc., 2000: pp. 187–194.

[Moller99] Moller, Tomas, and Haines, Eric, *Real-Time Rendering*, A K Peters, Ltd., 1999.

[Gardner70] Gardner, Martin, "Mathematical Games," *Scientific American*, vol. 223, no. 4, October 1970, pp. 120–123.

[Neider93] Neider, Jackie, et al, *OpenGL Programming Guide*, Addison-Wesley Publishing Co., 1993: pp. 407–409.

[Witting99] Witting, Patrick, "Computational Fluid Dynamics in a Traditional Animation Environment," Computer Graphics Proceedings (SIGGRAPH 1999) pp. 129–136.

[Feynman85] Feynamn, Richard P., *QED: The Strange Theory of Light and Matter*, Princeton University Press, 1985, pp. 37–76. Although he does not label it a "Fresnel integral," this is the name for the calculation he explains in Chapter 2. This powerful mathematics accounts for all phenomena in the propagation of light by a large sum of a few simple terms.

[Stam99] Stam, Joe, "Diffraction Shaders," Computer Graphics Proceedings (SIGGRAPH 1999) pp. 101–110.

Gomez, Miguel, "Implicit Euler Integration for Numerical Stability," *Game Programming Gems*, Charles River Media Inc., 2000: pp. 117–181.

# AUDIO PROGRAMMING

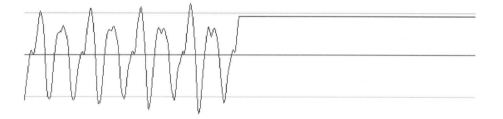

# Introduction

## *James Boer, Lithtech, Inc.*

jimb@lithtech.com

Welcome to the fascinating world of digital audio for game development! Graphics may bring an interactive digital world to life, but sound and music give a game its soul. A world without audio would seem hollow and empty indeed. Hyperbole aside, there are very few ways other than audio to so dramatically influence a player's emotions. Today's game designers are just starting to tap into this power, much in the same way Hollywood uses dramatic sound and music to play on the heartstrings of its theater-going audience.

In the past few years, advances in both hardware and software technology have brought new life to a once minor part of the game development process. Game audio is now a field of study and expertise in its own right, and we're now seeing dedicated audio programmers, much in the same way the industry currently uses AI, physics, and graphics specialists. Audio pipeline development, digital filters, 3D positional audio, occlusion and obstruction methods, API design, and interactive music techniques are all current design challenges for today's audio programmers. We'll be examining these topics and others in both this and upcoming *Game Programming Gems* titles.

For the original *Game Programming Gems*, we had hoped to have an audio section, but for various reasons, it never quite materialized. It finally came together for this, the second book in the *Gems* series, but it was still a bit of a challenge. Somewhat ironically, this happens to mirror the struggle for audio systems to emerge as a discrete field of game development. In the past, sound and music programming has too often been delegated to some junior programmer in the final months of a project. Now, games are expected to feature a bullet-point list of gee-whiz audio features much in the same manner as graphics.

Practical solutions for implementing these features, unfortunately, are still a bit elusive, with scattered resources and information across the Internet, and very few books dedicated to audio programming for games. Today, advanced digital audio techniques are finally being disseminated throughout the game programming community, including this selection of gems from noted industry professionals. I hope that you'll find them to be a valuable resource in solving your own game's audio programming challenges.

# 6.1

## Game Audio Design Patterns

### Scott Patterson

scottp@tonebyte.com

Design pattern concepts have achieved great popularity in recent years. Really, design patterns have been in use for a long time, and recently we have been getting better at categorizing and identifying them. Object-oriented programming languages are commonly associated with design pattern implementations, but even programming languages that are not identified as object oriented can provide effective object pattern implementations. Design patterns can also serve as an inspiration when building a code system. In this gem, we will use them as an inspiration for an audio interface design. This discussion assumes that we are audio interface designers and our clients are game programmers. We want to supply an audio interface to our clients that is convenient, flexible, and powerful. We will present brief summaries of some design patterns and how we can relate them to audio interface design.

## Bridge

"Decouple an abstraction from its implementation so that the two can vary independently."

### Sound Identifiers

An effective way of decoupling an abstraction from its implementation is to pass identifiers rather than things such as class pointers or references. Identifiers can be defined as numbers or strings. Since we are talking about audio, we are talking about an identifier for each particular sound. We can start and stop a sound by passing its identifier. How the audio system actually does the work to start and stop the sound is completely decoupled from the client of our API.

```
void StartSound( int nSoundId );
void StopSound( int nSoundId );
```

Also hidden is the way in which sounds are loaded and accessed. We can provide similar calls to load and unload a particular sound.

```
void LoadSound( int nSoundId );
void UnloadSound( int nSoundId );
```

Perhaps more useful is yet another identifier system for collections of sounds. Now we can load and unload many sounds at a time.

```
void LoadSoundCollection( int nSoundCollectionId );
void UnloadSoundCollection( int nSoundCollectionId );
```

It may be useful to know if a sound is currently loaded.

```
bool IsSoundLoaded( int nSoundId );
```

If we try to start a sound that is not loaded, the response could be to play no sound or play an error sound.

## Façade

"Provide a unified interface to a set of interfaces in a subsystem. Façade defines a higher-level interface that makes the subsystem easier to use."

### Subsystem Control

When writing an audio API for game programmers to use, the goal is to hide any tedious complexity of the audio system and cover the needs of all parts of the game. Writing an API with this type of goal is much like designing a class with the Façade design pattern. The complexity of the audio system is hidden from the complexity of the game code, and the connection between the two systems is our API.

We may have more than one method available to produce sounds, but having the same interface to control these sounds makes the audio subsystem easier to use. Calls to set and get master volume may look simple enough, but actually may update more than one audio subsystem internally.

```
float SetMasterVolume( float fVolume );
float GetMasterVolume();
```

Audio subsystems related to hardware synthesis, software synthesis, and streaming code may all be updated from calls such as these, but this complexity is hidden. Similar complexity may be hidden in a call that stops all sounds currently playing.

```
void StopAllSounds();
```

## Composite

"Compose objects into tree structures to represent part-whole hierarchies. Composite lets clients treat individual objects and compositions of objects uniformly."

### Engine Control

Something like a car engine may actually be composed of many different sounds. There may be rumbles, whines, clanks, and sputters all happening in concert. The volume and pitch and other parameters of these sounds may be mapped to various game parameters such as engine type, throttle level, power level, current speed, and many others. In this case, we may want to hide this complexity and provide functions specific to the type of engine we are controlling.

```
void StartEngine( CarInstance_t *pObject );
void UpdateEngine( CarInstance_t *pObject );
void StopEngine( CarInstance_t *pObject );
```

Now the internal audio code can interpret the states and parameters available in the given *CarInstance_t* object and translate them into the control of one or more sounds. Our client is able to treat engine control the same way, whether we are controlling an individual sound object or compositions of sound objects.

### Ambience Control

Control of ambient sounds can also be a situation that exhibits composite behavior. If we want to simulate an environment such as a jungle, we may be randomly playing many animal sounds. In this case, we may not have a structure in the game called *Jungle_t*, but we may know our distance from the jungle area and how excited the animals are.

```
void StartJungle( float fDistance, float fActivity );
void UpdateJungle( float fDistance, float fActivity );
void StopJungle();
```

## Proxy

"Provide a surrogate or placeholder for another object to control access to it."

### Handles

Handles provide just such a placeholder for another object to control access through. When we start a particular instance of a sound, we may want to continue to control that instance over time. Our control parameters may be anything from 3D position information to direct control over things such as volume, pitch, pan, or effects. Our start function returns a handle, and our update and stop functions use this handle to access the sound instance.

```
Handle_t StartHandledSound( int nSoundId, const ControlParams_t &cp);
void UpdateHandledSound( Handle_t hSound, const ControlParams_t &cp);
void StopHandledSound( Handle_t hSound );
```

A discussion on handles can be found in [Bilas00].

# Decorator

"Attach additional responsibilities to an object dynamically. Decorators provide a flexible alternative to subclassing for extending functionality."

### User Data

One way to allow dynamic responsibilities and associations to be given to an object is to provide user data access. If we provide a user data field that clients can set per instance of a sound, we can help clients link other responsibilities with sound instances. We can add user data access functions to our handled sound interface.

```
void SetHandledSoundUserData( Handle_t hSound, UserData_t UserData );
UserData_t GetHandledSoundUserData( Handle_t hSound );
```

### Callbacks

We can also provide a callback field that clients can set per instance of a sound. This callback could be defined to be triggered when a sound loops or has played for a certain amount of time.

```
void SetHandledSoundCallback( Handle_t hSound, CallbackFuncPtr_t pCB );
void ClearHandledSoundCallback( Handle_t hSound );
```

# Command

"Encapsulate a request as an object, thereby letting you parameterize clients with different requests, queue or log requests, and support undoable operations."

### Command Queues

We can put some or all calls to our audio API in a command queue that is processed once per game frame. We could look through this queue to determine if the same sound is being called more than once per frame, or whether a sound has been started and stopped before it had a chance to play. Viewing this queue can provide an important aid during debugging.

### Speech Systems

A speech system benefits from command queuing. Since more than one character may want to talk at one time, we can look through the queue of requests to determine who should speak next. There may also be times when we want to stop any further speaking so we clear the queue.

```
void PostSpeechRequest( int nSpeakerId, int nPhrase );
void ClearSpeechQueue();
```

## Memento

"Without violating encapsulation, capture and externalize an object's internal state so that the object can be restored to this state later."

### Pause and Restart

When we want to pause all sounds, we could return a handle to a state that can be used to restart those sounds later.

```
StateHandle_t PauseAllSounds();
void RestartAllSounds( StateHandle_t hState );
```

## Observer

"Define a one-to-many dependency between objects so that when one object changes state, all its dependents are notified and updated automatically."

### Dynamic Types

If we can pass a type number to a sound that we are starting, we could later reference that sound and any others that have been given the same type. For example, if we start all the sounds for a particular character with the same type number, then we can later turn off those sounds with one call.

```
void StartSoundWithType( int nSoundId, int nTypeId );
void StopAllSoundsWithType( int nTypeId );
```

We can also update all sounds of a particular type.

```
void UpdateSoundsWithType( int nTypeId, const ControlParams_t &cp);
```

We can also associate behaviors such as default priority and default volume with types.

```
void SetDefaultPriorityForType( int nTypeId, int nDefaultPriority );
void SetDefaultVolumeForType( int nTypeId, float fDefaultVolume );
```

It is assumed here that a priority system is in place to determine which sounds should play if limited buffers are available.

## Big Ball of Mud   (also known as *Spaghetti Code*)

The last design pattern I want to mention is the *Big Ball of Mud*. The paper with this title, written by Brian Foote and Joseph Yoder, is a witty and insightful categorization of patterns that can creep into a project quite naturally. In a way, the Big Ball of Mud is the pattern we all want to avoid, but conversely it is a pattern that may be impossible to avoid. Therefore, the wisdom here is that whether you know design patterns or not, you may be implementing the patterns that can lead to a Big Bull of Mud anyway, namely: Throwaway Code, Piecemeal Growth, Keep It Working, Shearing Layers, and Sweeping It Under the Rug.

So, how does the Big Ball of Mud pattern relate to audio and game programming? Our first goal might be to keep our audio system's internal code from being a Big Ball of Mud. Our second goal might be to keep the rest of the game code from being a Big Ball of Mud. We have some influence over the code organization by providing useful features in our audio API. We can also provide API features to help debug audio problems. Therefore, even if Mud prevails, our audio API can provide features for swamp navigation.

### Status Functions

Providing status functions can help us find common problems. We can return specific values in response to specific requests such as the number of voices playing. We can also return a string ready for display in response to more general requests such as sound status.

```
int GetNumberOfSoundsPlaying();
bool IsSoundPlaying( int nSoundId );
string GetAudioStatus();
void GetDescriptionsOfSoundsPlaying( list<string> &StringList );
```

### Logging Functions

We can provide a logging system that records audio system activity. The logging records could be directed to different types of output such as stdout or a file or a display. We can also provide a detail-level control to determine how much information is recorded. One detail level might just record all audio API calls and parameters passed. Another detail level might include internal sound buffer allocation information and other internal state information.

```
void EnableLogging();
void DisableLogging();
void SetLoggingDetailLevel( int nDetailLevel );
void SetLoggingOutputType( int nOutputType );
```

### System Disable

Sometimes the easiest way to determine if the audio system is causing problems with the game is to disable the audio system completely. When the audio system is disabled, all calls to audio API functions simply do no work. If problems still persist after disabling the audio system, then we can eliminate it as a cause. Disabling a system such as this can also make some game debugging situations less complicated.

```
void AudioSystemEnable();
void AudioSystemDisable();
```

## Conclusion

Using design patterns as an inspiration, we have outlined useful features for a game audio API. Whether we are revving engines, on a jungle safari, or just navigating the swamps, we want to make our clients happy.

## References

[Gamma94] Gamma, et al., *Design Patterns,* Addison-Wesley Longman, Inc., 1994.
[Foote99] Foote, Brian, and Yoder, Joseph, *Big Ball of Mud,* www.laputan.org/mud/
[Bilas00] Bilas, Scott, "A Generic Handle-Based Resource Manager," *Game Programming Gems,* Charles River Media, 2000: pp. 68–79.

# A Technique to Instantaneously Reuse Voices in a Sample-based Synthesizer

## Thomas Engel, Factor 5

tengel@factor5.com

**S**ynthesizers typically offer a limited number of voices that can be active at any given time, so complex allocation schemes are used to make the best use of the voices that are available. Allocating a voice at any given time is easy as long as free voices are available, but becomes quite tricky when this is not the case, requiring voices to be reused. The difficulty results from the amplitude difference between the current active sample and the next sample to be played, resulting in a sharp pop or click sound (see Figure 6.2.1). This gem presents a technique to accomplish this without any major calculation time or memory overhead.

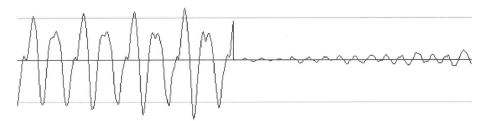

**FIGURE 6.2.1** *The amplitude difference between samples can create a distracting click.*

## The Problem

To reuse an active voice for playback of another sample, you might try slowly lowering the volume of the current sample and immediately starting the playback of the new sample. This would nicely avoid any clicks or pops caused by abruptly stopping the old sample, and would start the new sample promptly.

This is unfortunately not very practical since two voices are needed to handle this properly—and all this at a time when voices are no longer available. A possible solution to this problem would be to reserve a number of voices for just this case. Unfortunately, this also has major drawbacks. First, hardware resources are lost since you have to guarantee the availability of some extra voices at all times. Second, the number of voices that could be reallocated at once would be limited by the number of extra voices reserved for this purpose, making this a rather impractical solution.

You can remove the need for two voices by serializing the method: first fade out the old sample, and then start the new sample on the same voice. This delays the start of the new voice and lowers the volume of the old voice quite a bit earlier than one would like. It also can be very problematic when playing back a musical composition because the delay is very noticeable. The effect of the delay can be minimized by delaying *all* voice starts, no matter if reusing voices or not. This nevertheless introduces an extra global delay to the audio pipeline, and makes it more difficult to handle the voices due to added complexity.

A more elegant solution is needed.

## An Idea for a Solution

The basic idea for the solution is found within a simple question, or rather, the answer to it: What is sound? Answer: sound is a change in air pressure and, therefore, a change in the amplitude of the output signal. A constant output signal, no matter what the amplitude, will not be audible. Reallocating a voice results in a sudden, unwanted change in amplitude that generates a sharp pop sound. This sound would also be audible if one were to switch off the old sample even without starting a second sample.

The idea now is not only to stop any change or oscillation of the old sample, but also to keep its last amplitude active in the output sum. A single sample being stopped would look something like Figure 6.2.2.

This output would not generate any click or pop since there is no sudden amplitude change.

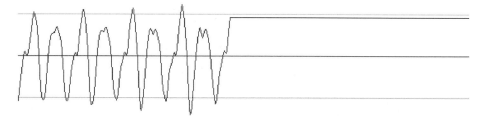

**FIGURE 6.2.2** *Holding the last amplitude from a sample prevents an undesired pop sound.*

## The Solution

The effect outlined previously can be put to good use to solve our problem. Halting the oscillation of a voice but not dropping its last amplitude simplifies things quite a bit, since all logic concerned with fetching new samples or handling the pitch for the old voice can be dropped as soon as the new sample is started.

The output would look something like Figure 6.2.3.

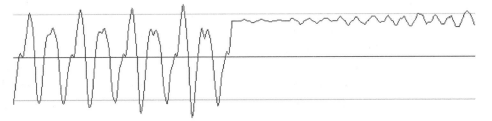

**FIGURE 6.2.3** *Starting the second sample at the final amplitude of the first.*

This has an obvious drawback: by simply halting the old voice we introduce a potentially high DC offset to the output signal, which, due to the limited maximum amplitude of the output sample, may cause the output quality to drop significantly because of clipping artifacts.

Two simple approaches can limit, and, in most cases, completely remove such artifacts. First, one should use a mix buffer of more than 16 bits to generate the final output signal. This extends the maximum amplitude, which can be internally handled. Since the DC offset will be handled together with other voices that again can lower the amplitude, this actually reduces artifacts quite dramatically. The most important step nevertheless is to lower the DC offset quickly to zero. One basically has to fade out the halted old sample (Figure 6.2.4).

All this would still require separate logic to handle the halted old sample for each voice to avoid limiting the number of voices that can be reused at once. But is this really true? In fact, one could handle all DC offsets introduced by voices being reused in one very simple handler.

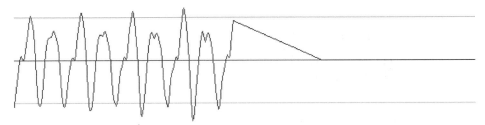

**FIGURE 6.2.4** *Fading the initial sample to zero.*

The logic is as follows: each time a voice is reused, the last value mixed into the sum by the old sample on this particular voice will be added to a global DC offset value. This value in turn will be added to the output signal once all voices are processed.

To get rid of this DC offset, which as outlined previously is necessary but unwanted, one lowers the DC offset sum on a per-sample basis over a certain time. This can be very efficiently done and does not introduce any further artifacts if not performed too rapidly. A period of about five milliseconds is usually slow enough to lower even a full amplitude DC offset to zero (Figure 6.2.5).

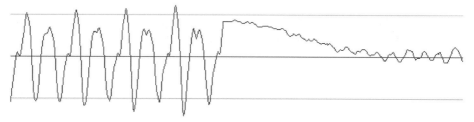

**FIGURE 6.2.5** *Fading the initial sample to zero while playing the second sample.*

## Conclusion

In practice, the theoretical negative side effects caused by the DC offset are close to inaudible. One would have to reuse extreme numbers of voices at high amplitudes to achieve some audible effect when using at least a 24-bit mix buffer.

At the same time, the benefits of this method are huge. One can reuse a voice on a moment's notice with no delay and with no audible artifacts in the output signal. The overhead needed to implement this method is minimal. The method can, with some extra work, be used in systems that feature multichannel hardware playback of samples. Just one voice has to be set aside to contain the DC offset values to be added in the form of a sample data stream generated by the CPU following the algorithm outlined in this gem.

# 6.3

## Software-based DSP Effects

### Ian Lewis, Acclaim Studios
ilewis@acclaim.com

**T**his gem introduces basic DSP concepts and techniques that can be cheaply implemented on today's PCs and next-generation consoles, including filtering, convolution, delay, and interpolation.

| DSP Technique | Purpose |
|---|---|
| Filtering | Occlusion and 3D sound effects |
| | Physical modeling effects such as strain on engines |
| Convolution | Head-Related Transfer Functions (HRTFs) |
| | Accurately simulating real acoustic spaces |
| Delay | Echoes from walls or terrain |
| Interpolation | Pitch shifting |
| | Sample rate conversion |

## Filtering

Filtering is actually a special case of convolution, but merits its own section because it is far simpler to implement quickly than general convolution.

To filter an audio signal is to emphasize or deemphasize certain frequency components, much like the "bass" and "treble" knobs on your stereo. The effect of this is extremely difficult to see on a graph of the waveform, but is immediately recognizable to the ear. For instance, applying a low-pass filter tends to make the wave sound muffled, and applying a high-pass filter tends to make the wave sound thin.

The general form of a filter is a loop where a set of values (filter coefficients) are multiplied with the incoming samples, and then added together. The first filter coefficient is multiplied with the current sample, the second with the previous sample, and so forth, so the code looks something like this:

```
for (k = 0; k < nCoefficients; k++)
{
    output+=coefficient[k] * (*(input-k));
}
```

This type of filter is called an FIR, or Finite Impulse Response filter, because its output will always decay to zero in a predictable amount of time after the input decays to zero. A slightly less acoustically "stable," but more powerful filter is the IIR, or Infinite Impulse Response filter. This design feeds the filter outputs back into the input in a form something like this:

```
for (k = 0; k < nCoefficients; k++)
{
    output+=coefficient[k] * input[n-k] +
    feedback_coefficient[k] * previousOutput[n-k];
}
```

After each sample is computed, of course, the contents of the previous *Output[]* array are shifted up by one, and the current output is placed into the bottom position. This looks more complex, but the upside is that the number of coefficients can be much smaller than the equivalent FIR implementation.

Although there are hundreds of filters available, most have musical purposes and tend to be more complex than what you need for games. The sample code uses a variant of the music-DSP source code archive's simple Chamberlin filter [DeJong01], which in its full form provides a high pass, low pass, notch, and bandpass filter that is extremely cheap and easy to implement.

Filters work really well with SIMD hardware and even vector hardware, because they're nothing but strings of multiply-accumulates.

## Convolution

Convolution is the process of taking two signals and multiplying them together so that the first signal takes on the characteristics of the second. For instance, say you had a level set in an old cathedral. You could literally make a recording of an "impulse" (a very short sound spike, like a balloon popping) in any handy Gothic cathedral, convolve that impulse with your game sounds, and presto!—your game sounds like it's inside that very cathedral. Unfortunately, convolution is extremely expensive—mostly because each output sample is the sum of one input sample multiplied by ALL of the impulse samples. To understand the code, think of each sample in the impulse file as being a coefficient in the FIR filter described earlier. This only really works for very short impulses.

A good collection of short impulses is the set of Head Related Transfer Functions (HRTFs) available at the MIT media lab [Gardner94]. Convolving with the appropriate HRTF gives the illusion of placing the sound in three-dimensional space.

A faster method of convolution involves translating both signals into the frequency domain (where each sample represents a frequency like on a spectroscope, rather than an amplitude like on an oscilloscope) using the Fast Fourier transform [Press92]. This can be useful if you're already storing samples in the frequency domain. Some methods of compression do use the FFT or one of its variants; for instance, MP3 compression uses a variant called the Discrete Cosine Transform (DCT).

## Delay

A digital delay is probably the easiest DSP effect to generate. It takes very little CPU, but it does require some RAM. The algorithm is simple: for each sample, push a copy of the sample onto a queue or circular buffer. Then read the oldest sample out of the buffer and mix it with the output.

```
DelayBuffer.push(input);
Output=input + DelayBuffer.pop() * delayGain;
```

The length of the buffer determines the length of the delay. Usually you'll want to scale the delay volume by some factor (*delayGain* in the preceding example). A simple delay can add an echo to a big outdoor scene, for instance.

More interesting delays are regenerative. In a regenerative delay, the scaled delay output samples are fed back into the delay buffer, producing a multiple echo effect that more accurately simulates natural spaces. Since the gain of each sample is reduced every time it gets recycled, eventually the echoes die away into nothing. The time it takes for the delay to die away is determined by the amount of attenuation you apply to each sample. Apply a lot, and you get a "slap-back" effect with very little presence, like you would at the edge of a canyon or near the wall of a very large building. Apply less attenuation, and you get a dense stream of echoes more like what you'd hear inside a cathedral or an echoing cavern.

An even more sophisticated reverb effect is the multi-tap reverb. In the multi-tap algorithm, a copy of the input sample is not only pushed onto the tail of the delay buffer, but inserted into other locations ("taps") in the buffer as well. This allows for much denser echoes and more realistic effects. For instance, a sound made in a large rectangular room might be pushed into the delay buffer four times, one for each wall the sound bounced off. The exact position of each tap in the buffer could be dynamically determined based on how far the source of the sound is from each wall.

The ultimate in spatial realism comes from DSP reverberation algorithms, which are an even more complex variation on the basic delay theme. Reverberation algorithms are generally too expensive to implement in software. With a growing trend to implement hardware reverb processors on PC soundcards (for example, Creative's EAX extensions) and next-generation game consoles, this article will not try to describe reverb algorithms in depth.

## Interpolation

Interpolation is the art of determining values for nonexistent samples, based on the values for known samples. That might seem a little esoteric, but the principle is one you use all the time in many areas of game programming. For instance, bilinear texture filtering is a form of interpolation, where you might use as few as 4 or 5 texels to cover 10 or 20 onscreen pixels. Resampling is the primary use of interpolation in audio. One of the most effective ways to compress audio is to reduce its sample rate, especially if the audio contains very few high-frequency components.

Sample-rate conversion (and pitch shifting, which is by and large the same thing) can use one of several algorithms. They are listed here from least to most expensive:

- **Sample doubling**, used when the ratio between the target sample rate and the source sample rate is a multiple of two.
- **Sample averaging**, where the target sample is computed to be the average of the values of the two closest points.
- **Linear interpolation**, similar to sample averaging except that the average is weighted—more weight is given to the value of the closer point.
- **Cubic interpolation**, where the nearest 3–7 points (reportedly 5 points gives the best results [DeJong01]) are approximated using a spline function, and the value of the target point is the value of the spline at that point.

Cubic interpolation does give a decidedly better result than the other forms of resampling, although surprisingly, all of the other forms sound about the same. In a case where the resample ratio is not a power of 2, simple sample averaging is the best choice if CPU cycles are at a premium. This gives a reasonable result for pitch shifting where the ratio between the source and target sample rates is between .75 and 1.5.

Cubic sampling can get you higher ratios without sounding terrible, but no simple resampling algorithm will ever avoid the dreaded "Mickey Mouse" effect. To get rid of "Mickey Mouse," you've got to do formant-corrected pitch shifting, which involves some extremely complicated calculations that are far beyond the scope of this gem.

# References

[Bores01] "Bores Signal Processing. Introduction to DSP," www.bores.com/courses/intro/ (4 March 2001)

[DeJong01] DeJong, Bram, "The Music-DSP Source Code Archive," www.smartelectronix.com/musicdsp/ (4 March 2001)

[Gardner94] Gardner, Bill, and Martin, Keith (1994). "HRTF Measurements of a KEMAR Dummy-Head Microphone." *MIT Media Lab,* http://sound.media.mit.edu/KEMAR.html (4 March 2001).

[Iowegian99] Iowegian International Corp. (1999), DSPGuru, www.dspguru.com/ (4 March 2001).

[Kosbar98] Kosbar, Kurt L. (1998), "Introduction to Digital Signal Processing (DSP)," www.siglab.ece.umr.edu/ee301/dsp/intro/index.html (4 March 2001).

[Press92] Press, William H., et al, *Numerical Recipes In C,* Cambridge University Press, 1992, www.ulib.org/webRoot/Books/Numerical_Recipes/ (4 March 2001).

[Sprenger01] Sprenger, Stephan M, "The DSP Dimension," www.dspdimension.com/ (4 March 2001).

# 6.4

# Interactive Processing Pipeline for Digital Audio

## *Keith Weiner, DiamondWare Ltd.*

keith@dw.com

## Introduction

Algorithms for Digital Signal Processing (DSP) have been readily available for a long time. Games haven't used them much, probably because of the high CPU cost. Today, however, gigahertz processors are cheap and are getting cheaper. They allow room for a certain amount of audio processing, even after the graphics engine, AI engine, and physics engine all get their share.

Games (and other applications) have a need for an audio processing pipeline. The goal is to allow a set of DSP functions with corresponding parameters to be specified for a sound. Other sounds may pass through a different set of DSP functions and/or use a different set of parameters.

A block diagram of an audio system is shown in Figure 6.4.1. A full architecture would stream sounds from any source, decrypt if necessary, decompress if necessary, process, mix, and then output. This gem describes the block labeled "Processing."

This gem presents a lightweight, but general-purpose architecture. "General purpose" is meant in two respects here. First, it allows any type of processing, even a speed changer. Speed changers are tricky because they necessitate a buffer length change. It gets even trickier if you want to allow parameter changes on the fly. Second, it's completely OS independent, and could be used on Linux as easily as Windows. The architecture demonstrated in this article has been used in device drivers, a general-purpose audio API/engine, and a telephony media control component.

### Constraints

In thinking about, and designing a system, a good way to get focused is to define the problem and all of the constraints for the solution. We've already begun, but I'd like to spell out all of the requirements in one list, and then discuss each item.

- Supports *N* sounds.
- Each sound can pass through *N* DSP functions.

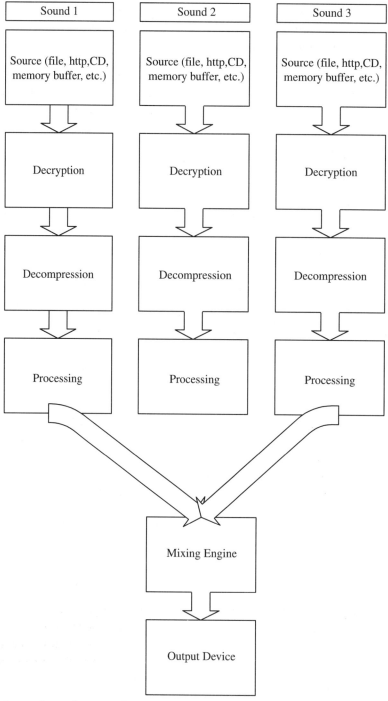

**FIGURE 6.4.1** *An audio processing system.*

- Any parameter for any DSP function may be changed at any time.
- Any function may impose a length change.
- Efficient, this is for games on PCs, not scientific research on supercomputers.
- Makes it easier to write DSP functions.

Let's drill down into each item. First, we said $N$ sounds. Monophonic sound engines have been obsolete since around 1994. If we store all DSP function and parameter information in the instance data of each sound, this will allow us to handle an unlimited number of sounds without having extra complexity.

Next is the requirement to support $N$ DSP functions per sound. This is the essence of the gem. If we wanted to pass a sound through only a single DSP function, we wouldn't need a pipeline!

Parameters may be changed at any time. This is the heart of interactivity. In a game, the sound designer doesn't know what will happen, or when it will happen. At any time, the user could enter the concrete pipe, and then certain sounds would have to have a reverb.

Perhaps it's not that often that you want to slow down or speed up a sound you're playing, but sometimes you do. As long as we're building a general-purpose engine, we may as well support this operation. A speed-changing DSP function, in the context of our pipeline, is any function that outputs a different number of samples than it uses for input. The classic example of a DSP function which slows down music is only one type of speed changer. A reverb function may be categorized as a speed changer (though it is actually more of a length changer) if it can generate output past the end of its input; in other words, it allows the last reverberations to fade to silence before stopping.

The audio system should be efficient. Hopefully the pipeline itself doesn't consume a lot of CPU cycles, but we can be careful not to cause any unnecessary copying of memory; for example, if a DSP function returns "I have no work to do," no memory copying should be performed.

The goal of any general-purpose API is to save work, not create work. An audio engine is built only once. There are many types of DSP functions. We should handle as much ancillary work as possible, so that each DSP function implements an algorithm and not much else.

## Discussion

Throughout this section, I will discuss what happens for one sound. Multiple sound support does not become a relevant factor until the mix stage.

Looking again at Figure 6.4.1, we see that the audio input to our little world comes from the decompressor (if present, or else from the input stream manager). The output goes to the mixing engine (which may be DirectSound or another system).

This is asymmetrical. While the input side is relatively flexible (it should be able to supply us with as many samples of audio as we request, within reason), the output side is inflexible. The mixing engine needs a certain number of samples from our stream; it cannot handle anything more, and if we try to pass it anything less it will continue mixing—without our sound, which will have a gap in it.

This is so important a rule that it should be stated again: the output of the audio processing pipeline must be determined by the needs of the mix engine. That's what determines how many samples we are to output.

There is only one type of inflexibility imposed by the input stream: EOF. When the stream reaches the end, the processing engine needs to know.

So, let's say the mix is done in a fixed buffer of 16,384 samples. This means that it waits until it needs that many samples, and then triggers the audio processing. Therefore, the audio processing pipeline must output 16,384 samples.

How many samples does the pipeline need for input? We don't know that yet. So far, we know only that the last function in the chain must output 16,384 samples. How many samples does this function need for input?

We don't know that either, but we can find out. We can ask it! The mixer wants 16,384 samples. The last function in the chain, with its current parameter set, says it wants 24,576 samples of input to produce 16,384 of output. To determine how many samples of input to obtain from the stream, we continue traversing the chain of DSP functions backward. We go backward because we know the number of samples output at the end, but not the number of samples input at the beginning.

Once we're done with this phase, we can obtain the requested number of samples from the input stream, and pass them to the first function in the chain. We can take its output and pass it to the second function, and so forth. At the end, theoretically, we have the right number of samples to send to the mix engine.

What if that assumption is broken? What if a DSP function produces fewer samples than it was supposed to? The next DSP function in the chain must be given the new, smaller buffer. It must produce output as well as it can. At the end, there may be a shortfall. We treat this shortfall as the desired output for a second iteration, query backward up the chain, and then process data a second time. We do this until we either run out of input samples, or fill the output buffer. For the sake of efficiency, DSP functions should be implemented in a manner such that they don't frivolously misreport their expected input requirements. This is a feature that should only be used if computing the exact number of input samples required would require substantial processing (for example, if the DSP function would have to actually process the audio to know exactly how many samples it would need).

What if a DSP function "eats" fewer samples than requested? This is a trickier case to program. The pipeline must provide a buffer between each pair of DSP functions in the chain. The buffer between function #2 and function #3 holds underflow data from function #3.

What if a DSP function produces too many output samples? Well, it shouldn't do that! Seriously, the obvious way to handle this case is to buffer it, but that is not demonstrated in the code for this gem.

This raises a point: DSP functions are not commutative. Order matters. This is not merely a limitation of the buffering system I just proposed, but also of the nature of processing. If one changes the pitch of a sound and then imposes a reverb, the result will sound different than if one applies a reverb and then changes the pitch. Therefore, we're not worried that our proposed architecture imposes this requirement as well.

### Details

We're envisioning an audio processing pipeline that's called whenever the mixing engine needs more data for a sound channel. It may be implemented as a callback, if the mix engine is driven by interrupts, or as a regular function if the status of the mix buffer is polled.

The processing engine must call the input stream manager to request raw data for the sound channel. It may return a full buffer, or less if the sound has reached the end.

The processing engine can call each DSP function with several messages. So far, we've discussed a query to determine how many input samples are needed to produce the required output, and of course the output call itself.

We ought to add two more: *firstcall* and *lastcall*. Firstcall is the first message sent to a DSP function, to let it allocate instance data, and lastcall allows it to free that data.

To implement a DSP function to plug into this architecture, the programmer must provide a single entry point that's capable of properly handing firstcall (initialization), lastcall (shutdown), query, and output messages. This entry point is given a single struct that contains the command number, input and output buffers and lengths, and two other items. One of these is a pointer to DSP-specific parameters, which is passed down from the application (presumably controlling all of this). Examples of DSP-specific parameters would be room size for a reverb, ratio for a speed changer, and so forth. The other item is private instance data allocated and maintained by the DSP function itself.

Implementing the engine is somewhat more complex, but this was our intent. Make this one piece intelligent so that the many DSP pieces are quick and easy to implement.

The processing engine uses three buffers: a source, a destination, and an accumulation buffer. During processing, the buffers swap roles, so the engine uses buf[0], buf[1], and buf[2]. The reason is that the destination (output) of DSP function #1 becomes the source (input) of DSP function #2.

Similarly, if the last DSP function in the chain outputs less than the amount required by the mixing engine, its destination buffer becomes the accumulation buffer. After the next iteration of the chain, the accumulation buffer is prepended to the new destination buffer.

## The Code

Let's look at the source code to the main entry point.

```
void dsp_ProcessAudio(dsp_AUDIO *audio)
{
  audio->src = 0;
  audio->dst = 1;
  audio->acc = 2;

  bfbuf_WIPE(audio->buf[audio->src]);
  bfbuf_WIPE(audio->buf[audio->dst]);
  bfbuf_WIPE(audio->buf[audio->acc]);

  audio->samps = 0;

  while ((audio->samps < audio->sampsneeded) && (!audio->done))
  {
    SWAP(audio->acc, audio->dst);

    QueryDSPIn(audio);
    stream_GetData(audio);
    DoDSP(audio);

    bfbuf_MoveAll(audio->buf[audio->dst], audio->buf[audio->acc]);
  }
}
```

One last explanation is necessary before this code makes sense. A *bfbuf* is a data structure of my own invention. A *backfill buffer* is a memory buffer designed to make it easy to prepend data. The contents are always aligned flush with the end, so that prepending is done with a simple memcpy(). The source code to BFBUF.C is included on the companion CD-ROM.

It turns out that the prepend operation is the one we need to handle the underflow buffers in the DSP chain itself. Therefore, I've implemented the outer loop to use a prepend to take the partial buffer from the previous iteration and add it to the current partial buffer. This could just as easily have been implemented to append the current partial buffer to the previous partial buffer. When you make yourself a new hammer, and you feel clever about it, you have a tendency to see everything as a nail.

Let's walk through the function. Its sole parameter is a pointer to a struct defined in the code on the CD. There are three backfill buffers, which we initialize to empty, and assign their initial semantics.

We have a loop that iterates until we run out of source data, or until the output buffer is full. For the first iteration, the swap is meaningless and does nothing.

The rest is simple. First, we determine how many input samples are needed, get them, and process. Then, we prepend the accumulated samples from previous iterations (if any) to the current destination.

stream_GetData() is the call to the input stream manager (external to DSP.C). It's important to understand that this function must put the samples in the *destination* buffer. As we'll see, DoDSP() swaps the source and destination buffers at the beginning.

Now let's look at the query function.

```
static void QueryDSPIn(dsp_AUDIO *audio)
{
  dsp_PARAMS params;
  dsp_DSP *dsp;
  DWORD underlen;
  DWORD x;

  params.cmd      = dsp_QUERYACTIN;
  params.actualin = audio->sampsneeded - audio->samps;

  for (x=0;x<audio->numdsps;x++)
  {
    dsp = &(audio->dsp[audio->numdsps - x - 1]);
    params.dstlen = params.actualin;

    (*dsp->callback)(&params);
    underlen = bfbuf_GETDATALEN(dsp->underbuf);

    dsp->inreq  = (underlen < params.actualin) ?
                     params.actualin - underlen : 0;
    dsp->outreq = params.dstlen;
  }
}
```

Notice how the function begins by knowing how many samples remain (`audio-> sampsneeded − audio->samps`). It sets this up where the code in the loop expects to find it from a previous iteration. Alternatively, I could have coded this with a `goto` to enter the loop in the middle, but that seemed a less elegant solution.

The loop itself traverses all the DSP filters used by the sound in reverse order. For each, it sets up a parameter to specify the desired number of output samples, and makes the call. Then it subtracts the number of samples stored in the underflow buffer from a previous iteration of processing. The result may be zero, if the previous iteration had sufficient samples left over. In this case, the filter needs no more input; all the input it requested is already waiting for it in our underflow buffer!

Each DSP stores how many input samples it needs, and the expected output (the number of samples requested by the next item in the chain).

The meat of the Gem is the `DoDSP()` function.

```
static void DoDSP(dsp_AUDIO *audio)
{
  bfbuf_BUFFER *srcbuf;
  bfbuf_BUFFER *dstbuf;
  dsp_PARAMS params;
  dsp_DSP *dsp;
  DWORD x;

  params.cmd = dsp_OUTPUT;

  for (x=0;x<audio->numdsps;x++)
  {
```

```
    dsp = &(audio->dsp[x]);

    SWAP(audio->src, audio->dst);

    srcbuf = audio->buf[audio->src];
    dstbuf = audio->buf[audio->dst];

    bfbuf_MoveAll(srcbuf, dsp->underbuf);
    bfbuf_SetDataLen(dstbuf, dsp->outreq);
    bfbuf_GetBufStart(srcbuf, &(params.lsrc), &(params.rsrc));
    bfbuf_GetBufStart(dstbuf, &(params.ldst), &(params.rdst));

    params.srclen      = bfbuf_GETDATALEN(srcbuf);
    params.dstlen      = bfbuf_GETDATALEN(dstbuf);
    params.dspspecific = dsp->dspspecific;
    params.privdata    = dsp->privdata;

    (*dsp->callback)(&params);

    if (params.nowork)
    {
      bfbuf_WIPE(dstbuf);
      SWAP(audio->src, audio->dst);

      params.actualout = params.srclen;
    }
    else
    {
      if (params.actualout < bfbuf_GETDATALEN(dstbuf))
      {
        bfbuf_ChokeUp(dstbuf, params.actualout);
      }
      if (params.actualin < bfbuf_GETDATALEN(srcbuf))
      {
        bfbuf_Eat(srcbuf, params.actualin);
        bfbuf_MoveAll(dsp->underbuf, srcbuf);
      }
      else
      {
        bfbuf_WIPE(srcbuf);
      }
    }
  }
  audio->samps += params.actualout;
}
```

At first, the initial swap of source and destination looks funny. Each DSP function is given the previous function's output (destination) for its own input (source). This also makes it easy to handle the case when a DSP reports that it has done no work.

There's some variable setup, and then four calls to this mysterious backfill buffer manager. First, we fetch all underflow samples from the previous iteration. Note: this is stored on a per-DSP basis. The underflow for DSP function #1 is different from the underflow for DSP function #2, and must be kept separate.

Next, we set up the expected size of the destination backfill buffer. If this turns out to be wrong, we'll fix it later. Finally, we obtain pointers to the current beginnings of the buffers. Notice that left and right are stored separately. This makes DSP processing easier, as well as the eventual move to multichannel audio (for example, 5.1).

We do some straightforward parameter setup. Notice how we provide the DSP with both a pointer to function-specific parameters, and its own instance data for this sound.

After the call, if the function did no work, we set the destination buffer to empty, and swap destination with source (so the destination is now the one with samples in it) to prepare for the next iteration, which will swap again.

Otherwise, something was done by the function, so we check to see if the DSP generated less than a full buffer. The *choke up* is the only BFBUF operation that must do a memory move.

Then we check to see if the function consumed less than all of the input data supplied to it. If so, we buffer it as underflow. Otherwise, we just mark the source buffer as empty.

## Extra Commentary

This isn't the easiest code to read, but it's nice and efficient, which is what counts! No cycles are wasted unless a DSP generates too little data, and there's not much to do about that except iterate the whole chain again hoping we'll get enough data.

Notice how each time dsp_ProcessAudio() is called, the parameters for all of the DSP functions could have changed. This code forms the core of an audio processing engine that meets all of the criteria we enumerated earlier.

Building it was not only possible, but it wasn't as hard as it seemed it would be.

Two functions have been omitted from the text (they're on the CD). dsp_New-Sound() must be called when a new sound is added to the system, and dsp_Delete-Sound() must be called when a sound is removed from the system. This is important because it's not obvious from the code presented thus far. There is a call to the stream manager, and that call sets audio->done if the stream reaches the end.

Whatever code calls dsp_ProcessAudio() must check this bit, and then call dsp_DeleteSound() if appropriate. The tricky part is to wait until the sound is done (in other words, audio->samps is 0). DSP functions (such as echo) may retain their own internal buffers. Regardless of how they determine when to eat input samples and produce nothing (when given a request for output and when provided with less input than requested) they must output whatever they can. This way, the DSP engine knows that when a stream reaches the end, *and* the DSP function chain produces no output, the last reverberations or echoes of the sound are done, and the sound may safely be deleted without causing an audible truncation.

From an architectural standpoint, this is admittedly somewhat weak. It is possible to design a more elegant, self-contained solution to this problem inside DSP.C. A related limitation is that the dsp_AUDIO struct and its dsp_DSP array are allocated outside as well. There is entirely too much management of DSP-related memory structures, parameters, and so forth, outside the DSP engine. This is done primarily to keep the code clean and easy to understand.

There are two functional limitations (the previous are considered to be structural or architectural) to discuss. First, the code doesn't handle the case of when a DSP function overflows. The quick excuse is that no function should ever output more data than is requested of it. It could also be argued that those few functions that would want to, can simply maintain an internal buffer. This isn't satisfactory because we've gone to great lengths to make sure that DSP functions are small, lightweight, and easy. The real answer is that this would add considerably to code size and complexity (including in BFBUF.C), and provide a (comparatively) marginal value. This code is not really a robust commercial implementation, and adding something like overflow protection (including the algorithms to determine how big is big enough, etc.) just wouldn't make sense before putting in DEBUG error-checking, for example.

The other missing feature is that there is no way to add or remove DSP functions after a sound is created. This can be worked around as long as all DSP functions have a parameter to indicate "passthru." Then, just make sure each sound is created with all of the DSP functions that you'll possibly want to use on it at any point during its lifetime. It's not inefficient, and it works (although it is a bit clunky).

It would be a bad kludge, but you could actually add new DSP functions to the end of the list (as long as you provided a way to do firstcall processing for them).

## Conclusion

The essence of this gem demonstrates how to build a basic DSP pipeline that supports passing a sound channel through a chain of DSP filters, each of which can do anything to the stream that it wants.

In order to support DSPs that may wish to change the size of the buffer as they process, we need a query call to ask the DSP "if we want $N$ samples of output, how many samples of input do you estimate you'll need?" We do this query in reverse order.

ON THE CD

In addition, we added support for two underflow conditions: generating too little data, and eating too little input. These weren't too hard to support with the help of an innovative data structure: the backfill buffer. The concept is the most difficult thing with this. As you'll see on the CD, the code is straightforward, if not trivial.

With this engine, and some glue logic, it's possible to do any type of audio processing that a game will need. Indeed, it could support a whole professional audio studio for music production and performance.

# 6.5

# A Basic Music Sequencer for Games

## Scott Patterson

scottp@tonebyte.com

This gem describes how to make a basic music sequencer. First, we will start with a comparison of music streaming and music sequencing. Then, we will review some important concepts from the MIDI music language, outline a basic computer music language implementation, and then discuss the coding issues that relate to timing and synthesis control.

## Streaming vs. Sequencing

Music in games is generally played back in one of two ways: either as a stream of sample data or as a sequence of instructions to an audio synthesis system. It is also possible that music playback may involve a combination of both methods. Individually, the methods have some pros and cons that depend on the hardware systems available. To be combined, synchronization issues must be addressed as well.

### Streaming Method Pros

- Audio hardware requirements are minimal.
- Music development and integration with the game is easy.
- Music quality is only limited by the sample rate and number of channels of the stream data.

### Streaming Method Cons

- Music data plays the same way each time.
- There can be latency in the start and stop of the stream.
- There may be latency problems when looping a stream or switching streams.
- There may be large memory buffer requirements.
- Certain resources may be tied up during playback such as DMA hardware and storage device hardware.
- If the stream data is not compressed, it will take significant storage space.
- If the stream data is compressed, it will require hardware or software decompression resources.

- It may not be possible to cross-fade two different streams depending on hardware limitations, so the only choice available may be fading to or from silence.

### Sequencing Method Pros

- No latency problems when starting or stopping the music.
- No latency problems when looping or switching music.
- If audio memory is available, sample data memory will not compete with game data memory.
- Resources such as DMA hardware and storage device hardware may not be required for music playback and will be free for the game to use at any time.
- A great deal of music styles and variations can be produced from a relatively small sample data set.
- Music data can be dynamically altered at runtime to create unique game and music interactions.

### Sequencing Method Cons

- Voices for music may compete with voices needed for other game audio.
- Music development and integration with the game is more complex.
- Music quality may be limited by synthesis capabilities.
- Music quality may be limited by available sample memory.

## Core Computer Music Concepts

Let's now review core computer music concepts, and build our music command language.

### Event Blocks

Music can be described as events or commands occurring over time. Therefore, we can build our music command language with "event blocks" composed of three elements: time, event type, and event details. We will store the time relative to previous events and call it a delta-time. The event type will be identified with a number, and the event details will be zero or more parameters that are defined by the event type (Figure 6.5.1).

By using a sequence of event blocks we can describe any combination of events and time intervals. Therefore, building our computer music language is now a task of

---

**Delta Time   /   Event Type   /   Event Parameters**

**FIGURE 6.5.1** *Event block.*

choosing how to store the delta time, choosing the event types to support, and choosing the parameters supplied for each event type.

### MIDI (Musical Instrument Digital Interface) Music

The MIDI specification has been around for a long time. Most music composition and sequencing software provides compatibility with MIDI input and output ports for recording and playback. These software products also provide options to save and load MIDI files. Since we are creating our own computer music language, a good place to start will be learning the MIDI specification and its file format. We can then convert MIDI file data to our own custom data.

The word *interface* in MIDI refers to the fact that it is a specification for communication between musical devices. In making a music sequencer for games, we aren't as interested in musical device communication as we are in music playback on a particular machine. Therefore, my introduction to MIDI will include only the parts that relate directly to making our music sequencer for games.

### MIDI Event Types

The MIDI specification defines several events called the channel voice messages. MIDI originated as a virtual piano keyboard communication language, so terms such as attack velocity, release velocity, pitch wheel, and key pressure all refer to actions applied to a virtual piano keyboard (Table 6.5.1).

The channel voice messages are the core musical control events defined by MIDI. The Program Change event defines what instrument definition to use. The Note On and Note Off events do as they suggest, and the remaining events update various audio playback parameters to new values. Since the Control Change event specifies a

**Table 6.5.1 MIDI Channel Voice Messages**

| Event Type | Event Parameters |
|---|---|
| Note Off | Note Number<br>Release Velocity |
| Note On | Note Number<br>Attack Velocity |
| Pitch Wheel | Pitch Bend LSB<br>Pitch Bend MSB |
| Control Change | Controller ID<br>Controller Value |
| Program Change | Program Number |
| Poly Key Pressure | Note Number<br>Pressure Value |
| Channel Pressure | Pressure Value |

Controller ID parameter, it can be used for many different types of audio control. Two of the most commonly used Controller IDs are 7 for Volume and 10 for Pan.

There are also meta-events defined in the MIDI file format 1.0 specification. Table 6.5.2 lists a selection that will be important to us.

The End of Track meta-event defines the end of a series of event blocks, and the Set Tempo meta-event defines how fast to step through the delta time values of event blocks. The Time Signature and Key Signature meta-events do not change the way that MIDI music plays, but are commonly used for organizing the visual display of music data. We can use these meta-events as special markers for our own organization or synchronization purposes. The remaining meta-events I have listed store string data. We can store custom information in these strings to be used in our conversion from the MIDI format to a custom format.

### MIDI Channels and Tracks

The "channel" in MIDI channel voice messages refers to the fact that each MIDI event block also contains a channel number from 1 to 16 (0 to 15). The channel concept makes it possible to send MIDI commands to more than one target over a serial connection. It would also be possible for us to store our music data as a single serial stream and assign channels to each message. An advantage of this method is that pro-

**Table 6.5.2 Selected MIDI Meta-Event Types**

| Meta-Event Type | Meta-Event Parameters |
| --- | --- |
| End of Track | |
| Set Tempo | Tempo Number |
| Time Signature | Numerator |
| | Denominator |
| | MIDI clocks per metronome click |
| | 32$^{nd}$-notes in a MIDI quarter-note |
| Key Signature | Sharps/Flats Indicator |
| | Major or Minor Indicator |
| Text Event | String Length |
| | String Data |
| Sequence/Track Name | String Length |
| | String Data |
| Instrument Name | String Length |
| | String Data |
| Lyric | String Length |
| | String Data |
| Marker | String Length |
| | String Data |
| Cue Point | String Length |
| | String Data |

cessing a single stream of data would work well for CPU caching. A disadvantage of this method is that track data organization would not be flexible and independent.

It so happens that the MIDI file format 1.0 specification defines "format 0" files that have all information combined in one track, and "format 1" files that have any number of tracks.

The basic music sequencer that we will present processes any number of tracks independently and does not have a channel concept.

## Computer Music Sequencer Implementation

Now we are at the point where we can determine our own custom computer music language. For the purposes of this gem we will choose to implement event types that are very similar to MIDI event types. You can create your own additional event types for your own needs.

### Sequences, Tracks, Events, Instruments, and Voices

Let's quickly cover the terminology used in the rest of this paper. A *sequence* is a collection of *tracks* that run simultaneously. Each track is a series of *event* blocks that we defined earlier. There is always a single current *instrument* on each track. Every Note On event in a track will start a *voice* of the current instrument. The corresponding Note Off event will turn this voice off. Many types of events in a track will modify the state of the track's voices.

The sequencer data structures described later show an implementation of these relationships.

### Sequencer Event Types

As a first step in creating our basic music sequencer we will come up with a list of event types that we want to support. These are displayed in Table 6.5.3.

### Table 6.5.3.  Event Type Ideas

| Event Types | Notes |
| --- | --- |
| **Note Control** | These work like the traditional MIDI events |
| Note Off | Key |
| | Release velocity (optional) |
| Note On | Key |
| | Attack velocity |

*(continues)*

**Table 6.5.3.** *(Continued)*

| Event Types | Notes |
|---|---|
| **Immediate Modifications** | These work like the traditional MIDI events |
| SetVolume | Value |
| SetPitchBend | Value |
| SetPan | Value |
| SetEffect | Any effect type |
|  | Value |
| SetInstrument | Program change |
| SetTempo | Value |
| **Target Modifications** | Target an event value rather than setting it |
| SetTarget | Time format and duration to target value |
|  | Basic modification type and data |
| **Arrangement** |  |
| Track End | Ends track playback |
| Track Marker | Additional entry points, sync points. |
| Jump to Track | Jump to new track data |
| Gosub to Track | Jump to new track data, returns when done |
| **Callback** |  |
| Callback | Calls game code, could change test values |

### Note Control

It is pretty hard to make music without notes. Following the MIDI tradition, we associate a key number and velocity with notes. The MIDI Note Off message includes a release velocity, but it is our option to include this for our sequencer.

### Immediate Modifications

These event types are quite similar to certain MIDI messages. This will make conversion from MIDI files for these events easy. These events also represent immediate updates of synth hardware. Values may be absolute or relative depending on the event type.

### Target Modifications

These event types interpolate from current value to destination value over a given time rather than changing settings immediately. Target modifications have the advantage of being able to describe a curve of parameter values with a single command rather than the many immediate modification commands needed to achieve the same effect.

### Arrangement

These event types switch us to different sections of music data.

### Callback

These event types generate callbacks to functions that have been registered with the music sequencer.

### Sequencer Data Structures

The abbreviated data structures that we could use for our music sequencer are listed in Listing 6.5.1.

## Listing 6.5.1  Music sequencer data structures

```
typedef list< Sequence_t * > SequencePtrList_t;
typedef list< Track_t * >    TrackPtrList_t;
typedef list< Voice_t * >    VoicePtrList_t;

class MusicSequencer_t {
    MusicSequencerState_t State;
    SequencePtrList_t     ActiveSequencePtrList;
    SequencePtrList_t     FreeSequencePtrList;
    TrackPtrList_t        ActiveTrackPtrList;
    TrackPtrList_t        FreeTrackPtrList;
    VoicePtrList_t        ActiveVoicePtrList;
    VoicePtrList_t        FreeVoicePtrList;
};

class SequenceState_t {
    Tempo_t  Tempo;
    Volume_t Volume;
};

class Sequence_t {
    SequenceState_t State;
    TimeUnit_t      TimeElapsed;
    TimeUnit_t      TimeStep;
    TrackPtrList_t  TrackPtrList;
};

class TrackState_t {
    Volume_t    Volume;
    PitchBend_t PitchBend;
    Pan_t       Pan;
    Effect_t    Effect;
};

class Track_t {
    TrackState_t   State;
    Sequence_t     *pOwner;
    char           *pEvent;
    Instrument_t   *pInstrument;
    VoicePtrList_t VoicePtrList;
};

class VoiceState_t {
```

```
    SynthVolume_t Volume;
    SynthPitch_t  Pitch;
    SynthPan_t    Pan;
    SynthEffect_t Effect;
};

class Voice_t {
    VoiceState_t  State;
    Track_t       *pOwner;
    int           nKey;
};
```

Here we show the *MusicSequencer_t* class that holds the lists of active and free sequences, tracks, and voices. We also see that sequences, tracks, and voices each have a notion of state and some example parameters of those states are shown. A *Sequence_t* has a *TrackPtrList* that holds the tracks owned by the sequence. A *Track_t* has a *VoicePtrList* that holds the voices owned by the track. A *Voice_t* has a *pOwner* that points to the track that owns the voice. A *Track_t* has a *pOwner* that points to the sequence that owns the track. These parent and child data structures help us query and update information up and down our hierarchy, whether we are operating on sequences, tracks, or voices.

### Event Data Structures

To implement the event type commands, we can have the event type command numbers correspond to an array lookup that holds the relevant function pointer and the byte length of the event type and parameters. Listing 6.5.2 shows this code. The function pointers give us a quick way to get to the code associated with each event type. The byte lengths give us a quick way to step to the next event block.

## Listing 6.5.2 Event type data structures

```
// Example Note Off Event Block
typedef struct {
    char nEventType;
    char nKey;
    // no release velocity
} NoteOff_EventBlock_t;

void NoteOff_Function( Track_t *pTrack )
{
    // the pEvent is pointing at our event block
    NoteOff_EventBlock_t *pNoteOffEB =
        (NoteOff_EventBlock_t *)pEvent;

    // walk through this track's voices and turn off
    // any that have pVoice->nKey == pNoteOffEB->nKey
}

// Example Note On Event Block
```

```
typedef struct {
    char nEventType;
    char nKey;
    char nVelocity;
} NoteOn_EventBlock_t;

void NoteOn_Function( Track_t *pTrack )
{
    // the pEvent is pointing at our event block
    NoteOn_EventBlock_t *pNoteOnEB = (NoteOn_EventBlock_t *)pEvent;

    // try to get a voice from the free list or
    // try to get a voice from the active list if possible
    // if we have a voice, turn it on with the pNoteOnEB->nKey
    // and pNoteOnEB->nVelocity and other state information
}

enum enumEventType
{
    EVENT_TYPE_NOTEOFF,
    EVENT_TYPE_NOTEON,
    .
    .
    .
    EVENT_TYPE_COUNT
};

typedef void (*EventFuncPtr_t)(Track_t *);

typedef struct {
    EventFuncPtr_t pFunc;    // pointer to command function
    int            nLength; // byte length of command
} EventTypes_t;

static EventTypes_t aET[EVENT_TYPE_COUNT] = {
    { NoteOff_Function, sizeof(NoteOff_EventBlock_t) },
    { NoteOn_Function, sizeof(NoteOn_EventBlock_t) },
    .
    .
    .
};
```

Here we show that we can give each event type a number that can be used to call up an *EventTypes_t* structure from an array. The *EventTypes_t* structure contains the function pointer to call for the given event type and the length of the command ID and parameters. Being able to define our own command numbers and have them correspond to array entries like this provides an alternative to switch statements.

### The Audio Frame and Update Interval

Different computer systems have different ways of providing timing callbacks or threads that wake up at specific intervals. I will simply assume that we can have a function called at a specific interval referred to as the audio callback. We can think of the time between these callbacks as the audio frame. During each callback, we need to update our notion of how much time will pass during the next audio frame, and we need to send out all of the commands that are due to occur over this time.

Independent of the audio callback rate we will also have an update interval. The update interval determines the amount of time we will step when sending out low-level commands. For example, we could have an audio callback that occurs once every second with the update interval at 120 times a second, which would require stepping through 120 time intervals per callback. Another possibility is that we could have an audio callback that occurs 60 times a second with the update interval at 120 times a second, which would require stepping through two time intervals per callback.

Listing 6.5.3 is an outline of the audio callback code.

## Listing 6.5.3  The audio frame

```
// This function is called by the timer callback
static void OSys_AudioCallback(void)
{
    // protect against callback reentrance

    // determine the number of update intervals required
    // to deliver during this callback

    // begin critical section
    OSys_BeginAudioCriticalSection();

    // for the number of update intervals required on this frame
    // {
    //      iterate over sequences
    //          perform per sequence operations

    //          iterate over tracks
    //              perform per track operations
    //
    //      send low-level commands for this time step
    //      move to next time step
    // }

    // end critical section
    OSys_EndAudioCriticalSection();
}
```

Since our callback may happen while other code is executing, this means it might happen when we are changing data structures for the music sequencer. We protect against this by using the critical section method specific to our operating system.

### Timing Calculations

In order to play our music data at different rates, we need to work out how to step through our music data based on three parameters: the music tempo, the update interval, and the resolution of our music time format.

- Music tempo is described in beats per minute (BPM).
- The update interval is described in updates per second (UPS).
- Music time resolution is described in parts per quarter note (PPQ).

We are looking for the amount of music time to increment for each audio callback. We can call this parts per update (PPU).

If we consider beats per minute (BPM) to be the same as quarter notes per minute (QPM), then the equation is:

PPU = QPM * PPQ * (1/UPS) * (1Minute/60Seconds)

If we store this PPU number as a 16.16 fixed point number, the final code is (Listing 6.5.4):

## Listing 6.5.4  Time step calculation

```
unsigned long CalcTimeStep( unsigned short qpm,
                            unsigned short ppq,
                            unsigned short ups)
{
    unsigned long ppu;
    unsigned long temp;
    temp = (unsigned long)qpm * (unsigned long)ppq;
    if( temp < 0x10000 )
    {
        ppu = ((temp * 0x10000) / 60)
                / (unsigned long)ups;
    } else {
        ppu = ((temp / 60) * 0x10000)
                / (unsigned long)ups;
    }
    return(ppu);
}
```

Our calculation here does a little range checking during the calculation to make sure that we obtain as accurate a 16.16 result as possible given that the input numbers can range in value.

We recalculate the parts-per-update value any time that a sequence's tempo changes. This parts-per-update value is placed in our *TimeStep* variable in our sequence structure. Since these time parameters are in the sequence structure, we can only change the tempo for the entire sequence. If we wanted to change tempo for each track individually, we could put these parameters and the tempo setting in the track structure.

## Audio Synthesis Control

### Connecting Synth to Sequencer

An important issue for our music sequencer implementation is how music event parameters are mapped to audio synthesis parameters. This is where music sequencer code can get very platform specific. In order to keep the code as cross-platform as possible, I will call a software synthesizer interface from our sequencer code.

One important part of connecting our audio synthesis to our music sequencer is the SetInstrument event type. The Program Change parameters of *SetInstrument* Command is used as an index into a table of instrument definitions. The address of this table entry is used to set the *pInstrument* field of our Track data structure. When a Note On command occurs, the parameters from the *pInstrument* are transferred to the voice to be started. You can view these details in the accompanying source code.

The capabilities of the audio synthesis system that we are using will determine instrument definition and even definition details. As a result, there will be certain types of control we will have available and music will have to be written with these control issues in mind.

## The Code

ON THE CD

The example code on the CD-ROM shows how to play music using our custom music sequencer language. This includes how to step through the music data of each track of each sequence, and how to code the event types for a particular synth interface. Of the event type ideas presented, the code implements the *NoteOn*, *NoteOff*, *SetPan*, *SetInstrument*, and *TrackEnd* commands.

ON THE CD

The example code uses a cross-platform audio engine called CSyn. The CSyn library provided on the CD-ROM is for demonstration purposes only.

## Conclusions

We covered the details of a basic music sequencer. Important MIDI concepts have been presented, as well as our custom music language. Implementation details of data structures, event types, and timing were presented. Finally, the code is there to play with and customize for your own needs. Enjoy!

## References

CSyn audio engine, www.softsynth.com/csyn.

# 6.6

# An Interactive Music Sequencer for Games

## *Scott Patterson*

scottp@tonebyte.com

**G**ames are interactive. This means that a player has control over the game in some way, and the game asks the player to use his or her control to interact in some way. This control and interaction is the foundation of gameplay that is immersive and entertaining.

It is natural to want to mix the immersiveness of control and interaction in computer games with the immersiveness of music. How do we control music? How can we create musical interaction? What kind of musical meanings can we generate? This is the motivation for this gem.

Building on the concepts and code from the basic music sequencer, we now will discuss features that provide interactive control. Specifically, we will discuss the ability to modify parameters on the sequence level and track level.

Making interactive music can be viewed as controlling a puppet. We need to pull the right strings to make it seem alive. And if we pull the right strings to control the way the music plays, we may even pull the emotional strings of our game player. In order to discuss what types of emotional strings might be available, we've generated a list of associations and meanings that music can convey. We then cover transitions, transition types, control granularity, and target control. Finally, we present a few design examples.

## Musical Associations

Music is its own form of entertainment. We listen for styles, attitudes, technology, improvisation, composition, and skilled performances and interpretations. Our memories associate music with past situations, friends, and places. While some associations may be personal and specific, others are quite common and generally accepted. We may associate a particular song with a particular person. We may associate a particular style of music with a particular geographical location. We may associate the "mood" of some music with love, hate, contentment, or anger (Table 6.6.1).

**Table 6.6.1 Music Associations**

| Category / Type | Description |
| --- | --- |
| Age Groups | Children, teenage, college, mature |
| Activities | Sports, chase, battle, puzzles |
| Cultures | Themes, styles, anthems |
| Time Periods | Historical, futuristic |
| Locations | Geographical, magical, space exploration |
| Mood | Humor, serious |
| Tension | Relaxed, tense |
| Strength | Powerful or weak |
| Reward | Pride, confident and energetic |
| Defeat | Ridicule, goofy and taunting |

## Musical Meaning

If we want our music to be interactive, we should know the different meanings that we wish to convey with the music. Some of the meanings that we might want to attach to the control of music are categorized in Table 6.6.2.

**Table 6.6.2 Musical Meanings**

| Category / Type | Description |
| --- | --- |
| **Self** | What state is the player in? |
| Health | Confidence in the music. |
| Power | Strength in the music. |
| Skill | Sharpness and agility in the music. |
| Mood | Heaviness or lightness in the music. |
| Familiar | Music that is familiar to certain player states in the game. |
| **Others** | What state are nonplayer characters in? |
| Friends | Pleasing attitude in the music. |
| Enemies | Harsh attitude in the music. |
| Love | Sweetness in the music. |
| Hate | Violence in the music. |
| Familiar | Music that is familiar to certain nonplayer character states in the game. |
| **Location** | What is our current location like? |
| Secrets | Occasional secret melodies or instruments play. |
| Hints | Sudden burst when looking the right way. |
| Safety | Even, predictable music. |
| Danger | Irregular, ominous music. |
| Magic | Chimes, and echoes, and sprinkles in the music. |
| Familiar | Music that is familiar to a common location in the game. |

**Table 6.6.2** (*Continued*)

| Category / Type | Description |
|---|---|
| **Situation** | What kind of situation are we in? |
| Safety | Even, predictable music. |
| Danger | Irregular, ominous music. |
| Magic | Chimes, and echoes, and sprinkles in the music. |
| Preparation for Battle | Drums of war. Mechanized beats. |
| Tension | Sharp tones and dynamic changes. |
| Adrenaline | Tempo is up. Mechanized beats. |
| Time is Running Out | Tempo is up. Chaotic passages. |
| Challenge Level | Complicated layering, added effects. |
| Reward | Triumphant music. |
| Failure | Whimpering or taunting music. |
| Familiar | Music that is familiar to a common situation in the game. |

## Transitions

Transitions can be defined as one or more changes occurring over a time interval. A transition might mean an interpolation of some type of state data done over a specific time interval. In addition, a transition might mean a new track section, musical cadence, key change, or other compositional technique. A transition could be a combination of these things.

Transitions may be triggered by a combination of game logic and music language logic. It is useful to provide API functions for game code to directly set target states. These types of implicit and explicit controls over transitions are another key element of the interactive control of music.

## Transition Types

Some of the many transition types are mentioned in Table 6.6.3.

The simplest way to use music interactively is to simply switch music. If we have one composition that is considered traveling music, and one composition that is considered battle music, then when we stop traveling in the game to have a battle, the music switches at the same time. This type of musical interactivity is very common and very useful. We could even use a basic music sequencer to simply stop one tune and start another. If we want our transitions between tunes to be more musical or subtle, then we need more sophisticated functionality from our music sequencer. We might want to overlap the two tunes so that one is heard to be fading off as the other fades in. We might want to have the tunes synchronized in some way as they go through this transition.

To use music interactively is not the same as making interactive music. This would mean that we actually change the character of a music composition through various control methods. What if we want to gradually switch the timbres of instruments in

**Table 6.6.3 Music Transition Types**

| Transition Type | Description |
| --- | --- |
| Quick | Music that stomps on previous music |
| Slow | Subtle alterations and state changes |
| Fading | Fading whole sequences or just some tracks |
| Intensity | Instrument dynamics |
| Effects | Any synthesis parameter changing |
| Key | Compositional changes |
| Chord | Compositional changes |
| Harmony | Compositional changes |
| Melody | Compositional changes |
| Accompaniment | Compositional changes |
| Percussion | Compositional changes |
| Transposing | Compositional changes |
| Layering | Compositional changes |
| Fills | Enter from any beat position, push music decoration events in to a queue |
| Rhythmic | Lagging, ahead, modified swing |
| Randomness | Controlled randomness of varying parameters |
| Instrument | Switching instruments |
| Timing | Switching tempo |

the music to make it seem more dangerous? What if we also want to gradually change the mix of the music to emphasize our new instrument timbres and bring up the percussion? Now we are talking about interactive music. If we can design manageable ways to control this complexity, we will have something pretty impressive.

## Control Granularity

The many ways to define and control volume are a great example of the levels of granularity available for music parameters. These volume control types are listed in Table 6.6.4.

We can see that there can be many levels of control for certain audio parameters. We might even want to group controls. It is useful to define the set of track volumes in a sequence as a *mix*. We can then command a sequence to switch to a given mix definition either immediately or gradually. We might want to externally control something like a sequence volume to turn it down while a character is talking. In addition, we might want to set up internal relationships such as ducking one sequence's volume when another sequence is playing.

**Table 6.6.4 Volume Types**

| Volume Controls | Description |
|---|---|
| Master | Controls all audio. |
| Music | The music volume controls all musical sequences. |
| Sequence | A sequence volume can be used to do fade in or fade out or ducking. |
| Track | Each track of a sequence has a volume. It is useful when creating music to be able to define the balance between tracks and to control crescendo and decrescendo. |
| Instrument | Instrument definitions may include volume. When defining instruments, we may want a volume control so that the instrument can be programmed to have similar volume range characteristics as other instruments. |
| Note | The velocity parameter of a note. It is useful when creating music to have this built-in volume control per note. |
| Voice | The value we pass to a particular synthesis voice. This value is determined from a combination of the other volume types. |

## Target Control

When we switch any parameter, we may want to do so immediately or gradually. To choose the gradual behavior, we set a target volume and timeframe for the transition. Internally, the parameter is interpolated from its original level to its target level over the given timeframe.

When audio synthesis is involved, even if you are setting immediate parameter values, the internal synthesis behavior might actually result in a quick interpolated transition from the original value to the "immediate" value over a short period of time. In addition, some synthesis parameters might only allow modification before a voice has been turned on and not while it is playing.

The abbreviated data structures for our music sequencer with new target controls are shown in Listing 6.6.1

## Listing 6.6.1 Sequencer data structures with target control

```
typedef list< Sequence_t * > SequencePtrList_t;
typedef list< Track_t * >    TrackPtrList_t;
typedef list< Voice_t * >    VoicePtrList_t;

class MusicSequencer_t {
    MusicSequencerState_t State;
    SequencePtrList_t      ActiveSequencePtrList;
    SequencePtrList_t      FreeSequencePtrList;
    TrackPtrList_t         ActiveTrackPtrList;
    TrackPtrList_t         FreeTrackPtrList;
    VoicePtrList_t         ActiveVoicePtrList;
    VoicePtrList_t         FreeVoicePtrList;
};

class SequenceState_t {
```

```
        Tempo_t   Tempo;
        Volume_t Volume;
};

class Sequence_t {
    SequenceState_t        State;
    SequenceState_t        TargetState;        // Interactive feature
    SequenceInterpolator_t Interpolator;       // Interactive feature
    TimeUnit_t             TimeElapsed;
    TimeUnit_t             TimeStep;
    TrackPtrList_t         TrackPtrList;
};

class TrackState_t {
    Volume_t     Volume;
    PitchBend_t PitchBend;
    Pan_t       Pan;
    Effect_t     Effect;
};

class Track_t {
    TrackState_t        State;
    TrackState_t        TargetState;        // Interactive feature
    TrackInterpolator_t Interpolator;       // Interactive feature
    Sequence_t     *pOwner;
    char           *pEvent;
    Instrument_t    *pInstrument;
    VoicePtrList_t  VoicePtrList;
};
```

Here we show new additions to our sequence and track data structures that allow us to interpolate from our current states to new target states. The *TargetState* and *Interpolator* members define what the target values are and how fast to step toward them.

## Design Examples

There are four important factors in the discussion of interactive music: game design, game programming, music design, and music programming. Music programming is influenced by the other factors in the following ways:

- Game design will influence music design.
- Music design will influence music programming.
- Game design will influence game programming.
- Game programming will influence music programming.

To point out these influences, I will describe some interactive music design examples.

### Design Example #1

**Game design**: Through player skill, a character can achieve a powered-up state. This state can last a very long time and a sound effect might get monotonous. We want to hear his energy in the music.

**Music design**: Transition the melody and percussion track instruments to add DSP effects that add color and depth to the instruments.

**Programming design**: Two sequence states are created, and the game can choose when to set each target state.

**Summary**: The music responds to the player's attributes. This way, the music tells the player how he or she is doing.

## Design Example #2

**Game design**: When our player goes near a dangerous location in a level, we may want to hint at that approaching danger, using the music to do so.

**Music design**: Fade down the main melody track and fade up the danger melody track.

**Programming design**: Based on distance from the location, set the track target states for volume.

**Summary**: The music responds to the player's location. This way, the music tells the player that there are new things to expect from this place.

## Design Example #3

**Game design**: Let's say we have a game design where we change from day to night. Assuming that the player's role is more offensive in the day and more defensive at night, we'll want energy music during the day, and tense and scary music at night.

**Music design**: To keep it simple, we will describe three tracks of the music: melody, accompaniment, and percussion. We will define "energy," "mellow," and "creepy" versions of each of the three tracks. Again, keeping it simple, we will define "energy," "mellow," and "creepy" versions of each of the instruments for each track.

We could describe our transition table like Table 6.6.5.

Stop at each column in the table and you can see a different stage of the music. We can consider each column a keyframe for our music control parameters. We can use the control value shown to interpolate between the keyframes.

**Table 6.6.5 Day-to-Night Transitions**

| Game Time | 12noon | 3pm | 6pm | 9pm | 12midnight |
|---|---|---|---|---|---|
| Control Value | 0.0 | 0.25 | 0.50 | 0.75 | 1.0 |
| Melody Track | Energy | Energy | Creepy | Creepy | Creepy |
| Melody Instrument | Energy | Mellow | Mellow | Creepy | Creepy |
| Accompaniment Track | Energy | Mellow | Mellow | Mellow | Creepy |
| Accompaniment Instrument | Energy | Energy | Mellow | Creepy | Creepy |
| Percussion Track | Energy | Energy | Energy | Mellow | Creepy |
| Percussion Instrument | Energy | Energy | Energy | Mellow | Creepy |

**Programming design**: We generate our control value based on the game time. This control value is used to interpolate between instrument states and track states. Therefore, when our game time reaches 3 P.M., the melody instrument has fully transitioned to the "mellow" state. When our game time reaches 6 P.M., the "energy" melody track has faded down and the "creepy" melody track has faded up.

**Summary**: The music responds to the game state. This way, the music tells the player something about how to play the game, or how the game is progressing, or what to expect next.

## The Code

ON THE CD

Building on the code presented in the basic music sequencer gem, the example code shows how to play music that can be interactively modified to new target states.

The example code uses a cross-platform audio engine called CSyn. The CSyn library provided on the CD-ROM is for demonstration purposes only.

## Conclusion

The reasons for developing your own interactive music sequencer code are the same as the reasons for any code development. You may want standard features across many platforms. There may not be systems available that meet your needs. You may want an implementation that you can optimize for delivering the particular features you need. You may want control over your own code to provide improvements, enhancements, and reliability in line with internal scheduling requirements.

In this discussion, we covered many motivations and implementation ideas for interactive music. We presented some core programming concepts that can give us the flexibility and control we need. We pointed out the design influences, meanings, and transition types. The next thing to do with all of these ideas is to implement your own interactive music sequencer and make sure interactive music is part of your game's design.

## References

CSyn audio engine, www.softsynth.com/csyn.

# 6.7

# A Low-Level Sound API

## Ian Lewis, Acclaim Studios

### ilewis@acclaim.com

This gem describes a platform-independent, low-level sound API suitable for games. This API could be a wrapper for DirectSound, OpenAL, or console-specific APIs. A DirectSound reference implementation is provided on the CD.

The goal of the API is to provide a platform-independent, extensible API in C++. The basic functionality must support:

- Hardware-accelerated mixing
- Software mixing and processing
- One-shot and looping sounds
- Wave caching

In addition, each feature must be extensible to support new platforms and features.

## Core Classes

| | |
|---|---|
| CWave | Wraps a wave audio source. Waves are always accessed indirectly by the output stage, so they can be cached and reused. |
| CWavePtr | Iterator class for indirectly accessing a CWave. CWavePtr's main function is to fill a user-supplied buffer with bytes from the wave to which it points. CWavePtr maintains a current position and a loop flag to make sure the bytes come from the correct place in the wave. |
| | The base class is fully functional, but it can be extended if extra processing is needed. For instance, you might extend CWavePtr to convert a 16-bit PCM input source into floating-point data, or to convert an ADPCM-encoded source into standard PCM. CWavePtr can also be extended to provide platform-specific memory functions. For instance, some console platforms contain both areas of memory that are directly CPU-accessible, and memory areas that cannot be directly accessed by the CPU. A CWavePtr-derived class might automatically move memory from non-CPU-accessible to CPU-accessible RAM. |

| CMixer | Encapsulates channel allocation and updating. Has a virtual *tick()* routine that should be called once per frame. (This is perhaps less elegant than running the mixer on a separate thread, as DirectSound does, but threads are hardly cross-platform... and since most threading OSs have a thread timeslice that is greater than the length of a 60-Hz frame, threading can often cause more problems than it solves.) <br><br> The mixer can be extended to handle various hardware architectures. The base class mixer does not allocate any memory for channels, since derived class mixers may want to use their own channel implementations. |
|---|---|
| CMixer::channel | The base channel class is tightly coupled with CMixer, so it's implemented as an inner class. Channels are responsible for managing a CWavePtr, which is the input to that channel. The channel class extracts data from the CWavePtr on demand, keeps track of whether the CWavePtr is still playing or has (in the case of one-shot sounds) finished, and deletes the CWavePtr when it is done <br><br> The channel class can also be extended to meet varying needs. The sample source for this article contains implementations for a DirectSound accelerated channel and a software-based mixer channel. <br><br> CMixer::channel also contains a virtual *tick()* function, which is called from the base CMixer::*tick()*. This allows platform-specific channel implementations to perform hardware housekeeping. For instance, the CDirectSoundAcceleratedChannel implementation uses *tick()* to apply the channel's gain and pan parameters to the hardware buffer. |
| CAudioBuffer | Encapsulates a pointer to audio data and a length. Used to pass data around the system. |
| CWaveDesc | Encapsulates a platform-independent wave description. It strongly resembles Microsoft's WAVEFORMATEX, but contains some extra fields for platform independence. |

ON THE CD

The sample source on the CD contains implementation classes for various DirectSound-based classes, showing how hardware acceleration, software mixing, and DSP-style processing can be worked into the base classes. This implementation is, of course, *not* optimized and is written more for readability than for performance.

# APPENDIX

## About the CD-ROM

The CD-ROM that accompanies this book contains a wide variety of useful information designed to make your life easier as a game developer. Here are some of the things that are included on the disc:

- **All of the gem source code listed in the book**
- **Demos of many of the techniques described in the book**
- **The DirectX SDK**
- **The glSetup Monolithic version**
- **The OpenGL Utility Toolkit (GLUT)**
- **High-resolution versions of the color plates**
- **Links to useful and interesting game development sites**

Complete installation and usage instructions are included on the CD-ROM in the AboutThisCD.htm file. Please read this first.

Also, be sure to visit the Web site www.GameProgrammingGems.com, for more information about the series and about game programming!

# Index